Studies on Aby Warburg, Fritz Saxl and Gertrud Bing

Originally published in German, Italian and French these articles have been translated into English for the first time by the author, the former archivist of The Warburg Institute, London. Aby Warburg's research and writings centred on images, their origins and metamorphoses, and their explanations and interpretations. The articles include discussions of Warburg's academic work with colleagues such as James Loeb, the American Hellenist and philanthropist, and founder of the Loeb Classical Library, and with Josef Strzygowski, the Polish-Austrian art historian of the Vienna School of Art History. Further articles include notes on Warburg's Serpent Ritual lecture of 1923; his politico-cultural initiative in 1914–1915; his work on caricature, in particular the *Struwwelpeter* topic; and discussions on the topic of Judaica.

The Viennese art historian Fritz Saxl became his trusted friend and collaborator helping to gather Warburg's large collection of books and photographs into the foundation of an academic institution in Hamburg in the 1920s, and then for a second time in London in the 1930s. The Warburg Institute has become one of the world's leading centres of intellectual history.

Dorothea McEwan was appointed the first archivist of The Warburg Institute Archive, London in 1993. Her research interests include Aby Warburg and Fritz Saxl and Ethiopian illuminated manuscripts and Ethiopian history. In 2008 she was awarded the Austrian Cross of Honour for Science and Art, in 2017 she was elected Associate Fellow of the Ethiopian Academy of Sciences and in 2021 she was awarded the Grand Decoration of Honour for Services to the Republic of Austria.

Also in the Variorum Collected Studies series

EVELLEEN RICHARDS
Ideology and Evolution in Nineteenth Century Britain
Embryos, Monsters, and Racial and Gendered Others in the Making of Evolutionary Theory and Culture (CS1089)

DAVID S. BACHRACH
Administration and Organization of War in Thirteenth-Century England (CS1088)

GÉRARD GOUIRAN, edited by Linda M. Paterson
From *Chanson de Geste* to Epic Chronicle
Medieval Occitan Poetry of War (CS1087)

JOHN A. COTSONIS
The Religious Figural Imagery of Byzantine Lead Seals II
Studies on the Images of the Saints and on Personal Piety (CS1086)

JOHN A. COTSONIS
The Religious Figural Imagery of Byzantine Lead Seals I
Studies on the Image of Christ, the Virgin and Narrative Scenes (CS1085)

WENDY DAVIES
Christian Spain and Portugal in the Early Middle Ages
Texts and Societies (CS1084)

PEREGRINE HORDEN and NICHOLAS PURCELL
The Boundless Sea
Writing Mediterranean History (CS1083)

MOHAMED EL MANSOUR
The Power of Islam in Morocco
Historical and Anthropological Perspectives (CS1082)

JOHN MARSHALL, edited by Philip Butterworth
Early English Performance: Medieval Plays and Robin Hood Games
Shifting Paradigms in Early English Drama Studies (CS1081)

JENNIFER O'REILLY, edited by CAROL A. FARR and ELIZABETH MULLINS
Early Medieval Text and Image II
The Codex Amiatinus, the Book of Kells and Anglo-Saxon Art (CS1080)

For more information about this series, please visit:www.routledge.com/Variorum-Collected-Studies/book-series/VARIORUM

Studies on Aby Warburg, Fritz Saxl and Gertrud Bing

Dorothea McEwan

VARIORUM COLLECTED STUDIES

Routledge
Taylor & Francis Group
LONDON AND NEW YORK

ZukunftsFonds
der Republik Österreich

First published 2023
by Routledge
4 Park Square, Milton Park, Abingdon, Oxon OX14 4RN

and by Routledge
605 Third Avenue, New York, NY 10158

Routledge is an imprint of the Taylor & Francis Group, an informa business

British Library Cataloguing-in-Publication Data
A catalogue record for this book is available from the British Library

Library of Congress Cataloging-in-Publication Data
Names: McEwan, Dorothea, author, translator.
Title: Studies on Aby Warburg, Fritz Saxl and Gertrud Bing / Dorothea McEwan.
Description: Abingdon, Oxon : Routledge, 2023. | Series: Variorum collected studies ; CS 1109 | Includes bibliographical references and index.
Identifiers: LCCN 2022045337 (print) | LCCN 2022045338 (ebook) | ISBN 9780367769413 (hardback) | ISBN 9780367769444 (paperback) | ISBN 9781003169024 (ebook)
Subjects: LCSH: Warburg, Aby, 1866-1929. | Saxl, Fritz, 1890-1948. | Bing, Gertrud. | Art—Historiography.
Classification: LCC N7483.W36 M33 2023 (print) | LCC N7483.W36 (ebook) | DDC 707.2/2—dc23/eng/20230113
LC record available at https://lccn.loc.gov/2022045337
LC ebook record available at https://lccn.loc.gov/2022045338

ISBN: 978-0-367-76941-3 (hbk)
ISBN: 978-0-367-76944-4 (pbk)
ISBN: 978-1-003-16902-4 (ebk)

DOI: 10.4324/9781003169024

Typeset in Times New Roman
by Apex CoVantage, LLC

VARIORUM COLLECTED STUDIES SERIES CS1109

CONTENTS

PREFACE

Aby Warburg, art historian, scholar, founder and director of the *Kulturwissenschaftliche Bibliothek Warburg* (KBW)[1] in Hamburg, worked on a great variety of research topics on cultural history in its widest sense. His collection of books, 55.000 volumes, was transferred to London in 1933 and forms part of the library of The Warburg Institute in London, a member institute of the School of Advanced Study of the University of London. His extensive correspondence with scholars in Europe and America is extant in the archive of The Warburg Institute, some 37.000 letters and postcards.[2] They throw light on the topics in which he was interested, from the history of the Renaissance in Florence to postage stamps and playing cards, from art-historical influences of northern European art on southern European art to the Native American serpent ritual, from the peregrination of astrology from east to west, through to Reformation pamphlets, satires, caricatures and much more – all to analyse the creation and shaping to the 'European mentality'.[3]

The volume presents material from The Warburg Institute Archive in London. Warburg is known for having researched the survival of classical antiquity, the area of research which encompassed the history of literature, religion, astrology and art history. In lectures and articles Warburg investigated the 'path ways of culture', which found their most important documentation in Warburg's *Mnemosyne Atlas*.[4]

Warburg kept everything: business cards and private letters, scholarly requests and his correspondence with universities, libraries, archives and publishers in

1 Cf. Diers, M. (ed), *Porträt aus Büchern*; Galitz, R. and Reimers, B. (eds), *Aby M. Warburg*; Stockhausen, T. von, *Die Kulturwissenschaftliche Bibliothek Warburg*; Saxl, F., 'The History of Warburg's Library, 1886–1944'. Gombrich, E. H., *Aby Warburg. An Intellectual Biography*, 325–338.

2 A volume of a selection of Warburg's correspondence has been published by Diers, M., *Warburg aus Briefen*; McEwan, D., *Ausreiten der Ecken. Die Aby Warburg – Fritz Saxl Korrespondenz 1910–1919*; Eadem, *Wanderstrassen der Kultur. Die Aby Warburg – Fritz Saxl Korrespondenz von 1920 bis 1929*.

3 Cf. Warburg, A., 'Orientalisierende Astrologie'; Britt, D., 'Astrology under Oriental Influence', 699–702 and 775.

4 Warnke, M., and Brink, C. (eds), *Aby Warburg (1866–1929)*; Ohrt, R., and Heil, A. (eds), *Aby Warburg: Bilderatlas Mnemosyne*.

Germany and abroad. The archive, therefore, is a rich source in general for the history of scholarship in Warburg's time and in particular for researching Warburg's own work and the work of his colleagues from 1880 to Warburg's death in 1929. In addition, the archive is an important resource for intellectual history in Hamburg until its transfer to London in 1933 and the integration of the new institute, then called The Warburg Institute, in the British academic landscape.

As the author of the original articles and author of this volume, I wish to thank all the journal publishers for having kindly granted me permission to re-use my published articles and illustrations in an expanded English version. The original places of publication for the chapters in this collection are listed with each chapter and in the bibliographical references to published chapters. I wish to express my gratitude to the Director of The Warburg Institute for allowing me to publish selected correspondence in the archive in full by authors for which the Archive holds copyright conditions. All other correspondence is published in agreement with copyright holders. Where copyright holders have not been established, every effort has been made to trace them and obtain permission to reproduce their materials. I therefore welcome any enquiry or information relating to copyright holders.

The chapters in this book are based on articles, originally published in German, Italian and French, and are now presented in an updated English version. They were the fruit of my work as director of the archive of The Warburg Institute in London and as a researcher in a number of archives in Germany. Depending on the subject matter they were published in different specialist journals and book publications in Germany and Austria, Italy and France. I therefore wish to thank Routledge for their interest and encouragement to publish these articles in an English-language volume.

The chapters are arranged according to topics, not chronologically. This seemed to me a more organic presentation but, as of needs, source material is sometimes mentioned or referenced twice. It goes without saying that a large part of the source material is taken from Warburg's and Fritz Saxl's correspondence, the mirror of their collaboration for some 20 years. Saxl, perhaps like no one else, with the exception of his librarian colleague Gertrud Bing, understood Warburg and collaborated with him on many research topics. All but one chapter are microhistories, research essays on specific questions, many involving the genesis and legacy of a particular research concern of Warburg's or Saxl's. The exception is the chapter about Alfons Augustinus Barb, who joined The Warburg Institute only in 1949, but worked on similar topics as Warburg and Saxl.

Over the years and parallel to articles in German, Italian and French, I published articles in English on Warburg and Saxl, which have also appeared in a variety of periodicals. A list with titles of these articles is included in the bibliography. They complement the original articles in German, French and Italian, having as their point of departure the same source material and the same aim, to produce research on particular topics which were addressed in the correspondence of both scholars. In the intervening years a number of topics have been revisited by colleagues and further developed. For their bibliography, please consult the online catalogue of the library holdings of The Warburg Institute in London. I would be very happy if these articles were also republished in one volume one day.

Finally, I would like to thank Nicola Bigwood very much for editing the initial draft of this volume. Her very nuanced command of English stopped the translation from jarring what I was trying to say. Colleagues in this country and abroad discussed with me finer points of translations, and I am indebted to their patience and knowledge. Members of The Warburg Institute, in particular Dr. Clare Lappin and Dr. Richard Gartner, Library; Dr. Claudia Wedepohl and Dr. Eckart Marchand, Archive; and Dr. Paul Taylor, Photographic Collection, generously gave their time for advice and assistance. I wish to express my great gratitude to Oleg Sokolyuk, IT engineer and computer expert, who, with great patience and even greater technical know-how, expertly guided me to avoid a number of pitfalls with IT. Finally, I wish to thank the publishers who encouraged me in taking up this project and saw it to fruition.

Dorothea McEwan

ACKNOWLEDGEMENTS

The publishers and I wish to thank the following for permission to reprint articles in this collection: Ferrara: Franco Cosimo Panini Editore (chapter 1); Torino: Nino Aragno Editore (chapter 2); Tübingen: Tübinger Vereinigung für Volkskunde (chapter 3); Berlin: Akademie-Verlag (chapter 4); Brno: Moravské zemské museum (chapter 5); Murnau; Schloßmuseum des Marktes Murnau (chapter 6); Vienna: Wiener Jahrbuch für Kunstgeschichte (chapter 7); Wiesbaden: Harrassowitz Verlag (chapter 8); Vienna: European University Press (chapter 9); Milan: Mimesis (chapter 10); Berlin: De Gruyter (chapter 11); Dornbirn: Vorarlberger Landesverlag (chapter 12); Berlin: Zeitschrift des Zentrums für Literaturforschung (chapter 13); Eisenstadt: Burgenländisches Landesarchiv und Burgenländische Landesbibliothek (chapter 14); Münster, New York, Munich, Berlin: Waxmann, Zeitschrift für Volkskunde and Oxford: Blackwell (chapter 15); Hamburg: Zeitschrift des Vereins für hamburgische Geschichte (chapter 16); Paris: Revue germanique internationale (chapter 17).

BIBLIOGRAPHICAL REFERENCES TO PUBLISHED CHAPTERS

Chapter 1, (2002), 'Corrispondenze zodiacali e personali. I commenti di Warburg in margine alla conferenza su Palazzo Schifanoia', in Bertozzi, M. (ed) (2002), *Aby Warburg e le metamorfosi degli antichi dei*. Ferrara: Franco Cosimo Panini Editore, 99–113. (2002).

Chapter 2, (2005), '"IDEA VINCIT – Die siegende, fliegende, Idea". Ein künstlerischer Auftrag von Aby Warburg'. Flach, Sabine/Münz-Koenen, Inge/Streisand, Marianne (eds), *Der Bilderatlas im Wechsel der Künste und Medien*. München: Wilhelm Fink Verlag, 121–151. The Italian translation by Benedetta Cestelli Guidi, Benedetta Cestelli (2004), '"Idea Vincit", la volante e vittoriosa Idea. Una commissione artistica di Aby Warburg', was published in Cieri Via, C., Monzani, P. (eds.), *Lo sguardo di Giano. Aby Warburg fra tempo e memoria*. Torino: Nino Aragno Editore, 345–375.

Chapter 3, (2007a), 'Ein Kampf gegen Windmühlen. Warburgs pro-italienische publizistische Initiative'. Korff, Gottfried (Hsg.), *Kasten 117. Aby Warburg und der Aberglaube im Großen Krieg*. Untersuchungen des Ludwig-Uhland-Instituts der Universität Tübingen im Auftrag der Tübinger Vereinigung für Volkskunde. Vol. 105. Tübingen: Tübinger Vereinigung für Volkskunde, 135–163. ISBN 9783932512445. See for a much shortened bilingual English and Italian translation McEwan, D. (2013), 'Due missioni politiche di Aby Warburg in Italia nel 1914–15', in Bertozzi, M., Venturi, G. (eds.), *I molti Rinascimenti di Aby Warburg. Schifanoia*. A cura dell'Istituto di Studi Rinascimentali di Ferrara, vol. 42–43, 2012. Pisa-Roma: Fabbrizio Serra Editore, 2013, 57–79.

Chapter 4, (2007b), 'Zur Entstehung des Vortrages über das Schlangenritual, Motiv und Motivation/Heilung durch Erinnerung'. Bender, Cora Bender/Hensel, Thomas/Schüttpelz, Erhard (eds), *Schlangenritual. Der Transfer der Wissensform vom Tsu'ti'kive der Hopi bis zu Aby Warburgs Kreuzlinger Vortrag*. Forschungskolleg 435 der Deutschen Forschungsgemeinschaft 'Wissenskultur und gesellschaftlicher Wandel'. Vol. 16, Berlin: Akademie Verlag, 267–281.

Chapter 5, (2008), 'Die Pospisil – Warburg Korrespondenz im Warburg Institute'. Hana Dvořákova (ed.), *Hanák na Pacifiku. Zapomenutá osobnost Františka Pospíšila. A Man from Haná on the Pacific Coast. The forgotten figure of František Pospíšil*. Brno: Moravské zemské museum, 197–206. (The additional Czech

Translation by *Hana Dvořákova*, 'Korespondence Pospíšil – Warburg uložená ve Warburgově institute,' 183–196, with the text of his lecture to the Folklore Society in London, untitled, English and Czech, 207–218.)

Chapter 6, (2000), 'Façetten einer Freundschaft: Aby Warburg und James Loeb. Verwandte, Freunde, Wissenschaftler, Mäzene', in *James Loeb, 1867–1933. Kunstsammler und Mäzen*. Exhibition Catalogue, ed. by Brigitte Salmen, Murnau am Staffelsee, April 2000, 75–98.

Chapter 7, (2004a), 'Fritz Saxl und Aby Warburg: Würdigung einer Zusammenarbeit'. Bundesdenkmalamt Wien und Institut für Kunstgeschichte der Universität Wien (eds.): *Wiener Schule. Erinnerung und Perspektiven*. Wiener Jahrbuch für Kunstgeschichte. Wien-Köln-Weimar: Böhlau Verlag, vol. LIII, 139–151.

Chapter 8, McEwan, D., Burtea, B. (2013), 'Eine Trouvaille aus dem Warburg Institute Archive zu Mandäismus und Gnosis'. Voigt, Rainer (ed), *"Durch Dein Wort ward jegliches Ding!" "Through Thy Word All Things were Made!" 2. Mandäistische und samaritanistische Tagung/2nd International Conference of Mandaic and Samaritan Studies. Zum Gedenken an Rudolf Macuch (1919–1993)/ In Honour of Rudolf Macuch (1919–1993)*. Wiesbaden: Harrassowitz Verlag, vol. 4, Mandäistische Forschungen, 137–153.

Chapter 9, (2015), 'Strzygowski im Spiegel der Aby Warburg Korrespondenz. Der Strzygowski-Briefbestand im Warburg Institute London'. Scholz, Piotr/Dlugosz, Magdalena (eds.), *Von Biala nach Wien. Josef Strzygowski und die Kunstwissenschaften. Zum 150. Geburtstag von Josef Strzygowski. Akten der Konferenz Bielsko-Biala (27.-30.3.2012) und Wien (12.10.2012)*. Vienna: European University Press, Dept. für Vergleichende Kunstgeschichte am Kulturwissenschaftlichen Institute an der Maria Curie-Sklodowska Universität in Lublin and Gesellschaft für Vergleichende Kunstforschung in Vienna, 2015, 53–69.

Chapter 10, (2016), 'Far luce nel buio. Aby Warburg e Fritz Saxl discutono su Mitra'. Barale, Alice/Desideri, Fabrizio/Ferretti, Silvia (eds.), *Energia e rappresentazione. Warburg, Panofsky, Wind*. Milano: Mimesis, 119–132. [Italian translation of the English online publication 'Bringing light into darkness. Aby Warburg and Fritz Saxl in conversation on Mithras'. *Aisthesis. rivista on-line del Seminario Permanente di Estetica*. Florence: Firenze University Press. Anno VIII, numero 2, 27–39, publ. November 2015. www.fupress.com/aisthesis.]

Chapter 11, (2021), 'Karikatur als Kriegsdienst: Aby Warburgs "neuer Stil in Wort und Bild", 1914–1918'. *Zeitschrift für Kunstgeschichte*. Berlin: De Gruyter, 2021, vol. 84, issue 1, 78–95.

Chapter 12, (1999), '". . . wahrscheinlich latenter Antisemitismus"', *in Montfort. Vierteljahresschrift für Geschichte und Gegenwart Vorarlbergs*, Dornbirn: Vorarlberger Landesverlag, 51.Jg., 1999, Heft 2, 197–198.

Chapter 13, (2004b), 'Gegen die Pioniere der Diesseitigkeit' and McEwan, D., Treml, M. (2004), 'Aby an Gisela Warburg'. Weigel, Sigrid (ed), *Trajekte*. Berlin: Zeitschrift des Zentrums für Literaturforschung, 2004, 4. Jg., Heft 8, 4–7 und 8–11.

Chapter 14, (2020), '"Das, was ich als Jude vertrete, kann ich auch als Katholik vertreten". Zu Alfons Augustinus Barbs wissenschaftlicher Laufbahn und seinem

Glaubenswechsel'. *Burgenländische Heimatblätter*, 82. Jg., *nos*. 3 und 4, 2020. Eisenstadt: Burgenländisches Landesarchiv und Burgenländische Landesbibliothek, 102–147.

Chapter 15, (2006), 'Der gute Bischof Nikolaus'. Aby Warburg's Interpretation der russischen Übersetzung von *Struwwelpeter* und die politischen Parodien *Struwwelhitler – A Nazi Story Book* und *Schicklgrüber'. Zeitschrift für Volkskunde*. Münster, New York, München, Berlin: Waxmann, 2006/I, 67–90. This article was slightly extended with material from McEwan, Dorothea (1997), 'Aby Warburg und die Figur des Nikolaus im "Russischen Struwwelpeter"'. *German Life and Letters*. Oxford: Blackwell, 1997, vol. L, no. 3, 354–364.

Chapter 16, (2004c), 'Der Palazzo Potetje. Zum Triptychon von Mary Warburg'. *Zeitschrift des Vereins für hamburgische Geschichte*, Hamburg, Band 90, 75–95.

Chapter 17, (2018), 'La *Kulturwissenschaftliche Bibliothek Warburg* à la lumière de ses archives. Entretien avec Dorothea McEwan', in Carole Maigné, Audrey Lieber, Céline Trautmann-Waller (eds.), *La* Kulturwissenschaftliche Bibliothek Warburg *comme laboratoire*. Paris: Revue germanique internationale, 28, 199–209.

ABBREVIATIONS

The following abbreviations and translations have been used throughout:
Tagebuch = Diary

Warburg's personal diary: Notebook, Diary:
'Diary': 1914–9.9.1915: III.10.4.
'Kriegszibaldone': 10.9.1915–27.8.1916: III.10.5.
'Kriesgzibaldone': 28.8.1916–31.12.1916: III.10.6.
'Diary': 1.1.1917–7.1917: III.10.7.
'Diary': 24.7.1917–26.1.1918: III.10.8.
'Kriegszibaldone': 27.1.1918–31.8.1918; III.10.9.

Bibliothekstagebuch = *Journal*, from 1926 onwards. Michels/Schoell-Glass: Michels, Karen, Schoell-Glass, Charlotte (eds.) (2001), *Aby Warburg. Tagebuch der Kulturwissenschaftlichen Bibliothek Warburg. Mit Einträgen von Gertrud Bing und Fritz Saxl.* Berlin: Akademie Verlag.

Zettelkasten = Index card box
Kopierbuch = Copy book
Warburg = Aby Warburg
Saxl = Fritz Saxl
Bing = Gertrud Bing
BFPP *Journal* = Barb Family Private Papers
WIA = Warburg Institute Archive
WIA, GC = General Correspondence
WIA, FC = Family Correspondence
KBW = Kulturwissenschftliche Bibliothek Warburg

n.d. = not dated
n.p. = not paginated

FIGURES

Part I

ARTICLES ON A SELECTION OF WARBURG'S MAIN RESEARCH TOPICS

1

PERSONAL AND ZODIACAL. WARBURG'S COMMENTS ON THE PALAZZO SCHIFANOIA LECTURE IN 1912[1]

Aby Warburg's research into the frescoes in Palazzo Schifanoia, culminating in his lecture 'Italienische Kunst und internationale Astrologie im Palazzo Schifanoia zu Ferrara' ('Italian Art and International Astrology in the Palazzo Schifanoia in Ferrara') at the Tenth International Congress on the History of Art in October 1912 in Rome,[2] was a topic which demonstrated exemplarily the triad of his research foci 'art, religion and history'. In 1924 Warburg expressed his research interests, the interpenetration and cross-fertilisation of art, religion and history with this pithy statement in a letter to his young friend Percy E. Schramm.[3] He brought the same elements together in a letter to Professor Rudolf Larisch of the School for Arts and Crafts in Vienna, using the example of the frescoes in Palazzo Schifanoia and in particular the *Sphaera Barbarica* to demonstrate 'that strange world of the stars, which was made up of elements from Greek wisdom and Oriental fantasy'.[4] In his studies of astrology he looked for correlations between images, on the flux and flow of their shapes and meanings. Astrology, the pre-eminent field for explaining influences which are outside the physical realm of experience yet at the same time are said to affect the physical realm of humanity, was generally thought to be a link between the present and the future and more: that the future would align with some pre-ordained pattern.

This chapter quotes from Warburg's correspondence to show the impact of the art historical Congress in Rome in 1912 and the publication of his lecture in 1922, the reactions by friends and colleagues at the very end of Warburg's

1 Originally published in McEwan, D., 'Corrispondenze zodiacali e personali. I commenti di Warburg in margine alla conferenza su Palazzo Schifanoia', 99–113.

2 Warburg, A., 'Italienische Kunst und internationale Astrologie im Palazzo Schifanoja zu Ferrara', 179–193 and plates XXXVII-XLVII; Britt, D., 'Italian Art and International Astrology in the Palazzo Schifanoia, Ferrara', 563–592 and 732–758.

3 WIA, GC, Warburg to P. Schramm, 11.11.1924. Aby Warburg, German art historian, 1866–1929; Percy, E., 'Schramm German Historian', 1894–1970.

4 WIA, GC, Warburg to R. Larisch, 19.09.1924, whom he commissioned to design a bookplate for the books from the library of the late Franz Boll. Rudolf Larisch, Austrian calligrapher, 1866–1919.

DOI: 10.4324/9781003169024-2

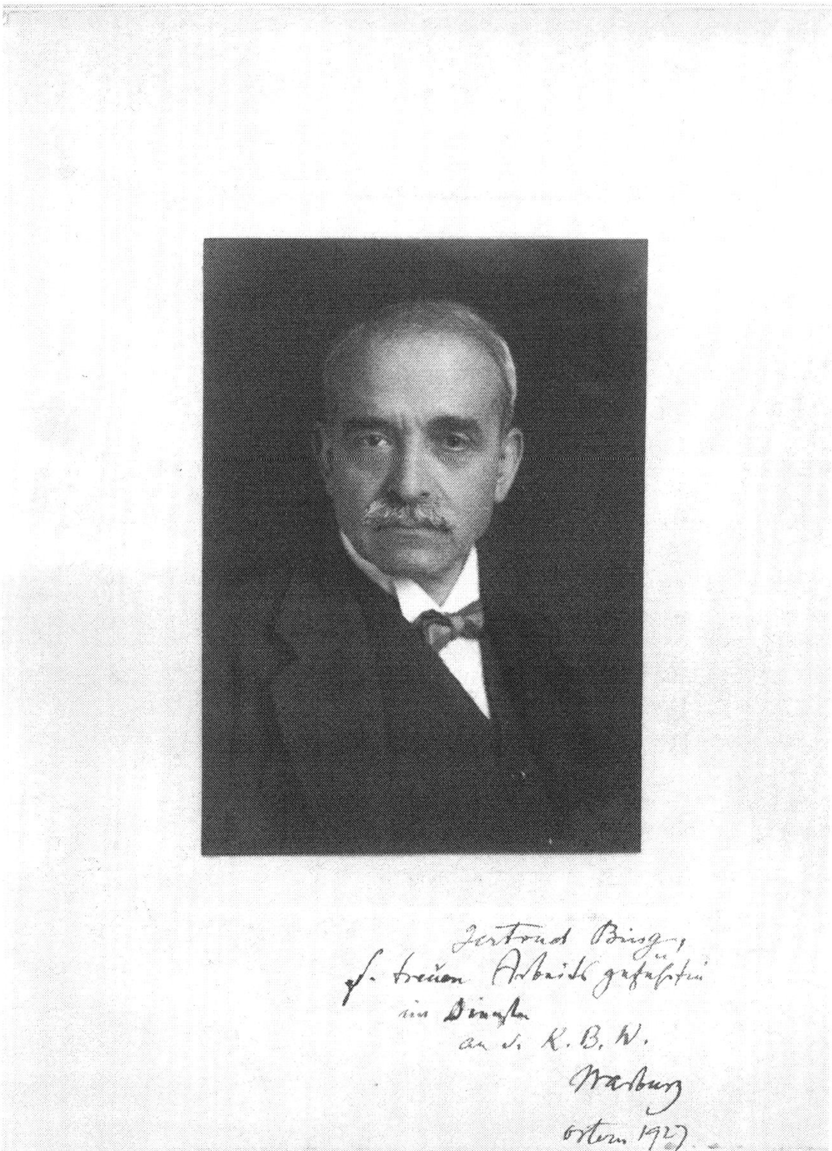

Figure 1.1 Aby Warburg. WIA, Portrait collection. Gertrud Bing, s.[einer] treuen Arbeitsgefährtin im Dienste and.[er] K. B. W. Warburg Ostern 1927'['To Gertrud Bing, his faithful colleague at work in the K, B. W. Warburg Easter 1927'].

Source: © Photo: The Warburg Institute.

stay at the Kreuzlingen sanatorium, Switzerland, and after his return to Hamburg. The publication of the lecture triggered renewed vigour which was to bear fruit in articles on orientalising astrology and the Quattrocento in years to come. Ludwig Binswanger, the director of the Kreuzlingen sanatorium, after having read Warburg's long letter full of news of all his activity in Hamburg in 1925, in particular his lecture course on a research topic first begun twenty years before, agreed: 'This bridge-building to the past, which at the same time always means a move forward, and upward, seems to me the most beautiful aspect of a scholar's career'.[5]

The Correspondence and Diary collections in The Warburg Institute Archive provide: first, the links between the public events and the personal appraisals and reactions to them, the letters to and from his family and close friends at the two pivotal points and locations in his life immediately before, during and after the lecture in 1912; and then secondly, after the publication of the lecture in 1923 and 1924.

In October 1912, before and during the Congress, Warburg just about found time to keep up his correspondence as an artistic consultant with artists and officials of the Hamburg America shipping line who were busily building and decorating the steamship *Imperator*. Further, he exchanged letters with his brother Max on the moves to establish a university in Hamburg. Mostly, however, the correspondence dealt with official Congress matters – publicity, organisation, receptions, programme, matters of protocol, translations and expenses – as Warburg was the treasurer of the organisation of the Congresses and, after the Congress, with letters of thanks, and the letters he exchanged with his wife Mary in Hamburg.

Warburg was highly ambivalent in his own self-assessment. At times he was self-assured, but more often he felt misunderstood, even undervalued both by his family and by the community of scholars in Hamburg and elsewhere. Having read thousands of letters in the General and Family Correspondences and hundreds of pages of Diary entries, I can quote many instances when he expressed doubt and anger, even despair. The exception is the Schifanoia lecture.

The preparations for the Congress taxed Warburg to his limits. He had been a loyal participant of the art history congresses in Germany and knew exactly what he was taking on when he was voted onto the Congress board as treasurer in 1906. He took his task seriously; scores of letters written before and after the Congress testify to his untiring efforts to raise money to publicise the event in Germany and abroad. Warburg was a conscientious board member, keeping in touch with the other members and with the local Italian committee in Rome; he was a good organiser, feeding his ideas into programme-making, into preparations for the receptions, publications, voting procedures and much

5 WIA, GC, L. Binswanger to Warburg, 28.12.1925. Dr. Ludwig Binswanger, Swiss psychiatrist, 1881–1966.

more.[6] He was satisfied when the organisation and framework he had suggested were accepted:

> It is true, that my organisational and scientific ideas have been victorious all along the line. I know there will be problems, but the main thing is: the Congress lives . . . despite the fact that many wise and powerful people in Germany have declared it to be dead.[7]

After his arrival in Rome in early October 1912 he wrote to his wife Mary that, while there were still difficulties to be settled, he did not see that they would be 'insurmountable'. Some 500 participants had registered for the Congress, official subsidies had been obtained, civic honours had been prepared. 'Now then, cool head and calm stomach!'[8] was his prescription for getting through the ordeal that the Congress was for him.

He had travelled to Rome without his wife, despite the fact that his colleagues Paul Clemen, J. A. F. Orbaan[9] and others had arrived with their wives and that Mary was celebrating her 46th birthday on 13 October. Warburg sent her birthday greetings and an apology: 'pity that we cannot celebrate your birthday together but it is more practical like this'. He obviously wanted to concentrate on the task ahead and proceeded to describe the twists and turns of committee discussions.[10] Mary Warburg celebrated by taking her three children on a day trip to Mölln, north of Hamburg, and in the next letter asked her husband whether the expenses could be considered a birthday present for her. She also wrote about the project of a children's opera and asked him to consent to their children Max Adolf and Frede taking part. Finally, she informed him that Pia di Mayo-Gelati would visit her and both would finish the translation of the opening address to the Congress by the president, Rudolf Kautzsch, from 1911.[11] Two days later the translation was finished and dispatched to Rome.[12] On the same day, however, Warburg wrote a short message on a postcard: he was getting anxious, he feared cancellations and deplored the poor organisation and lack of understanding between the Germans and Italians.[13] To add to his anxiety, two days later he was stuck for three quarters of an hour in a lift in the Palazzo Corsini – an experience that made Warburg

6 The collection of letters in WIA, GC, from 1909 to 1913 is dominated by the topic of the Congress in Rome.

7 WIA, FC, Warburg to Mary Warburg, 23.10.1912. Mary Warburg, German Painter and Sculptor, 1866–1934.

8 WIA, FC, Warburg to Mary Warburg, n.d.; after 3.10.1912.

9 Clemen, P., German Art Historian, 1866–1947; Orbaan, J.A.F., Dutch Art Historian, Independent Researcher, 1874–1933.

10 WIA, FC, Warburg to Mary Warburg, 10.09.1912.

11 WIA, FC, Mary Warburg to Warburg, 10.10.1912. Pia di Mayo-Gelati, Italian writer and translator; Rudolf Kautzsch, German art historian, 1868–1945.

12 WIA, GC, Mary Warburg to Warburg, 12.10.1912.

13 WIA, FC, Warburg to Mary Warburg, 12.10.1912.

ask himself 'whether the Congress will be very much more exhausting'. He was pleased that the day trip of his family to Mölln had been such a success and reported that he had spent the afternoon in the Campagna.[14] Apart from these two cards revealing anxiety, the rest of the correspondence was upbeat.

Despite Warburg's lecture being scheduled for 19 October, Mary, surprisingly, asked him how it had gone already on 14 October. She also mentioned that Morris Loeb had died.[15] Professor Morris Loeb, a physical chemist and philanthropist in New York and brother of James Loeb (founder of the Loeb Classical Library), was a member of a banking family with family connections to Warburg: Warburg's brother, Paul Moritz Warburg, had married James's sister Nina Loeb in 1895 and Warburg had sailed to New York for their wedding.[16] Why Mary asked him prematurely about his lecture is not quite clear. She was very supportive and certainly knew the date of Warburg's lecture; she may have made a mistake, or she may have wanted to pad out her letter, which she did quite regularly in her correspondence.

The Congress did not start until 16 October. The days and hours before the opening were spent in committee and private meetings. Warburg was delighted that 'my old Schmarsow', August Schmarsow,[17] professor of art history in Leipzig, turned up at the meetings. This meant that he had an ally on the board and the two managed to defeat the discussion on a change of the bye-laws raised by Paul Clemen.[18] On the day before the official opening Warburg wrote of a 'cosy dinner' with the *Presidenza*, Roberto Papini, Paul Clemen, Federico Hermanin, J. A. F. Orbaan and their wives, Adolfo Venturi, Wilhelm Waetzoldt, Wilhelm Printz, Henry Thode, Max Dvořak and C. Hofstede de Groot.[19] The organisation was 'capable of improvement', but the overall atmosphere among 'us workers' was one of mutual trust, even when there were some 'egotistical blockheads' among the official German delegates. He thanked his wife and Pia di Mayo-Gelati for their translation of the Kautzsch address and signed off: 'Your superhusband, in haste.'[20]

A short postcard on 17 October simply records that the first day of the Congress had gone well, that Kautzsch had bravely given his lecture in Italian and

14 WIA, FC, Warburg to Mary Warburg, 14.10.1912.

15 WIA, GC, Mary Warburg to Warburg, 14.10.1912. Morris Loeb had died of typhoid on 8.10.1912, cf. III.10.3., Diary 1903–1914, n.p., entry for 1912. Morris Loeb, American physical chemist and philanthropist, 1863–1912. See Chapter 2; McEwan, D., 'Façetten einer Freundschaft: Aby Warburg und James Loeb. Verwandte, Freunde, Wissenschaftler, Mäzene'.

16 WIA, GC, Max Warburg to Warburg, 16.10.1912. Max Warburg, German banker, 1867–1946; Paul M. Warburg, German-American Investment Banker, 1868–1932; Nina Loeb, 1870–1946.

17 Founder of the Kunsthistorisches Institut in Florenz, the art history institute in Florence, in 1888. August Schmarsow, German art historian, 1853–1936.

18 WIA, FC, Warburg to Mary Warburg, 14.10.1912.

19 Roberto Papini, Italian art historian and critic, 1883–1957; Federico Hermanin de Reichenfeld, Italian art critic, 1868–1953; Adolfo Venturi, Italian art historian, 1856–1941; Wilhelm Waetzoldt, German art historian, 1880–1945; Wilhelm Printz, German Indologist, 1887–1941; Henry Thode, German art historian, 1857–1920; Max Dvořak, Czech-Austrian art historian, 1874–1921; C. Hofstede de Groot, Dutch art historian, 1863–1930.

20 WIA, FC, Warburg to Mary Warburg, 15.10.1912.

that Warburg had gone to bed late.[21] By now Mary was really impatient. She was waiting for a cable informing her of the success of Warburg's lecture.[22] On 19 October, immediately after his lecture on 'Italian Art and International Astrology in Palazzo Schifanoia in Ferrara', Warburg sent a cable, and his friends, Adolph Goldschmidt, Botho Graef, Alfred Doren, Carl Georg Heise, Wilhelm Waetzoldt, J.A.F. Orbaan, Jan Veth, Paul Kehr and André Aubert, 'overjoyed', sent a postcard to Mary still 'shaken by the huge success of Aby'.[23] Fritz Saxl wrote in his unpublished biography of Warburg:

> Warburg's lecture was unquestionably the climax. . . . Certainly a number of people went away with the impression that they had witnessed the dawn of a new era in the history of art. Wide horizons seemed to open up, the narrow isolationist was challenged, the history of art was linked to the history of religion, the creative genius of the artist was given his place, monumental and popular art treated as a unit, the epoch from antiquity to modern times considered as one whole, and geographical barriers had been broken down.
>
> The Congress had certainly justified the expectations of those who had worked for it, and Warburg had reason to believe that he had not wasted his energies . . .[24]

The next day, Sunday, Warburg wrote a short report to his wife:

> A few quick words before I go and have breakfast with Kehr in Frascati. Yesterday afternoon I spoke for three quarters of an hour (not more) and was completely successful: I even kept the attention of those who did not understand German, and all colleagues were really grateful how I saved the situation because the two previous lectures had been hidebound. The atmosphere at the banquet afterwards was very good. I was not apprehensive.

Immediately after Warburg's lecture Hermanin had summarised it in Italian. Kehr, the sceptic, director of the Royal Prussian Historical Institute, praised his lecture as an 'example of erudition'. He took his place at the banquet next to Warburg and 'we then ruled the scholarly world of Germany and beyond'.[25]

21 WIA, FC, Warburg to Mary Warburg, 17.10.1912.

22 WIA, GC, Mary Warburg to Warburg, 19.10.1912. Adolph Goldschmidt, German art historian, 1863–1944; Alfred Doren, German economic historian, 1869–1934; Botho Graef, German economic historian, 1869–1934; Carl Georg Heise, art historian, 1890–1979; Jan Veth, Dutch painter, 1864–1925; Paul Kehr, German historian, 1860–1944 and André Aubert, Norwegian art historian, 1851–1913.

23 WIA, FC, the friends, as mentioned, to Mary Warburg, 19.10.1912.

24 F. Saxl, Unpublished biography of Warburg, 1944, typed version, WIA, III, 111.1., 72–73. Fritz Saxl, Austrian art historian, 1890–1948.

25 WIA, FC, Warburg to Mary Warburg, 20.10.1912.

Once the Congress had ended, Warburg had time for a thorough appraisal. He wrote to Mary that during his second address to the Congress, he showed a Lumière photograph of the Johann Anton Ramboux watercolour copy of the badly decayed Piero della Francesca fresco in the church of San Francesco in Arezzo, and handed it as the '*ricordo*', the gift of the Conference committee to the editors of the editorial committee proceedings.[26] In the evening there was a concert of old Italian music in Palazzo Corsini. It can be assumed that he enjoyed it as it is a rare mention of musical matters in his entire correspondence. The end of the Congress showed that the board had succeeded in everything, that there was a future for international art history congresses, that there was honest enthusiasm for work.

> I think I can say without exaggeration that I have been victorious in the direction of my policies since 11 November 1908 in Vicollo de' Savelli[27]and confess that the enormous efforts no longer seem pains suffered pointlessly, because they have earned me the sincere friendship of Venturi, Hermanin, Papini, Orbaan and many others. Total strangers have thanked me in most touching ways for the lecture.

It remained for the board to invite the committee to dinner, and it was left to Warburg to decide the menu and the seating order which was 'a friendly business in comparison to the previous days'. He did not feel particularly exhausted and hoped to be in full vigour by the end of the week.[28] Carl Georg Heise, then a young student, noted half a century later that Warburg was 'serene and relaxed'.[29]

Mary congratulated him with cables and letters;[30] she was very proud of his achievements and the esteem in which he was held by others.[31] Warburg surmised that she must have received glowing reports from his friends, notably Waetzoldt, for which he expressed his gratitude.[32]

However, a week after the lecture, when he was still in Rome and packing for his return journey to Hamburg, a change of mood can be detected. He wrote to Mary, 'Rome has shown me clearly what I can do if I am given trust and a space

26 Warburg, A., 'Piero della Francescas Constantinschlacht in der Aquarellkopie des Johann Anton Ramboux', 326–327; Britt, D., 'Piero della Francesca's *Battle of Constantine* in the Watercolor Copy by Johann Anton Ramboux', 339–342 and 490–493. Johann Anton Ramboux, German painter and lithographer, 1790–1866.

27 The administrative headquarters for the congress in Rome. WIA, GC, Warburg to H. Brockhaus, 12.11.1908, Copy book II, 436, 435, 437, 438; Warburg to H. Brockhaus, 12.11.1908 with the detailed report of his trip to Rome and the meeting on 10 November 1908, at which he had been able to solve some organisational problems. Heinrich Brockhaus, German art historian, 1858–1941.

28 WIA, FC, Warburg to Mary Warburg. The letter has three pages: the first two are dated 22.10.1912, the third 23.10.1912.

29 Heise, C.G., *Persönliche Erinnerungen an Aby Warburg*, 40. See also the commented edition, Björn and Schäfer, *Carl Georg Heise*.

30 WIA, GC, Mary Warburg to Warburg, 24.10.1912.

31 WIA, GC, Mary Warburg to Warburg, 23.10.1912.

32 WIA, FC, Warburg to Mary Warburg, 27.10.1912.

in which to manoeuvre. Both are lacking in Hamburg'.[33] Contrary to his lifelong habit of keeping a diary, there is only one short statement referring to the Congress, not on the events or people he had met, but on how he appraised the situation in Hamburg after returning from Rome. On 8 October he had noted the death of Morris Loeb; immediately afterwards he simply recorded, without giving dates, 'Gardone with Fritzens', the meeting in Gardone on Lake Garda, where he interrupted his return journey to Hamburg for two days to meet his brother Fritz and Anna Beata, Warburg's sister-in-law. Back in Hamburg, he wrote, after complaining of toothache, 'It is difficult to endure these feelings of uselessness in the gloom of Hamburg. Ageing is all around me, in contrast – place for the young. . . . The university memorandum – summer courses'.[34] This reaction, after the experience of the 'Roman rejoicing' as Saxl put it thirty years later,[35] reveals Warburg's deep dissatisfaction with the intellectual situation prevailing in Hamburg. Saxl spelt it out: 'It was hard to give up Italy once again, to resume volunteering in Hamburg as a sick-nurse, whenever the symptoms of spiritual illness showed'.[36]

What were those symptoms? The realisation of the university project, for which the Warburg family had donated a large sum of money, dragged on and Warburg was extremely impatient. The golden glow of his experience in Rome had given way to the gloom of political realities in autumnal Hamburg. Higher education was supplied by the so-called Colonial Institute without the full range of academic subjects in the humanities. For Warburg this meant that he had to continue with his work outside a university framework. The decision by the Senate in Hamburg in 1913 not to establish a university was a hard blow, but Warburg wrote a defiant letter to his friend Franz Boll,[37] scathing in his condemnation of 'wire pullers', 'obstructionists' and 'Philistines':

> In the end it will not matter whatever they do. The bridge will be constructed and we shall have served as the material of which it is built. We are like the stone which is ground to dust. Others will walk across our concrete bridge without realizing that it conceals the painful preparation by the sand mill.[38]

In November 1912, however, not everything was gloomy. There were letters which reminded Warburg of his triumph. Participants of the Congress wrote to him expressing their gratitude for his devotion and the lecture to the Congress.

33 WIA, FC, Warburg to Mary Warburg, 26.10.1912.

34 WIA, III, 10.3, Diary 1903–1914, entry for 1912, n.p.

35 Saxl, F., Unpublished Biography of Warburg, handwritten version, dated 1944. WIA, III, 111.1, p. 72. In the typed version, the sentence reads 'How difficult it is to endure one's futility in the Hamburg crepuscule'. WIA, III, 111.2, 'D'.

36 Saxl, F., Unpublished Biography of Warburg, 1944, typed version, WIA, III, 111.1., 72–73.

37 Franz Boll, German classicist, 1867–1924.

38 WIA, GC, Warburg to F. Boll, 13.11.1913. Saxl's English translation in the typed version of his unpublished biography of Warburg, 1944, WIA, III, 111.1., 69–70.

André Aubert was the first person who thanked Warburg after his lecture, called him the scholar who had never lost sight of the idea of the Congress, who had fought for it and had won. He sent him the text of the toast made to Warburg at the banquet in the Palace Hotel in Rome on 23 October 1912:

> . . . Caro Amico. Amico carissimo, diamante del nero carbone! . . . Your beautiful black eyes, beautiful above all else because of your soul, they glitter dazzlingly with white sparks of wit and gracious, meaning-laden malice. But in their deep black shadows I have sensed and felt a pain. I explained it thus: Your well-furnished mind has fought a hard fight to find the expression – you have won! You have won gloriously! And, from now on, you will spread the victory inside you and outside, from victory to victory. Not only for your friends, who believe in you. But for the world, for scholarship. For me the lecture by Aby Warburg was the highlight of the congress. I invite you, ladies and gentlemen, to give a toast in the Norwegian way, three times three "Long live Aby Warburg"!!![39]

Adolph Goldschmidt wrote that the success of the Congress was due to Warburg;[40] Venturi thanked him,[41] to which Warburg replied that he and his German colleagues truly appreciated and enjoyed the 'vitality' of the Congress in Rome.[42] Even Richard Kautzsch, who had gone to Rome with undisguised misgivings, confessed that the Congress was Warburg's achievement and that everybody was deeply indebted to him. He touched on the unease which he had felt towards the end of the Congress, because Warburg managed to turn factual differences of opinion into objections on moral grounds. He hoped that Warburg would accept him as he was just as Kautzsch accepted Warburg.[43] Wilhelm Waetzoldt, his erstwhile assistant, thanked him for having made it possible for him to travel to Rome; he had enjoyed the Congress and had learnt a great deal,[44] and Alfred Doren wrote in a similar vein.[45]

Warburg himself repeatedly stated that he was content with the Congress. In a letter to Roberto Papini he admitted that he had fond memories of it and that everything had gone very well.[46] In a letter to Franz Boll he declared that he was happy with his lecture. He thanked him for his help,[47] since Boll's and Carl

39 WIA, GC, A. Aubert to Warburg, 23.10.1912.
40 WIA, GC, A. Goldschmidt to Warburg, 4.11.1912.
41 WIA, GC, A. Venturi to Warburg, 14.11.1912.
42 WIA, GC, Warburg to Venturi, 18.11.1912.
43 WIA, GC, R. Kautzsch to Warburg, 16.11.1912.
44 WIA, GC, W. Waetzoldt to Warburg, 23.11.1912.
45 WIA, GC, A. Doren to Warburg, 15.12.1912.
46 WIA, GC, Warburg to R. Papini, 3.11.1912, Copy book V, 84.
47 WIA, GC, Warburg to F. Boll, 9.11.1912, Copy book IV, 383, 385, 384.

Bezold's zodiacal research[48] had explained the system of decans which helped Warburg to make the link, to 'read' the frescoes in Palazzo Schifanoia. In a letter to his good friend 'Alfresco', Doren, he wrote,

> I am pleased that despite everything you cherish the memory of Rome and I am really happy that I have not involved my friend in a tiring and thankless adventure. I, like you, cherish the memory although I returned from Rome with influenza that troubled me for weeks.[49]

He realised that the Congress in Rome, in which he had invested so much enthusiasm, committee work as well as money, and which he had urged his friends and colleagues from Germany and abroad to attend, was a high point of his life. Indeed, a great success. To Otto Friedrich Theodor Lewald, director at the Ministry of the Interior, he expressed his satisfaction with the Congress;[50] he thanked Federico Hermanin for all his work[51] and Paul Kehr for his support of the art history Congress and the skilful way he had guided the German delegation.[52]

Yet, at the same time, the work to plan and run the Congress with the committee had taken a heavy toll on Warburg. Both in the run-up to the Congress and afterwards, Warburg's letters to Arthur Haseloff[53] of the Royal Prussian Historical Institute in Rome, a member of the local committee, were full of requests, questions, admonitions, and mostly complaints: in mid-November 1912 he complained that he had heard from no one since returning from Rome. He requested news of Orbaan and asked him for a financial statement so that he could release funds to settle expenses incurred. The only really weak point in the organisation had been the Congress office – a complaint which Haseloff was to hear more than once.[54]

A long article in the prestigious *Vossische Zeitung* gave a thorough description of the Congress. Warburg was credited with having done more than perhaps any other lecturer to make the Congress come alive. Thoroughly and with an acute mind he had charted the influence of astrological views and illustrations on the art of the early Renaissance, as shown in the cycle of frescoes by Cosmé Tura, Francesco del Cossa and Galasso Galassi for Duke Borso d'Este in Ferrara. It

48 Boll, F., *Sphaera*; See also Bezold, C., *Zenit- und Aequatorialgestirne am babylonischen Fixsternhimmel*; Boll and Bezold, *Sternglaube und Sterndeutung*. Carl Bezold, *German orientalist*, 1859–1922.

49 WIA, GC, Warburg to A. Doren, 18.11.1912.

50 WIA, GC, Warburg to O.F.T. Lewald, 17.11.1912, Copy book V, 87. O.F.T. Lewald, German administrator and civil servant, 1860–1947.

51 WIA, GC, Warburg to F. Hermanin, 6.12.1912, Copy book V, 92, 93.

52 WIA, GC, Warburg to P. Kehr, 28.12.1912, Copy book IV, 431, 432.

53 Arthur Haseloff, German art historian, 1872–1955.

54 WIA, GC, Warburg to A. Haseloff, 12.11.1912.

was Warburg who had explained the link between all the figures in the paintings, which had only been surmised as representing astrology until then.[55]

However, this newspaper cutting of 26 October 1912 (sent by Wilhelmine Oppenheim, a distant relative who had attended the Congress) might not have reached Warburg until August 1925, as there is no post from Oppenheim extant after the Congress. It is filed together with Warburg's copy of the Congress Proceedings, the *Atti del X Congresso internazionale di storia dell'Arte*, which he received on 20 November 1923 and into which he entered in pencil 'after eleven years'. Below the printed title he wrote 'On the metamorphosis of pagan gods. A fairy tale from reality'. The outbreak of World War I had put a stop to the work of editing and publishing the Proceedings. Only after the end of the war was work resumed and completed in 1923. When the Proceedings finally arrived, the world had changed as had Warburg: he was now a sick man. The initial joy and success he experienced had long given way to despair and illness.

The publication of the Schifanoia lecture, late as it was, appeared when Warburg was in the Sanatorium Bellevue in Kreuzlingen, Switzerland. From time to time from January 1922 onwards, there had been sporadic letters from Rome to Fritz Saxl and Warburg with requests for photographic plates, for explanations as to who would pay for the costs of printing the colour plate of the Ramboux copy, with promises of the impending completion of the publication, etc.[56] Saxl was by then director of the KBW library and Warburg's trusted friend.[57] By August 1923 Saxl had received a copy of the whole publication and three months later the long-awaited offprints of Warburg's lecture, which he speedily dispatched on behalf of Warburg to friends and colleagues, such as G. Agnelli in Ferrara[58] and Wilhelm Niemeyer in Hamburg,[59] among others.

Coming in the autumn of 1923, after the important lecture on the Pueblo Indians on 21 April 1923, the publication of the *Atti* was a boost to Warburg, another impetus to continue writing and lecturing. In a letter from April 1924 he explained the Schifanoia frescoes to his daughters, Marietta (25) and Frede (21): 'I will try to show you with the aid of a table the way from Cossa to Kepler'. He wrote clearly and vividly about Manilius[60] and Mars, about Perseus, 'the activity monster'

55 Schöner, R., 'Von den römischen Kongressen', 26.10.1912, 7, kept with copy of *Atti*, WIA, 83.5. with a note that Wilhelmine Oppenheim sent it to Warburg on 05.08.1925. Cosmé Tura, Italian painter, 1430–1495; Francesco del Cossa, Italian painter, 1430–1477; Galasso Galassi, Italian painter, 1423–1473; Borso d'Este, Duke of Ferrara, 1413–1471.

56 WIA, GC, for instance Vittorio Moschini to Warburg, 18.01.1922. Vittorio Moschini, Italian art historian, 1896–1976.

57 See Chapter 12, Figure 12.1., Warburg's portrait photograph with the dedication to his friend Fritz Saxl, 2.9.1916.

58 WIA, GC, G. Agnelli to F. Saxl, 9.8.1923. Giuseppe Agnelli, Italian bibliographer, 1856–1940.

59 WIA, GC, W. Niemeyer to F. Saxl, 18.9.1923. Wilhelm Niemeyer, German art historian, 1874–1960.

60 Marcus Manilius, Roman astrologer, 1st century CE.

and about groups of stars, such as the 'stellar divinity' and Agostino Chigi.[61] He referred to the frescoes in a letter to his brother Max, calling the lecture on the frescoes 'a historical psychology of human expression'. He stated that he himself had healed his troubled mind in the twelve months from April 1923, starting with the lecture on the Pueblo Indians and culminating in Ernst Cassirer's visit to Kreuzlingen in April 1924[62] and, one should add, the publication of his Schifanoia lecture. Warburg sent one offprint with the personal dedication to Saxl: 'To Fritz Saxl, his faithful helper, in gratitude Warburg, Kreuzlingen, 12 April 1924'.[63] Astrology, the intersection of the world of symbols with the world of images, the worldview of religion or myth with the worldview of reason, had originally brought Fritz Saxl and Warburg together in 1910.[64]

He also explained the frescoes in the Palazzo Schifanoia in a letter to Professor U. von Wilamowitz-Moellendorff,[65] providing a lucid synopsis of the topic, which Saxl called 'a work of art'.[66] Warburg was very pleased that Wilamowitz was going to speak on 'Zeus' in the Warburg library lecture series in May 1924 and reminded Wilamowitz of a conversation they had had some fifteen years earlier. Wilamowitz had agreed with Warburg, that Hamburg needed an academic institution like a cultural-historical library. This had been achieved and more so, the university had been established 'which really made the library an organ, which plays a vital part in the circulation of ideas'. Warburg proceeded in his seven-page letter to give a summary of the process of recognition and acceptance of classical symbols in the cosmological cycle of frescoes in the Palazzo Schifanoia and the Farnesina.[67] In particular he highlighted the figure of Perseus, the essence of power, depicted as the heroic winged saviour in the sky who changed into the dark figure of the executioner, the bringer of fate to heavily burdened humanity. 'The fate of Perseus reveals the problem which is posed by the process of re-establishing classical antiquity from its post-classical servitude. How do the monsters win back their wings for the ether?' At the very end, Warburg encouraged Wilamowitz to put the branch of an olive tree on the altar of 'Minerva memor', as he put it, the goddess of the arts, for her 'to send Perseus to liberate the prisoner of Kreuzlingen, so that he can offer thanks to Minerva Medica at home' (the goddess Minerva worshipped in her temple in Rome).[68] The Proceedings with the article on the frescoes

61 WIA, GC, Warburg to daughters Marietta and Frede Warburg, 18.4.1924. Johannes Kepler, German astronomer, 1571–1630; Agostino Chigi, Italian banker, 1466–1520. Marietta Warburg, eldest child of Aby Warburg, married Braden, 1899–1973; Frede Warburg, youngest child of Aby Warburg, married Prag, 1904–2004.

62 WIA, GC, Warburg to Max Warburg, 16.4.1924. Ernst Cassirer, German philosopher, 1874–1945.

63 WIA, III.83.6.13.

64 cf. McEwan, D., *Ausreiten der Ecken*.

65 WIA, GC, Warburg to U. von Wilamowitz-Moellendorff, 23.04.1924. Ulrich von Wilamowitz-Moellendorff, German classicist, 1848–1931.

66 WIA, GC, F. Saxl to Mary Warburg, 23.4.1924.

67 The Villa Farnesina in Rome.

68 WIA, GC, Warburg to U. von Wilamowitz-Moellendorf, 23.4.1924.

of the astrological cycle in the Palazzo Schifanoia had more than art-historical or zodiacal importance to him: its publication had marked a special point in his recovery.

Reactions to the Schifanoia article from his friends and colleagues, though not instant, were favourable. In the course of 1924, after his return to Hamburg, Warburg continued to send out copies of his articles and received letters of thanks and appreciation from Robert Eisler,[69] Franz Dornseiff,[70] and Alfred Doren.[71] Wilhelm Gundel expressed his hope that Warburg would soon publish his research on the Salone in Padua.[72] The pianist and friend of the family Julia Sauer wrote that there was no doubt that thoughts of classical antiquity entered medieval Europe in calendar pictures.[73] Carl Melchior thanked him.[74] By October 1924 Warburg took up the subject of the Schifanoia lecture with Federico Hermanin saying he wanted to add a short, important piece of information to Hermanin's book on the Farnesina, namely the date of birth of Agostino Chigi, as calculated by the late Franz Boll, K. Graff of the planetarium in Bergedorf/Hamburg and Warburg himself.[75] Richard Reitzenstein thanked him for the article and praised his work and his research into the survival of classical antiquity, an approach which he, as a philologist, welcomed.[76]

From a distance of twelve years, after World War I had started and finished, at the very end of his years in various sanatoriums, Warburg's self-assessment was clear. In the spring of 1924, in a letter to his friend, the historian Robert Davidsohn in Florence, to whom he had sent a copy of the *Atti*, Warburg wrote how pleased he was with Davidsohn's favourable reaction and simply stated that the lecture was 'my best'.[77] It had stood the test of time. And the publication, coming as it did during his stay in a sanatorium, infused him with new vigour and health. The lecture was thus of twofold importance to Warburg's life: firstly, it explained the iconographical programme of the frescoes in the Palazzo Schifanoia: the 36 decans, the astrological images, which had developed and changed over the centuries and cultures, a prime example of 'the pathways and networks of thoughts',[78] the journeys of ideas, images, and their metamorphoses. Secondly, it gave him the impetus to continue with his work of research, writing and giving lectures, which he was to

69 Robert Eisler, Austrian polymath, 1882–1949.

70 WIA, GC, F. Dornseiff to F. Saxl, 12.6.1924. Franz Dornseiff, German art historian, 1888–1960.

71 WIA, GC, A. Doren to F. Saxl, 6.7.1924.

72 WIA, GC, W. Gundel to Warburg, 1908.1924. Wilhelm Gundel, German classicist, 1880–1945.

73 WIA, GC, J. Sauer to Warburg, 28.08.1924. Julia Sauer, wife of Emil von Sauer, both German pianists.

74 WIA, GC, C. Melchior to Warburg, 30.9.1924. Carl Melchior, German banker, 1871–1933.

75 WIA, GC, Warburg to F. Hermanin, 1.10.1924. Kasimir Graff, Polish-German astronomer, 1878–1950.

76 WIA, GC, R. Reitzenstein to Warburg, 19.11.1924. Richard Reitzenstein, German classicist, 1861–1931.

77 WIA, GC, Warburg to R. Davidsohn, 29.4.1924. Robert Davidsohn, German historian, 1853–1937.

78 E.g. WIA, GC, Saxl to Warburg, 23.4.1913 and 29.4.1913.

term 'cultural-historical exercises', an expression carrying the flavour of religious exercises as practised in retreats.[79] One had to undergo them, endure them, like a ritual cleansing and invigoration. The past had caught up with him. In the Serpent lecture of April 1923 he drew on the American journey of 1895–1896, and in his correspondence after the publication of the Schifanoia lecture in November 1923 he drew on his research of planets and planet children begun some twenty years before. There is a certain parallelism in this to Lessing's metaphor of working hard and digging deep, which became Lessing's famous characterisation of himself: 'I do not feel that living spring within me that wells up by its own power, and by its own power gushes forth in such rich, fresh, and pure jets. I must pump it all out of me through applying pressure and pipes'.[80] This image of working hard to 'pump it all out' may be said to apply to Warburg as well. His devotion to mundane tasks like administrative work for the Congress committee or his intense thoroughness and meticulous research, culminating in public lectures, sapped his strength. But in 1923–1924, with the publication of the Schifanoia lecture, he knew that he had 'pumped out' a piece of research which he himself for once accepted as his 'best'.

79 WIA, GC, Warburg to Mrs. Toni Lüders, 1.6.1926. Toni E.W. Lüders, née Tönnießen, director of a speech and language school in Hamburg, 1893–1979.

80 Gotthold Ephraim Lessing, *Hamburgische Dramaturgie*, vol. XLIII, 209, 19.04.1768. Quote in Gombrich, E., 'Lessing', 133. Gotthold Ephraim Lessing, German philosopher and author, 1729–1781; Ernst Hans Gombrich, Austrian-British art historian, 1909–2001.

2

'IDEA VINCIT', 'THE VICTORIOUS, FLYING IDEA'. AN ARTISTIC COMMISSION BY ABY WARBURG[1]

Introduction

'Machine art' or 'art expressed by machines' was the modern-sounding, yet ultimately quite helpless, comment from James Loeb when the linocut 'Idea Vincit' winged its way from Hamburg to his residence in Murnau am Staffelsee. Loeb, an American ex-banker, living in southern Germany, founder of the prestigious Loeb Classical Library, philanthropist and life-long friend of Aby Warburg, to whom he was related by marriage, received a print of the 'Idea Vincit' linocut like a good number of Warburg's friends, family members and colleagues. Loeb sounded genuine in his acceptance note, albeit a bit hesitant: 'The likes of us first have to look at it and get inside it'. He mused that 'machine art' or graphic art, with its depiction of machines and steel constructions, was a symptom of the times, which art historians in the 25th century would find as justifiably typical of our times as we today find the mathematical and related symbols in Dürer's 'Melencolia I' typical of his time. Loeb, however, in his comment on the written words appearing on the linocut, applauded Warburg's choice of three names, Briand, Chamberlain, Stresemann, as a highly apposite motto and more, 'really inspired'.[2]

1 Originally published in German in McEwan, D., 'IDEA VINCIT – "Die siegende, fliegende 'Idea', 121–151, based on the Italian translation by Benedetta Cestelli Guidi, in Guidi, B.C., '"Idea Vincit", la volante e vittoriosa Idea. Una commissione artistica di Aby Warburg', 345–375.

2 WIA, GC, J. Loeb to A. Warburg, 14.1.1927. James Loeb, American-German philanthropist, 1867–1933. Gustav Stresemann, German statesman, 1878–1929; Aristide Briand, French statesman, 1862–1932; Joseph Austen Chamberlain, British statesman, 1863–1937. The German Foreign Minister Gustav Stresemann saw in a political rapprochement the best opportunity for Germany to achieve its main goal, namely a revision of the Treaty of Versailles. Stresemann, French Foreign Minister Briand and British Foreign Secretary Chamberlain, the signatories of the Locarno Pact, were jointly awarded the Nobel Peace Prize in 1926.

The Warburg Institute does not hold a copy of the linocut, but from descriptions in the manuscript sources a copy of the linocut was located in The William Hayes Fogg Art Museum of Harvard University, kept in the Papers of Paul J. Sachs collection. See figure 2.3. I am indebted

DOI: 10.4324/9781003169024-3

Warburg, however. was not convinced by or satisfied with Loeb's appraisal. In his reply to Gertrud Bing, the librarian of the KBW in Hamburg and a trusted friend and secretary, who had sent the linocut to Loeb, Warburg spelt it out that Loeb had not understood the symbolism.[3] Warburg worked, particularly in the five years before his death in 1929, on the life of symbols.[4] He investigated the meaning of symbols, both ancient images, determining meaning even in much later settings, and modern images, assembling archetypical motifs. During this period he worked on three projects. First, the 'Bilderatlas' or 'Mnemosyne Atlas', mapping the pathways of images from classical antiquity onwards. To demonstrate the movement of images he used photographs of paintings, medals, sculpture, architecture, all assembled on movable screens, a superb teaching aid as he could alter the composition of one screen easily and quickly. The second project was an exhibition in connection with the establishment of the Planetarium in Hamburg. In order to understand astronomy, one has to look at its forerunner, astrology and the history of astrology. The third topic arose from his life-long love of stamp collecting and was based on his interest in the psychological make-up of different cultures and their self-image through the medium of the postage stamp, a new channel expressing symbolic traditions.

The basic premise that an 'idea', the mental concept, comes first and that its visual representation, its image, is its result, making the 'idea' victorious, had long been advocated by Warburg and found expression in the arrangement of the books in his library: he created four main categories in which books were shelved, ascending from Orientation to Image, from there to Word and finally to Dromenon ('Action'). This arrangement, in use in Hamburg with its many sub-divisions, was reversed when the books of the KBW were finally arranged in a purpose-built library building in London. In London they started with Image followed by Word, Orientation and Action.[5] Underlying both arrangements is the concept of an 'idea' winning through, the place of the 'mental space' being the goal: 'It is the way from the monster to the idea' ('Es ist der Weg vom Monstrum zur Idee'.)[6] The 'idea' then is not an abstract, but a living entity, a thought which brings to bear and fruition other thoughts and thereby leads to actions.

One example of an 'idea' taking off is demonstrated in this linocut, which Warburg commissioned from the artist Otto Heinrich Strohmeyer.[7] What was the context for Warburg approaching Strohmeyer and what did he want to demonstrate with the linocut?

In 1926 Warburg was engaged in researching postage stamps as a documentation of culture, as art representing a country and symbolising its achievements.

to Karen Michels and Ian B. Jones for their advice and assistance in this matter. Albrecht Dürer, German painter and printmaker, 1471–1528.

3 WIA, GC, Warburg to Bing, 16.1.1927.

4 cf. Gombrich, E.H., *Aby Warburg*, 260–282.

5 cf. Settis, S., 'Warburg continuatus. Description d'une bibliothèque', 122–169.

6 WIA, III.82.5, last sentence of draft paper, not featured in the printed version by Britt, D., 'Italian Art and International Astrology in the Palazzo Schifanoia, Ferrara', 563–592.

7 Otto Heinrich Strohmeyer, German architect, graphic artist and sculptor, 1895–1967, working from 1925 onwards in Hamburg; cf. Italiaander, R., *Gleise und Nebengleise des O. H. Strohmeyer*.

As such, postage stamps signalled something different from medals, posters, landscapes, paintings. They revealed the 'psychology of a state',[8] exemplified by representing heads of state[9] or artists, inventors or memorable events in the life of a country or landscapes and buildings. Warburg explained to Franz Fuchs of the Deutsche Museum, Munich, in support of setting up a section on postage stamps in the museum, that the picture on a postage stamp was the mirror of the contemporary culture of a country. As such, the stamp was the most important object for a history of art which attempted to interpret art by looking at symbols.[10]

The *Graf Zeppelin* and the aviator Hugo Eckener

Warburg's pursuit of understanding and interpreting symbols led him early on to the stories postage stamps tell. Before World War I he mooted a publication project with the publishers B. G. Teubner in Leipzig to document the historical art development of the postage stamp. Teubner did not take up the suggestion, rather – with an eye to sales – suggested a book which would also feature information on stamp collecting[11] and cover all aspects of philately,[12] something which Warburg did not take any further. Warburg did collect stamps; he sent stamp collection catalogues to sons of friends, notably Wulf Rohland;[13] and he wrote to publishers of catalogues pointing out the shortcomings of editions and suggesting improvements for further editions.[14] In 1924, in the first winter after his return to Hamburg from years in a sanatorium in Kreuzlingen, Switzerland, Warburg speedily took up his work, scouring newspapers and book catalogues, purchasing books for the library, reacting to daily news in the

8 'Die Bildersprache des Weltverkehrs' ['The metaphorical language of world traffic'] was the title of Warburg's lecture in the KBW on 13 August 1927. 'Die Briefmarke als Kulturdokument' ['The postage stamp as cultural document'] was the title of the dual lecture by E. Redslob and Warburg in the KBW on 14 August 1926, published in *Philatelisten-Zeitung* (1.9.1927), Gössnitz, Heft 9, 118. Edwin Redslob, German art historian, 1884–1973.

9 On the theme of the importance of people shown on a postage stamp: Warburg kept a photograph of a house in the country, in Blankenese, near Hamburg, and made a picture postcard out of it. It has no message, signature or addressee, but the 'stamp' is a small oval photograph showing the heads of two children, one of them his daughter Marietta, the other could be James Paul Warburg, American banker, 1896–1969. WIA, GC, Anonymous, 1900.

10 WIA, GC, Warburg to F. Fuchs, 10.2.1927. Franz Fuchs, German scientist, 1881–1971.

11 WIA, GC, B.G. Teubner to Warburg, 30.12.1913.

12 WIA, GC, B.G. Teubner to Warburg, 3.1.1914.

13 Wulf Rohland (1911–1989), son of his friend Milly Becker-Rohland, was a sickly child and for a long time bed-ridden. Warburg sent him chocolates and postage stamps for many years. After Warburg's postage stamp lecture in August 1927 Wulf thanked him and explained the difference in Warburg's approach to postage stamps and his own approach: Warburg was the art historian, whereas Wulf was the collector, looking for the value of the stamp, the details. Nevertheless, he took the lesson of Warburg's lecture to heart: he had learnt not to see in the portrait of a ruler the person, but the symbol for the state. WIA, GC, W. Rohland to Warburg, 11.09.1927. Milly Becker-Rohland, sister of German painter Paula Becker-Rohland, 1874–1949.

14 WIA, GC, Warburg to Herbert Munk, 7.3.1927. Warburg suggested urgently a second edition of Bungerz's book on philately (see Bungerz, A., *Grosses Lexikon der Philatelie*), as the first edition (1923) was riddled with mistakes. Herbert Munk, German philatelist, 1875–1953.

city of Hamburg and the state of Germany and following general developments in art, industry and inventions. The airship *Graf Zeppelin*, a feat of German engineering, caught his imagination. He read about the airship, urged members of his family to attend lectures by Dr. Hugo Eckener, pilot of the first trip by an airship to America,[15] tried to secure tickets for himself[16] and asked his brother Felix in New York to confirm reports that the first air freight was a box of toys.[17]

Years before, he had seen two 'arazzi', wall hangings, in the private rooms of the Palazzo Doria in Rome, which he had visited on the occasion of the Tenth International Congress on the History of Art in Rome in 1912, depicting scenes from the life of Alexander the Great, conquering the world (see figure 2.1). The wall hanging

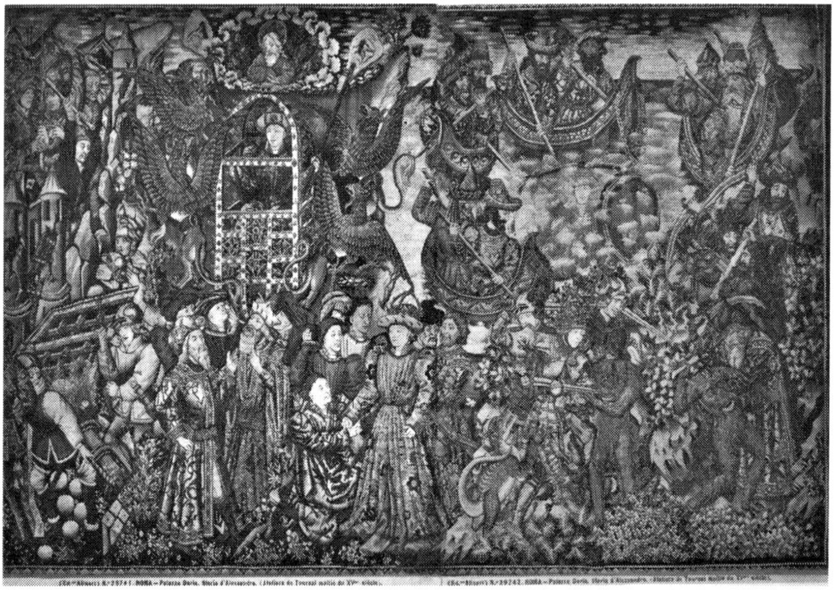

Figure 2.1 Wall hanging, 15th century, Rome, Palazzo Doria. Warburg (1913). Britt, D. (1999), 'Airship and Submarine in the Medieval Imagination', vol.1, 333–337 and 487–490, Figure 64. WIA, III.107.6, panel 34, no.9. Left: Alexander's ascent with the griffins. Right: The journey to the depths of the Sea.

Source: Photo: The Warburg Institute.

15 WIA, GC, Warburg to his brother Max M. Warburg, 10.12.1924. Hugo Eckener, manager of the airship *Zeppelin*, 1868–1954.

16 WIA, GC, Warburg to Gesellschaft für Auslandskunde, 4.2.1925.

17 WIA, GC, Warburg to his brother Felix M. Warburg, 5.11.1924. The 1928 book by Hugo Eckener (see Eckener, H., *Die Amerikafahrt des "Graf Zeppelin"*), does not mention the contents of the payload. Felix M. Warburg, German-American banker and philanthropist, 1871–1937.

depicted two scenes from the life of Alexander the Great, conquering the world, Alexander's journey into heaven and under the sea. In 1913, Warburg had published an essay, 'Airship and Submarine in the Medieval',[18] in which he explained the visual representation of the *Romance of Alexander*, the flights of fancy when Alexander ascended into the skies with a pair of griffins and dived down into the depths of the sea in a crystal boat: 'The king is seen flying aloft, to the amazement of the bystanders, in a metal cage drawn by four griffins; nearby, we see him lowered into the sea in a glass tub'.[19] In the final paragraph of his article he stressed the 'inner energy', the will inherent in people to master their universe.[20] In 1913 he had used picture postcards in his private correspondence to his wife, showing the airship, the pilot-in-chief Gluud and the crew.[21] He also sent picture postcards to Arndt von Holtzendorff of the Hamburg America Line, one for the addressee and one to be forwarded to Hugo Eckener as an invitation to discuss with him steps to popularise the idea of air travel[22] – if need be with a story from the *Romance of Alexander*.

When presidential elections were looming, Warburg mentioned Eckener's name as a possible contender to Hans Luther, Finance Minister from 1923 to 1925 and Prime Minister from 1925 onwards,[23] and to Walter Kluge of the Reich Chancellory[24] and requested background information on Eckener from Felix von Eckardt, editor-in-chief of the *Hamburger Fremdenblatt*.[25] Von Eckardt did not think that Eckener would make a good president; he was too ponderous and inflexible.[26] Warburg berated the *Vossische Zeitung* for printing an article, 'probably by Mr. Loebell', which amounted to nothing but a very superficial rejection of a name suggested for the presidential election; it could only have been directed against Eckener. As Warburg thought highly of Eckener, he wanted to know the name of the organisation which had proposed Eckener's candidacy so that he could get in touch with them.[27]

18 First published in *Hamburger Fremdenblatt, Illustrierte Rundschau*, Vol. 85, no. 52, 2.3.1913. Britt, D., 'Airship and Submarine in the Medieval Imagination', 332–337 and 487–490.

19 Britt, D., *Aby Warburg. The Renewal of Pagan Antiquity*, 332.

20 Britt, D., *Aby Warburg. The Renewal of Pagan Antiquity*, 338.

21 WIA, FC, Warburg to Mary Warburg, undated postcard after 29.9.1913, without any comment on the landing of Zeppelin IV in Lunéville. Ferdinand Gluud, German airship pilot, 1875–1913.

22 WIA, GC, Warburg to A. von Holtzendorff, 14.12.1924. Arndt von Holtzendorff, director of the Hamburg America Line, 1859–1935.

23 WIA, GC, Warburg to H. Luther, 30.3.1925. Warburg was impressed by Eckener, who he felt would be a capable captain of all those in the boat, the boat community, that is the state. Hans Luther, German politician, 1879–1962.

24 WIA, GC, Warburg to W. Kluge, 16.5.1925. Walter Reinhold Kluge, German civil servant, b. 1901.

25 WIA, GC, Warburg to F. v. Eckardt, 27.4.1925. Felix von Eckardt, editor-in-chief of the *Hamburger Fremdenblatt*, 1866–1936.

26 WIA, GC, F. v. Eckardt to Warburg, 2.5.1925.

27 WIA, GC, Warburg to Vossische Zeitung, 5.5.1925. Friedrich Wilhelm von Loebell, 1855–1931, conservative politician, Prussian Minister of the Interior 1914–1917, from 1920 onward president of the Reichsbürgerrat. When this organisation was dissolved, he regrouped in the 'Loebell committee' conservative organisations who campaigned for Hindenburg for president. Paul von Hindenburg, German statesman, 1847–1934.

He would continue to speak up for Eckener, as he avowed to the Berlin publishers Julius Springer.[28]

Warburg wrote to the publishers B. G. Teubner to mobilise them to publish a book on Eckener's flight to America,[29] but Alfred Giesecke of B. G. Teubner did not think there was sufficient interest in the flight of the airship, and preferred a book on Eckener's projected expedition to the North Pole.[30] The invention of the aeroplane, the airship, the scientific new ground which could be explored by air traffic, and the discussion about financing Eckener's North Pole expedition had gripped Warburg; in it he saw a possibility for Germany to become leaders in world politics, 'in the air the (medieval), intellectual and economic policy of the tollgate (irrespective of the national soulfulness) has to fall: the United States of Europe lie – despite everything – in the air'.[31]

Warburg did not let up: Eckener's achievement, his trip, had 'not yet been understood as a revolutionary turn in people's mindset towards the cosmos and has certainly not yet become common knowledge of the German man of culture'. Warburg tried to interest Alfred Giesecke in a 'boys' book for adults' on German aviation. The reasons: a historical survey and a description of the instruments would provide an encyclopaedia of a Germany of the intellect at a time when a complete change in humanity's views of the cosmos was being given impetus by European and Anglo-American science.[32] A book on the flight to America, a gushing account of heroic deeds, was eventually published by Eckener in 1928.

When appeals for donations to fund Eckener's North Pole expedition were published throughout Germany, Warburg grumbled that there were not enough paying in centres and that newspapers ought to publish their addresses.[33] Even from his holiday retreat in Noordwijk, in the Netherlands, Warburg impressed on von Eckardt that airspace had to be viewed as international since a nationalist interpretation no longer worked; with a flourish he confessed that, when it came to airspace, he no longer could advocate an 'economic policy of the tollgate', for 'the united states of Europe lie in the air'.[34] Warburg asked W. de Gruyter & Co, the publishers of *Kürschners Deutscher Gelehrten-Kalender*, the German *Who's Who*, to include an entry on Hugo Eckener[35] and they duly promised to send a form.[36] The airship and Eckener caught Warburg's imagination. He jotted down the words 'Eckener', 'Lakehurst' and 'Alexander transported by griffins' on notes to be kept in Warburg's

28 WIA, GC, Warburg to J. Springer, 4.7.1925. Julius Springer, academic publishing house in Berlin.

29 WIA, GC, Warburg to A. Giesecke, 31.7.1925. Alfred Giesecke, German publisher, 1868–1945.

30 WIA, GC, A. Giesecke to Warburg, 13.8.1925.

31 WIA, GC, Warburg to F. v. Eckardt, 10.9.1925.

32 WIA, GC, Warburg to A. Giesecke in B.G. Teubner file, 19.8.1925.

33 WIA, GC, Warburg to F. v. Eckardt, 2.9.1925.

34 WIA, GC, Warburg to F. v. Eckardt, 10.9.1925.

35 WIA, GC, Warburg to W. de Gruyter, 12.10.1925. Walter de Gruyter, owner of the German publishing house, 1862–1924.

36 WIA, GC, Walter de Gruyter & Co. to Warburg, 14.10.1925. H. Eckener did not feature in the 1928/29 edition of *Kürschners deutscher Gelehrtenkalender*.

own subject catalogue.[37] Thus, the intellectual pedigree of the modern concept of aviation comprised the ideas and visions of those tellers of historical narratives who invented, embroidered and embellished the Greek text and put it into international circulation under the title of the *Romance of Alexander*. Warburg understood Eckener's flight to America as another example of mind over matter, of a technical solution to deal with problems such as gravity and distance. The political solution, the 'united states of Europe', albeit only for airspace, is surprising, given Warburg's strong nationalist feelings and pride. Even so, it signals a desire to give value to a technology which could overcome boundaries drawn by narrow nationalisms.

Postage stamp queries and the Alexander Liebmann Commission

In the autumn of 1926, Warburg was in correspondence with officials at the Post Museum in Berlin. His letter is not extant, but their reply is. They informed him that there was a collection of books on postage stamps, but none of them gave the names of artists designing stamps. However, they did know the name of the Swiss artist who had designed the Swiss airmail stamp of 1924, the illustrator and painter Pierre Eugène Vibert.[38] On the other hand they did not know the names of the artists who had designed the various Lenin memorial stamps.[39] A few days later, the Post Office in Berne informed Warburg that the Zurich painter Karl Bickel had designed the four Swiss airmail stamps of 1923.[40] Warburg also approached E. Goulburn Sinckler in London, who together with C. P. Bowen had written *Royal Visits to Barbados* (1887). Introducing himself by mentioning his research into writing 'a history of art on stamps', Warburg asked him about E. F. S. Bowen's design of a stamp for Barbados with Queen Victoria as Britannia ruling the waves. Did Sinckler know where E. F. S. Bowen got 'the lucky idea' from of representing the Queen as Britannia ruling the waves 'in that "antick" shape'?[41] He also wrote to William Wallace Cathcart

37 WIA, III.2.1., index card box [3], 042967, dated 30.11.1926.

38 Pierre Eugène Vibert, Swiss painter, 1875–1937.

39 WIA, GC, Reichspostmuseum in Berlin to Warburg, 3.12.1926. Warburg followed this up with a letter to L. E. Eichfuss in Moscow, 14.1.1927, in which he averred how impressed he was with the postage stamp issued at Lenin's death. L. E. Eichfuss to Warburg, 22.2.1927, replied that there was no book on the history of Russian revolution stamps and did not mention the name of the designer of the Lenin stamp. Leonhard E. Eichfuss, All-Russian Society of Philatelists, Secretary General 1924–25. The *Lenin Mourning Stamp 1924* was designed by Ivan Ivanovich Dubasov, Russian artist, 1897–1988.

40 WIA, GC, Oberpostdirektion in Berne, Switzerland, to Warburg, 09.12.1926. Karl Bickel, Swiss artist, 1886–1982.

41 WIA, GC, Warburg to E. G. Sinckler, 12.12.1926; on same sheet draft of Warburg's letter to W.W.C. Dunlop. Edward Goulburn Sinckler, British author, 1856–1922; Charles Parker Bowen, British author, dates unknown; Ernest F. S. Bowen, British Superintendent of the Public Works Department in Barbados, civil servant, designer of the Barbados 1897 Diamond Jubilee issue of Queen Victoria postage stamp, d. 1926; William Wallace Cathcart Dunlop, Barbadian classicist, d. 1938. For E. F. S. Bowen see Morel, 'From Neptune to Trident. How the Colonial Deputed Seal for Barbados Evolved into a National Symbol'. I am grateful for information by Richard Scott Morel, Curator of the Philatelic Collection, British Library.

Dunlop, who held the Chair of Classical Philology at the Codrington College in Barbados, asking about the sources for E. F. S. Bowen's design: 'I suppose that he found the archetype composition in some old print representing an "entrée" of royal persons at Barbados or in an old-fashioned illustration of Virgil'. In the course of a long correspondence Warburg became very friendly with Dunlop, who, 'in faultless German', thanked Warburg for his explanations of the Barbados postage stamp.[42]

Alexander Liebmann, by his own account 'a penniless artist', and friend of Warburg's from his days of military service, sent sixtieth birthday wishes to Warburg in 1924, two years too early.[43] His first letter to Warburg had been in 1896, on the dearth of artistic advertisements in Germany, in contrast to advertisements in American and English newspapers.[44] After having been highly decorated in World War I, he lived in poverty. When he apologised, two and a half years after his letter with the mistaken birthday date, he did so by stressing that it was proof that he was still thinking of Warburg; he reminded him of their time together in Gottesaue near Karlsruhe as young men doing their military service. He tried to get Warburg to interest German newspapers in adopting advertisements, no doubt with a view to receiving commissions. What he really wanted were contacts in America: he, a painter and etcher, was broke, he had sold all his property, he needed to sell his graphic art and forwarded sample photographs.[45]

It so happened that three weeks earlier Warburg had written an entry in the *Journal* of the KBW (the logbook kept by Warburg and his librarians Fritz Saxl and Gertrud Bing of appointment schedules, queries, replies to queries, etc.) that he had looked at postage stamps which compared favourably with the 'stupid new stamp'.[46] The photographs of Liebmann's etchings, which Warburg found 'tasteful', must have prompted him: he promised to try to help him find commissions not only by asking his brothers Felix M. and Paul M. Warburg in New York – although the US market was difficult, still very much dominated by French taste – but also by commissioning him to design a German airmail stamp. He suggested the following specific features: 'An aeroplane with the caption "idea victrix", below it the sea, behind the aeroplane a red sky in the morning. The whole sky enclosed by a flat arc'.[47] The next day he sketched the image himself (see figure 2.2).[48] In his summary of the events in the *Journal* Warburg phrased it slightly differently: he had asked Liebmann 'to draw for

42 WIA, GC, Warburg to W. W. C. Dunlop, 1.2.1927.

43 WIA, GC, A. Liebmann to Warburg, 26.7.1924. Alexander Liebmann, German Artist, Called 'Seal', 1871–1938.

44 WIA, GC, A. Liebmann to Warburg, 25.12.1896.

45 WIA, GC, A. Liebmann to Warburg, 2.12.1926.

46 Michels/Schoell-Glass, *Journal* (*Aby Warburg. Tagebuch*), 12.11.1926, 25. There is one stamp in his collection of stamps, a French red 2 centime stamp, which annoyed him so much that he wrote on 22.12.1926, 'this monster of a postage stamp . . . Instead of scales, one should put a cut-off head into the clutches of the woman'. WIA, III.2.1., index card box [3], 043595.

47 WIA, GC, Warburg to A. Liebmann, 4.12.1926. Felix M. Warburg, German-American banker, 1871–1937; Paul M. Warburg, German-American investment banker, 1868–1932.

48 WIA, III.2.1., index card box [3], following 042792, dated 5.12.1926.

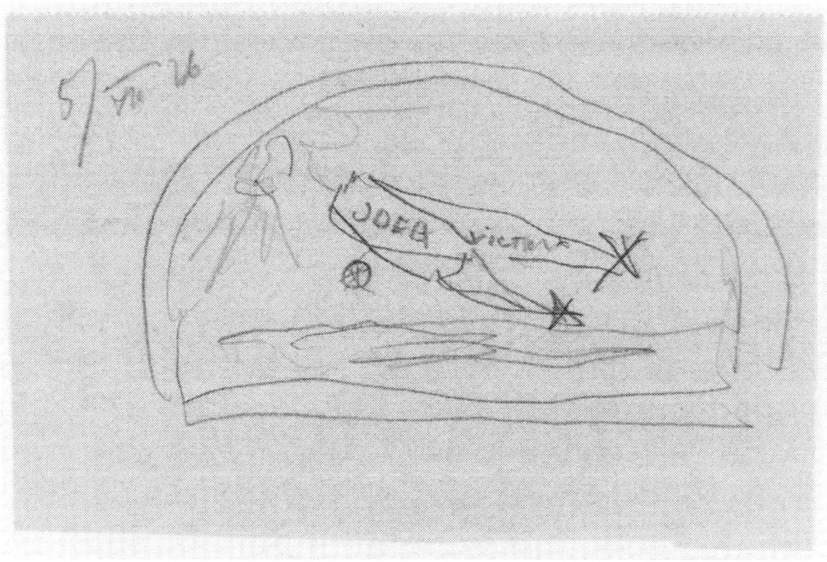

Figure 2.2 Warburg's design for IDEA VICTRIX. WIA, III.99.12.1. fol. 1., dated 5.12.1926.
Source: © Photo: The Warburg Institute.

me first of all a new German postage stamp in landscape format, which should show at the bottom the sea and above it the steeply ascending aeroplane'.[49]

With the help of a new German airmail stamp Warburg hoped to signal to the world that Germany was interested in peaceful cooperation. It was not the first time that Warburg had approached a graphic artist with a view to interesting him in a drawing project. In 1915 Warburg suggested that Olaf Gulbransson, who worked for the satirical magazine *Simplicissimus*, caricature the line 'Britannia rules the waves' by substituting 'waves' with 'slaves'.[50] He offered his explanations for this pun – Italy entering the war on the side of the Allied powers – and described what he thought the illustration should feature.[51] Two years later, he wrote to Thomas Theodor Heine, the co-founder of *Simplicissimus*, and again supplied a pun, 'Fata Morgana', in order to illustrate the peace feelers by President Thomas Woodrow Wilson and the banker John Pierpoint Morgan Jr.[52] Since nothing came of these

49 Michels/Schoell-Glass, *Journal*, 21.12.1926, 24.

50 WIA, GC, Copy book VI, 132, Warburg to O. Gulbransson, 18.8.1915. Olaf Gulbransson, Norwegian painter and designer, 1873–1958.

51 WIA, GC, Copy book VI, 147, Warburg to O. Gulbransson, 29.8.1915.

52 WIA, GC, Copy book VI, 282, Warburg to Th. Heine, 6.1.1917. John Pierpoint Morgan Jr., American banker, 1867–1943; Thomas Theodor Heine, German painter, 1867–1948. Thomas Woodrow Wilson, American president, 1856–1924.

suggestions, he wrote to Professor Max Slevogt in Berlin, the painter and graphic artist, with the request 'to illustrate the ideas of other people', in this case to draw the damaged Statue of Liberty, holding aloft a bloody stump with the motto 'Liberty Enlightening the World'.[53]

These and other suggestions by Warburg were not realised during World War I; however, the wish to transpose a phrase or pun into a visual medium, to find an artist who would help Warburg with this process, must have led Warburg to commission his illustrator friend in 1926. Liebmann duly sent six designs, which look somewhat stiff and strangely static.[54] Warburg, however, reacted positively, 'You have made this really very beautifully!' and selected the third one for Liebmann to develop further; in particular, he suggested two motifs, one with dark blue wavy lines and another without writing; but most importantly of all – he forwarded 100 marks.[55] Liebmann replied a week later with thanks for the cheque and forwarded two draft designs as ordered by Warburg as well as a Swiss postage stamp showing an aeroplane soaring high over mountains. Liebmann, who had heard that Foreign Minister Stresemann was visiting Hamburg on 20 December 1926, suggested to Warburg that the three 1926 Nobel Peace Prize winners, Briand, Chamberlain and Stresemann, commission him to design a stamp. He also informed Warburg that he had made etchings of clipper ships – could they be bought by the prestigious Hamburg America Line as souvenirs for their passengers?[56] Nothing more is extant of a Liebmann – Warburg correspondence until March of the next year.

Otto Heinrich Strohmeyer

By the time Liebmann referred to Stresemann's visit to Hamburg, Warburg was already in negotiations with another artist, Otto Heinrich Strohmeyer, whose style of architectural drawing, clean lines and expressive design gripped Warburg more than Liebmann's work. Referring to Liebmann's etchings of clipper ships, he confessed, 'you have strong competition in this genre'.[57] Liebmann resigned himself to the fact that he was not selling his etchings of clipper ships. He decided to accept work in property management – at least he would be offered free accommodation![58] – but he still remained a member of the Munich-based artist society Münchener Künstler-Genossenschaft.[59]

Amid Warburg's correspondence on postage stamp matters at the end of 1926, the name Otto Heinrich Strohmeyer emerged in mid-December. There was no

53 WIA, GC, Copy book VI, 297, 298, 299, Warburg to M. Slevogt, 23.4.1917 M. Slevogt to Warburg, 25.4.1917. Max Slevogt, German painter, 1868–1932, declined the commission. For a detailed appraisal of Warburg's attempts see Chapter 11.
54 WIA, IV.87, Envelope 'Liebmann Correspondence, Sent 10.12.1926'.
55 WIA, GC, Warburg to A. Liebmann, 10.12.1926.
56 WIA, GC, A. Liebmann to Warburg, 17.12.1926.
57 WIA, GC, Warburg to A. Liebmann, 2.3.1927.
58 WIA, GC, A. Liebmann to Warburg, 26.3.1927.
59 WIA, GC, A. Liebmann to Warburg, 26.1.1928.

preceding correspondence with friends requesting names of artists and there was no specific enquiry regarding Strohmeyer's art. In the *Journal* Warburg simply mentioned that he had wanted to ask Fritz Schumacher, the architect, and Gustav Pauli, director of the 'Kunsthalle' in Hamburg, to help him put flesh on his 'Idea Victrix' idea (as he called it before he accepted the suggestion of 'Idea Vincit' by Fritz Saxl, librarian of KBW and director after 1929), but had refrained from doing so.[60] Dr. Gustav Stresemann, the German Foreign Minister, had been awarded the Nobel Peace Prize in 1926 together with Aristide Briand and Joseph Austen Chamberlain for negotiating the treaty of Locarno which was hoped to usher in a new order for peace in Europe after the horrific war. Stresemann had been invited to Hamburg by the Hamburg Senate but postponed his visit from 14 December to 20 December. Warburg, keen to invite Stresemann to the KBW, rang the Foreign Office and learnt that Stresemann would be visiting the KBW after a breakfast with the mayor, Carl Petersen.[61] Presenting him with a suitable gift became imperative. Warburg, who knew Strohmeyer's works and liked his 'fantastically real statics',[62] arranged a meeting with him to discuss his 'Idea Victrix' project and added in his entry in the *Journal* the word 'discretion' for the benefit of Saxl and Bing.[63] In his Diary he simply stated 'Strohmeyer accepts the "Idea Victrix" enthusiastically'.[64]

Three sketches, variations on the theme of an aeroplane flying up into the sky, against a backdrop of the sun rising out of the sea, are dated 15 December. The first sketch shows a flat arc enclosing the scene, the initials 'I' and 'V' for 'Idea Victrix' on the wings of the aeroplane and the words 'Deutsches Reich' on the seashore in the foreground. The second sketch has the date '1926' in the two top spandrels, the initials 'I' and 'V' on the wings of the aeroplane and waves indicating the setting. The third sketch has the three names Chamberlain, Briand and Stresemann written into the arc, the words 'Idea Victrix' along the fuselage of the aeroplane, the number '25' in the left and right spandrels and 'Deutsches Reich' left and '1926' right on the bottom line. They are certainly Warburg's drawings, showing the development of the design, still clearly a postage stamp, complete with year and country. The first and second drawings are dated 'Wednesday. 15/XII, 5pm',[65] the third, crucially with the three names 'Briand, Chamberlain, Stresemann', is not dated. It is unclear whether the three names have been inserted in response to Liebmann's suggestion of 17 December, which must have arrived on 18 December, or whether Warburg thought of it independently of Liebmann.

60 Michels/Schoell-Glass, *Journal*, 21.12.1926, 23. Fritz Schumacher, German architect, 1869–1947; Gustav Pauli, German art historian, 1866–1938.

61 WIA, III.11.75., Diary, 15.12.1926, 8314. Carl Petersen, German lawyer, 1868–1933.

62 Michels/Schoell-Glass, *Journal*, 21.12.1926, 23.

63 Michels/Schoell-Glass, *Journal*, 15.12.1926, 33.

64 WIA, III.11.75., Diary, table of contents, 15.12.1926.

65 WIA, IV.87, folder 'Liebmann Correspondence'.

What is certain is that on 17 December Warburg summarised the conversation he had had with Strohmeyer the previous day: he thanked Strohmeyer for 'the brilliant execution of my amateur idea'. He, his wife and Saxl decided to commission him to produce an 'IDEA VINCIT' linocut for a fee of 200 marks. Warburg ordered six more prints for 50 marks each and asked Strohmeyer to add in the lower right corner 'Strohmeyer fecit' and in the lower left corner 'Warburg inv.'.[66] There is no longer any talk of a design for a postage stamp, simply a 'linocut', a work of art designed to be used as a present.

The next day, Strohmeyer brought the reworked and finished drafts 'in brilliant style. The aeroplane is really victoriously taking off'.[67] The police called to prepare for Stresemann's visit. On Sunday, 19 December 1926, Strohmeyer delivered 'the illustrated "idea vincit" in perfect shape and by the evening in seven copies!'[68] Saxl saw to it that the linocut was framed, or rather mounted in a folder.[69] Warburg's commission for a stamp design expressing his hope for a future not hemmed in by narrow nationalisms had metamorphosed into a commission for a work of art which, by using the same symbolic language, would express the same hopes thanks to worthy statesmen who had done so much to bring Europe together.

However, Warburg was not impressed by Stresemann: 'So. The big event, Stresemann's visit. He came much too late and showed gross restlessness. I could not show my finest nuances! Only the blunt chunk of Strohmeyer's linocut saved the situation'.[70] Warburg's final judgment was 'ah, well'.[71] But according to Max M. Warburg, Stresemann was very impressed 'by the way I was tied up with the library'. Warburg informed Strohmeyer that he handed a copy of the print to Foreign Minister Stresemann, who was very impressed with it.[72]

To underline the occasion every print of the linocut (see figure 2.3) which Warburg was to send to his friends had the inscription 'This linocut by Otto Heinrich Strohmeyer was presented to the German Minister Dr. Stresemann on the occasion of his visit in the KBW in Hamburg on 20 December 1926 – "Reproduction only with permission"'.[73] Stresemann stated at the reception given in his honour that 'Treaties concluded at Locarno would remain dead letters if we do not succeed in building upon them in a large spirit of understanding, and so at last erect a structure that will enable the nations to live and work side by side in peace'[74] – Warburg's concept of the united states of Europe. In the next few days there were

66 WIA, GC, Warburg to O. H. Strohmeyer, n.d.; must be 17.12.1926.

67 WIA, III.11.75., Diary, 18.12.1926, 8318–8319.

68 Michels/Schoell-Glass, *Journal*, 19.12.1926, 36.

69 WIA, III.11.75., Diary, 18.12.1926, 8319.

70 WIA, III.11.75., Diary, 20.12.1926, 8321.

71 WIA, III.11.75., Diary, table of contents, 20.12.1926.

72 WIA, GC, Warburg to O. H. Strohmeyer, 21.12.1926.

73 cf. verso of print sent to Professor Paul J. Sachs, kept in The William Hayes Fogg Art Museum of Harvard University. Cf. also inscription written on piece of card, kept in WIA, Minuta, III.22. Paul J. Sachs, American art historian, 1878–1965.

74 Sutton, E., *Gustav Stresemann*, 81.

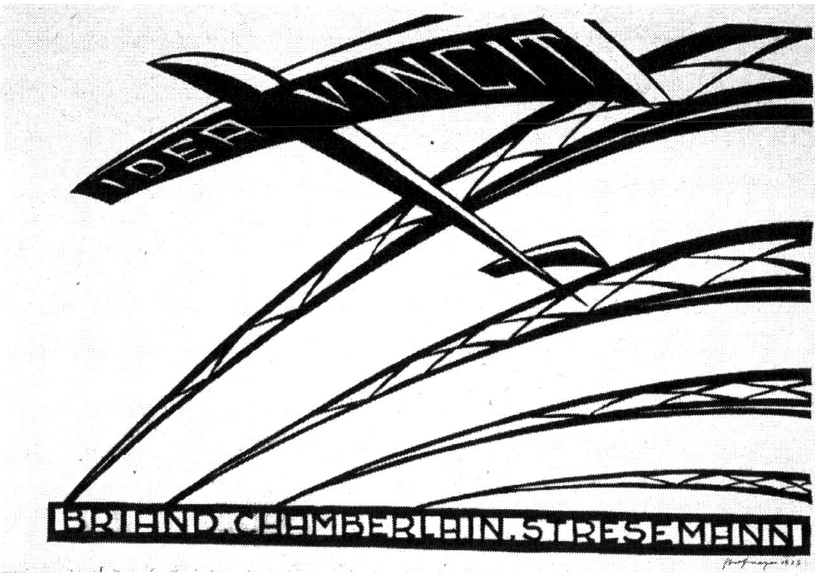

Figure 2.3 IDEA VINCIT. Linocut by Otto Heinrich Strohmeyer. Fogg Art Museum, Harvard University, Gift of Paul J. Sachs. Macintyre, Allam Copyright: 2004.

Photo: Harvard Art Museums/Fogg Museum. President and Fellows of Harvard College.

discussions on how to proceed with Stresemann's suggestion of sending copies of the print directly to Briand and to Chamberlain[75] or to the Consuls General of France and Great Britain in Hamburg,[76] in which case Warburg's name should be omitted,[77] or to the former mayor of Hamburg and current German ambassador in London Dr. Friedrich Sthamer, as 'This man from Hamburg has really shown himself for once as German'.[78] Finally Warburg suggested that Strohmeyer himself, and not the Senate of Hamburg, should forward the linocut on the instructions of Stresemann.[79]

By 26 December 1926 Warburg had ordered 46 copies of the print from Strohmeyer and had already presented some 20 to his friends and family, among them his son Max Adolf.[80] Two weeks later he ordered ten more copies and informed Strohmeyer that he had handed Strohmeyer's material to Theodor Brodersen of the Hamburg

75 Michels/Schoell-Glass, *Journal*, 21.12.1926, 24.
76 WIA, GC, Warburg to H. Merck, 21.12.1926. Heino Merck, German civil servant, 1877–1958.
77 WIA, GC, Warburg to Carl Wilhelm Petersen, the mayor of Hamburg, 22.12.1926.
78 WIA, GC, Warburg to Max M. Warburg, 21.12.1926. Friedrich Sthamer, German lawyer and diplomat, 1856–1931.
79 WIA, GC, Warburg to C. W. Petersen, 23.12.1926; and Michels/Schoell-Glass, *Journal*, 21.12.1926, 25.
80 WIA, GC, Warburg to C. W. Petersen, 23.12.1926; and Michels/Schoell-Glass, *Journal*, 26.12.1926, 40. Max Adolf Warburg, classical philologist, 1902–1974.

Kunstverein with a view to launching a Strohmeyer exhibition.[81] Brodersen was keen to exhibit Strohmeyer in an exhibition of works by the German painters Gert Wollheim and von Schölley and French watercolour painters.[82] This was Warburg's last contact with Strohmeyer. No records of later meetings or letters are extant.

Reception

Warburg had chosen an artist with imagination and a draughtman's skills to produce a cameo work of art which expressed admirably Warburg's ideas about 'the victorious idea'. Proof of his esteem is the high number of prints which Warburg purchased and, as with offprints of his articles, sent to friends and colleagues. They doubled up as New Year cards, as is shown in the dedication written on the card to Paul Sachs: 'To Professor Paul Sachs, the highly esteemed colleague on the other side of the big pond, presented on behalf of the KBW by A. Warburg with best wishes for 1927'.[83] There are 19 letters of thanks extant in the correspondence collection of The Warburg Institute, ranging from polite thanks to confessions of a lack of understanding to rapturous praise for the idea behind 'Idea' and its execution.

Warburg, when sending offprints of his articles to friends, expected to receive their reactions in the post. He would then go on to explain a particular point raised. The same happened with the linocut. The first extant letter was directed to Axel Gauffin, director of the art gallery in Stockholm. Warburg had been in touch with him over the years on account of the Rembrandt painting *Claudius Civilis*, which he called a 'marvel'[84] and which was copied for Warburg in Stockholm by Carl Schuberth and delivered shortly before Christmas 1926.[85] As a token of his sincere gratitude Warburg forwarded the 'print of a new linocut from Hamburg'.[86] Two months later, albeit with an apology, Gauffin acknowledged, soberly, receipt of the 'beautiful linocut'.[87]

81 WIA, GC, Warburg to O.H. Strohmeyer, 07.01.1927. Theodor Brodersen, German art manager, b. 1874.

82 WIA, GC, O. H. Strohmeyer to Warburg, 28.01.1927. Gert Wollheim, German expressionist painter, 1894–1974; Ruth von Schölley, German painter, 1893–1969.

83 See this Chapter, note 73.

84 WIA, GC, Warburg to W. Stechow, 26.9.1925. In a letter WIA, GC, to H. Schneider, 13.10.1925, Warburg talked about his particular *Claudius Civilis* research direction, not a historical art investigation, but the history of the influence of the topic from classical antiquity to the 17th century. Axel Gauffin, Swedish art historian, 1877–1964; Wolfgang Stechow, German-American art historian, 1896–1974; Hans Schneider, Swiss art historian, 1888–1953; Rembrandt, Dutch painter, 1606–1669.

85 For an extended discussion of Warburg's commission of the Rembrandt *Claudius Civilis* copy see McEwan, D., 'IDEA VINCIT – "Die siegende, fliegende 'Idea'"', 121–151, here 127–129. Today the oil painting hangs in the staircase of the Warburg Institute London, see figure 5.1. Carl Schuberth, Swedish painter, 1860–1929.

86 WIA, GC, Warburg to A. Gauffin, 26.12.1926.

87 WIA, GC, A. Gauffin to Warburg, 27.2.1927.

Warburg's lifelong friend Robert Davidsohn, whom he had introduced to James Loeb many years before, sent a New Year's card with thanks for the 'aeroplane of Idea'.[88] Wilhelm Gundel, who had, funded by Warburg, prepared the third edition of the Franz Boll – Carl Bezold book *Sphaera*, thanked him likewise for New Year greetings and the linocut of 'Vincit Idea' [sic!] with Warburg's dedication. He planned to hang it next to Warburg's portrait photograph in his study.[89] The philosopher Ernst Cassirer was very pleased to have a copy of the print[90] and his son George was very impressed.[91] Jacques Mesnil, art historian in Paris and friend of Warburg since their days in Florence, whom Warburg had helped find writing commissions, thanked him for his copy[92] and his wife Clara thanked Warburg on a separate postcard, mentioning that she had shown it to an artist who found it very well executed.[93] Paul Harris Jr., the secretary of the National Council for the Prevention of War in the USA, requested and duly received a copy.[94] John Palmer Gavit wanted to publish it in an article on Germany in the New York paper *Survey*, but although three copies were sent it is unclear whether the article was ever written.[95]

Gladys Bronwen Stern called the print 'Cubist'. She described her study and its furnishings in order to give Warburg a feeling of where she had hung the print: there was a silk curtain which used to drape the piano in the drawing room of the Rakonitz family, a family she had written about, a picture of Mammon, a statuette of the Madonna and child, carved from a single elephant tusk like the one in the church at Villeneuve-les-Avignon, a Max Beerbohm caricature and a picture of her husband,[96] to which Warburg replied two months later that he only hoped that 'IDEA' did not disturb her ensemble.[97] In the *Journal*, however, he entered immediately upon receiving her 'very amusing letter' that she showed understanding for 'Idea Vincit'.[98]

In response to a letter from Cyrus Adler, Principal of the Dropsie College for Hebrew and Cognate Learning in Philadelphia, acknowledging receipt of 'the beautiful reproduction' but confessing that he could not 'make out the

88 WIA, GC, R. Davidsohn to Warburg, 30.12.1926. Robert Davidsohn, German historian, 1853–1937.

89 WIA, GC, W. Gundel to Warburg, 30.12.1926. Wilhelm Gundel, German classicist, 1880–1945.

90 WIA, III.11.75., Diary, 24.12.1926, 8324. Ernst Cassirer, German philosopher, 1874–1945.

91 WIA, GC, G. Cassirer to Warburg, 13.1.1927. George Cassirer, theatre photographer, 1904–1958.

92 WIA, GC, J. Mesnil to Warburg, 15.1.1927. Jean-Jacques Dwelshauvers, known as Jacques Mesnil, Belgian art historian, 1872–1940. See also McEwan and Scafi, 'Warburg and D'Annunzio in Defence of Truth: On Modern Literature and Alleged Jewishness', 259–279.

93 WIA, GC, C. Mesnil to Warburg, 18.1.1927. Clara Mesnil, wife of Jacques Mesnil.

94 WIA, GC, P. Harris to Warburg, 20.3.1929 and C. Hertz to Warburg, 6.4.1929. Paul Harris Jr., director of the Peace Action Service 1932–1939. Clara Hertz, employee in the KBW, 1871–1950.

95 Michels/Schoell-Glass, *Journal*, 19.8.1928, 332; cf. also WIA, GC, Warburg to Mary Warburg, 16.3.1929. John Palmer Gavit, American journalist, 1868–1954.

96 WIA, GC, G. B. Stern to Warburg, 16.1.1927. Gladys Bronwen Stern, British author, 1890–1973; Max Beerbohm, English essayist, 1872–1956.

97 WIA, GC, Warburg to G. B. Stern, 13.3.1927.

98 Michels/Schoell-Glass, *Journal*, 1.2.1927, 47; WIA, GC, Warburg to W. W. C. Dunlop, 1.2.1927.

symbolism',[99] Warburg explained it by referring to international understanding in general and European understanding in particular, as exemplified by the Locarno Conference when Briand, Chamberlain and Stresemann met, despite encountering enormous resistance in their respective countries. The idea that immaterial values will triumph, can and will lead to a 'prolonged pause of reason'. Precisely because the political situation was so brittle, 'we Hamburgers' wanted to strengthen Stresemann's conviction to believe in reason with the help of the symbol of 'Idea Vincit', he said. Whether it helped Stresemann objectively was not Warburg's business. It was enough to have tried it – 'in magnis voluisse sat est'.[100]

Mona-Lisa Steffen, daughter of the economist and social scientist Gustaf Steffen in Gothenburg, thanked Warburg, 'leader in the aircraft of ideas', for the print with the dedication to her father; she liked it so much that she had hung it up in her study.[101] The head of Waldpark Sanatorium in Baden-Baden, Friedrich Heinsheimer, thanked him for the 'beautiful and interesting etching'[102] and Sten Konow, editor of *Acta Orientalia* in Oslo, was going to put it next to a photograph of Rabindranath Tagore.[103] He went on to discuss the political message of the print in greater detail as he was convinced that Briand had never been an imperialist, but Chamberlain had certainly been one and Stresemann used to be an 'Annexionist'. Had these two really been convinced by the idea of an end to nationalism? The idea of an idea being victorious and crossing political borders seemed stronger to him than the idea itself. The idea as a means of war was so potent that he was not convinced that the idea had won. The three statesmen had only done their duty; they should not have been awarded the Nobel Peace Prize.[104]

The sinologist Otto Franke, who had given a lecture in KBW, in the 'proud temple of scholarship', thanked him for the 'splendid image', which in his eyes was such an outstanding artistic achievement, 'that I think any escalation above and beyond hardly possible'.[105] Max Warburg ordered more copies of the print;[106] Paul Warburg thanked him for 'your Stresemann card'[107] in January and a second time – more appreciatively – in July 1927: he found the linocut '. . . immensely interesting und impressive'.[108] Warburg, who had made it his business to keep

99 WIA, GC, C. Adler to Warburg, 17.1.1927. Cyrus Adler, American scholar, 1863–1940.

100 WIA, GC, Warburg to C. Adler, 1.2.1927. Propertius, *Elegiarum liber 2*, X, 6, 208: 'to once have wanted is enough in great deeds'. Sextus Propertius, Latin, elegiac poet, 50/45 BCE – 15 CE.

101 WIA, GC, M. Steffen to Warburg, 19.1.1927. Gustaf Steffen, Swedish sociologist, 1864–1929.

102 WIA, GC, F. Heinsheimer to Warburg, 20.1.1927. Friedrich Heinsheimer, director of the Waldpark sanatorium, 1873–1935.

103 Sten Konow, Norwegian indologist, 1867–1948; Rabindranath Tagore, Bengali polymath, 1861–1841.

104 WIA, GC, S. Konow to Warburg, 22.1.1927. 'Personally, I do believe in the power of the idea, because the idea, if it is genuine, is sustained by the masses. But I also fear that precisely the leading politicians have been made immune to the influence of the idea'.

105 WIA, GC, O. Franke to Warburg, 1.3.1927. Otto Franke, German sinologist, 1863–1946.

106 WIA, GC, G. Bing to Warburg, 14.1.1927.

107 WIA, GC, P. Warburg to Warburg, n.d., January 1927.

108 WIA, GC, P. Warburg to Warburg, 12.7.1927.

his brothers abreast of developments in KBW, also had the slight suspicion that they did not understand him and did not fully value his work. He must have been requesting a fuller appreciation from his brother Paul after the rather matter-Of fact acknowledgement of January.

While the majority of these appraisals, together with the one by James Loeb mentioned at the beginning, were rather short and insubstantial, the correspondence with Oscar Ollendorff brought the intellectual exchange of ideas which Warburg cherished. Ollendorff, from Hamburg but living in Wiesbaden, was an old friend and art historian, working on his own, not connected with an academic institution. He had been ill in his youth, could not finish his degree, married late and lacked recognition for books which Warburg found most engaging; he congratulated Ollendorff on finishing the book 'Liebe in der Malerei' and promised that he would do everything in his power to draw the attention of his colleagues to Ollendorff's books. In Warburg's opinion, those who did not review Ollendorff's books suffered from 'inner blindness of the soul'. Ollendorff's book 'Andacht in der Malerei' was especially precious to Warburg, 'because I want to make the pictorial element in its widest sense the basis of the unwritten doctrine of human expression'.[109] In 1928 he initiated a process for Hamburg University to award an honorary doctorate to Ollendorff, which, however, did not come to fruition.

In his postcard of thanks for the print Ollendorff gave his opinion: 'There is spirited power and at the same time subtlety in the shapes of the lines and everywhere elastic inner movement'. This was what he admired, but he did not understand the link with the 'Idea vincit' motif 'despite my inclination towards the symbolic'.[110] Ten days later he sent another postcard, cheerily proclaiming that, upon closer inspection, he had understood how 'Idea Vincit', rising ever higher, had to be interpreted: 'Draughtsmen of earlier times, like Menzel, who fully understood to follow symbolism, did so with human shapes. Strohmeyer does so with a network of lines, and nobody can deny its expressive, characterful essence'.[111] He regretted having missed Warburg's address to members of the Congress of Orientalists,[112] but was pleased to see from publications sent by Warburg that what drove Warburg was 'the cursed general human'.[113] Warburg reacted swiftly, sending him offprints on long loan as both of them pursued research along the same lines. He thanked Ollendorff for what he had written about 'the human'; Ollendorff's phrase reminded him of their discussions walking under the branches of the Red Tree – an allusion to Rothenbaumchaussee, a well-to-do part of Hamburg, now the University district. In the final paragraph of the letter, however, he confesses to disillusionment: 'I feel that Strohmeyer's linocut is in itself an unerringly balanced symbol, but I do

109 WIA, GC, Warburg to O. Ollendorff, 31.5.1926. Oscar Ollendorff, German art historian, 1865–1939.

110 WIA, GC, O. Ollendorff to Warburg, 16.1.1927.

111 WIA, GC, O. Ollendorff to Warburg, 26.1.1927.

112 Warburg, A., 'Orientalisierende Astrologie'; Britt, D., 'Astrology under Oriental Influence', 699–702 and 775.

113 WIA, GC, O. Ollendorff to Warburg, 7.3.1927.

understand that for the time being it will not succeed because the public at large has been painstakingly conditioned by modern art criticism to reject content-related art as literary'.[114] Ollendorff, in his reply, summarised that both shared the same view with regard to Strohmeyer's print, 'art scholarship and intellectual contents!'.[115] Did he allude to Plato's ideal of 'beautiful and good'? A clue might lie in Warburg's own appraisal written in the *Journal*, as a reminder to himself and explanation to Saxl and Bing.[116] Warburg had wanted Liebmann to translate the concept of the open skies, something good, into a clearly legible symbol which was beautiful, a work of art which also had, as a postage stamp, a practical application. The first Liebmann designs, however, did not match up to the Strohmeyer designs with their elegant and thought-provoking strikingly modern lines.

The Edwin Redslob – Aby Warburg postage stamp lecture

The commission for Strohmeyer was not a distraction from Warburg's postage stamp research. It was a particular method for realising an idea. At the same time, inveterate letter writer that he was, he approached a number of people in pursuit of his interests, among them Edwin Redslob, whose title was 'Reichskunstwart' or superintendent of German art, a civil service position like a minister for the arts.

Warburg had asked his son Max Adolf in Berlin to purchase the catalogue of the exhibition 'Die künstlerische Formgebung des Reiches' in the lobby of the Parliament building, curated by Edwin Redslob.[117] But by the time Max Adolf went there, it had been taken down, to be exhibited again in the university building in Hardenbergstrasse.[118] Warburg therefore introduced himself by writing, emphasising his postage stamp research, and promptly complained that a book ordered two weeks earlier had not been delivered.[119] In his very polite reply, Redslob sent him the book *Die künstlerische Formgebung des Reiches* together with a stamp catalogue and promised to send him more material as Warburg was supporting Redslob's efforts in an important way.[120] Warburg tried to find out more about Redslob: did Carl Georg Heise, director of the arts and crafts museum in Lübeck, know him? Was Redslob responsible for the 'hideous' recently issued stamps or did he hide behind Hugo Rudolf Zabel?[121] Heise promised to speak with Redslob[122] and reported back that Redslob was interested in everything to do

114 WIA, GC, A. Warburg to O. Ollendorff, 9.3.1927.
115 WIA, GC, O. Ollendorff to Warburg, 11.3.1927.
116 Michels/Schoell-Glass, *Journal*, 21.12.1926, 23–25.
117 WIA, FC, Warburg to M. A. Warburg, 15.11.1926. Edwin Redslob, German civil servant, 1884–1973; Max Adolf Warburg, classical philologist, 1902–1974.
118 WIA, FC, M. A. Warburg to Warburg, 20.11.1926.
119 WIA, GC, Warburg to E. Redslob, 14.12.1926.
120 WIA, GC, E. Redslob to Warburg, 21.12.1926.
121 WIA, GC, Warburg to C. G. Heise, 27.12.1926. Hugo Rudolf Zabel, German journalist, 1876–1939. Carl Georg Heise, German art historian, 1890–1979.
122 WIA, GC, C. G. Heise to Warburg, 3.1.1927.

with postage stamps,[123] and so Warburg kept him informed on further developments. Redslob visited KBW on 7 April 1927 and Warburg showed him the stamp albums, displayed on the tables. Both men talked about forgeries, technical skills, artistic possibilities, historical symbols; Warburg used the term 'crossing point' to illustrate the value the meeting had for him. He was particularly impressed with Redslob's characterisation of the Lenin stamp as 'an illustrated obituary of great force, albeit no postage stamp'.[124] Redslob suggested a joint lecture at the KBW on the problems of making stamps on the occasion of the forthcoming 'Design of Empire' art exhibition in Hamburg in August 1927. Warburg agreed keenly, because he felt that Redslob valued artistic creations if they corresponded to the aims of a postage stamp.[125]

Warburg quickly informed Heise of the planned joint lecture at the KBW and added that he was very pleased that Heise had agreed to purchase some of Strohmeyer's prints as Warburg was cross that only he himself, but neither his family nor his friends, had supported Strohmeyer so far.[126] Heise duly reported to Warburg that he had ordered Strohmeyer folios, but was more interested in finding out Warburg's view on the Emil Nolde exhibition in Hamburg.[127] Warburg rose to the occasion and sent an 'Easter epistle' on Emil Nolde: although Warburg was convinced that he was 'among the leaders on the front', he was less convinced by Nolde's symbols. Animals, clouds, landscapes were enchanting, but Warburg confessed he was not gripped by his treatment of tragic human scenes and compared them to Tyrolean passion paintings.[128]

Warburg, who had already given a lecture on postage stamps to a small circle in the KBW on 11 December 1926,[129] wanted to use the exhibition in Hamburg on designs of official art in August 1927 as an excellent opportunity to underline the importance of work on official art: in his next letter to Redslob he complained about 'Americanisms' like the use of the official German coat-of-arms on advertising materials, and asked what could be done about it.[130] Warburg now wrote from Karlsbad to Saxl and asked for his help in finding the source for the scene of Neptune taming horses, as shown on the postage stamp of Barbados featuring a conch-shaped chariot drawn by horses in the sea. Did Saxl know of scenes of Neptune in the Vatican Museum? Why did fasces become Mussolini's symbol?[131]

123 WIA, GC, C. G. Heise to Warburg, 26.1.1927.
124 WIA, III.99.7.2. Warburg's Account of Redslob's visit to KBW on 7.4.1927.
125 WIA, GC, E. Redslob to Warburg, 13.4.1927.
126 WIA, GC, Warburg to C. G. Heise, 8.4.1927.
127 WIA, GC, C. G. Heise to Warburg, 14.4.1927. There is no Strohmeyer print in the collections of the museums in Lübeck, according to a communication from Dr. Brigitte Heise, 31.3.1999. It is just possible that Heise did purchase a print for his private use and not for the museum. Emil Nolde, Danish-German painter, 1867–1956.
128 WIA, GC, Warburg to C. G. Heise, 18.4.1927.
129 WIA, III.11.75., Diary, 11.12.1926, 8310.
130 WIA, GC, Warburg to E. Redslob, 27.4.1927.
131 WIA, GC, Warburg to Saxl, 11.5.1927. Benito Mussolini, Italian politician, 1883–1945.

The use of a classical symbol like the old river god, Neptune, on a stamp from the New World indicated the survival of symbolic language in totally new surroundings and therefore was for Warburg, focused on the Mnemosyne Atlas of images and their migration from classical antiquity, proof of the importance of symbols.

Redslob suggested the title 'Postage stamp art as cultural endeavour?' for the joint lecture at the KBW,[132] which was altered slightly to 'The postage stamp as a document of culture'. Warburg wanted to know whether Redslob would talk about the new Hindenburg stamp by the arts and crafts artist Sigmund von Weech. Warburg did not like that Hindenburg was represented in uniform and Warburg, 'as every reasonable German man', admired Hindenburg the civilian, sporting his famous top hat.[133] Redslob assured him that the stamp would not be printed, only another one, showing Hindenburg in civilian clothes. Redslob used the opportunity to draft an outline of his lecture: he would stress the importance of commercial art, the competition of 1919/20, the collaboration with S. von Weech, the airmail stamp with the image of an eagle by Otto Hermann Werner Hadank, professor at the academy of arts and crafts in Berlin, Redslob's own suggestion of cityscapes. This would leave Warburg free to concentrate on the cultural and philatelic points of view and to discuss the German stamps in detail.[134] Warburg replied that his lecture would simply be 'emotional outpourings of an art-loving stamp collector',[135] toning down the contents of his illustrated lecture, but not the method: showing the development of images and symbols by pointing to photographs on mobile walls, the 'Mnemosyne Atlas', thus charting the route of artistic developments.

In his lecture Warburg used the same multi-media approach to his methodology of teaching as in his tutorials and seminars, focusing on the route 'From a History of Art to a Science of the Image', as explained in a letter to his friend Moritz von Geiger, professor of philosophy in Göttingen, who recommended a student of his, Klaus Berger, to Warburg.[136] The newspapers duly reported on the lecture under the title 'the language of images in world traffic' and 'the postage stamp as cultural document', which was, in fact, Warburg's definition of a postage stamp and a superb example of linguistic precision yoking art and science,[137] but none of the authors specifically mentioned 'Idea Vincit'. And yet it was the last exhibit which Warburg showed in his lecture and which was commented upon favourably in letters of thanks after the lecture. Benno Diederich, a grammar school teacher, who

132 WIA, GC, E. Redslob to Warburg, 15.7.1927.

133 WIA, GC, Warburg to E. Redslob, 1.8.1927. Paul von Hindenburg, German statesman, 1847–1934; Sigmund von Weech, German graphic artist, 1888–1982.

134 WIA, GC, E. Redslob to Warburg, 3.8.927. Otto Hermann Werner Hadank, German artist, 1889–1965.

135 WIA, GC, Warburg to E. Redslob, 7.8.1927.

136 WIA, GC, A. Warburg to M. v. Geiger, 17.11.1925. Moritz von Geiger, German philosopher, 1860–1937. Klaus Berger, editor of Geiger's writings, German art historian 1901–2000.

137 Warburg, A., 'Bildersprache des Weltverkehrs'; and Warburg and Redslob, 'Die Briefmarke als Kulturdokument.'

wrote that he was neither convinced by Warburg's explanation of the lion on the Bavarian stamp nor by Redslob's explanation of the eagle, found the last exhibit, IDEA, 'of extraordinary power'.[138]

Most touching of all tributes was Redslob's. He thanked Warburg for the evening in the KBW, enlightened by Warburg's lecture 'through which a ray from space was projected onto the small postage stamp'. He had already spoken with Dr. Eberhard Hölscher, chair of the Association of German Commercial Artists [Bund Deutscher Gebrauchsgraphiker], who had suggested having Warburg's lecture published in the Journal of the organisation.[139] Nothing came of it, however. Warburg forwarded a copy of the newspaper article on the lecture to Gladys Amanda Reichard, an American anthropologist,[140] to his brother Felix Warburg in New York,[141] to William Wallace Dunlop in Barbados,[142] mentioned the lecture to his friend Jacques Mesnil in Paris,[143] to Wilhelm von Bode in Berlin,[144] and refused the request by A. E. Glasewald, the editor of *Philatelisten-Zeitung* in Gössnitz, that Warburg lend him his lecture slides, on the grounds that he should encourage people to attend the actual lectures.[145]

Idea Vincit

Warburg followed politics by reading newspapers and by discussing events with members of his family, mainly his brother, the banker Max Moritz Warburg, and friends. Indeed, during World War I, he was hard at work scouring newspapers, selecting articles for cuttings and cataloguing them in his War Archive, ostensibly to have the sources ready to tell the world the truth after the war as to why Germany had to go to war. Sources would also be entries in the *Journal*, his correspondence and his working papers on a variety of research topics. Warburg never did write the history of the truth of the origins of the war and its propaganda horror stories. Incidentally, when the KBW was packed up to be shipped to London in December 1933, the only substantial collection of papers which stayed behind in Hamburg was his War Archive. It is believed that it was destroyed in World War II.[146]

138 WIA, GC, B. Diederich to A. Warburg, 14.8.1927. Benno Diederich, German philologist, 1870–1947.
139 WIA, GC, E. Redslob to A. Warburg, 15.8.1927. Eberhard Hölscher, German graphic artist, 1890–1969.
140 WIA, GC, A. Warburg to G. A. Reichard, 16.8.1927. Gladys Amanda Reichard, American anthropologist, 1893–1955.
141 WIA, GC, A. Warburg to Felix Warburg, 27.8.1927.
142 WIA, GC, A. Warburg to W. W. C. Dunlop, 5.9.1927.
143 WIA, GC, A. Warburg to J. Mesnil, 18.8.1927.
144 WIA, GC, A. Warburg to W. v. Bode, 29.8.1927. Wilhelm von Bode, German art historian, 1845–1929.
145 WIA, GC, A. Warburg to A. E. Glasewald, 6.9.1927. Arthur Ernst Glasewald, German stamp dealer, 1861–1926.
146 For details on the war archive see Chapter 3.

Still, his lifelong interest in politics, the way it shaped views and hatreds, ambitions and defeats, made him comment on great events and political heavyweights not merely from a day-to-day point of view, but from the standpoint of symbols. The potency of symbols, as shown, for instance, by the Fascists when they appropriated imperial Roman symbols to serve their purpose, their lust for power in the 20th century, was juxtaposed by Warburg with the symbol of the 'Idea': 'Classical antiquity on a postage stamp (fasces) reveals the schizophrenic power craze in Italy: in contrast to it is Strohmeyer's IDEA VINCIT a protest of the "impractical" idea'.[147]

In August 1928, when Erich Warburg, Aby Warburg's nephew, was on his way to meet Frank Billings Kellogg, the US Foreign Secretary, Warburg gave him three copies of 'Idea Vincit' with a message: when handing them over, Erich was to tell Kellogg that a copy had been presented to G. Stresemann and that the motto 'Idea Vincit' should be seen as the leitmotif of things to come in Germany.[148] With the signing of the Kellogg – Briand Pact in August 1928, Warburg saw his initiative, the representation of victory of (technological and thereby political) ideas, justified.[149] He entered in the *Journal* Stresemann's message to a French newspaper after signing the Kellogg – Briand Pact: 'the power of the idea stands higher than material might, which carries humanity along with it'.[150] In his view Stresemann had rightfully received the 'Idea Vincit' in 1926.

In another context, in connection with the establishment of the Planetarium in Hamburg, Warburg toyed with the idea of adding a copy of the linocut to the exhibition gallery of the history of astronomy and astrology.[151] It was important for him to show the development of thought breaking free from the grip of fantastic monsters ruling the universe to embrace technological and scientific explanations of the mechanics of the universe. Once again Warburg referred to an important political event: the speech by the British Prime Minister Ramsay MacDonald to the Assembly of the League of Nations in Geneva on 3 September 1929. The speech on disarmament and peace, on reducing armament and finding a solution for Palestine, 'the risks of peace', ended with an acceptance of reason:

> The greatest test of enlightenment in these days is to show our willingness to reduce armaments, to banish from our mind all ideas of security, and to throw ourselves, with courage unflinchingly into this position, that we trust men and women and nations who come and make bargains with us.

147 Michels/Schoell-Glass, *Journal*, 31.12.1926, 96.

148 WIA, GC, Warburg to Erich Warburg, 18.8.1928. Frank Billings Kellogg, American statesman, 1856–1937. Erich, later Eric M. Warburg, German and American banker, 1900–1990.

149 Michels/Schoell-Glass, *Journal*, 28.8.1928, 337. On 27 August 1928 the US and France signed the Kellogg – Brian Pact, in which they and 13 other nations outlawed war as tool of national politics and pledged to settle conflicts with peaceful means.

150 Michels/Schoell-Glass, *Journal*, 9.9.1928, 340.

151 Michels/Schoell-Glass, *Journal*, 17.9.1928, 343.

> We will carry out our part, and they will carry out their part, and in order that that may be done without break, we set up Courts to take the place of arms and conciliation to take the place of threats, and we agree that reason is the greatest creative power in the universe.[152]

Warburg approved this turn of events and commented upon it by writing 'Idea Vincit' in the *Journal*[153] and by writing 'Briand speaks in Geneva. Still, "Idea Vincit"'.[154] The phrase even entered his private communications: he presented a copy of Jean Paul's *Werke* to his daughter Frede, with the by now often used dedication 'Everything is possible. Idea Victrix. To his dear Frede. Father'.[155]

The victory of the idea had become a hope, like a beacon with which to illuminate the future.[156] It had become possible to grasp it by limiting it to a pictorial, visual language which expressed that which was remembered, which was conventionally called tradition, which had become collective social memory. Images on postage stamps, or for that matter on a deck of cards or emblems embroidered on a sleeve, were the leitmotifs yoking the past to the future. As an art historian Warburg saw his role as interpreting pictorial representations of ideas. Surprisingly, he did not often comment on musical reminiscences of one composer in the work of another. Once, when he did, it served to underpin his view of the importance of symbol-making and symbol repetition, for instance classical antiquity being transformed into 'opera or the musical drama of the soul' or into a 'piece of aeronautical engineering'.[157] In modern times the postage stamp, the most economic manifestation of specificity of purpose and totality of application, became the carrier of symbols: political power was signalled by the use of traditional national emblems, the notion of one's home country was expressed by landscapes on stamps, and the energy and dynamism of travel and transport as shown on the airmail stamp replaced the application of narrow national political will.[158] The idea that airspace was international, this was the victory of the mind, of the idea. The symbol of something which in itself is hard to represent, the idea, like the soul, had been pressed into the shape of a soaring aeroplane. The idea had not so much become flesh and bone but steel and machine. It was an advertisement of greatness and prestige, a pointer to the coming technological age. But Warburg did not use the phrase 'Idea Vincit' for technology alone: we see it in his *Journal* – 'Idea vincit'

152 From *The Times*, see Reuters News Agency, 'Disarmament and Peace. Mr. MacDonald's Speech at Geneva', 11 c – d. Ramsay MacDonald, British statesman, 1866–1937.

153 Michels/Schoell-Glass, *Journal*, 5.9.1929, 521.

154 WIA, III.11.82., Diary, 5.9.1929, 9463, wrongly dated 5.10.1929.

155 Jean Paul, *Jean Pauls Werke*, vol. 4–6. Dedication on flyleaf, '6/V/1929'. Jean Paul, German writer, 1763–1825.

156 Warburg frequently made use of tower similes, likening the KBW to a tower, a receiver, a focal point picking up developments long before everybody else or an aerial capable of transmitting ideas, cf. McEwan, D., 'Mapping the Traderoutes of the Mind: The Warburg Institute', 37–50.

157 Michels/Schoell-Glass, *Journal*, 3.5.1928, 253.

158 Michels/Schoell-Glass, *Journal*, 28.2.1927, 62.

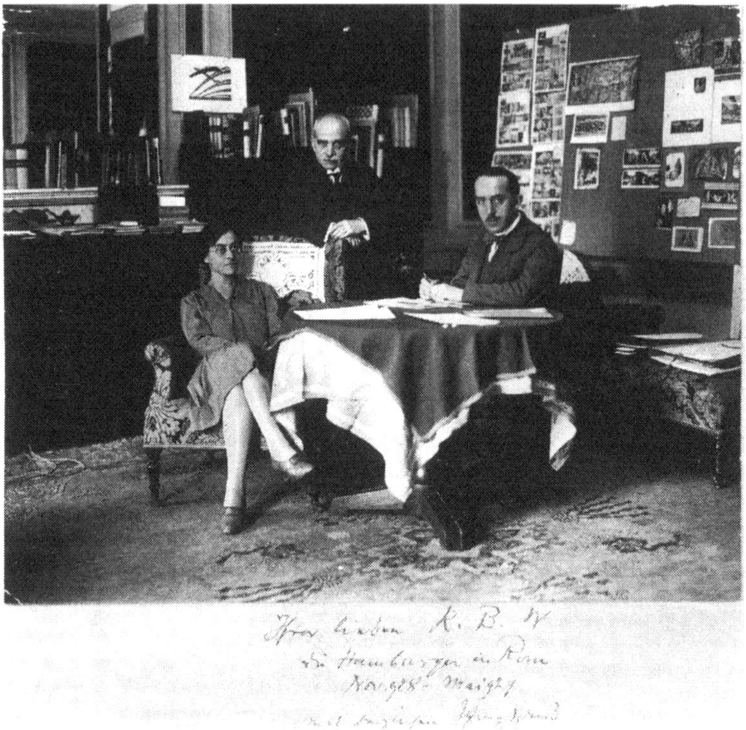

Figure 2.4 From left to right: Gertrud Bing, Aby Warburg (standing), Franz Alber. Rome, Palace Hotel, May 1929. In the background the mobile walls with the photographs for the Mnemosyne exhibition, next to them on the wall a copy of IDEA VINCIT. WIA, Portrait collection. 'Ihrer lieben K.B.W. Die Hamburger in Rom. Nov. 928-Mai 929'. ['To dear K.B.W. The Hamburgers in Rome, Nov. 1928 to May 1929'].

Photo: The Warburg Institute.

below the illustration of three postage stamps, showing the heads of Gustav Stresemann, Foreign Minister, and Paul von Hindenburg, President, and below them in Warburg's hand 'everything is possible'.[159] He had a copy of the print pinned up in his rooms in the Palace Hotel in Rome (see figure 2.4) and used this phrase again after returning from the very long stay in Italy in July 1929. He wrote with tangible relief, encouraging or possibly comforting himself, that getting used to life in Hamburg had been made unexpectedly easy: 'Everything is possible, Idea vincit'.[160] Did he, three months before his death, really see the victory of the 'idea'? The political situation in the following years would have bitterly disappointed him.

159 Michels/Schoell-Glass, *Journal*, 10.7.1929, 470 and 471 (image).
160 Michels/Schoell-Glass, *Journal*, 18.7.1929, 470.

3

A FIGHT AGAINST WINDMILLS. ON *RIVISTA ILLUSTRATA*, WARBURG'S PRO-ITALIAN PUBLISHING INITIATIVE[1]

Introduction

'Support for the War effort. In the afternoon Samson and Lo Verde with me because of planned Italian journal' (see figure 3.1).[2] The pithy entry in Warburg's Diary states that he attended a meeting of the Hamburg committee for war aid and in the afternoon met two friends, the banker Martin Samson und the journalist Felice Lo Verde. It was, in fact, the first meeting of an editorial committee, which was to publish two editions of the publication *Rivista Illustrata I* and *II*.[3]

In the summer of 1914 the political alliances among the dominant European powers were complex. The Habsburg monarchy, the German Empire and the Kingdom of Italy, an uneasy partner in the so-called Triple Alliance, faced the big colonial powers of the British Empire, France and Russia. In addition, there were secret treaties between the British Empire, France, Russia and Italy, which meant that Italy was not wholeheartedly anchored in the Triple Alliance. Military manoeuvres, revolutionary acts, strikes, rumours, political killings, they all created fertile ground for defamations, half-truths, nationalistic showing off and threatening behaviour. The situation was not peaceful, the Balkans were restless, the circumstances in Russia decidedly bad. And yet, in the summer of 1914 nobody could foresee that a few years later the map of Europe would be radically altered.

On 29 July 1914 Warburg entered into his Diary that Germany was threatened by war. He still expressed this bleak vision only as a possibility – 'all of Germany would burn!' – and asked himself, 'Can this be stopped?' and 'What is England doing? Everything depends on it for us'.[4]

1 Originally published in McEwan, D., 'Ein Kampf gegen Windmühlen. Warburgs pro-italienische publizistische Initiative', 135–163. For a much shortened bilingual English and Italian translation, see McEwan, D., 'Due missioni politiche di Aby Warburg in Italia nel 1914–15', 57–79.

2 WIA, III.10.4, Diary, 3.10.1914, 49. Martin Samson, of the Gebrüder Samson bank in Berlin, b. 1870; Felice Lo Verde, Italian journalist, b. 1876.

3 WIA, IV, 63.1.2.

4 WIA, III.10.3., Diary, 29.7.1914, 92. WIA, III.10.4., Diary, 4.8.1914, 2.

DOI: 10.4324/9781003169024-4

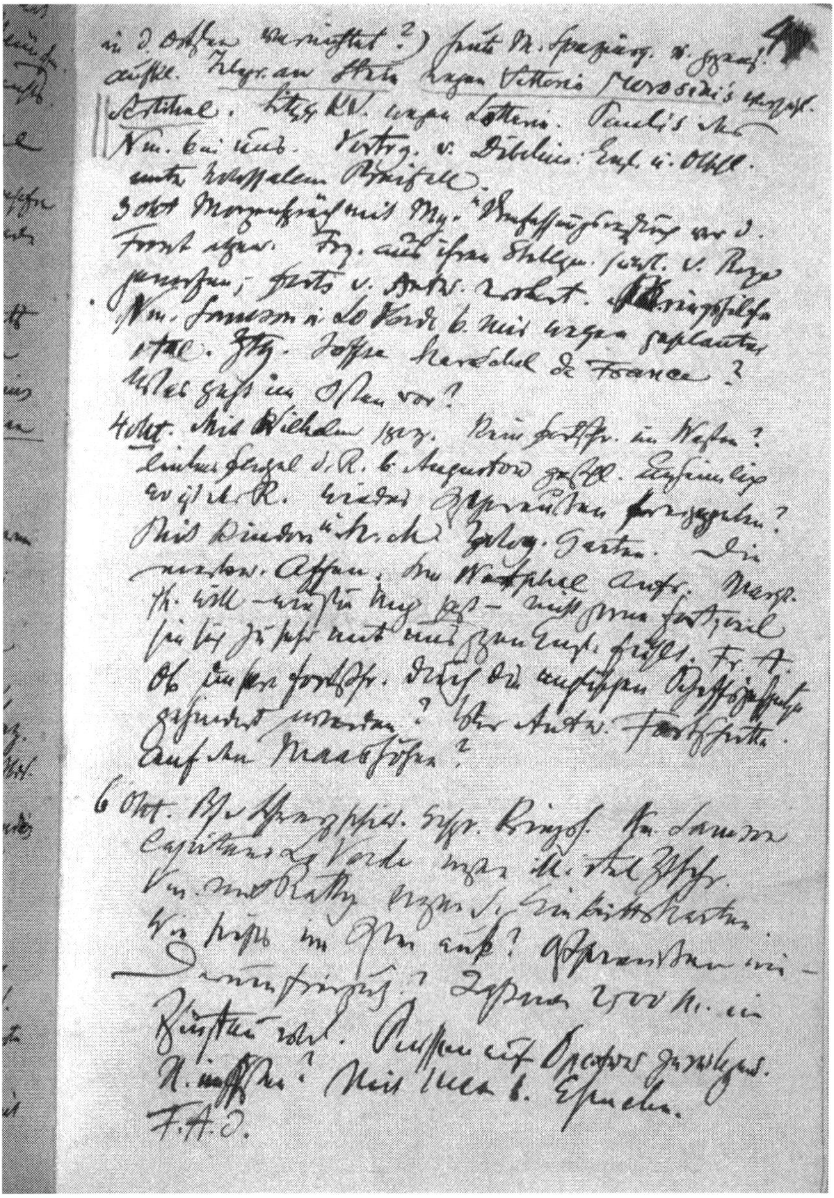

Figure 3.1 WIA, III.10.4, Diary, 3.10.1914, 49.

Source: © Photo: The Warburg Institute.

The intensely detailed entries in his Diary give insight into Warburg's thoughts, fears, and conviction that it would become imperative to stop Italy entering the war and to unveil the lies which led to the outbreak of war. He meticulously kept records of battles fought, ships sunk, prisoners taken, which airships were downed and where, how many guns were captured on both fronts, in the West and in the East, troop movements, road conditions, whether bridges were destroyed and supply routes attacked; these pieces of information were augmented by observations on the inertia of diplomacy, the ineptitude of politicians and, inevitably, which of his friends and neighbours had been captured and killed. But the Diary entries also reveal something personal: the confessions of his own exhaustion, frustration, unease and hunger for news. Almost daily he recorded whom he visited, what he heard when having lunch or dinner with friends and family members. Not everybody had a telephone; it was therefore important to visit people to hear whether they had received news from family members serving in the army. A network of information developed, which was reflected in his extensive correspondence. In many letters to colleagues he knew from his years in Florence, he confessed he felt called upon to stop Italy falling victim to the enemies of Germany: the 'slave drivers',[5] namely Great Britain and France.

Another source for analysing Warburg's intellectual and practical activities in World War I are the so-called index card boxes, the subject catalogue, in particular boxes 18, 'Religion', and 117, 'Superstition in war' (see figure 3.2).

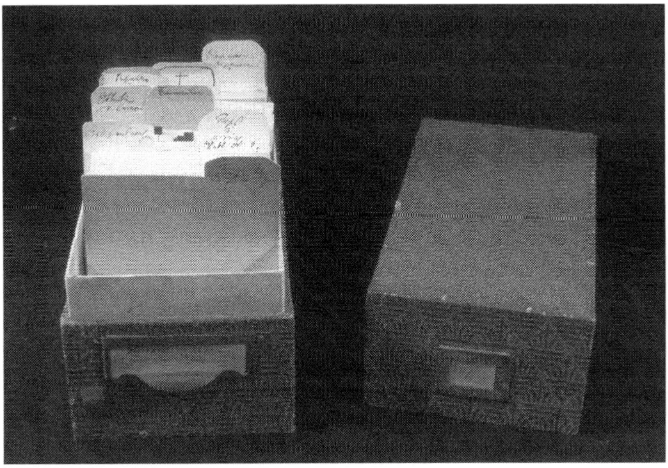

Figure 3.2 WIA, III.2.1., Index card box 117, Superstition in war.

Source: © Photo: The Warburg Institute.

5 WIA, GC, Warburg to F. Saxl, 29.6.1915.

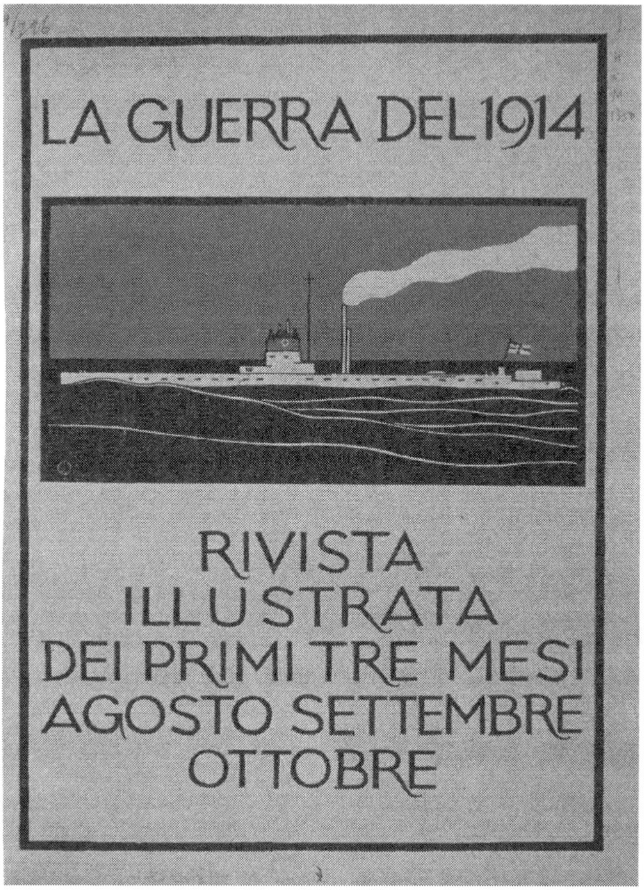

Figure 3.3 WIA, IV.11.1.1.1., Wilhelm von Beckerath, Title illustration for *La Rivista I.*

Source: © Photo: The Warburg Institute.

Over the course of many years Warburg had collected a wealth of bibliographical references in box 117 on prophecies in wartime, prejudices, Nostradamus, Plato, visions, soothsayers, telepathy, kabbalism, research into souls, magic bells, interpretation of dreams, talismans, amulets, spiritualists, sick children, amputations, atrocities. He often added his own comments to bibliographical references, like 'might for the sake of might',[6] 'states talking freedom and bleeding dividends'[7] or 'On the freedom of Entente man',[8] a clear echo of

6 WIA, III.2.1., index card box, 117, 009122.
7 WIA, III.2.1., index card box, 117, 009112.
8 WIA, III.2.1., index card box, 117, 009123.

Martin Luther's writing in 1520 *On the freedom of a Christian.*[9] Warburg is not only cynical and shocked, but also spurred on by patriotism, believing that the good combination of 'disciplina tedesca and Roman genius'[10] could be strengthened by a book about the truth behind the causes of the war and the behaviour of Germany.

The fight for the truth about the reasons for war is a common thread in Warburg's work during World War I. The states at war were to him like wheels in a fantastic machinery of lies, blindly thudding and thumping and using false arguments to force the treaty partners to fight. In order to document this campaign of lies after the end of the war Warburg started his war archive project.[11] He roped in his whole family to assist him; they had to select articles from ten newspapers and cut them out to be catalogued in a detailed subject catalogue. The very large collection of cut-outs has not survived; neither did Warburg write the planned book about the campaign of lies.[12] What has survived are the headings in his boxes, his thoughts about cataloguing and three boxes of contemporary propaganda photographs.

The fight against lies

The three-day battle in Leuven at the end of August 1914 had been a blood bath. To Warburg it was as if 'the seven deadly sins' ruled.[13] The single individual and his wish for peace were as nothing. Horror-struck, he commented that it took only eight days to turn an educated, gentle young man into a hatred-filled bloodthirsty beast: 'The Germans won themselves to death' in Belgium; they would not be able to keep Belgium should the people revolt, it would spell 'finis Germaniae' – the end of Germany.[14] It was tragically wrong to believe that Belgium could be taken rapidly, and to disregard the psychology of peoples was a conceptual error. Therefore, Warburg believed at the beginning of the war that the USA would stay neutral towards Japan; if not, it would portend 'the affliction of the Nibelungs'. He was, like many of his contemporaries, aghast at the news that the British deployed Indian troops in France.[15]

The daily entries, the harsh language, the many questions over who supported whom, they all were directed at the dreadful state of affairs perpetrated

9 Preuss, H., *Von der Freiheit eines Christenmenschen/Martin Luther*. Martin Luther, German Reformer, 1483–1546.

10 WIA, III.2.1., index card box, 117, 009246.

11 WIA, GC, Warburg to Frankfurter Zeitung, 2.2.1915. In this letter Warburg criticised missing or faulty source references in newspaper articles, which would only complicate Warburg's task after the war, namely the writing of a thorough *Handbook of falsehoods*.

12 For the unexplained fate of the collection see Biester, B., *Der innere Beruf zur Wissenschaft: Paul Ruben (1866–1943)*, 174–176, in particular the comments by Alfred Vagts, German historian, 1892–1986 and Carl A. Rathjens, German geographer, 1887–1966.

13 WIA, III.10.4., Diary, 26.8.1914, 19.

14 WIA, III.10.4., Diary, 29.8.1914, 21.

15 WIA, III.10.4., Diary, 30.8.1914, 24.

by the official, semi-official, military and journalistic propaganda machines. They all delivered false pieces of information; they all unleashed an epidemic of lies. The planned book, a bibliography of falsehoods, and the planned museum of falsehoods[16] would, after the war, analyse terms like 'sedition' and 'global conflagration'.[17]

Warburg hoped that his Italian friends, among them the art historian Federico Hermanin would support him. At the same time he also feared that Italy, blinded by French successes, would turn against Germany. 'It really seems that a nationalist Catholic Renaissance is under way in France, which I think is very dangerous, because it has a moral-ascetic core'.[18] He mused that the neutrality of Italy was not clear nor was a politics of neutrality acceptable to the majority of Italians. Seen from a German point of view, such a position was dangerous because there was an explosive element in it. Thoughts like these explain Warburg's frequent outbursts against defamation, lies and covert insinuations by politicians like René Viviani, the French prime minister and foreign minister in 1914, whose speeches were 'the epitome of a pack of lies and phrase-mongering'.[19]

The editorial committee and the first edition

The belief in his mission drove him on; the results were two periodicals called *Rivista Illustrata*. The first one was published in November 1914, the second in April 1915. Further editions were planned, but Italy's entry into the war against the Habsburg empire in May 1915 stopped any further work in its tracks.

The first days and weeks of war reports were a rude awakening. Suddenly everybody suspected everybody else of being a spy. Rumours proliferated. People wanted to get facts, but only got lies.[20] The bulletins from the army were 'fatally curt'.[21] Warburg bought himself a revolver and learnt to shoot; his younger brother Max Warburg, the banker, and Albert Ballin, director of the Hamburg-American shipping line HAPAG, were taken to Berlin by car, commandeered by the army, to attend urgent meetings.[22] What shocked the Germans was that the British contravened the neutrality of Belgium. For Warburg, as well as for Fürst Bernhard von Bülow, a friend of the family, diplomat and former imperial chancellor, this was the most brutal and shocking show of might.[23] Ultimately it turned out to be a question of whom to believe, the reports from abroad or the German newspapers: 'one wakes up every morning and thinks: this is not possible! The collapse of

16 WIA, GC, Warburg, Memorandum, 20.12.1914.
17 WIA, III.10.4., Diary, 22.9.1914, 39.
18 WIA, III.10.4., Diary, 21.8.1914, 13.
19 WIA, III.10.4., Diary, 25.12.1914, 106. René Viviani, French politician, 1863–1925.
20 WIA, III.10.4., Diary, 16.8.1914, 7.
21 WIA, III.10.4., Diary, 22.11.1914, 88.
22 WIA, III.10.4., Diary, 6.8.1914, 3.
23 WIA, III.10.4., Diary, 8.8.1914, 4. Fürst Bernhard von Bülow, German statesman, 1849–1929.

Europe'. Despite the vitriolic comments coming via the 'telegraphic network of lies' he was convinced that Germany would win.[24]

At the end of August 1914 Georg Thilenius, Professor at the Colonial Institute in Hamburg, had started to publish a series of notes, *Announcements for foreign countries*, in order to defend the German point of view abroad. At the end of September 1914 Warburg and Martin Samson had taken the decision to improve German-Italian relations by publishing an Italian-language periodical giving space to all the above-mentioned views. It was hoped that the issues of *Rivista Illustrata*, the result of the collaboration of Warburg and his friends, would stop Italy ruining itself on the side of the enemies of Germany. The team of assistants comprised Georg Thilenius, Giulio Panconcelli-Calzia, the head of the phonetic laboratory of the Colonial Institute in Hamburg, Fritz Saxl, Warburg's young librarian, Käthe Embden, sister of Warburg's medical doctor who worked in field hospitals, and other helpers.[25] Warburg's contribution was the selection of illustrations as well as the German texts. Panconcelli-Calzia and other Italian friends were responsible for the Italian translations. None of them had any journalistic training or experience. As a project, it seems overly daring to found a periodical in the midst of a war, destined to be sold cheaply in newsstands in Italy. An issue was planned every fortnight, to be produced without journalists, without a news agency, without picture sources or a sales organisation in Italy. It was an ambitious enterprise, but ultimately doomed. The prestigious Hamburg newspaper *Hamburger Fremdenblatt*, whose editor-in-chief was Warburg's friend Felix von Eckardt, put the newspaper's printing house at Warburg's disposal, but did not allow the *Rivista Illustrata* to use the masthead of the *Fremdenblatt*. Even for an existing newspaper printer and distributor it would have been extremely difficult to launch a new title.[26] Still, Warburg was not to be deterred by logistical considerations. He hoped to print between 20,000 and 100,000 copies every fortnight in the printing house of the *Hamburger Fremdenblatt*. A request to the marine news services for financial support remained unanswered.[27] On the very next day after Warburg's request, Thilenius sent a bundle of articles to Warburg to be discussed at the first editorial meeting.

At the beginning of October 1914 events moved fast. There was an endless series of meetings and negotiations with the printing house of the *Hamburger Fremdenblatt* after the first editorial meeting.[28] Warburg sent a list with the names of his contacts

24 WIA, III.10.4., Diary, 19.8.1914, 8.

25 WIA, III.10.4., Diary, 12.10.1914, 53. Georg Thilenius, German ethnologist, 1868–1937. Giulio Panconcelli-Calzia, Italian phonetician, 1878–1966; Fritz Saxl, Austrian art historian, 1890–1948; Käthe Embden, nurse in the Barmbeck hospital, Hamburg, sister of Marianne Embden. Their brother Heinrich Embden was Aby Warburg's general physician.

26 WIA, III.10.4., Diary, 13.10.1914, 53. Felix von Eckardt, German journalist, 1866–1936.

27 WIA, GC, Warburg to Heinrich Löhlein, captain and director of the marine intelligence service in Berlin, 1.10.1914.

28 WIA, III.10.4., Diary, 13.10.1914, 53.

in Italy to the Colonial Institute.[29] He had asked his friends to send him articles, as he wanted to produce an illustrated chronicle of the war, 'in order to calmly enlighten' people.[30] After selection by the committee, articles would be translated into Italian[31]; in fact, Saxl and Panconcelli-Calzia had started by translating an article by Umberto Gnoli, who 'personifies the type, rather unknown in Germany, of the noble Italian from former times' and the 'incorruptible Italian idealist'.[32]

Paul Gustav Hübner, assistant at the Bibliotheca Hertziana library in Rome, sent newspapers, periodicals and reports on the mood in Italy.[33] The Italian consul in Hamburg, Giuseppe Count Giacchi, who had been Francesco Crispi's secretary when Crispi signed the Triple Alliance, penned an introductory dedication to everybody who wanted to know what Germany thought about the war.[34] On 11 November 1914 Warburg proudly entered into his Diary that the first issue was ready and made a good impression, but – would it be successful?[35]

The title illustration of *La Guerra del 1914. Rivista Illustrata dei primi tre mesi agosto, settembre, ottobre*, was made by Willy von Beckerath, head of the school of arts and crafts in Hamburg (see figure 3.3). The issue, with its 24 pages, contained 30 Italian articles and 31 black and white illustrations. The price was 15 cents.[36] The archive copy in The Warburg Institute Archive in London has corrections in the text and a further two pages, a table of illustrations and a table listing the distribution of topics under the headings 'German news', 'Italian news' and 'news from neutral countries', each subdivided into politics, war on land, war at sea, economy, Russia, the Orient. It goes without saying that the issue featured pictures of crusty old soldiers, smiling fathers in uniform holding the hands of their children, prisoner-of-war transports, wounded prisoners, action-packed pictures of soldiers aiming their guns at the enemy, trenches, soldiers making music, etc. The articles were not much better: patriotic appeals, translations of clips in English newspapers, psychological observations, financial statements of the cost of war.

The initial reactions from friends in Hamburg, like Senator Gottfried Holthusen, were positive.[37] Carl von Weinberg from Frankfurt am Main suggested more sentimental illustrations and less text for the next issue: 'We should never lose sight of

29 WIA, GC, Warburg to G. Thilenius, 5.10.1914.
30 WIA, GC, Warburg to F. Hermanin, 13.10.1914.
31 WIA, III.10.4., Diary, 7.10.1914, 50. Warburg had asked Senator Otto Westphal for articles. Otto Westphal, German merchant, 1853–1919.
32 WIA, GC, Warburg to P.G. Hübner, 21.10.1914. Umberto Gnoli, Italian art historian, 1878–1947.
33 WIA, GC, P.G. Hübner to Warburg, 31.10.1914. Paul Gustav Hübner, German art historian, from 1929 onwards Director of the Prussian Art Department, b. 1888.
34 WIA, III.10.4., Diary, 5.11.1914, 76. Page 1 of the first edition was signed 'G. G.'. Giuseppe Count Giacchi, Italian Consul General in Sarajevo in 1910, later in Hamburg, 1860–1931; Francesco Crispi, Italian statesman, 1819–1901.
35 WIA, III.10.4., Diary, 11.11.1914, 80.
36 WIA, IV.11.11.1.1. Willy von Beckerath, German painter, 1868–1938.
37 WIA, III.10.4., Diary, 21.11.1914, 87. Gottfried Holthusen, Hamburg senator, 1848–1920.

the fact, that all the Italians are big children after all'.[38] There was a trickle of orders, some of them cautiously critical, stating that the articles, mainly translations from newspapers and news agencies, had to be correctly referenced.[39] True enough, as a number of articlcs in *Rivista Illustrata* were printed without precise references.

Distribution and distribution problems in Italy

The editorial board had, indeed, managed to produce an issue, had translated articles, had them printed and had the first issue sent out. This was doubtlessly an organisational success. Hübner und Arthur Haseloff, secretary of the Prussian Historical Institute in Rome, were the contacts for Italy[40] and charged with building up a distribution network, so that the *Rivista Illustrata* would be available all over Italy.[41]

It was not clear what impression the first issue made on Italian readers. There were a number of other pro-German publications, cheap brochures that had flooded the market, so that nobody seemed to be interested in more of them. Pietro Silvio Rivetta in Rome suggested to Panconcelli-Calzia that it would be better to support the large pro-German Italian newspapers like the *Italia Nostra* group than to come up with a second issue.[42] Warburg agreed and, on subscribing to *Italia Nostra*, observed that it was '. . . the irrefutable duty to help in any way possible the marvellous people who commit themselves for us'.[43] Hübner speculated that the *Rivista Illustrata* might be too 'cultivated' for Romans and therefore did not sell well.[44]

Warburg wrote to Fürst Bülow to ask whether he could publicise *Rivista* in Italy,[45] and to the publishing firm and bookstore Leo S. Olschki in Florence to ask whether they could do the same. Olschki liked *Rivista* very much and predicted that the demand for it would be great once it was available at newsstands.[46] What became clear was that it was only after the publication of the first issue that serious considerations as to the sale and distribution of *Rivista* entered into the discussion. It seems as if the logistics had not been thought through. It was a project undertaken by well-meaning academics, friends of Italy, who hoped to dictate the flow of events. It was rather like tilting at windmills. The first issue found few buyers; the second issue was simply given away.

And yet, there were a number of very positive reports from German firms doing business in Italy. The German-Italian marketing board had ordered 1,000 copies,

38 WIA, GC, C. v. Weinberg to Warburg, 20.11.1914. Carl von Weinberg, German industrialist, 1861–1943.
39 WIA, GC, G. Gronau to Warburg, 3.12.1914. Georg Gronau, German art historian, 1868–1938.
40 WIA, GC, Warburg to P. G. Hübner, 22.11.1914. Arthur Haseloff, German art historian, 1872–1955.
41 WIA, GC, Warburg to A. Haseloff, 25.11.1914.
42 WIA, GC, P. S. Rivetta to G. Panconcelli-Calzia, 17.12.1914. Pietro Silvio Rivetta, Italian journalist, 1886–1952.
43 WIA, III.10.4., Diary, 30.12.1914, 109.
44 WIA, GC, P.G. Hübner to Warburg, 25.12.1914.
45 WIA, GC, Warburg to B. v. Bülow, 22.11.1914.
46 WIA, GC, L. S. Olschki to Warburg, 7.12.1914. Leo S. Olschki, Italian bookdealer, 1861–1940.

the Italian chamber of commerce 50 copies.[47] Many letters were appreciative, but there were also critical comments.[48] Hübner was one of them. Early on he was convinced of the uselessness of the enterprise: he was unable to find buyers.[49]

The second issue and Warburg's assignment in Italy

At the end of November 1914 an opportunity presented itself for Warburg to travel to Italy. Wilhelm von Bode, art historian, president of the German art history institute in Florence, first director of the Kaiser-Friedrich-Museum in Berlin – which had been built according to his plans – and director general of the royal, after 1918 national, museums from 1905 to 1920, asked for Warburg's advice with the German historical institute in Florence. The German nationals had to enlist for military service, among them the director, Hans von der Gabelentz-Linsingen; the institute was without a leader. It was imperative to consider whether the institute in Florence could be kept open during the war. Warburg spontaneously agreed to travel to Florence, to introduce a new director and to chair an academic meeting.[50] He wrote to the institute that German-Italian relations occupied a key position in world politics and stressed that Bernhard von Bülow, as German ambassador in Rome, did his best to remove Italian prejudice against Germany. It followed that the institute should do its bit and – sell the *Rivista Illustrata*. He announced his arrival in January 1915 in order to introduce Dr. Kurt N. Zoege von Manteuffel as the new deputy director.[51]

Already in December 1914, immediately after the publication of the first issue and irrespective of whether it was a commercial success or not, Warburg was thinking of publishing the next issue. Otto Runge, the editor of *Norddeutsche Allgemeine Zeitung* in Berlin, was particularly pleased that Warburg wanted to use an article about the breach of Belgium's neutrality.[52] The campaign of lies against Germany had to be documented; the pro-German circles in Italy had to be given reasons to argue against Italy's entry into the war.

Warburg travelled to Berlin, where he had meetings with the military brass, civil servants, and friends. Immediately after his return suggestions to improve the second issue were discussed in the editorial meetings. Giacchi was against articles on the whole topic of neutrality,[53] the translator Pia di Mayo-Gelati as well. But even members of Warburg's own family, such as his cousin Anna Blumenfeld, who had returned from Rome in December 1914, had doubts about the success

47 WIA, GC, G. Hedler of the Colonial Institute in Hamburg to Warburg, 7.12.1914.

48 WIA, IV.11.1.2., from 24.11.1914 to 23.4.1915, orders for *Rivista Illustrata I* and *II*.

49 WIA, GC, P. G. Hübner to Warburg, 6.1.1915.

50 WIA, III.10.4., Diary, 26.11.1914, 91. Wilhelm von Bode, German art historian, 1845–1929; Hans von der Gabelentz-Linsingen, German art historian, 1872–1946.

51 WIA, GC, Warburg to the committee of the art history institute in Florence, 4.12.1912. Kurt N. Zoege von Manteuffel, Baltic German art historian, 1881–1941.

52 WIA, GC, Warburg to O. Runge, 25.11.1914 and Runge's reply 26.11.1914. Otto Runge, German journalist, 1864–1940.

53 WIA, III.10.4., Diary, 14.12.1914, 102.

of the operation. Three months afterwards, Warburg wrote in his Diary that he had had a chat with his mother and his cousin and stated: Anna Blumenfeld was 'against German discipline, which destroyed ability'.[54] On the other hand, the German news agency in Berlin promised to send aerial photographs of French positions behind a cathedral and permitted their reprint in the *Rivista*.[55]

Today it is very difficult to comprehend the feelings, expectations and disappointments of patriotic Germans celebrating their first Christmas during the war. Warburg, loyal to the emperor, no longer observed the Jewish religion of his parents and did not precisely share the Christian practices of his wife, but tolerated them. He recorded in his Diary that the family set up the Christmas crib made by his wife; they did not sing Christmas carols but the national anthem 'Deutschland, Deutschland über alles' ('Germany, Germany, above all'). A long list of events followed, beginning with the words 'if someone had said last year . . .', in which Warburg listed the inexplicable facts of the war, many friends killed in action, Warburg's own activities as editor of *Rivista* as well as his new tasks, the trip to Italy and the production of the second issue of *Rivista*.[56]

The decision to go ahead with a second issue of *Rivista* meant that Panconcelli-Calzia, who was to travel with Warburg to Florence, would continue on to Rome to

54 WIA, III.10.4., Diary, 23.12.1914, 105 and 26.3.1915, 159. Anna Blumenfeld, née Warburg, wife of Martin Blumenfeld, 1866–1929.

55 WIA, GC, Hansen of the Deutscher Überseedienst to Warburg, 14.12.1914. Dr. Hansen, journalist in the German news agency. See also Schwartz, P.J., 'Aby Warburg and Cinema Revisited', 105–140.

56 WIA, III.10.4., Diary, 26.11.1914, 107–108:
'If somebody had said last year: 1914
You will have paper money
And Miss Th.[urnham] will have 'fled' to England
And Wilh.[elm Hertz] will wear the uniform of first lieutenant,
Graefe, Wegehaupt, Strack will have been killed in action
And Waetzoldt wounded in Bochum!
And I would ask [ill.; possibly 'von' abbreviated] Basse for eye-witnesses of Strack's death in Flanders
And I will prepare myself for a trip to Italy.
And Embden will suffer in Russia,
Käte Embden will be a nurse in the Barmbecker hospital,
C. G. Heise writes an article against Hunzinger
And I have edited Rivista Illustrata della Guerra 1914 with Thilenius and Calzia!
Ballin, admiral ashore
Franz Blumenfeld, Erich Lachmann killed in action'.
Explanation of names: Miss Margaret Emily Thurnham, nanny to Warburg's children, b. 1882; Wilhelm Hertz, Dr. jur., judge, 1873–1939; Erich Graefe, Orientalist, d. 1914; Hans Wegehaupt, philologist, 1872–1914; Max L. Strack, historian, 1867–1914; Wilhelm Waetzoldt, art historian, 1880–1945; Hans von Basse, senior lieutenant, 1887–1979. (The abbreviation in front of his name may be 'von' or possibly his title. I thank Steffen Haug for his explanation.); Heinrich Embden, German neurologist, 1871–1941; Carl Georg Heise, art historian, 1890–1979; August Wilhelm Hunzinger, theologian, 1871–1920; Albert Ballin, soldier, 1857–1918; Franz Blumenfeld, 1892–1914, son of Anna Blumenfeld, née Warburg; Erich Lachmann, non-commissioned officer, 1891–1914, son of Caroline Lachmann, née Rosenbacher. I am grateful for Steffen Haug's help.

set up appointments for Warburg, referring to 'Bauchi' for Fürst Bülow, 'Tari' for Rivetta and 'Paoli' for Hübner.[57] The use of noms de plume seems conspiratorial, but was certainly necessary. Warburg travelled to Florence at the end of January and stayed there for one month, with one weekend in Rome. He met with friends from his time in Florence from 1897 to 1902, including the English poet and art historian Herbert Horne, who was very pleased to see him. All these activities filled Warburg with a sense of purpose: his contribution and convictions seemed to matter; there were people who shared his ideas. However, Warburg did not underestimate 'the mendacious world of our enemies' to whom his friends were exposed.[58] He reprimanded Count Stein, whom he called a 'brutish type', after having read his memorandum 'Germany's greatness and Italy's wickedness'. Warburg saw the situation differently: nation states with their principles of hegemony would not solve anything; the solution would be the creation of the 'United States of Western Europe'.[59]

The academic meeting, or *adunanza*, took place in the art history institute in Florence on 20 February 1915 (see figure 3.4). Warburg introduced the new deputy director and afterwards returned to Hamburg convinced that he was able to influence the situation in Italy. There were plans for more academic events; the last one took place on 17 April 1915. The Italian declaration of war against Austria-Hungary on 23 May 1915 stopped any further activities. Based on the cancellation of the Triple Alliance on 3 May 1915 the institute was closed on 16 May 1915. It was put under the protection of the Swiss consul Carlo A. Steinhäuslin. Fritz Baron von Marcuard,[60] a Swiss national living in Florence and member of the local committee of the art history institute, was charged with the interim administration.[61] Work in the institute resumed only after the end of the war.

The sojourn in Italy boosted Warburg's belief in the need to produce a second issue of *Rivista*. It was completed on 17 March 1915 and was produced in the printing house of the *Hamburger Fremdenblatt*.[62] However, two days later, Warburg received a cable from Hübner in Rome that said to stop publishing more issues.[63] This time the message did not use noms de plume, but medical terms: the 'patient' was in a critical situation, the 'temperature curve' fluctuated. This stopped Warburg from packing up the issue ready for despatch.[64]

57 WIA, GC, G. Panconcelli-Calzia to Warburg, 11.2.1915.

58 WIA, FC, Warburg to Mary Warburg, 5.2.1915. Herbert Horne, English art historian, 1864–1916.

59 WIA, III.10.4., Diary, 15.2.1915, 137. No further details about Count Stein are known.

60 WIA, GC, Zoege von Manteuffel to Warburg, 28.5.1915. Carlo A. Steinhäuslin, Swiss diplomat; Fritz Baron von Marcuard, Swiss national, resident in Florence.

61 Hubert, H.W., *Das kunsthistorische Institut in Florenz*, 36.

62 WIA, III.10.4., Diary, 17.3.1915, 154.

63 WIA, III.10.4., Diary, 19.3.1915, 156.

64 WIA, III.10.4., Diary, 20.3.1915, 157.

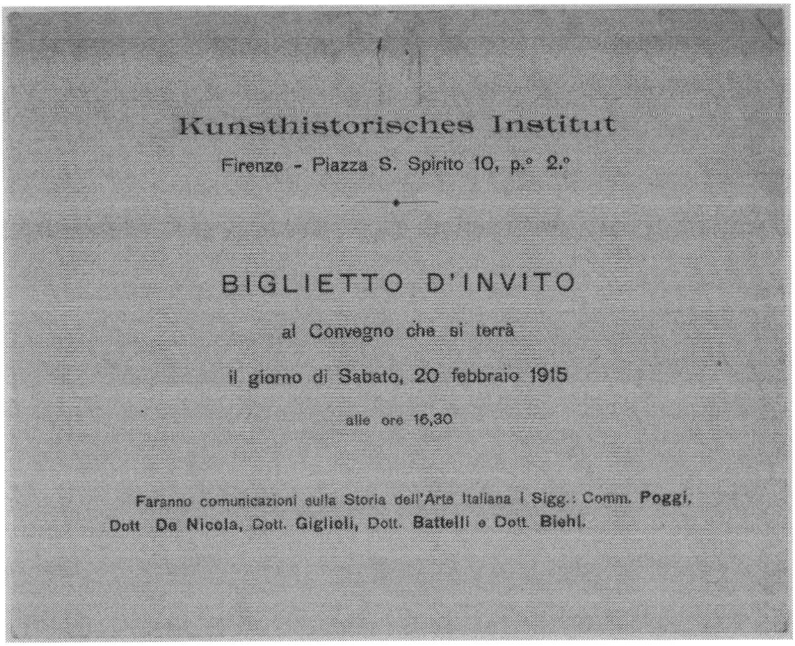

Kunsthistorisches Institut
Firenze - Piazza S. Spirito 10, p.° 2.°

BIGLIETTO D'INVITO
al Convegno che si terrà
il giorno di Sabato, 20 febbraio 1915
alle ore 16,30

Faranno comunicazioni sulla Storia dell'Arte Italiana i Sigg.: Comm. Poggi, Dott De Nicola, Dott. Giglioli, Dott. Battelli e Dott. Biehl.

Figure 3.4 WIA IV.3.1.4.4.10, fol.1, Entrance ticket for the meeting on 20.2.1915.
Source: © Photo: The Warburg Institute.

What did this issue look like?[65] This time, there was a price printed on the title page, 20 cents. Beckerath again designed the artistic title illustrations (see figure 3.5). There were 24 pages with 17 articles and 33 illustrations, for instance the use of Indian elephants in Flanders (see figure 3.6). The main arrangement followed the arrangement in the first issue. The copy in The Warburg Institute features manuscript corrections as well as one sheet, a later addition, noting that both issues of *Rivista* had been exhibited in the 'War Exhibition' in Hamburg in June 1916. The caption of the exhibited object repeated Warburg's dictum of the 'lies of our enemies', unmasked by a periodical like *Rivista*.

Undeterred, Warburg sent out copies of *Rivista* with letters to his friends and colleagues in which he explained that his views about the war presented a view of German culture. In his letter to Werner Weisbach, an art historian in Berlin, he expressed his conviction that Germany after the war had to return to Fichte and Kant's 'categorial imperative'.[66] To Carl Mönckeberg, who wrote for the *Neue Hamburger*

65 WIA, IV.11.1.1.2. La Guerra del 1914–15. *Rivista Illustrata dei mesi novembre, dicembre, gennaio, febbraio.*

66 WIA, GC, Warburg to Werner Weisbach, 3.4.1915. Werner Weisbach, German-Swiss art historian, 1873–1953.

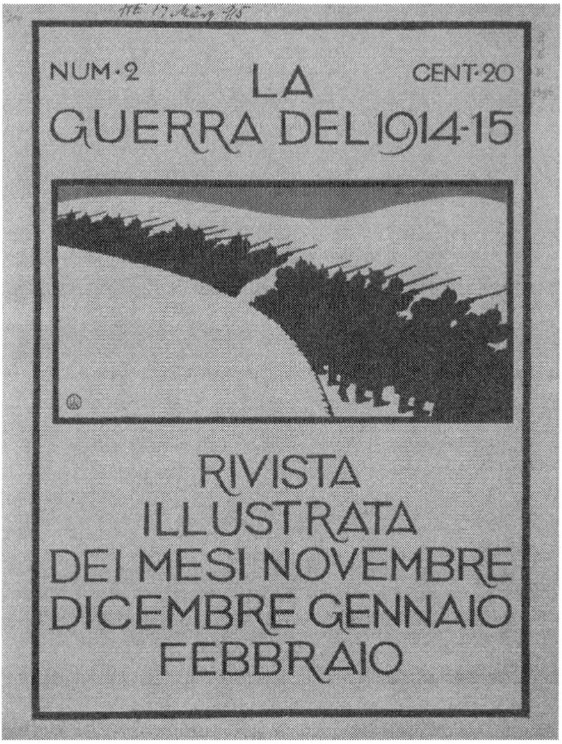

Figure 3.5 WIA, IV.11.1.1.2, Wilhelm von Beckerath, Title illustration for *La Rivista II*.
Source: © Photo: The Warburg Institute.

Zeitung, Warburg explained the situation which neutral Italy had to assess: 'The difference between our war and the war of our enemies is the fact that the Entente wages a cabinet war with the aim of making loot and we wage a people's war to protect the fatherland . . .'. Certainly, after the war Germany would have to introduce reforms, but the country would be morally superior to the allied powers.[67]

In April and May 1915 the situation in Italy had not improved, even when Warburg received an encouraging cable from Panconcelli-Calzia: 'Bauchi', that is Bülow, was enthusiastic about the second issue and an unnamed American found it the best published so far.[68] However, shortly afterwards Panconcelli-Calzia wrote of his poor health; the majority of doctors had advised he have an operation immediately, which meant his return to Hamburg.[69]

67 WIA, GC, Warburg to C. Mönckeberg, 20.4.1915. Carl Mönckeberg, German historian, 1873–1939.
68 WIA, III.10.4., Diary, 9.4.1915, 167–168.
69 WIA, III.10.4., Diary, 14.4.1915. 170–171.

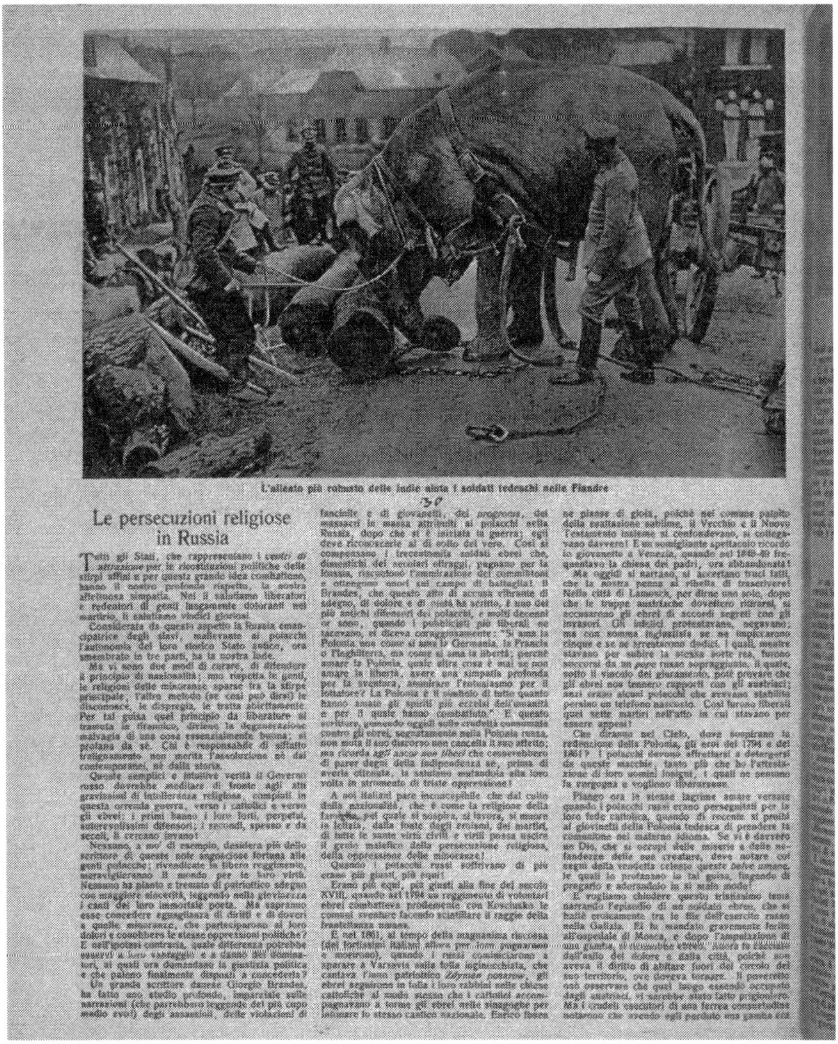

L'alleato più robusto delle Indie aiuta i soldati tedeschi nelle Fiandre

Le persecuzioni religiose in Russia

Figure 3.6 WIA, IV.11.1.1.2., *La Rivista II*. The strongest ally from India, an Elephant in action, helping German soldiers in Flanders [L'alleato più robusto delle Indie aiuta i soldati tedeschi nelle Fiandre], 22.

Source: © Photo: The Warburg Institute.

Warburg had conflicting feelings: he oscillated between satisfaction over work done well and despair that it was all in vain, that the project was a failure and had not stopped Italy going to war. His brother-in-law Wilhelm Hertz was called up, while he himself complained that he could hardly stand it to stay at home, with the women, 'in this henhouse'.[70] He wanted to play his part, but he also knew that he was not well enough. When his sister-in-law Alice Warburg reproached him, telling him he should not always exaggerate and he should ultimately learn to take things more lightly, he entered sarcastically in his Diary, 'He lived, exaggerated and died'.[71] He was annoyed that his own family did not take him seriously.

War was coming. Gabriele d'Annunzio's speeches became ever more belligerent to the point that by 4 May Warburg believed that Victor Emanuel III had no other option but to march on Austria, which he did twenty days later.[72] D'Annunzio spoke of the earthquake in the Abruzzo region and other events as portents of things to come, which Warburg commented on with the word 'omina!' The significance of omens and comets, freaks of nature and natural disasters would be analysed by Warburg in his Luther research later in the war.[73] Activities like D'Annunzio kissing the sword of Bisio in the Forum Romanum and Principe Colonna kissing the Italian flag were for Warburg important rituals for the emotional wellbeing of the people.[74] Shortly later Warburg translated an article from the politically left Journal *Avanti*, which he published under the title 'From the deathbed of Italian conscience' with his own comments in the *Hamburger Echo*.[75]

The developments over many weeks and months, the diplomatic manoeuvres, the political dramas, the personal beliefs of Warburg, they all surface in the Diary and the correspondence along with the ever more frantic attempts to sell copies of the two issues of *Rivista*. Long after Italy's entry into the war, in July 1915, Warburg sent free copies to Theodor A. Bögeholz in Lugano in the hope that he could sell them in Switzerland.[76] Martin Samson asked Warburg for free copies as he wanted to send them to Italians living in Argentina.[77]

70 WIA, III.10.4., Diary, 22.4.1915, 176. Wilhelm Hertz, German lawyer, 1873–1939.

71 WIA, III.10.4., Diary, 22.4.1916, 176–177. Alice Warburg, wife of the banker Max M. Warburg, 1873–1960.

72 WIA, III.10.4., Diary, 4.5.1915, 187. Gabriele d'Annunzio, Italian novelist, 1863–1938; Victor Emanuel III, King of Italy, 1869–1947. On Warburg's view of D'Annunzio see McEwan and Scafi, 'Warburg and D'Annunzio in Defence of Truth: On Modern Literature and Alleged Jewishness', 259–279.

73 Warburg, A., *Heidnisch-antike Weissagung in Wort und Bild zu Luthers Zeiten*; Britt, D., 'Pagan-Antique Prophecy in Words and Images in the Age of Luther', 597–697 and 760–775; McEwan, D., 'Making a Reception for Warburg: Fritz Saxl and Warburg's Book *Heidnisch-antike Weissagung in Wort und Bild zu Luthers Zeiten*', 93–120.

74 WIA, III.10.4., Diary, 19.5.1915, 198. Prospero Colonna, Duke of Rignano, Prince of Sonnino, Italian politician, 1858–1937.

75 WIA, III.86.5.1.2. *Hamburger Echo*, 21.5.1915, 1.

76 WIA, GC, Warburg to Th. A. Bögeholz, 13.7.1915. Theodor A. Bögeholz, Swiss businessman.

77 WIA, GC, M. Samson to Warburg, 27.07.1915.

Warburg's view of his Italian mission

At the beginning of the war, in September 1914, Warburg felt that the 'balancing pole of my professional work' had suddenly been shot to pieces.[78] He had gone to Berlin to find out what he could do to contribute to the war effort; he had taken up riding and shooting determined to do his bit. Eight months later, at the beginning of April 1915, he had to note that Count Stein in Rome had sent his family back to Germany, which gave Warburg cause for alarm. The talks over Trieste were at a stalemate; Warburg confessed he would prefer to perish with the Austrians than lose Trieste. He offered to work as translator in prisoner-of-war camps, from which his former librarian Wilhelm Waetzoldt quickly dissuaded him.[79] He was too old, not well enough, but very proud that his librarians, Wilhelm Printz and Fritz Saxl, served in the German and Austrian armies.[80]

With hindsight, it is hard to accept that Warburg could actually have believed that by publishing two issues of a periodical he would have helped prevent a war with Italy; it was a complete misjudgement of the situation, the will of the government and the will of the people. But for Warburg, as he explains in a letter to his friend Senator Werner von Melle, later Mayor of Hamburg, it had been a question of keeping at one's post until the end. Italy had been dragged into war by a small group of traitors. It was therefore Germany's duty to see to it that they would be punished.[81] Warburg was deeply disappointed. In his view Italy, 'the steward of the highest goods of faith, law and art in all of Western Europe' had become incurably rotten; the unrestrained Italian press, with its diet of lies, had pushed the country into war. His own work, the two issues of *Rivista* 'which were published for our friends in Italy; they are not dead, only mutilated and oppressed',[82] had come to nothing. It must have been bitter for Warburg who, in 1901, had called himself 'Ebreo di sangue, Amburg[h]ese di cuore, D'anima Fiorentino',[83] to concede that his judgment had been wrong.

In the weeks immediately before the declaration of war, Warburg concentrated on his research on superstition, on German freedom and 'disciplina tedesca',[84] continued his correspondence with colleagues in the field of research into the history of astrology, decans and the astrologer Abu Ma'shar,[85] and set to work excerpting newspaper articles on the true reason for the war. His hopes to turn Italy away from the allies had not materialised, and so he stressed all the more his own role as 'the old pioneer for the good European', who was passionately interested in the 'rebirth of the German conscience'.[86]

78 WIA, FC, Warburg to Mary Warburg, 25.09.1914.
79 WIA, GC, W. Waetzoldt to Warburg, 06.05.1915.
80 WIA, GC, Warburg to F. Saxl, 29.06.1915.
81 WIA, GC, Warburg to W. von Melle, 2.6.1915. Werner von Melle, German jurist, 1853–1937.
82 WIA, GC, Warburg to Otto Lanz, 27.6.1915.
83 WIA, III.10.3., Diary, 1.6.1906, 95. His declaration translates as 'Jew by blood, Hamburger at heart, Florentine in spirit'.
84 WIA, III.10.4., Diary, 13.4.1915, 170.
85 Abu Ma'shar, Persian Muslim astrologer, 787–886.
86 WIA, III.10.4., Diary, 2.5.1915, 185–186 in conversation with Senator Max Schramm and Werner Weisbach. Max Schramm, German politician, 1861–1928.

Rivista had not turned out to be the hoped-for propaganda vehicle, and so the greater the importance for German newspapers to use correct bibliographical references when reporting on the Italian lies in the press. Alas, his planned book, 'a psychology and history of the lies in the press of our enemies', was never written.[87]

Despite the feared declaration of war there were discussions to produce a third issue of *Rivista* in April 1915. All this was scuppered with the declaration of war, although Warburg planned, but did not publish, more issues as records of the history of public opinion after the war.[88] After the end of the war the two issues of *Rivista* were sent for reference purposes to the specialised 'Library of World War I' in Stuttgart.

After the outbreak of the war the tone of Warburg's letters became sarcastic. Finding out 'Who is our greatest enemy?' was like a quiz game.[89] Warburg promised Fritz Saxl, who was a pacifist and socialist, to become more 'democratic' when he saw that the 'aristocracy of conscience' had to draw upon Social Democrats; they had been the only group which had worked against Italy falling prey to enslavement by the English. As an officer, Saxl was able to inculcate in his troops diligence and fanaticism for order, whereby they would beat the Italians. He expected that a revolution of 80 percent of the population, reluctant to take part in the war, would sweep away the regime of Prime Minister Antonio Salandra and Foreign Minister Giorgio Sidney Sonnino.[90]

Warburg continued to send out copies of *Rivista*, in May 1917 to Selma Fliess, who wrote for *Gazette des Ardennes*. He fulminated against the 'temporary triumph of the enslavement of the world by England'. The war was not a war of the machine, but in reality a war of the idea. The destruction of works of art, memories of the past, no longer made an impression on him.[91]

On the day of the declaration of war he confided to his Diary:

> The question 'are we too decent' will become urgent on the occasion of the Italian betrayal; following Kant I transpose it into the language of rules of morality in active service: <u>decency is the official attitude of the human subordinate towards the unknown god of history. Transgression of respect will be punished with exclusion</u>.[92]

Warburg had honestly thought that with *Rivista*, a journalistic tool, he could make a difference. He also honestly thought that it was possible to carry on business as usual in the German art history institute in Florence and that it would become a beacon of hope to the intelligentsia and Italy's friends in Germany. It did not happen, but what mattered to him was having tried.

87 WIA, GC, Warburg to P.G. Hübner, 27.4.1915.
88 WIA, GC, Warburg to G. Thilenius, 26.7.1915.
89 WIA, III.10.4., Diary, 24.6.1915, 226.
90 WIA, GC, Warburg to F. Saxl, 29.6.1915. Antonio Salandra, Italian prime minister, 1853–1931; Giorgio Sidney Sonnino, Italian statesman, 1847–1922.
91 WIA, GC, Warburg to S. Fliess, 7.5.1917. Selma Fliess, German academic in France.
92 WIA, III.10.4., Diary, 25.5.1915, 202.

4

ON THE ORIGINS OF THE SERPENT RITUAL LECTURE. MOTIVE AND MOTIVATION. HEALING THROUGH REMEMBRANCE[1]

Introduction

A number of events coincided for Warburg to think about giving a lecture in Kreuzlingen Sanatorium in 1923.[2] Using a methodological interpretation I wish to present side by side the intellectual milieu in Kreuzlingen as well as the projects which Saxl had initiated in Hamburg. The source material is fragmentary: on the one hand the volume of information is large, on the other hand personal limits dictated by the medium of letters formed a barrier to the public use of information until now. Also, the correspondence between Warburg and Fritz Saxl stopped for the weeks when Saxl was in Kreuzlingen, most importantly the weeks and days before Warburg's lecture in April 1923.

In addition to the correspondence between Warburg and Saxl, there are a number of letters, by Saxl to Mary Warburg and friends, which point to Warburg's occupation with the topic, not yet visible to outsiders, and show how the research by the two scholars coalesced to bring it to the surface. The correspondence corpus, therefore, is an important source, but only one segment with which to chart the development of the lecture text and the collaboration between Warburg and Saxl, as well as Warburg's preparation for his lecture. The correspondence, however, permits insights into the way in which the task, the research, and then the drawing up and presentation of the lecture comes to the fore, with Warburg and Saxl as protagonists. A beautiful example for this fusion is the poem 'Among School Children' by William Butler Yeats, in which the great Irish poet put it thus: 'how can we know

1 Originally published in McEwan, D., 'Zur Entstehung des Vortrages über das Schlangenritual, Motiv und Motivation/Heilung durch Erinnerung', 267–281.

2 For information on the Sanatorium Bellevue and the generation of medical doctors Ludwig, Robert and Otto Binswanger see Strauss, H., *Kreuzlinger Mosaik*. I am grateful to Claudia Wedepohl and Erika Klingler for their comments.

DOI: 10.4324/9781003169024-5

the dancer from the dance?'[3] He evokes a picture of total integration, a picture of the multiplicity of ideas, events, impressions, which bring about the shape of the final product. It is in this sense that I see Warburg's lecture, when his experiences, gained on his travels in America, received new significance during his stay in Kreuzlingen. These experiences and their contemplation, that is the memories and the research distilled from them, intertwined with each other. The travels in America as the dance and Warburg as the dancer bring motive and motivation together.

Warburg suffered from a mental illness which manifested itself at the end of World War I. After stays in various sanatoriums in Germany he moved to Kreuzlingen, to the sanatorium of Dr. Ludwig Binswanger in Switzerland, from 1921 to 1924. As part of his treatment he was encouraged to write down his observations, which led him to work on and deliver a lecture.

In 1923 Warburg had two big successes: on 21 April he presented in front of doctors and nurses, patients and friends in the sanatorium his lecture 'On logic in the magic of primitive man' ('Über die Logik in der Magie des primitiven Menschen'), also known today as the 'Serpent Ritual' ('Schlangenritual'). And in the autumn of 1923 he was sent the proceedings of his lecture in Rome from October 1912.[4] Both lectures are seminal pieces of research. The lecture on the serpent ritual was first printed in 1938, nine years after Warburg's death, in a shortened version in English[5] and in German only in 1988.[6] The lecture in Rome was published in 1922 and only reached Warburg in 1923. The lecture in Kreuzlingen as well as the publication of the lecture in Rome were made possible by Saxl's active assistance and became steps on the road to Warburg's recovery. Saxl's share in Warburg's recuperation and re-integration in his work in Hamburg were gratefully recorded by Warburg still years later.[7] This chapter will limit itself to the genesis of the text of the serpent lecture.

American impressions

It was in September 1895 when Warburg, 29 years of age, sailed to New York for the wedding on 1 October 1895 of his brother Paul Moritz with Nina Loeb.[8] Apart from family commitments and society invitations he found time to visit the

3 Yeats, W.B., 'Among School Children', 242–245. William Butler Yeats, Irish poet, 1865–1939. Yeats wrote the poem after inspecting a school and linked his impressions to his thoughts on the development of the children and, beyond that, the world. It ended with the image of the rhythm of the dance merging with the dancer.

4 Warburg, A., 'Italienische Kunst und internationale Astrologie im Palazzo Schifanoja zu Ferrara', 179–193 and plates XXXVII – XLVII; Britt, D., 'Italian Art and International Astrology in the Palazzo Schifanoia, Ferrara', 563–592 and 732–758.

5 Warburg, A., 'A Lecture on Serpent Ritual', 222–292.

6 Warburg, A., *Schlangenritual*. See also Fleckner, U., *Aby Warburg. Bilder aus dem Gebiet der Pueblo-Indianer: Vorträge und Fotografien*.

7 Cf. WIA, GC, Warburg to L. Binswanger, 18.11.1924, file 'W24'; WIA, GC, Warburg to Saxl, 8.12.1928, 'W/S' file; WIA, GC, Warburg to Saxl, 1.6.1929, 'W/S' file.

8 Paul M. Warburg, German-American investment banker, 1868–1932; Nina Warburg, née Loeb, 1870–1946.

Smithsonian Institute in Washington, where he saw exhibits from Native American peoples. Shortly afterwards he headed to the West, armed with letters of recommendation to the military authorities and friends of the family, as he wanted to see for himself the paintings and ornaments of the Hopi and Zuni.[9] For Warburg, having been raised in a big city, it was an encounter with cultures which were diametrically opposite to his range of experience. Small rural communities, where missionaries and teachers had been active for many years, were in the transitional phase from traditional culture to the erosion of their cultures under the influence of 'modern' values. He noted in his travel Diary, 'I read Stevenson's story Dr. Jekyll and Mr. Hyde. Deeply symbolic. Everybody has such a Mr. Hyde'.[10] He felt placed in a situation which he could not, or could not yet, fathom.

He was gripped by a feeling of dislocation, alienation, transformation. His travels through Arizona, New Mexico and California were physically arduous, but Warburg accepted everything, the cold, the poor food, the bad lodgings, the rutted roads[11] – the resulting reports, photographs, collections of works of art and utensils were to prove important to him. He made lists of words[12] in order to communicate directly with Native Americans, for 'here I learn more about the history of the human soul than staying at home in Europe for years'.[13] He confessed when writing to his future wife that he had embarked on an 'immortal work':

> 'Symbolism as function of the force of gravity in the mental household'. Really, I should not produce some nonsensical writing about my insights, because, in fact, they are quintessentially my thoughts . . . My experiences in America present me with living experiences for religious symbolism, but taken as a whole I will have to wait for a long time until this work is completed.[14]

He bought a camera in order to photograph the dances around the totem poles; he bought cooking pots, utensils, pieces of clothing, which he sent to Hamburg[15] and later deposited them as permanent loans in the ethnological museum there in

9 WIA, FC, Warburg to Felix Warburg, 18.12.1895. The Hopi are a Native American population who live primarily on the Hopi reservation in north-eastern Arizona. The Zuni are Native American Pueblo peoples, living in the Zuni river valley in New Mexico and Arizona.

10 WIA, III.10.1., Diary, 7.4.1896, 52. See also Stevenson, R.L., *The Strange Case of Dr. Jekyll and Mr. Hyde*.

11 WIA, FC, Warburg to Charlotte and Moritz Warburg, 12.1.1896. Moritz M. Warburg, German banker, 1838–1910 and his wife, Charlotte Esther Warburg, née Oppenheim, 1842–1921.

12 Cf. WIA, III.2.1., index card box, 40, 'Americana', Moki Vocabulary booklet, 040/020435. Hopi, formerly called Moki or Moqui, are the westernmost group of Pueblo Native Americans, in north-eastern Arizona.

13 WIA, FC, Warburg to Charlotte and Moritz Warburg, 12.1.1896.

14 WIA, FC, Warburg to Mary Hertz, 3.3.1896. 'M/H' file.

15 WIA, FC, Warburg to Charlotte and Moritz Warburg, 31.1.1896.

1902.[16] He read modern American journals, like *The Lark* and *Chap Books*, about which he wrote articles after his return to Europe.[17] His sister Olga added to her welcome letter a passage by Nietzsche, 'Daybreak: Thoughts on the prejudices of morality', dealing with superstition, fear and the history of culture, hoping that Warburg would find it interesting.[18]

After his return to Hamburg he prepared lectures with photographs about his travels: 'I have happily written down the dance of the Indians with the help of the stenographer Marta Martens, but have arrived at a dead point again'.[19] He did lecture twice in Hamburg and once in Berlin in 1897.[20] As he had not seen the so-called Hopi serpent dance, he was invited by William H. Bean at the end of 1896 to return to America. Bean offered to organise the trip for Warburg.[21] It did not happen then and it did not happen when he wanted to travel to America in the late 1920s. Despite his interest in and intensive occupation with Native American culture during his stay in the southwest of the USA, and despite his correspondence with Philipp N. Lilienthal in San Francisco – who waited eagerly for Warburg's book about it[22] – with James Loeb – on Warburg's research on Native American symbols[23] – and with Karl Lamprecht in Leipzig – who worked on drawings by Hopi children in 1905[24] – Warburg had started working on other research projects. But he let slip his feelings for America: when Warburg contrasted a lecture by Professor Richard Muther on Rembrandt in Hamburg in 1907, 'a verbal exhibition of dry professorial messianic fake diamonds', with an 'eminently appreciative letter about my Sassetti'[25] by Max Weber, which gave him an 'emotional uplift', he

16 WIA, GC, K. Hagen to Warburg, 3.1.1902. Karl Hagen, German ethnologist, b. 1866.

17 Warburg, A., 'Amerikanische Chap-Books'; Britt, D., 'American Chapbooks', 703–710 and 776.

18 WIA, FC, Olga Kohn-Speyer to Warburg, 1.8.1896. Friedrich Nietzsche, German philosopher, 1844–1900. Olga Warburg, sister of Aby Warburg, married to Paul Kohn-Speyer, 1873–1904.

19 WIA, III.10.1., Diary, 11.10.1896, 63.

20 On 21 January 1897 Warburg gave a lecture at the photography association Gesellschaft zur Förderung der Amateur-Photographie in Hamburg. For a short summary, see the two articles by F. Goerke. For Warburg's first lecture see Goerke, F., '"Projektionsabend – A. Warburg, Eine Reise durch das Gebiet der Pueblo-Indiane in Neu-Mexiko und Arizona". Bilder aus dem Leben der Pueblo-Indianer in Nordamerika', 38.

Warburg gave a second lecture on 10 February 1897 in Hamburg at the 'Amerikanistenclub'; I have not come across printed reports about this lecture.

Warburg gave a third lecture in Berlin on 16 March 1897. See Goerke, F., '"Projektionsabend – A. Warburg, Eine Reise durch das Gebiet der Pueblo-Indiane in Neu-Mexiko und Arizona". Bilder aus dem Leben der Pueblo-Indianer in Nordamerika', 61.

21 WIA, GC, W.H. Bean to Warburg, 30.12.1896. William H. Bean, American officer, 1839–1909.

22 WIA, GC, Ph. Lilienthal to Warburg, 1.10.1897. Philipp Nettre Lilienthal, American banker and philanthropist, 1850–1908.

23 WIA, GC, J. Loeb to Warburg, 23.4.1897. James Loeb, German-American philanthropist, 1867–1933.

24 WIA, GC, K. Lamprecht to Warburg, 5.12.1905. Karl Lamprecht, German historian, 1856–1915.

25 Warburg, A., 'Francesco Sassettis letztwillige Verfügung', 129–152; Britt, D., 'Francesco Sassetti's Last Injunctions to His Sons', 223–262 and 451–466. Richard Muther, German art historian, 1860–1909; Max Weber, German sociologist, 1864–1920.

admitted that he would have 'sold myself to America long ago'.[26] It is anybody's guess how honestly Warburg meant what he wrote, given that the topic of Native American art and culture was mentioned only rarely. In 1910, on the occasion of the International Hygiene Exhibition in Dresden, Warburg sent three objects from his American travels to the exhibition, one of them the paper bread which the Pueblo Indians used at rituals.[27]

Only in 1921 did Native American topics surface again. Saxl regularly wrote to Warburg about books, lectures and developments in Hamburg, and he mentioned a lecture at the Society of Religious Studies where Cassirer spoke about F. H. Cushing's article on the Zuni.[28] According to Saxl, the Zuni linked their cosmology not to astrology, but to the totem animal, a finding which Cassirer could only have studied in Warburg's library.[29] Half a year later Warburg thanked Saxl for Cassirer's lecture text, which he found 'very good', but in contrast to Saxl he failed to find a reference to the Zuni.[30] This was the first time that Warburg picked up the topic again, which in the space of one year would solidify into his lecture on the serpent ritual.

Motif and motivation

The travels in America were the motif which Warburg took up again in September 1922, 15 months into his treatment in the sanatorium in Kreuzlingen. As part of the treatment Dr. Ludwig Binswanger, head of the sanatorium, encouraged Warburg to write down his 'self-observations' about his illness. It was Warburg himself who had, on the occasion of one of Saxl's frequent visits, expressed the wish to be allowed to do so.[31] Warburg stayed in Kreuzlingen from 1921 to 1924 and during that period Saxl visited him a few times per year, as often as Dr. Binswanger permitted it.[32] For his trips to Kreuzlingen, Saxl, as acting director of the Warburg library and lecturer in the university,[33] was granted leave of absence from Hamburg university by the dean of the Philosophy Faculty, Conrad Borchling, who agreed with Saxl that it was important 'to our university' for Warburg to

26 WIA, GC, Warburg to Max Warburg, 13.10.1907, Copy book II, 165–168.

27 WIA, GC, Warburg to O. Neustätter, 1.6.1910, Copy book III, 349–351. Otto Neustätter, German physician, 1871–1943. The International Hygiene Exhibition, Dresden, 1911, a show on the history of hygiene.

28 WIA, GC, Saxl to Warburg, 5.12.1921, 'Saxl to Warburg' file. Meeting at the 'Religionswissenschaftliche Gesellschaft', the Deputy President was Ernst Cassirer. Frank Hamilton Cushing, American anthropologist, 1857–1900. Ernst Cassirer, German philosopher, 1874–1945.

29 WIA, GC, Saxl to Warburg, 8.12.1921.

30 WIA, GC, Warburg to Saxl, 5.6.1922.

31 WIA, GC, Saxl to Fritz Warburg, 'Bruder' file, 21.9.1922.

32 Cf. the correspondence on visitor permits, WIA, GC, Saxl to L. Binswanger, 25.3.1922.

33 McEwan, D., *Fritz Saxl. Eine Biografie*, 53–54, 62–63.

return healed to Hamburg some day.[34] Close cooperation continued despite the geographical distance.

The doctors treating Warburg had noticed that each visit by Saxl had a calming influence on Warburg,[35] so they allowed Warburg to dictate his observations, among which his travels to the Native Americans was a high point.[36] In October 1922 he expected a visit from his brother Fritz and asked him to bring him 'my American material'.[37] Two days later he repeated his request, this time to his son Max Adolf,[38] and explained to his wife that his 'American material' was kept with his documents and in the subject catalogue 'Americana'. He wondered whether anybody would come to a lecture of his in Kreuzlingen and requested more postage stamps from Mary, as his friends were no longer able to keep up their correspondence due to the raging inflation.[39]

The therapeutically prescribed writing exercise very quickly turned into something quite different: he no longer wanted to write for himself, but for an audience, possibly triggered by the lecture programmes of Saxl and Binswanger. Saxl had started a lecture programme in Hamburg, which initiated discussions about the research agendas as well as the research methods in the KBW. Saxl knew that book publications of lectures were the appropriate visiting cards to show and explain to colleagues the function of the KBW. Such publications were also vital for Warburg to see what was going in in his library despite his absence. In October 1921 Saxl had been able to send a programme of lectures in the Warburg Library to editors of a number of academic journals requesting wider distribution.[40] To Warburg he wrote, 'Your library has completely turned into a scholarly institute with productive results'.[41] In the first lecture Saxl explained the rationale for the lecture programme, Warburg's work and Saxl's belief in Warburg's work,[42] which Warburg should not dismiss as 'gentle persuasion'.[43] When the article appeared in 1923 it went without saying that Saxl sent a copy to Warburg.

34 WIA, GC, C. Borchling to Saxl, 16.4.1923. Conrad Borchling, German philologist, 1872–1946. See also McEwan, D., '"The Enemy of Hypothesis": Fritz Saxl as Acting Director of the Warburg Library', 75–86.

35 WIA, GC, Kurt Binswanger to Saxl, 19.10.1922.

36 WIA, GC, Warburg to Max Warburg, 21.9.1922.

37 WIA, FC, Warburg to Mary Warburg, 19.10.1922.

38 WIA, FC, Warburg to Mary Warburg, 21.10.1922.

39 WIA, FC, Warburg to Mary Warburg, 26.10.1922.

40 WIA, GC, Saxl to G. Sarton, editor of *Isis* in Brussels, 20.10.1921 or to J. Ilberg, editor of *Neue Jahrbücher* in Leipzig, on the same day. George Sarton, Belgian-American chemist and historian, 1884–1956; Johann Ilberg, German educationalist, 1860–1930.

41 WIA, GC, Saxl to Warburg, 8.8.1921.

42 WIA, GC, Saxl to Warburg, 28.12.1921. See McEwan, D., 'Why Historiography? Saxl's Thoughts on History and Writing History', 97–107 and 224–227, here 106.

43 Saxl, F., 'Die Bibliothek Warburg und ihr Ziel', 1–10. Apart from the *Vorträge* (*Lectures*) series Saxl started a second series, *Studien* (*Studies*), in which topics were published which had not been presented as lectures in the KBW.

In October 1922, after having started on his own case history, the lecture idea had taken shape. The topic would be the Hopi, an eminently important topic for Warburg's case history. At the end of the month Saxl regretted that he could not be in Kreuzlingen for Warburg's lecture because the academic year had begun in Hamburg. 'What a pity that I cannot be with you and hear the American lecture, how much I could learn!'[44] This did not mean that Warburg's lecture was imminent, only that Saxl could not get away from Hamburg again to assist Warburg. Saxl knew how significant the project was for Warburg and therefore tried to help him from Hamburg by, for instance, supplying articles about the Zuni in the *Census Report*,[45] and he promised to collaborate with him on his next visit.[46]

The lecture project followed in the footsteps of another event. On 16 November 1922 Binswanger spoke in the sanatorium to patients, colleagues and friends about Husserl's 'Phenomenology' lecture, in particular about the difference between the arts and the sciences, about 'the cathedral style of music', the *Blue Horses* painting by Franz Marc and the term 'speech room', 'which was coined by a mentally ill person as collective noun for voice hallucinations'.[47] Warburg was enthusiastic about the lecture, claiming the topic was 'the real topic of my psyche' and called it in his summary to his wife 'Image and Sign' with the subtitle 'Phobic selection of the function of image memory'.[48] The reference to Franz Marc's famous horse paintings must have made Warburg sit up, because he had bought the Marc painting *Mare with Foal. 1912* in 1916.[49]

The lectures, that is speaking and sharing as a method of scholarship, the lecture programme started by Saxl in Hamburg, and the lecture programme on offer in Kreuzlingen, spurred Warburg on to work on a lecture of his 'American material'. He asked Carl Georg Heise in Lübeck to visit and bring him slides. Heise, although not very well, was having to travel to Switzerland for two lectures and did not want to make a detour to Kreuzlingen with heavy glass slides. He wrote to

44 WIA, GC, Saxl to Warburg, 30.10.1922.

45 WIA, GC, Saxl to W. Printz, 1.11.1922. Census Reports, United States Census Office, 1900. Wilhelm Printz, German Indologist, 1887–1941.

46 WIA, GC, Saxl to Warburg, 13.11.1922, 'W/Saxl' file.

47 Cf. Schindler, T. *Zwischen Empfinden und Denken*, 8 and footnotes 23 and 24. Edmund Husserl, German philosopher, 1859–1938.

48 WIA, FC, Warburg to Mary Warburg, 'Saxl-Warburg' File, 24.11.1922. This document, although begun as a letter, is the beginning of Warburg's biography. Pages 1 to 4 dated 5.10.1922. Franz Marc, German painter, 1880–1916.

It is unresolved whether Binswanger referred with his term 'speech room' to the educationalist Siegfried Bernfeld and the Journal *Sprechsaal* he established in 1912/1913, which saw itself as a 'small spiritual centre' for the youth. Cf. Lohmann, I., 'Siegfried Bernfeld: Sisyphos oder die Grenzen der Erziehung. Der geheime Zweifel der Pädagogik', 180–192. Siegfried Bernfeld, Austrian psychologist, 1892–1953.

49 *Stute mit Fohlen*, 1912. The painting, in a private collection in Switzerland, was exhibited in the Franz Marc exhibition in the summer of 2000 in Staatsgalerie Stuttgart, cat. no. 73, illustration 107. Cf. Heckscher, W.S., 'The Genesis of Iconology', 529–547.

Saxl for advice,[50] who replied that he would take the glass slides on his next visit to Warburg.[51] Shortly afterwards Warburg asked Saxl to visit him in Kreuzlingen in January 1923 for his lecture about the Native Americans,[52] but Saxl had not yet received Binswanger's permission.[53]

Warburg's lecture in Kreuzlingen in context

In January 1923 Saxl was preparing to travel to Kreuzlingen as well as to attend lectures in Zurich[54] und Basle,[55] but the plans did not work out: his mother in Vienna suffered a stroke and he had to travel to Vienna.[56] This was hard for Warburg; he pressed Saxl, 'You do know that my return to Hamburg depends to a certain degree on the promise of your extended presence here'.[57]

Saxl arrived in Kreuzlingen on 12 March. From now onwards it was the librarian Gertrud Bing's task to supply Warburg with books from Hamburg, maps of America, the paper bread of the Zuni which Cushing had sent.[58] Mary Warburg advised Saxl in her first letter that he should not blame himself if he could not achieve anything in Kreuzlingen.[59] But as early as the next day Saxl was able to reassure her: Saxl had typed up 40 pages which Warburg had dictated. The notes were mainly aphorisms, thoughts which had occupied Warburg in San Francisco, symbolism, topics which connected his illness with his research work, the liberation of the human being from magical fear, a topic with which he was confronted every day of his treatment. In his Diary Warburg wrote, 'To my surprise [I find] much of value in the old notes. Hunting magic, by mimetic change weather magic in the Kiva'.[60] Ernst H. Gombrich wrote that Warburg doubtlessly had

> . . . sensed that his own mental illness had given him new insights into these 'primitive' states and he was confident that in describing them he would again acquire sufficient 'distance' to achieve that poise which he had always known to be precarious.[61]

50 WIA, GC, C. G. Heise to Saxl, 25.11.1922.
51 WIA, GC, Saxl to C. G. Heise, 27.11.1922.
52 WIA, GC, Warburg to Saxl, 6.12.1922.
53 WIA, GC, Saxl to Warburg, 13.12.1922.
54 WIA, GC, Saxl to A. Stern, 20.12.1922 and Saxl to H. Bodmer, 4.1.1923. Alfred Stern, German historian, 1846–1936; Heinrich Bodmer, Swiss art historian, 1885–1950.
55 WIA, GC, Saxl to F. Rintelen, 20.12.1922. Friedrich Rintelen, German art historian, 1881–1926.
56 WIA, GC, Saxl to Warburg, 29.1.1923.
57 WIA, GC, Warburg to Saxl, 1.2.1923.
58 WIA, GC, Bing to Saxl, 19.3.1923.
59 WIA, GC, Mary Warburg to Saxl, 2.3.1923.
60 WIA, III. 11, no. 54a. Diary, 23.3.1923, 5887. 'Kiva' is the name for the ritual space of the Pueblo peoples.
61 Gombrich, E.H., *Aby Warburg. An Intellectual Biography with a Memoir on the History of the Library by F. Saxl.*

Saxl was pleasantly surprised that the work went well, noting 'the impetus for work is incredibly strong in the hope to get away from Kreuzlingen'. True, he complained about the lack of specialist books, which made it difficult to get Warburg away 'from philosophising' and to get him to work on the material. In Saxl's mind, it was only 'actual work' which would lead Warburg 'to come out of this ghost world into the world of physical health'.[62]

The next day Warburg and Saxl went for a walk and visited St Ulrich, the old church of Kreuzlingen. Warburg showed Saxl the baroque side chapel with a crucifix hanging from the ceiling and a painting above it depicting the scene with the brazen serpent on a pole. He entered in his Diary, 'Moses – the serpent miracle directly above the crucifixion (Augustinian erudition. Library)' (see figure 4.1).[63] He spoke to Binswanger about 'the *serpent cult*, "suppressed" by Christianity, yet typologically

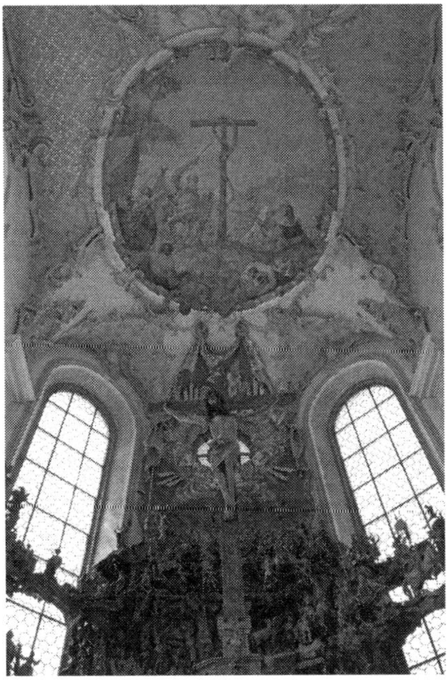

Figure 4.1 Kreuzlingen, St Ulrich church. Fresco of the Mount of Olives chapel. The erection of the brazen serpent, wall painting in the background, the large crucifix in the foreground. © Kreuzlingen, Pfarramt, St. Ulrich.

Source: Photo: Andreas Schwendener.

62 WIA, FC, Saxl to Mary Warburg, 23.3.1923. 'Saxl to Mary Warburg' file.
63 WIA, III.11, no. 54a. Diary, 24.3.1923, 5893.

conscious (4,21)' and 'about the serpent in Kreuzlingen'.[64] In his daily letter to Mary he referred to his finding of the serpent in Kreuzlingen, 'where I showed Saxl the ceiling painting of the miracles of the brazen serpent in the Old Testament parallel to the crucifixion' as an example of banning fear. Warburg wanted to know more about it: he asked his friend Paul Ruben for an explanation from the point of view of Orthodox Judaism of 'this idolatrous renunciation, sanctioned by Moses'.[65] Soon afterwards he told Mary that he and Saxl had studied the book by Fewkes about the serpent dance, 'doubtlessly the most interesting enclave of pagan nature religiosity in the midst of European culture from earlier centuries (Spain/Mexico) and present time'.[66] And: 'I resumed work on Laocoön as a symbol of the great affliction by serpents and am myself a roaring serpent-Laocoön. What I have to endure!'[67]

Aside from assisting Warburg in Kreuzlingen, Saxl kept up his correspondence with scholars, in particular Ernst Cassirer. Cassirer, who frequented the Warburg library in Hamburg, remarked that every day he understood better the arrangement of the books and the 'harmony' in the library, so that he was able to see in language the link between myth and logic.[68] In a heartfelt letter Warburg thanked Cassirer:

> Recently, hardly anything gave me such great joy as your letter. It made me sense the knocking on the other side of the tunnel, the attempt of a breakthrough, so that I take up again my tools, which I had put down, and try to find the courage to clear up the old debris.[69]

It was important for Warburg to be understood by Cassirer. Bing replied to a question on the brazen serpent,[70] Saxl updated Mary Warburg on the progress of work, and by the end of March Warburg had dictated more than 50 pages and selected 80 slides, primarily pictures of dances he had witnessed in America. The framework for the lecture was ready: Warburg would present a geographical introduction, show pictures of landscapes – 'so that one can see that the people live in villages in the steppe' – of pottery and of weaving, through which he wanted to show 'that they are the symbolic expressions of magical imagination', followed by pictures of dances 'as the mimic expression of magical imaginations'. He was certain that with the pictures of the life of the Hopi he would establish what was essential, what 'primitive thinking distinguishes from our thinking'.[71]

64 WIA, III.11, no. 54a. Diary, 24.3.1923, 5894–5895. Hebrew Bible, Numbers 21:4–9; 2 Kings 18:4.

65 WIA, FC, Warburg to Mary Warburg, 24.3.1923. Paul Ruben, German Hebraist, 1866–1943.

66 WIA, FC, Warburg to Mary Warburg, 8.4.1923. Cf. Fewkes, J.W., 'A Comparison of Sia and Tusayan Snake Ceremonials', 118–141; Fewkes, J.W., 'Tusayan Snake Ceremonies', 273–326. Jesse Walter Fewkes, American anthropologist, 1850–1930.

67 WIA, FC, Warburg to Mary Warburg, 11.4.1923.

68 WIA, GC, E. Cassirer to Saxl, 24.3.1923.

69 WIA, GC, Warburg to E. Cassirer, 27.3.1923.

70 WIA, GC, Bing to Warburg, 27.3.1923.

71 WIA, FC, Saxl to Mary Warburg, 29.3.1923. 'Saxl – Mary Warburg' file.

Alfred Doren's lecture in the Warburg Library on 24 March 1923 on 'Fortuna in the Middle Ages and in the Renaissance' was extensively summarised by Bing and equally extensively commented on by Warburg. He found in Doren's subject matter an echo of his own: the goddess of destiny, Fortuna, with her sail, rudder and horn of plenty, and the god of luck, Caerus, with his forelock, were images for making tangible intangible and incomprehensible events. 'In this way Fortuna's rudder and Caerus's lock of luck are the graspable handles for those who fight the demonic powers of life'. The language of symbols, in which incomprehensible events are explained by causal connections, the 'purely mythically anthropomorphic causation of the things generally', comprises the essence of pagan-religious symbols on the one hand and on the other the possibility for the faithful 'to grapple with this quasi human cause not only through adoration and sacrifice'.[72] Investigations into pagan-religious tropes stretched from Europe to America. Warburg's use of the word 'pagan' was ambiguous; what he meant was a spiritual condition, 'the state of the surrender to the impulses of frenzy and of fear'. Warburg wanted to study, according to Gombrich, 'this fateful heritage . . . and in this quest he freely identified the life of the individual and that of the collective mind'.[73]

The intensive work proved very positive for Warburg: he concentrated on his research and no longer on his own musings. He wanted to understand and get to grips with the 'primitive', or magically oriented thinking, into which he had lapsed.

The doctors were impressed with his progress,[74] and even Warburg himself must have been aware of it, for he praised Saxl in a letter to Doren, calling him his 'best friend'.[75] Saxl knew he had not done enough work for the library and that he had not written regularly enough, but he worked tirelessly with Warburg in the few days left before the lecture 'On logic in the magic of primitive man', a topic which was 'doubtlessly an attempt to save oneself from magic'.[76]

Ludwig Binswanger wrote to Warburg's general physician in Hamburg, Dr. Heinrich Embden, to say that he wanted to talk with him about discharging Warburg from the sanatorium. Embden had mentioned it to Mary, but Mary had written to Saxl that it would be a very difficult period for Saxl after Warburg's return to Hamburg. She added that she could not thank Saxl adequately enough for his touching dedication to Warburg,[77] for standing by Warburg in his battle, which, years ago, she had termed the battle of 'astral' nature against 'swamp' nature.[78]

72 WIA, GC, Warburg to A. Doren, 31.3.1923, 'W Private' file.

73 Gombrich, E.H., *Aby Warburg. An Intellectual Biography with a Memoir on the History of the Library by F. Saxl*, 308.

74 WIA, GC, Saxl to Mary Warburg, 8.4.1923.

75 WIA, GC, Warburg to Saxl, 6.4.1923.

76 WIA, GC, Saxl to KBW, 8.4.1923, 'Über die Logik in der Magie des primitiven Menschen'.

77 WIA, GC, Mary Warburg to Saxl, 8.4.1923, 'Saxl – Mary Warburg' file. Heinrich Embden, German neurologist, 1871–1941.

78 WIA, FC, Mary Hertz to A. Warburg, 29.5.1892.

An 'incredible occurrence'

Saxl stayed in Kreuzlingen until 24 April, after the lecture on 21 April. Mary Warburg felt it important to write to Saxl before the lecture that, if everything went as well as Saxl hoped, it would be due to Saxl's influence.[79]

On the evening before the lecture Saxl wrote a note of thanks to Warburg; he confessed that he found it beautiful that Warburg had been able to finish the task. Despite Warburg's illness he had made a great impression on Saxl, so that he wanted to end with a Goethe quote – 'Wär nicht das Auge sonnenhaft! Die Sonne könnt es nie erblicken!', 'Were not the eye itself a Sun / It could never perceive the Sun'[80] – which gave the proof of Saxl's understanding of Warburg.

On the same evening Warburg wrote to Mary full of doubts, commented that it was all in all an 'incredible occurrence' that he would speak in front of the audience in the sanatorium, but in the second part of his letter (dated the next day) he sounded upbeat and reported that everything had gone really well. His son, Max Adolf, who also attended, added a postscript that the lecture was enthusiastically received:

> Father, of course, used only sporadically his nearly word-for-word drafted manuscript and otherwise spoke freely and with brilliant appraisement of the audience, for whom, as a matter of fact, he had to make sacrifices with many a phrasing and instead had to 'show' more . . . One can only say 'hurrah'.[81]

In his report to Hamburg, Saxl stressed that after a rehearsal on the afternoon of 21 April, the lecture in the evening went very well. The dining room of the sanatorium was filled with patients, doctors, nurses, friends and members of 'intellectual' Kreuzlingen. On the lectern Warburg's typescript lay close at hand, but he did not need to use it; he spoke freely. The evening was improved by this; it lost its academic tone and turned into a 'more or less good-humoured causerie'. To Saxl it was impressive to see the command Warburg had of his topic, recasting it in a totally new form. The audience would not have been able to follow a scholarly manuscript.[82] When at some stage one slide got stuck, Warburg did not panic, but waited in a jovial mood until the glitch was fixed.[83] The audience was gripped by the passion with which he spoke and discussed the question, 'how does humankind save itself from primitive magic and arrive at spiritual devotion on the one hand and logical thinking on the other hand?'[84] What the reaction of

79 WIA, GC, Mary Warburg to Saxl, 15.4.1923.

80 WIA, GC, Saxl to Warburg, 20.4.1923. Goethe, *Zahme Xenien, III*. Johann Wolfgang von Goethe, German poet, 1749–1832.

81 WIA, FC, Warburg to Mary Warburg, part one dated 20.4.1923, part two 21.4.1923.

82 WIA, GC, Saxl to Mary Warburg, 23/04/1923, 'Saxl – Mary Warburg' file.

83 WIA, GC, Saxl to staff in Hamburg, 24.4.1923.

84 WIA, GC, Saxl to Mary Warburg, 23.4.1923, 'Saxl – Mary Warburg' file.

'intellectual' Kreuzlingen was is anybody's guess; so far I have not found reviews about it in any local newspapers.

Five days later Warburg made Saxl promise not to show the lecture text to anybody except Mary, his friend Embden, his brother Max and Ernst Cassirer. He also specified that the lecture text must not be published, as Warburg, to whom it was 'the frightening deadly spasms of a decapitated frog', had to revise it thoroughly. He thanked Saxl for his services as 'birth assistant' of his 'monstrosity'.[85]

Warburg's injunction is the reason for the late publication of this lecture. Saxl had kept his promise to Warburg not to publish it straightaway. Back in Hamburg he read the text with Embden[86] and Cassirer.[87] He apologised to his Viennese friend Dagobert Frey for the late return of the corrected proofs of his article 'Frühes Christentum und spätes Heidentum' and explained the delay was due to his seven weeks of work in Kreuzlingen. 'You can imagine how important it would be to help this man on a human and scholarly level to succeed and, if possible, help this man to provide scholarly works again'.[88] After Saxl had departed from Kreuzlingen, Warburg thanked him again and lamented about pains,[89] impressed on him once more not to show the lecture text to anybody[90] and wondered why Cassirer did not visit him – were Warburg's ideas too weak?[91] Saxl was able to reassure him that Cassirer was impressed by the serpent ritual lecture,[92] but could not yet give him a date for his visit.[93]

Warburg felt isolated. The lecture had not brought him back to Hamburg,[94] although Cassirer wrote to him that Embden would soon allow him a short stay in Hamburg. After having read Warburg's lecture, he was very much looking forward to meeting Warburg, as he realised how closely aligned their research interests were.[95]

The topic of the serpent ritual surfaced a few more times. At the end of 1923 Saxl sent Warburg Fendt's description of a Gnostic church service, stating: 'it is simply marvellous how these things converge with the Zuni ceremonies'.[96] In his reply Warburg explained his research in Kreuzlingen as the 'struggle with the monster', as 'an archetypal act of pictorial symbolic cosmological causation' and illustrated his view with examples from his earlier research on 'Ferrara

85 WIA, GC, Warburg to Saxl, 26.4.1923.
86 WIA, GC, Saxl to Warburg, 30.4.1923.
87 WIA, GC, Saxl to Warburg, 7.5.1923.
88 WIA, GC, Saxl to D. Frey, 2.5.1923. Dagobert Frey, Austrian art historian, 1883–1962. See Saxl, F., 'Frühes Christentum und spätes Heidentum in ihren künstlerischen Ausdrucksformen', 63–121.
89 WIA, GC, Warburg to Saxl, 8.5.1923.
90 WIA, GC, Warburg to Saxl, 15.5.1923.
91 WIA, GC, Warburg to Saxl, 31.5.1923.
92 WIA, GC, Saxl to Warburg, 26.6.1923.
93 WIA, GC, Saxl to Warburg, 5.6.1923.
94 WIA, GC, Warburg to Saxl, 1.6.1923.
95 WIA, GC, E. Cassirer to Warburg, 15.6.1923.
96 WIA, GC, Saxl to Warburg, 14.12.1923. Cf. Fendt, L., *Gnostische Mysterien*. Leonhard Fendt, Protestant theologian, 1881–1957.

(Perseus)-Fortuna-Luther-Oraibi'.[97] Warburg felt in himself 'an ascending power . . . for liberation from emotional dysfunction' in the time between his lecture on 21 April 1923 and Cassirer's visit on 10 April 1924; he had healed his destroyed spirit and beaten the monster himself.[98]

Warburg was able to return to Hamburg for good in August 1924. He read Th. W. Danzel's 1922 books *Mexiko I: Grundzüge der altmexikanischen Geisteskultur* and *Mexiko II: Kultur und Leben im alten Mexiko*,[99] entered into a correspondence with him about a shepherd's crook with a piece of wood in human form tied to it and asked Danzel to find the drawings by Native American children, which Warburg had loaned to the ethnological museum where Danzel worked.[100] He wrote to Franz Boas about his assumption that the shepherd's crook with the human form pointed to an animal sacrifice. Via Boas he also sought to get in touch again with James Mooney at the Smithsonian Institution,[101] with the Mennonite missionary and Hopi expert Henry H. Voth,[102] and with Richard Wetherill, his guide in Mancos, Colorado.[103] His friends Paul and Else Hildebrandt in Berlin sent him the article 'The Red Indians invoke the rain. Great festival with the Pueblo-Indians' and asked Warburg to check it prior to its publication in the youth magazine *Jugendinsel*.[104] In 1928 Warburg seriously entertained the idea of travelling for a second time to America, but his brothers were against it and Warburg went on his extended trip to Italy instead. Nevertheless, when in Rome, he wrote to church authorities to ask whether the missionary Pater Guillard, whom he had met among the Pueblos, was still alive.[105]

The lecture in Kreuzlingen was printed only after Warburg's death and the move of the KBW to London. It is fitting to end with Warburg's thanks to Saxl for his 'devoted support', which led him back to scholarship.[106] Saxl, who understood like nobody else what linked Warburg to the Zuni, promised to write a book titled 'From the Zunis to Rembrandt's *Claudius Civilis*. A. Warburg on his 70th

97 WIA, GC, Warburg to Saxl, 13.1.1924, 'Saxl/W' file. Oraibi, the unofficial capital of the Hopi reservation in Navajo County, Arizona, on the third mesa.

98 WIA, GC, Warburg to Max Warburg, 16.4.1924.

99 Danzel, T.W., *Mexiko I*; idem, *Mexiko II*. Theodor Wilhelm Danzel, German ethnologist, 1886–1954.

100 WIA, GC, Warburg to Th. W. Danzel, 4.10.1924.

101 WIA, GC, Warburg to F. Boas, 13.12.1924. James Mooney, American ethnographer, 1861–1921; Franz Boas, German-American anthropologist, 1858–1942.

102 WIA, GC, Warburg to G. A. Reichard, 1.9.1928. Henry Richert Voth, Reverend, 1855–1931.

103 WIA, GC, C. L. Bernheimer to Paul Warburg, 23.3.1925. Charles Leopold Bernheimer, American businessman, 1864–1944; Richard Wetherill, American archaeologist, 1856–1910.

104 WIA, GC, Else Hildebrandt to Warburg, 2.11.1926. Warburg and Saxl, 'Die Indianer beschwören den Regen. Großes Fest bei den Pueblo-Indianern'. Paul Hildebrandt, German classical philologist, 1870–1948. His wife Else, German writer, 1878–1945.

105 WIA, GC, Warburg to B. Nogara, 5.3.1929. Bartolomeo Nogara, Italian director of the papal museums, 1868–1954. The correct spelling of George Guillard is Julliard; George Julliard, missionary in Arizona, dates unknown.

106 WIA, GC, Warburg to Saxl, 23.12.1923.

birthday', which, however, was never written.[107] Saxl once more came to talk about the serpent ritual lecture on the occasion of his lecture at the KBW to the International Americanist Congress from 7 to 13 September 1930. He spoke about the relation of anthropology and art history, 'as the professor had understood it', and read a passage from Warburg's lecture about the relationship of the serpent symbol and Laocoön. Bing ended her report of Saxl's lecture to Mary Warburg wistfully, confessing that 'Saxl and I both had the feeling that it was the last piece of the direct legacy of the professor, and I believe, he would have been happy with the progress of the evening'.[108]

107 Warburg died aged 63.
108 WIA, GC, Bing to Mary Warburg, 19.9.1930.

5

THE FRANTIŠEK POSPÍŠIL – ABY WARBURG CORRESPONDENCE IN THE WARBURG INSTITUTE[1]

Introduction

Looking at the research of the ethnologist František Pospíšil[2] one might wonder what linked his research to Warburg's. The ethnologist from Brno, who travelled with his film camera through Europe to film folk dances, shared Warburg's interest in a special form of folk dance, the sword dances, in which the old ritual of oath-taking was expressed. The leitmotif of swearing an oath was a very old judicial practice, a quasi-religious affirmation of the truth of an assertion. It was a legally binding custom, its validity strengthened by laying hands on an object which was held to be holy or important, like the Bible or the weapons used to defend the fatherland, the swords. It was the intersection of idea and action where both scholars met – the sword dance with its climax of swearing an oath on the sword.[3]

Rembrandt's oil painting *The Conspiracy of Claudius Civilis*

Aby Warburg was passionate about collecting books – his library of cultural history in its widest sense grew to 55,000 volumes until his death – as well as passionate about his correspondence. He exchanged letters with experts in Europe and America and discussed the wide field of the history of 'the European mentality' with examples from the Renaissance in Florence, art history influences of the Orient on the Occident and of northern Europe on southern Europe, postage stamps, playing cards, the Native American serpent ritual, pamphlets from the

1 Originally published in McEwan, D., 'Die Pospíšil – Warburg Korrespondenz im Warburg Institute', 197–206. (The additional Czech translation is by Hana Dvořákova, 'Korespondence Pospíšil – Warburg uložená ve Warburgově institute,' 183–196, with the text of Pospíšil's lecture to the Folklore Society in London, untitled, English and Czech, 207–218.)

2 František Pospíšil, Czech ethnologist, 1885–1958.

3 See also WIA, III.2.1., index card box, 67, 'Ur-Dances'. Warburg was interested in this topic; he collected notes about it, books, and images in general on dance, but also in particular, to wit the following subdivisions: Moresca, sword dance, Moresca and art, the danza de mattachines, Oraibi, the unofficial capital of the Hopi reservation in Navajo County, Arizona, on the third mesa, Pospíšil.

DOI: 10.4324/9781003169024-6

Reformation, satires, caricatures and the peregrinations of astrology from east to west, and many more.[4]

He worked in his library, an independent scholar, assisted by librarians. After World War I, when Warburg suffered from a mental illness, Fritz Saxl, the Viennese art historian, Rembrandt scholar and expert in the history of astrology, was employed as librarian. Saxl introduced and built up a lecture series and two publication series, *Vorträge* (*Lectures*) and *Studien* (*Studies*). When Warburg returned to Hamburg in the late summer of 1924 he was able to resume his work as head of the library and scholar in a fully functioning academic institute.

For Warburg leadership was an important topic: the leader who determines the outcome of the struggle, the leader of men in the same boat, the leader who does not lose sight of his goal. He saw an example of this in the historic event of the rebellion of the Batavians. The Germanic tribes of the Batavians provoked a rebellion under their leader Gaius Claudius Civilis against the Roman occupying forces in CE 69–70. It was crushed, but Civilis was able to negotiate a truce acceptable to both sides. Warburg understood the momentousness of the event when he saw Rembrandt's painting *The Conspiracy of Claudius Civilis* in the Rembrandt exhibition in Amsterdam in September 1925 and was thrilled.

What fascinated Warburg was the topic of nationalism, swearing an oath on swords, the binding together of a community in order to take decisions. He decided to commission a copy of the painting from the National Museum in Stockholm for his new library building that was under construction in Hamburg.[5] The copy, painted by Carl Schuberth, is displayed in the staircase of The Warburg Institute in London (see figure 5.1).[6]

Moresca dances

His interest in the oath-taking of the Batavians intersected with his research into *Moresca* dances, which Warburg had analysed in his article 'Flemish and Florentine Art in Lorenzo de' Medici's Circle around 1480' in 1901.[7] He worked on the so-called 'panni dipinti' ('painted cloths') in the inventory of Lucrezia de Medici,

4 Cf. Warburg, A., 'Orientalisierende Astrologie'; Britt, D., 'Astrology under Oriental Influence', 699–702 and 775, here 699: 'The Warburg Library took particular pleasure in accepting the invitation to participate in the Fourth Congress of German Orientalists, because the Congress coincided with the publication of Wilhelm Gundel's new third edition of *Sternglaube und Sterndeutung*, by Franz Boll (who died in 1924), and this offered an opportunity to draw the attention of Orientalists to Boll's importance in involving Oriental studies in the attempt to establish solid philological and historical foundations for a history of the European mind'.

5 WIA, GC, A. Gauffin, Director of the National Museum, to Warburg, n.d., received 3.10.1925. Axel Gauffin, Swedish art historian, 1877–1964.

6 Carl Schuberth, Swedish painter, 1860–1929.

7 Warburg, A., 'Flandrische und florentinische Kunst im Kreise des Lorenzo Medici um 1480'; Britt, D., 'Flemish and Florentine Art in Lorenzo de' Medici's Circle Around 1480', 305–307 and 483; 'panni dipinti', 307.

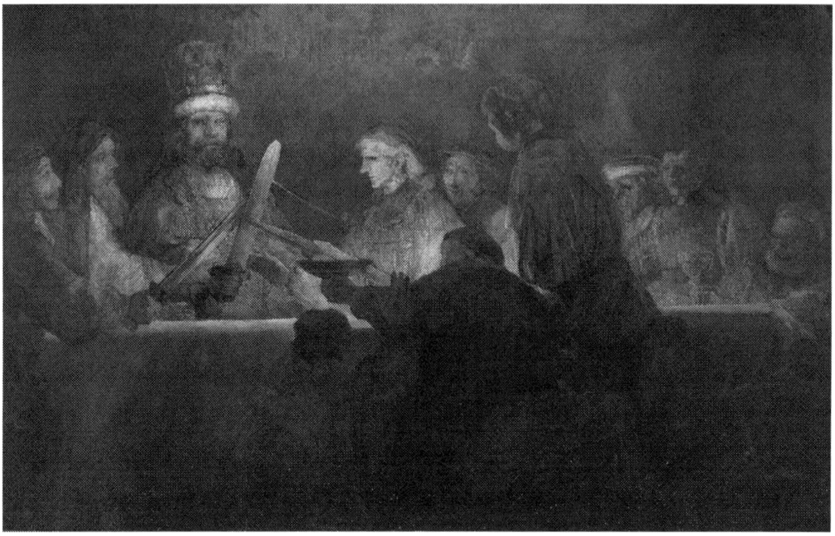

Figure 5.1 Rembrandt Harmensz van Rijn, *The Conspiracy of Claudius Civilis*. Oil copy.
Source: © Photo: The Warburg Institute.

and one of these painted cloths showed a group of people dancing a *Moresca*. He did not investigate this dance any further at the time, but later on Warburg turned to colleagues for information on this dance. Gustav von Bezold, the director of the German National Museum in Nuremberg, found no images of morris dancers in his museums, but referred him to an ivory pyx with carvings of dancers.[8] In 1905 in his article 'Artistic Exchanges between North and South in the Fifteenth Century' he did not describe the ivory pyx, but a Norwegian wooden box or container known as a 'Tine', used to keep butter and cheese fresh, with its colourful images of the so-called *Battle of the Breeches* ('Hosenkampf'). It was the motif of the carnival play about seven wives who quarrelled about the trousers of a man.[9] Despite the fact that the images on the wooden box did not explicitly show a dance, Warburg was convinced that the motif was a link in the development of the *Moresca* dance.[10] In 1914 Warburg published in his article 'The Emergence of the Antique as a Stylistic Ideal in Early Renaissance Painting' the same motif

8 WIA, GC, G. v. Bezold to Warburg, 16.11.1903.
9 Warburg, A., 'Austausch künstlerischer Kultur zwischen Norden und Süden im 15. Jahrhundert'; Britt, D., 'Artistic Exchanges between North and South in the Fifteenth Century', 275–279 and 468–469.
10 WIA, FC, Warburg to Mary Warburg, 19.2.1905, after Max Lehrs, of the Department of Prints and Drawings in Berlin, has shown him an engraving by Master E. S. of the *Battle of the Breeches*. Max Lehrs, German art historian, 1855–1938. Master E. S., unidentified German engraver, 1420–1468.

with two images: young girls performing a 'round dance' on an engraving by Baccio Baldini and a male foil, the *Battle of the Nudes* ('Männerkampf') on a copper engraving by Antonio Pollaiuolo. The latter depicted six armed men in a circle, holding their weapons aloft with three of those swords ready to attack, and two men bent down, killing with their draggers two men lying on the ground. They formed a fighting scene which Warburg interpreted as 'escalation of temperament' and 'an almost baroque muscular rhetoric'.[11]

In the course of World War I Warburg returned to the *Moresca* topic, to sword dances, in particular to a sword richly decorated and once owned by Gustav II Adolf, but the topic did not solidify into an article then.[12] Only after Warburg's

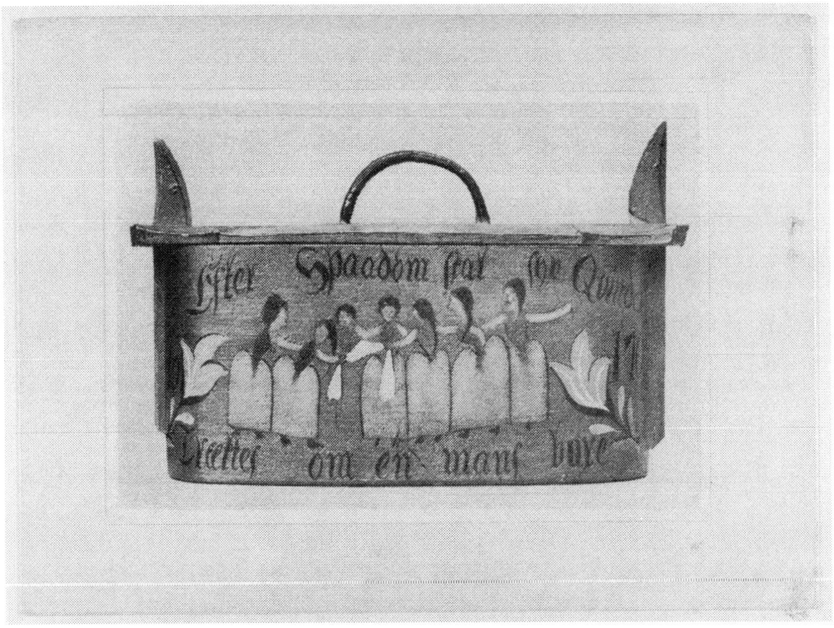

Figure 5.2 Battle of the Breeches. Norwegian 'Tine'. WIA, III.107.6, panel 32, no. 22. Britt, D. (1999), Norwegian 'tine' (Figure 45, 272).

Source: © Photo: The Warburg Institute.

11 Warburg, A., 'Der Eintritt des antikisierenden Idealstils in die Malerei der Frührenaissance'; Britt, D., 'The Emergence of the Antique as a Stylistic Ideal in Early Renaissance Painting', 271–273 and 468–469. In this chapter there are three examples of *The Battle of the Breeches* explained: a) a painted Norwegian 'Tine' (there Figure 45, here figure 5.2), b) an engraving by the Master of the Banderoles (there Figure 46) and c) a Florentine engraving (there Figure 47). Baccio Baldini, Italian engraver, c. 1436–1487; Antonio Pollaiuolo, Italian painter, 1429 or 1433–1498.

12 WIA, GC, Copy book VI, 182, Warburg to E. Panofsky, 20.1.1916. Gustav II Adolf, king of Sweden, 1592–1632.

return from the sanatorium in Switzerland in 1924 did he continue with questions of swearing an oath. His friend, the Hebraist Paul Ruben, confirmed that swearing an oath on a sword had a long tradition, which expressed a particular point of view or idea and by which the high value of the sword as weapon was emphasised.[13] Warburg wrote to the ethnologist Julius Schwietering in Leipzig for literature on sword dances,[14] who sent him Hans Naumann's book *Primitive Gemeinschaftskultur* (1921).[15] He asked his friend Jacques Mesnil about plays by the baroque poet Jan Bara and instructions for stage design on the theme of swearing an oath.[16] Saxl supplied information on the Dutch playwright Joost van den Vondel and his play *Batavian Brothers or Suppressed Freedom*,[17] that is, the *Claudius Civilis* topic. Saxl complemented his information with further explanations: the scene of swearing an oath by laying hands on crossed swords was frequently painted on popular paintings in the 17th century in order to disguise contemporary political events, for instance the conspiracy of the Arminians against the stadtholder Prince Maurice in the early 17th century. Another example from literature was Hamlet, who challenged Horatio to swear an oath on his sword.[18]

Research was carried out not only into literature on the swearing of oaths on swords but also, most notably, into images. Warburg was sent a photograph of a painting of a sword dance referred to in the *Geschichte der deutschen Literatur in der Schweiz* from the Central Library in Zurich.[19] When an ensemble of morris dancers performed *Moresca* dances in the open-air theatre in the Hamburg Stadtpark in the summer of 1926, Saxl attended their performances and photographed them (see figure 5.3). He was very impressed and quickly informed Warburg, who was at the spa in Baden-Baden.[20] Additional performances were announced for July. The whole Warburg family, albeit without Aby Warburg, attended to see the English sword dances, morris dances, German folk dances and traditional folk song performances on 3 July 1926. Saxl's photographs in the collection of photographs in The Warburg Institute provide proof of these performances, which

13 WIA, GC, P. Ruben to Warburg, 27.8.1924.

14 WIA, GC, Warburg to J. Schwietering, 17.11.1924. Julius Schwietering, German ethnologist, 1864–1962.

15 WIA, GC, J. Schwietering to Warburg, 20.11.1924. Hans Naumann, German folklorist, 1886–1951.

16 WIA, GC, Warburg to Jacques Mesnil, 23.2.1925. Jan Bara, Dutch poet, 1627–1706.

17 Vondel, *Batavische Gebroeders*. Joost van den Vondel, Dutch playwright, 1587–1679.

18 WIA, GC, Saxl to Warburg, 16.5.1925. The rebellion of Arminians or Remonstrants in The Netherlands was directed against Prince Maurice and his Calvinist leanings. For Shakespeare, *Hamlet*, Act 1, scene 5 see Dowden, E., *The Tragedy of Hamlet*. Maurice of Nassau, Prince of Orange, 1567–1621.

19 Baechtold, J.M., *Geschichte der deutschen Literatur in der Schweiz*, here 64, with a note explaining an instructive colour image of sword dances in Zurich in 1578 in the *Wickschen Sammlung* of the Zurich city library. Another sword dance is mentioned, from Winterthur in 1555, with forty dancers wearing white shirts with gold collars, black hats with golden stars, and bells on feet and shoes. WIA, GC, B. Hirzel to Warburg, 10.3.1926. Jacques Baechtold, Swiss writer, 1887–1984; Bruno Hirzel, Swiss librarian, 1876–1936.

20 WIA, FC, Mary Warburg to Warburg, 5.6.1926.

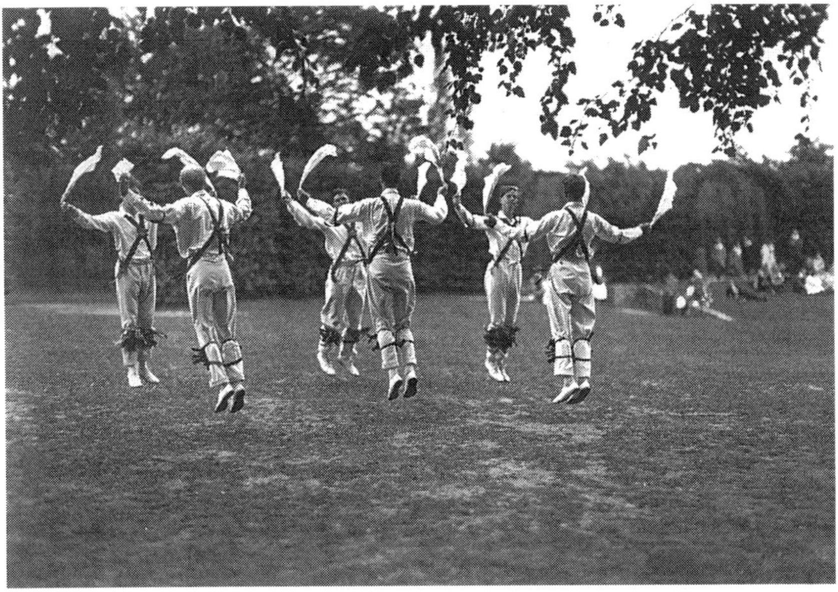

Figure 5.3 *Moresca* Dance. Performance of the Geestland folk dance ensemble in Stadtpark, Hamburg, 4.7.1926.

Source: Photograph by F. Saxl. Photographic collection. © Photo: The Warburg Institute.

delighted everybody. Mary saw in the morris dances the vestiges of the original *Moresca* dances, with the little bells on the legs, the leaps in the air, the white handkerchiefs in the hands of the dancers.[21] Next day Gertrud Bing, the librarian, wrote a detailed report of it to Warburg, describing the foot movements of the dancers, the figures, the little bells on the dancers' legs and in particular the sword dance, where a man in the middle of the circle was apparently beheaded.[22] In Warburg's reply to Mary he added his own explanations: the white handkerchiefs were something like a forfeit, which sometimes was wound around the helmet. He wanted to know more about the performances – who had organised them, who had taken photographs – and regretted not having seen them for himself.[23] In his letter to Bing he added that the white cloths were 'courtly favours' of now unrecognisable origin.[24] Mary Warburg replied that the performances had been organised by the Geestland folk dance ensemble, which performed 'country dances' like the English and morris dances in the hall of the Sagebiel Restaurant and the open

21 WIA, FC, Mary Warburg to Warburg, 4.7.1926.
22 WIA, GC, Bing to Warburg, 5.7.1926. Gertrud Bing, German art historian, 1892–1964.
23 WIA, FC, Warburg to Mary Warburg, 5.7.1926.
24 WIA, GC, Warburg to Bing, 7.7.1926.

air theatre in the Stadtpark. Saxl had photographed all dances from all possible angles.[25] Max Adolf, Warburg's son, who had been presented with a gramophone for his birthday, promised to buy gramophone records of sword dances.[26]

Contact with František Pospíšil

Shortly afterwards, Giulio Panconcelli-Calzia, director of the phonetics laboratory at Hamburg University and a friend of Warburg's, met Pospíšil in Hamburg, who showed him a Czech print of a 'Dusak', a wooden tournament sword. It was then that Panconcelli-Calzia told Pospíšil that Warburg was interested in sword dances. All this figured in Pospíšil's first letter to Warburg when he introduced himself as an author of a book on sword dances.[27] He enclosed a small brochure and told him that he had also made films of sword dances in Bohemia, Moravia, Slovakia, Poland, Russia, Ukraine, Dalmatia, Italy, Germany and Austria. He offered for sale copies of his films and ended by saying that he was interested in all materials on sword dances.[28] This was the cue for Warburg. By return of post Warburg thanked him and propounded his view on sword dances – they were games, sacrificial games, as he had also witnessed in New Mexico. He enclosed an article by Gustav Kowalewski[29] and entered in the *Journal*, 'I have written to Mr. Pospíšil, who plans a book on sword dances'.[30]

At the same time, Thomas Walker Arnold, an expert in Islamic painting, sent him a book with images of morris dances in England.[31] Saxl, who had interested Warburg in the *Claudius Civilis* painting,[32] wanted to write an article about it with Warburg in which the topos of the 'last supper' would be linked to the topos of the 'sacred oath'.[33] He therefore continued to collect literature on the idea of swearing an oath.[34] The topics of oath-swearing and sword dances were in the wind – and this was the very circumstance in which Pospíšil turned up at the KBW and talked to Saxl about his research work and the 1,900 metres of film he had made. He hoped that Warburg would visit him in Brno: Warburg's expert knowledge, based

25 WIA, FC, Mary Warburg to Warburg, 7.7.1926.

26 WIA, FC, Max Adolf Warburg to Warburg, 14.7.1926. Max Adolf Warburg, classical philologist, 1902–1974.

27 Pospíšil, F., *'Mečový (zbrojný) tanec naslovanské půdě'*, 25–55 ('Sword dances among Slavic peoples'). Giulio Panconcelli-Calzia, Italian phonetician, 1878–1966.

28 WIA, GC, F. Pospíšil to Warburg, 3.10.1926.

29 WIA, GC, Warburg to F. Pospíšil, 6.10.1926; Kowalewski, 'Der Schwerttanz'. Gustav Kowalewski, b. 1858, d. before 1926.

30 Michels/Schoell-Glass, *Journal*, 6.10.1926, 16.

31 WIA, GC, T. W. Arnold to Warburg, 11.10.1926. Thomas Walker Arnold, British orientalist, 1858–1930.

32 WIA, GC, Warburg to C. Neumann, 22.1.1927. The letter, 11 pages, is an impressive text on Warburg's thoughts on the *Claudius Civilis* topic. Carl Neumann, German art historian, 1860–1934.

33 WIA, GC, Saxl to Warburg, n.d., before 25.1.1927.

34 WIA, GC, Saxl to Warburg, 8.6.1927.

on the research centre of the KBW, would be important to Pospíšil.[35] It was Saxl, putting together the lecture series for 1928, who suggested that Warburg invite Pospíšil to lecture in Hamburg.[36] The invitation was sent and Pospíšil accepted the date of 25 February 1928 for a lecture on *pyrrhiché*, a dance with weapons originating in Greece and used as part of military training, for instance in Sparta. It forms the basis of Socrates' claim that the best dancers were also the best fighters. Pospíšil requested a slide projector and a film projector for showing his films, but only to a small number of people, namely Warburg, Giulio Panconcelli-Calzia and the ethnologists Arthur Byhan and Georg Thilenius. He asked how many images would be included in a print version of his lecture.[37]

It is possible that Warburg mentioned his invitation to Pospíšil to the founders of the *Reallexikon der deutschen Literaturgeschichte*, Wolfgang Stammler and Paul Merker, because they told Warburg of one of their students, Kurt Meschke. Meschke had written a dissertation on sword dances, which they would recommend to Warburg for publication in the *Studien* series.[38] By return of post Warburg invited them and Meschke to the lecture by Pospíšil on 'Ancient Dances in the Basque Region', so that Saxl and Warburg could discuss with them their suggestion of publishing the dissertation. Warburg even offered to pay for Meschke's railway ticket.[39] Professor Stammler was delighted to accept.[40]

Ever more building blocks were put together, among them drawings for theatre plays and ballets, which unambiguously presented a sword dancer who, for the final act of his apotheosis, was lifted high up in the air on the shields of the other dancers.[41] Saxl found a copper engraving by the French engraver Daniel Marot of a scene of swearing an oath on a sword.[42] In the meantime the lecture date was changed to 17 March 1928; requests and bookings arrived;[43] Kurt Meschke was looking forward to the lecture and promised to bring an article of his on sword

35 WIA, GC, Saxl to Warburg, 6.10.1927.

36 WIA, GC, Saxl to Warburg, 9.11.1927.

37 WIA, GC, F. Pospíšil to Saxl, 6.12.1927. Neoptolemus, also Pyrrhus, son of the famous Homeric hero Achilles, was an excellent dancer and was thought of as the inventor of the Greek war dance, which is known under his name, Pyrrhichos. Arthur Byhan, German ethnologist, 1872–1942.

38 WIA, GC, W. Stammler and P. Merker to Warburg, 19.1.1928. Meschke, K., *Schwerttanz und Schwerttanzspiel im germanischen Kulturkreis*. Wolfgang Stammler, German literary historian, 1886–1964; Paul Merker, German literary historian, 1884–1945; Kurt Meschke, German ethnologist, 1902–1971.

39 WIA, GC, Warburg to W. Stammler, 21.1.1928.

40 WIA, GC, W. Stammler to Warburg, 30.1.1928.

41 WIA, GC, Warburg to M. Arnim, University library Göttingen, 3.2.1928. Max Arnim, German librarian, 1889–1946.

42 WIA, GC, Saxl to Warburg, 19.2.1928. Daniel Marot, French-Dutch engraver, 1661–1752.

43 WIA, GC, E. G. Tarnow to Warburg, 28.2.1928. Mrs E. G. Tarnow, dates unknown member of Queen's College, London, and a friend of Warburg's friends in Florence. WIA, GC, W. Stammler to Warburg, 12.3.1928. In the entry in the *Journal* the Czechoslovak consul was mentioned as having been told that the KBW would not desire a report in the press. Michels/Schoell-Glass, *Journal*, 14.3.1928, 225. Mrs. E. G. Tarnow, dates unknown member of Queen's College, London.

dances.[44] Warburg sent ten tickets to Pospíšil, was looking forward to meeting him, and invited him for lunch on Sunday, 18 March 1928.[45] Pospíšil had invited the Spanish and Czechoslovak consuls in Hamburg to the lecture, which was scheduled to last for half an hour with an additional hour for showing 50 slides and 1,500 metres of film.[46]

A few days before the lecture, Meschke arrived in Hamburg. Warburg guided him through the KBW and showed him the *Moresca* panel,[47] which he had put together for the Mnemosyne Atlas, with its images from the north and south, the engraving with the round dance or *Battle of the Breeches* from the 15th century. In particular, panel 32 in the published atlas shows images of *Grotesques, Dance around the woman in the centre, Vœux du Paon, Quaresima, Monkey cup, Grotesque of monkeys, Dance of the women around the trousers [cf. Dance of the priest, Death of Orpheus], Tool as vehicle*.[48] Warburg, who was able to assess people quickly and accurately, was not impressed by Meschke; in the *Journal*, where all visitors were mentioned, Warburg called him a 'conceited ass'. True, he was trained as a theologian, knew the available pieces of information about sword dances and wanted to be cautious in the context of religious studies, but Warburg found that Meschke resented the link between *Moresca* and sword dances and could not really discuss the origin of the dance.[49] Meschke, for his part, was enthusiastic about the KBW, which he called a 'paradise of scholarship', in which the books were arranged according to the principle 'from mythology to logic'.[50] Warburg did not really take delight in him and his colleague, Miss Anker, whom he called 'silly little girl'.[51]

František Pospíšil's lecture at the KBW in Hamburg

On the morning of Pospíšil's lecture Stammler arrived at the KBW in a state of agitation. He wanted to show Warburg a letter from Pospíšil in which he had complained about Meschke. Warburg took no notice. Shortly afterwards, when Pospíšil arrived and Stammler heard that Meschke's research was well received by Pospíšil, he changed his tone. He was glad to hear the lecture had gone well and attributed it to Warburg's help leading Meschke 'to the exact reception of German sword dances'. Warburg shrugged it off as 'private defamation'.

Warburg summarised the lecture in the *Journal*: 'The lecture was energetically saturated and worked convincingly despite the dialect. What I added later on was

44 WIA, GC, K. Meschke to Warburg, 8.3.1928.
45 WIA, GC, Warburg to F. Pospíšil, 8.3.1928.
46 WIA, GC, F. Pospíšil to Warburg, 15.3.1928.
47 Ohrt and Heil, *Aby Warburg*.
48 Warnke and Brinck, *Aby Warburg (1866–1929)*, 54–55, plate 32.
49 Michels/Schoell-Glass, *Journal*, 14.3.1928, 224–225.
50 WIA, GC, K. Meschke to Warburg, 28.3.1928.
51 Michels/Schoell-Glass, *Journal*, 14.3.1928, 224–225.

"instructive", but I lacked real freshness'.[52] 'Energetic', showing vitality, heightening perception, related to or characterised by energy, was one of Warburg's favourite terms, a technical term from physics. Normally Warburg introduced the speaker before the lecture and summarised it afterwards. But this time, although he was impressed by Pospíšil's lecture, he seemed not to be really content with the form or content.

Pospíšil wrote to Saxl after the lecture to say he was happy to see that Warburg had taken an active interest in his lecture and films. He thanked Saxl for putting him in touch with Warburg as he was the only person who understood Pospíšil's sword dance research. The folklorist A. R. Wrighte had invited him to London to lecture on 20 September 1928. Further, Pospíšil wanted to sell copies of his films and regretted that there was no film archive in Germany about local customs. Would Saxl know someone who might buy his films? He wanted to make more films, particularly in the Balkans, where one could still see the 'most primitive dances'.[53]

Pospíšil stayed a few more days in Hamburg, mostly at the KBW, and waited for the arrival of Albrecht Knust. Knust, an acquaintance of his from Lubeck, was a dancer and leader of a dance school, the 'Hamburg Movement Choirs Rudolf von Laban', who had attended Pospíšil's lecture.[54] Knust had choreographed a sword dance, with the leaders being lifted up in the air in the centre of a circle, and had sent photographs to Warburg and told him that he had enjoyed Pospíšil's lecture and Warburg's explanatory words.[55] Warburg was pleased to hear that the dancers felt the connection between the past, present and future, a continuum of culture.[56]

Warburg met Pospíšil shortly before Warburg's trip to Berlin and Pospíšil's return to Brno. A memo about this meeting is extant in the *Journal*. Pospíšil was 'really glad about me being still alive', which gave him the opportunity to explain his plans to Warburg. He wanted to continue with his research work, but needed a car, 'if only he could import a small Ford car tax free into his country!' Perhaps Professor Hahne in Halle or a ministry would buy copies of the sword dance films – Warburg wanted to think about it.[57]

At the beginning of April Warburg replied to a letter from Stammler, saying that he regretted not having had time enough to talk to Stammler and the two students, Miss Busse und Miss Anker. He hoped that they enjoyed the atmosphere in KBW and 'were comfortable in the life-giving circulation of observation, willing to look

52 Michels/Schoell-Glass, *Journal*, 18.3.1928, 227–228.

53 WIA, GC, F. Pospíšil to Saxl, n.d., after 17.3.1928. Arthur Robinson Wrighte, British folklorist, 1862–1932.

54 WIA, FC, Mary Warburg to Warburg, 21.3.1928. Albrecht Knust, German ballet master, 1896–1978. Rudolf von Laban, Hungarian dance artist, 1879–1958.

55 WIA, GC, A. Knust to Warburg, 22.3.1928.

56 WIA, GC, Warburg to A. Knust, 28.3.1928.

57 Michels/Schoell-Glass, *Journal*, 27.3.1928, 232. Hans Hahne, German ethnologist, 1875–1935. Warburg had wrongly written 'Hahn'.

back, and sensitive to the present'. He confessed his honest admiration for Pospíšil and his lecture:

> Even if the chopping knife of time may detrimentally interfere at some stage, the research of cultural history will delight in saving social movements in images, which will be preserved by using the utmost energy and superior intelligence. They are singularly valuable to the psychology of European festivals and will keep processes, which are about to wither away, in the memory.[58]

And this very commendable judgment on Pospíšil's personality as well as the precisely outlined research topics of both scholars is all we have from Pospíšil's lecture – the text was never published.

Meschke's review of Pospíšil's lecture for newspapers in Hamburg never happened either.[59] Still, Meschke asked Warburg for funding to travel from East Prussia to see the performances by the English ensemble 'Travelling Morris' in Holland and Germany in the summer[60] and Warburg sent him money again, 100 marks.[61] This time Meschke sent a very detailed report about the performance of 'English dances' in Bonn on 6 July 1928. He saw contradances, square dances, and the so-called Ampleforth sword dance. According to Meschke the handkerchiefs were originally weapons, as one can still see with the battle dances in the Basque region as filmed by Pospíšil. Sword dances and hoop dances were something quite different, because the dancers were linked to each other for the duration of the whole dance by an object, a hoop or a sword. Morris dances were something else again: they showed the courting of and fight for a woman.[62] Warburg was not impressed by this; he scribbled the note 'inferior' on Meschke's letter and said that Meschke should become a preacher as soon as possible and retire from scholarship.

Warburg also reacted sharply when Meschke asked whether his dissertation on sword dances and sword dance games would be published in the *Studien* (*Studies*) series.[63] Warburg obviously did not want to do so, so he wrote that he was not a sword dance expert, advised that Meschke's doctoral supervisor Stammler should write an appraisal, and that Meschke should first contact the president of the Emergency Association of German Science [Deutsche Notgemeinschaft], Friedrich Schmidt-Ott, in Berlin.[64] Even so, Warburg himself wrote to Schmidt-Ott. The letter was a long examination on the necessity to

58 WIA, GC, Warburg to W. Stammler, 2.4.1928.
59 WIA, GC, K. Meschke to Warburg, 4.5.1928.
60 WIA, GC, K. Meschke to Warburg, 23.6.1928.
61 WIA, GC, Warburg to K. Meschke, 4.7.1928.
62 WIA, GC, K. Meschke to Warburg, 24.7.1928.
63 WIA, GC, K. Meschke to Warburg, 8.4.1929.
64 WIA, GC, Warburg to K. Meschke, 27.6.1929. Friedrich Schmidt-Ott, German lawyer, 1860–1956.

take part in the intellectual life outside Germany. He spoke of the 'torpedo boat of culture', that is, an institution pursuing the goal to fund the research of German scholars abroad. He mentioned three scholars. First, Alfred Neumeyer, who was researching Johann Anton Ramboux, and second, Ludwig Heinrich Heydenreich, who was researching Leonardo. Warburg recommended them both. Third, he also mentioned the pastor Kurt Meschke, who was researching sword dances, but Warburg was not certain about Meschke's scholarship. He advised Schmidt-Ott to contact the doctoral supervisor, Wolfgang Stammler, for more information.[65]

Pospíšil lectured on battle dances at the Second Congress of Dance in Essen in July 1928 and wrote to Warburg about it.[66] His English colleagues from the Folklore Society had invited him to a conference in England and thought wrongly that sword dances were only danced in England. He asked Warburg again whether he had found people who would like to buy copies of his films. He was in a difficult situation, he wanted to continue with his research, but could not get funding because he was not a member of a party. He asked Warburg to write to the Czechoslovak foreign minister Edvard Beneš and the education minister Milan Hodza to inform them how badly he was treated. He showed Slavic films abroad, but was not recognised by his own government. He came back from abroad with gifts, among them Benin bronzes from the Museum of Ethnology in Hamburg, which meant that it was Pospíšil who brought the first Benin bronzes to Czechoslovakia.[67]

Where was Pospíšil's article?

Pospíšil's invitation to lecture in Hamburg was contingent on his submitting his lecture text for publication and sending it as soon as possible to Saxl. Pospíšil did not do so. Five months after the lecture, Bing reminded him that they were

65 WIA, GC, Warburg to F. Schmidt-Ott, 29.6.1929. Meschke's doctoral dissertation was only printed in 1931, the KBW contributed 300 marks to the printing costs. WIA, GC, Saxl to Meschke, 1.7.1931. Meschke's letter of thanks in WIA, GC, 16.9.1931 with a copy of his volume. Alfred Neumeyer, German-American art historian, 1901–1972; Johann Anton Ramboux, German painter, 1790–1866; Ludwig Heinrich Heydenreich, German art historian, 1903–1978. Leonardo da Vinci, Italian polymath, 1452–1519.

66 WIA, GC, F. Pospíšil to Warburg, 1.7.1928.

67 WIA, GC, F. Pospíšil to Warburg, 1.8.1928. I thank Bernd Schmelz, Museum für Völkerkunde Hamburg, for his kind communication: the correspondence between Arthur Byhan, Museum für Völkerkunde Hamburg, and Pospíšil, Moravské Zemské Museum Brno, is kept in the archive of the museum in Hamburg. Two letters of 1.12. and 3.12.1928 deal with the consignment of a crate of Benin bronzes, which were sent to Pospíšil in Brno and their receipt was acknowledged by Pospíšil. A letter of 20.3.1927 to Pospíšil mentions two bronze objects from Benin, a bird and a mask. Whether it was these two objects which were sent to Brno in 1928 is not proven. Edvard Beneš, Czech statesman, 1884–1948; Milan Hodza, Slovak politician, 1878–1944.

still waiting for the typescript of his lecture.[68] Another four months later a cable was sent to Pospíšil. The KBW needed his typescript to be sent to the publishers for the next issue of *Vorträge* (*Lectures*);[69] one month later Saxl sent an urgent reminder.[70] Pospíšil was quick when he requested financial support, but simply neglected to fulfil the conditions of his lecture appointment in Hamburg. Warburg, who was with Gertrud Bing on an extended trip in Italy for nine months from the autumn of 1928 to the summer of 1929, was displeased. He urged Saxl,[71] Saxl urged Pospíšil,[72] but Pospíšil did not react.

One can understand the surprise when Warburg and Bing were in Naples in May 1929, on their way to San Martino to visit the sepulchral monument of the poet Jacopo Sannazaro, and bumped into Pospíšil there, which elicited Warburg's comment in the *Journal* that Pospíšil's face turned purple. Pospíšil, who had attended the Folklore congress in Florence, extended his trip by travelling through Italy and accidentally ran into Warburg and Bing in San Martino. Pospíšil took photographs of Warburg and Bing in the cemetery of the monastery on 28 May 1929 and sent three of them to Hamburg (see figure 5.4).[73] However, his typescript remained outstanding, despite renewed reminders, to the extent that Pospíšil delayed the publication of the entire volume.[74] Warburg had to apologise to German philologist Karl Vossler in mid-October 1929 that printing was delayed because Pospíšil's article had still not been submitted. As the editors could no longer wait, they took the decision to print the volume without it.[75]

Two weeks later Warburg had died. When Pospíšil heard about it, he was shocked. He wanted to know whether the KBW would continue its work and enclosed photographs he had taken of Mary Warburg, Bing and Saxl. He referred to his letter of 1 August 1928 which, in his words, had been confiscated by a 'cursed soul in the KBW' and had therefore not reached Warburg. In this letter he had called his lecture manuscript 'insignificant' and, further, had expressed his disappointment, because Saxl knew that he had given the lecture 'just for the amusement' of Warburg. Now Pospíšil complained that Warburg had promised him whatever help he needed when they had met in Berlin on 27 March 1928, so that Pospíšil had counted on making a second film of sword dances. Sadly, Warburg had never mentioned it again and only sent reminders for the typescript.[76]

68 WIA, GC, Bing to F. Pospíšil, 17.8.1928.
69 WIA, GC, KBW to F. Pospíšil, 14.12.1928.
70 WIA, GC, Saxl to F. Pospíšil, 23.1.1929.
71 WIA, GC, Warburg to Saxl, 23.1.1929.
72 WIA, GC, Saxl to F. Pospíšil, 5.2.1929.
73 The photographs are in the Portrait Collection, WIA. The meeting in San Martino was mentioned in *Journal*, see Michels/Schoell-Glass, *Journal*, 28.5.1929, 461. Jacopo Sannazaro, Neapolitan poet, 1458–1530.
74 WIA, GC, Warburg to F. Pospíšil, 12.8.1929.
75 WIA, GC, Warburg to K. Vossler, 12.10.1929. Karl Vossler, German philologist, 1872–1949.
76 WIA, GC, F. Pospíšil to Saxl, 16.12.1929. See also Kessner, L., *Aby Warburg*.

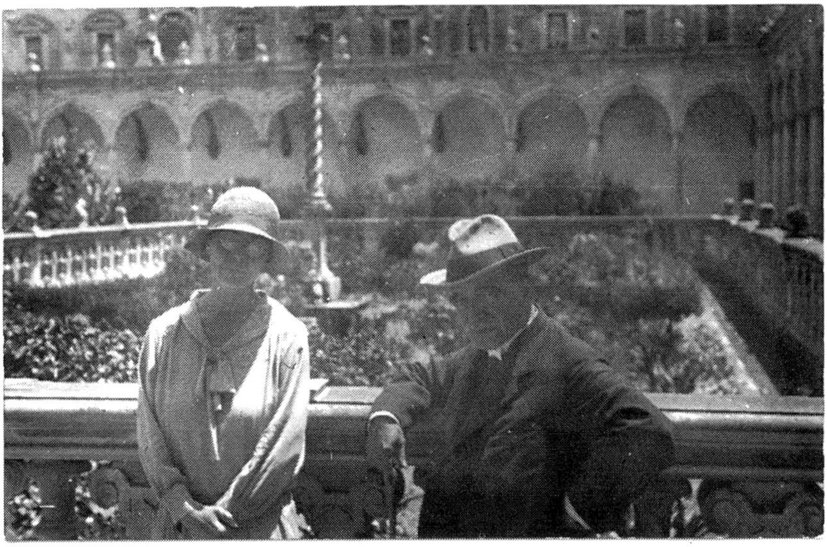

Figure 5.4 Aby Warburg and Gertrud Bing in the cemetery of the monastery Certosa San Martino, Naples.

Source: Photograph by F. Pospisil. WIA, Portrait collection. Photo: The Warburg Institute.

Bing replied by return of post, thanking him for seven 'wonderful' photographs, saying they were the best they had of Warburg. The photographs from San Martino in May 1929 especially showed how happy Warburg had been in Italy. She asked whether she could have prints made of the photographs and, if so, asked Pospíšil to send her the negatives. She also assured him that the KWB would publish his article, that work in the KBW would continue under Saxl's directorship and that Bing would publish Warburg's literary estate.[77] Bing's letter was friendly, whether or not Pospíšil's typescript would turn up.

Saxl also liked Pospíšil's photographs; he claimed they ranked 'among the best photographs' of Warburg.[78] Pospíšil only replied in September 1930, when he was staying in Hamburg on the occasion of the International Americanist Congress, lecturing on American choreography. He stressed that he would return the volumes on loan to him from the KBW, as well as bring the negatives of his photographs, and asked whether he could spend a night in a small room in the KBW.[79] Bing provided him with a quiet and cheap room.[80] Again, Pospíšil tried to find

77 WIA, GC, Bing to F. Pospíšil, 19.12.1929.
78 WIA, GC, Saxl to F. Pospíšil, 4.3.1930.
79 WIA, GC, F. Pospíšil to Saxl, 30.8.1930.
80 WIA, GC, Saxl to F. Pospíšil, 3.9.1930.

funding for his work. As Warburg had asked him to analyse American dances and had assured him of the assistance of the Warburg family in America, Pospíšil was now ready to bring the topic of sword dances in Europe and America to completion. However, he needed funding for this, since 'the entire capital of my wife and my parents have been used for filming'. Could Saxl interest Warburg's brothers in America? Pospíšil had promised Warburg to dedicate his book to Warburg; he wanted to tie his life's work to the name of Warburg.[81]

One month later he again asked Saxl to write to Warburg's relations in America, as he was on his way to New York shortly.[82] Saxl had indeed spoken to Warburg's brother Max, the head of the bank M. M. Warburg & Co. in Hamburg, and Max had written to his brother Paul in New York; however, Paul did not want or could not do anything for Pospíšil and referred him to his brother Felix. For Saxl this whole matter was embarrassing; everything had happened too fast, which precluded thoroughly preparing the brothers in America.[83] Pospíšil thanked him and hoped for the publication of his article on sword dances and battle dances in the *Vorträge* volumes of the KBW, adding rather presumptively that with this article Warburg's work 'would become more immediate and more comprehensive'.[84] Again, this did not happen. Pospíšil never published a book on sword dances. Pospíšil's stalling tactics were the reason that the lecture was not drawn up in writing and therefore not printed. The correspondence ceased. Warburg and Pospíšil were both interested in sword dances, but, ultimately, their research agendas went different ways.

81 WIA, GC, F. Pospíšil to Saxl, 10.9.1930. For supplements to the programmes of conferences with illustrations and summaries of Pospíšil's lectures see the Polish Ethnographical Congress 1927, the Folklore Congress in Amsterdam, 20. – 29.9.1927, the Folklore Society Jubilee Congress in London, 19. – 25.9.1928 and the Folklore Congress in Florence, 8. – 12.5.1929.

82 WIA, GC, F. Pospíšil to Saxl, 14.10.1930.

83 WIA, GC, Saxl to F. Pospíšil, 16.10.1930. Felix M. Warburg, German-American banker, 1871–1937; Max Warburg, German banker, 1867–1946; Paul M. Warburg, German-American investment banker, 1868–1932.

84 WIA, GC, F. Pospíšil to Saxl, 22.10.1930.

Part II

ABY WARBURG'S COLLABORATION WITH JAMES LOEB AND FRITZ SAXL

6

FACETS OF A FRIENDSHIP

Aby Warburg and James Loeb. Friends, scholars, relatives, patrons of the arts[1]

Introduction

Warburg was related to James Loeb,[2] a banker, scholar and philanthropist in New York, who moved to Germany in 1905. But it was not family relations alone which linked Warburg with Loeb, but also matters of research. Warburg appreciated 'with special satisfaction' the importance of Loeb's research when he was awarded an honorary doctorate from the University of Cambridge in 1925. The two of them, in collaboration with their assistants, got 'something like a Renaissance of relationships of the European to classical antiquity' going. He repeated what he had written to his publishers, B. G. Teubner in Leipzig, as shorthand for his library, 'The heritage of classical antiquity as an element of European culture', and added, 'I believe that also you would agree to this wording as motto of your aspirations'.[3] Loeb's 'aspirations' had been the driving force to start the famous *Loeb Classical Library*, that is, editions of classical authors in English, called 'classical envoys' by Warburg.[4] Loeb himself called it his life's work.[5]

Family contacts

Warburg was one year older than Loeb. After completion of his studies[6] and one year of military service in Karlsruhe and extended stays in Berlin and Florence, he went to America. Like Loeb, he came from a Jewish family of bankers, both of which had not only business but also familial ties. Warburg's brother Felix Moritz had married Frieda Schiff, daughter of Jacob Schiff, in New York on 19

1 Originally published in McEwan, D., 'Façetten einer Freundschaft: Aby Warburg und James Loeb. Verwandte, Freunde, Wissenschaftler, Mäzene', 75–98.
2 For James Loeb's biography see Burgmair and Weber, '"... daß er sich nirgends wohler als in Murnau fühle ..." James Loeb als Förderer der Wissenschaft und philanthropischer Mäzen', 77–128.
3 WIA, GC, Warburg to J. Loeb, 6.3.1925.
4 WIA, GC, Warburg to J. Loeb, 23.8.1926. See also www.loebclassics.com/ (accessed June 2022).
5 WIA, GC, J. Loeb to Warburg, 16.9.1910.
6 Warburg, A, '*Sandro Botticellis "Geburt der Venus" und "Frühling"*'; Britt, D., 'Sandro Botticelli's *Birth of Venus and Spring*', 89–156 and 405–431.

DOI: 10.4324/9781003169024-8

March 1895. Warburg's sister Olga, who had gone to Felix's wedding with her brother Paul Moritz, met James Loeb on this occasion. Despite her fondness for him she did not marry him, but Paul Kohn-Speyer of the bank Kuhn, Loeb und Co. in August 1898 in New York (see figure 6.1). Tragically she committed suicide in 1904. The flow of family correspondence around this event is markedly slim and non-existent in Loeb's correspondence.[7]

Warburg's brother Paul Moritz Warburg married Nina Jenny Loeb in New York on 1 October 1895. She was the sister of James Loeb, who then still worked in the family bank in New York. The wedding was the reason for Warburg's trip to America in September 1895, where he met members of the Loeb and Kohn-Speyer families and their business partners. Warburg stayed for six months in the

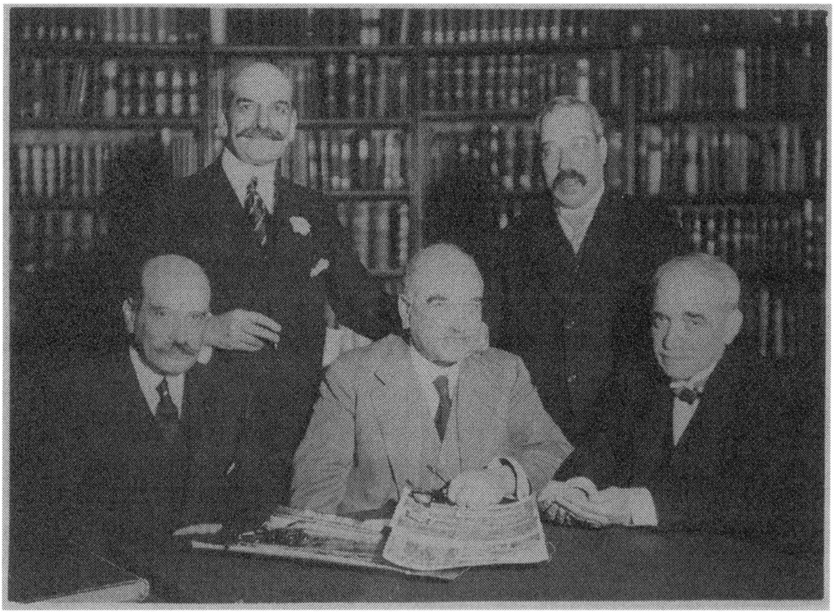

Figure 6.1 The five Warburg Brothers in KBW, 1929. WIA, Portrait collection. James Loeb file.

Source: © Photo: The Warburg Institute.

7 The five Warburg brothers, from left to right: Paul, Felix, Max, Fritz and Aby Warburg, 21.8.1929. Hamburg. For Gisela Warburg's travels with Felix Warburg in Palestine see Chapter 13. Felix Warburg, German-American banker, 1871–1937; Frieda Warburg, née Schiff, 1876–1958; Paul Moritz Warburg, German-American investment banker, 1868–1932; Olga Charlotte Kohn-Speyer, née Warburg, 1873–1904; Paul Henry Kohn-Speyer, British merchant banker, 1868–1942.

USA. The trip to the Native Americans in Arizona, New Mexico and Colorado in the winter of 1895/96 would turn out to be of great importance to Warburg and give him long-lasting stimuli for his cultural science research.

We owe to this trip to the Native Americans the first letter in the long Warburg – Loeb correspondence. Following the festivities around the wedding in New York, Warburg visited museums and libraries on the east coast of the USA in order to prepare himself for his trip to the west. Travelling into Native American reservations necessitated letters of recommendations – Loeb was supposed to bring them to the train, but came too late. A letter with an introduction for Warburg by Hoke Smith, the Secretary of the Interior,[8] to the agent of the Native American reservations, with a box of cigars and chocolates, reached him in Chicago as well as letters to Mr. Freund in Chicago, Mr. Guggenheim in Denver[9] and William H. Bean, commander of von Fort Wingate in New Mexico.[10]

Loeb enjoyed reading Warburg's description of the life in the southwest, which he called 'our barbaric country' in English, although he normally wrote in German.[11] Similar descriptions of Warburg's impressions of his travels surface in his diary and letters to family members in Hamburg. Loeb's replies were often humoristic, using language not deemed appropriate now; he hoped for Warburg's speedy 'return to the whites' after his 'life among the reds';[12] he wanted to know what Warburg experienced living with 'natives'[13] and did not forget to mention that he had cleaned Warburg's letter before reading it to avoid catching an infectious disease.[14] The tone was cordial. Loeb spoke about Warburg to his teacher Charles Eliot Norton, an art historian at Harvard, who promised to send articles from the Institute of Archaeology to Warburg.[15]

Family links had brought them together; their scholarly contact on art history and the history of classical antiquity continued throughout their lives. After Warburg's return to Hamburg in 1896 Loeb sent him a book 'with pretty pictures of American Indians',[16] requested a copy of Warburg's doctoral dissertation and other articles,[17] and, in short, corresponded about everything from New Year greetings[18] to appraisals of Warburg's academic articles – such as on the relief with the seven planets on the fireplace in the Italian room of the residence in Landshut[19] – or

8 Hoke Smith, American politician, 1855–1931. Ernst Freund, American lawyer, 1864–1931.

9 WIA, GC, J. Loeb to Warburg, 14.11.1895. John Simon Guggenheim, American politician, 1867–1941.

10 WIA, GC, J. Loeb to Warburg, 21.11.1895.

11 WIA, GC, J. Loeb to Warburg, 16.12.1895.

12 WIA, GC, J. Loeb to Warburg, 9.1.1896.

13 WIA, GC, J. Loeb to Warburg, 18.1.1896.

14 WIA, GC, J. Loeb to Warburg, 24.1.1896.

15 WIA, GC, J. Loeb to Warburg, 11.2.1896. Charles Eliot Norton, American art historian, 1827–1908.

16 WIA, GC, J. Loeb to Warburg, 20.8.1896.

17 WIA, GC, J. Loeb to Warburg, 22.9.1896.

18 WIA, GC, J. Loeb to Warburg, 5.1.1897.

19 WIA, GC, J. Loeb to Warburg, 3.5.1908 and 13.7.1908. Warburg, A., 'Kirchliche und höfische Kunst in Landshut'; Britt, D., 'Church and Court Art at Landshut', 561 and 732.

requests for supporting poor friends, such as Oskar Bulle in 1909 or Margaret Thurnham in 1915 (see below).[20]

From 1905 onward Warburg used a so-called Copy Book for copies of outgoing correspondence.[21] Earlier on, he did not always make copies of outgoing correspondence, so his requests can only be reconstructed by checking replies; one example in the Loeb – Warburg correspondence, where Warburg's outgoing letter has not survived, was Warburg's letter about his project to write an article about Native American symbols. However, letters from Morris Loeb as well as James Loeb about this topic are extant. James Loeb wrote that he was keenly interested in Warburg's article.[22] Warburg gave lectures with slides about his trip to the southwest of America one year after his return from America, see Chapter 4, n. 20. However, his research on the symbols of Native Americans was only presented to an audience in the lecture about the serpent ritual in 1923.[23]

When Loeb thought about moving to Germany, he asked Warburg for his views. He was thinking of moving either to Bonn or to Munich, to be near his friend Adolf Furtwängler.[24] Again, there is no reply extant, but Loeb's inquiry shows how close the contacts were between both Loeb and Warburg and Loeb and Warburg's wife Mary, who was a painter and sculptress. In one of his letters he asked her advice about modelling:

> Dear Mary, may I ask you for a great favour? I want to fill my time here with making models. As I do not know where to obtain plasticine from, I would be very grateful to you if you could ask your supplier to send me a large amount as well as utensils and the invoice. Felix told me full of admiration of the bust of little Paul which you have made. May I have a photograph?
>
> Please give my greetings to Aby. What is he working on right now? Would he agree to write a monograph about the dependence of Renaissance art on the motifs which we find on Arretine pottery? I plan to publish a volume, following the model of the publications of the Monument Piot, with the contributions of three or four more articles about my Arretine collection, very richly illustrated.
>
> Incidentally, I have sent a request to Boston to send plaster copies of the most important objects of my collection to Aby, as I have promised him some time ago.

20 On Bulle and Thurnham see this Chapter, notes 109–111 and 112–114 respectively. Oskar Bulle, German writer, 1857–1917. Margaret Emily Thurnham, English nanny to Warburg's children, b. 1882.

21 There are six volumes of Copy Books in the WIA, from 1905 to 1918, with some 2,300 copies of outgoing correspondence; all volumes underwent a process of conservation in 1998. See also Diers, M., *Warburg aus Briefen*; McEwan, D., 'Millennium-feuilles from Half-Eaten Wafers', 2.

22 WIA, GC, M. Loeb to Warburg, 18.02.1897 and WIA, GC, J. Loeb to Warburg, 23.4.1897. Morris Loeb, American Philanthropist, 1863–1912.

23 For a comprehensive bibliography of this lecture see the two books by Guidi and Mann, *Photographs at the Frontier* and *Grenzerweiterungen*. See also Chapter 5.

24 WIA, GC, J. Loeb to Warburg, 1408.190li2. Adolf Furtwängler, German archaeologist, 1853–1907.

Thanking you in advance for your assistance and with cordial greetings to you, Aby and the dear children as well as all Kösterbergers.

Your devoted friend
James Loeb.[25]

Whether Mary sent utensils for modelling is not known. The hoped-for collaboration with Warburg did not materialise either. At this time Warburg was occupied with his own research on the Renaissance in Florence.

Loeb moved to Munich in 1905 and had a large house and garden built in Murnau in Bavaria in 1912/13, and members of the Warburg and Hertz families went on holidays there.[26] Walther Hertz, Mary Warburg's nephew, read law in Munich and spent the Christmas holidays in 1922 with Loeb in Murnau.[27] Hertz became a professional musician, however, but music lover Loeb must have been happy about this. He wrote that Walther's choice of profession reminded him of the bad times his maternal grandfather, Simon Gallenberg, had had to weather as first violinist in the Grand Ducal Opera house in Mannheim.[28] Musical topics were rare in the correspondence, but when Loeb learnt that Warburg and his wife would be on holiday in Partenkirchen, he invited them to an evening of music-making with Loeb playing in a string quartet. It remains unknown whether the Warburgs attended; there is no entry about it in the diary.[29]

A feeling of familial warmth characterised the relationship of the two friends. When Warburg sent a photograph of his three children and congratulated Loeb for his work on the *Loeb Classical Library* despite World War I, Loeb expressed beautifully what was important to him in life:

> Dear Aby, thank you very much for the charming picture of your three splendid children. The three are distinctly different little children. Your favourite word 'surrogate' cannot be used with them! I am very glad for the picture. For somebody like me who has to live for many more months without people and dear friends, photographs have a special intimate value. In my thoughts I live a little bit in the company of such pictures!
>
> Thank you very much for congratulating me on my 'cultural activity', the L. C. L. [Loeb Classical Library]. However, how much happier I would be if I had achieved such a cultural activity as you have achieved with your three children! Do you understand this?

25 WIA, GC, J. Loeb, in Villa Hainstein, Eisenach, to Mary Warburg, 4.9.1905. On Kösterberg, a hillock near Hamburg, a number of members of the Warburg family, 'Kösterbergers', had houses. Little Paul, recte Paul Felix, was the first child of Felix and Frieda Warburg, born 1904. Monument Piot was a series of publications, see Fondation Eugène Piot, *Monuments et mémoires de la Fondation Eugène Piot*. Frieda Warburg, née Schiff, 1876–1958; Mary Warburg, née Hertz, German painter and sculptor, 1866–1934.

26 See Mayer et al., *James Loeb*.

27 WIA, GC, W. Hertz to Warburg, 21.12.1922.

28 WIA, GC, J. Loeb to Warburg, 18.11.1924. Simon Gallenberg, violinist in Mannheim, 1803–1872.

29 WIA, GC, J. Loeb to Warburg, 17.1.1912.

Here it is always quiet; I do not meet any friends, as the difficulties of obtaining provisions nip hospitality in the bud. If one returns home with a bunch of the finest ceps, as Hanna and I did this afternoon, one feels as if the challenges of feeding have partly been solved!

My best greetings to you, Mary and the children, Your Jim.[30]

Loeb, who did not have children, valued the three Warburg children. When Warburg's oldest child, Marietta, known as Detta, spent a few days with Loeb, he wrote full of joy to Warburg:

> I have to write to you and tell you what great joy it has been to have Detta with us for a few days. What a dear, sensible girl she is! You have every reason to be very proud of and very happy about her and with her. We both enjoyed very much to see such a cheerful sunny disposition behind her serious nature. To cultivate this and give it ample opportunity to apply itself will surely be your aim.[31]

Scientific contacts

Throughout his life Warburg sent his articles and books to Loeb and posed him detailed questions or expected comments from Loeb, who did likewise. Loeb's name was in the list of 33 recipients – the list makes impressive reading – who received Warburg's article on 'The Art of Portraiture and the Florentine Bourgeoisie' from the bookseller G. W. Niemeyer Nachfolger in Hamburg, among them names of colleagues with whom Warburg kept up a correspondence all his life.[32] After having read Warburg's article on 'Peasants at Work in Burgundian

30 WIA, GC, J. Loeb to Warburg, 25.7.1916.

31 WIA, GC, J. Loeb to Warburg, 23.11.1925.

32 WIA, GC, G. Wolfhagen, G.W. Niemeyer Nachfolger, to Warburg, 24.2.1902.

Warburg, A., 'Bildniskunst und florentinisches Bürgertum'; Britt, D., 'The Art of Portraiture and the Florentine Bourgeoisie', 185–221 and 435–450; WIA, GC, G. Wolfhagen, G. W. Niemeyer Nachfolger, to Warburg, 24.2.1902.

Copies were sent to the publishers and to Sidney Colvin in London, British art critic, 1845–1927; Alice Hallgarten Franchetti in Rome, American philanthropist, 1874–1911; Anton Dohrn in Naples, German zoologist, 1840–1909; Paul Kohn-Speyer in London, merchant banker, 1868–1942; Morris Loeb, American philanthropist, 1863–1912; James Loeb in New York, 1867–1933; Felix Moritz Warburg in New York, German-American banker, 1871–1937; Eugène Müntz in Paris, French art historian, 1845–1902; Jan Pieter Veth in Bussum, Dutch painter, 1864–1925; Charles Eliot Norton in Cambridge, USA, American art historian, 1827–1908; Lewis Einstein in New York, American historian, 1877–1967; Theobald Ziegler in Strasbourg, German philosopher, 1846–1918; Carl Robert in Halle, German classical philologist, 1850–1922; Johann (John) Hertz in Helmstedt, Aby Warburg's brother-in-law, 1869–1908; Karl Lamprecht in Leipzig, German historian, 1856–1915; Paul Hensel in Heidelberg, German philosopher, 1860–1930; Cornelius von Fabriczy in Stuttgart,

Tapestries',[33] Loeb told him that woodcutters did not feature on the tapestries in the emperor pavilion on the occasion of the parade for Emperor Wilhelm II in Maximilian Street in Munich in 1906. Warburg asked him about American slang words[34] or about his family or Jewish affairs and continued to send him his latest articles. Loeb was impressed with 'Francesco Sassetti's Last Injunctions to His Sons',[35] which he commented on favourably after having read it in Hamburg on the occasion of Warburg's 40th birthday:

> I now have read your article with enjoyment. It prompts me to tell you and your dear colleague how excellent I find your achievement. The whole presentation of the material, the closely fitting line of argument of your thesis are admirable and work convincingly. I found the psychological interpretation of the documents and the different visual presentations highly interesting and original and particularly valuable as adjustment to the antique-like interpretations, of which there are far too many already. Such a strictly scientific, deductive treatment of art-historical material would greatly contribute to turning the attention of the reading public, which is not really sympathetic to pure aesthetics, to the inner value of art history. I can only say, we wish this article many male descendants![36]

He asked Warburg for a copy and another copy for Professor Norton, only to tell him shortly afterwards that Norton had died on 21 October 1908.[37]

Part of their collaboration included making contact with scholars, for instance when Loeb needed professional advice on English painting in the 18th century and

German art historian, 1839–1910; Henry Thode in Heidelberg, German art historian, 1857–1920; Max L. Strack in Bonn, German historian, 1867–1914; Henry Simonsfeld in Munich, German medievalist, 1852–1913; August Schmarsow in Leipzig, German art historian, 1853–1936; Artur Weese in Munich, German art historian, 1868–1934; Marc Rosenberg in Karlsruhe, German art historian, 1862–1930; Emil Schaeffer in Bielitz, Austrian art historian, 1874–1944; Wilhelm Vöge in Hanover, German art historian, 1868–1952; Ernst Schwedeler-Meyer in Cologne, German art historian, 1867–1934; Joseph Neuwirth in Vienna, Austrian art historian, 1855–1934; Adolf Michaelis in Strasbourg, German art historian, 1835–1910; Hermann Oldenberg in Kiel, German scholar of Indology, 1854–1920; Erich von Hornbostel in Vienna, Austrian ethnomusicologist, 1877–1935; Oscar Ollendorff in Wiesbaden, German art historian, 1865–1939; Moritz Nathan Oppenheim in Frankfurt, German businessman, 1848–1933.

33 WIA, GC, J. Loeb to Warburg, 14.11.1906. Warburg, A., 'Arbeitende Bauern auf Burgundischen Teppichen'; Britt, D., 'Peasants at Work in Burgundian Tapestries', 315–323 and 484–485. Wilhelm II, German emperor, 1845–1886.

34 WIA, GC, J. Loeb to Warburg, 6.12.1906.

35 WIA, GC, J. Loeb to Warburg, 14.8.1907. Warburg, A., 'Francesco Sassettis letztwillige Verfügung'; Britt, D., 'Francesco Sassetti's Last Injunctions to His Sons', 223–262 and 451–466.

36 WIA, GC, J. Loeb to Warburg, 14.8.1907.

37 WIA, GC, J. Loeb to Warburg, 26.10.1908.

wondered whether he could write to privy councillor Wilhelm von Bode.[38] Another time he needed expertise on '15 very strange bas reliefs', which he sent to Warburg. Morti Schiff, father-in-law of Felix M. Warburg, had bought them from the art dealer Goldschmidt in Frankfurt, who told Morti that they were original works of the 16th-century maiolica potter Giorgio di Gubbio.[39] Loeb was not so sure:

> in inventiveness as well as execution the objects appear to be very suspicious. Some of them look clumsy like the work of incompetent persons in the 18th century, other objects, however, show a certain charming freshness and simplicity, as one is used to find in earlier times.[40]

By return of post Warburg confirmed that Morti had bought forgeries.[41] Still another time, Loeb sent Warburg a copy of the Bulletin of the Metropolitan Museums in New York with the image of a 'rather insufficient copy of the front of a cassone', which Loeb had donated to the museum a short time before.[42]

A large part of their correspondence dealt with requests for expert opinions when purchasing works of art, whether it was on behalf of Warburg's brother Paul[43] or whether it was checking if prices were reasonable or not.[44] Loeb sent a photograph of a relief, attributed to Jacopo della Quercia, to Warburg, who did not accept the attribution and dated the relief circa 1470.[45] Yet another time Loeb asked whether Warburg was interested in the purchase of 3,000 volumes from the library of Robert R. von Schneider, director of the Austrian archaeological institute.[46]

During the Tenth International Congress on the History of Art in Rome in October 1912, which was to become a scholarly high point in Warburg's life with his research on the frescoes in Palazzo Schifanoia in Ferrara and resultant lecture, 'Italian Art and International Astrology in the Palazzo Schifanoia, Ferrara', Mary Warburg informed him of the death of Morris Loeb.[47] Warburg could not attend the funeral, but his brother Max went to a family gathering in London where he and his wife Alice met Ike Seligman and his wife Guta, James Loeb's sister, as

38 WIA, GC, J. Loeb to Warburg, 22.3.1908.

39 Giorgio di Gubbio or Maestro Giorgio, Italian potter, 1465–1555.

40 WIA, GC, J. Loeb to Warburg, 13.7.1908.

41 WIA, GC, J. Loeb to Warburg, 18.7.1908.

42 WIA, GC, J. Loeb to Warburg, 28.10.1908.

43 WIA, GC, J. Böhler, court antiquarian in Munich, to Warburg, 7.12.1908. Julius Böhler, German art dealer, 1883–1966.

44 WIA, GC, J. Loeb to Warburg, cable, 14.8.1902 requesting information on a good copy of *Hypnerotomachia* by Francesco Colonna. Colonna, Italian priest, credited with the authorship of *Hypnerotomachia*, 1433–1527.

45 WIA, GC, Warburg to Rudolf Borchardt, 18.3.1912. Jacopo della Quercia, Italian sculptor, c. 1374–1438; Rudolf Borchardt, German writer, 1877–1945.

46 WIA, GC, J. Loeb to Warburg, 18.2.1910. Robert R. von Schneider, Austrian archaeologist, 1854–1909.

47 WIA, GC, Mary Warburg to Warburg, 14.10.1912, see Chapter 1, n. 15.

well as Paul and Nina Warburg and James Loeb, and they all went to the funeral in New York together.[48]

With regard to the university project in Hamburg before World War I, in which the Warburg family was involved as advisers and supporters, there was also talk of support by James Loeb. But when it became clear that the university would not be established in 1913 and that this would have consequences for the Warburg library, Max Warburg counselled patience in his letter to Warburg: 'I was very interested in your news of the library. However, we cannot request anything from James Loeb at the moment, we have to arrange it ourselves'.[49] He was referring to the fact that Loeb was very ill at the time and could not be asked to busy himself with problems in Hamburg. However, again and again there were letters in which Warburg told his brother Fritz, a banker in Hamburg, that Loeb had made donations to the Warburg library account.[50]

In the first winter of World War I Warburg had tried to stop Italy joining the Allies and had started the periodical *Rivista* with the help of Thilenius and Panconcelli-Calzia in Hamburg and Hübner in Rome.[51] He sent out copies to friends in Germany and abroad and donors like Loeb.[52] Loeb appraised the situation differently, much more realistically than Warburg or a committee which had started work in Munich and

> which tries to work in Italy for the benefit of Germany. . . . I fear that everything will be to no avail. In times of lack of conscience every country simply does what serves her own advantage or what she sees will serve her own advantage and one day even Italy will abandon her allies![53]

– which happened with the declaration of war by Italy to the Axis Powers in May 1915 and hit Warburg badly.

Loeb's friendship with the historian Robert Davidsohn was an important one, in terms of their scholarly collaboration as well as personal art patronage. Davidsohn, a German scholar who worked in Florence, had visited Loeb a few days before the Italian declaration of war in 1915 and was extremely pessimistic about the situation.[54] But this visit ushered in a long and enduring friendship, one which Warburg had initiated.[55] The Davidsohns spent their holidays in Murnau in 1915,

48 WIA, GC, Max Warburg to Warburg, 16.10.1912. Isac ('Ike') Newton Seligman, American banker, 1855–1917; Max Warburg, 1867–1946, German banker.

49 WIA, GC, Max Warburg to Warburg, 31.12.1913.

50 For instance WIA, GC, Copy book VI, 56, Warburg to Fritz Warburg, 14.4.1915.

51 WIA, IV.63.2.1. *La Guerra del 1914. Rivista illustrata dei primi tre mesi agosto, settembre, ottobre*; WIA, IV.63.2.2. *La Guerra del 1914–15 dei mesi novembre, dicembre, gennaio, febbraio*, Hamburg: Broschek & Co. Panconelli-Calzia and Hübner, see Chapter 3.

52 WIA, GC, Copy book VI, 67, Warburg to J. Loeb, 29.4.1915.

53 WIA, GC, J. Loeb to Warburg, 21.11.1914.

54 WIA, GC, J. Loeb to Warburg, 30.4.1915.

55 WIA, GC, J. Loeb to Warburg, 17.5.1915. Robert Davidsohn, German historian, 1853–1937.

the first of many.[56] Davidsohn, who had to return to Munich during the war, had found a colleague and friend in Loeb.[57] After the war the Davidsohns reciprocated and placed their villa in Florence at Loeb's disposal.[58] Visits to Florence, to the 'really delightful villa',[59] where both scholars could spend a lot of time together, were commented on with particular affection. And just as Warburg had bookplates made for books from the estates of friends and colleagues[60] – which, through Warburg's efforts, entered public institutions, such as those for professors Robert Münzel in 1918 und Franz Boll in 1925 – so Loeb had a medal with Davidsohn's portrait made and sent a copy to Warburg:

> With the same post I send you the portrait medal of our dear friend, Professor Davidsohn. It was a great joy for me to commission the very talented Professor Georgii, the son-in-law of Hildebrand. We, as well as Davidsohn and his wife, find the portrait splendid and I hope that this medal will bring you and Mary as much pleasure as it has us.[61]

Before having seen it, Warburg wrote that he and his wife were very much looking forward to receiving it.

> Mary remembers from the times in Florence[62] that she found Davidsohn's characterful head simply inviting to being sculpted. In his face one sees the achievements of Atlas, which carry masterfully the heritage of orient and occident and are at the same time unwaveringly obedient.[63]

And Loeb again thanked Warburg for having introduced Davidsohn to him:

> I saw with great joy from Mary's kind letter and your epilogue that you as well consider the Davidsohn medal as very accomplished. It is dear to me that you, through whom I met the dear and treasured man, now own it.[64]

The Loeb – Davidsohn friendship enriched Loeb's life in spite of, or perhaps because of, the war. Warburg and Loeb experienced the war as a catastrophe. Although Warburg was a patriotic German and loyal to the German emperor, recording every twist and turn in the war, he had to realise that many years of

56 WIA, GC, J. Loeb to Warburg, 14.6.1915.
57 WIA, GC, R. Davidsohn to Warburg, 15.7.1915 and 24.6.1917.
58 WIA, GC, J. Loeb to 'Maraby' i.e. Aby and Mary Warburg, 18.11.1924.
59 WIA, GC, J. Loeb to Warburg, 11.11.1924.
60 See also McEwan, D., 'Arch and Flag: Leitmotifs for the Aby Warburg Bookplate', 95–110.
61 WIA, GC, J. Loeb to Warburg, 3.3.1925. Adolf von Hildebrand, German sculptor, 1847–1921. Theodor Georgii, Russian sculptor, 1883–1963.
62 Aby and Mary Warburg lived in Florence from 1898 to 1902.
63 WIA, GC, Warburg to J. Loeb, 06.03.1925.
64 WIA, GC, J. Loeb to Warburg, 21.3.1925.

sacrifice and deaths would bring neither victory nor truth. Warburg was distraught about Italy's declaration of war against the Axis Powers in 1915. Shortly before it he noted with satisfaction that Loeb, although an American national, had decided to stay in Germany.[65] After the declaration of war Warburg was so shocked by the attitude of the USA, with their talk of peace and simultaneous building up of arms, that he positively congratulated Loeb 'that you do not have to sit on the steps of the temple of peace with the money changers'.[66] His successor as director of the library, Fritz Saxl, wrote much later that Warburg did not hold on to the idea of German hegemony, but believed in the 'United States of Europe'.[67]

Loeb encouraged Warburg in the second year of the war to continue with his project of the war archive, the collection of newspaper cuttings. 'The war archive cannot fail to thrive and be completed considering your staff of collaborators'.[68] He also informed Warburg that the Samson Foundation of the Bavarian Academy of Sciences had set up a prize of 6,000 marks for the best work on 'Ethical feelings of nations in the world war'. Would Warburg be interested in applying, 'given your large newspaper archive, which is without equal . . .'?[69] Although the two friends did not come back to this suggestion, Loeb knew that Warburg was passionately interested in making public the true reasons for the war, the domestic and foreign policies, as he saw them. Warburg, for instance, wrote in May 1916 to the press department of the 18th army corps in Frankfurt that he wanted to publish a letter by the American president Thomas Jefferson in the neutral countries and in the USA, in order to turn public opinion against the USA entering the war in 1917.[70] He sent a copy of this letter to Loeb asking him to dispatch it from a neutral country to the USA.[71] Again Loeb did not let himself get carried away by Warburg's ideas. He found such an endeavour simply too late; in his own opinion the war would not be ended by the attitude of neutral countries.[72] Finally, in 1923, when the lack of space for the ever-growing library in Warburg's house was discussed, Loeb suggested Max Warburg sell or give away the war archive in order to create space for books.[73]

65 WIA, GC, Copy book VI, 60, Warburg to J. Loeb, 18.4.1915.

66 WIA, GC, Copy book VI, 92, Warburg to J. Loeb, 12.6.1915.

67 WIA, 111.2, 11. Unpublished biography, 1944. Saxl most probably remembered Warburg's phrase, which he had used in a letter to Felix von Eckardt. In it Warburg stressed that an English nationalist interpretation, at least for air traffic, was no longer possible. See Chapter 2, note 31, WIA, GC, Warburg to F. v. Eckardt, 10.9.1925.

68 WIA, GC, J. Loeb to Warburg, 13.10.1915.

69 WIA, GC, J. Loeb to Warburg, 27.10.1916.

70 WIA, GC, Copy book VI, 227, Warburg to the Press Department of the Deputy General Command of the 18th army corps in Frankfurt, 18.5.1916. Cf. Warburg's efforts to send texts for political caricatures to *Simplicissimus* and *Kladderadatsch* in McEwan, D., 'Karikatur als Kriegsdienst: Aby Warburgs "neuer Stil in Wort und Bild", 1914–1918', 78–95; see Chapter 11. Thomas Jefferson, American president, 1743–1826.

71 WIA, GC, Copy book VI, 229, Warburg to J. Loeb, 18.5.1916.

72 WIA, GC, J. Loeb to Warburg, 21.5.1916.

73 WIA, GC, Max Warburg to Saxl, 26.2.1923. See Chapter 3 for details on the war archive.

Though Loeb and Warburg differed in their appraisal of the war, their scholarly work continued undiminished. Loeb, for instance, sent a copy of the Bulletin of the Boston Museum of Fine Arts to Warburg with an article about engravings of star sign allegories. He also announced that a catalogue of an exhibition of early Italian engravings in the Fogg Museum, curated by Paul Sachs, would be sent to Warburg.[74] Another instance of cooperation was when Warburg thanked Johannes Sieveking in Munich for having forwarded a catalogue of Loeb's terracottas.[75]

The post-war years

For Loeb as well as for Warburg World War I was a caesura, which deeply affected both of them. The end of the war with its profound, political changes did not bring the desired solution and much less the 'truth'. For Warburg, years of illness followed. Loeb fell ill in 1917; he suffered from depression and was able to continue with his writing and collection work only in 1920. From 1918 onwards Warburg could no longer run the library in Hamburg. His family, as the funding network, employed Fritz Saxl, Warburg's former assistant, as librarian and interim director in 1919. He continued with Warburg's work, but intensified it by introducing innovations through which the library of a private scholar graduated to become a research institute: he organised lectures in the library, he arranged seminars in the library as part of the curriculum of the newly established Hamburg University's art history institute, and he established two publication series, *Vorträge* and *Studien*, which presented topics within the research agenda of the library. He sent copies of the publication series to Loeb as a matter of course,[76] and in return received the volumes of the *Loeb Classical Library* for free. Saxl was very happy with this arrangement, as he had to be careful with the annual purchase budget granted by the Warburg family.[77]

The Warburg – Loeb correspondence was interrupted in the years of Warburg's stay in sanatoriums, at first in Hamburg, then in the Bellevue sanatorium, run by Dr. Ludwig Binswanger, in Kreuzlingen on the shores of Lake Constance in Switzerland. But with Warburg's return to Hamburg in 1924, their correspondence started up again. Warburg had sent Loeb the text of his introduction and words of thanks that was inserted into volume 2 of *Vorträge* on the occasion of Karl Reinhardt's lecture on 'Ovid's Metamorphoses'. Loeb and his wife Tony, Marie Antonie Hambuechen-Loeb, thanked him warmly for his 'succinct, heartfelt, splendid address' and congratulated him that what he had

74 WIA, GC, J. Loeb to Warburg, 3.12.1915.

75 WIA, GC, Warburg to J. Sieveking, 30.11.1916. Johannes Sieveking, German classical archaeologist, 1869–1942.

76 WIA, GC, Saxl to J. Loeb, 14.9.1923 with *Vorträge 1*, 1922/22.

77 WIA, GC, Saxl to J. Loeb, 2.10.1923. On Saxl's pioneering work from 1920 to 1924 see McEwan, D., '"The Enemy of Hypothesis": Fritz Saxl as Acting Director of the Warburg Library', 75–86.

started with his doctoral dissertation on Botticelli in 1888 had been completed with Reinhardt's article.[78]

Loeb was right: Warburg had found a modicum of stability and strength to continue with his academic work. Warburg's return to Hamburg marked the start of a particularly fertile period for Warburg's work, which he himself called 'harvesting hay during a thunderstorm', a simile with which he expressed the urgency to reap the harvest, to complete his life's work.[79] One aspect of this was the need for a purpose-built building for the library. So far, his library had been housed in his family home and was bursting at the seams. In the autumn of 1924 a new library was planned on the adjoining piece of land, in 1925 building started and in the spring of 1926 the library moved into the new building (see figure 6.2).

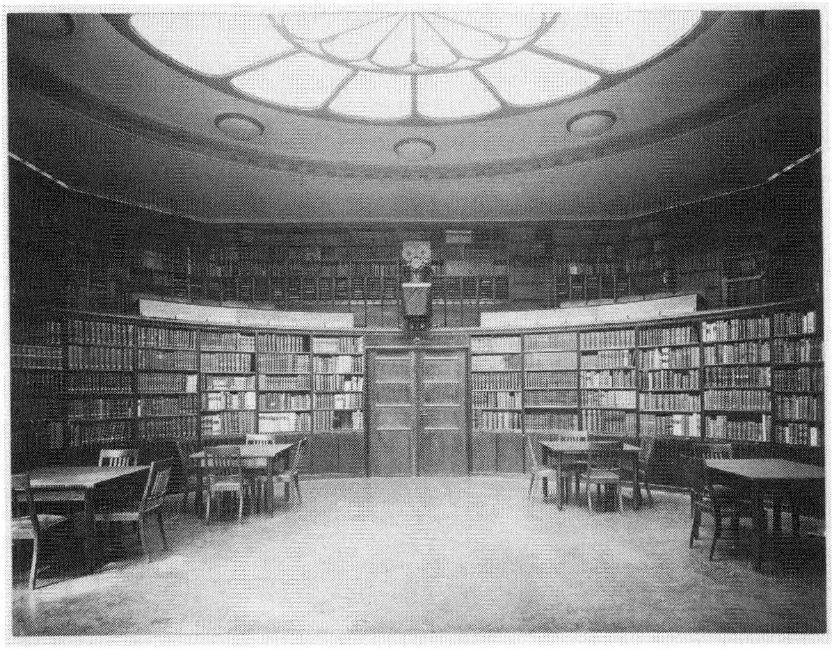

Figure 6.2 KBW, Elliptical Reading Room, 1926. WIA, I.4.20.3, no.12.

Source: © Photo: The Warburg Institute.

78 WIA, GC, J. Loeb to Warburg, 11.11.1924. The address was given on 24 October 1924. See also Stimilli and Wedepohl, *Aby M. Warburg "Per Monstra and Sphaeram"*. Karl Reinhardt, German classical philologist, 1886–1958.

79 WIA, GC, Saxl to J. Loeb, 18.01.1932.

Loeb also suggested to Max Warburg technical innovations, such as fitted cupboards for the books, and Max asked him for technical drawings,[80] which Loeb supplied with descriptions.[81] He wanted to make sure that his 'patent shelves' were correctly measured:

> I want careful scrutiny of whether my patent shelves are possible. Since a third of the measure of length could be saved with my suggestion it would contribute to a noticeable reduction of the building costs.[82]

Nothing more was heard of the 'patent shelves', but Loeb was the first to be invited to the opening of the library.[83] He could not attend, but thanking Loeb for his congratulations gave Warburg the opportunity to explain the legal status of the library: 'I own it, partly as proprietor, partly as administrator of a maintained family property'. There was no word of donating the library to the state or the university, but the intention to make the KWB 'the museum of the soul', accessible to the public, which did not change the legal situation.[84] Earlier on he had used descriptions like 'laboratory' for the library;[85] this time he called it a place for scholars to pose as 'cannon fodder for respectable question marks'[86] and invited Loeb to inspect it on his next visit to Hamburg.[87]

Warburg, who had often invited friends and colleagues to visit his library in order to realise its value as a research library, was disappointed that Loeb instead travelled to Sicily in the summer of 1926:

> . . . if you can travel to Sicily, you also have to come to the North, even if it is not as pleasurable. I confess openly that I feel fate has dealt me a blow, that you, who are, like me, a desperado of idealism, do not muster the energy of friendship to have a look at my institute. If we were not related, I believe that you would long have cared for this organism lovingly. The dark side of kinship is that one says: you know him and he stays with you. Is this objectively true??[88]

Loeb in his reply, which is not extant, must have contradicted Warburg, which gave Warburg the chance to develop further what he had meant with his phrase 'desperado of idealism'.

80 Bankhaus Warburg, Hamburg, Archiv, Max Warburg to J. Loeb, 25.5.1924.
81 Bankhaus Warburg, Hamburg, Archiv, J. Loeb to Max Warburg, 1.6.1924.
82 Bankhaus Warburg, Hamburg, Archiv, J. Loeb to Max Warburg, 30.12.1924.
83 WIA, GC, Warburg to J. Loeb, 22.1.1925.
84 WIA, GC, Warburg to J. Loeb, 31.8.1926.
85 WIA, GC, Warburg to A. Doren, n.d. 1910.
86 WIA, GC, Warburg to Saxl, 23.12.1911.
87 WIA, GC, Warburg to J. Loeb, 21.5.1926.
88 WIA, GC, Warburg to J. Loeb, 23.8.1926. The last sentence of the quote is a handwritten addition to the typed letter. For 'desperadoes of idealism' see also Chapter 13.

> After all, one also speaks of 'energy of despair' or a 'desperately energetic person', which means that one does not use the adjective in the sense of inactive internal despair, but rather in the sense of utmost determination for better or worse, which now can be directed at the good or the bad. In our case it only means that we have burnt the ships of crass egotism behind ourselves and now preach to the journalistically contaminated audience about the blessing of our treasure of memory, that is, the internal cultural mission. You disseminate the little treatises in simply astonishing numbers and for them I have built the chapel, which awaits you and your wife for prayers. With this prospect I live impatiently, but in the gratifying hope that, in the event you come, you will not allow yourself to be used as fodder for stupid family breakfasts.[89]

Warburg's unique exactness of expression did not move Loeb and nothing further was heard of a visit. Both continued to send each other books, requesting comments and congratulating each other for successes. Loeb wrote about the project of translating the Jewish historian Flavius Josephus – 'It contains incredibly interesting details about the trustworthiness of the Jewish historian in contrast to the lying-prone Greek!'[90] – to which Warburg did not reply. Another time Loeb marvelled at the programme of interesting lecture series at the KBW: 'I congratulate you on the rich meal which the Warburg library will serve its guests in its lectures this year',[91] but this rich meal was not consumed by Loeb either.

Loeb only rarely commented on current affairs, although he was very capable of assessing them. One exception were his comments on events in Munich in 1926:

> The protest meeting, where Thomas Mann played a leading role, is said to have been very impressive. Our good friend, City Councillor Kieselbach (sic!), the leading spirit among the women of the democratic party in Munich, has told us about it enthusiastically. I refer you to a letter which I wrote to Max [Warburg] last night with the authentic details of the unpleasant events at the University of Munich.[92]

89 WIA, GC, Warburg to J. Loeb, 31.8.1926. Only in January 1928 there was talk of Loeb's visiting the KBW, WIA, GC, Warburg to Loeb, 5.1.1928. Loeb's own reaction to the guided tour through the library is not extant; in its stead he gives thanks for Warburg's having given Luise Kiesselbach a very interesting tour through the library. WIA, GC, J. Loeb to Warburg, 2.5.1928. Luise Kiesselbach, German social policy maker, 1863–1929

90 WIA, GC, J. Loeb to Warburg, 6.11.1926. The Loeb Classical Library 186, *Josephus*. Flavius Jospehus, Romano-Jewish scholar and historian, AD 30 – c. 100.

91 WIA, GC, J. Loeb to Warburg, 27.11.1926.

92 WIA, GC, J. Loeb to Warburg, 7.12.1926. On the topic of the Thomas Mann lecture in Munich, 'Kampf um München als Kulturzentrum' on 30 November 1926, see Kolbe and Bittel, *Heller Zauber*. Thomas Mann, German writer, 1875–1955.

Warburg recognised the importance of Mann's speech. Spontaneously he sent him the third edition of the book by Boll and Bezold, published on Warburg's instigation in 1926. He couched his thanks in words like 'resolute thrust into the infinite in the midst of Bavarian narrowness' in the name of all of those 'who suffer from possible heliotropism'. And he used the phrase again, writing of himself as the 'long time desperado of heliotropism'.[93] Thomas Mann very quickly expressed his thanks, saying the book fitted into his own research on 'early oriental, Babylonian-Canaanite-Egyptian topics'. He congratulated himself that

> the little earthquake, which we have stage managed here recently, has driven its waves so far that is has brought me this beautiful gift from the shores of the sea.[94]

Unfortunately, Warburg's response to the 'earthquake' is not extant. In his last years Loeb wrote more letters to Warburg than vice versa. But, as a matter of course, Warburg continued sending him invitations to lectures, publications of the KBW or the linocut 'Idea', which Loeb commented on as follows:

> The victorious flying 'Idea' came from the Warburg library today. Many thanks. The likes of us first have to look at it and get inside it. Machine art, or let us say graphic art, in which machines and iron braces play the main role, doubtlessly belong to the symptoms of our time. It may be that art historians in the 25th century find all this as justifiable as we find the mathematical and very necessary symbols of Dürer's 'Melencolia' as being typical for his intellectual orbit today. In any case the motto of your linocut and the sequence of the names Briand, Chamberlain and Stresemann is really inspired.[95]

For Loeb's 60th birthday Warburg sent him a book[96] and Mary a bronze sculpture, which greatly impressed Loeb.

> Dear Mary, I see in your gift of a little bronze, despite its small size, a great work of art, because of its format, rhythm, fidelity to nature, poetry, absolute mastery of shape and true artistic devotion.[97]

93 WIA, GC, draft for a letter, Warburg to Thomas Mann, n.d., before 7.12.1926. Boll and Bezold, *Sternglaube und Sterndeutung*. Franz Boll, German classicist, 1867–1924; Carl Bezold, German orientalist, 1859–1922.

94 WIA, GC, T. Mann to Warburg, 7.12.1926.

95 WIA, GC, J. Loeb to Warburg, 14.1.1927. See Chapter 2 for details on 'Idea'.

96 Inventory no. 5058 in Schloßmuseum Murnau.

97 WIA, GC, J. Loeb to Aby and Mary Warburg, 8.8.1927; Hedinger et al., *Mary Warburg*, V 46, 475. Small nude. WIA, GC, Mary Warburg to Frede Warburg, 7.5.1927, in which Mary writes about working in her studio on the small nude.

The correspondence remained cordial but lost its frequency. When the aged art historian Adolph Goldschmidt planned a trip to America in 1927, Warburg felt encouraged to do the same. 'If he risks it, why can I not risk it?' He expanded on his reasons:

> My standpoint is that I now have to have a period of renaissance of my intellectual powers or I have to go into my retirement home and find my mental oracle in a test tube, which I am not going to do. Since having jumped through the hoops of my 60 years I have only one wish, to produce the power of illumination and care for others as much as possible. This is connected to my plan to visit Florence with my whole family for a few weeks in the autumn, so that once more I can explain to them the world in which the main roots of my mental existence are embedded.[98]

In a very affectionate reply Loeb warned Warburg of the risk 'inherent in the hurried American life for people of your nature and mine' of travelling to America. Deciding not to travel would not mean doing nothing, for Warburg had achieved great success in training disciples in Europe, which was more beautiful and calmer than America.[99]

And so Warburg did not travel to America in 1927. When Loeb was supposed to travel to Harvard University in 1928 to receive an honorary law doctorate, he told Warburg that he was going to forgo the award ceremony and stay at home, otherwise he would risk not being allowed back into Germany because of his American passport. In the same letter he thanked Warburg for another volume of *Vorträge* from the KBW, in particular as Paul Hensel's article on 'Montaigne and Classical antiquity' had been published in it. He reminded Warburg that Grace Norton, the sister of Charles Eliot Norton, was a Montaigne specialist.[100] As Mary Warburg had told Loeb that Warburg would like to have a picture of Charles Eliot Norton for his Carlyle room, Loeb sent him as a birthday present the photograph of an oil painting of Norton that was kept in the Widener Library in Harvard. Loeb had donated the bust of Norton to the Fogg Museum.[101] Warburg confessed that the photograph of Norton had really given him great pleasure and explained that he would hang the picture in the reception room below the painting of Carlyle, which was the highest place of honour in his house.[102] Long before their marriage,

98 WIA, GC, Warburg to J. Loeb, 7.9.1927; Warburg, A., 'Francesco Sassettis Letztwillige Verfügung'; Britt, D., 'Francesco Sassetti's Last Injunctions to His Sons', 223–262 and 451–466. Adolph Goldschmidt, German art historian 1863–1944.

99 WIA, GC, J. Loeb to Warburg, 10.9.1927.

100 WIA, GC, J. Loeb to Warburg, 2.5.1928. Hensel, P., 'Montaigne und die Antike', 67–94. Grace Norton, American Montaigne specialist, 1834–1926; Michel de Montaigne, French writer, 1533–1592.

101 WIA, GC, J. Loeb to Warburg, 8.6.1928. The Carlyle room was named for Thomas Carlyle, Scottish cultural critic, 1795–1881.

102 WIA, GC, Warburg to J. Loeb, 14.6.1928.

Mary Warburg had asked Warburg to read Carlyle.[103] Loeb sent him a second photograph of Carlyle,[104] which Warburg mounted above the photograph of Boll in the small reception room of his house.[105]

This marked the end of the Loeb – Warburg correspondence. Letters from Warburg from his trip to Italy in 1928 to 1929 are not extant. After Warburg's death on 29 October 1929 the KBW kept up correspondence with Loeb, in particular on practical topics such as Loeb's requests for reader permits for colleagues,[106] for another copy of Warburg's Sassetti article,[107] and the plates for Warburg's *Bilderatlas*.[108]

Support and philanthropy

Artists and scientists repeatedly turned to supporters, intellectuals, philanthropists – circles in which both Loeb and Warburg moved. Artists offered their works of art for sale, young people requested letters of recommendation, members of charitable committees asked them to become members or donors, publishers invited them to take out subscriptions, students wanted information on employment – in short, the reasons why support was sought were manifold.

Loeb was a philanthropist all his life, in Munich and in Murnau. Among the people who were helped by Loeb or Warburg were some who received help anonymously, mostly via requests, which either Warburg himself granted or which he forwarded for consideration to Loeb.

Two projects merit further discussion. Warburg sent to Loeb a request by Oskar Bulle and his wife Elisa. Elisa was a painter; she painted wall hangings, which Warburg called 'painted tapestries'. Oskar Bulle needed money to continue with his studies.[109] One month later, Loeb wrote to Warburg that Bulle was over the worst and Bulle did not know that it was Loeb who had helped him financially.[110] Elisa Bulle contacted Warburg after the death of her husband in 1917 and offered her painting 'Goethes Gartenhaus' for sale, which Warburg purchased.[111]

103 Cf. WIA, GC, Mary Hertz to Warburg, 8.6.1894 and 20.6.1894.

104 WIA, GC, J. Loeb to Warburg, 19.6.1928.

105 WIA, GC, Warburg to J. Loeb, 23.6.1928.

106 WIA, GC, A. Loeb to Saxl, 21.6.1930 introducing Dr. Hans Wühr, assistant to Professor Max J. Friedländer in Berlin; WIA, GC, G. Bing to J. Loeb, 5.2.1931 introducing Miss Berta Segall. Max Jakob Friedländer, German art historian, 1867–1958; Berta Segall, German art historian, 1902–1976; Hans Wühr, Austro-Hungarian art historian, 1891–1982.

107 WIA, GC, J. Loeb to Saxl, 8.11.1931 requesting a volume and WIA, GC, Bing to J. Loeb, 16.11.1931 that a volume has been sent.

108 WIA, GC, J. Loeb to Bing, 20.11.1931; WIA, GC, Bing to J. Loeb, 1.12.1931; WIA, GC, J. Loeb to Bing, 6.12.1931.

109 WIA, GC, Copy book III, 14,13,15. Warburg to J. Loeb, 16.3.1909. Elisa Bulle, née Rigutini, Italian painter, 1859–1940.

110 WIA, GC, Warburg to J. Loeb, 15.4.1909.

111 WIA, GC, Elisa Bulle to Warburg, 26.12.1917.

A different project concerned Miss Margaret Thurnham, the English nanny in Warburg's house. After the outbreak of war, she was no longer able to live in Germany as an 'enemy alien'; she wanted to return to England and train as a nurse. Warburg wanted to help her financially but could not send money to England. He also must have been afraid of being found out, as his diary entries never mentioned her full name, only 'Marg.' or 'T'.[112] Loeb, who had decided to stay in Germany despite holding an American passport, arranged for money to be sent to Thurnham via New York,[113] but shortly afterwards payments were discontinued.[114]

The sale of Franz Boll's library was another example of collaboration. Boll had influenced Warburg's research greatly, so Warburg wanted to avoid Boll's library being broken up and sold piecemeal after Boll's death on 3 July 1924. Loeb offered Max Warburg his financial help,[115] duplicates were bought by Warburg, the bulk of the books were sold to university institutes, and additional funding went to Boll's nephew to finish his studies[116] and to Wilhelm Gundel to prepare the third edition of the Boll – Bezold book.[117]

A very important exchange of letters between Saxl and Loeb in the years after Warburg's death dealt with the ever more pressing question of the future of the KBW. The political situation was bleak. Saxl contacted Max Warburg, the head of the Warburg bank, and Loeb to discuss with them the option of moving the entire library to Rome.[118] Saxl, the mastermind behind the transformation of the library of a private scholar into a research institute in its own right in contact with the university of Hamburg, saw the transfer as doable and 'in many instances even desirable'. He wrote admiringly of Warburg's wealth of ideas, precision of expression, his stupendous universality, which was more strikingly expressed in discussions than in his publications, his way of dealing with history, and his power of deduction, which had led to the intellectual structure of his library. All this was unique and in danger, if the university in Hamburg could be dismantled by the ongoing political and financial developments in which the atmosphere towards scholarship was 'brittle'. He brought up Loeb's support of the KBW and listed three points to safeguard the work in the library: Firstly, the library had to continue its work in all its areas of research. Secondly, in order to do so, it was necessary to employ staff to catalogue the books according to KBW standards. Thirdly, the staff had to have the funds to publish their own research findings and that of their colleagues.

112 cf. WIA, III.10.4. Diary 1914–1915, 26, 107, 154.

113 WIA, GC, Copy book VI, 60, Warburg to J. Loeb, 18.4.1915.

114 WIA, GC, Copy book VI, 112, Warburg to Bankhaus M.M. Warburg & Co. in Hamburg, 21.7.1915.

115 Bankhaus Warburg, Hamburg, J. Loeb to Max Warburg, 27.7.1924. Franz Boll, German classicist, 1867–1924.

116 WIA, GC, Warburg to J. Loeb, 19.1.1925.

117 WIA, GC, Warburg to J. Loeb, 22.11.1924. Boll and Bezold, *Sternglaube und Sterndeutung*. Wilhelm Gundel, German classicist, 1880–1945.

118 WIA, GC, Saxl to J. Loeb, 18.1.1932.

> In the event these three demands are not met, the library cannot survive. Either its collections become incomplete and can no longer be working tools for the scholars, or the scholars are no longer there to work on the collections, which therefore will become useless. Or, finally, if the library can no longer publish, it no longer has a sounding board and is dependent on much too narrow a circle in Hamburg. The existing funds can no longer guarantee the requirements.

Saxl was clear that, following the development of the library in Hamburg, they could no longer go with 'young Warburg' to Florence, but would have to go to Rome. Warburg himself, who had loved Florence, said if he could no longer direct the library, it should be moved to Rome.[119]

Loeb thanked him for his thoughts and admitted that the KBW would be orphaned if the university of Hamburg really were dismantled. He also admitted that a transfer to Rome would be a logical step, but he could not imagine how the move to and the work in Rome would be financed. He advised dismissing personnel and reducing the book purchasing budget but conceded that everything he said was as a dilettante and not a scholar. He therefore advised the KBW to stay in Hamburg.[120] In his reply, Saxl methodically responded to every reason put forward by Loeb and explained why he was convinced by the plan to move to Rome. He appealed to Loeb to help him build, on the existing intellectual ground plan, the house which might develop a science of culture for the next generations, a true synopsis of diverse research areas. Saxl finished by stressing that Loeb was one of the few people who had from the very beginning believed in Warburg and his work.[121]

Formally speaking, this was right. But events led to a different development. The political situation, as well as the death of Loeb on 27 May 1933, prompted further discussions, and possibly the solution favoured by Saxl. The library was shipped to London in December 1933, where it was incorporated into the University of London in 1944.[122] In this way the lifetime achievements of both scholars, Warburg's library and the Loeb Classical Library, continue. Both reflect the way of thinking of both founders, both are examples of the intellectual landscape at the beginning of the 20th century.

119 WIA, GC, Saxl to J. Loeb, 18.1.1932. The Hamburg University had been established in 1919.

120 WIA, GC, J. Loeb to Saxl, 23.1.1932.

121 WIA, GC, Saxl to J. Loeb, 1.2.1932.

122 On the transfer of the library see Saxl, F., 'The History of Warburg's Library, 1886–1944'; Gombrich, E.H., *An Intellectual Biography with a Memoir on the History of the Library by F. Saxl*, 325–338.

7

FRITZ SAXL AND ABY WARBURG

Appreciation of a friendship. Evaluating collaboration, tracing contacts to the 'Vienna School'[1]

Introduction

The attitude of the Viennese art historian Fritz Saxl (1890–1948) and the Hamburg art historian and cultural scientist Aby Warburg (1866–1929) towards the 'Vienna School of Art History'[2] merits an investigation beyond the pioneering works of both scholars and their appraisal in specialist literature. The scientific methodology of both scholars and members of the 'Wiener Schule', or 'Vienna School', pursued different aims. Warburg, a private scholar and proprietor of a large collection of books and photographs, used both like a laboratory to unlock textual and visual source material for his research on the 'survival of classical antiquity'.[3] Saxl, an art historian at home in the most important archives and museums in Europe, academic teacher, and collaborator with, and later successor of Warburg, understood himself and Warburg as being not so much scholars keeping within the boundaries of disciplines, but as men crossing borders. For them, as well as a group of experts, the library in Hamburg was a focal or crystallisation point, which enabled them to pursue their own research methodology.

In the interwar years the group of scholars in contact with the KBW in Hamburg and the circle of researchers in Vienna, which referred themselves as the 'school', were regarded as the leading art history research centres. An investigation into their mutual contacts and interests, how far one of them influenced or wanted to influence the other or, indeed, was spurning a narrow school methodology, is the

1 Originally published in McEwan, D., 'Fritz Saxl und Aby Warburg: Würdigung einer Zusammenarbeit', 139–151.

2 Cf. Michalski, 'Zur methodologischen Stellung der Wiener Schule in den zwanziger und dreißiger Jahren', 83–90; Hofmann, W., 'Was bleibt von der "Wiener Schule"?', 4–8; Seiler, M., 'Aspekte theoretischer Kongruenz von Wiener Schule und Warburg-Kreis: Edgar Wind und Julius von Schlosser', 44–50; Seiler, M., 'Empiristische Motive im Denken und Forschen der Wiener Schule der Kunstgeschichte', 49–86.

3 cf. Meier et al., *Kulturwissenschaftliche Bibliographie zum Nachleben der Antike*; WIA, GC, Saxl in Baden bei Wien to Warburg, 13.9.1913.

DOI: 10.4324/9781003169024-9

topic of his chapter. Heinrich Dilly's formulation, the 'strict systems of Riegl and Wölfflin' in contrast to the 'system blasting' insights of Warburg, offers a fruitful distinction. What he meant was that Warburg and Saxl were less keen on treating questions of aestheticism and attribution, but more keen on the scientific groundwork of an intellectually rigorous cultural historiography.[4] Warburg called himself an 'action man' in a letter to Mesnil, where he stressed that he could work with much less disturbance in Hamburg than in Florence, 'where the aesthetic phrases throw a smoke screen over the documentary value of image-making' and therefore rather 'wanted to do without aestheticism than lack energy and courage'.[5] In this context I want to investigate what it meant to the Viennese art historians to have an Austrian colleague in Hamburg and later in London. What did it mean for Saxl to anchor his own research work in the Hamburg milieu?

I take as my source the two important sections of the correspondence collection in The Warburg Institute Archive in London, the so-called Aby Warburg General correspondence and the Family correspondence, some 37,000 letters and postcards. Cataloguing the archive holdings took from 1993 to 2010, following the postulate of Gombrich, then director of The Warburg Institute, from some forty years previously. He found it imperative to catalogue the Warburg correspondence in order to understand truly Warburg's personality.[6] This request proved right not only for the Warburg research, but also particularly for the scholars who collaborated with Warburg: Fritz Saxl, Gertrud Bing, Erwin Panofsky, Ernst Cassirer and many more.[7]

Fritz Saxl and the first years of collaborating with Aby Warburg

Saxl descended from a family which had come from Bohemia to Vienna, where his father, Ignaz, became a distinguished lawyer. Saxl pursued his art history studies in Vienna with Max Dvořak[8] and in Berlin with Heinrich Wölfflin. He was awarded his degree in 1912 with the dissertation on *Rembrandt-Studien* with Professor Dvořak. In the same year he published four articles on topics which would accompany him throughout his life: Rembrandt research, art history, art education, that is methodology, and images of planets in the Orient and Occident.[9] He studied Indo-European

4 Dilly, H., *Altmeister moderner Kunstgeschichte*, 13. Heinrich Dilly, German art historian, 1941–2019; Alois Riegl, Austrian art historian, 1858–1905; Heinrich Wölfflin, Swiss art historian, 1864–1945.

5 WIA, GC, Warburg to Jacques Dwelshauvers, later Mesnil, 31.12.1910. Jean-Jacques Dwelshauvers, known as Jacques Mesnil, Belgian art historian, 1872–1940.

6 Gombrich, E.H., 'Festvortrag', 15–36, here 17.

7 McEwan, D., *Ausreiten der Ecken*; eadem, *Wanderstraßen der Kultur. Die Aby Warburg – Fritz Saxl Korrespondenz von 1920 bis 1929. Mit einem Vorwort von Martin Warnke*. Gertrud Bing, German art historian, 1892–1964; Erwin Panofsky, art historian, 1892–1968; Ernst Cassirer, German philosopher, 1874–1945.

8 For Max Dvořak, art historian, 1874–192, see also Chapter 9.

9 Saxl, F., *Rembrandt-Studien*; idem., 'Ein neues Buch von Carl Larsson', 96–99; idem., 'Kunstgeschichte und künstlerische Erziehung'; idem., 'Beiträge zu einer Geschichte der Planetendarstellungen im Orient und im Okzident', 151–177.

deities, astrology, natural sciences in the Middle Ages, art of the Renaissance and cosmology. He contrasted Oriental belief in stars with the Christian understanding of wisdom as well as the Renaissance understanding of universal man. The focus for these very diverse disciplines was research into the transformation of ideas and symbols, as Warburg was to enter them in his 'map of the pathways of the mind';[10] they were maps which showed the routes on which the celestial constellations were depicted on their peregrinations from Greece to India and back to Europe and North Germany. Saxl said of himself that he was a vagabond through the museums, libraries and archives of Europe. He called himself an art historian but refused to recognise the boundaries of academic disciplines, because a work of art needed to be studied within the totality of cultural frameworks, and historical processes needed to be interpreted through pictures and the impressions they made. Their contrasting and ambivalent motifs had to be released from the canon of aesthetics.

What brought Warburg and Saxl together was their shared interest in how the astrological religious-magical imagination was transposed into pictures, an area of research which had until their time been insufficiently addressed by historians and art historians. The philosopher Ernst Cassirer saw in astrology the link between a mythical and a rational worldview, between 'the world of the symbol and the world of the image',[11] both large fields of application for art historians as well as scientists of culture. Together with Cassirer's research on symbols and symbolism,[12] Warburg's work contributed to building the bridge to psychological developments, 'from grasping by physical force to grasping by the intellect'.[13] It was about understanding the conceptual space between reaction and reflection, the evolutionary process from archetypical fear to overcoming fear, first with the help of fetishes, later by thought processes, which demystified the value of symbols and rationalised causal connections. Neither scholar wanted to work on provenance and connoisseurship, but on the 'why?' of a work of art, not on the collective of styles, but on the systematic, scrupulously precise pluridisciplinary application of research.

When Saxl met Warburg in 1910, Warburg was middle-aged while Saxl was a young man who had not yet finished his studies. Nobody could know then that Saxl would care for Warburg devotedly in the 1920s and, according to Gombrich, that Saxl would be rightfully called the real founder of the KWB as a research institute. Further, that it would be Saxl as successor to Warburg who would ship Warburg's life's work, the famous library, from Hamburg to London and anchor it in the academic life of Great Britain.[14]

10 See for instance WIA, GC, Warburg to Saxl, 31.12.1921, W/Saxl file, 'Wanderstraßen des Geistes'.

11 cf. Cassirer, E., 'Microcosm and Memory', 277.

12 Cassirer, E., *Philosophie der symbolischen Formen*.

13 Cf. also Chapter 14, note 165; Warburg, A., 'Zum Vortrag von Karl Reinhardt über "Ovids Metamorphosen"'. Preface on a loose leaf inserted into Saxl, F., *Vorträge 5, 1924/1925*, with Reinhardt's lecture in KBW on 24 October 1924. See Stimilli and Wedepohl, *Aby M. Warburg "Per Monstra and Sphaeram"*, 59–61.

14 Gombrich, E.H., 'Festvortrag', here 30.

In 1910, Saxl had approached Warburg after having heard of the specialist library of the private scholar on medieval astrological illustrations.[15] Warburg must have been impressed by the enthusiasm of the young student, because he suggested to Saxl a work schedule 'in connection with research on images of planets'[16] and placed the library that he called his laboratory at Saxl's disposal.[17] Warburg's library, his 'intellectual public convenience'[18] was expanded by both scholars into a unique research tool. In particular, during the economically bad years after World War I, the library was able to concentrate on the specialist questions pursued by a large circle of scholars and friends. According to Warburg in a letter to Hans Tietze, the buying of books had never been interrupted – theoretical texts, social psychological writings, reference books, detailed pieces of research as well as photographs – in order to probe into and investigate the 'still missing history of culture'.[19] The library was arranged in sections, which in their completeness became of great value to questions on the science of culture, for instance the collections on astrology, festivals, mythography, literature of legends, history of humanism, education, religion, philosophy, early history of natural sciences, ethnography, history of morality and art history based on all of these.

Josef Strzygowski, who, like Warburg, was a member of the committee of the art history congresses and, incidentally, was not esteemed by Warburg, was the only professor at Vienna university who did not award Saxl with the highest grade for his dissertation, which meant that he could not receive the accolade 'sub auspiciis imperatoris'.[20] Instead Saxl's doctoral supervisor, Max Dvořak, had promised him he would talk to Wilhelm von Bode in Berlin about employment for Saxl. As Saxl's father was Jewish, Saxl could never count on a position in one of the imperial museums in the Austrian monarchy.[21]

Warburg had come to know and appreciate Saxl as a thoroughgoing and most importantly enthusiastic researcher.[22] Warburg urged Saxl to finish his studies

15 Gombrich, E.H., *Aby Warburg. An Intellectual Biography with a Memoir on the History of the Library by F. Saxl*, 191.

16 WIA, GC, Warburg to B. Fuchs, 17.3.1910. Warburg cabled an invitation to Fuchs in Munich, in order to work out a schedule for the planet research. Fuchs, B.A., *Die Ikonographie der sieben Planeten in der Kunst Italiens bis zum Ausgang des Mittelalters*.

17 WIA, GC, Warburg to Saxl, 24.9.1910. See also Johnson and Wedepohl, 'From the Arsenal to the Laboratory', 106–124.

18 WIA, GC, Warburg to Max Warburg, 13.2.1901. Warburg called his collection of books an 'intellectual public convenience' ['geistige Bedürfnisanstalt'] in contrast to the 'reading fodder dispenser' ['Lesefutterautomat'] of the city library. WIA, GC, Warburg to Max Warburg, 20.11.1910.

19 WIA, GC, Warburg to Hans Tietze, 15.6.1917. Hans Tietze, Austrian art historian, 1880–1954.

20 WIA, GC, Saxl to Warburg, 20.7.1912. This accolade, meaning 'under the auspices of the Emperor', was a rare title bestowed by the Austro-Hungarian Emperor only on students who graduated with distinction. Josef Strzygowski, Polish-Austrian art historian, 1862–1941. On Strzygowski see Chapter 9.

21 WIA, GC, Saxl to Warburg, 11.8.1912. Wilhelm von Bode, German art historian, 1845–1929.

22 Saxl, F., 'Beiträge zu einer Geschichte der Planetendarstellungen im Orient und im Okzident', 151. WIA, GC, Copy book IV, 300, Warburg to Saxl, 17.4.1912. Warburg thanked him for the dedication and offered to help him when Saxl worked on the children of the planets, the classical notion that men and women are born under the influence of a planet.

so that afterwards the two of them could collaborate: 'I cannot rate your time and your life higher than mine: cannon fodder for respectable questions marks'.[23] After Saxl had been awarded his doctorate, it was Warburg who got Saxl a research scholarship from the Heidelberg Academy of Sciences for producing a catalogue of astrological and mythological illustrated medieval manuscripts.[24] After the end of the Heidelberg scholarship Warburg offered additional funds to Saxl, which he declined at first,[25] but then accepted, because his work had not been concluded and he realised that his research was of the greatest importance for his and Warburg's own collaboration: 'Your find urb. 899 is simply wonderful'.[26] Warburg encouraged Saxl, Warburg invested in Saxl, and Saxl found ever more parallels and links, predecessors and copies, which documented the pathways of the mind (see figure 7.1).[27] This led Saxl to formulate his research agenda: '. . . My question is the

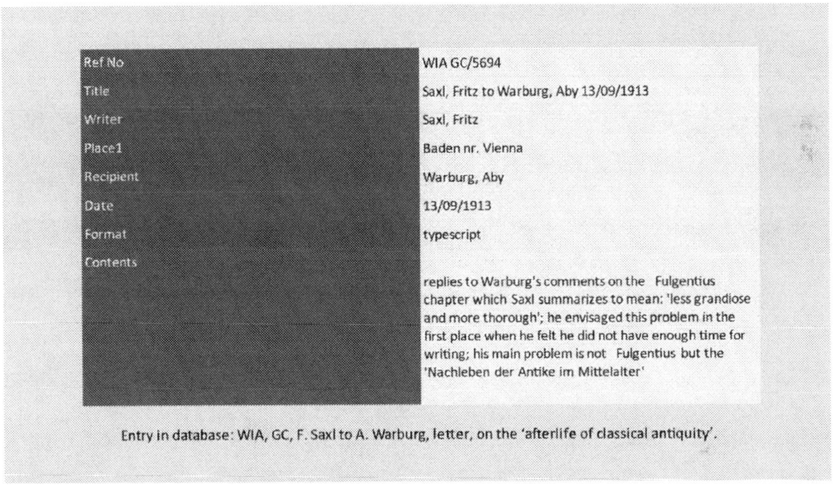

Ref No	WIA GC/5694
Title	Saxl, Fritz to Warburg, Aby 13/09/1913
Writer	Saxl, Fritz
Place1	Baden nr. Vienna
Recipient	Warburg, Aby
Date	13/09/1913
Format	typescript
Contents	replies to Warburg's comments on the Fulgentius chapter which Saxl summarizes to mean: 'less grandiose and more thorough'; he envisaged this problem in the first place when he felt he did not have enough time for writing; his main problem is not Fulgentius but the 'Nachleben der Antike im Mittelalter'

Entry in database: WIA, GC, F. Saxl to A. Warburg, letter, on the 'afterlife of classical antiquity'.

Figure 7.1 WIA, GC, Saxl to Warburg, 13.9.1913. Letter on the 'afterlife of classical antiquity'.

Source: © Photo: The Warburg Institute.

23 WIA, GC, Warburg to Saxl, 23.12.1911.

24 Saxl, F., *Verzeichnis astrologischer und mythologischer illustrierter Handschriften des lateinischen Mittelalters in römischen Bibliotheken*. Two more volumes were published, the manuscripts in the National Library in Vienna in 1925–1926 and the manuscripts in English libraries in 1953 (posthum).

25 WIA, GC, Copy book V, 145, Warburg to Saxl, 13.4.1913.

26 WIA, GC, Copy book IV, 152, Warburg to Saxl, 27.4.1913. The Codex Vaticanus Urbinas Latinus 899 is a manuscript with illustrations of festivals, floats etc., which were of particular interest to Warburg for the history of festivals, theatre and the artistic performances in the interludes, called intermezzi.

27 WIA, GC, Saxl to Warburg, e.g. 23.4.1913 and 29.4.1913.

survival of classical antiquity in the Middle Ages',[28] the well-known phrase which became the leitmotif of Warburg, his library and the institute (see figure 7.2).

In 1914 Warburg employed Saxl as librarian in his private library in Hamburg, stating expressly that his library would attempt to adapt to Saxl's research requirements.[29] It was an ideal setup for a young academic, like the stars aligning for a young academic, but it would not last. At the end of the year Saxl had to report to the army in Austria and spent World War I at the Italian front. Remarkably, both kept up their correspondence: Warburg sent Saxl reference books; Saxl commented on them, read proofs and wondered about academic work after the war.

Saxl agreed with the pamphlets on 'Theories of War' by the eminent economist Friedrich von Wieser and his views that 'the cleansing fight against the hatred of peoples' was the most important fight of the time.[30] He sent brochures and theoretical articles on socialism to Warburg with the request to place them in the

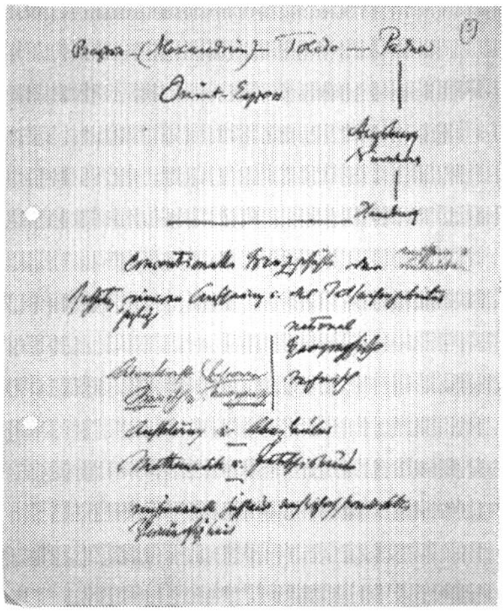

Bagdad – (Alexandrien) – Toledo – Padua
Orient-Express
Augsburg
Nürnberg
Hamburg
Conventionelle Grenzpfähle der mühsam und undenkbar
subjektiven geistigen inneren Aufklärung und des
Tatsachengebietes
national
geographisch
technisch
Lebenskraft
Organisch u. besondere[?] unorganisch
Aufklärung u. Aberglauben
Mathematik u. Fetischismus
imponderable höchstens mäßiglich ponderable
Vernünftigkeit

'Baghdad – (Alexandria) – Toledo – Padua
Orient Express
Augsburg
Nuremberg
Hamburg
conventional boundary posts of arduous and unthinkable
the subjective mental interior
enlightenment and the facts national
geographical
technical
vitality
organic and especially [?] inorganic
enlightenment and superstition
mathematics and fetishism
imponderable at most moderately ponderable
rationality'

Figure 7.2 WIA, III.87.4.[5]. Orientexpress. 1913.

Source: © Photo: The Warburg Institute.

28 WIA, GC, Saxl in Baden bei Wien to Warburg, 13.9.1913.

29 WIA, GC, Copy book V, 322, Warburg to Saxl, 10.1.1914.

30 WIA, GC, Saxl to Warburg, 31.8.1915. Wieser, F. Freiherr von, 'Die Lehren des Krieges'. Friedrich Baron von Wieser, Austrian economist, 1851–1926.

Idealism section.[31] Saxl's ability to become engrossed in a topic despite the fact that the hatred of peoples raged all around him, enabled him, as Gombrich wrote, 'to find in the past a refuge from the pressures and perplexities of the present'.[32] His intellectual work was not only a mental space for him, where he could safely survive, but also a method of survival. J. A. F. Orbaan, the Dutch art historian, inquired of Warburg in 1916 'whether the very intelligent and nearly suicidally overworking Saxl was still with Warburg',[33] an accurate characterisation of Saxl.

In a letter of October 1915, which one can term a programmatical letter, Saxl told Warburg of his plan to set up something like the Warburg Library in Vienna, in order to

> make Vienna aware of and understand its past, to make way for a new great Vienna full of self-consciousness. Do you think the authorities have the courage to trust me with large amounts of money for an institute of Austrian culture and art history? Or even for such a collection of Austrian culture. It goes without saying, it will not happen, we young scholars will not be admitted. But what it would mean to me! Or to give lectures in the whole of Austria for the Central Commission, to save everywhere what can be saved from our precious old life, would this not be good for me![34]

It would take two further years before Saxl could make concrete suggestions to Warburg: he envisaged collaborating on the Austrian art-historical bibliography, continuing the works by Thieme and Becker or collaborating on the editorial team of the Yearbooks of the Central Commission[35] and setting up a literary office of the Central Commission for relevant literature. Saxl, a convinced socialist who had joined the army and sat his officer's examinations, hoped that his suggestions for employment might find him work in post-war Vienna.[36]

Immediately after the end of the war he was employed by the state[37] as an art historian in the German-Austrian Office for the army, in the department of the educational authority of the Peoples' guard. He organised touring exhibitions[38] in Austria for adult education on topics such as garden cities, small apartments and wall decorations, thereby trying to plant small seeds of culture.[39] He had no illusions – under the prevailing situation he could not hope for much – but expressed his

31 WIA, GC, Saxl to Warburg, 27.10.1915.
32 Gombrich, E.H., 'Introduction', 9–10.
33 WIA, GC, J.A.F. Orbaan to Warburg, 12.1.1916. J.A.F. Orbaan, Dutch art historian and researcher 1874–1933.
34 WIA, GC, Saxl to Warburg, 14.10.1915. The imperial and royal Central Commission for research and maintenance of art and historical monuments.
35 Thieme, U. / Becker, F., *Allgemeines Lexikon der bildenden Künstler: von der Antike bis zur Gegenwart: unter Mitwirkung von 300 Fachgelehrten des In- und Auslandes*.
36 WIA, GC, Saxl to Warburg, 15.2.1917. WIA, III.2.1., index card box, 64, 065/037871.
37 WIA, GC, Saxl to Warburg, 13.2.1919.
38 Rappl, W., 'Fritz Saxls Ausstellungen nach dem Ersten Weltkrieg in Wien', 40–52.
39 WIA, GC, Saxl to Warburg, 15.7.1919.

content at bringing colour into flats; he also ran drawing classes for many talented people among the soldiers.[40]

This work ended with his offer of employment in Hamburg at the end of 1919. Aby Warburg, who grew ill after the war and spent the years until 1924 in sanatorium, could no longer pursue his work on the survival of classical antiquity. The Warburg family, as the funding body for the library, trusted in Saxl and employed him as director. Max Warburg knew how much his brother valued Saxl.[41]

Saxl's appointment in Hamburg

Saxl's field of work had moved away from Vienna only geographically, but thematically continued and was expanded in Hamburg. Apart from his own research interests he was now charged with carrying on Warburg's work in the library, with the cataloguing system according to the so-called Prussian Instructions.[42] Added to this was the coding of book sections with a three-colour scheme as the library's system of press marks, as in operation in Vienna, which proved extraordinarily helpful to searchers[43] because the book cases were full of colours 'like a parrot'.[44] Saxl was also instrumental in expanding and integrating the Warburg library in the operations of the newly founded University of Hamburg. The library was used by the university for lectures and seminars as part of the art history institute. Added to this was Saxl care for Warburg, which decisively contributed to his recovery.[45] Saxl qualified as a professor at the University of Hamburg, kept up extensive correspondence with Warburg as well as with leading German and foreign scholars, mainly in connection with the two publication series which Saxl had started and edited. The library hosted circa ten lectures for the general public per year, which were published in the *Vorträge* series. In addition, in the *Studien* series, monographs were published which either expanded a lecture topic or presented new research.

These two publication projects were the discussion starter that, in the bad post-war years, led many an Austrian colleague to turn to Saxl and request the offer of an invitation to Hamburg. Hans Tietze spoke on 26 March 1927 on 'Romanesque art and Renaissance', Julius von Schlosser on 30 April 1927 'On the modern cult

40 WIA, GC, Saxl to Mary Warburg, 4.11.1919.

41 WIA, GC, Max Warburg to Saxl, 3.11.1919. Max Warburg, 1867–1946, German banker.

42 The Prussian Instructions were a set of cataloguing rules drawn up for alphabetical catalogues in Prussian libraries. First published in 1899, the rules were retained in The Warburg Institute Library after its move to London until the card catalogue was replaced with the computer catalogue in 1991, when the Anglo-American Cataloguing Rules, 2nd ed. (AACR2) were adopted in their place.

43 On the colour-coding system see Mazal, O., *Bibliotheca Eugeniana: die Sammlungen des Prinzen Eugen von Savoyen. Ausstellung der Österreichischen Nationalbibliothek und der Graphischen Sammlung Albertina*; Gombrich, E.H., 'Gertrud Bing zum Gedenken', 7–12, here 9, stated, however without source indication, something else: 'The witty classification system in the library, with its correlation of letters and coloured strips of paper, is partly her [Bing's] work'.

44 WIA, GC, Saxl to Warburg, 23.9.1922.

45 Saxl, F., 'Die kulturwissenschaftliche Bibliothek Warburg in Hamburg', 355–358.

of monuments'.[46] Dagobert Frey, art historian, curator of monuments and Saxl's friend from his time in Vienna, spoke on 23 June 1923 on 'The epistemological problem in Renaissance art'. Back in Vienna he thanked and congratulated Saxl for his successful work. He credited Saxl with having created an intellectual centre, full of thriving energy, which was of the highest importance for the German history of thought. He wished for a closer cooperation between the Vienna School and the Warburg library and offered himself to contribute to such a cooperation.[47]

The Vienna School and the circle of scholars in the Warburg library

It was not the first time that there was talk of the Vienna School in Warburg's and Saxl's correspondence. Warburg, however, was always his own man, he had no use for a 'School'. Carl Neumann, Professor of art history, who had sent Warburg his review of Hans Tietze's article 'On the method of art history: an essay'[48] did not esteem the Vienna School either. He was confirmed in his criticism by Warburg,

> Thank you very much for sending me your telling-off of the 'Wiener Schule'. Tietze's book is one of those which I buy, leaf through and do not read. I also do not believe in the discovery of general laws of art on such a narrow foundation and limited outlook. Every day, when I can trick my aching body into work, I ever more become an image historian. Saxl's Catalogue of astrological and mythological manuscripts in Roman libraries is a product of my school of thought.[49]

It was not so much Tietze's book which Warburg did not find especially striking, but much more the fact that the Viennese colleagues did not have an idea of Warburg's work. Three months later, Warburg made no secret of his disappointment:

> I confess freely that although I have learnt to forgo the recognition of the nearest circle of colleagues, I have always found it objectively senseless that the Wiener Schule, which in contrast to the others in Germany is nearest to my work, has never made the effort of evaluating more thoroughly the method which I follow.[50]

46 Both lectures were published in Saxl, F., *Vorträge 7, 1926/27*, von Schlosser, 1–21 and Tietze, 43–57. Julius von Schlosser, Austrian art historian, 1866–1938.

47 WIA, GC, D. Frey to Saxl, 29.6.1923. Dagobert Frey, Austrian art historian, 1883–1962.

48 Neumann, C., 'Zur Theorie der Geschichte und Kunstgeschichte', 484–494.

49 WIA, GC, Copy book VI, 289, Warburg to C. Neumann, 20.3.1917. At the end of the letter Warburg mentioned the two issues of his periodical, Warburg et al, *La Guerra del 1914*. WIA, IV, 63.2.1. and *Rivista llustrata, La guerra del 1914–15*. WIA, IV, 63.2.2. With these periodicals Warburg had tried to enlighten the Italians that her enemies were not the Axis powers, but the Allied powers; see Chapter 3. For 'image historian' see also Chapter 14.

50 WIA, GC, Warburg to H. Tietze, 15.6.1917.

He spoke of a relationship of method, not of concept. He, 'the most humble thinker', as he was called years later in an article in the *Vossische Zeitung* on 'New history of art',[51] was not convinced by the absolute accuracy and conclusiveness of the method of the Vienna School, but recognised the 'conditionality of all human knowledge and experience'. To Warburg the work of art was not an artistic product which, seen on its own, had to be investigated. It acquired its supporting components in the interaction with the surrounding world from which it was made. Despite this contrast of his views to the Vienna School, Warburg expressed his joy that his friend Saxl had opened a route between Hamburg and Vienna and hoped that Tietze and his wife Erika, one of the first women to study art history, would come to Hamburg.[52] They would then see

> that the library was organised in such a way as to allow you to discover that life itself is the style-forming power. Let us hope that we live to see art history helping to discover the still missing cultural history of Europeans in modern times[53]

– a concern dealt with by Warburg's library, but not by the Vienna School.

Tietze thanked him for the kind invitation, especially welcome in times of war. However, he was not able to get leave from the army and he was not helped with a short trip to Hamburg. He saw in Warburg's library an 'external-internal symbol' and pinned his hopes on it. He countered Warburg's reproach against the illogical attitude of the Vienna School. He had only recently started to analyse Warburg's writings and only just realised the need for a thorough expansion of art research in the way pursued by Warburg. He wrote that he wanted to do so after the war and hoped to open up a field of research with like-minded scholars.[54] He did not dispel the illogicality of the Vienna School and he apologised for his lack of knowledge of Warburg's writings, precisely what Warburg had complained about. But Tietze promised to till the 'joint field of work', which did happen in the next 20 years.

Collaboration with other scholars in Vienna, however, did not happen. Saxl had, on behalf of Julius von Schlosser and Karl Swoboda, written to Warburg with Ludwig Münz's suggestion to publish the last lecture cycle by Alois Riegl, 'The History of Flemish and Dutch art', in a *Vorträge* volume together with articles by Warburg and Wolfgang Stechow on Dutch art history. Initially Warburg consented, but then back-pedalled; he could not imagine anything of a homogeneous

51 Article signed by '-ch.', *Vossische Zeitung*, no. 536, 18.11.1933.

52 Tietze-Conrat, E., 'Zur höfischen Allegorie der Renaissance', 25–32; Tietze-Conrat, E., *Die Bronzen der fürstlich Liechtensteinschen Kunstkammer*. Erika Tietze-Conrat, née Conrat, Austrian American art historian, 1883–1958.

53 WIA, GC, Warburg to H. Tietze, 15.6.1917.

54 WIA, GC, H. Tietze to Warburg, 23.6.1917.

nature under the triumvirate Riegl, Warburg and Stechow.[55] This publication project was not accomplished. At least Gertrud Bing valued Riegl's books, as she wrote in the *Journal* of the library, when she worked with Warburg in Rome from 1928 to 1929, noting that Riegl's book had opened her eyes 'in relation to the finer differences' of baroque Rome.[56]

In order to remedy the fact that not even colleagues like Dvořak knew of Warburg's writings, Saxl published an article after his move to Hamburg in 1920 entitled 'The Survival of classical antiquity: Introduction to the Warburg library'[57] and dedicated the same topic to the first lecture in the newly founded lecture series, 'The Warburg Library and its Aim'.[58] He sent a copy of the lecture text to Josef Strzygowski and mentioned in the accompanying letter that he would be happy if Strzygowski found it valuable. 'Warburg and I travel on ways different from yours and your school, but I believe that in many ways we meet each other in our results'.[59] The letter, devoid of any polemics, captivates with its calm language.

What Saxl expressed with 'meeting each other' surfaced as a desideratum in the extensive correspondence of Dagobert Frey to Saxl in the years 1924 to 1925. Frey had sent offprints of Saxl's article 'Early Christianity and late Paganism' to Hamburg.[60] Its publication had long been delayed by the negotiations over the *Wiener Jahrbuch für Kunstgeschichte*'s change in publishers from Hölzel to Krystall-Verlag. Frey apologised for the late publications and regretted that due to the bad economic situation their work had been seriously impeded. Nevertheless, he asked Saxl to write for the *Wiener Jahrbuch für Kunstgeschichte* again, saying he valued Saxl's input: Saxl was part of the Vienna School and Dvořak's programme stressed what the *Wiener Jahrbuch für Kunstgeschichte* represented. Frey went even further: he averred that if necessary he would 'woo the Hamburgers [Panofsky and Saxl] like Jacob for seven years'.[61] Panofsky had already declined and Saxl went on to publish only two more articles in *Belvedere* in Vienna.[62]

Although Saxl was a student of Max Dvořak, the now deceased head of the art history and second chair in Vienna, his letter to Strzygowski, the incumbent head of the art history and first chair and mentioned above, was relevant. The scholars in

55 Michels/Schoell-Glass, *Journal*, Saxl's suggestion on 1.7.1927, 110 and Warburg's comment on 1.7.1927, 110–111. Ludwig Münz, Austrian art historian, 1889–1957; Karl Swoboda, Austrian art historian, 1889–1977; Wolfgang Stechow, German-American art historian, 1896–1974.

56 Michels/Schoell-Glass, *Journal*, 6. – 11.1.1929, 393.

57 Saxl, F., 'Das Nachleben der Antike: zur Einführung in die Bibliothek Warburg', 244–247.

58 Saxl, F., 'Die Bibliothek Warburg und ihr Ziel', 1–10.

59 WIA, GC, Saxl to J. Strzygowski, 11.7.1922. On Strzygowski see Chapter 9.

60 Saxl, F., 'Frühes Christentum und spätes Heidentum in ihren künstlerischen Ausdrucksformen', 63–121.

61 WIA, GC, D. Frey to Saxl, 23.3.1925.

62 Saxl, F., 'Studien über Hans Holbein d. J: I. Die Karlsruher Kreuztragung I. Vorgeschichte und Vorbilder', 139–154; idem., 'Die Karlsruher Kreuztragung des Meisters H. H. (Hans Holbein d. J.?)', 205–15.

Hamburg conducted themselves in a strictly neutral manner towards their colleagues in Vienna. They did not wish to be co-opted by one chair in Vienna or the other.

Another time Felix Horb, editor of the art periodical *Belvedere* wrote to Saxl: Hans Sedlmayr, the 'most talented' of the younger generation of Viennese scholars, had written a book on the architectural thinking of Borromini,[63] which was too long for *Belvedere*. Also, Sedlmayr was unable to offer it for publication to the *Wiener Jahrbuch für Kunstgeschichte* after having written a polemical criticism of Dagobert Frey's book *Fischer von Erlach der Ältere*. Could Saxl help them out and publish Sedlmayr's book in Hamburg?[64] Saxl declined, saying the topic was not one of interest to the KBW.[65]

Saxl kept up contact with friends and colleagues in Vienna, not necessarily as part of the agendas pursued by the colleagues, but rather more in affinity with their research topics. One example will suffice: Saxl's letter to the medical doctor Emil Klein in Vienna. Saxl spent a few weeks in Vienna in the winter of 1925/1926 and met Klein. They talked about Warburg's work on the belief in astrology and Saxl's own works on astrology. After his return to Hamburg, Saxl sent him a few articles and thanked him for the evening spent together. Saxl confessed that he was surprised to be able to speak with scholars, far away, who were dealing with the same questions as the Hamburgers. He had the feeling that 'after all, the common features between the two "schools" were profound'.[66]

An example of how Saxl's employment and contacts in Hamburg were viewed is the letter by Otto Benesch, who lost his post as trainee in the art history museum after Dvořak's death in 1921. Benesch asked Saxl whether he could recommend him as assistant to Panofsky.[67] Panofsky, however, at that time associate professor in Hamburg, was not in a position to employ an assistant, so Saxl could not be of any help to Benesch.[68] Dvořak's death had affected Saxl deeply. He offered help to Erika Tietze and hoped that the 'damned Viennese circle of cliques' would not make mistakes which were irreparable. It would be a mammoth task to edit Dvořak's estate, a work which had to be done and on which he mentioned to her that he would, as a matter of course, be ready to collaborate.[69] It did not happen.

Finally, Friedrich Antal, who worked in Berlin in 1926, tried to get into closer contact with Saxl by asking him for book reviews for the projected new periodical called *Kritische Berichte zur kunstgeschichtlichen Literatur*. Antal voiced what Frey only hinted at: 'You must not abandon us in our task either to get recognition

63 Sedlmayer, H., *Die Architektur Borrominis*. Felix Horb, Austrian art historian, 1890–1956; Hans Sedlmayer, Austrian art historian, 1896–1984; Francesco Borromini, Italian architect, 1599–1667.

64 WIA, GC, F. Horb to Saxl, 9.10.1925.

65 WIA, GC, Saxl to F. Horb, 13.10.1925.

66 WIA, GC, Saxl to E. Klein, 5.2.1926. Emil Klein, Austrian medical doctor, 1873–1950.

67 WIA, GC, O. Benesch to Saxl, 17.3.1922. Otto Benesch, Austrian art historian, 1896–1964.

68 WIA, GC, Saxl to O. Benesch, 3.4.1922.

69 WIA, GC, Saxl to E. Tietze, 23.2.1921.

for the Wiener Schule in Germany or to continue with the hopeless state of affairs of anarchical art history here for ever'.[70]

Saxl complied and sent him a review for the first volume of the new periodical.[71] He confessed that he had no time for more, adding it was not his objective to help the prestige of the Vienna School in Germany. Despite this, he stayed in touch with Antal, who had spent some months in Florence in 1928, researching Baccio Baldini for Warburg, even if Warburg's and Antal's working relationship was not always perfect.[72]

The Vienna School with its analysis of form was for Saxl and for Warburg, as 'image historian', too narrow. Both were interested in images. Saxl had gained valuable exhibition experience in Vienna, which he was to continue through his work for Warburg's *Mnemosyne Atlas*. This main work of Warburg's was programmatic, a series of images which documented metamorphoses, triggered associations, invited reflection – in short, they were the very personal tools used by Warburg, which did not come across as a school, but with which the ambivalence, transformation, alternatives of interpretation were visualised. Even in Saxl's earliest letters he praised Warburg's 'exemplary' art criticism of modern art, because it told him that profound knowledge was required to talk about it. It was not a matter of 'an ephemeral judgement of taste' or of 'linking knowledge with social feeling'.[73] He criticised lectures which were not sufficiently broad in their synthesis.[74] Warburg's method was concentrated on the reciprocal validation of images and texts. Saxl's method, in particular his Mithras research, concentrated on investigating form to come to relevant results in the history of religion, even when there was no or very little textual source material. He practised analysis of form in an area, namely late antique art, in which scholars of the Vienna School had, indeed, done outstanding work. In the preface to his book *Mithras: Typengeschichtliche Untersuchungen*[75] he wrote a concise treatise on how to discuss the history of form of monuments.[76] He went methodologically beyond Warburg in exploring a number of different interpretative options and referred in this context to Riegl's *Spätrömische Kunstindustrie* and Wickhoff's *Römische Kunst*,[77] which discussed fundamental art-historical problems of the epoch to which the Mithras monuments also belonged. This seems to be a strong hint that Saxl here was guided by Riegl.[78] But despite the fact that Saxl's book on Mithras could be termed the most Viennese book of the

70 WIA, GC, F. Antal to Saxl, 30.11.1926. Friedrich Antal, Hungarian art historian, 1888–1954.

71 Saxl, F., 'Review of August Mayer's *Dominico Theotocopuli El Greco*', 86–96.

72 WIA, GC, Warburg to F. Antal, 14.1.1928. Baccio Baldini, Italian engraver, 1436–1487.

73 WIA, GC, Saxl to Warburg, 17.5.1910, previously III.2.1., index card box, 50, 028007.

74 On the lecture of Ludwig Curtius on 12.12.1928 in Rome see the comments in Michels/Schoell-Glass, *Journal*, 12.12.1928, 382–383. Ludwig Curtius, German archaeologist, 1894–1954.

75 Saxl, *Mithras: Typengeschichtliche Untersuchungen*.

76 Saxl, *Mithras: Typengeschichtliche Untersuchungen*, vii.

77 Riegl, A., *Die spätrömische Kunst-Industrie nach den Funden in Österreich-Ungarn*; Wickhoff, F., *Römische Kunst: die Wiener Genesis*. Franz Wickhoff, Austrian art historian, 1853–1909.

78 I am grateful to Rainer Donandt, Hamburg, for his observations on these questions.

Warburg scholars, one cannot derive a Vienna School in Hamburg from it. The art historians Schlosser, Strzygowski and Wickhoff were in touch with Warburg[79] and Saxl. In addition, Ernst Kris, Otto Kurz, Johannes Wilde, Otto Pächt, Leo Planiscig and Stella Kramrisch were in touch with The Warburg Institute in London, and Ernst Gombrich became its director from 1959 to 1976. There were contacts with librarians in Vienna, with museum curators, university teachers, scholars like Betty Kurth, art historians like Ludwig Münz, Kurt Rathe, Fritz Eichler, Gustav Glück, Hermann Egger, Erika and Hans Tietze, Karl Graf Lanckoronski, Josef von Karabacek, Robert Eisler, Lili Fröhlich-Bum, Karl von Tolnai, and many more, so that researchers in Hamburg as well as in Vienna knew of each other and commented on each other's works – a fact which was important to them.[80] The circle of scholars in Hamburg was interested in the echo of their colleagues in the most diverse disciplines, as attested to by the extensive correspondence and the entries in the accession books of the KBW in the 1920s.

The Vienna School and the Warburg Circle

The project in the shape of a Viennese Warburg Institute, of which Saxl had spoken during World War I, remained an unrealised pipedream, or a project which Saxl did not realise in this form. Despite this, one reads often enough of a Warburg School.[81] The Vienna School was in the first instance interested in the visual, whereas Warburg and Saxl were interested in the intellectual or, according to Warburg, his work consisted of 'cataloguing the clown jumps of the human spirit'.[82] Saxl was interested in theoretical and historical research questions, which went

79 WIA, GC, Warburg to A. Goldschmidt, 9.8.1902 [previously WIA, III.57.2.2] on their discussion on the methodological history of artistic styles with the art historians Julius von Schlosser, Josef Strzygowski and Franz Wickhoff.

80 For correspondence with the following scholars check the database of the WIA throughout: Betty Kurth, Austrian art historian, 1878–1948; Ernst Kris, Austrian psychoanalyst and art historian, 1900–1957; Otto Kurz, Austrian British art historian, 1908–1975; Johannes Wilde, Hungarian art historian, 1891–1970; Otto Pächt, Austrian art historian, 1902–1988; Leo Planiscig, Austrian art historian, 1887–1951; Stella Kramrisch, Austria art historian, 1896–1993; Kurt Rathe, Austrian art historian, 1886–1952; Fritz Eichler, Austrian archaeologist, 1887–1971; Gustav Glück, Austrian art historian, 1871–1952; Hermann Egger, Austrian art historian, 1873–1949; Karl Graf Lanckoronski, Polish art collector, 1848–1933; Josef von Karabacek, Austrian Orientalist, 184–1918; Robert Eisler, Austrian polymath, 1882–1949; Lili Fröhlich-Bum, Austrian British art historian, 1886–1981; Karl von Tolnai, Hungarian art historian, 1899–1981.

81 See for instance Szönyi, G., 'Warburg's Intuitions in Light of Postmodern Challenges'; cf. also Landauer, C.H., *The Survival of Antiquity: The German Years of the Warburg Institute*, 104: 'Except for a year of study with Heinrich Wölfflin in Berlin, Saxl learned his art historical methodology from Max Dvořak and Julius Schlosser in Vienna. Often called the "Vienna School", the group of art historians led by Schlosser had a penchant for the documentary history of art, as Schlosser's own *Quellenbuch zur Kunstgeschichte and Material zur Quellenkunde der Kunstgeschichte* would suggest. The "Vienna School" and Warburg's "Hamburg School" would later stand as the two major sources of opposition to the formalistic methodology of Heinrich Wölfflin.'

82 WIA, GC, Warburg to Jacques Dwelshauvers, later Mesnil, 31.12.1910.

beyond the objectives of a School. Warburg and Saxl, in their work as cultural historians, did not stay within a technique or discipline, but operated with people and their inventions, thoughts and works of art. The study of culture in its widest sense is, to borrow Gombrich's phrase, is the 'study of continuities':[83] the exploration of all that which is passed on and how it is passed on and not the uncritical acceptance of an event or a work of art. And so the two groups of scholars grouped around the Vienna School and the Warburg Library remained at an amicable distance, but nothing more.

Saxl, who during his studies in Vienna was influenced by the Vienna School but was not its trailblazer in Hamburg, maintained contact with members of the Vienna School in the 1920s, even if he was partly critical and remained equidistant to the two chairs of art history in Vienna. He invited scholars to give lectures in Hamburg, as discussed, and published with Erwin Panofsky *Melencolia I* in 1923, the study begun by German scholar Carl Giehlow, who spent many years in Vienna and whose research had remained unfinished ever since his death.[84] Saxl could be critical in his appraisal of books by the Vienna School, like his colleague Edgar Wind, who was 'against this unarticulated tendency to standardisation, which under the name of intellectual history still makes difficulties today' or Warburg when speaking against the troubles inflicted by the academic 'frontier guards'.[85] With his deployment and work in the KBW Saxl was able to launch a brilliant academic career in Hamburg and continue it in London – the takeover by the National Socialists had made the work of the KBW in Hamburg impossible. The library, with all its books, photographs, book binding machines and academic personnel, moved to London in 1933, where Saxl had to build it up as an institute again. Following the political turmoil which forced many scholars to emigrate, The Warburg Institute in London became the focus for hundreds of scientists from Central Europe. They, and the Austrian colleagues among them, were able to count on assistance from Gertrud Bing and Saxl.[86]

83 Gombrich, E.H., *In Search of Cultural History*, 49.
84 Saxl and Panofsky, *Dürers 'Melencolia I'*. Carl Giehlow, German art historian, 1863–1913.
85 Wind, E., 'Einleitung', v–xvii, here vii. Edgar Wind, German British art historian, 1900–1971.
86 McEwan, D., 'A Tale of One Institute and Two Cities: The Warburg Institute', 25–42.

Part III

TOPICS WHICH CAUGHT WARBURG'S INTEREST

8

A TROUVAILLE FROM THE WARBURG INSTITUTE ARCHIVE ON MANDAEISM AND GNOSTICISM[1]

Introduction

Gnosticism and Mandaeism were research topics which generated lively discussions like no other topics of religious history had since the famous 'Bible-Babel' controversy over the Babylonian influence on the Hebrew Bible.[2] Western scholars, Semitists, Orientalists, historians of religion, and theologians alike were fascinated by Mandaeism, the last existing Gnostic religious community with its own language. This fascination lives on in the still-unsettled problematic nature of a history of the Mandaeans, which cannot be treated without analysing the so-called Mandaeism question: the controversy of the origin of the Mandaeans, opened by Reitzenstein's book in 1919 and Lidzbarski's volume on Mandaean liturgies in 1920.[3] The main aspects of the controversy centred firstly on the relationship of the Mandaeans' self-designation as the *Nazarene* (Mandaean *naśuraiia*) to the Ναζωραίοι (Nasoraioi) of the Greek Bible, Mt. 2:23, and secondly, on the question of whether these names encompass the pre-Christian 'Observants', those who follow the law, to whom Jesus belonged at one time.[4]

Further, scholars tried to tie the original Mandaeans[5] to the disciples of John the Baptist, as he figures in the Mandaean tradition, so that the Mandaean baptism was considered a precursor of the Christian baptism. An important place in the discussion was given to the evaluation of Mandaean mythology:

1 Originally published in McEwan and Burtea, 'Eine Trouvaille aus dem Warburg Institute Archive zu Mandäismus und Gnosis', 137–153.

2 Johanning, K., *Der Bibel-Babel-Streit. Eine forschungsgeschichtliche Studie.*

3 Reitzenstein, R., *Das mandäische Buch des Herrn der Größe und die Evangelienüberlieferung*; Lidzbarski, M., *Mandäische Liturgien*. Richard Reitzenstein, German classical philologist, 1861–1931; Mark Lidzbarski, Polish philologist, 1868–1928.

4 See Schaeder, H.H., 'Nazarenos, Nazoraios', 161–165.

5 Widengren, G., 'Einleitung', 1–17, here 11–12.

DOI: 10.4324/9781003169024-11

on the one hand the connection between the Son of Man in the gospels and the Mandaean *Anōš-Uthra*, one of the saviours in Mandaean mythology, and on the other hand the relationship of Christology in the Gospel of John to the Mandaean-gnostic teaching of a redeemer. These questions could be seen as parallels to the Bible-Babel quarrel, which viewed as Panbabylonism[6] the Babylonian influence on the Hebrew Bible and its environment. In the case of Mandaeism (and Gnosticism in general) these aspects were interpreted as proof of a religious movement spanning from Iran to the Near East. This movement was further thought to be the background for the old Jewish and early Christian religions, which commentators like the Orientalists Reitzenstein, Lidzbarski and Franz Rosenthal, the historian of religion Hans Heinrich Schaeder and theologians Hans Lietzmann, Erik Peterson and Rudolf Bultmann discussed and later termed Paniranism.[7] Bultmann wrote in his commentary to the Gospel of John that only with Gnostic and in particular Mandaean texts could light be shed on John's role and importance.

In the collections of The Warburg Institute in London letters on Mandaeist topics are extant from 1922 to 1929. They give witness to the very broad spectrum of topics and interests pursued by the scholars around Aby Warburg[8] and Fritz Saxl, and the fact that the discussions about Gnosticism and Mandaeism did not only affect experts. Saxl had met Warburg in the course of his research on the history of astrology and consequently published on topics of medieval astrological illuminations as well as on early Christian art.[9] Warburg found in Boll's book *Sphaera*[10] important insights into art history and history of religion, which he linked to his own research.

The following exchange of correspondence between Warburg, Saxl, Reitzenstein and Lidzbarski documents the research interests in the years after the publication of Warburg's and Saxl's quoted articles, which gave significant momentum

6 Panbabylonism considers the cultures and religions of the Middle East as deriving from Babylonian mythology.

7 This is the main tenet of the so-called 'Religionsgeschichtliche Schule'. The term gnosis, Greek for knowledge, is used by various religions and philosophies. It is of Iranian origin and might have directly influenced Jewish and Christian ideas with its mythological primordial man – saviour system. See also Colpe, C., *Die religionsgeschichtliche Schule. Darstellung und Kritik ihres Bildes vom gnostischen Erlösermytho*. Franz Rosenthal, German-American Orientalist, 1914–2003; Hans Heinrich Schaeder, German Iranologist, 1896–1957; Hans Lietzmann, German Protestant theologian, 1875–1942; Erik Peterson, German Catholic theologian, b. 1890; Rudolf Bultmann, German Protestant theologian, 1884–1976.

8 Warburg, A., *Heidnisch-antike Weissagung in Wort und Bild zu Luthers Zeiten*; Britt, D., 'Pagan-Antique Prophecy in Words and Images in the Age of Luther', 597–697 and 760–775.

9 Saxl, F., 'Frühes Christentum und spätes Heidentum in ihren künstlerischen Ausdrucksformen', 63–121.

10 Boll, F., *Sphaera*.

to the research of Gnosticism. Reitzenstein[11] and Lidzbarski both influenced Mandaeist research in the first three decades of the 20th century.

1st letter

Saxl, in Hamburg, to Warburg, in Kreuzlingen, on 31 October 1922. Typed with manuscript corrections, see 8.1a and 8.1b.

[p. 1] Dear Professor,

I have to report on the second lecture by Reitzenstein, which was possibly better than his first lecture at the KBW; Reitzenstein spoke freely and was therefore mentally much freer when he propounded complicated formulations quite solemnly. He spoke in the university on the invitation of Plasberg;[12] 30 to 40 people were not present, which was really scandalous. Reitzenstein spoke about two papyri, the first one, a historical Alexander drama, deals with Antipater and Alexander's mother [manuscript insert: Olympia]. It is a prose text written on eight sheets [insert: two] in different hands and both stop in the middle of the page before the end of the story. Reitzenstein delivered a highly ingenious explanation: the text might be a school exercise, re-narrating a play in prose, which had to be finished in a given time. One of the students broke off in the middle of a word because his exercise book was taken away from him at the end of the allotted time. Reitzenstein had presented the story beautifully, which is important, as we do not have any other fragments of secular dramas. For us the second papyrus is essentially more important. It deals with animal novellas [underlined by Saxl: novella]. And now something really remarkable happens, as Reitzenstein could prove a direct translation of Egyptian stories, the Egyptian religious character [underlined by Saxl: religious]. The Greek translator

[p. 2]

of the Egyptian text de-deified it and turned the myth into a novella.

It was wonderful to see how this man [Reitzenstein], quite apart from his mind, masters his tools. If one is born again, one can only become a classical philologist.

After the lecture Reitzenstein came to me and Panofsky,[13] told beautiful stories of Robert[14] and other clever people. Later we also talked about Melencolia[15] and similar topics. Reitzenstein was very enthusiastic about the KBW and offered right

11 Cf. Koch, C., 'Richard Reitzensteins Beiträge zur Mandäerforschung', 49–80.

12 Otto Plasberg, German classical philologist, 1869–1924.

13 Erwin Panofsky, German-American art historian, 1892–1968.

14 Carl Robert, German classical philologist and archaeologist, 1850–1922.

15 See Saxl and Panofsky, *Dürers 'Melencolia I'*.

away to return next year and give a lecture. It goes without saying that I agreed with the old gentleman. With Reitzenstein one always has the feeling, how really dreadful it would be, if one day his weak organism stopped working. For the sheer number of facts piled up and processed in his brain in 62 years is so marvellous that it really should never be allowed to perish.

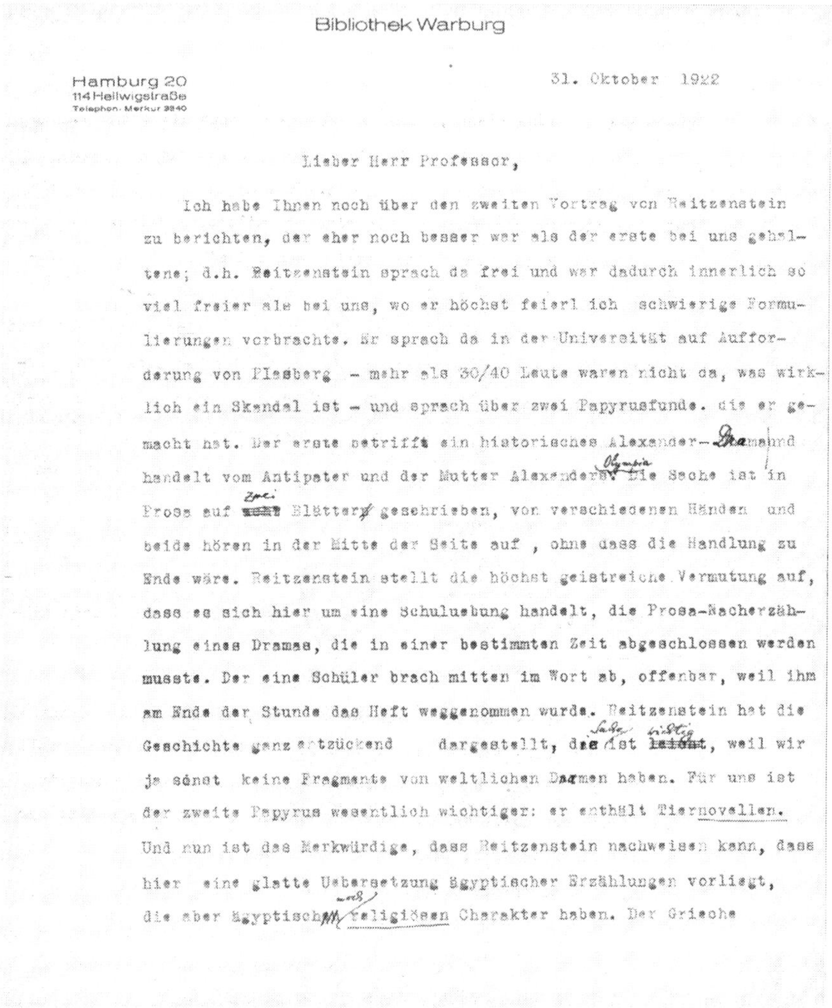

Bibliothek Warburg

Hamburg 20
114 Heilwigstraße
Telephon: Merkur 3840

31. Oktober 1922

Lieber Herr Professor,

Ich habe Ihnen noch über den zweiten Vortrag von Reitzenstein zu berichten, der eher noch besser war als der erste bei uns gehaltene; d.h. Reitzenstein sprach da frei und war dadurch innerlich so viel freier als bei uns, wo er höchst feierlich schwierige Formulierungen vorbrachte. Er sprach da in der Universität auf Aufforderung von Plasberg – mehr als 30/40 Leute waren nicht da, was wirklich ein Skandal ist – und sprach über zwei Papyrusfunde. die er gemacht hat. Der erste betrifft ein historisches Alexander-[Dra]ma und handelt vom Antipater und der Mutter Alexanders [Olympia]. Die Sache ist in Prosa auf [zwei] Blätter gesehrieben, von verschiedenen Händen und beide hören in der Mitte der Seite auf, ohne dass die Handlung zu Ende wäre. Reitzenstein stellt die höchst geistreiche Vermutung auf, dass es sich hier um eine Schuluebung handelt, die Prosa-Nacherzählung eines Dramas, die in einer bestimmten Zeit abgeschlossen werden musste. Der eine Schüler brach mitten im Wort ab, offenbar, weil ihm am Ende der Stunde das Heft weggenommen wurde. Reitzenstein hat die Geschichte ganz entzückend dargestellt, [die Sache] ist [wichtig], weil wir ja sonst keine Fragmente von weltlichen Dramen haben. Für uns ist der zweite Papyrus wesentlich wichtiger: er enthält Tiernovellen. Und nun ist das Merkwürdige, dass Reitzenstein nachweisen kann, dass hier eine glatte Uebersetzung ägyptischer Erzählungen vorliegt, die aber ägyptisch [noch] religiösen Charakter haben. Der Grieche

Figure 8.1 a and b, WIA, GC, Saxl to Warburg, 31.10.1922.

Source: © Photo: The Warburg Institute.

entgöttlicht es
übersetzt das Aegyptische, und macht aus dem Mythus die Novelle.

Wunderbar war zu sehen, wie dieser Mann, ganz abgesehen von
seinem Geist sein Werkzeug beherrscht. Wenn man noch einmal auf die
Welt kommt, kann man doch nur klassischer Philologe werden.

Nach dem Vortrag war Reitzenstein noch bei mir, wo auch Panofs-
ky war, hat reizende Geschichten von Robert und anderen Gelehrten
Leuten erzählt. Dann sprachen wir noch über die Melancholie und sonst
allerlei. Er war so begeistert von der B.W., dass er sich sofort er-
bötig gemacht hat, im nächsten Jahr wieder zu kommen und einen Vor-
trag zu halten. Selbstverständlich bin mit grösster Dankbarkeit auf
diesen Vorschlag des alten Herrn eingegangen. Bei Reitzenstein hat
man immer die Empfindung, ~~wie~~ besonders furchtbar es wäre, wenn
dieser doch sehr schwache Organismus eines Tages nicht mehr funktio-
nierte; denn was dieses Gehirn in den 62 Jahren aufgestapelt und ver-
arbeitet hat, ist so herrlich, dass es eigentlich nie zu Grunde geh-
en dürfte.

Eine sehr wichtige Anregung hat mir noch Reitzenstein gegeben:
Lidzbarski hat das heilige Buch der Mandäer, die Ganze, übersetzt
und kann es ~~noch~~ nicht drucken. Es handelt sich nicht um sehr viel,
nur um 190 Seiten. Ob <u>wir</u> das nicht drucken sollten? Ich muss mir
die Sache noch durch den Kopf gehen lassen. Es gibt eine uralte Ueber-
setzung von Petermann, die aber shr schlecht sein soll, so dass
alles, was auf ihr beruht, falsch ist.

Figure 8.1 (Continued)

Reitzenstein has suggested to me something very important: Lidzbarski has translated the holy book of the Mandaeans, the Ginza[16] and is unable to have it published. It is not a big book, some 190 pages only. Should we [underlined by Saxl: we] have it printed? I have to think about it a bit more. There is only a very old translation extant by Petermann,[17] which is said to be very poor, so that everything which rests on it is wrong.

Your Saxl [handwritten].[18]

Commentary on the 1st letter

Reitzenstein's second lecture at the KBW, 'Augustine as ancient and medieval man', which Saxl mentions in this letter, was published in the second volume of *Vorträge*, edited by Saxl, only in 1925. In it Reitzenstein talked about the role of Manichaeism for the theological development of the later St Augustine. The end of the letter gave witness to Reitzenstein's interest in and commitment to translating and publicising Mandaean sources, after Lidzbarski had translated one part of *Ginza*, most likely the left part (*Ginza smala*), into German. In 1921 Reitzenstein made reference to this part and used it to construct his theoretical arguments in his book *Das iranische Erlösungsmysterium. Religionsgeschichtliche Untersuchungen.*[19]

The reference to Petermann's 'very old translation' needs further explanation. Petermann did not publish translations of Mandaean texts, but published the first, and until then the only, *Ginza* edition in 1867. The Swedish Orientalist Matthias Norberg translated the *Ginza* into Latin in 1815–16; it is possible that Saxl did not know of the Norberg translation; it does not feature in The Warburg Institute catalogue. Norberg held the Mandaean language to be poor Syriac and consequently corrected the Mandaean text to agree with Syriac grammar, which based the translation on false assumptions.[20]

16 *Ginza*, the 'treasure' or *Sidra Rabba*, 'the great book', is the comprehensive and significant book of the Mandaeans. It consists of two main parts: *Ginza iamina*, the right *Ginza*, and *Ginza smala*, the left *Ginza*. The right *Ginza* is a collection of 18 treatises, according to the classification by M. Lidzbarski, of mainly mythological, cosmological and theological subject matter. The left *Ginza* consists of three books, two with hymns and songs about the soul's ascent to the world beyond after death, which, in part, is recited during the Mandaeans' service for the dead. The book traditionally contains the right *Ginza* on one side, and, when turned upside down and back to front, contains the left *Ginza* (the left *Ginza* is also called 'The Book of the Dead').

17 Heinrich Petermann, German Orientalist, 1801–1876. See Petermann, J.H., *Thesaurus sive Liber Magnus*.

18 WIA, GC, Saxl to Warburg, 31.10.1922.

19 Reitzenstein, R., *Das iranische Erlösungsmysterium*, in particular 43–76; see Lidzbarski, M., *Ginzā. Der Schatz oder das große Buch der Mandäer* for the (German) translation of both parts of Ginza, the right part 3–419, the left part 423–596.

20 Matthias Norberg, Swedish Orientalist, 1747–1826. Norberg, M., *Codex Nasaraeus*.

2nd letter

Saxl, in Hamburg, to M. Lidzbarski, in Göttingen, on 9 November 1922, typed copy.

[p. 1] Dear Professor,

Permit me to make a suggestion. I know from Reitzenstein's publications that you have worked on a translation of the Genzer [sic!], which so far has not been published. The Warburg library publishes a *Studien* series. The volumes essentially address topics from the history of religion and art history linked to the survival of classical antiquity. The first volume is devoted to the research by Ernst Cassirer under the heading of 'Conceptual form in mythical thought'.[21] A book by Norden follows, 'The birth of the child',[22] then a book by Dr. Panofsky and myself on 'Dürer's Melencolia' and an edition of the great Hellenistic-Arabic book of magic by Professor Ritter of Hamburg university.[23]

I do know that the Mandaean worldview has actually nothing to do with the classical Hellenic worldview; however, the relationship between these two became more and more apparent in the last few decades and so it would be fitting for a translation from Mandaean to be published in our series. [by B. G. Teubner in Leipzig, asterisk in the margin: missing in the text.]

[p. 2:]

Presumably, it might be possible to publish in the first instance only the left Ginza, a part which is not too large. In case you decide to publish your translation with us, I would be grateful for further details about extent etc. Royalties amount to 20 % of each sold copy.

I am looking forward to your news with thanks,

Yours sincerely
[signature missing]
To Professor Dr. Mark Lidzbarski
Göttingen
Merckelstrasse 4a[24]

Commentary on the 2nd letter

Saxl wrote the letter to Lidzbarski a few days after his report to Warburg on 31 October 1922. Although there is no word from Warburg on Saxl's suggestion to publish Lidzbarski's research, Saxl went ahead with asking Lidzbarski about his

21 Cassirer, E., *Die Begriffsform im mythischen Denken*.

22 Norden, E., *Die Geburt des Kindes*. Eduard Norden, classical philologist and historian of religion, 1868–1941.

23 Ritter, H., *Picatrix*. Hellmut Ritter, German Orientalist, 1892–1971.

24 WIA, GC, Saxl to M. Lidzbarski, 9.11.1922.

Ginza translation, a research topic that was typical for the 1920s, establishing the contacts, relationships and exchanges between the classical Hellenistic and Oriental worlds. Not only an expanding Christianity, but also Gnosticism, with its heterogeneous trends, became research topics on mutual fertilisation as well as mutual isolation.

3rd letter

Richard Reitzenstein, in Göttingen, to Saxl, in Hamburg, on 12 December 1922, handwritten.

[p. 1:] Göttingen Dahlmannstr. 16. 12.12.22

Dear Doctor,

I do not know whether you remember that we spoke in Hamburg about research by Mrs. Luise Troje[25] in Königsberg [today Kaliningrad], which you were thinking about publishing in the *Studien* series. A lengthy correspondence between her and me ensued, because the article which I had in mind then, her analysis of an Indian sacrificial ceremony as an Aion mystery, will be published by the Archiv für Religionswissenschaft after continued funding from Sweden. It would also have been too short on its own.[26]

However, she now asks me whether there would be any possibility of publishing a larger piece of work with you. Her work has been accepted for publication elsewhere, in the series of volumes on the history of religion in Bonn (I do not know the title, the heads are Professors Clemen and Kirfel),[27] but they declared that they cannot print in 1923 and cannot say whether they will have funds later.

Under these conditions it is understandable that Mrs. Troje would be extremely happy to find another opportunity to publish. I will try to give a short description.

[p. 2] The title is 'Dogmas in number formulas, a contribution to the basis of Manichaeism'.[28] Her research is based on the only lengthy original treatise by Manichaeans, extant in Chinese. Chavannes and Pelliot published it in the Journal Asiatique in 1910 and '11, without really knowing what to do with it.[29] Larger parts of a Turkish-Manichaean version have been added by Le

25 Luise Troje, also Louise Troje, née Stein, German historian of religion working with the Deutsche Morgenländische Gesellschaft, 1867–1954.

26 Troje, L., *Die Geburt des Aion – ein altes Mysterium*. Aion is a Hellenistic deity, the personification and god of indefinitely extending time.

27 Carl Clemen, professor for New Testament and history of religion, Bonn, 1865–1940. Willibald Kirfel, German Indologist, 1885–1964.

28 Troje, L., *Die dreizehn und die zwölf im Traktat Pelliot (Dogmen in Zahlenformeln). Ein Beitrag zu den Grundlagen des Manichäismus*.

29 Édouard Chavannes, French sinologist, 1865–1918; Paul Pelliot, French sinologist, 1878–1945. Chavannes and Pelliot, 'Un traité manichéen retrouvé en Chine traduit et annoté', 499–617.

Coq.[30] I myself know the first part and can judge it. Mrs. Troje has far outstripped my own attempts with her subtle interpretation starting with Indian sources. She partly contradicted my findings and corrected them. She continued this part following the series of twelve and the series of seven Aions in Gnosticism, where, according to her, the religious symbolism of stars has been superimposed over an older oriental (Indian) teaching, which is simple for every believer to imagine and easy to understand. With the evidence of this older stratum Troje wants to bring to light the religiosity of Gnosticism, in itself already a mix of a number of Indian systems. The proof

[p. 3] will be presented in images and words. The worldview of Hellenistic religiosity with its seven layers and its twelve-gate, twelve-part hell and heaven will be proved as being partly inherited from Samkya and Buddhism.[31] Samkya influences more the perceptions of Gnosticism as a way to salvation, whereas Buddhism stresses the personal saviour. Professor Franke (Königsberg, University) will no doubt write a short reference; admittedly he also only knows some parts.[32] The article will cover eight sheets and be as long as Troje's Adam und Zoe (Heidelberger Sitzungsberichte. 1916.Tract 17).[33]

You see, I cannot state much yet. The writer is very intelligent and profoundly well-read, and, like all of us and as a matter of course, in danger of deducing too much from one source. But the connection between Persian and Indian, later expanded by Hellenistic, ideas has finally to be taken up in earnest. The interpretation of these images which closely relate to astral theology is a topic of research in the *Studien* series. This was brilliantly shown again by the lecture of Professor Ritter, who finally gave me an understanding of Picatrix. Unfortunately, I will only be able to thank him in the holidays. At present, I am nearly dying

[p. 4] from the burden of daily committee meetings. They have also stopped me completing the addendum to Augustine and as Teubner only wants to print when everything is together, I have time. In the meantime I thank you for returning this part. The address of Mrs. Troje is Königsberg Pr.[Prussia] Tiergartenstr. 40.

I conclude by thanking you once more for your kindness and remain in deep respect

Your very loyal
R. Reitzenstein
I am sure that Mrs. Troje will not object to a review
by the Hamburg expert.
May I ask you to convey my best regards to Mrs. Warburg.[34]

30 Albert von Le Coq, German archaeologist, 1860–1930. Le Coq, A., *Die buddhistische Spätantike in Mittelasien.*

31 *Samkya*, one of the six schools of classical Indian philosophy.

32 Rudolf Otto Franke, German indologist, Königsberg, 1862–1928.

33 Troje, L., *Adam und Zoe.*

34 WIA, GC, Reitzenstein to Saxl, 12.12.1922.

Commentary on the 3rd letter

Reitzenstein's letter once more confirmed that his approach to research on the history of religions matched his interest in not only the origins of Gnosticism as well as the links to the Hellenistic religions, but also their links to the Persian, Indian and Far Eastern religions. In this context it was a matter of course to speak up for Troje. Her article on 'Dogmas in number formulas' was published in Leipzig only in 1925; her contribution on the prehistory of Christian baptism was published in Reitzenstein's volume in 1929.[35] He dedicated the volume to Troje; she contributed two pieces of research: to chapter IV, on the nature of God, and to chapter V, on the Mandaean and Christian baptism, of which the second one is especially important. Under the heading 'Sanbat'[36] she investigated in an extensive treatise what linked the Jewish-Christian speculations about holy/ritual times in the old Ethiopian text 'Tə'əzazä Sänbät', the 'Commandment of the Sabbath',[37] to the Mandaean 'Habšabba':[38]

> Behind the idea of God as the personification of Sabbath, 'the Seventh', stands the Aion idea of 'the Seventh as a code', in which the role of the leader and divine mediator falls to the Sabbath God. The seventh day should equally be the first day. In this concept it became the Mandaean Habšabba, who in contrast to the Sabbath is a young creation, and has not run through a number of phases of development, so that name and connotation have to concur. With Habšabba the link to the theology of Aion becomes apparent.[39]

4th letter

Richard Reitzenstein, no place given, to Fritz Saxl, in Hamburg, on 28 February 1923, handwritten.

> [p. 1:]28 Febr. 23
>
> Dear Doctor,
>
> I return with thanks the addendum to my lecture, enclosed, from my sickbed. I hope that you were able to finish printing the first volume of Vorträge.[40]

35 Troje, L, *Die dreizehn und die zwölf im Traktat Pelliot (Dogmen in Zahlenformeln). Ein Beitrag zu den Grundlagen des Manichäismus.*

36 Sanbat (Amharic Sänbät) is the Ethiopian word for the Jewish Sabbath. The Ethiopian Orthodox Church uses this word for Saturday, also called the 'small' or 'first' Sabbath, as well as for Sunday, also called the 'great' Sabbath.

37 The book *Tə'əzazä Sänbät*, 'Commandments of the Sabbath', is a Betä 'Əsrael literary work, which stresses the importance of the Sabbath for the Ethiopian Jews: it is the mediator day personified, which intercedes with God on behalf of the believers. Kaplan, S., 'Tə'əzazä Sänbät', 885a–b.

38 *Habšabba* is the Mandaean word for Sunday, literally 'the first [day] of the seven [days]'.

39 Voigt, R., *"Durch Dein Wort ward jegliches Ding!"*; Reitzenstein, R., *Die Vorgeschichte der christlichen Taufe* with the chapter 'Sanbat' by L. Troje, 328–377, here 349.

40 Reitzenstein, R., 'Augustin als antiker und als mittelalterlicher Mensch', 38–75.

I have been on *the lookout out for Norden's book for a long time, likewise Prof. Junker's lecture* on Zarvan.[41] Referring to the alchemist object which you sent me, I would ask your kindness in forwarding the copy [of Vorträge] for Plasberg, either to the library or the seminar [of the university].[42] But it is not urgent. I presume it will be easier for you to see Professor Ritter in your library.

I heard that you asked Lidzbarski [to publish in the series of the KBW] and I thank you very much for doing so. If only we could find a place where poor Mrs. Troje could publish. Norden sent me

[p. 2] a very appreciative letter about her.

With my best thanks for your gracious letter,

Yours,
respectfully
R. Reitzenstein[43]

Commentary on the 4th letter

Zarvan refers to the Iranian god Zurvan, and hence the essence of Gnosis and the links to Iran. As mentioned above, this addresses Aion ideas, specifically the Zoroastrian idea of 'infinite' time (Iranian *zurvan akarana*), which was deified and became the god Zurvan. With the help of Iranian magi, the idea spread all over the Hellenistic world, as is shown by Junker's book, which is still well worth reading. For Reitzenstein this topic was valuable for a different reason: it provided a plausible argument for the Iranian background of not only Gnosticism, but also other religious currents of the time, as becomes clear from the following quotes:

> . . . 6th January, the day on which Jesus was baptised, because previously [it was] the birthday of Aion or the primordial man, of that godly man who becomes Moses in Philo, and among the Christians has become Jesus.[44]
>
> Among the Mandaeans this first day belonged to Mandā d'Haijē, the knowledge of God; but he ruled under a different name and a different interpretation of his essence on the following six days. He is Aion, the messenger of God in the world and the primordial man. The contrast to Judaism reveals itself strangely in the name for the day, which can stand for the name of God. Judaism also assesses a seven-day week in

41 Norden, E., *Die Geburt des Kindes*; Junker, H., 'Über iranische Quellen der hellenistischen Aion-Vorstellung', 125–178. Zarvan or Zurvan is the Persian creator god. Heinrich Junker, scholar in Iranian studies, 1889–1970.

42 Reitzenstein, R., *Helidori carmina quattuor ad fidem codicis casselani edidit Günther Goldschmidt*.

43 WIA, GC, R. Reitzenstein to Saxl, 28.2.1923.

44 Reitzenstein, R., 'Augustin als antiker und als mittelalterlicher Mensch', 38–75, here 31.

a religious way. The day is called 'One after the seven', the new unified Aion starts with a new creation and not with rest.[45]

Not only Junker researched the perception of the Aion idea, but also Eduard Norden, which explains Reitzenstein's interest in both their books.

5th letter

Mark Lidzbarski, in Göttingen, to Fritz Saxl, in Hamburg, on 8 July 1923, handwritten.

[p. 1:] Göttingen, 8th July 1923. Merkelstr. 7.

Dear Sir,

In the autumn we corresponded about publishing the Mandaean Ginza. The steep costs of printing caused difficulties. I therefore ask you whether the volume could be accommodated in the collection of the KBW. Some time ago you wrote to me about the left Ginza, probably following Professor Reitzenstein's suggestion as he is most interested in this part because of his research on Psyche. By itself there is no reason to publish just this part. I think it desirable
[p. 2:]
to make available the entire Ginza, which is of utmost importance for the knowledge of Gnosticism. Such a volume with the translation and a linguistic and factual comment, as concise as possible, would comprise some 35 sheets. Judging by the interest in religions of late antiquity I believe that such a publication would also sell well. The two volumes which were published earlier on the 'Johannesbuch' and the Liturgy sell very well.
[continued in the margin:] For further discussions of these two books see the Zeitschrift für Assyriologie and the Theologische Rundschau.

Yours sincerely
M. Lidzbarski.[46]

Commentary on the 5th letter

Lidzbarski wanted to publish the entire Ginza corpus; it would have been the completion of two decades' worth of translation and editing work. He worked from 1905 to 1915 on his book *Johannesbuch der Mandäer*[47] and in 1920 his book *Mandäische Liturgien*,[48] which were not only the most important ritual texts of this religious community, but also significant for introducing Mandaean questions. Notes in the margin of Lidzbarski's letter referred to reviews

45 Reitzenstein, R., 'Augustin als antiker und als mittelalterlicher Mensch', here 37.
46 WIA, GC, M. Lidzbarski to Saxl, 8.7.1923.
47 Lidzbarski, M., *Das Johannesbuch der Mandäer. Text, Einleitung, Übersetzung und Kommentar*.
48 Lidzbarski, M., *Mandäische Liturgien*.

by Th. Nöldeke in *Zeitschrift für Assyriologie* and W. Bousset in *Theologische Rundschau*.[49]

6th letter

Richard Reitzenstein, in Kiesewald, Post Petersdorf, Riesengebirge, to Fritz Saxl, in Hamburg, on 4 September 1924. Handwritten, extract from the letter.

Reitzenstein suggested a lecture on 'Philosophy and the history of religion' to Saxl. He wanted 'to separate the philological, historical nature of research into religion from the theological and folkloristic nature and to present it as the essential task for present times'.

Commentary on the 6th letter

The topic addressed here was about continuity of spiritual life. Reitzenstein had published two articles about it in the series of the KBW: 'Ancient Greek theology and its sources' in *Vorträge 1924–1925* and 'Plato and Zarathustra' in the same volume.[50] Hans Heinrich Schaeder also published a long and important article on 'Original form and developments of the Manichaean System' in the same volume, in which he touched on Mandaeism.[51]

7th letter

Fritz Saxl, in Hamburg, to Aby Warburg, in Rome, on 2 January 1929, part of a typed letter, insertions in handwriting.

> The lecture by Reitzenstein ['Sacred Act'] was in my estimation a triumph of the library as if from you personally![52] It was not very full, which I always welcome, but unfortunately both philologists [one of them Lidzbarski] were absent from Hamburg.
>
> Reitzenstein's personality being unconditionally consumed by questions, the incisive diction, borne by an eminently religious emotion, simply casts a magic spell which listeners cannot escape. This personality is the criterion for the benchmark of what ought to happen in these rooms.[53]

49 For Nöldeke's review of *Das Johannesbuch* by Lidzbarski, see Bezold, C., *Zeitschrift für Assyriologie*, XXX, 139–162; for Nöldeke's review of *Mandäische Liturgien* by Lidzbarski, see Bezold, C., *Zeitschrift für Assyriologie*, XXXIII, 72–80; for Bousset's review of *Das Johannesbuch*, see Bousset, W., 'Die Religion der Mandäer', 185–205; see also Brandt, W., *Die Mandäer. Ihre Religion und ihre Geschichte*. Theodor Nöldeke, German Orientalist, 1836–1930; Wilhelm Brandt, German Orientalist, 1855–1915. Wilhelm Bousset, German theologian, 1865–1920.

50 Reitzenstein, R., 'Alt-griechische Theologie und ihre Quellen', 1–19; and idem, 'Plato und Zarathustra', 20–37.

51 Schaeder, 'Urform und Fortbildungen des manichäischen Systems', 65–157.

52 Reitzenstein, R., 'Holy Deed', 21–41. Reitzenstein's lecture was held in the KBW in Hamburg on 29 December 1928.

53 Saxl summarises here the academic work in the KBW, the publication series *Vorträge der Bibliothek Warburg* (9 vols.) and *Studien der Bibliothek Warburg* (23 vols.).

Whether Reitzenstein's thesis was correct in its details is something I cannot judge. He started with the [Insert: 'liturgy'] of baptism with the Mandaeans, in which an ascension to the heavens ['ascension to the heavens' underlined in blue, possibly by Warburg] is described, and attempted to show that the three different acts of baptism, which are accounted for in early Christianity, lose their incomprehensibility if one knows their explanations in connection ['in connection' underlined in black, possibly by Saxl] with the Mandaean religion.

Now, Mandaean culture has only been attested to since the 8th century and Reitzenstein's task was to prove that the roots of Mandaeism go back to much earlier times. He tried to supply this evidence from Indian and Persian sources ['Indian and Persian' underlined in blue, possibly by Warburg].

He started his lecture by saying that he was happy to open the cycle of lectures on the ascension into the heavens at one single point, etc.,

[p. 3:] and then in his very personal way he talked about his relationship to the library and in particular to you. He called his lecture 'Holy deed', the title of Usener's book,[54] mentioned that Warburg had been a student of Usener's and that was precisely the characteristic of this deed, was the spirit [insert: 'Usener live', crossed out: 'different']. I believe that Reitzenstein has hit upon something essential with this explanation. Afterwards Ruben and I accompanied the old gentlemen to Curiohaus.[55] Reitzenstein is so ill, he is not very mobile down from one shoulder to his foot, so that I think he will not lecture again. I have especially regretted that a personal contact by Cassirer or other celebrities had not been sought. But you do know how it is here. [Insert: 'Years ago'] I once invited Reitzenstein to come to Cassirer's and the matter went horribly wrong. Cassirer cannot deal with this fervent personality. So much the more Ruben, who was comfortable and had Reitzenstein speak about Usener, Mommsen etc. for a long time.[56]

His son, who had to bring the father, made a very good impression.[57] He has qualified as professor in Bonn. Your son Max knows him from Heidelberg and likes him. He is writing

[p. 4:] a piece of research on 'Leptos', which he is following through the whole of Greek atomism [insert 'and natural philosophy'] and then trying to clarify the change in the stylistic concept of the more delicate tone in Alexandrinian verse. He is a student of Boll's and his first research piece is on [Insert: 'Theophrastus in Lucretius and Epictetus'].[58]

54 Usener, H., *Heilige Handlung*. Hermann Usener, German philologist and comparative religion scholar, 1834–1905.

55 The Curio House in Rothenbaumchausee, Hamburg, built for the Society of Friends for the patriotic school and education system, was a meeting place for artists and intellectuals. Peter Paul Ruben, German Hebraist, 1866–1943.

56 Theodor Mommsen, German historian and classicist, 1817–1903.

57 Erich Reitzenstein, German classical philologist, 1897–1976.

58 WIA, GC, Saxl to Warburg, 2.1.1929. Reitzenstein, E., *Theophrast bei Epikur und Lukrez*. Theophrastus, Greek philosopher, BC 371–BC 287; Lucretius, Roman philosopher, BC 99–BC 55; Epictetus, Greek stoic philosopher, c. 50–c. 135.

Commentary on the 7th letter

Saxl reported to Warburg about the splendid lecture by Reitzenstein which was published by the KBW. He praised Reitzenstein's exemplary approach when talking about the history of religion, namely that he no longer speaks of religions which are different from each other, but of religion in the singular as the most profound spiritual life in humans. On the other hand, Mandaeism is the starting point for his arguments of an Iranian myth of salvation which forms the basis of this one religion:

> I take as my starting point a pagan baptism ritual, which with small changes in very different usages is to be understood as acts of acceptance, as communal celebrations at the beginning of this period of time, as dedications before important phases of life, as last rites and finally as a funeral mass for the deceased. This ritual has been evidenced by a small religious community on the lower Euphrates ever since the 8th century – it existed until the Great War and perhaps still exists. The Mandaeans, who are called after the baptismal God Mandā d'Haijē, which means knowledge of life, which is their name for God. Their other name is Nāśōräer, the keeper of a mystery, that is baptism, the ascension, as they term it.[59]

However, it seems that Reitzenstein does not tell apart the two main rituals of the Mandaeans, baptism and the ascension of the soul, but views both as one whole. Also the fact of his late dating of the Mandaeans to the 8th century reveals that he did not know the earliest proofs of the Mandaeans, the magic cups and amulets.[60]

This short overview of the literature on the topic of transformation of the old into a new religion affords us today a glimpse into the research topics at a time of political change, the start of something new. The continuity of the original concern of humanity, the question of the meaning of life, the – religious – linkage – to supra-individual dimensions and guidance to hope-filled life, was dealt with at the time of Lidzbarski and Reitzenstein by a number of scientific disciplines. The perspective of the universe, that is, continuity in times of discontinuity, gave new emphasis to research into the history of religion. It seemed reasonable to scholars around Warburg and Saxl that they also study these topics, to wit Warburg's research on Luther[61] and Saxl's research on early Christianity.[62] Schaeder expressed this strikingly in the last sentence of his article: 'Our goal in this field remains a history not of religions, but of *the* religion'.[63]

59 Reitzenstein, R., 'Heilige Handlung', 21–41, here 22. F. Saxl, *Vorträge 9*, 1930/31.

60 cf. Lidzbarski, M., 'Ein mandäisches Amulett', 349–373.

61 Warburg, A., *Heidnisch-antike Weissagung in Wort und Bild zu Luthers Zeiten*. Martin Luther, German reformer, 1483–1546.

62 Saxl, F., 'Frühes Christentum und spätes Heidentum in ihren künstlerischen Ausdrucksformen', 63–121.

63 Schaeder, H.H., 'Urform und Fortbildungen des manichäischen Systems', 65–157, here 157.

9

WARBURG'S VIEW OF STRZYGOWSKI AS REFLECTED IN THE ABY WARBURG CORRESPONDENCE[1]

Preparing the Congress on the History of Art in 1907

Aby Warburg (see figure 9.1), the famous art historian and cultural historian in Hamburg, kept very extensive correspondence with colleagues, friends and members of his family, which has been accessible in a database since 2010.[2] The topic of this chapter is an investigation of the contacts between Professor Josef Strzygowski, Professor in Graz, later in Vienna, Austria, on the one hand and Dr. Aby Warburg, private scholar in Hamburg, on the other hand. Both served on the committee of the art history congresses in Germany in the years from 1906 to 1908.

August Schmarsow, the founder in 1888 of the German art history Institute in Florence, today the Kunsthistorisches Institut in Florenz (KHI) and part of the Max Planck Institute, knew Warburg from his student days when Warburg and his student friends Ernst Burmeister, Hermann Ullmann, Ernst 'Pepi' Zimmermann and Max Friedländer stayed with Schmarsow for four months in Florence in the winter of 1888–1889.[3] The art history institute was founded on the private initiative of independent scholars and Warburg kept up links with the institute all his life.

In 1906 Schmarsow wrote to Warburg that the next congress would not take place in Stockholm as planned and that Warburg had been elected unanimously to the permanent committee of the art history congresses together with Henry Thode, Josef Strzygowski, Wilhelm Vöge, Rudolf Kautzsch and Karl Koetschau. Thode

1 Originally published in McEwan, D., 'Strzygowski im Spiegel der Aby Warburg Korrespondenz. Der Strzygowski-Briefbestand im Warburg Institute London', 53–69.

2 McEwan, D., *Correspondence of Aby Warburg, General Correspondence and Family Correspondence, from 1882 to 1929*. The online database is available at: https://wi-calm.sas.ac.uk/calmview/ (accessed June 2022).

3 WIA, FC, Warburg to Charlotte Warburg, 28.10.1222. August Schmarsow, German professor of art history 1853–1936; Ernst Burmeister, German art historian, d. 1894; Hermann Ullmann, German art historian, 1866–1896; Ernst 'Pepi' Zimmermann, German art historian, 1866–1940; Max Friedländer, German art historian, 1867–1958; Josef Strzygowski, Polish-Austrian art historian, 1862–1941.

DOI: 10.4324/9781003169024-12

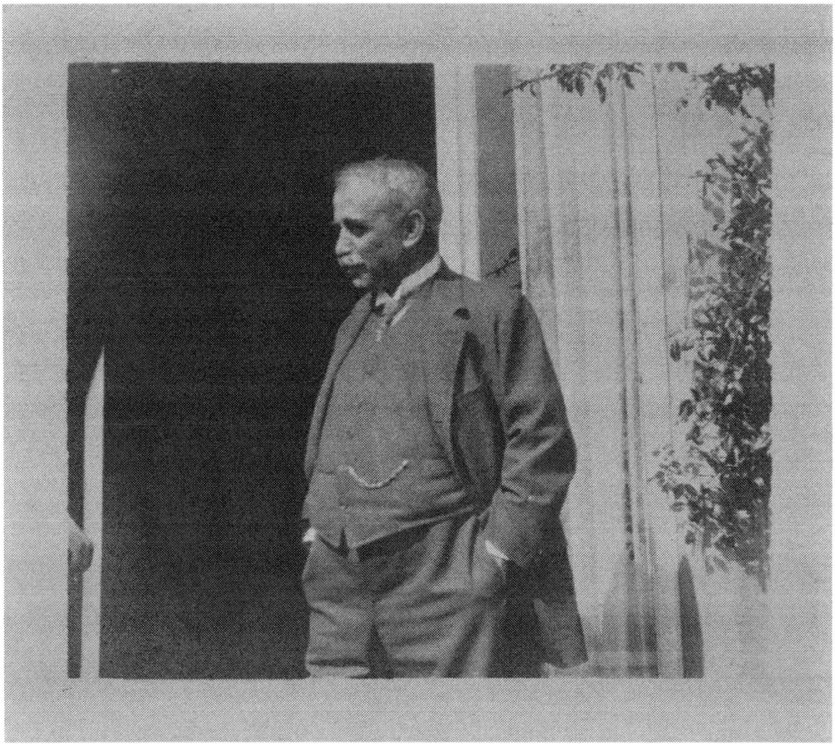

Figure 9.1 Portrait of Aby Warburg in the 1920s. WIA, Portrait collection.
Source: © Photo: The Warburg Institute.

was professor in Heidelberg, Strzygowski in Vienna, Vöge was then still employed at the royal museum in Berlin, Kautzsch was professor at the technical university in Darmstadt, and Koetschau was director of the royal historical museum in Dresden. Schmarsow went on to ask Warburg whether he would stand for the post of treasurer in view of his contacts to the world of banking and business.[4]

Warburg accepted and took his work in the committee very seriously; he rendered a particularly important service to the congresses congress on the history of art with his initiative for an art history congress in Italy in 1912, see Chapter 1. But that was in the future. Warburg threw himself into the preparations right away. In June 1906 he

4 WIA, GC, A. Schmarsow to Warburg, 1.6.1906. Henry Thode, German art historian, 1857–1902; Wilhelm Vöge, German art historian, 1868–1952; Rudolf Kautzsch, German art historian, 1868–1945; Karl Koetschau, German art historian, 1868–1949. The *National-Zeitung* in Berlin advertised the names of the new committee members on 20 July 1906.

wrote to Kautzsch that a committee meeting was urgently required,[5] in a letter to Koetschau he suggested dates of either 14 or 15 July, and added that Strzygowski, as first chair, would have to be urged to take part, for without a committee meeting Warburg would not stay on the committee.[6] Schmarsow wanted to maintain the continuity of and preparations for the congresses with the new committee,[7] after the cancellation of the congress in Stockholm, when Dresden was chosen to host the congress in October 1907. However, the congress did not take place in Dresden, but in Darmstadt in September 1907. In a letter from Dresden to his wife Mary, Warburg told her his ideas: he advocated a 'stricter organisation of art history with the help of a handbook of art history' and the creation of annual reports. He was clear after the first meeting that he could work with his colleagues, demonstrating a 'mature friendship among men': Strzygowski was in his best years at the age of 46, Warburg was 40, Koetschau and Kautzsch were both 38 years of age. All of them wanted to put a stop to the amateurish organisation of the congress. He characterised the committee in the following way: Strzygowski was a pioneer in the field of Orient-Occident research, Kautzsch was an expert in illuminated manuscripts, Koetschau was a practical man and Warburg was an expert in classical antiquity, Florence, Flanders, festivals.[8]

In Strzygowski's first letter to Warburg he thanked him for articles; there was talk of the committee work of a first chairman and suggested changes to the by-laws.[9] Warburg was against changing the rules before a full meeting.[10] His reasoning was that the new members of the committee were only the 'trustees' of previous congresses until being formally appointed as the new members of the committee. Only when they all cooperated properly would they prove to be better than the old committee or members like Franz Wickhoff, for instance, whom Warburg referred to as a 'Viennese bogyman'.[11] Warburg did not like Wickhoff's article on Botticelli's *Primavera*, in which Wickhoff, only out of vanity, wanted to present a new interpretation of a topic which Warburg had treated in his doctoral dissertation.[12] Koetschau, who, like Warburg, was a new member of the committee, also discussed the merits of a change in congress rules, with a view to establishing an art history handbook or a Society, but as early as September 1906 he commented that he had trust in Warburg and Kautzsch, but not in Strzygowski.[13]

5 WIA, GC, Copy book I, 225. Warburg to R. Kautzsch, n.d., between 18. and 21.6.1906.
6 WIA, GC, Copy book 1, 226. Warburg to K. Koetschau, 18.6.1906.
7 WIA, GC, A. Schmarsow to Warburg, 21.6.1906.
8 WIA, FC, Warburg to Mary Warburg, 16.7.1906, second letter of the day.
9 WIA, GC, J. Strzygowski to Warburg, 29.7.1906.
10 WIA, GC, Copy book 1, 258, 259. Warburg to J. Strzygowski, 4.8.1906.
11 WIA, GC, Copy book 1, 282, 283. Warburg to J. Strzygowski, n.d., either 18. or 19.8.1906.
12 WIA, GC, Copy book 1, 258, 259. Warburg to J. Strzygowski, 4.8.1906. Wickhoff, F., 'Die Hochzeitsbilder Sandro Botticellis', 198–207. Warburg found Wickhoff's article deplorable, a 'senile flight of ideas'. Warburg, who had written his PhD dissertation on *Sandro Botticellis "Geburt der Venus" und "Frühling"*, continued to work on the questions discussed, see Treml et al., *Werke in einem Band*, 114.
13 WIA, GC, K. Koetschau to Warburg, 3.9.1906.

Strzygowski sent a number of letters to Warburg on the subject of congress rules,[14] which Warburg commented upon and criticised in a number of points.[15] Warburg informed Koetschau about Strzygowski's approach and that he had cautioned Strzygowski not to foreground the attitude of a 'vice squad' and a 'bureaucracy of councils'. Warburg did not want to stay on the committee without Koetschau, 'for, if we allow Strzygowski to manage things alone the result will just be unpredictable'.[16]

Difficulties and misunderstandings

The style of Warburg's letters to Strzygowski was rather professorial and pedantic, but definitely not unfriendly, while Strzygowski did not easily tolerate criticism. He quickly let Warburg know that he did not appreciate his tone and warned that Warburg should pull in the same direction as the others and send the list of names of scholars who were ready to cooperate on the annual report (see figures 9.2a and 9.2b).[17] Again Warburg, talking about the organisation and work of the committee, stressed that the new board could only call a preparatory meeting, because the new members had still not been appointed officially. He further suggested Berlin as the next venue for an art history congress in 1908 and supplied the names of scholars Caroline Fröhlich, Ferdinand Laban and Ernst Wilhelm Bredt as having volunteered to cooperate on the annual report.[18] They were experienced colleagues, especially when seen in contrast to the unsatisfactory contributions by the likes of Wickhoff or Ernst Steinmann.[19] All this because Warburg took his work seriously, made suggestions, understood organisational bottlenecks and blocked suggestions which did not seem expedient to him.[20]

He took the same approach when commenting on the draft for a classification scheme, prepared by Strzygowski. After carefully considering it, he reached the conclusion that it was an important document but that he, as a matter of principle, was against its publication. He saw it as private communication on the part of Strzygowski and explained again that its publication before the next congress would only confuse the participants and paralyse the course of the congress. A number of organisational questions would have to be aired, for instance the

14 E.g. WIA, GC, J. Strzygowski to Warburg, 6.9.1906.

15 WIA, GC, Copy book 1, 388, 389, Warburg to J. Strzygowski, 6.12.1906.

16 WIA, GC, Copy book 1, 417, 148, Warburg to K. Koetschau, 18.12.1906.

17 WIA, GC, J. Strzygowski to Warburg, 19.12.1906.

18 WIA, GC, Copy book 1, 484. Warburg to J. Strzygowski, 21.2.1907. Ferdinand Laban, author, German art historian, 1856 1910; Ernst Wihelm Bredt, German art historian, 1869–1938; Caroline Fröhlich-Bum, Austrian art historian, b. 1886 d. after 1975.

19 WIA, GC, Copy book 1, 492. Warburg to J. Strzygowski, 10.3.1907. Ernst Steinmann, 1866–1934, founder and director of the Bibliotheca Hertziana, Rome, who was also a Botticelli and Ghirlandajo scholar.

20 WIA, IV.53.2., Congress in Darmstadt, 1907. Manuscript note re. appointment of provisional committee in September 1906 in preparation for the next congress in September 1907.

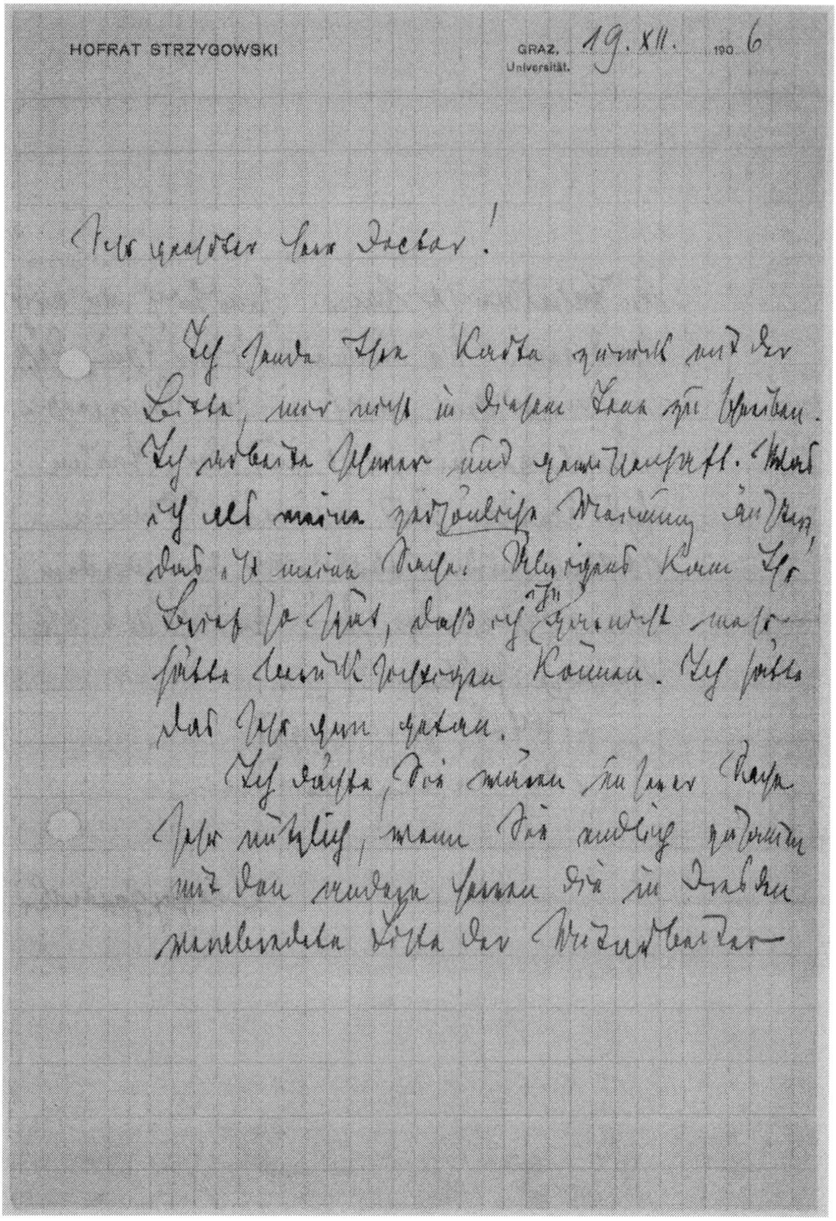

HOFRAT STRZYGOWSKI

GRAZ, 19. XII. 1906
Universität.

Sehr geehrter Herr Doctor!

Figure 9.2 a and b WIA, GC, Strzygowski to Warburg, 19.12.1906.

Source: © Helga Strzygowski, Vienna.

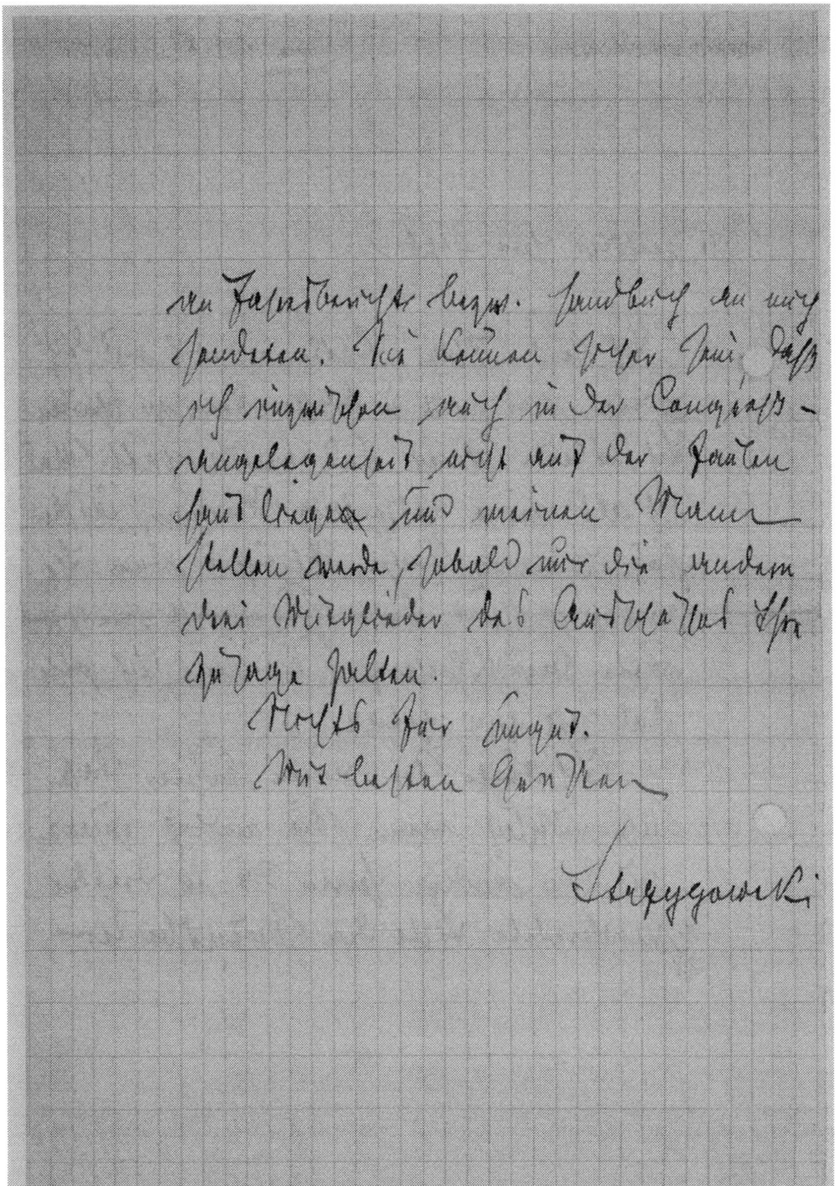

Strzygowski

Figure 9.2 (Continued)

appointment of the new board and the steps to create an art history Society,[21] as suggested by Koetschau the previous year.[22] Strzygowski gave in,[23] but followed this up by sending a letter to all members of the committee in which he stressed that the workload had to be shared by all.[24] In Warburg's case he posed a direct question as to Warburg's family connections in England[25] as well as about his own contacts with art historians in general.[26] Warburg replied that he would send the preliminary congress programme to his colleagues abroad.[27] Strzygowski then asked him to inform the German and Austrian colleagues as well and asked him for the names of the colleagues who had replied so far.[28] There is a certain impatience to be felt in Strzygowski's correspondence with Warburg: he urged him repeatedly to send names, to send drafts for the annual report, to speed things up, which Warburg did not do or did not do fast enough. Strzygowski sent a letter saying that Schmarsow would only attend if the elections to the committee were dealt with in the very first congress session,[29] doubtlessly to highlight that time was of the essence. By return of post Warburg sent a list of 16 registrations and assured him that he would persuade Max Friedländer, of the Museum of Prints and Drawings in Berlin, to attend.[30] These questions show clearly that Strzygowski was focused on the details but did not want to tackle the larger issues or had already ruled out doing so.

In his correspondence with Koetschau and Kautzsch, Warburg emphasised his good standing with Wilhelm von Bode, who for his part was on good terms with W. M. Schmid and Friedrich Althoff, practically the kingmaker for civil service posts. This was important, because Warburg was already uneasy as to whether Strzygowski would remain chair of the committee.[31] Warburg asked Koetschau whether Koetschau wanted to become president of the planned German Society for Studies of Art History.[32] Warburg was exasperated by Strzygowski's article on 'National art history and international art history' and commented

21 WIA, GC, Warburg to anonymous recipient, possibly K. Koetschau, 27.4.1907.
22 WIA, GC, Copy book 1, 276. Warburg to K. Koetschau, 16.8.1906.
23 WIA, GC, R. Kautzsch to Warburg, 16.5.1907.
24 WIA, GC, R. Kautzsch to Warburg, 23.5.1907.
25 WIA, GC, J. Strzygowski to Warburg, 31.5.1907.
26 WIA, GC, J. Strzygowski to Warburg, 7.6.1907.
27 WIA, GC, Copy book, 2, 62. Warburg to J. Strzygowski, 9.6.1907.
28 WIA, GC, J. Strzygowski to Warburg, 13.6.1907.
29 WIA, GC, J. Strzygowski to Warburg, 20.6.91907.
30 WIA, GC, Copy book 2, 74, 75. Warburg to J. Strzygowski, 22.6.1907.
31 WIA, GC, Copy book 2, 114–118. Warburg to R. Kautzsch and K. Koetschau, 8.8.1907. Wilhelm von Bode, German art historian, 1845–1929; Friedrich Althoff, 1839–1908, head of the university department in the Prussian ministry of culture; Wolfgang Maria Schmid, German art historian, 1867–1943, treasurer of the 9th art history congress in Munich.
32 The German Society for Studies of Art History (Deutscher Verein für Kunstwissenschaft) was founded on the initiative of Wilhelm von Bode and Friedrich Althoff in Berlin in 1908, inspired by the edition of historical documents on German medieval history, Monumenta Germaniae Historica.

curtly that 'every word [was] a faux pas'.[33] Koetschau shared Warburg's opinion.[34] Warburg reacted against Strzygowski's fundamental mindset in the article because he was propagating a 'psychological basis', which in Warburg's eyes had nothing to do with fine arts as science. Strzygowski advocated a comparative art history, not one engaged in a chronological sequence. Warburg held that this would mean, from the point of view of quality, a modern work of art could stand immediately next to a Japanese or antique work or art. It was therefore not a critical discourse analysis; what Warburg advocated was rather the demand for art history as a legitimate history of science. Indeed, questions of comparison and evolution did become topics of international congresses because these were scholarly topics for which no 'boundary posts' should be erected.[35] Warburg furnished his letter with lines and exclamation marks in the margin: clearly the overall tenor of international art history exercised Warburg. Some 18 years later, Warburg did adopt internationalisation in general: airspace did not know any state boundaries for 'the economic politics of the boundary posts' had come to an end with the invention of air travel – 'the United States of Europe are in the air', as he put it in a letter to his friend and editor-in-chief of the *Hamburger Fremdenblatt*, Felix von Eckardt.[36]

Back to the manoeuvring in 1907: it seems that a month before the congress Warburg had already formed his opinion that Strzygowski could not remain the chair of the congress organisation. Strzygowski exhorted Warburg to send at long last the part of the annual report for which he was responsible, that is early Renaissance, festivals, etc.[37] Warburg countered that there were too few collaborators to do justice to reports from the specialist literature. Warburg added that he and his colleagues would only present a provisional survey of the specialist Renaissance literature.[38] Koetschau also complained about Strzygowski's blundering attacks;[39] he advised that 'the man from Graz' should be taught a lesson.[40] Warburg, on a trip to the Hartz Mountains, mentioned all of this to his wife. He took it on himself to calm the tempers and said he would speak to Koetschau at the meeting of the committee in Berlin.[41]

The congress in Darmstadt, from 23 to 26 September 1907, did not proceed smoothly (see figure 9.3). Warburg complained that he had to look after events

33 WIA, GC, Copy book 2, 119–120. Warburg to K. Koetschau, 15.8.1907. WIA, IV, 53.1., Warburg's notes in red on Strzygowski, J., 'Nationale Kunstgeschichte und internationale Kunstwissenschaft', 3.8.1907, 573–578.

34 WIA, GC, K. Koetschau to Warburg, 23.8.1907.

35 Strzygowski, J., 'Nationale Kunstgeschichte und internationale Kunstwissenschaft', 573–578, here 577.

36 WIA, GC, Warburg to F. von Eckardt, 10.9.1925. Felix von Eckardt, German journalist, 1866–1936. See also Chapter 2.

37 WIA, GC, J. Strzygowski to Warburg, 28.8.1907.

38 WIA, GC, Copy book 2, 140. Warburg to J. Strzygowski, 31.8.1907.

39 WIA, GC, K. Koetschau to Warburg, 3.9.1907.

40 WIA, GC, K. Koetschau to Warburg, 8.9.1907.

41 WIA, FC, Warburg to M. Warburg, 9.9.1907.

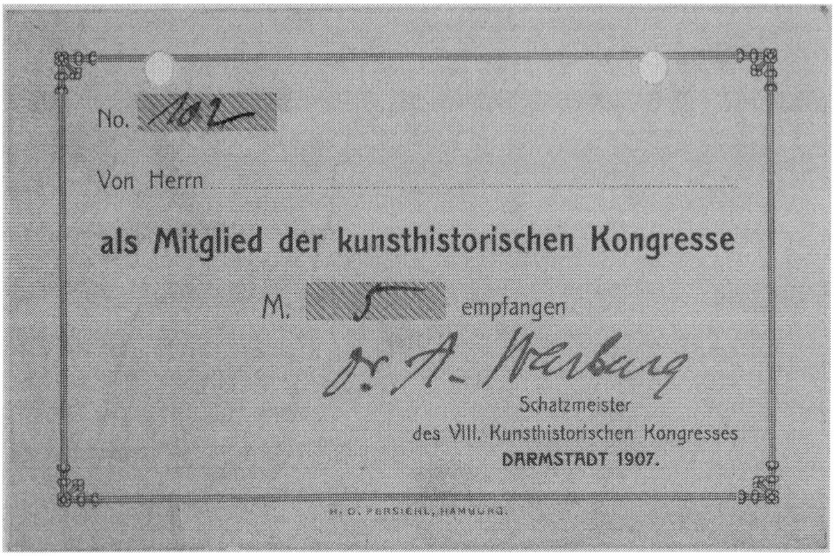
No. 102

Von Herrn

als Mitglied der kunsthistorischen Kongresse

M. 5 empfangen

Dr. A. Warburg

Schatzmeister

des VIII. Kunsthistorischen Kongresses

DARMSTADT 1907.

H. O. PERSIEHL, HAMBURG.

Figure 9.3 WIA, IV.53.3.1. Printed form to acknowledge payment for the Darmstadt congress fee in 1907, signed by Warburg as treasurer.

Source: © Photo: The Warburg Institute.

which should have been organised by others, mainly the members of the local committee – for instance preparing the seating plan and list of speakers – and that it was left to him to entertain the assembly. Strzygowski had by his 'dreadfully clumsy schoolmasterly inferior conduct' turned out to be an inadequate president. Otto Erich Deutsch, a student of Strzygowski's, confessed to Warburg that Strzygowski had never done anything like that so far.[42]

Nothing further about the course of the congress was reported in Warburg's correspondence. However, the post-congress work showed grave disagreements. Strzygowski had written a document on the classification of the annual reports and bibliography as the first tangible results of the congress, which he had sent to a number of scholars and which he hoped would be adopted by the constitutive meeting of the German Society for Studies of Art History.[43] Koetschau forwarded it to Warburg, but mentioned that while it contained a few good ideas, the overarching fundamental idea was still missing.[44] Warburg, who forwarded this document with other suggestions for a cataloguing system to Oskar Wulff, found that these

42 WIA, FC, Warburg to M. Warburg, 27.9.1907. Otto Erich Deutsch, art historian and musicologist, 1883–1967.

43 WIA, GC, J. Strzygowski to Warburg, 19.10.1907.

44 WIA, GC, K. Koetschau to Warburg, 25.10.1907.

suggestions were either alphabetical and simple or 'whimsically complicated'.[45] He sent his part of the congress report, the finance part, to Koetschau to shorten it and to correct all reports, in particular Strzygowski's.[46] Koetschau replied that it might be necessary to postpone the constitutive meeting of the German Society for Studies of Art History until the following year because of Althoff's illness,[47] which prompted Warburg to inform him that due to the quick reaction against antisemitic utterances by W. Schack, 'the preacher of hate', Warburg would be able to curb Schack's influence in Hamburg. Warburg promised to continue his work on the new committee, although he was annoyed by Strzygowski's talk of an 'imperial institute'.[48]

Strzygowski's resignation

On the same day Kautzsch wrote to Warburg that Strzygowski had resigned from his post as chair and asked who should become his successor. Kautzsch immediately ruled himself out as not diplomatic enough and not witty enough. He suggested Paul Clemen, although Clemen had strongly argued against an internationalisation of the congresses. Should a committee member talk to Clemen? Henry Thode could be taken into consideration, but the best thing would be to continue with the present members of the committee and to wait until the founding of the German Society for Studies of Art History.[49]

Despite everything which had gone beforehand, Warburg wanted to persuade Strzygowski to stay on the committee. He avowed he did not understand Strzygowski's arguments, but the congress needed him. He suggested steps the committee had to take to ensure Strzygowski stayed on the committee, particularly because the committee was a 'collegial council', whose president was the chair of the committee and not a supervisor.[50] In his reply Strzygowski showed himself impatient with Warburg, who, although apparently having received the shorthand transcripts of the congress minutes from Koetschau, only wanted to publish an article in *Allgemeine Zeitung* after the constitutive meeting of the German Society for Studies of Art History. He requested the shorthand transcripts of the minutes and Warburg's own draft on cataloguing systems;

45 WIA, GC, Copy book 2, 181. Warburg to Oskar Wulff, 31.10.1907. Oskar Wulff, German art historian, 1864–1946, worked in the Kaiser Friedrich Museum in Berlin.

46 WIA, GC, Copy book 2, 202, 203. Warburg to K. Koetschau, 17.11.1907.

47 WIA, GC, K. Koetschau to Warburg 19.11.1907.

48 WIA, GC, Copy book 2, 208. Warburg to K. Koetschau, 21.11.1907. Wilhelm Schack, German politician, 1869–1944. He was a board member of various national and economic associations, member from 1899 to 1907 of the Hamburg Citizenship and from November 1905 member of the German Reichstag for the German Social Party, also known as the German Social Antisemitic Party. Warburg, in mentioning Schack, who had nothing to do with art-historical developments but with antisemitic activities, showed his alertness and opposition to 'national' or 'imperial' attitudes. In Warburg's Diary, WIA, III.10.3, 65–73 there are no entries for Schack in 1907.

49 WIA, GC, R. Kautzsch to Warburg, 21.11.1907. Warburg, however, replied that Kautzsch would be a very competent president. WIA, GC, Copy book 2, 217–218. Warburg to R. Kautzsch, 25.11.1907. Paul Clemen, German art historian 1866–1947.

50 WIA, GC, Copy book 2, 213–215. Warburg to J. Strzygowski, 25.11.1907.

as for the rest, he could not accept Warburg's advice for Strzygowski's not resigning. Strzygowski admitted that he had done Koetschau wrong when claiming that he was postponing work on the congress report in favour of the German Society for Studies of Art History,[51] whereupon Warburg again suggested a meeting, as he found Strzygowski's complaints against Koetschau and procedural matters unjustified.[52] Warburg, as a member of the Bibliographical Commission, also asked Strzygowski, as chair of the Congress Committee and of the Bibliographical Commission, to call a meeting to discuss the work standards of this Commission; the best occasion would be at the inaugural meeting of the German Society for Studies of Art History.[53]

Gradually Warburg used more critical words in his communications when writing about Strzygowski. To Koetschau he called him 'subordinate', not exactly flattering for a leader.[54] In his letter to Otto Erich Deutsch he confessed that he did not understand Strzygowski – Warburg had suggested steps which would guarantee him an honourable resignation, but Strzygowski did not engage in these discussions and fixated only on details.[55] He found Kautzsch's report on Strzygowski's resignation[56] confusing and distrustful of the committee. Strzygowski feared a rapprochement between Koetschau and von Bode and suggested writing a conciliatory letter to von Bode.[57] Koetschau was angry about Strzygowski's 'dawdling', saying he had only offered to resign because he was not having any success and could no longer use the congress for his personal aims.[58]

Deutsch defended Strzygowski, stating that he had to be pedantic and not slapdash. It was up to Warburg to find an amicable solution, because he, Deutsch, could not really believe that Thode or Wölfflin would be better chairs than Strzygowski.[59] Strzygowski replied to Warburg, expressing how dissatisfied he had been and how he could not accept Warburg's suggestions. He had just about tolerated the 'surprise attack' during the congress in Darmstadt,[60] but now he had had enough and confirmed his decision to resign for a second time.[61] The correspondence intensified. Warburg

51 WIA, GC, J. Strzygowski to Warburg, 28.11.1907. Koetschau commissioned Warburg to write an article about the congress in the *Allgemeine Zeitung* newspaper (Munich) with the title 'Results of the 8th International Congress on the History of Art' ('Ergebnisse des 8. Internationalen kunsth.[istorischen] Kongresses'); however, Warburg's article is not extant, but an article with the same title was published by the four committee members in July 1908, see this Chapter, note 74.

52 WIA, GC, Copy book 2, 225–226. Warburg to J. Strzygowski, 30.11.1907.

53 WIA, GC, Copy book 2, 247. Warburg to J. Strzygowski, 14.12.1907.

54 WIA, GC, Copy book 2, 227–228, Warburg to K. Koetschau, 30.11.1907.

55 WIA, GC, Copybook 2, 229. Warburg to O.E. Deutsch, 30.11.1907.

56 WIA, GC, J. Strzygowski to Warburg, 3.12.1907.

57 WIA, GC, R. Kautzsch to Warburg, 1.12.1907.

58 WIA, GC, K. Koetschau to Warburg, 2.12.1907.

59 WIA, GC, O.E. Deutsch to Warburg, 3.12.1907. Heinrich Wölfflin, 1864–1945, art critic, art historian.

60 WIA, IV.53.2.27. Congress in Darmstadt, 1907. There is a reference to Strzygowski's shortcomings under the title 'Work of the section': In it Strzygowski's method as the chair was termed 'irrelevant'. On a separate sheet: 'The system is supposed to emerge from the specifics of the congress and the congress is not supposed to be squeezed into the system'.

61 WIA, GC, Copy book 2, 255, 256, 257. Warburg to Paul Warburg, 18.12.1907.

wrote to the committee members and suggested a meeting with Strzygowski.[62] He then informed Strzygowski that Koetschau was busy getting the congress papers printed and stated that Strzygowski's attitude – in neither replying to Warburg's suggestions nor forwarding them to the other committee members – would have consequences.[63] Kautzsch agreed to a meeting with Strzygowski,[64] but Warburg thought it no longer necessary. He characterised Strzygowski as an 'inflated loner', without any 'sensibility', 'distrustful', a 'confusion monger', who was not trustworthy when he, 'under the influence of the Orient', started to insist on authority.[65]

Shortly afterwards Warburg wrote to Deutsch again about Strzygowski's conduct: in Warburg's eyes, he could go far if only he would give up his vanity.[66] In a private communication to his brother Paul Warburg in New York he painted a picture of the difficulties in the committee work and the need for Strzygowski's removal from the committee.[67] What annoyed Warburg was the fact that Strzygowski asked for speedy work on the transcriptions of the shorthand notes, but did not forward correspondence: 'To begin with he plays the president and then leaves the work to everybody else! Polish man!' Warburg confessed that he needed a few days to recover from Strzygowski's most recent announcement, his second letter of resignation.[68] Warburg had requested he return all his letters, as they would be archived with all the papers of the art history congress. He also asked him whether he would remain in the Bibliographical Commission if Warburg withdrew from it.[69] Kautzsch sent more explanations on the aftermath of Strzygowski's complaints: Strzygowski, possibly because he had accused Koetschau of conspiring with von Bode and not sending off the transcripts of the congress proceedings, had written to von Bode that he had no option but to resign. He did so in order to trap Koetschau, who in turn wrote to Strzygowski, which was proof to Strzygowski of a conspiracy on the part of the museum experts against the university teachers.[70]

Strzygowski returned Warburg's letters and confirmed that he had resigned from the chairmanship of the committee.[71] It seems that no further letters to the members of the committee were forthcoming, because Warburg commented angrily that the 'Polack' had not even replied.[72] At a committee meeting in Frankfurt in March 1908 his resignation was accepted.[73]

62 WIA, GC, Copy book 2, 236. Warburg to R. Kautzsch, 5.12.1907.
63 WIA, GC, Copy book 2, 238. Warburg to J. Strzygowski, 7.12.1907.
64 WIA, GC, R. Kautzsch to Warburg, 7.12.1907.
65 WIA, GC, Copy book 2, 240. Warburg to R. Kautzsch, 10.12.1907.
66 WIA, GC, Copy book 2, 243. Warburg to O.E. Deutsch, date illegible, probably 12.12.1907.
67 WIA, GC, Copy book 2, 255, 256, 257. Warburg to Paul Warburg, 18.12.1907. Paul M. Warburg, German-American investment banker, 1868–1932.
68 WIA, GC, Copy book 2, 272. Warburg to K. Koetschau, 7.1.1908.
69 WIA, GC, Copy book 2, 273, 274. Warburg to J. Strzygowski, 7.1.1908.
70 WIA, GC, R. Kautzsch to Warburg, 9.1.1908.
71 WIA, GC, J. Strzygowski to Warburg, 9.1.1908.
72 WIA, GC, Copy book 2, 297. Warburg to K. Koetschau, 2.2.1908. Here we see Warburg's frustration in his use of the pejorative term 'Polack' instead of 'Polish man' as previously.
73 WIA, IV.53.3.5. Draft manuscript, 8.3.1908, not signed.

Finally, the topics discussed at the Darmstadt congress were published in *Kunstchronik* only in July 1908, signed by four committee members. Strzygowski's signature was missing; Adolph Goldschmidt signed in his stead.[74]

Two years later, Warburg wrote to Gustav Glück in Vienna and, among other matters, asked him for news on Strzygowski – 'I cannot stand him'[75] – and Glück told him that Strzygowski was busily writing newspaper articles, which was not fitting for a professor, and was 'being shunned to the best of everybody's ability'.[76] Warburg avowed that he was not surprised by Strzygowski's behaviour and lack of character.[77] In a letter on the same day Warburg reprimanded Koetschau for still not having published the congress proceedings, which, however, was not as bad as not having replied to questions about the layout and the publishing of the missing annual reports. Warburg wanted to avoid Strzygowski laughing about the ineptitude of the leadership.[78]

Further remarks turn up scattered throughout the correspondence. When Strzygowski's name came up in 1911 in connection with the vacancy of a chair in Göttingen University, Warburg explained that he would be prepared to give information on his suitability or lack of suitability for the post.[79] In 1912 it was Fritz Saxl who told Warburg that Strzygowski had been the only professor in Vienna who did not give the highest mark to Saxl's doctoral dissertation, so that Saxl was not awarded the 'sub auspiciis imperatoris' accolade.[80] In the midst of World War I Strzygowski wrote to Warburg that he was sorry he had never been invited to lecture in Hamburg, because he would be able to tell the Hamburg scholars many a thing.[81] When Saxl was employed as deputy director of the Warburg library by the Warburg family in Hamburg in 1920, Saxl proved himself conciliatory. In order to explain Warburg's writings and work to colleagues like Max Dvořak, Saxl wrote the article 'The Survival of Classical Antiquity: Introducing the Warburg Library'[82] and devoted the first chapter, 'The Warburg Library', in the newly founded series *Vorträge der*

74 WIA, IV.53.3.4. Congress in Darmstadt, 1907. Goldschmidt et al., 'Ergebnisse des VII. [sic] internationalen Kunsthistorischen Kongresses zu Darmstadt'. The article in *Kunstchronik*, 17 July 1908, 1–2, simply reported the topics addressed at the congress, while Deutsch, O. E., 'Kunstblatt. Der internationale Kunsthistorikerkongreß in Darmstadt' cited the names of the lecturers and the titles of their lectures, 7 December 1907.

75 Österreichische Nationalbibliothek, 1095/12–2, Warburg to G. Glück, 24.1.1910. Gustav Glück, Austrian art historian, museum director, 1871–1952.

76 WIA, GC, G. Glück to Warburg, 26.2.1910.

77 Österreichische Nationalbibliothek, 1095/12–3, Warburg to G. Glück, 7.3.1910.

78 WIA, GC, Copy book 3, 328. Warburg to K. Koetschau, 7.3.1910.

79 WIA, GC, Copy book 4, 53. Warburg to Lili Du Bois-Reymond, friend of the family, author and editor, 26.5.1911.

80 WIA, GC, Saxl to Warburg, 20.7.1912. This accolade, meaning 'under the auspices of the Emperor', was a rare title bestowed by the Austro-Hungarian Emperor only on students who graduated with distinction. Saxl's statement was not correct, however, because the average marks from grammar school reports were also used to establish eligibility for the award. I thank Erika Klingler for this information, see Chapter 7.

81 WIA, GC, J. Strzygowski to Warburg, 22.11.1917.

82 Saxl, F., 'Das Nachleben der Antike: zur Einführung in die Bibliothek Warburg', 244–247. Max Dvořak, Czech-Austrian historian and curator of monuments, 1874–1921.

Bibliothek Warburg ('Lectures of the Warburg Library') to the same topic.[83] He sent an offprint to Strzygowski and invited him to lecture in Hamburg in the Warburg library.[84] However, Saxl's lecture report to Warburg did not mince words:

> Strzygowski was here, he was very interested in your library; but his lecture in the evening on 'Revolution in art history' was so bad that I was cross with the man. This was why I did not report the whole affair to you. An obnoxious type!

It went without saying that the lecture was not published in the *Vorträge* series.[85]

Warburg's commitment to the art history congresses and his experience with the chair of the committee, as with other colleagues, is a case study of two different directions. The two key players were too different to collaborate properly; they had too-different sensibilities. Whether it was Warburg's bureaucratic approach which clashed with Strzygowski's autocratic tendencies might be too general a question. The details of two people being incompatible when supposed to work together exercised the minds of other committee members as well. Certainly, the chair was unable to cope with the committee members: he, as an academic teacher, faced with looking after organisational matters which were normally done by somebody else, was overchallenged. On the other hand, Warburg was a powerfully eloquent speaker and writer, who could deliver extra precise or even exaggerated phrasing in his correspondence. Temperamentally they were contrary, academically they did not appreciate each other particularly well. Sometimes Warburg's stinging remarks went beyond the professional tone and hurt the recipient personally. Although Warburg was not a professor then, he behaved like professors frequently did: he was always right, which at times alienated people. Strzygowski remained a controversial scholar. The volume which was published on the occasion of his 150th birthday, *Von Biala nach Wien*, in 2015 presents a very rich collection of chapters on his life and the history of the reception of his works. He was a man of his time, an excellent rhetorician whose research and publications were ideologically and politically determined by stressing German and conservative views. Mathias F. Müller called him a person who dazzles, blinds others, an impostor, somebody who ultimately failed.[86] Both Warburg and Strzygowski tried, for the first time in their lives, to steer a grand organisational event and on this occasion, Warburg proved to be the scholar with the greater support and vision.

83 Saxl, F., 'Die Bibliothek Warburg und ihr Ziel', 1–10.

84 WIA, GC, Saxl to J. Strzygowski, 11.7.1922.

85 WIA, GC, Saxl to Warburg, 13.11.1922.

86 Müller, M.F., 'Die positivistisch-politische Kunstgeschichtsschreibung von Josef Strzygowski. Eine kritische Analyse seines chauvinistischen Denkens', 308–320, here 318.

10

BRINGING LIGHT INTO DARKNESS. ABY WARBURG AND FRITZ SAXL IN CONVERSATION ON MITHRAS[1]

Introduction

Warburg's and Saxl's research interests intersected in a number of areas, among them ancient religions and astrology. As early as 1910 the Viennese student Saxl, reading art history for one term in Berlin, found his way to Warburg in Hamburg to talk to him about astrological images and Warburg shared with him his ideas about the peregrinations of ancient images.

In the early 1920s Saxl, by then acting director of the Warburg Library in Hamburg, continued to pursue the topic of how in late antiquity art and images melded into early Christian presentations of the new faith. In Hamburg in 1922, for his postdoctoral qualification, the so-called 'Habilitation', Saxl presented his research on the images of gods of antiquity in the late Renaissance.[2] In a lecture to the Religionswissenschaftliche Gesellschaft ('religious studies society') in Berlin, also in 1922, he spoke about images of Oriental and Greek mystery cults[3] and, notably, in his inaugural lecture at Hamburg University in 1922 he concentrated on 'The Dialogue in Christian Art'.[4] In the article 'Early Christianity and late Paganism in their artistic expressions'[5] he discussed three major research topics: firstly, the pictorial presentation of dialogue in Christian art, especially the dialogue

1 Originally published in McEwan, D., 'Far luce nel buio. Aby Warburg e Fritz Saxl discutono su Mitra', 119–132. (This is an Italian translation in 2016 of the original English article in 2015, McEwan, D., 'Bringing Light into Darkness. Aby Warburg and Fritz Saxl in Conversation on Mithras', 27–29, here updated.)

2 Saxl, F., *Antike Götter in der Spätrenaissance. Ein Freskenzyklus und ein Discorso des Jacopo Zucchi.*

3 WIA, GC, O. Dempwolff to Saxl, 24.5.1922. Dempwolff forwarded the minutes of the meeting of the Religionswissenschaftliche Gesellschaft, Berlin on 11 May 1922 with a summary of Saxl's lecture 'Griechisches und Orientalisches in Kultbildern hellenistischer Mysterienreligionen und des frühen Christentums'. Dempwolff's view was that the individualising aspect of Christianity triumphed over other salvation mystery religions. Otto Dempwolff, German anthropologist, 1871–1938.

4 Saxl's lecture 'Der Dialog in der christlichen Kunst' was held on 26 July 1922.

5 Saxl, F., 'Frühes Christentum und spätes Heidentum in ihren künstlerischen Ausdrucksformen', 63–121.

DOI: 10.4324/9781003169024-13

of philosophers; secondly, Greek and Oriental influences and expressions in cult images of Hellenistic mystery religions, Mithraism and Christianity; and thirdly, how the idea of the king of the world was presented in images.

He pursued his research into mystery cults further, in particular Babylonian and Iranian cosmogonies and the Christian creation story, in order to understand the origin of image types. He corresponded with a number of experts on the history of religion, on comparative religion, on early Christianity, and exchanged with them his views on images and practices of Mithraism.[6] Mithraic cult images show the birth of Mithras from a rock, the sun chariot, the bull-slaying scene, a lion-headed figure entwined by a serpent, the meal of the Blessed, i.e. the banquet of the initiates with Sol/Helios as well as the twelve scenes of the zodiac surrounding the central motifs. As written sources of the cultic practices or the theology of Mithraism are nearly non-existent, it is a matter of explaining the images, their arrangement, their development, either painted or sculpted, in order to find meaning in them. Even today there is no firm body of evidence of the precise meaning of a number of images, so that Saxl's interpretation remains one of a number of possible interpretations. Saxl commented in a letter to Professor Franz Boll, a friend of Warburg's and Saxl's, on the research into Assyrian seal cylinders by Otto Weber. There he had found images which paralleled the representations on Mithras reliefs of the bull sitting in a hut; for the first time, it would be possible to demonstrate in effigy how Oriental thought flowed into Occidental thought.[7]

Warburg and Gertrud Bing, the deputy librarian of the KBW, stayed for many months in Italy in 1928 to 1929. The exchange of letters between Warburg and Saxl permits us a close look at the research work and interests of both scholars at that time. Warburg, surrounded by his books and pictures in the Palace Hotel in Rome, was engaged in his work on the *Mnemosyne Atlas*, a huge collection of images to document the movement of images, of ideas, of concepts.[8] Mithras and Mithraea were included into this collection in Table 8, 'Auffahrt zur Sonne' ('Ascent to the sun').[9] It

6 In addition to Dempwolff, Hugo Greßmann, German biblical scholar, 1877–1927; Richard Reitzenstein, German classicist, 1861–1931; Bernhard Schweitzer, German classical archaeologist, 1892–1966: Franz Boll, German classicist, 1867–1924; Valentin Müller, German classical archaeologist, 1889–1945; Robert Eisler, Austrian polymath, 1882–1949. Saxl had discussed the Mithras topic with Erwin Panofsky for many years and Panofsky, in fact, read the final drafts of Saxl's lecture on 'The Ascension of Mithras and the Ascension of Christ' in 1929. Erwin Panofsky, German-American art historian, 1892–1968.

7 WIA, GC, Saxl to F. Boll, 25.11.1920. Weber, O., *Altorientalische Siegelbilder*. Otto Weber, German librarian, 1877–1928.

8 Photographs pinned on mobile walls were the vehicles used by Warburg to present images related by form or contents. This method gave Warburg the opportunity to arrange and re-arrange images in new sequences to make visible the development of an image, its transformation, metamorphoses and connections. See Warnke and Brinck, *Aby Warburg (1866–1929). Gesammelte Schriften* and Ohrt and Heil, *Aby Warburg: Bilderatlas Mnemosyne*.

9 Warnke and Brink, *Aby Warburg (1866–1929)*, 28–29.

was clear to Warburg and Saxl that without an in-depth study of the Mithras mysteries the fight between paganism and Christianity could not be understood.[10]

Exchange of research findings

In 1929, Saxl, juggling his duties as librarian and academic teacher in Hamburg, was revising his 'Early Christianity' article of 1923, which he thought needed updating. He wanted to respond to recent scholarship to show how, or discuss whether, pagan and Christian architecture were related.[11] Prompted by Warburg's request to send him the book by the German archaeologist Friedrich Behn on the Mithras shrine in Dieburg in Southern Hesse, Germany,[12] Saxl mentioned the surprising, or not so surprising, synchronicity in Warburg's request with Saxl's own renewed Mithras studies. He went on to state what interested him most, apart from the 'hundreds of unsolved problems of Mithras research': the reception of classical antiquity by the mystery cults in late antiquity. He saw examples of the reception of classical topics into Christianity in the baptism of Christ, which followed the model of the Eleusinian initiation rites and the presentation of Christ, which could be traced back to the presentation of Orpheus. The question regarding architecture was: which of the new religions used solutions from classical antiquity? Saxl found the images in the basilica-type underground building in Viale Manzoni in front of the Porta Maggiore in Rome as foreign to Christianity as the Mithraic, Isis and Attis cult images. These traditions gave priority to naturalistic elements and this idea did not seem to Saxl to have entered Christianity. However, there was one tradition which had accepted the same symbols as Christianity: Buddhism, when Buddha was represented as Rhetor, that is, as philosopher, talking to his disciples, or when the pictorial language for the death of Buddha were the same as that shown on reliefs of the lament for the death of Christ or the death of Mary. In short, the principle of selection had been effective – different religious currents had selected different symbols or images for similar cultic practices.[13]

At the same time, apart from the Mithras research shared by both scholars, the exhibition project on the *History of Astrology and Astronomy* in the newly built Planetarium in Hamburg was keenly discussed. Warburg suggested frequently that models should be made to illustrate how humankind grappled with understanding its place in the cosmos. This could – in Warburg's view – best be done by replicas of cult places, like a Chinese temple of the heavens, a Mithras sanctuary, the

10 WIA, FC, Warburg to Mary Warburg, 29.3.1929.

11 WIA, GC, Saxl to F. Drexel, 7.1.1929. Friedrich Drexel, German archaeologist, 1885–1930.

12 Behn, Friedrich, *Das Mithrasheiligtum zu Dieburg*. German archaeologist, 1883–1970.

13 WIA, GC, Saxl to Warburg, 18.2.1929. Despite Saxl's enthusiasm for Buddha in this letter, Buddha was mentioned only once by him in Saxl, F., *Mithras: Typengeschichtliche Untersuchungen*, 107, when he simply stated that both the image of Christ and the image of Buddha had its origin in the image of the pagan philosopher.

Sphaera Barbarica in the Salone in Padua, an Egyptian grave chamber, etc.[14] For the Mithras sanctuary he wanted to commission a model of the two-sided relief in red sandstone in the Mithraeum in Dieburg (see figures 10.1 and 10.2).[15] This stone was particularly interesting not only for its iconography, but also for the fact that a hole was carved out in the middle of the lowest register of the stone.

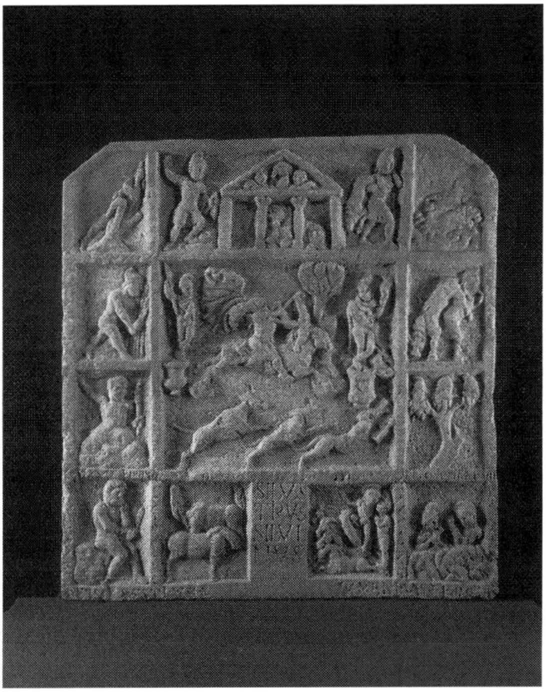

Figure 10.1 The Mithras stone in Dieburg, front view.

Source: © public domain: www.tertullian.org/rpearse/mithras/display.php?page=cimrm1247

14 Cf. WIA, GC, Warburg to Saxl, 11.2.1929 and WIA, GC, Warburg to Saxl, W. Gundel and E. Wind, 26.3.1929. The exhibition was opened on 15 April 1930 in the Hamburg Planetarium.

15 Red sandstone with carvings on front and back. Figure 10.1 shows the front view of the stone: in the centre, a hunting scene with three dogs and Mithras, in a cape, on a horse and shooting an arrow, and Cautes and Cautopates with torches. Surrounding this central scene are episodes from the cosmic and terrestrial life of Mithras: his birth from a stone; creation of water and fire; hunting and killing of the bull; Mithras' struggle with Sol; the crowning of Sol by Mithras; the meal of the blessed served on the slain body of the bull; their ascent to Heaven. At the bottom is an opening for an implement, a pivot, with which to turn the stone slab around and show the other side to the worshippers. Figure 10.2 shows the back view of the stone: Phaeton requests the solar chariot from Sol; Sol descends from his throne and receives Mithras/Phaeton. Opposite him is a woman, personifying summer. Behind Sol are three women, representing from left to right autumn, spring and winter. At the bottom is a head, Caelus ('sky'), in the space created by two figures holding

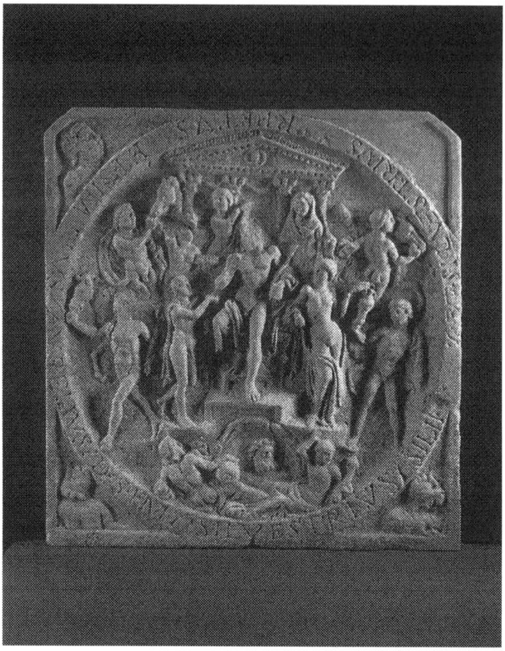

Figure 10.2 The Mithras stone in Dieburg, back view.

Source: © public domain: www.tertullian.org/rpearse/mithras/display.php?page=cimrm1247 (accessed June 2022).

According to Warburg, it might have been the place into which a pivot or swivel pin could be inserted to turn the stone around in order to show the onlooker the other side.[16] He asked Saxl's view, what he thought of the pivot or swivel pin, and whether it was permissible to conclude that initiates were first shown the relief side with the fall of Phaeton and afterwards the other side, with Mithras' victorious chase and his conquest of the sun god.[17]

In the spring of 1929, the exchange of research queries and research findings on Mithraism intensified. Greek and Oriental influences in cult images in mystery religions took up a large part of the discussion. The image of Mithras killing the primordial bull, thereby releasing the seeds of creation, was well-known. Less

garlands, on the left Oceanus, on the right a female figure, possibly Tellus. In the corners of the relief are the gods of the winds.

16 WIA, GC, Warburg to Saxl, W. Gundel, E. Wind, 26.3.1929. Also WIA, GC, Warburg to Saxl, 17.4.1929.

17 WIA, GC, Warburg to Saxl, 2.5.1929. Warburg was sure that his discovery about the stone with the two reliefs and the hole at the bottom, for inserting a handle to turn the stone from one side to the other, would stand up to research and went as far as asking Saxl whether he had credited Warburg for the solution to the riddle of the hole in the Dieburg reliefs. WIA, GC, Warburg to Saxl, 4.6.1929.

well-known was the image of Nike – the Greek goddess of victory – killing the bull, which in Saxl's understanding could be traced back to the fights of the centaurs: when Nike grabs the snout of the bull, it correlates to gripping the head of the centaur. The motif of bracing one's knee against the falling opponent, of grabbing his head with the left hand and striking him with the right hand, was interpreted as the 'basic motif of Greek cruelty'. However, this motif – like the Mithras motif of killing the bull – harked back to Oriental motifs. Equally important was the fact that the sacrifice, the killing of the bull, had to be shown to take place in a natural landscape. In this respect, the scenes on Mithras reliefs strikingly resembled Alexandrian fountain reliefs. Thus the cult of nature in which nymphs play a large part, with grottoes as their cultic sites, found expression in the Mithraic cult.[18] Saxl regarded the cult in Italy as being more bucolic and less didactic than in northern Europe. The reason for this was that Mithras monuments in Italy were basically monuments showing the killing of the bull and did not fulfil the didactic use of the myth.[19]

Only three days later, Saxl sent observations on a relief of Mithras tauroktonos (tauroctony, or the slaughter of the bull) of the usual type in the Palazzo dei Conservatori in Rome, originally found on the Esquiline Hill, Rome, which had been discussed by F. Cumont and H. S. Jones. Saxl wondered whether the two men standing at the lower right at an altar and holding a knife showed a Persian fraternisation scene, a blood brotherhood, and whether the semi-circular marking on the body of the bull might present a half moon. The sculpture also featured Sol (the sun) in the upper left, Luna (the moon) in the upper right, and the dog, serpent and scorpion. If his interpretation proved right, he would have documentary evidence that the scene of the killing of the bull meant the fight between sun and moon.[20]

The KBW in Hamburg had a monthly lecture programme; an invitation to give a lecture there was sought-after and prestigious. Occasionally the proposed lecturer had to cancel and arrangements for a replacement had to be made. Arduino Colasanti[21] had been invited to talk about 'Giovanni Pisano and his encyclopaedia of images' on 27 April 1929 but cancelled his lecture two weeks beforehand. As Saxl was in the midst of his Mithras research he volunteered to give a lecture on 'The Ascension of Mithras and the Ascension of Christ' ('Die Himmelfahrt des Mithras und Christi Himmelfahrt') without further ado.[22] Warburg, despite his quip to Saxl that he 'gives too much sugar to his black horse' or over-interprets Mithras images,[23] was excited. For him, it went without saying that Mithras was a legend

18 WIA, GC, Saxl to Warburg, 19.3.1929.

19 WIA, GC, Saxl to Warburg, 22.3.1929.

20 WIA, GC, Saxl to Warburg, 26.3.1929; Cumont, F., *Die Mysterien des Mithra*, 88–89; Jones, H.S., *A Catalogue of the Ancient Sculptures Preserved in the Municipal Collections of Rome*, 4. Franz Cumont, Belgian archaeologist, 1868–1947; Henry Stuart Jones, British historian, 1867–1939.

21 Arduino Colasanti, Italian art historian, 1877–1935.

22 WIA, GC, Saxl to Warburg, 16.4.1929. Giovanni Pisano, Italian sculptor, c. 1250–1314.

23 WIA, GC, Warburg to Saxl, 3.4.1929.

of salvation: 'But who is saved by whom?' Warburg gave his opinion that the carvings on the back of the stone relief in Dieburg showed the legend of the fall of the driver of the sun chariot, Phaeton, the son of the sun god Helios. Mithras, the bull killer, somehow managed to liberate Phaeton and appointed him in turn to become the 'real driver of the chariot of light'.[24] This interpretation was also Saxl's view.[25]

Saxl's lecture report

It was only natural that Saxl sent a summary of his lecture in a letter to Warburg. The lecture text is not extant, if ever it existed. The following letter is therefore the most complete version of Saxl's thoughts:

> Dear Professor,
>
> Thank goodness, the lecture is over and once again I start to reply to letters and to do everything a librarian has to do; but the last week I have done nothing else but only attended to blessed Mithras.
>
> He is blessed, indeed, or better, holy, because he occupies a strange in-between position, as he is first the messenger of Helios and then conquers him and become Helios himself. I hope that with Panofsky's assistance I have left behind the time when I found it impossible to interpret the reliefs consistently and with them the myth. You see, one can get quite far in interpreting the myth without Cumont's[26] fertile imagination, if one enlists the myth of Heracles as prototype. Preceding his myth is a cosmogony, beginning with chaos and ending with the fight of Zeus with the giants. Without doubt, these things were called chaos, Zeus and giants in the Occident. The cosmogony was Greek, even if it represented – perhaps only partly – Iranian thought in Greek form. In essence, this is how Cumont saw it, a disguised Persian scene only instead of a Greek one. However, I believe that in this time of syncretism one has to stress the Greek element much more than the Oriental.
>
> Be that as it may, what followed after this cosmogony was the next act, the birth of Mithras from a rock, then the travels into the land of Helios, where he collects the fruits of the tree (of knowledge) – the apples of the Hesperides. Thereafter he reaches the land of the moon and there he finds the bull of light, the carrier of the seed and of the light. Mithras brings him down to earth, where he sacrifices him at the command of Helios. And now, the main difference I have with Cumont, but which leads me to believe that the story becomes intelligible, is the following: when I say to myself, if this scorpion on earth devours the seed of the bull, as it

24 WIA, GC, Warburg to Saxl, 21.4.1929.

25 Saxl, F., *Mithras*, 78. Saxl further explained that the reliefs in other mithraea on the Danube showed the creation of the world, the entrapment of light by darkness, baptism, ascent to heaven and the banquet, that is, the symbolic acts of Mithras through which he becomes the sun god and through which he brings certain salvation.

26 Cumont, F., *Die Mysterien des Mithra*.

is shown on all monuments, then it means that in this act of creation the light is brought down into the dark cave on earth and mixes there with darkness. It is no coincidence that the early Christian opponents of Mithras railed against the view that this sun god accomplishes the deed in a dark cave on earth. But this, indeed, is supposed to be the unfathomable mystery, that the creation of the world means the mixing of light and dark.

Until this point Mithras is the agent of the sun god, merely the hero who, following the example of Theseus or Heracles, has to catch and kill a bull; but now he takes up the fight with Helios, baptises him, ascends with him to heaven and celebrates with him the meal of the Blessed. In the same way apotheosis and the meal in heaven stand at the end of Heracles' career. Now, this Mithras is a redeemer god, who again ascends with the human being from earth to heaven, as he has ascended to heaven with Helios.

The development is also easily explained if looked at from a genetic point of view. In the Iranian context Ormuzd[27] creates the primeval bull in the first break of the fight with darkness. In the second fight this primeval bull is killed by evil and Ormuzd can do nothing else but administer a narcotic to soothe the dying. The soul of the bull ascends to heaven in order to complain bitterly. However, after Ormuzd has made it clear that he cannot avert evil, the soul consents and plants sprout from the dead body of the bull.

Here, in fact, evil kills the bull, the good element only drugs the bull; and it is now that the myth travels to the West, where Mithras becomes identical to the sun god. In the Avesta[28] Mithras is only the god of the wide pastures, a military god together with lighting, which gives power and might and which gives the soul the power of resurrection after death.

In the Babylonian context Mithras becomes identical to the sun god and here he is also under the spell of a religiosity, which presented the killing of the bull as one of the main topics in sculpture just as in literature, where Gilgamesh kills the bull of heaven.

The two motifs, the connection with the sun god and with the myth of the hero killing the bull, enter the Iranian cosmology and travel further west. Now the myth of the deeds of Mithras reaches an area where the deeds of Heracles were alive, where Heracles was identical with the sun, where his deeds took place in the zodiac; new traits are now added, like the travels to the Hesperides. Most importantly, this religion has to face up to the religion of Helios. In this way the myth is born which first comprises the motif of the bull of light, who is brought down to earth and thereby creation comes about, secondly presents the killing of the sun by a hero (instead of by evil) and finally thirdly the strange re-duplication of these two presentations of Helios. In this way the myth of the killing of the bull is stuck onto the myth of the Persian sun god who first fights

27 Also known as Ahura Mazda, the god or higher divinity in the old Iranian religion.

28 The Avesta are the sacred texts of Zoroastrianism, in the Avestan language.

the Greek myth and then gets reconciled with it: together they ascend to heaven in the solar chariot.

The points of contact with Christianity are astonishingly manifold. Christ is the sun of salvation, god from the very beginning, who by command of his father (dove) descends to earth (in the Mithras cult the messenger of Helios is the raven), enters into suffering and returns to heaven. In the same way Mithras descends with the bull from the realm of the sun to earth, where he has to kill the bull and where he links him to evil, where he enters into matter and later ascends to heaven.

The recurring motifs with the ascension into heaven are always the three pictorial topoi: baptism, ascension and meal of the Blessed.

But here is also the essential difference between the symbols. In the cosmological religion of Mithras, the heaven of light has to sacrifice the bull of the moon in order to perform the creation. Mithras is a god of light in this Iranian world in which evil is divinely strong, as is goodness. He is a god mediating between light and darkness. The element of the light, which Mithras brings down and which is in the seed of the bull, is putrefied here below by the poisonous scorpion. In this way creation contains the mixture of darkness and light, but Mithras becomes the sun god and helps the human being after death to lead parts of light up to total light.

In Mithraism the suffering is the creation. In the old Iranian understanding, the spirit of the bull sacrifices itself consciously: there the spirit is the divine voluntary suffering. In the Greek-Roman understanding it is hunted and suffers death reluctantly. The hero, who fulfils the sacrifice und thereby creates the fruit, is the god of cultivation, not the bull. This god of cultivation fulfils the sacrifice in a divine feast. He becomes the sun god, the light symbol of power and fertility, the symbol of the eternal equal exchange of light and darkness, of birth and resurrection.

In Christianity the god is he who sacrifices himself on earth; he takes on the suffering of the creatures on earth and thereby redeems the world.

In the life of Mithras, his ascension into heaven as the sun god follows the descent into the cave on earth and the accomplishment of the creative sacrifice. Christ unites both in himself: he is Mithras the god as he is himself the suffering creation.

I think that everything here is logically as well as historically explicable from the types of images, so that my interpretation could be correct.

Panofsky has helped me surprisingly much. I had all the elements covered, but then it was a question of establishing the sequence of images. Panofsky with his unerring logic has helped me and in one evening has achieved it superbly. It is a fact that at this moment he is, not only in Hamburg but possibly anywhere in the world, the only person who has a feeling for the history of an image and the history of ideas and can combine both. . . .29

29 WIA, GC, Saxl to Warburg, 30.4.1929. An untitled and undated collection of papers, pp. 16, first line 'Ausgehen von einem Bild des erhöhten Herrn', is kept in WIA, Saxl Cupboard, for the images used in this talk. Helios, sun god in Greek mythology; Heracles, divine hero in Greek mythology; Hesperides, nymphs of the evenings in Greek mythology; Theseus, mythical king and founder-hero of Athens; Gilgamesh, semi-mythical king in Mesopotamia.

This summary skilfully tied together a number of research findings and topics discussed between Warburg and Saxl. Warburg by return of post congratulated Saxl and addressed him with the title of a figure found on many Mithraic cult images, the 'Dadophoros' or torch bearer, who illuminated the way into the grotto so graphically and convincingly. Surely nobody in Hamburg was sorry not to hear Colasanti, 'the fascist fanfare'![30]

Many of the lectures in the KBW were published in the *Vorträge* series. However, Saxl did not think that his Mithras lecture would fit. He had formed the opinion that he should rather write a new article with good photographs from the important Mithraic monuments in Ostia, Vienna, Osterburken[31] and Neuenheim.[32] More importantly, he was convinced that some of the views he held previously, for instance on the Mithraic ascent into heaven, did not play as great a part in contrast to the title of his lecture.[33]

Two weeks after Saxl's lecture, Warburg visited the subterranean Mithraeum in Capua. It made a deep impression on him.[34] He found the experience of going down into the dark space below street level 'inhumanly interesting' and forthwith wanted to scrap the architectural models of Chinese and Babylonian cult structures for the Planetarium exhibition in Hamburg and concentrate on models of Mithras and the Salone in Padua.[35] Saxl's 'expedition to the unknown sources of heliotropism' – originally or mainly a botanical term for the motion of plants in response to the direction and stimulus of the sun, but used here for explaining the Mithraic creation myth, flowing from heaven to earth and back to heaven – stunned him. Warburg supplied in great detail his explanations of the paintings, not sculptures, which he had seen in Capua, paintings of Mithras killing the bull and a woman in a chariot drawn by two wild asses. The expedition had the strongest impact on Warburg; he ranked it amid the greatest results of his time in Italy.[36]

Saxl attested the woman in a chariot drawn by two wild asses in the Mithraeum in Capua, as described by Warburg, as being Luna, whose chariot was often shown as being pulled down into the abyss. The catacombs or hypogeum of the Aurelii in Viale Manzoni were 'fairly unambiguously' not Christian; the images there were the product of an interesting interpretation of Homer by a writer of allegories.[37] In short, he knew his subject and understood the messages in their visual languages. Overall, Saxl, in his lecture report to Arturo Farinelli, summarised his research progress – he mentioned that he had written 50 pages – and said that he could attempt to produce convincing explanations: Mithras is called down from heaven

30 WIA, GC, Warburg to Saxl, 2.5.1929.
31 In the Neckar/Odenwald District of Baden-Württemberg, Germany.
32 A district of the city of Heidelberg, in southwest Germany.
33 WIA, GC, Saxl to Warburg, 2.5.1929.
34 WIA, GC, Warburg to F. Hermanin, 22.5.1929. The visit took place on 17.5.1929.
35 WIA, GC, Warburg to Saxl, n.d., after 17.5.1929.
36 WIA, GC, Warburg to KBW, 21.5.1929.
37 WIA, GC, Saxl to Warburg, 27.5.1929.

to the cave in the earth in order to create the world by killing the bull. Mithras is the hero; he overcomes the sun god and becomes a second Helios who ascends to the heaven with Helios. The myth is the model for the fate awaiting humans – the soul is forced down from heaven to the earth, but in the end, with the help of God, it can get back to heaven again.[38] Or, in Warburg's words, 'You were killed and you were awakened to life again'.[39]

And so the arguments accumulated, going to and fro; some were discarded, others were developed further. Panofsky advised him to lengthen the text and Saxl agreed as he himself was not yet satisfied with his 'coffee house product'.[40] Warburg urged him to send the research findings to Teubner publishers right away.[41] Lengthening the research text resulted in Saxl's book *Mithras*, which he published in 1931.[42]

After Warburg's return from Italy to Hamburg in June 1929 the correspondence dies down, only to resume when Saxl spent some time in London in the autumn of 1929. Saxl once more identified the two main theses of his work: first, that the origin of the representation of Mithras in the cave can be found in the image of the grottoes of the nymphs, and second, that the altar tablets with their additional scenes on the sides of the altar offer something fundamentally new, which is related to Christianity – pictures of the life of the saviour. It is no coincidence that there are no Greek images of the life of Zeus. Mithras thereby becomes, on the one hand, more human, as close as Jesus, but through his ascent into heaven becomes, on the other hand, as distant as Christ. Saxl was certain that the whole idea of the ascent of the soul had *ex post* been read into the syncretistic mixture of Persian and Asia Minor bodies of thought under Greek influence.[43]

Warburg replied with his own interpretation:

> It seems to me that the tertium comparationis lies in the idea of the sacrifice between father and son. Sol relinquishes in sinful clemency the reins of the regiment to his son, and Mithras, the conqueror of Sol, joins the world together again through the sacrifice of the bull. The element of the sacrifice of the bull must have been introduced by the soldiers who, before the battle and before the slaughter, requested more than a myth: a blood-splattered cultic reality.[44]

38 WIA, GC, Saxl to A. Farinelli, 31.5.1929. Arturo Farinelli, Italian literary critic, 1867–1948.

39 WIA, GC, Warburg to KBW, 21.5.1929.

40 WIA, GC, Saxl to Warburg, 1.6.1929.

41 WIA, FC, Warburg to Mary Warburg, 2.6.1929, telling her to give Warburg's request to Saxl.

42 Saxl, F., *Mithras*. See also Russell, J.R., *Zoroastrianism in Armenia*; idem, 'On the Armeno-Iranian Roots of Mithraism', 183–193.

43 WIA, GC, Saxl to Warburg, 18.9.1929.

44 WIA, GC, Warburg to Saxl, 26.9.1929. See Cumont, F., *Die Mysterien des Mithra* for 'taurobolium', the sacrifice of a bull and thereafter the blood baptism, the ritual dousing with the blood of the slaughtered bull, in order to allow the strength of the animal to enter the person, 136–137; ibid., for heliolatry as the worship of the sun, 139.

Saxl did not develop this thought further but continued with his detailed research into the relationship of Mithraism with the old mystery religions. He realised that there were points of overlap between Mithras and Dionysus: the images of the krater[45] and the lion and snake on the Mithras images led straight into Dionysian thought.[46] And then, in October 1929, Saxl wrote from London that his work was nearly finished, although he admitted he could continue for much longer. While not having been able to solve the role Phaeton played, the Prometheus motif had become clear to him: 'The bull, which Mithras takes with him from heaven to earth, is essentially nothing else but the heavenly fire of Prometheus'. This explained why Helios was involved in the story – Mithras succeeded in his theft of the bull, but Helios demanded its slaughter on earth. The ethical corollary was, 'Work, so that the light is liberated heavenwards again'.

In a handwritten addition to the typed letter Saxl commented on the decision by Panofsky to stay in Hamburg and not to accept the call to Heidelberg University. With Panofsky in Hamburg, the University was 'consolidated', the foundation of 1919 had developed enough weight to convince professors like Ernst Cassirer and Erwin Panofsky to stay in Hamburg. Saxl suggested to Warburg one single step which would show Panofsky that 'we like him, need him and regard him with favour': would Warburg know a way to get Panofsky an invitation to lecture in America? It was a personal quest for Panofsky as well as for his wife, and Saxl knew how grateful Panofsky would be and that Panofsky himself would never approach Warburg.[47] Two weeks later, Saxl wrote to Panofsky that Warburg would forward Panofsky's lecture request to his contacts in the USA, when a good opportunity arose.[48]

Panofsky continued to assist Saxl with the illustrations;[49] Warburg was pleased that Saxl's work had progressed so much and promised to do everything to have it published as soon as possible,[50] but nine days later Warburg had died. Warburg's death brought many changes, not least on the personal level for Saxl, as the intensive exchange of ideas between these two scholars had come to an end. Saxl published his book on Mithras in 1931. In it he expounded that the Mithras images had turned into cyclical presentations where the killing of the bull constituted both the triumphal beginning of the cosmic events and the triumphal high point of

45 Krater, a Greek word for a vessel used to dilute wine with water.

46 WIA, GC, Saxl to Warburg, 26.9.1929.

47 WIA, GC, Saxl to Warburg, 13.10.1929. Prometheus, in Greek mythology, a Titan god of fire. WIA, GC, E. Panofsky to Saxl, 20.9.1929 and 6.10.1929. The request by Saxl to Warburg for Panofsky is neither mentioned in the correspondence of Panofsky, see Wuttke, D., *Erwin Panofsky. Korrespondenz 1910–1968: Eine kommentierte Auswahl in fünf Bänden.* nor in the *Journal*, see Michels/Schoell-Glass, *Journal*, 10.10.1929, 546, where Warburg mentions that he needed to thank Panofsky for his loyalty in staying in Hamburg.

48 WIA, GC, Saxl to E. Panofsky, 23.10.1929.

49 WIA, GC, E. Panofsky to Saxl, 16.10.1929.

50 WIA, GC, Warburg to Saxl, 17.10.1929.

the life of the saviour.[51] Since then, a number of Mithraea have been discovered and/or further investigated and not all of Saxl's findings and hunches have been vindicated. What is left – apart from the book publication – is the enthusiastic correspondence between two scholars which shows how both wrestled with the images of Mithras in the absence of literary monuments of the cult, apart from the writings of their opponents. The multi-layered images found in Mithraea had to suffice to construct the origins, transformation and pathways of the cult.

51 Saxl, F., *Mithras*, 53. In this book Saxl discussed most methodically the various forms of Mithras images: the representation of the victorious god, the bull fight and the Nike images, variations of the Mithraic bull sacrifice, Mithras symbols, the historical effects of Mithraic symbolism, the mise-en-scène of the central image, the composition of the Mithras reliefs, the religious meaning of the images of Mithras, the character of the cultic god, Mithras as an Olympic and a heroic figure, Mithras as the god of nature, Mithras as saviour, Mithras stealing the bull, Mithras sacrificing the bull, the myth of the creation of the world and the myth of the sun, Mithraic elements in Christian art, the subject of salvation in the development of Mithraism and Christianity, cosmological presentations in Mithraic and Christian art and the restitution of old motifs in the art of late antiquity.

11

CARICATURE AS WAR EFFORT

Aby Warburg's 'new style in word and image', 1914–1918[1]

It is well-known that Aby Warburg concerned himself at length during World War I with the reception of astrological pamphlets and political satires in the time of Martin Luther.[2] Less well-known is that due to his inner unrest and sheer exasperation about the war he tried his hand at being a political cartoonist. He understood cartoons as mutually escalating symbioses of word and image, that is as doubly strong carriers of messages. He saw a means to achieve this through his proclivity for strident puns, incisive neologisms and reworked proverbs, less so through his talent for drawing. Satirical comments, jokes and funny names were all used in Warburg's family, to wit 'Malice', the abbreviation for the couple Max and Alice Warburg, or the many nicknames by which Warburg was known in his family, 'Pet[t]ich', 'Pfater', 'Baubu', to name but a few. In a way, biting humour or unerring characterisations or trenchant observations or reprimands were all part of the ammunition used by Warburg when talking or writing about other members of the family or scholars or students or Hamburg authorities which had triggered Warburg's ire. These names were a sort of shorthand and positioned the addressed person or authorities immediately in one of two camps: either the family, or annoying fellow citizens and authorities. One example is the label he gave to the Hamburg 'Bücherhalle', the lending library for the people of Hamburg, which he termed 'reader feeder', in German 'Lesefutterautomat', in contrast to the academic research library, the Stadtbibliothek, in Hamburg, which he termed 'the pride of Hamburg'.[3]

Incisive wit cannot be detected in a tiny addition to a staidly humorous programme for his military unit in 1893 on the occasion of the birthday of Emperor Wilhelm II (see figure 11.1). The gunner bottom left, cheekily styled 'I' by Warburg and wearing epaulettes that were painstakingly added by Warburg in black

1 Originally published in McEwan, D., 'Karikatur als Kriegsdienst: Aby Warburgs "neuer Stil in Wort und Bild", 1914–1918', 78–95.

2 Warburg, A., *Heidnisch-antike Weissagung im Wort und Bild zu Luthers Zeiten.* Cf. Wedepohl, C., '"Agitationsmittel für die Bearbeitung der Ungelehrten": Warburgs Reformationsstudien zwischen Kriegsbeobachtung, historisch-kritischer Forschung und Verfolgungswahn', 325–368.

3 WI A, GC, Copy book III, 437, 438, 439. Warburg to Max Warburg, 20.11.1910.

DOI: 10.4324/9781003169024-14

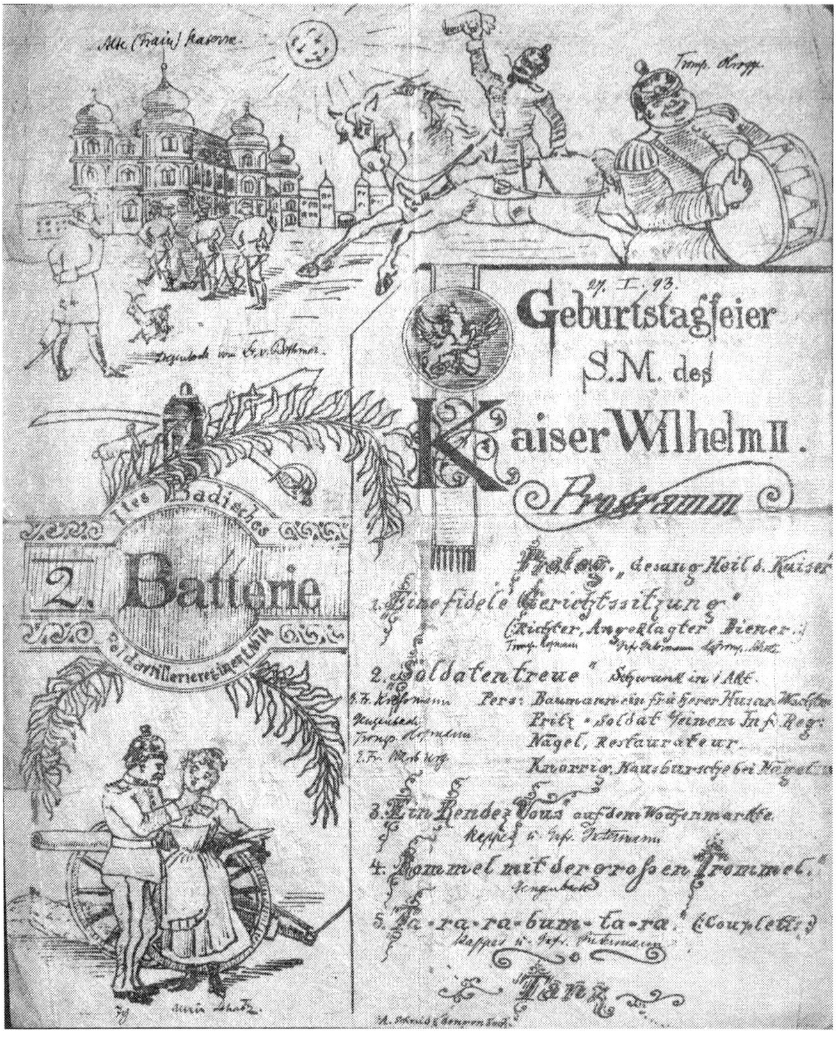

Figure 11.1 WIA, III.7.1, Aby Warburg, *Aus dem Tagebuch eines Artilleristen, Karlsruhe, 1892–1893* [*From the Diary of an Artillerist, Karlsruhe, 1892–1893*]. Lithograph of the drawing for the celebrations of the birthday of the German Emperor William II on 27.1.1893. With additions in black ink by Warburg.

Source: © Photo: The Warburg Institute.

ink, stands next to his sweetheart. It is not a great effort, while the news of his promotion to Private is reported by him with obvious ironic delight in military language as 'highest rank of baseness', a pun in German expressing meanness and disgrace.[4]

The first hint of a growing interest in caricature painting and literature appears in a letter from his brother Fritz. In 1904, when Warburg was absent from Hamburg, Fritz forwarded his correspondence and offered to pre-order the privately printed book on caricatures by Eduard Fuchs.[5] Warburg, a punctual reader of newspapers, regularly got on to the subject of the day's events and their presentation in the different newspapers in his correspondence with family members and friends. Political caricatures offered entertainment on the one hand and triggered a state of shock on the other hand. They dramatized the day's events with a clarity that textual messages could not convey so fast. They showed politics, they drew politics, they exaggerated authorities and identities in new, often surprising contexts, and had an effect on the public at large by being published in satirical periodicals.

The outbreak of World War I preoccupied Warburg to such a degree that he started his personal political mission: with the help of new periodical, he wanted and hoped to influence neutral Italy for Germany's benefit. Together with two professors from the Hamburg Colonial Institute, the ethnographer Georg Thilenius and the phonetician Giulio Panconcelli-Calzia, he published two issues of *Rivista Illustrata* in 1914 and 1915.[6] Fritz Saxl, who had to serve in the Austrian army, found the self-righteous tone of voice of these two periodicals counterproductive, but Warburg hoped to convey with the new periodical Germany's alleged innocence.[7] However, this journalistic initiative, run with the utmost effort, could not bring about the desired change of mood and so Warburg and his collaborators, frustrated, had to accept the inevitable catastrophe in May 1915: Italy's entry into the war on the side of the Allied powers.

4 WIA, III.7.1, *Aus dem Tagebuch eines Artilleristen, Karlsruhe, 1892–1893*; WIA, FC, Warburg to his mother Charlotte, 7. 3.1893. See also Roeck, B., *Der junge Aby Warburg*, 88.

5 WIA, FC, Fritz Warburg to Warburg, 3. 4.1904. It is not clear whether this was a subscription for Fuchs, *Die Frau in der Karikatur*, a volume which was published in 1906 but is not in the accession books of the library. Fuchs, E., *Der Weltkrieg in der Karikatur*, was published later, in 1916. Eduard Fuchs, German political activist, 1870–1940.

6 WIA, IV.63.2.1: *La Guerra del 1914: Rivista illustrata dei primi mesi agosto, settembre, ottobre*. WIA, IV.63.2.2: *La Guerra del 1914–15: Rivista illustrata dei mesi novembre, dicembre, gennaio, febbraio*, see Chapter 3 Cf. Diers, M., *Schlagbilder: Zur politischen Ikonologie der Gegenwart*, 25–31; McEwan, D., 'Ein Kampf gegen Windmühlen: Warburgs pro-italienische publizistische Initiative', 135–163; McEwan and Scafi, 'Warburg and D'Annunzio in Defence of Truth: On Modern Literature and Alleged Jewishness', 259–279; Haug, S., 'Bildpropaganda im Ersten Weltkrieg: Aby Warburg als Redakteur der illustrierten Zeitschrift La Guerra del 1914', 104–109.

7 WIA, GC, Saxl to Warburg, 8.4.1915. See McEwan, D., *Ausreiten der Ecken: Die Aby Warburg – Fritz Saxl-Korrespondenz 1910–1919*, 36, 82.

The war archive

Warburg also embarked on another project in 1914: to catalogue news of the war from the daily press in texts and images, a so-called war archive.[8] For him the newspaper cut-outs would serve after the end of the war as tools to tell the world the truth about the enemies of Germany and their deeply felt dishonest motivations. Ever since his university days Warburg had operated with index card boxes, which were subdivided thematically and contained bibliographical references on little slips of papers, a sort of subject catalogue. Aided by his secretary and library assistant Clara Hertz, a relative of his wife Mary, he catalogued more than 12,000 references from July to December 1917 alone.[9] Warburg's efforts to find a buyer after the war for the war archive, which had grown to over 90,000 slips, were not successful. Similar collections and cataloguing activities had been undertaken by individuals and institutions, some of them extant in the archive in Stuttgart.[10] After the transfer of the library to London in 1933, Warburg's war archive was the only collection of the former KBW to remain in Hamburg and it was destroyed in 1943, presumably during a bombing raid.[11]

Warburg was convinced that the German Empire, by virtue of its intellectual and moral predominance, would triumph over the other European and non-European powers. Fuelled by this conviction he entered into his diaries and miscellaneous writings, for 1915 and 1916 all collected under the heading *Kriegszibaldone*[12] for 1915 and 1916, 'ideas for images': 'L'Entente, international business for the export of the French Revolution',[13] 'Pictorial broad sheet of the war' and 'George the Fifth offers George the Lloyd his demission',[14] 'Financial News 5/IV 17: "for the last three centuries or so we have been the financiers of European liberty"',[15] 'Joke of world history' and 'The Turks come via the Balkans to help the Austrians'.[16] These were witty ideas, puns, caustic remarks, which he found suitable for journalistic support to the German war effort.

8 WIA, III.2.4, table of contents of the second series of index card boxes, put together between 1930 and 1933. Previously this collection was catalogued with the presssmarks III.21.1. and IV.64.1 ('Die Kriegssammlungen: Ein Nachweis ihrer Einrichtung und ihres Bestandes'). See Schwartz, P.J., 'Aby Warburgs Kriegskartothek: Vorbericht einer Rekonstruktion', 39–69.

9 WIA, GC, Warburg to A. Buddecke, 23.12.1917. Hertz's task was to cut out articles from newspapers and fit them to pieces of paper with bibliographical details. Albert Buddecke, Prussian military historian, 1858–1931.

10 Stuttgart, Landesarchiv Baden-Württemberg, Zeitungsausschnittsammlungen des Kriegsministeriums, M 731, Druckschriften und Zeitungsausschnittsammlungen.

11 See Heise, C.G., *Persönliche Erinnerungen an Aby Warburg*, 47–59, here 50.

12 Literally 'a heap of things' in Italian, miscellany.

13 WIA, III.10.7, Diary 1917, 995, n.d.

14 WIA, III.10.7, Diary 1917, 994, n.d. *The Financial Times* is quoted as source, 5.4.1917. George V, King of the United Kingdom and the British Dominions and Emperor of India, 1865–1936; David Lloyd George, British statesman, 1863–1945.

15 WIA, III.10.7, Diary 1917, 994, n.d. *The Financial Times* is quoted as source, 5.4.1917. George V, King of the United Kingdom and the British Dominions and Emperor of India, 1865–1936; David Lloyd George, British statesman, 1863–1945, 994, n.d.

16 WIA, III.10.5, *Kriegszibaldone 1915/16* (n.d.; between September 1915 and August 1916).

Warburg had military training as a private, but he was 48 years of age when war broke out and so was too old to serve in the army, which he regretted very much. Despite this, he sent inquiries to his younger colleagues serving in the army, asking how he could put himself at the disposal of the army. He was thinking of working as an intelligence officer in Italy. He asked the journalist Otto Röse, who had been detailed to the Austrian Southern headquarters,

> [. . .] that you inform me shortly, if somebody like me, who has perfect command of Italian, is required anywhere; my special areas of deployment might be journalism and the interrogation of prisoners. Although I am unfit for military service, I would, provided I am treated properly, voluntarily serve as interpreter only, with the rank of Officer (in 1893 I left the army with the rank of non-commissioned officer, I was not asked to undertake further exercises because I travelled to America and afterwards lived in Italy). I tell you these personal details only for the sake of completeness: in the main I am guided by the thought of making myself useful in the war, wherever I can do it best.[17]

One month earlier he had written to the neurologist Rudolf von Hößlin for a medical certificate to prove his fitness.[18] Unfortunately, this initiative did not yield the desired result. And, although his health left a lot to be desired, he still thought of deployment abroad two years later – his first assistant in the library, Wilhelm Printz, advised him strongly against it.[19] Warburg had to accept the fact that he would have to find another field to become useful *pro patria*. His development of the war archive, his work on *Rivista Illustrata*, his extensive correspondence with friends at home and abroad, they all became his alternative military service.

Olaf Gulbransson and Warburg's ideas

Among the paper slips in Warburg's war archive were slips from satirical periodicals, like *Simplicissimus*, published since 1896, and *Kladderadatsch*, founded in 1848.[20] In *Simplicissimus*, for instance, Eduard Fuchs' *Der Weltkrieg in der Karikatur* was advertised to be the 'most interesting deluxe book of the war', with its drawings by the Norwegian artist Olaf Gulbransson.[21] *Kladderadatsch*, originally the periodical for the liberal-democratic educated middle class, became, like *Simplicissimus*, a very

17 WIA, GC, Copy book VI, 97, Warburg to Röse, 23.6.1915. Otto Röse, German journalist, 1853–1925.

18 WIA, GC, Warburg to Hößlin, 21.5,1915. Rudolf von Hoßlin, German neurologist, 1858–1936.

19 WIA, GC, W. Printz to Warburg, 21. 11.1917. Wilhelm Printz, German Indologist, 1887–1941.

20 Cf. Roth, E., *Simplicissimus: Ein Rückblick auf die satirische Zeitschrift*; Heinrich-Jost, I., *Kladderadatsch: Die Geschichte eines Berliner Witzblattes von 1848 bis ins Dritte Reich.*

21 *Simplicissimus* 20, 1915, no. 26, 6 (28. 9.1915). Olaf Gulbransson, Norwegian painter and designer, 1873–1958.

angry journalistic defender of the fatherland in World War I. In both satirical papers there appeared appeals to subscribe to war bonds, anecdotes from the front, poems, letters to the editors, advertisements of all kinds – everything except serious war reports, which the daily papers printed or, at least, purported to print. The satirical weeklies fed and lived on sensationalism. Their contributions were not illustrated by photographs, but by drawings, falsifying or distorting facts, which in their blatancy appeared much more violent than photographs or photomontages. It goes without saying that Warburg appreciated the trenchant humour in these satirical publications; they made clear what was not necessarily apparent to every reader otherwise and they invited further comments and repetitions and new applications where necessary. Warburg's linguistic forte came to the fore when he coined neologisms, which were razor sharp, even if not often short enough to be understood instantly.

Gulbransson's drawings in *Simplicissimus* impressed Warburg very much, for instance the cover illustrations of 'the two eagles with the Bersagliere, which I hold to be one of the few really mentally mature creations of the war' (see figure 11.2a),[22] as well as a drawing by Gulbransson with the title *Italian Autumn Season* (see figure 11.2b):[23] it shows a waiter with watery eyes and drooping belly, eating his own meal of noodles, because tourists did not show up on account of the war. Crestfallen, he turns to the patron saint of his line of business: 'Oh, holy Baedeker, when will your star shine again on us?' As drawings by Gulbransson were exhibited side by side with 'utter Christmas rubbish' in the Commeter art shop – 'also the waiter with the macaroni is there' – Warburg wrote to the director of the Hamburg Kunsthalle art museum, Gustav Pauli, that his museum should purchase the Gulbransson drawings: 'I would be very happy to know that these drawings are in public ownership. The time for Gulbransson to be purchased by state collections has come and should not be passed over'.[24] The title illustration with the two eagles was, indeed, a gripping drawing, showing a black eagle sitting on the summit of a mountain, his head turned to the right, while the second eagle, a double-headed eagle, squats on a somewhat lower summit with one head turned to the left and one head turned to the right. Far in the background stands a small one-armed Bersagliere, a broad-brimmed hat on his head with long feathers swinging in the wind, in his hand a gun, his mouth wide open – an eye-catching presentation of the alliance between Germany and Austria-Hungary. The title of the drawing *The Alpine Watch* referred to the song *The Watch on the Rhine*, a German patriotic hymn conjuring up national unity.

In August of the same year, 1915, Warburg wrote four letters to Gulbransson, in which he submitted ideas for caricatures: 'Dear Sir, now, when everybody has to do something for Germany, I want to put at your disposal an idea to be executed by your

22 *Simplicissimus* 20, 1915, no. 10, Title page (8.7.1915). The 'And *he* wants to harm us? He is only capable of shooting songbirds!' alludes to the annual killing of migratory birds in Italy and suggests that the two main powers would not have to fear the military prowess of the Italians.

23 *Simplicissimus* 20, 1915, no. 10, no. 28, 11 (12.10.1915).

24 Baedeker is the name of a guidebook. WIA, GC, Warburg to G. Pauli, 1.12. 1915.

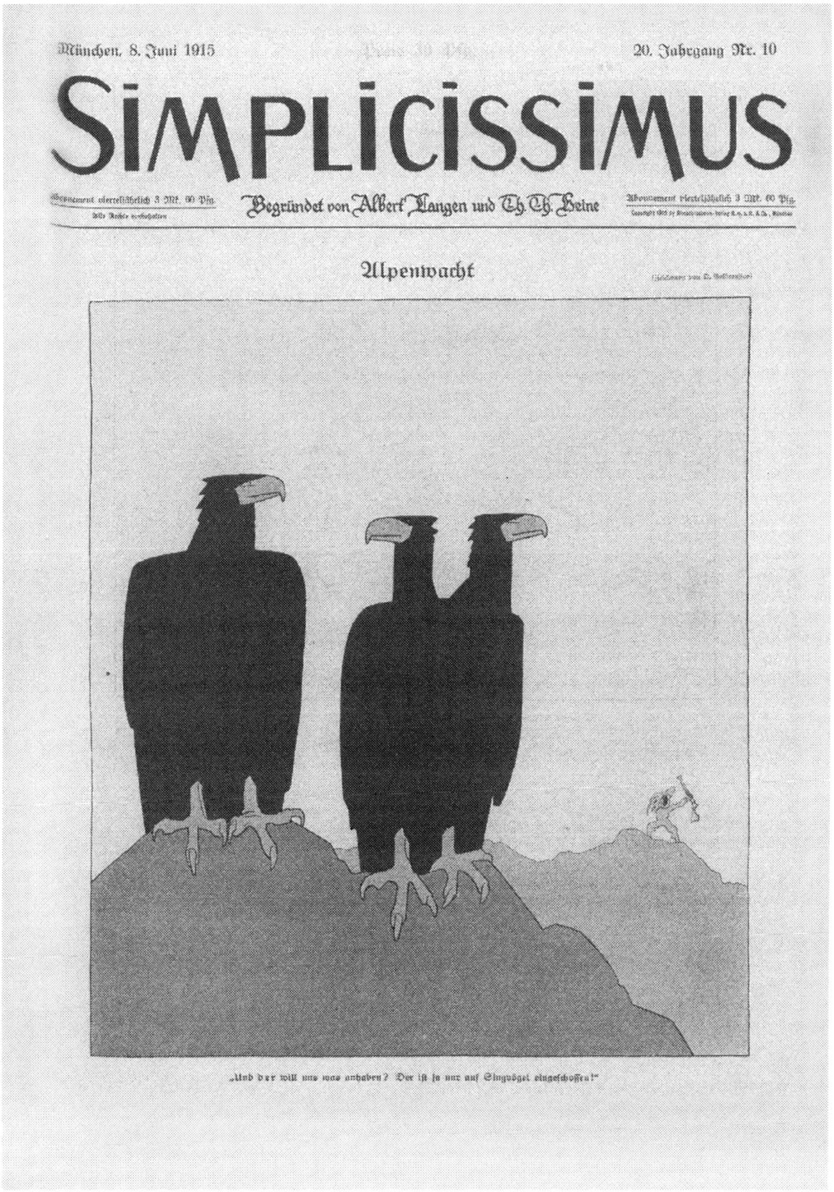

Figure 11.2a Olaf Gulbransson, *Alpenwacht*. Caption: 'Und *der* will uns was anhaben? Der ist ja nur auf Singvögel eingeschossen!' ['And *he* wants to harm us? He is only capable of shooting songbirds!']. Title page, *Simplicissimus* 20, 1915, no. 10 (8. Juni 1915).

Source: © Public domain: www.simplicissimus.info/uploads/tx_lombkswjournaldb/1/20/20_10_109.jpg (accessed 29 September 2020).

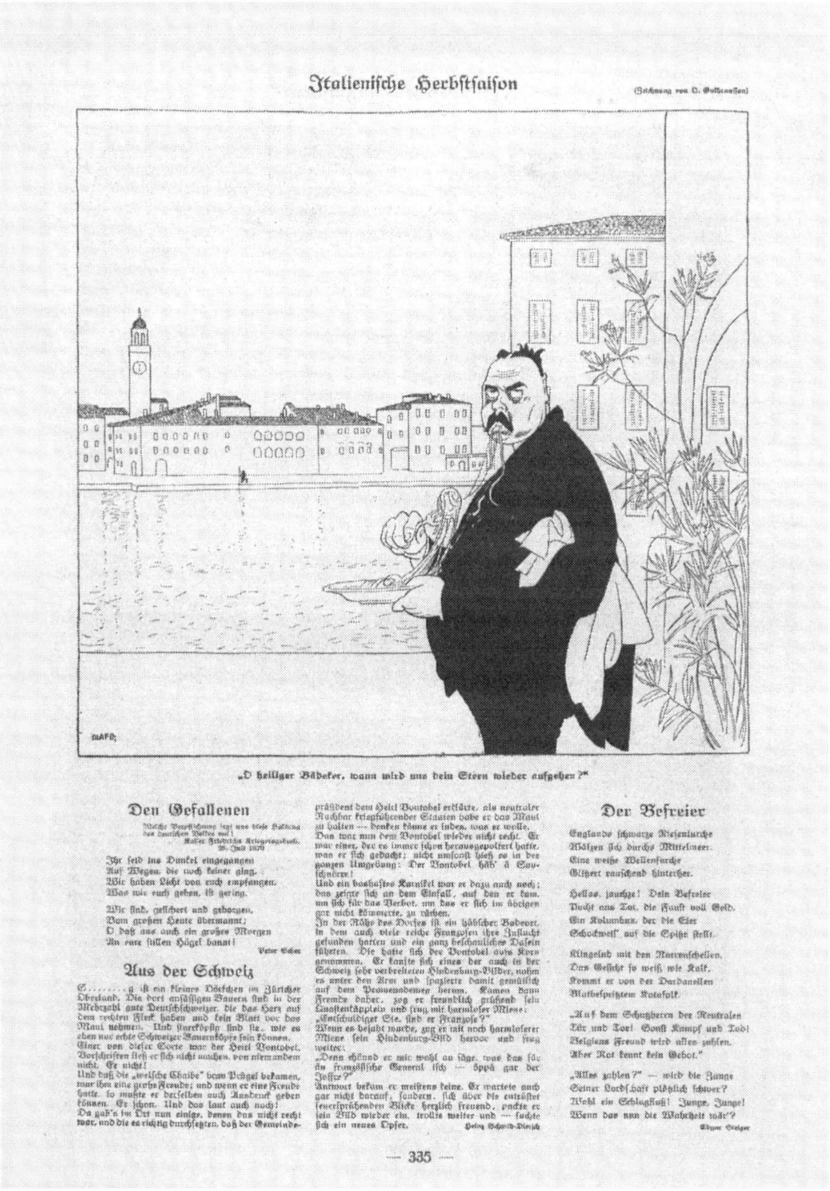
Italienische Herbstsaison

(Zeichnung von O. Gulbransson)

„O heiliger Bädeker, wann wird uns dein Stern wieder aufgehen?"

Den Gefallenen

Welche Verpflichtung legt uns diese Haltung des deutschen Volkes auf!
Kaiser Friedrichs Kriegstagebuch, [illegible] Juli 1870

Ihr seid ins Dunkel eingegangen
Auf Wegen, die noch keiner ging.
Wir haben Licht von euch empfangen,
Was wir euch geben, ist gering.

Wir sind, gesichert und geborgen,
Vom großen Heute übermannt;
O daß uns auch ein großes Morgen
An eure stillen Hügel bannt!

Peter Scher

Aus der Schweiz

S........g ist ein kleines Dörfchen im Züricher Oberland. Die dort ansässigen Bauern sind in der Mehrzahl gute Deutschschweizer, die das Herz auf dem rechten Fleck haben und kein Blatt vor das Maul nehmen. Und starrköpfig sind sie, wie es eben nur echte Schweizer Bauernköpfe sein können.
Einer von dieser Sorte war der Heiri Vontobel. Vorschriften ließ er sich nicht machen, von niemandem nicht. Er nicht!
Und daß die „welsche Chaibe" dem Prügel bekamen, war ihm eine große Freude; und wenn er eine Freude hatte, so mußte er derselben auch Ausdruck geben können. Er schon. Und das laut auch noch!
Da gab's im Ort nun einige, denen das nicht recht war, und die es richtig durchsetzten, daß der Gemeindepräsident dem Heiri Vontobel erklärte, als neutraler Nachbar kriegführender Staaten habe er das Maul zu halten — denken könne er indes, was er wolle.
Das war nun dem Vontobel wieder nicht recht. Er war einer, der es immer schon herausgepoltert hatte, was er sich gedacht; nicht umsonst hieß es in der ganzen Umgebung: Der Vontobel häb' ä Saufschnorre!
Und ein boshaftes Karnikel war er dazu auch noch; das zeigte sich an dem Einfall, auf den er kam, um sich für das Verbot, um das er sich im übrigen gar nicht kümmerte, zu rächen.
In der Nähe des Dorfes ist ein hübscher Badeort, in dem auch viele reiche Franzosen ihre Zuflucht gefunden hatten und ein ganz beschauliches Dasein führten. Die hatte sich der Vontobel aufs Korn genommen. Er kaufte sich eines der auch in der Schweiz sehr verbreiteten Hindenburg-Bilder, nahm es unter den Arm und spazierte damit gemütlich auf den Promenadewegen herum. Kamen dann Fremde daher, zog er freundlich grüßend sein Kuttenkäpplein und frug mit harmloser Miene:
„Entschuldiget Sie, sind er Franzose?"
Wenn es bejaht wurde, zog er mit noch harmloserer Miene sein Hindenburg-Bild hervor und frug weiter:
„Denn chönnd er mir wohl au säge, was das für än französische General isch — öppä gar der Joffre?"
Antwort bekam er meistens keine. Er wartete auch gar nicht darauf, sondern, sich über die entrüstet feuersprühenden Blicke herzlich freuend, packte er sein Bild wieder ein, trollte weiter und — suchte sich ein neues Opfer.

Heinz Schmidt-Dinzich

Der Befreier

Englands schwarze Riesenlurche
Wälzen sich durchs Mittelmeer.
Eine weiße Wellenfurche
Glitzert rauschend hinterher.

Hellas, jauchze! Dein Befreier
Pocht ans Tor, die Faust voll Geld,
Ein Kolumbus, der die Eier
„Schockweis" auf die Spitze stellt.

Klingelnd mit den Narrenschellen,
Das Gesicht so weiß wie Kalk,
Kommt er von den Dardanellen
Blutbespritzten Katafalk.

„Auf dem Schutzherrn der Neutralen
Tür und Tor! Sonst Kampf und Tod!
Belgiens Freund wird alles zahlen.
Aber Not kennt kein Gebot."

„Alles zahlen?" — wird die Zunge
Seiner Lordschaft plötzlich schwer?
Wohl ein Schlagfluß! Junge, Junge!
Wenn das nun die Wahrheit wär'?

Edgar Steiger

— 335 —

Figure 11.2b Olaf Gulbransson, *Italienische Herbstsaison*. Caption: 'O heiliger Bädeker, wann wird uns dein Stern wieder aufgehen?' ['Oh, Saint Baedeker, when will your star rise again for us?']. *Simplicissimus* 20, 1915, no. 28 (12. Oktober 1915), 11.

Source: © Public domain: www.simplicissimus.info/uploads/tx_lombkswjournaldb/1/20/20_28_335.jpg (accessed 29 September 2020).

pen, really only a title: Britannia rules the slaves (instead of waves)'. His pun referred to the jingoistic hymn *Rule, Britannia!* and its lyrics 'Rule Britannia, Britannia rules the waves, Britons never, never, never shall be slaves', which is still sung today on the last evening of the concert series of the 'Proms' concerts in the Royal Albert Hall in London, loudly accompanied by the audience. Rulership over slaves instead of over waves was, for Warburg, the hallmark of the outrageous politics of Great Britain to exploit other states commercially. He ended with the remark, 'I, as a matter of course, forgo any reference to my name; if you do not want to take up my idea, I am happy if you put it at the disposal of other fighters in *Simplicissimus* (for instance Th. Th. Heine)'.[25]

After waiting for one week, Warburg wrote again to lend weight to his suggestion with the addition that even Italy had sunk so low as to be a slave state dependent on Great Britain.[26] However, this communication remained unanswered. Warburg tried for a third time. He described the elements of the drawing that would best correspond to his text, denouncing Victor Emanuel III of Italy as a condottiere who had been bought by England:

> I wish to add to my letters of 18th and 24th of this month that the latest reports about the rape of Italy by England (for instance in the Lokalanzeiger of 29th with the report from Berne of 28th August), could not be better illustrated than by the suggested catchphrase 'Britannia rules the slaves', the embodiment of England, which drives the Italian mercenaries into war.
>
> Without anticipating anything, I imagine the illustration in such a way that fat Britannia with a black and a gold-coloured (money and coal) whip drives on the attack of the Italian condottiere ('Il condottiere dei milliardi') (Re Vittorio Emmanuele) or a very young Bersagliere. In the event you do not want to use my idea, I request a short note. I believe it expedient, for factual reasons, to publish this catchphrase, in any shape.[27]

Again, the letter remained unanswered. Warburg must have been bitterly disappointed, because four weeks later he wrote resignedly that he assumed that Gulbransson did not want to use his idea. 'In the event you do want to use this motto, I ask you for a reply on the enclosed reply card'.[28] This time he received a short reply from the editors of *Simplicissimus*: they thanked Warburg for his kindness, but could not use his idea.[29] This was a clear refusal, but his idea did not seem to go away because Warburg noted it once more in 1917 under the heading 'Ideas for illustrations'.[30]

25 WIA, GC, Copy book VI, 132, Warburg to O. Gulbransson, 18.8.1915. Thomas Theodor Heine, German painter and illustrator, 1867–1948.

26 WIA, GC, Copy book VI, 134, Warburg to O. Gulbransson, 24.8.1915.

27 WIA, GC, Copy book VI, 147, Warburg to O. Gulbransson, 29.8.1915. Victor Emanuel III, King of Italy, 1869–1947.

28 WIA, GC, Copy book VI, 159, Warburg to O. Gulbransson, 30.9.1915.

29 WIA, GC, Editor of *Simplicissimus* to Warburg, 8.10.1915.

30 WIA, III.10.7, Diary 1917, 995 n.d.

Warburg, whose meticulous care and methodology have produced the adjective 'Warburgian' in English, did not allow himself to be distracted from his task and objectives. His friends and some members of his family sent him cut-outs from newspapers, encouraged him to persevere and understood that his work was an important contribution to the history of the war.[31] Warburg exhorted newspapers like the *Hamburgischer Correspondent* to add precise source references to their reports, without which, unable to unmask the campaign of lies of their enemies, they could not write the psychology and history of press lies after the war.[32]

To Warburg caricature was a didactic medium which was used to thrill and impact on the reader. Caricatures, with their texts and images, used allegories; they hinted at ideas which went beyond the factual truth and thereby referred to unverbalised perceptions and possibilities. Individuals were grotesquely exaggerated, single small additional properties in the drawings expressed messages which became that much more legible and intelligible. The library, which Warburg had created with its sections for 'Image', 'Word', 'Orientation' and 'Dromenon' ('action'), attests to the many layers with which Warburg treated a proposition. Tellingly, he quoted in his article *Heidnisch-antike Weissagung in Wort und Bild zu Luthers Zeiten* the poet Jean Paul, who called image and word 'the dual branches of satirical jokes': 'The satirical joke can either animate the body or embody the spirit'.[33] Yoking image and word together duplicated their effect, so that minuscule changes in a well-known text lent credence to them in a new light. Juxtaposing known symbols in a new, contemporary interpretation like 'Britannia rules the slaves' was the best practice at the disposal of caricaturists.

The title illustration of *Simplicissimus* on 4 January 1916 – timely for Epiphany or the Three Kings' Day – showed *The three unholy kings* in swirling garments and with crowns on their heads, even then, when one king was a president of a republic: Tsar Nicholas II of Russia, King George V of Great Britain and Ireland, and the French president Raymond Poincaré wearing a top hat and a paper crown over it. All three of them walked with their gifts of money in their hands toward the star, which stood above the aptly named 'Bethlehem Steel Work'. The caption, 'Wie schön leucht' uns der Morganstern' or 'How beautifully shines the Morgan star' was a pun on the name of the banker John Pierpont Morgan Jr, who also operated as an American commercial agent for the British government (see figure 11.3).[34] The steel work was,

31 See for instance the letter from the banker and philanthropist and Warburg's relative by marriage James Loeb to Warburg, WIA, GC, 13.10.1915. For Loeb see McEwan, D., 'Façetten einer Freundschaft: Aby Warburg und James Loeb. Verwandte, Freunde, Wissenschaftler, Mäzene', 75–98. See Chapter 6.

32 WIA, GC, Warburg to *Hamburgischer Correspondent*, 26.6.1915. It was the first daily newspaper in Hamburg, appearing regularly since 1724, at times one of the most influential in Europe.

33 Müller, J., *Vorschule der Ästhetik*, 184, § 50; quoted after an older copy in Warburg, A., *Heidnisch-antike Weissagung in Wort und Bild zu Luthers Zeiten*, 6. Jean Paul, German writer, 1763–1825.

34 *Simplicissimus* 20, 1916, no. 40, Title page (4.1.1916; drawing by Ragnvald Blix). The caption was a modification of the hymn *Wie schön leuchtet der Morgenstern* [*How Beautifully Shines the Morning Star*] by Philipp Nicolai, which Johann Sebastian Bach set to music in his chorale cantata BWV 1. John Pierpoint Morgan Jr, American banker, 1837–1913; Nicholas II, Tsar of Russia, 1868–1918; Raymond Poincaré, president of France, 1860–1934.

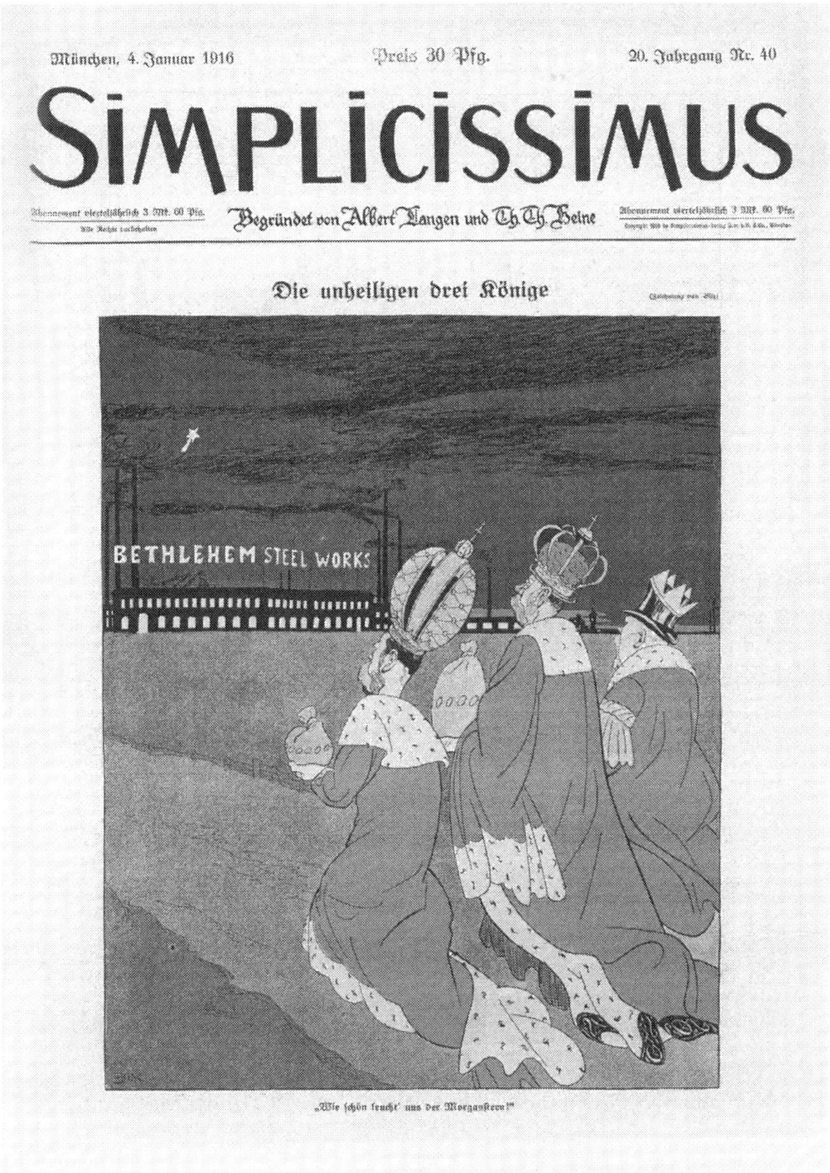

Figure 11.3 Ragnvald Blix, *Die unheiligen drei Konige*. Title page. *Simplicissimus* 20, 1916, no. 40 (4.1.1916).

Source: © Public domain: www.simplicissimus.info/uploads/tx_lombkswjournaldb/1/20/20_40_469 (accessed 29 September 2020).

as a matter of course, an arms factory, which, transposed into the caricature, was not the stable of the Christian prince of peace, but the goal for the rich potentates, which harboured the means of violence and destruction of the world.[35]

One year later Warburg entered in his diary another idea, an immediate reaction to the abdication of Tsar Nicholas II at the beginning of the Russian February Revolution, which once again took up the motive of the crowns:

> Balfour, seated in a box office, says to the King of Italy and Poincaré, who have secured their crown and top hat with chin straps, 'You better do'. In the background a poster above the entry to the theatre: Order your crowns before leaving the premises.[36]

A few more times Warburg came back to the topic of arms factories when he requested reference books, for instance from the second-hand book dealer Joseph Baer & Co. in Frankfurt or from art historian Frida Schottmüller at the library of the royal museums in Berlin.[37] Lili du Bois-Reymond, writer and friend of the Warburg family in Berlin, replied in her letter to Warburg's requests,[38] and finally Warburg ended a letter to his brother Fritz with the exclamation 'America! "From the stable in Bethlehem to Bethlehem Steel!"'.[39]

After the refusal from the publishers of *Simplicissimus*, Warburg continued to concern himself with how a catchphrase or pictograph could emerge from a text and image.[40] He tried again to interest Thomas Theodor Heine, the co-founder of *Simplicissimus*: 'I have pleasure in sending the following heading, "Fata Morgana", to illustrate Wilson's and Morgan Jr's ideal and real ideas for peace, at your or *Simplicissimus*'s disposal'. He did not add further details, only requested that his name not be mentioned: 'I will be happy if you use the idea freely pro patria'.[41]

35 The city of Bethlehem with its steel works in Pennsylvania, USA, ranked among the largest American armament factories. The president of the Bethlehem Steel Company, Charles M. Schwab, reported at the end of 1916, that is, before the declaration of war by the US to the Central Powers, that his factories produced 50% more machinery and ammunition than the famous Krupp-Werke in Essen, Germany, and one third of all shipbuilding. The Times, 3.1.1917, Capacity of US Ordnance Works, 7.

36 WIA, III.10.7. Diary, 18.3.1917, 909. Arthur Balfour, British prime minister, 1848–1930.

37 WIA, GC, Warburg to J. Baer, 24.4.1917; WIA, GC, Warburg to F. Schottmüller, 30.4.1917. Frida Schottmüller, German art historian, 1872–1936.

38 WIA, GC, L. du Bois-Reymond to Warburg, 5.7.1917. Lili du Bois-Reymond, German author, 1864–1948.

39 WIA, FC, Warburg to his brother Fritz, 17.7.1917. Warburg also entered his catchphrase in his Diary, WIA, III.10.7, Diary 1917, 993 n.d.

40 Gombrich, E.H., 'Magie, Mythos und Metapher: Betrachtungen über die satirische Graphik', 35–77, here 71.

41 WIA, GC, Copy book VI, 282, Warburg to T.T. Heine, 6.1.1917. In contrast to his brother Max, Warburg judged the attempts at negotiations by Wilson four months later (and then abandoned) very critically. 'Wilson's big message to the Senate of "War without victory". Max thinks we should eagerly accept the idea (because it is correct)'. Warburg also recorded that 'Wilson's ideas would be accepted in Germany only with protest'. WIA, III.10.7, Diary 1917, 23.1.1917 and 24.1.1917, 872.

But even this initiative was not successful, so that Warburg noted in his diary 'I came up with the title "Fata Morgana" (Morgan, fatum ['doom']) for a newspaper article'; however, this article was never written.[42]

Aby Warburg and Max Slevogt

Realising that his suggestions of witty headings were not getting him any further, Warburg tried approaching the painter and graphic artist Max Slevogt. His first letter is not extant, but Slevogt's reply, in which he told Warburg that due to his work on political caricatures he had no time to realise somebody else's ideas, is.[43] After the declaration of war by the USA to the Axis Powers on 6 April 1917, Warburg tried again. He justified his renewed attempt by simply saying that the fatherland demanded it. The reason for Warburg was the fact that the German art of drawing typified the events of the war in a higher sense only rarely and mostly unsatisfactorily.[44]

Although Warburg confessed that he saw the most eye-catching drawings and texts about the war in *Simplicissimus*, he found that the spirit of the periodical alone was not enough. He complained about Gulbransson and Ludwig Thoma, who regularly contributed their comments. He found Thoma wanting, as if talking to regulars at their reserved table, and Gulbransson was too dry for him, working as if with poisonous puppets and without a mind for the landscape. With his criticism of the leading vitriolic, satirical periodical he gave vent to his disappointment over the refusal for his suggestion of 'Fata Morgana'. He reprimanded the periodical because it was lacking 'attention to the transcendental absolute in the days' events'. This was his point of departure for suggesting a political topic with which he wanted to comment on the events in the war 'in a higher sense'. He wanted to commission Slevogt for a drawing of the damage caused to the Statue of Liberty in the harbour of New York on 30 June 1916 by an explosion of an ammunitions factory in New Jersey. To him this was the 'joke of world history'. The vision of 'damaged liberty' was, in any case, challenging. Warburg introduced his idea with the words 'Signs and wonders are yet to come, if one can feel them',[45] which conformed to his sense of the legibility of signs and wonders: clouds of smoke billowed from the bleeding arm stump, which had lost its torch, and the plinth of the statue glowed brightly like a furnace in full blast.[46]

The statue, this 'pretentious thing', the work of the Alsatian sculptor Frédéric Auguste Bartholdi, was in Warburg's eyes 'nothing less than the symbol of

42 WIA, III.10.7, Diary 1917, 29.1.1917, 875.

43 WIA, GC, M. Slevogt to Warburg, 25.1.1917. Max Slevogt, German painter, 1868–1932.

44 WIA, GC, Copy book VI, 297–299, Warburg to M. Slevogt, 23.4.1917.

45 Hebrew Bible, Exodus, Moses 7:19.

46 WIA, III.10.5, *Kriegszibaldone* 1915–1916, 396 n.d. Ludwig Thoma, German author, 1867–1921.

America'; it was the gift of the French Republic in memory of the centenary of the creation of the American republic in 1886, 'a monument to comradeship in the fight against freedom-threatening England'. The inscription *Liberty Enlightening the World* was mockery to Warburg: the USA had been recently enslaved by Great Britain when the Entente powers had urged the USA to enter the war on their side. Warburg added a sketch (no longer extant) and asked Slevogt, who had masterfully illustrated the *Leatherstocking Tales* by James Fenimore Cooper in their 'primeval power',[47] to create a drawing according to Warburg's suggestions. He said he would like to purchase the drawing, possibly to use later on. This commission, therefore, was no longer a textual proposal for a drawing: he wanted to make his own mark as journalistic broker with Slevogt's drawing. He was convinced that the Entente would perish because of its betrayal of the spiritual qualities of humanity. A business to export the French Revolution to Russia had already started; the conspirators trembled in the hands of 'Marianne', the nom de plume for France.[48]

This time, Slevogt replied promptly, the letterhead decorated with a lithograph of the new *Gesichte* portraits portfolio.[49] He wrote that he was sending the lithographed papers to his friends not to find buyers, but as evidence that, as Warburg had said, the art of German drawings certainly did not demonstrate the events of the war in a higher sense. In his drawings he had gone one step further; he refrained from explanations. He would welcome it if Warburg visited him in Berlin, as Warburg's judgment was valuable to him, but he said he could not draw Warburg's idea in as lively and spirited a manner as was necessary.[50]

47 WIA, III.10.7, Diary 1917, 930, 29.4.1917. In between news from the war about sunk ships and a trip on the Alster river, Warburg noted that his sister-in-law Alice Warburg had looked with her children at the book in its German translation (see Cooper, J.F., *Lederstrumpf-Erzählungen*) which contained the Slevogt lithographs. It is possible that Warburg, in his reception of the 'primeval power' of text and illustrations, was influenced by his own contact with the original populations of Northern America, cf. Guidi and Mann, *Grenzerweiterungen. Aby Warburg in Amerika 1895–1896*. Frédéric Auguste Bartholdi, French sculptor, 1934–1904; James Fenimore Cooper, American writer, 1789–1851; Alice Warburg, sister-in-law of Aby Warburg, 1873–1960; Paul Cassirer, German art dealer and editor, 1871–1926.

48 WIA, GC, Copy book VI, 297–299, Warburg to M. Slevogt, 23. 4.1917.

49 Slevogt, M., *Gesichte. 21 Stein- und Zinkdrucke*. The artist had an edition of 60 signed copies, of which Warburg ordered one folio on 21 April 1917 under the title Ein Kriegstagebuch ('a war diary'). See WIA, 10.1.2.1, Accession catalogue [*Zugangsverzeichnis der Bibliothek Warburg vom 1. Januar 1905–28. September 1918*]. In December Warburg ordered two further folios: WIA, GC, Warburg to M. Slevogt, 5.12.1917. In WIA, GC, Warburg to M. Slevogt, 27.4.1917, mentioned the order of 21 April 1917, but this letter was never sent. Slevogt's lithographs count as failed attempts to deal with the horrors of war in art. See Suhr, N., 'Max Slevogt als Graphiker', 75–93, here 82.

50 The letter is in WIA, GC, M. Slevogt to Warburg, 25.4.1917. The title of the header, a lithograph, was *Thesiphone Regem, Reginamque in Fuorem Agit* (Tisiphone, one of the three Furies, enraged King Athamas and Queen Ino, according to Ovid, see Ovid, *Metamorphoses* IV, 464–511). See also Haug, S./Wedekind, G., 'Max Slevogt's "Gesichte". Mit einem Nachtrag zu Aby Warburg', in press.

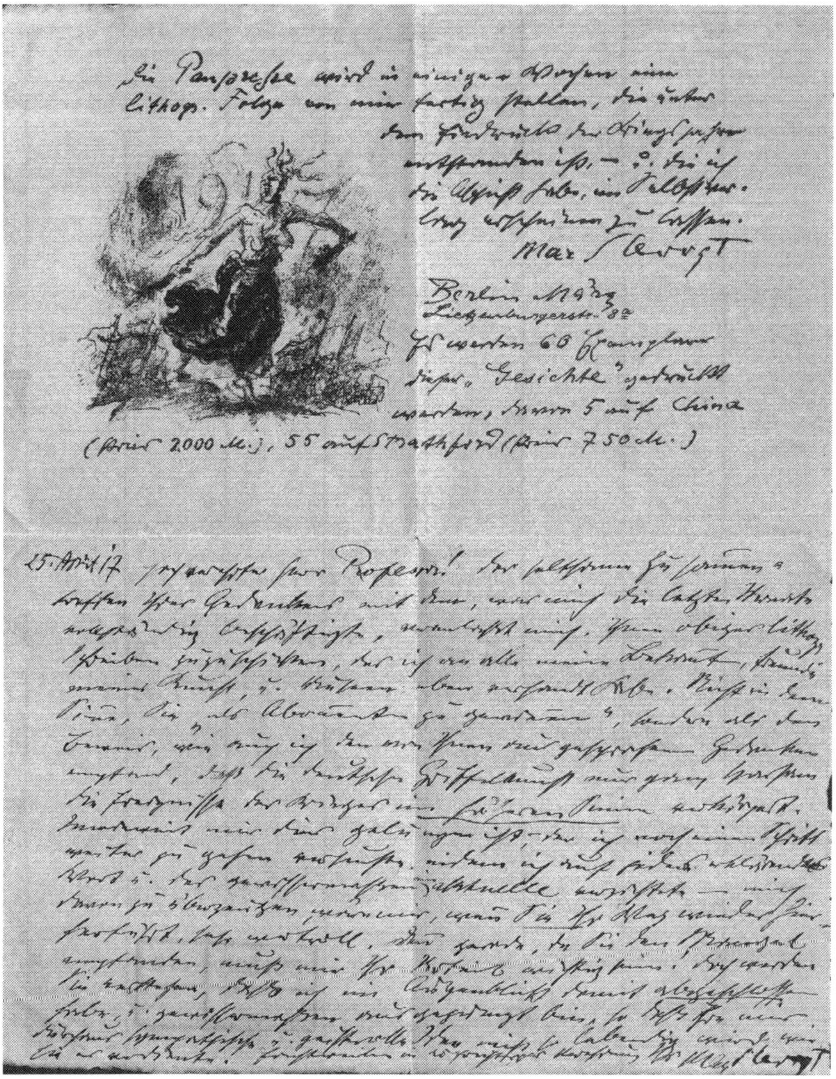

Figure 11.4 WIA, GC, Max Slevogt to Aby Warburg, 25.4.1917.

Source: © Photo: The Warburg Institute.

Slevogt valued Warburg's comments on the lack of ideas in the artistic war caricatures but was too busy to accept Warburg's ideas (see figure 11.4). By repeating Warburg's use of 'Griffelkunst' for 'art of drawing', a term coined by Max Klinger and used by him for drawings and printed graphic work, Slevogt signalled the appreciation both he and Warburg had for Klinger's considerations on art theory.[51] Warburg had no correspondence with Klinger, but his name is mentioned in a dozen of Warburg's letter.[52] Despite Slevogt's refusal, it elicited a joyful entry in the Diary: 'Very kind reply by Slevogt on "Prosperity enlightening the world", but has just lithographed *Gesichte*'.[53]

And there was more than just an entry in the Diary. Warburg wrote another letter on the same day but did not send it. It is illuminating about his plans in the matter of 'art in the service of the war effort'. Warburg informed Slevogt that he would visit him when next in Berlin in order to discuss something which was of importance to both of them – the damage to the Statue of Liberty in New York. He felt that a drawing about an actual event was appropriate for giving that event an ethical profile. He suggested first of all two pages of text, with a passage from the American Declaration of Independence, a passage from Lesseps' speech when the statue was handed over in 1886, statistics on the export of arms and ammunition in the war from 1914 onwards, then information about the explosion and damage to the statue, Wilson's speech with the assertion that America had entered the war out of pure selflessness, and Asquith's overtures of allyship. The word 'Liberty' should be substituted by the word 'Prosperity', because prosperity was the idol of the United States. The collective title for the series of sheets should be 'On the Freedom of an Entente man', derived from the famous letter by Luther 'On the Freedom of a Christian' in 1520. With this title Warburg wanted to show his conviction that Germany would win the war not by superior technical might – 'any industrial state can beat another' – but by the fact that 'we have not relinquished the spiritual qualities of humanity to the purpose of advertising on signboards'. The 'Entente man' in his Russian and French manifestations would be destroyed by the discrepancy between talk of liberty and capitalist enslavement. Money has no value where ethos rules and there is no ethos where brutal power prevails. Warburg regretted that he could not find a writer of satire like Rabelais 'to put together this book of the freedom of the Entente man based on Reuters cables'; however, he went on to make new suggestions for text-and-image series on the suppression of the Easter Rising in Ireland, on the February Revolution in Russia and the murder of the French socialist Jean Jaurès:

> Two torn out chapters: 'From the two capitals which have been conquered by the Entente, Dublin and St Petersburg'. For instance, the following topics are calling out to be illustrated with images of monumental irony: how Dublin was conquered and the good man Skeffington

51 See for instance Avenarius, F., *Max Klingers Griffelkunst: Ein Begleiter durch ihre Phantasiewelt*. The Griffelkunst-Vereinigung in Hamburg, a private art association which produces editions of original graphic art to this day, took up this term in 1925. Max Klinger, German artist, 1857–1920.

52 See for instance WIA, FC, Warburg's sister O. Kohn-Speyer to Warburg, 2.4.1894, on an exhibition in the Hamburger Kunsthalle, where she was impressed by the works of Max Klinger or WIA, FC, C. Warburg to Warburg, 5.4.1894.

53 WIA, III.10.7, Diary 1917, 928a, 27.4.1917.

> lost his life after a long bombardment by soldiers of his government and how Sir Roger Casement hangs on the gallows with a facsimile of the letter by Findley [sic] . . . or how St Petersburg was conquered with the printed article on the rights of soldiers . . . Also the Tsar, how he diligently reads the newspaper for the first time . . . and how Grand Duke Boris, destitute, will be captured by military policemen behind the front, Rasputin with one dead leg stares out from the ice because the Englishman commissioned with his murder has not drowned him properly . . . The Tsarina, the all-powerful of yesterday, encounters the revolutionaries as a nurse faces a nursery . . ., the murder of Jaurès (revolver sticking out of a curtain in a coffee house) still unpunished today in order to spare the Russians. Title illustration: The cave of the English lion, 'vestigia terrent',[54]and on the outside on coat racks hang the crowns of those who entered but did not return.

Warburg spoke of perfidy, admitting that even Rabelais and Goya would have been sorely tested to cope with the number of events. He closed his long and spirited letter to explain that he did not want to prompt Slevogt to illustrate Warburg's impressions, but to have an additional reason to talk to him one day.[55] The description of text and images broke off: Warburg either lost interest in the topic or did not find any artist who would fulfil it.[56] To his brother Fritz he spoke of Jaurès 'as the finest blossom' of French political humanity, which was sacrificed by the French to the 'Russian moloch' without pursuing the hangman's assistant.[57]

Simplicissimus and *Kladderadatsch*

Warburg's suggestions to Slevogt were not taken up and turned into satirical drawings. However, he was lucky with another textual suggestion he sent to *Kladderadatsch*. This periodical published every week, from the first year onwards, a dialogue between two men, Schultze and Müller, fictitious plain German 'Michels',

54 'vestigia terrent', meaning 'the tracks repel me'. (Horace, *Epistulae I*, 1, 74, after a fable by Aesop, in which the fox refuses to enter the cave of the sick lion because he sees the tracks of other animals leading into the cave, but not out of it.)

55 WIA, GC, Warburg to M. Slevogt, 27.4.1917. Ferdinand de Lesseps, French diplomat and entrepreneur, 1805–1894; Herbert Henry Asquith, British prime minister, 1852–1928; François Rabelais, French writer, 1483/94–1553; Jean Jaurès, French Socialist, 1859–1914; Francis Sheehy Skeffington, Irish suffragist, 1878–1916; Sir Roger Casement, Irish nationalist, 1864–1916; Mansfeldt Findlay, British diplomat, 1861–1932; Grand Duke Boris Vladimirovich of Russia, 1877–1943; Grigori Rasputin, Russian mystic, 1869–1916; Tsarina Alexandra Feodorovna of Russia, 1872–1918; Francisco Goya, Spanish painter and printmaker, 1746–1828.

56 WIA, III.10.7, Diary 1917, 995 n.d.

57 WIA, FC, Warburg to his brother Fritz, 17.7.1917.

stock figures of satirical journalism[58] who, from a worm's-eye view, commented on the day's events in Berlin dialect, for instance:

> Müller: For apartments with central heating it will be a cold winter. One has no other option but to change lodgings.
>
> Schultze: Nonsense! On the contrary, when it is cold one has to change into more clothes.[59]

Warburg must have found these little dialogues amusing because he sent a dialogue to the publishers, without form of address or signature, simply to the 'Letters to the editor' section (see figure 11.5). On acceptance he requested a reply in the 'Letters to the editor' section of 'Kladderadatsch 1848'. Only then would he supply his name and address.

> Schultze: So, Count Westarp has cut the tablecloth between himself and the Centre? This means the end of their collaboration.
>
> Müller: Oh no! As long as you have the tablecloth, I do not worry. Only when Westarp destroys the whole table and leaves the place for good –
>
> Schulze [sic]: Oh. You think that the brothers will meet again, when the new freedom meal is served to be polished off?
>
> Müller: Yep.[60]

Kuno Graf Westarp, conservative member of parliament, terminated the collaboration with the Catholic Centre Party after its representative Matthias Erzberger tabled a resolution for peace in the main committee of the parliament on 6 July 1917. Erzberger helped to bring about the dismissal of Prime Minister Bethmann Hollweg a few days later after resignation threats by Hindenburg and Ludendorff, because both had in principle rejected his failed attempts to reach an understanding in domestic and foreign politics.[61] In order to explain to the wider readership the momentousness of this domestic crisis Warburg transposed it to the level of a chat in the pub. The simile of the cut tablecloth signalled the end of a friendship. In 1874 *Kladderadatsch* commented on Bismarck's fight in parliament with the Centre Party in the same way:

> The tablecloth is cut./You know what this means for fraternity.
>
> According to gentlemanly customs/we will be enemies for eternity.[62]

58 The first dialogues were written by David Kalisch, see Heinrich-Jost, *Kladderadatsch*, 17.

59 *Kladderadatsch* 70, 1917, no. 26, 30.6.1917 (not paginated).

60 WIA, GC, Copy book VI, 308, Warburg to the editors of *Kladderadatsch*, with distorted handwriting, not signed, 12.7.1917.

61 Kuno Friedrich Viktor Graf Westarp, German conservative MP, 1864–1945; Matthias Erzberger, German politician, 1875–1921; Theobald Theodor Friedrich Alfred von Bethmann Hollweg, German prime minister, 1856–1921; Paul von Hindenburg, German statesman, 1847–1934; Erich Ludendorff, German army officer, 1865–1937.

62 *Kladderadatsch* 27, 1874, no. 57, 13.12.1874 (not paginated). Cf. Röhrich, L., *Lexikon der sprichwörtlichen Redensarten*, 1077. Otto von Bismarck, German statesman, 1815–1898.

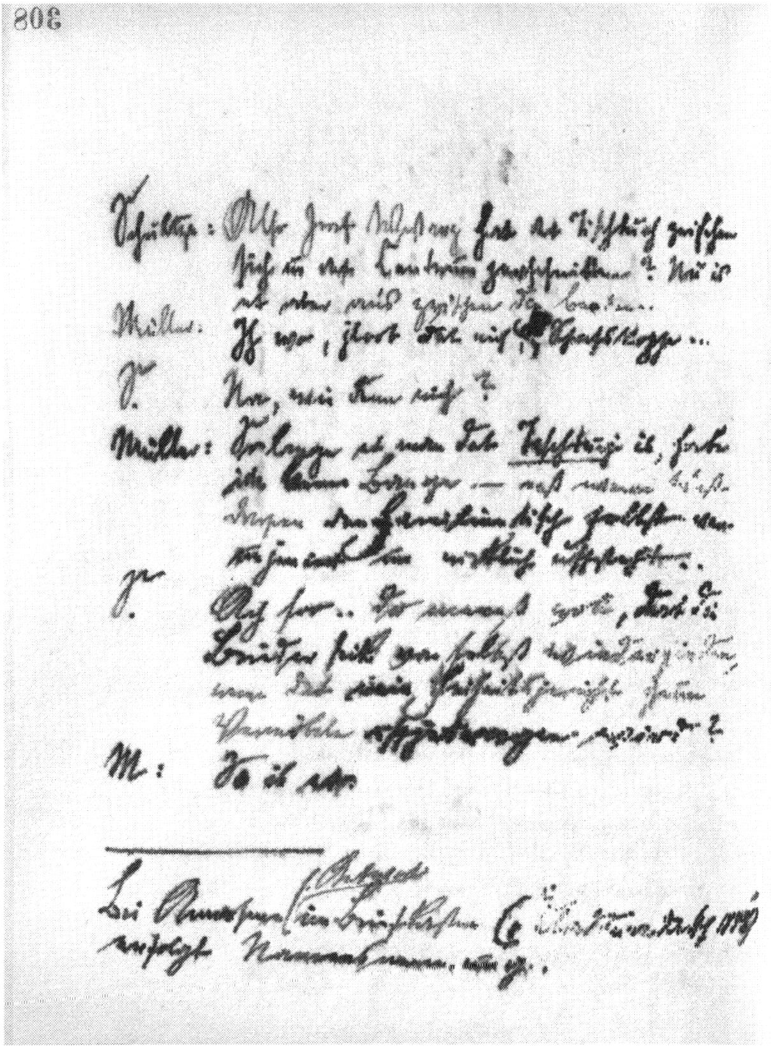

Figure 11.5 WIA, GC, Copy book VI, 308. Warburg to *Kladderadatsch* with distorted handwriting, 12.7.1917, 308.

Source: © Photo: The Warburg Institute.

It is possible that the title illustration in *Simplicissimus* of 5 June 1917 gave Warburg the idea of the cut tablecloth. It sported the heading *The Catastrophe* and showed two men, one of them cutting the tablecloth. The caption made the action clear: 'The French rentier cuts the tablecloth between himself and Russia with his redundant coupon scissors'.[63] And on the page with 'Ideas for drawings' Warburg noted in his Diary, 'Müller and Schultze on the cut tablecloth between the Conservatives and the Centre Party'.[64]

In Warburg's version of the dialogue Müller reassured Schultze that the situation was not dangerous, so long as only the tablecloth was cut between the Conservatives and the Centre Party. Only when Westarp stopped sitting with his family and left the table – that is, the parties which collaborated with him in the parliament – would it be dangerous. But then Schultze sounded less pessimistic: it would not come to pass because the 'brothers' would sit down at the same table again and the new freedom meal would be gobbled up.

Warburg must have been really happy when his dialogue was printed on 29 July 1917 and he found in the 'Letters to the editor' section the cryptic message 'Hamburg, Kladderadatsch 1848. Accepted'.[65] He replied as promised: 'As I have found my contribution in your issue of today, I'm sending you my name and address, as mentioned, without renouncing my request for anonymity'.[66] This success as satirical commentator was not further commented upon. But Warburg cut out the message from the periodical and slipped it into his Diary.

The dialect dialogues were always printed without authors' names. Warburg therefore must have felt safe not being found out as the author of such literary output. As he wanted to continue publishing satirical comments, it was important to him not to reveal his name and address. In 1917 two important events happened: the entry into the war of the USA and the two Russian revolutions. After the proclamation of the Russian Republic by the Mensheviks in September 1917, he turned again to *Kladderadatsch* with a new suggestion which he had entered in his Diary.[67]

> 'The liberation of Russia from the Entente'. Kornilow, dressed as a Cossack, on his head a nightcap, sitting on top of a safe, the words 'Fortune Russe' on its door, trying to crush a Russian who lies in his blood.[68]

And he sketched out what he described: Kornilow sitting on top of a safe, with a whip in his hand; below him a man desperately struggling not to be crushed by the heavy safe (see figure 11.6).

63 'Coupon scissors' were scissors with which to cut out coupons, which were printed on large sheets. When the rentier presented the cut coupons, dividends for matured stocks and shares were paid to him. *Simplicissimus* 22, 1917, no. 10, Title page, 5.6.1917.

64 WIA, III.10.7, Diary 1917, 993 n.d.

65 *Kladderadatsch* 70, 1917, no. 30, not paginated, 29.7.1917.

66 WIA, GC, Copy book VI, 314, Warburg to *Kladderadatsch*, 3.8.1917.

67 WIA, III.10.7, Diary 1917, 1150, not dated, but certainly in the second half of September 1917.

68 WIA, GC, Copy book VI, 329, Warburg to *Kladderadatsch*, 20.9.1917. The nightcap was described in the Diary as 'nightcap of a rentier'. General Lavr Georgievich Kornilow, who according to Warburg's thinking would act as enforcer, had been arrested on the command of the new Prime Minister Alexander Kerensky four days previously. Lavr Georgievich Kornilow, Russian general, 1870–1918; Alexander Kerensky, Russian lawyer and revolutionary, 1881–1970.

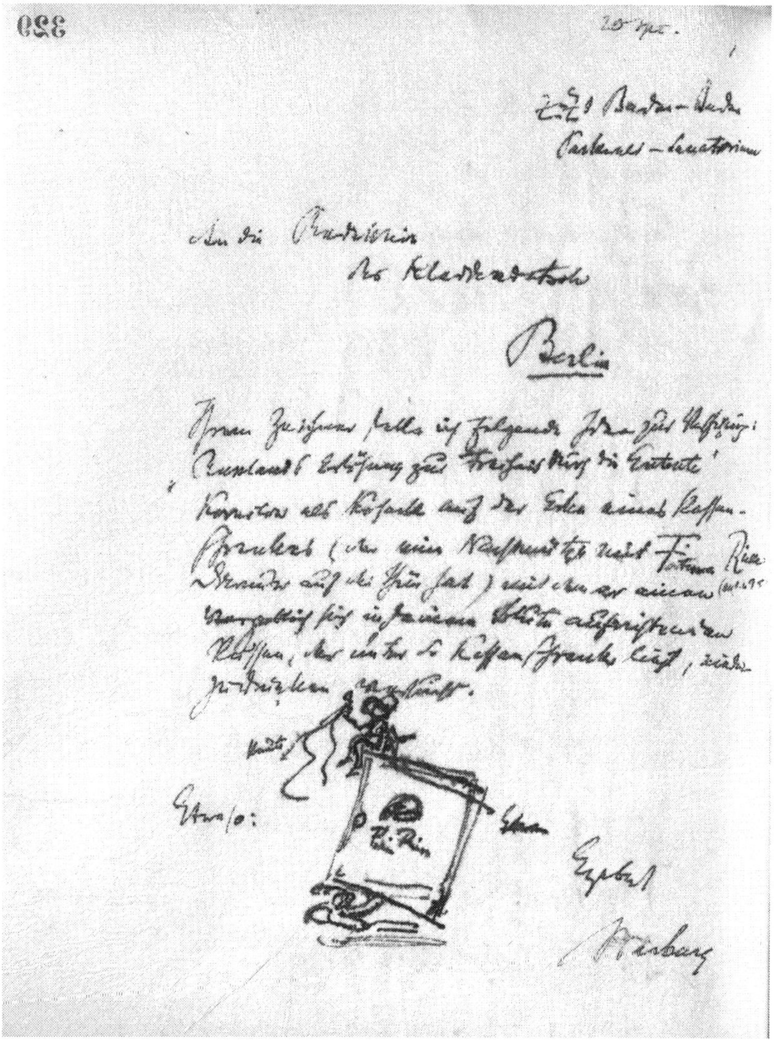

Figure 11.6 WIA, GC, Copy book VI, 329. Warburg to *Kladderadatsch* with a sketch of a textual and visual suggestion 'Russlands Erlösung zur Freiheit durch die Entente' ['Russia's salvation to freedom by the entente'], 20.9.1917.

Source: © Photo: The Warburg Institute.

Neither the text nor the image were taken up by the periodical. Warburg stopped approaching the periodicals with ideas for converting more events into political caricatures. Gustav Schiefler, who collected graphic art and edited the *Literarische Gesellschaft zu Hamburg*, invited Warburg to contribute to the January or February issues of 1919, carnival issues, not just with joke articles, but with serious material too – satire, jokes and deeper meaning[69] – and, if possible, to give him the names of other authors whom Schiefler could approach. Warburg drily replied that in view of the precarious situation he could not consider a carnival issue and only promised that he would think about it, but admitted that important things could not be said because of censorship.[70]

Schiefler softened his tone; he had not been intending a fun publication but 'wanted to parade bitterly serious things in a very subtle form in the mask of a joker or fool'. For Hamburg it would be something new, but at the same time that much more attractive. Schiefler reminded Warburg that he had asked him two years ago for an article about the Roman Pasquino, a topic which seemed suitable for the carnival issue.[71]

At this time Warburg was already too ill for such a task to appeal to him. He had understood his 'catchphrases' as contributing to the German war effort, but the war was lost. He did not waver in his conviction that education and culture would win and not brute force of arms, money or human sacrifice. Certainly, the opposite result at the end of war contributed to Warburg's mental breakdown. He spent the years from 1918 to 1924 in different sanatoriums and after his return to Hamburg devoted his time to academic research without further interest in caricatures. There was one exception: his admiration for Heinrich Hoffmann's *Struwwelpeter*. In the story of St Nicholas, who was called the evil 'magician' in the Russian translation, meaning Tsar Nicolas I, Warburg found the beginning of a satirical political worldview, which could not be detected in other versions of this story. They did exist in Warburg's lifetime, however, and later in many adaptions that denounced contemporary abuses, the most powerful being *Struwwelhitler*.[72]

69 WIA, GC, G. Schiefler to Warburg, 22.9.1918. Schiefler referred here to Christian Dietrich Grabbe's *Scherz, Satire, Ironie und tiefere Bedeutung*. Gustav Schiefler, German art collector, 1857–1835.

70 WIA, GC, Warburg to G. Schiefler, 28.9.1918.

71 WIA, GC, G. Schiefler to Warburg, 1.10.1918. Pasquino is the name for a Hellenistic-style statue which was unearthed in Rome in the 15th century. The statue is known as the first of the 'talking statues' of Rome, because of the tradition of attaching pieces of paper with anonymous criticisms to its base.

72 See McEwan, D., 'Aby Warburg und die Figur des Nikolaus im "Russischen Struwwelpeter"', 354–364; eadem, 'Der gute Bischof Nikolaus: Aby Warburgs Interpretation der russischen Übersetzung von *Struwwelpeter* und die politischen Parodien *Struwwelhitler – A Nazi Story Book* und *Schicklgrüber*', 67–90. Heinrich Hoffmann, German psychiatrist, 1809–1894; Nicholas I, Tsar of Russia, 1796–1855. See Chapter 15 for *Struwwelpeter* and his literary successors.

Part IV

JUDAICA

12

'. . . PROBABLY LATENT ANTISEMITISM'[1]

The Austrian art historian Fritz Saxl, professor of art history in the University of Hamburg and librarian at the KBW in Hamburg, met Warburg in 1910 during his one term of studies in Berlin (see figures 12.1 and 12.2). The academic interests of both scholars intersected and would prove game-changing for their lifelong collaboration. After finishing his studies in Vienna in 1912, Saxl obtained a research fellowship in Italy[2] with the help of Warburg and Franz Boll and thereafter was employed as Warburg's assistant in Hamburg. This employment was interrupted by World War I, when Saxl served in the Austrian army on the Austrian-Italian front.[3] After the war, when Warburg spent five years in sanatorium, the family re-employed Saxl to look after the library in Warburg's absence.

At Saxl's suggestion Warburg's private library was transformed into a research institute, in contact with the newly founded University of Hamburg. After Warburg's return to Hamburg, when his private house had become too small to accommodate the large library, a purpose-built building was constructed to house the collection of books, photographs and papers, financed by the Warburg family. In 1926 it was organisationally set up as the Kulturwissenschaftliche Bibliothek Warburg (KBW), the Warburg Library of Cultural Science, with Saxl as a member of the board. After Warburg's death in 1929 Saxl became director of the KBW and, in the wake of the widespread book burnings in Germany in 1933, it was Saxl who saved the entire collection of books, then 55,000 titles, by shipping the whole lot, including some of the furniture of the institute, for instance the bookbinding machines, to London. In 1944 it was incorporated into the University of London, where it is still today.[4]

Warburg's research corpus dealt with the influence of classical antiquity on European culture, in particular in the Renaissance. He was interested in the topic which Saxl outlined concisely in his phrase of 'the pathways of the mind',[5] namely

1 Originally published in McEwan, D., '"... wahrscheinlich latenter Antisemitismus"', 197–198.

2 See McEwan, D., 'Saxl and Boll'. Franz Boll, German classicist, 1867–1924.

3 McEwan, D., *Ausreiten der Ecken*.

4 Eadem., *Fritz Saxl. Eine Biografie*.

5 WIA, GC, Saxl to Warburg, e.g. 23.4.1913 and 29.4.1913. WIA, GC, Warburg to Saxl, 31.12.1921, W/Saxl file.

DOI: 10.4324/9781003169024-16

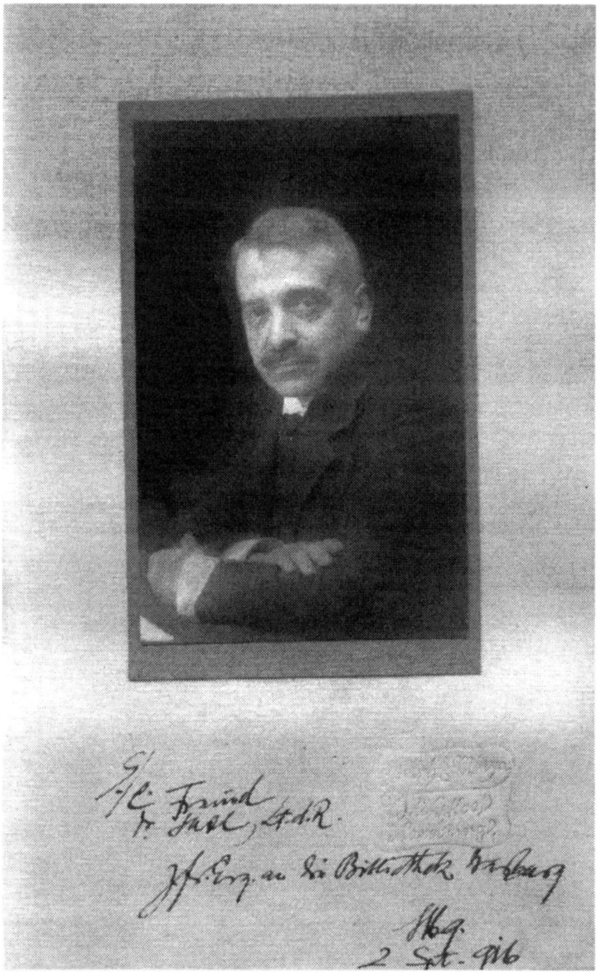

Figure 12.1 Aby Warburg. WIA, Portrait collection, 2.9.1916. 'S.[einem] l. [ieben] Freund Dr. Saxl, Lt.d.R. [Leutnant der Reserve] z.[ur] fr.[eundlichen] Erg.[Erinnerung] an die Bibliothek Warburg Hbg[Hamburg]'. '2. Spt.[September] 916. To his friend, Dr. Saxl, junior officer, in friendly memory of the Warburg Library, Hamburg, 2 September 1916'.

Source: © Photo: The Warburg Institute.

the way images and their metamorphoses were depicted in European thought and culture. Saxl worked on two large research areas, Rembrandt and medieval illuminated manuscripts, in particular the ancient classical and medieval beliefs in stars, which were expressed in the portrayal of planets. Warburg and Saxl understood that ideas and images from pagan and ancient sources, introduced by the Renaissance into Christian Europe, were of the utmost importance and contributed to the development of the history of ideas.

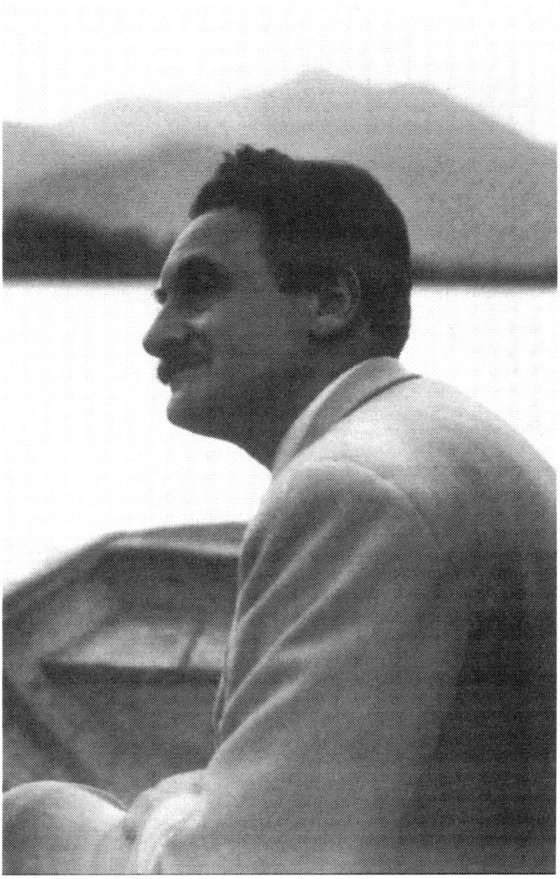

Figure 12.2 Fritz Saxl. WIA, Portrait collection, n.d., in the 1920s.
Source: © Photo: The Warburg Institute.

One example will suffice: when Saxl published his first book in 1915, *Catalogue of astrological and mythological manuscripts of the Latin Middle Ages in Roman libraries*,[6] Franz Ehrle from Vorarlberg, formerly a prefect of the Vatican library in Rome and later a cardinal, called it 'one of those pioneering works, which create the right foundation for researching a large, but so far barely studied, area. The volume will therefore prove a much needed important piece of research which the Vatican still has to accomplish'.[7] Years later Warburg acknowledged

6 Saxl, F., *Verzeichnis astrologischer und mythologischer illustrierter Handschriften des lateinischen Mittelalters in römischen Bibliotheken*.
7 WIA, GC, F. Ehrle in Feldkirch to Warburg. 7.6.1916. Franz Ehrle, Austrian cardinal, 1845–1934.

that it was Ehrle who had drawn Warburg's attention to a highly interesting manuscript, the translation and study of which would occupy Warburg for many years.[8] Warburg explained it was a book of magic, which was put together in Arabic from Oriental and Hellenistic elements under the title *Ghāyat al-Ḥakīm* or *The aim of the sage* in the 11th century and was translated at the court of King Alfonso X into Spanish. It was later known under the Latin title *Picatrix* – no longer thought to be a corruption of *Hippokrates* – and spread throughout Europe until the late Middle Ages. The text was first published, a translation from the Arabic into German, in the *Studien* (*Studies*) series of The Warburg Institute in 1962.[9]

As an Austrian living in North Germany, Saxl liked to spend his holidays in Austria and one of them took him and his family to Southern Germany and thence to Vorarlberg. In the postcard from his holidays in 1926 Saxl expressed his unease about latent antisemitism, he did not quote any specific incidents, he most probably overheard people talking. Warburg and Saxl were of Jewish extraction, but neither of them practised their religion. However, both of them were sensitive about any racist discrimination.

> Dear Professor,
>
> I do not write, because there was no reason to write. At first, I spent 10 days in Reichenau without doing much else than rowing and swimming. I have hardly spoken a word with a stranger because the public was impossible. I have not read anything else other than children's books.
>
> Yesterday we left Reichenau and went to Vorarlberg, into the mountains, to Schruns, where I stayed many years ago. The weather was not great. The place is dreadful – many people, two coffee houses, probably latent antisemitism – so that we moved on to Gargellen today. There is only one hotel there, altitude is 1,500m.
>
> We will stay here for a few days. On Monday we will be in Lindau where I hope to find your note concerning Leipzig. I am very grateful for the holidays, I had wonderful days on the lake [Constance] and hope to have wonderful days in the mountains, so that I have a store of memories of the great outdoors. I can live on these in the long winter and extract the scale for greatness and beauty.
>
> Many happy greetings from me, my wife and the children,
>
> Your old Saxl.
>
> Gargellen, Thursday.[10]

While Warburg's reply to this postcard and the quip about antisemitism is not extant, the tone of Saxl's card impresses: it is friendly, a true holiday card. Normally their correspondence is full of bibliographical references, research ideas, comments on colleagues' writings and rarely news or comments of antisemitic activities, but this time Saxl seems to have had time to relax with his family and prepare for the long winter.

8 WIA, FC, Warburg to Paul Warburg, Felix Warburg, L. Binswanger, 6.10.1926.

9 Ritter and Plessner, *Das Ziel des Weisen, von Pseudo-Maĝrīṭī*.

10 WIA, GC, Saxl to Warburg, dated only 'Thursday', that is 12.8.1926. Reichenau, a town on Lake Constance, Germany, Schruns, a town in southern Vorarlberg, Austria, Gargellen a village in the Montafon area of southern Vorarlberg, Lindau, a town on Lake Constance, Germany.

13

ABY TO GISELA WARBURG

Against the 'pioneers of this-worldliness'[1]

In the spring of 1929, in the autumn of the year in which Warburg would die, members of Warburg's family, brother Max and his wife, with his daughter Gisela and his brother Felix with his wife Frieda, undertook a trip to Palestine.[2] The correspondence which Warburg received from this trip provides an insight into the views of Warburg's perception of Jews who lived in Yishuv ('Settlements') in Palestine under the British Mandate as well as his enthusiasm about a newly excavated mosaic there in Beth Alpha. His niece's letter of 11 May 1929 gave Warburg the opportunity to write about '. . . the great, seemingly unbridgeable contrast between the Jews at the Wailing Wall and the Jews of the soil'.[3]

Gisela,[4] who was the fifth child of Max Moritz Warburg, head of the family bank M. M. Warburg & Co. in Hamburg, was still a schoolgirl when she accompanied her father, her uncle Felix and her aunt Frieda on this trip to Palestine in May 1929. Felix Warburg was friends with Chaim Weizmann, president of the World Zionist Organisation

1 Originally published in McEwan, D., 'Gegen die Pioniere der Diesseitigkeit', 9–11 and McEwan and Treml, 'Aby an Gisela Warburg', 4–8.

2 WIA, FC, G. Warburg to Warburg, 11.5.1929. Gisela was the daughter of Max Warburg, Aby Warburg's brother, and his wife Alice. Max Warburg, German banker, 1867–1946; Alice Warburg, née Magnus, 1873–1960; Gisela Wyzanski, née Warburg, Zionist leader, 1912–1991; Felix M. Warburg, German-American banker, 1871–1937; Frieda Warburg, née Schiff, American philanthropist, 1876–1958.

3 WIA, FC, Warburg to G. Warburg, 14.5.1929.

4 Gisela Warburg was active in the Zionist movement, although she never lived in Palestine. She worked in Berlin in positions of influence with the 'Jugend-Alijah' ('Youth Emigration'). This organisation had been founded in 1933 and was run by the US Zionist Henrietta Szold, who organised and coordinated the emigration of Jewish children to Palestine. Some 5,000 children were able to leave Nazi Germany before the beginning of the war and another 15,000 survivors of the Shoah after the war. Henrietta Szold, Jewish Zionist leader and founder of 'Hadassah', 1860–1945. In August 1938 Gisela moved with her family to the USA but wanted to return to Germany after the war to continue with her work. She was not able to do so, and only visited Germany once in 1949. See Chernow, R., *The Warburgs: A Family Saga*, 510–512, 567–568, 689. In the USA Gisela worked for 'Hadassah', the American Zionist Women's organisation, co-founded by her aunt Frieda Warburg in 1912 with the aim of setting up a health service in Palestine. See Spinelli, I.W., *Die Dringlichkeit des Mitleids und die Einsamkeit nein zu sagen. Erinnerungen 1910–1989*, 454.

DOI: 10.4324/9781003169024-17

and later the first president of the state of Israel.[5] Felix and Frieda were philanthropists, who had long since committed themselves to Jewish welfare and culture in America and had promoted Yishuv in Palestine since the beginning of the 1920s. Felix was travelling to Israel to purchase orange groves in order to finance the University of Jerusalem with their proceeds; his wife Frieda donated $100,000.00.[6]

Warburg, who stayed in Naples in May 1929, requested of his brother Max that Gisela send him her impressions of Palestine.[7] Gisela replied promptly from Venice on their return journey. She found the request of her uncle Aby a 'tough challenge'; she confessed that the impressions were overwhelming and she did not know where to start.

> Well, if one does not know where to start, one starts with the Jews!
>
> The Jews in Palestine are totally different. This is baffling. They are the best type of Jews in the world. They are gentlemen, natural, capable of sacrifice, tough and full of energy! Each one is nicer than the next, with blond, strong and Hebrew-speaking children on the farms. There are some 10,000 Jews in Jerusalem who are in sharp contrast: Ghetto Jews, with long hairlocks. Small traders or idlers. These are the Wailing Wall Jews. They speak Yiddish and a thousand different dialects, they refuse to speak Hebrew, because the language should remain sacred. They are the bitterest enemies of the Zionists, they wait for the Messiah and hold the routine purchasing of land, insofar it is connected to political goals, for a sin. – It is a pity that the few Jews in the world are not united; they would have conquered Palestine a long time ago, because the Arabs are totally divided and the Christians are represented by 37 different sects in Jerusalem alone. – The settlers have only one wish, that the hinterland understands them and, by supporting them, feels connected to their construction work.[8]

Gisela waxed lyrical about the beauty of the landscape, of the 'oriental life' in the old city. She admired the small industrial enterprises and finally felt 'connected' to everything, not least because Uncle Felix, the philanthropist, who had achieved great things for the land, 'was received with open arms'. She concluded enthusiastically 'that I would return rather today than tomorrow'.[9]

These are the key points that Warburg expressed in his reply. He confessed he had nearly awarded her the 'Grand Order of the golden mezuzah[10] with a wreath of onions and the tablets of the Ten Commandments', if only she had not filled two

5 Chaim Weizmann, Russian-Israeli biochemist, Israeli statesman, 1874–1952.

6 Chernow, R., *The Warburgs: A Family Saga*, 371–372.

7 WIA, FC, Warburg to his brother Max Warburg, 9.5.1929.

8 WIA, FC, G. Warburg to Warburg, 11.5.1929.

9 WIA, FC, G. Warburg to Warburg, 11.5.1929.

10 Mezuzah, a piece of parchment inscribed with verses from the Torah and mounted in a case on the right-hand doorpost to a house.

pages with 'gushing teenage prose'. However, he was happy with Gisela's letter, it was 'splendid' and exactly what Warburg had expected, the confirmation 'that the royal progress with picturesque people at their feet had turned into a pilgrimage for these people, who, as human beings, were all gripped by it', noting '. . . it is a fact that the epistemological values are transcendentally rooted and not only grounded in the shifting sands of a luxury travel'.[11]

What follows is Warburg's extensive commentary of Gisela's impressions of Palestine, as background, as it were, to the sensational news of the excavation of the newly discovered astrological mosaic in Beth Alpha[12] (see figure 13.1) in the *Vossische Zeitung* of 14 April 1929.

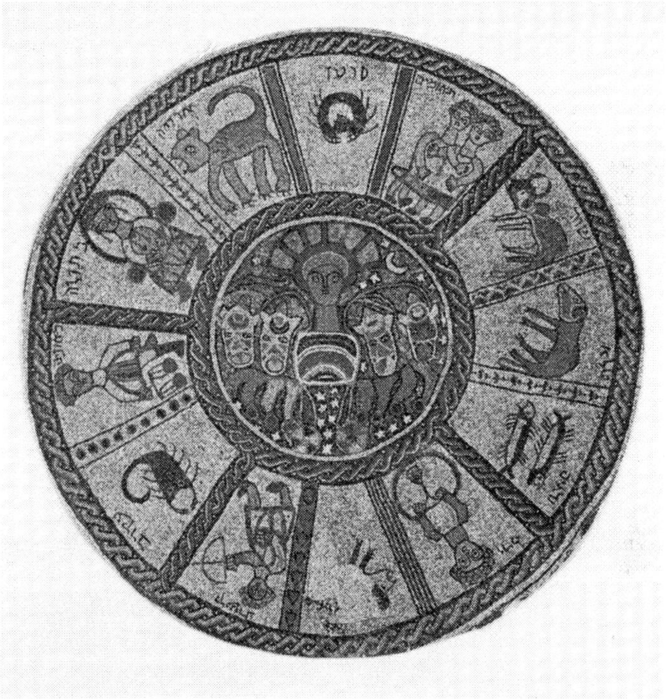

Figure 13.1 Beth Alpha, zodiac wheel with Hebrew captions. Mosaic.

Source: © Public domain.

11 WIA, FC, Warburg to G. Warburg, 14.5.1929.

12 Beth Alpha, thought to be a synagogue from the 6th century CE, is located at the foot of the Gilboa mountains, a mountain range overlooking the Jezreel Valley to the north and the Jordan Valley to the south-east.

1/ To Gisela Warburg

Copy Naples, Excelsior Hotel, 14.5.1929

You have clearly and convincingly felt the great, seemingly unbridgeable contrast between the Jews at the Wailing Wall and the Jews of the soil, in its destructive opposition towards those Jews who are longing to return home. On one side are the Chaluzim,[13] these desperadoes of this-worldliness, on the other side are the Ghetto Jews who, burdened by their heritage, have grown so fond of Yiddish, the secret language of their prison, that they cling to it as if to a magical religious dialect. What then do the pious prove? The loss of the temple? If it were allowed to be rebuilt, they could make sacrifices as they did in the heyday of the Jewish empire. You only need to read in 'Josephus', when the enemies laid siege to Jerusalem, how the high priests tried to bribe them in order to obtain the sacrificial animals for the altar (for, without the smell of burning blood and flesh God did not listen to their supplications).[14] Because of the destruction of the slaughter altar of Jerusalem, Judaism has finally been forced to accept a monotheistic spiritualisation, which is something one cannot get across to a Jew from the Ghetto, who believes that the Messiah will come only when the altars in Jerusalem smell of burnt flesh again. I would really like to know what the Rabbis of today and the Ghetto Jews in Jerusalem think about burnt offerings in practice.

2/In the development of the sacrificial cult (which is the mysterious centre of each religion) Judaism has occupied a heroic and facilitating position of enlightenment through the fact that Elijah inflicted an irremediable moral defeat on the child-killing Moloch priests;[15] however, animal sacrifices remained, and in this way the Jews remained pagans in the Mediterranean basin. Only the revolutionary inheritors of Judaism, the Christians, tried to cleanse the house of God of the thick smoke from the sacrificial altar by imagining a general replacement of blood sacrifices.[16] But in one instance the old and the new Jews did the same thing, they denied the incense offering to the deified human emperor at the cost of their lives.[17] The Chaluzim, if they won back the temple, would not be plagued by such religious Ghetto scruples. Maybe, these upstarts of this-worldliness would turn it into an agricultural academy. How, then, can one give these ambivalent homecomers a personal, fruitful sense of community? They need to be shown by academic teachers that historic consciousness (formed in a European style) can bring them

13 Pioneers.

14 See Whiston, W., *Flavius Josephus, Jewish Antiquities 6*, 91–111.

15 See the Hebrew Bible, Second Book of Kings, 23:10.

16 See the Greek Bible, Letter to the Hebrews, 9.

17 See Pliny the Younger, in Carrington, P., *The Early Christian Church*. This letter (c. 109–111) is the earliest account of Christian worship.

to a level-headedness about the spiritual place which they inhabit and by doing so open up to them a region where it is no longer necessary to bloody themselves with the harp of Zion[18] or the American spade.

It is precisely this spade which excavated a mosaic a short time ago, which showed those keen to return as if 'through a glass darkly'[19] one page of the diary of the eternal Jew, which initially they cannot read. Because of this an old Jewish lighthouse keeper on the North Sea has to decide to help out with an admittedly tentative interpretation.[20]

3/On 14th April an article was published in Vossische Zeitung about an excavated mosaic in Beth Alpha, followed by a partial and poor illustration in the 'Zeitgeist' section[21] on 28th April. By trying – not without some effort – to force myself to ignore the sensationalist tone and the unsavoury Ghetto sentimentality of the author, there arises for the historian of religion the following: the discovery of a mosaic and temple ruins in the shape of a basilica, which opens out to the south in a sort of almemar finished off by the ark of the Torah. A lion and a bull, flanking the ark of the Torah, finish the mosaic in the south.[22]

[Two footnotes by Warburg (1, 2) entered here in the original:

1, Is the lion the symbol of Judah and the bull the symbol of Israel? To which time do the small coins, which are cited as part of the hoard date back?

2, Whether Isaac is placed above or below the cosmos is not reported by the all-too awestruck journalist. [All words are crossed out except for 'Isaac' and 'below the cosmos'].

It ['the mosaic', crossed out] shows two images, one biblical and one seemingly pagan-cosmological. The first one shows the preparations for the sacrifice of Isaac, six people and the substitute, the ram.[23] The journalist, not versed in art history, allowed himself to be misled by the artistically unhelpful formal treatment of the zodiacal symbols to view the entire cosmos mosaic as a Byzantine incursion into autochthonous culture. However, if you look more carefully, you will notice a highly characteristic deviation in the iconological centring. It is not Helios – Sol,

18 See Psalm 137, 1–5.

19 See *The Jerusalem Bible*, 1 Cor. 13:12: 'Now we are seeing a dim reflection in a mirror; but then we shall be seeing face to face'. St Paul, Apostle, 5–64/67.

20 Warburg used terms like 'rotating tower' or 'lighthouse' to explain the wide-ranging research of his library in Hamburg and his role in it.

21 Warburg uses 'Zeitgeist' here, which is wrong, it should be 'Zeitbilder' in *Vossische Zeitung*.

22 For the report of the excavation see Sukenik, E.L., *The Ancient Synagogue of Beth Alpha*, 1932. An almemar is a raised platform for a lectern in a synagogue, similar to a pulpit in a church.

23 Warburg writes here about the solar chariot, which surrounds the zodiac, and about the sacrifice of Isaac, called 'the Binding of Isaac'. Gen. 22:1–18. In Jewish interpretations, the 'Binding' is either an affirmation of God's mercy or a confirmation of the covenant with Israel; in Christian interpretation it is a typological prefiguration of the crucifixion. Isaac, son of Abraham and Sarah.

who drives the quadriga in the centre, because the animals are not horses, but bulls.[24] And with this we arrive at the primeval-semitic moon religion.

4/God might be either the moon herself or Zebaoth, the lord of the astral heavenly host, hinted at by some 20 stars (stations of the moon?). For a long time people have tried to look at the moon for similar representations of the Cosmocrator, instead of the sun. Professor Saxl, for instance, has pointed to a Persian silver salver, which shows the moon in the guise of the driver of a quadriga pulled by bulls.[25]

[One footnote by Warburg, (3): Saxl, 'Planetendarstellungen', Islam, vol. III, ill. 6.]

The arrangement of zodiacal symbols corresponds completely to the Hellenistic model of depictions of the cosmos, as they are known mainly in the context of the sanctuaries of Mithras, the sun god of soldiers, whose cult, the most resistant enemy of Christianity, even overran Germany in the times of the migration of peoples.[26]

[One footnote by Warburg, (4): See the research by Cumont, Mysterien des Mithras; die orientalischen Religionen im römischen Heidentum. (A new French edition is being prepared and will be published soon.)]

The mosaic therefore emerges on the face of it as a schematic diagram, just like those in many other contemporary religions, but completely independent and claiming to be understood programmatically and ideologically.

A Hebrew inscription tells us that at the time of Emperor Justinian the temple was either endowed or built by Marianus, the son of Chanina. The same inscription is repeated in Greek.[27]

5/So, a man stands in front of us, here expressed in the shape of pagan cosmological science, contrary to the old prohibition on images of God, and included into the cult. But all this culminates in the reading of the Torah hinting at the intrinsic leitmotif of the religiosity of Isaac's sacrifice. If you know the literature of the typology of images, that is, the religious-philosophical-historical understanding of the Church Fathers, who saw in the activities of the Old Testament the precursors from the time of the unredeemed, we find in this a peculiarly demonstrative expla-

24 Research findings come to a different explanation today; the solar chariot is drawn by horses. See Sukenik, E.L., *The Ancient Synagogue of Beth Alpha*.

25 For the article Warburg is referring to, see Saxl, F., 'Beiträge zu einer Geschichte der Planetendarstellungen im Orient und Okzident', 151–177.

26 Warburg knew the book by Cumont on Mithras, see Cumont, F., *Die Mysterien des Mithra*. In the Roman cult Mithras was regarded as god, as Sol Invictus, unconquered sun. Franz Cumont, Belgian archaeologist, 1868–1947.

27 See Sukenik, E.L., *The Ancient Synagogue of Beth Alpha*, 43–47. Justinian I, Eastern Roman emperor, 482–565; Marianus, the son of Chanina, artisan, 6th century CE.

nation for the cult of sacrifices.[28] Not the human sacrifice, which Christianity puts into the centre of its mysteries, but the sacrifice of animals as substitute, is used here as the quote on the banner. The sacrifice of Isaac in the old belief was, indeed, the precursor, which the Christian church saw as the actual objective to be overcome.

So, what do we have in front of us? As long as I do not have more photographs of the mosaic and the temple remains with their measurements, I will under no circumstances pass judgment. But to you, who have been travelling through Palestine, I want to say only, without obligation, that we stand here in front of a totally novel, very courageous attempt at a 'new-fangled' characterful balancing act, attempting to express an ideology by making a compromise between Greek and Semitic cosmologies, bound with the old Jewish teaching of substitution sacrifice. Against this backdrop Marianus Ben Chanina would, in good conscience, have been able to have the Torah read to them. The word, not the sacrificial act, had the [last?] word.[29]

14. V. 929

Naples

Compare Cumont; La Théologie Solaire du Paganisme Romain, Paris 1909,[30] p. 5: 'En Chaldée, le soleil, Shamash, est une personnage secondaire qui suit Sin[31] comme son serviteur'. When reading this, who does not think of the shamash of the Chanukah candlestick? In the centre of its arrangement (according to the Chaldeans' arrangement of the planetary sphere) is the single little candle which lights all other candles and is called shamash, meaning servant. Years ago I discovered the ms Uffenbach, a Hebrew-German illustrated planetary calendar, in the Hamburg City Library.[32] It was owned by Susman Simon Warburg, who lived in the vicinity of Frankfurt and perhaps was one of our ancestors. The planet of the sun was represented as a man, wearing luxurious, long garments and bearing a bowl of fruits (?), with the Hebrew word 'shamash' next to him. In any case, the planet here is not shown as the king, but as the bringer of gifts.[33]

28 The sacrifice of Isaac as reference for the sacrifice of Jesus on the cross has since antiquity been held up as example for the Christian interconnection with and interpretation of the Old Testament.

29 This sentence, a handwritten addition to the typed text, breaks off without being finished.

30 Cumont, F., *La Théologie Solaire du Paganisme Romain*, part 2. In the original the page reference is 4, not 5. 'In Chaldea, the sun, Shamash, is a secondary character, who follows Sin like her servant'.

31 Sîn was the name for the moon, who was followed by her servant, Shamash; this word is written with the same consonants, but vocalised differently for the name of the sun, Shemesh.

32 Philipp Uffenbach, German painter, 1566–1636. Warburg, although mentioning a manuscript, refers to Uffenbach's book *Zeitweiser*, with a sun dial and gnomic world map. Uffenbach, P., *Bericht und Erklärung zweier beigefügten Kupferstücken, oder Zeitweiser der Sonnen über die ganze Welt*.

33 WIA, FC, Warburg to G. Warburg, 14.5.1929, typed copy with manuscript additions. For extensive comments see McEwan and Treml, 'Aby an Gisela', 4–8.

This, undoubtedly, was heavy stuff. It was not only meant for Gisela. On the same day he sent copies of the typed letter to his wife Mary and to Saxl.[34] He asked Saxl to find out more about Marianus, which Saxl promised to do, but Saxl also used the opportunity to spell out some corrections. He agreed with Warburg that in history blood sacrifices came to an end with the expulsion of the Jews. However, the tendency to 'turn Judaism into a pure logos religion' was older and the expulsion was only an external cause. It was also not the destruction of the temple that forced Judaism to accept monotheistic spiritualisation. There would have been centuries of preparation for this process. Saxl also interpreted the sacrifice of Isaac differently and placed it in the broad context of ancient hopes of salvation. Alongside representations of this event on the floors of ancient synagogues, other biblical narratives like Daniel in the lions' den (cf. Daniel 6:2–29) had been found:

> It is certainly no coincidence, that these images are also favourite topics in early Christian art. In early Christian art we are completely clear on how to interpret them. Daniel and Isaac are presented as symbols of salvation. They are illustrations of the age-old prayer formula: as you have saved Daniel, Isaac, Susanna etc., in the same way also save us. – These presentations correspond to the presentations of the apotheosis of Heracles, the resurrected Attis, etc. in pagan religions.[35]

Also the emblematic centre piece in Beth Alpha, with the chariot drawn by animals, was interpreted differently by Saxl: they were not bulls, but rather lions.

> What stops me from seeing bulls here is, first of all, the position of the crescent moon to the right of the head, which, in any case, would have to appear above the head of the main figure, and secondly the zodiac. The zodiac is, as a matter of course, the orbital of the sun. I therefore think that for the time being one should recognise in the main figure here the cosmocrator Yahweh.[36]

Warburg stuck to his guns: Saxl's objections had only confirmed his view that the figure stood in the courtyard. But he wanted to know in which other synagogues there were similar mosaics – 'How is it possible that the moon (sun) god, placed in the centre, is supposed to be Yahweh? That would offend every dress code'.[37]

Mary Warburg found Gisela's letter impressive and could not suppress her fear that Warburg's reply would give Gisela bellyache or she would understand only half of it.[38] In response Warburg decreed by cable that the whole family, which

34 WIA, GC, Warburg to Saxl, 14.5.1929; WIA, FC, Warburg to Mary Warburg, 14.5.1929.

35 WIA, GC, Saxl to Warburg, 22.5.1929, W/S.

36 WIA, GC, Saxl to Warburg, Yahweh, the national god of ancient Israel.

37 WIA, GC, Warburg to Saxl, 28.5.1929, W/S.

38 WIA, FC, Mary Warburg to Warburg, 17.5.1929.

had got together for the Whitsun holiday in their country houses in Kösterberg near Hamburg, should convene a family conference with Saxl and Paul Ruben, a Hebraist and friend of the family, in order for them to explain the mosaic and the illustration in *Vossische Zeitung*.[39] Two days later he sent a cable asking 'have you and Gisela understood Beth Alpha?'[40] and four days later another saying he was 'grateful for well-founded objections'.[41]

Warburg's interest in Beth Alpha persisted, because Gisela's report and her observations were expressive of a polarised Jewish world. On one side were 'the Jews of Wailing Wall' or the 'Ghetto Jews', on the other 'the Jews of the soil', both in the same country, both 'homecomers', both groups 'encumbered by their heritage'. Warburg admitted that his biological terminology made overcoming these divides improbable, unless one could find a cultural sphere in which change were possible. Warburg had discovered such a sphere in religion, more precisely in the reversal of the assumption that God could be won over by the smell of burnt meat God, which would lead to a cultic practice beyond burnt offerings. The Christians, who shared the divine tradition with the Jews, had taken the next step – they had cleansed the house of God of sacrificial smoke – and with the Jews, whether they clung to the smell of the sacrifices or not, had gone the next step and refused to obey a 'deified human emperor'. How would the 'desperadoes of this-worldliness', the new Zionist settlers in Palestine, develop a feeling for a fatherland with the old pious Ghetto Jews; how could they learn not to be strangers any more to each other?[42] A prophetic question which, today more than ever, characterises the situation.

There were traditionally pious people in Warburg's own family too. He had quarrels with his father, for instance about keeping the ritual dietary rules as a student in Bonn. His engagement to a Protestant Christian woman, Mary Hertz, was discussed in many a letter; even his siblings had different opinions. His sister Olga said that a woman who accepted the name of her husband should also accept his religion.[43]

Warburg's brother Max was more conciliatory. He understood his father's view, which he and his other siblings shared. On the one hand, he knew that his new sister-in-law Mary could not be forced to change her religion. On the other hand, he would insist that children born of this marriage should be brought up as Jews. However, the Warburg family had no right to expect the bride's family to meet this condition precisely because 'the Jewish race and religion' was wrongly interpreted to be lower than 'the race and religion of the bride'. A belief in God beyond dogmas would minimise frictions, because there was no difference between a pious Jew and a pious Christian.[44]

Brother Paul fell into line. The first five books of the Hebrew Bible were the same for Jews and Christians, so Mary would be able to hand on to their children

39 WIA, FC, Warburg to Mary Warburg, 20.5.1929. Paul Ruben, German Hebraist, 1866–1943.
40 WIA, FC, Warburg to Mary Warburg, 22.5.1929.
41 WIA, FC, Warburg to Mary Warburg, 26.5.1929.
42 WIA, FC, Warburg to G. Warburg, 14.5.1929.
43 WIA, FC, O. Warburg to Warburg, 5.4.1897.
44 WIA, FC, Max Warburg to Warburg, 11.4.1897.

a religion which resonated with her own, along the lines of 'Your father is a Jew and I, your mother, I am a Christian and yet the good which we strive for and in which we believe is the same'. Many Christians were only Christians because they despised the Jews, he said, and so it was nobler to be on the side of those who suffered injustice than to inflict injustice.[45]

All exhortations and pleas brought the opposite effect. Warburg had made a decision; he did not want to cave in to family pressure. It all smacked to him of 'a piece of heartless formality'.[46] He and Mary married in Wiesbaden in the absence of his parents, who met the young couple one day later. Warburg's father and mother loved their new daughter-in-law as dearly as their other daughters-in-law. The children were not raised as Jews; Warburg had left the Jewish community of Hamburg, and he did not keep the dietary rules, but through all his life he was sensitive when he read about pogroms in the newspapers. His brother Max had published a memorandum during World War I with the title 'The Jewish Question in the Context of German Politics',[47] which Warburg commented on at length. In his view it should be part of the 'personal file of the German nation'.[48] He explained Zionism to Max thus:

> I would not touch this sensitive point, rather wait until the question is put to you, as is unavoidable. The reference to Catholicism is particularly dangerous; its conflict with German culture has only been covered up.[49]

During his stay in the sanatorium Bellevue in Kreuzlingen on Lake Constance from 1921 to 1924, Warburg was encouraged as part of his therapy to write his autobiography, and so he wrote about impressions from his days as a schoolboy, when Darwinism had flourished and stood diametrically opposed to the religious practice of his family. He had found it unbearable that people should bow under the yoke of God. He therefore left school a staunch optimistic follower of the theory of evolution and in this way liberated himself from his past, as he avowed. He recalled how he had felt as if he had two heads like Janus.[50] Warburg had stopped his religious Jewish practice and yet had rediscovered his heritage in events and images,[51] which presented him with a spiritual ambivalence. This ambivalence shines through his writings on the excavation of Beth Alpha and his thoughts on the iconography of the mosaic. As a topic it lived on the KBW when Bing declared that she would not convert to Christianity and A. A. Barb had done just that.[52]

45 WIA, FC, Paul Warburg to Warburg, 16.4.1897.

46 WIA, FC, Warburg to Max Warburg, 31.5.1897.

47 Warburg, M., *Die Judenfrage im Rahmen der deutschen Gesamtpolitik*. Cf. Schoell-Glass, C., *Aby Warburg und der Antisemitismus. Kulturwissenchaft als Geistespolitik*, in particular 132–143.

48 WIA, GC, Copy book VI, 270–272, Warburg to Max Warburg, 25.11.1916.

49 WIA, GC, Copy book VI, 270–272, Warburg to Max Warburg, 25.11.1916.

50 WIA, GC, Warburg to Fritz Saxl, 24.11.1922. Janus is the Roman god of beginnings who, with his two faces, looks both forwards and backwards at once.

51 WIA, FC, Warburg to G. Warburg, 14.5.1929.

52 See Chapter 14. A. A. Barb, Austrian archaeologist, 1901–1979.

14

'WHAT I CAN REPRESENT AS A JEW, I CAN ALSO REPRESENT AS A CATHOLIC'. ON ALFONS AUGUSTINUS BARB'S SCHOLARLY CAREER AND HIS CHANGE OF RELIGION[1]

Alfons Augustinus Barb's academic career

Among the 116 entries of works by Barb (see figure 14.1) in the catalogue of The Warburg Institute only one third comprises titles of his works before World War II. However, these titles figure in the catalogue of the Burgenland Regional Museum in Eisenstadt, so that both catalogues attest to Barb's extraordinarily rich creative work.

Barb was born in 1901 and was listed in the register of the Jewish community of Vienna with the names Alphons Asher. In the Viennese circles of liberal Judaism it had become common place for children to be given German as well as Jewish names. Barb read classical and Oriental studies in Vienna, while at the same time training to become a goldsmith and jeweller. He was awarded his doctorate with his research on *The imperial coins of the city of Tarsos in Cilicia* in 1924.[2] In addition to this topic he was interested in the area of Pannonia, originally the province of the Roman Empire bounded on the north and east by the Danube, today western Hungary and the province of Burgenland in Austria, which became incorporated into the Republic of Austria in 1921. His publications covered excavations of Celtic, Roman and medieval burial grounds and articles explaining the finds he unearthed. His detailed research was appreciated by Aby Warburg as well as by Fritz Saxl and Gertrud Bing, director and deputy director respectively of The Warburg Institute (see figure 14.2).

1 Originally published in McEwan, D., '"Das, was ich als Jude vertrete, kann ich auch als Katholik vertreten". Zu Alfons Augustinus Barbs wissenschaftlicher Laufbahn und seinem Glaubenswechsel', 102–147.

I wish to thank the family of A. A. Barb profoundly for their interest in and support of my article as well as the WIA for the permission to quote from Barb's letters. My thanks also go to Dr. Timothy Jackson, Dublin, Professor Wolfgang Hahn, Vienna, and Fr. Philippe Luisier, SJ, Rome, for their helpful comments after reading the first draft.

2 Barb, A.A., *Die kaiserlichen Münzen der Stadt Tarsos in Kilikien.*

DOI: 10.4324/9781003169024-18

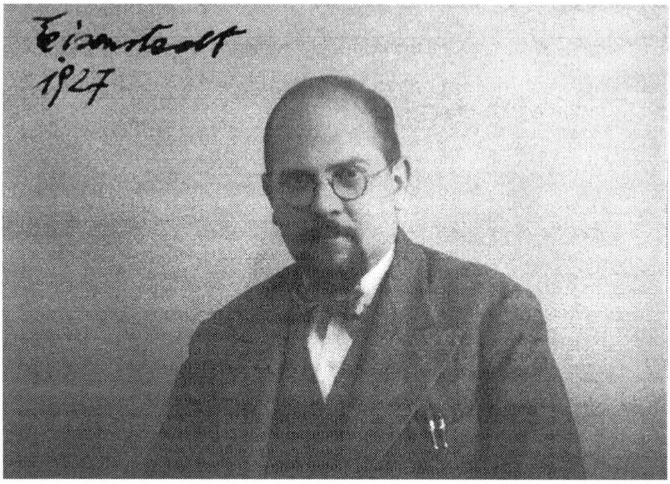

Figure 14.1 Portrait Barb, Eisenstadt, 1927.
Source: © Private collection, Barb Family, A – VI 55.

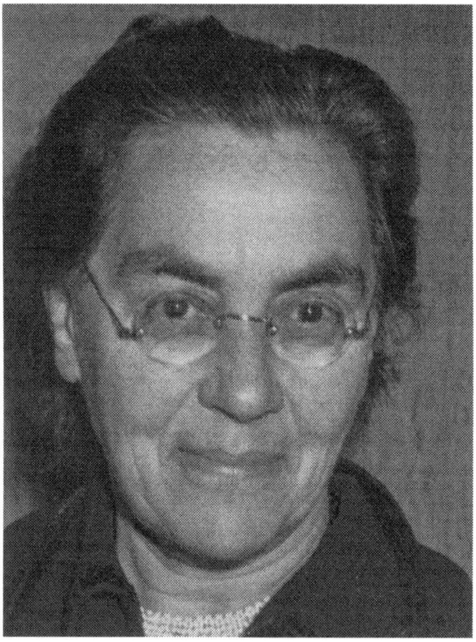

Figure 14.2 Gertrud Bing. WIA, Portrait collection, n.d., in the 1930s.
Source: © Photo: The Warburg Institute.

The political catastrophe of the annexation of Austria to the German Reich in 1938 threw him off course. A folder with Barb's personal papers, his curriculum vitae in German and English, highlights the solid practical training he underwent in order to earn a living: the copy of his goldsmith apprenticeship certification exam of 26 June 1922, the employer's report from the jeweller Karl Bauer in Vienna from 1919 to 1922, and the certificate from the Brothers Zirner, court jewellers on Graben, Vienna, of 24 October 1923 are impressive testimonials to Barb's work. Later, in his academic work on gemstones, his training would prove important to him.

Sandor Wolf, a wine merchant, art collector and honorary conservator of the Federal Monuments Office, had brought together a great collection of antiquities and was looking for a space to display the objects in Eisenstadt, the capital city of the new province of Burgenland.[3] While the province of Burgenland had been part of western Hungary, with its historic cities like Sopron and Moson, both in Hungary, and Bratislava, in Slovakia, Eisenstadt had remained a small city. However, after the referendum in 1921, which split the western part of Hungary, Eisenstadt flourished. Wolf put one of his houses, the 'Leinner-Haus', at the disposal of Eisenstadt in which to establish the new museum with his collection.

After finishing his degree at the university of Vienna, Barb worked as an unpaid assistant in the numismatic department of the university. After having published his first articles on archaeological finds in Pannonia and following discussions with his doctoral supervisor Wilhelm Kubitschek, Barb was employed by the newly established Burgenland Regional Museum, at first to catalogue the Wolf collection, and then from 1929 onwards as its director.[4] Barb's wife, Ilona Geiger, from Hungary, was related to Sandor Wolf. The museum soon gained an excellent reputation, not least through Barb's mission, his many excavations and research publications. But in 1938 he shared the same fate as all his coreligionists. Dr. Tobias Portschy, head of the local government in Burgenland, announced to Barb four days after the annexation, 'I suspend you from your office of director of the Regional Museum with immediate effect'.[5] It was completely clear to Barb that he had to write to his academic colleagues abroad. He started an extensive correspondence with colleagues in Europe, among them, as a matter of course, Saxl, the director of The Warburg Institute in London, the institute of intellectual history which had been able to make a name for itself in London in a short span of time.

3 Sandor Wolf, Austrian wine merchant and collector of antiquities, 1871–1946. His collection formed the basis of the new museum.

4 Hess, M., *Braver Beamter, Oppotunist, Verfolgter: die burgenländischen Spitzenbeamten von 1923 bis 1938*, 'Alphons Barb', 415–434, here 415, 416 and 420. Hess's chapter is a summary of Barb's personnel file in Eisenstadt. Wilhelm Kubitschek, Austrian classical historian, 1858–1936.

5 Barb Family Private Papers [BFPP], *Journal* no. 1, 2015. T. Portschy to A.A. Barb, 17.3.1938. Tobias Portschy, Austrian national socialist politician, 1905–1996.

Leaving Austria

Barb wrote to Saxl about his 'most urgent need to emigrate'.[6] It was Bing who would be on hand over the years with help and advice. Barb had been in touch with the institute a few times, sending his booklets to London, for instance *The craft of witches in classical antiquity originating from the decay of classical religions*[7] and *Austria at the time of the Romans*,[8] or asking for the loan of books not available to him in Eisenstadt or Vienna.[9]

Scholars like Balduin Saria, an Austrian historian studying ancient history, who wrote a reference for Barb[10] and whose articles and books are kept in The Warburg Institute, and Leo Aryeh Mayer, who had studied in Vienna and was Professor at the Hebrew University in Jerusalem, wrote to The Warburg Institute.[11] The Hebrew University, the second oldest university in Israel, was founded in 1918. Among the financiers was Felix Warburg, one of Aby Warburg's brothers, who lived in the USA and was the founder of *The American Friends of the Hebrew University* in June 1925. Since then, the family of Felix Warburg had supported the Hebrew University and in particular the Institute of Jewish Studies in remembrance of his parents, Moritz and Charlotte Warburg.

It stood to reason that scholars like Mayer supported Barb. They knew his academic work and his research findings, which fitted in with those of The Warburg Institute. The KBW in Hamburg was the creation of Aby Warburg, the German art historian or, more precisely, 'image historian', as he explained to the art historian Carl Neumann in 1917.[12] Strictly speaking, he was a cultural scientist, who had made it his life's passion to research the survival of classical antiquity in the history of the European mind. The commercial orientation of Hamburg hardly touched the young Warburg, who was the eldest son of a banker and thereby expected to succeed his father in the bank. He chose a different profession: he studied art history, not the narrow attribution of works of arts, but the explanation of symbols used in sculptures and images from antiquity to the Renaissance, which had undergone metamorphoses and transformations that were ever more difficult to understand.[13] This was, however, precisely the field of work that was

6 WIA, GC, A.A. Barb to Saxl, 1.6.1938. Fritz Saxl, Austrian art historian, 1890–1948.

7 Barb, *Klassische Hexenkunst aus der Verwesung antiker Religionen*, 1–32. Gertrud Bing, German art historian, 1892–1964.

8 Barb, *Österreich zur Römerzeit*, 1–33.

9 WIA, Bing to A.A. Barb, 27.6.1928.

10 BFPP, *Journal* no. 3, 1010, B. Saria to unnamed recipient, 15.12.1938. Balduin Saria, Austrian historian, 1893–1974.

11 WIA, GC, A.A. Barb to Bing, 16.11.1938. Leo Aryeh Mayer, Israeli scholar on Islamic art, 1895–1959.

12 WIA, GC, Warburg to Carl Neumann, 20.3.1917. See also WIA, III.10.7. Diary, 12.2.1917, 885, entry of a conversation by Aby Warburg with his son Max Adolf, in which Warburg called himself 'image historian', not 'art historian'. Carl Neumann, German art historian, 1860–1934.

13 For general as well as more specialised introductions to Aby Warburg's oeuvre, the KBW in Hamburg, Fritz Saxl and The Warburg Institute in London, see the website of The Warburg Institute and

important to Barb, who had been confronted with imagery, through his archaeological work, which so far had been difficult to interpret.

Both Warburg and Saxl grew up in liberal bourgeois families. Warburg's parents and siblings kept the rituals of their religion, while Aby Warburg discontinued his religious practice during his student days. Despite this, he was interested all throughout his life in research by Jewish scholars, news about Judaism, the fate of Jewish colleagues, and so on, and although he no longer practised his religion, there was no talk of converting to another religion.

In Warburg's library in Hamburg his librarian, Fritz Saxl, focused his research on the investigation of late classical antiquity and early Christianity.[14] He understood this area of research as closely related to the growth of the Christian religion, which, according to Hans Liebeschütz,[15] was tantamount to an 'analysis of European culture'.[16] For Saxl a juxtaposition of synagogue and church was not the way to pursue the development of cultures. His method was to understand both perspectives as human successes: from his own personal intellectual point of view and from his inherited point of view. As a Jewish man, everywhere an outsider, as it were, he could exercise his own mental independence and with it his study of religions without a tie-in to a particular religion or religious practice.[17]

The history of religion, literature and ideas, the migration of symbolic forms from Asia to Europe, the crossing of image elements to other regions and cultures, the artistic unfolding of an idea – all these aspects of human creative power were topics for Saxl as well as for Barb. It is therefore understandable that Barb turned to The Warburg Institute in London in his hour of need. Nearly all of the employees at the institute had been in a similar situation to Barb, affected by the Nazi laws on the non-admissibility of Jewish civil servants. Aby Warburg had died in 1929 and thus did not live to see the rise of Hitler. Saxl and Bing did see it and drew their conclusions: after the book burnings in Germany in 1933 they went to Great Britain and in bringing the entire library of 55,000 books with them, saved them. Helped by the Warburg bank as well as by British philanthropists, the group of continental academics were successful with their new start in London. At first their stay was only guaranteed for three years, then extended for seven years, and then made permanent when the Institute was incorporated into the University of London in 1944. One of the most significant reasons for this was the fact that some 40 per cent of books in the library were not available in any other public library in Britain.[18]

the books and articles by Dorothea McEwan in the catalogue of the Warburg Institute Library, as well as the bibliography in this volume.

14 For instance Saxl, F., 'Frühes Christentum und spätes Heidentum in ihren künstlerischen Ausdrucksformen', 63–121 or idem, *Mithras*.

15 See Liebeschütz, H, *Das allegorische Weltbild der heiligen Hildegard von Bingen*. With Saxl's help Liebeschütz was able to emigrate to Great Britain where initially he was interned on the Isle of Man, like Barb. Hans Liebeschütz, German medievalist, 1893–1978.

16 Liebeschütz, H., 'Aby Warburg (1866–1929) as Interpreter of Civilisation', 225–236, here 228.

17 Liebeschütz, H., 'Aby Warburg (1866–1929) as Interpreter of Civilisation', 228.

18 See McEwan, D., *Fritz Saxl. Eine Biografie*, Appendix II, Trust Deed, 28.11.1944, 301–302.

When all this happened, Barb had been in Great Britain for a number of years, still very much in touch in person as well as by correspondence with Saxl and Bing. After this leap ahead for the establishment of The Warburg Institute, it is important to come back to the personal situation for Barb in 1938. Saxl and Bing had championed German, Czechoslovak and Austrian colleagues for many years: they helped them with travel arrangements, visa matters and employment opportunities; they contacted authorities and private individuals for requests for assistance.[19] The archive of The Warburg Institute is witness to this humanitarian assistance. And all this was, as a matter of course, the case with Barb. As with so many others, Barb's requests sounded ever more urgent in 1938, the hopelessness of the situation became ever more desolate, the letters bulged with curricula vitae, letters of reference and texts for application for a post. On a picture postcard of the Burgenland Regional Museum, which shows the skeleton of a small dinosaur, Barb assured that he would be happy with any work, for his case in Eisenstadt was desperate (see figure 14.3)[20] and in November 1938 Barb sent a job application in

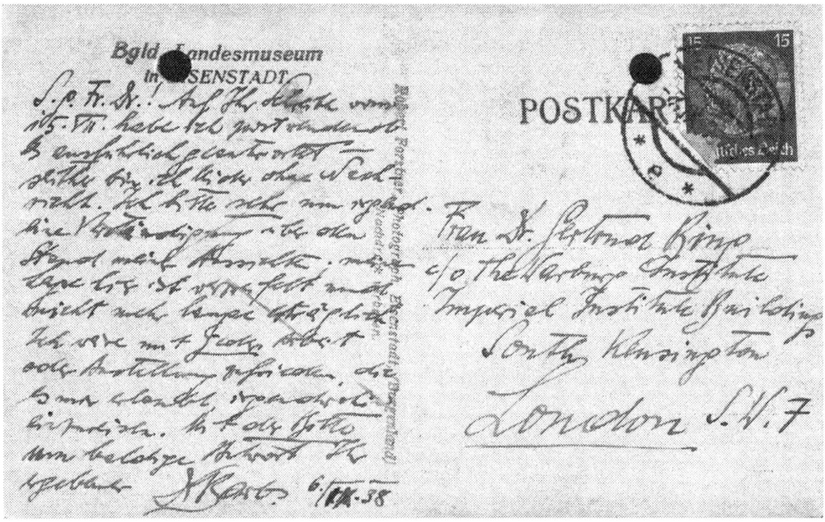

Figure 14.3 Picture postcard. WIA, GC, A. A., Barb to Bing, 6.9.1938.

Source: © Photo: The Warburg Institute.

19 Cooper, R., *Retrospective Sympathetic Affection*, supported immigrants with advice for employment worldwide.

20 WIA, GC, A.A. Barb to Bing, 6.9.1938.

English in which he stressed his training and determination to accept any work whatsoever:

> Married Couple; Austrian Jews; 37 and 34; two children, 11 and 8; wife excellent cook, nurse, very efficient in all household duties; man doctor of philosophy, experienced teacher, private tutor, librarian, but also most skillfull [sic] worker, trained goldsmith and jeweller, dexterous in all handicrafts; want position; go anywhere; excellent references. – Dr. Barb, Vienna I Ruprechtsplatz 1.[21]

After having been relieved of his post immediately after the annexation of Austria, he was appointed on 1 December 1938 as 'curator of archaeological finds in the administrative district Neusiedl am See in Burgenland (now Niederdonau)'. One month later, however, he was also relieved of this appointment in line with the dictate of the racist Nuremberg Laws. On behalf of Herbert Seiberl, president of the central office for the protection of monuments in the Ministry of the Interior and Culture, Dr. Willvonseder signed Barb's certificate of employment:

> The merits which you have earned as curator of the central office for the protection of historical monuments, as well as director of the Burgenland Regional Museum for prehistorical and early historical research, will always be appreciated here.

In the appendix Willvonseder praised Barb for his work as director of the Burgenland Regional Museum from 1926 to 1938 as he performed his duties to the fullest satisfaction of his superiors. Barb's successor assessed his work as 'the best'.[22] This meant that Barb was pensioned off as scientific assistant of the province of Burgenland on 1 February 1939.[23] In fact, Heinrich Kunnert wrote in his article on Barb that the pressure from the Gestapo was so great that Barb and his family were threatened with internment in a concentration camp if they emigrated to England without a prior work permit. On 20 March 1939 Barb informed the president of the State government of Niederdonau, eastern Austria, that he had moved to 214 Finchley Rd, London NW3.[24]

21 WIA, GC, A.A. Barb to Bing, 27.11.1938.

22 BFPP, *Journal* no. 3, EA 1006. Dr. Kurt Willvonseder, for the president of the central office for the protection of historical monuments in the Ministry of Internal and Cultural Affairs, to A.A. Barb, 4.1.1939. Herbert Seiberl, Austrian president of the Central office for the protection of monuments, 1905–1952; Kurt Willvonseder, Austrian prehistorian, 1903–1968.

23 BFPP, *Journal* no. 3, EA 1003. Karl Johann Vogel [styled 'Vogl' by Barb], for the presidium of the government of Niederdonau, to A.A. Barb, 1.2.1939. See also Eminger, S., 'Theresianisten, CVer, Burschenschafter. Spitzenbeamte in Niederösterreich 1918–1934–1938–1945', 239–270, here 255. Karl Johann Vogel, Austrian civil servant, member of the NSDAP, 1883–1945.

24 Kunnert, H., 'Alphons A. Barb. 75 Jahre', 3–6, here 4. I am grateful to Michael Hess for a copy of this document from Barb's personnel file. A.A. Barb signed as 'retired academic local government employee'.

Thus ended Barb's scientific career in Austria and more, his livelihood in Austria. It was the need of the hour to find a way out, to escape wherever possible, so that he could rebuild his life again. He was married, had two children, had a profession in hand, but the anxiety-filled weeks and months after the annexation of Austria brought severe burdens to Barb. It was during this time that Barb had contacted Saxl and Bing; in June 1938 he had pulled out all the stops to obtain an exit visa. In July 1938 Bing asked him whether he wanted to go to Palestine and become a goldsmith.[25] Barb replied immediately that he would like to do so, but he was 'completely penniless' and did not have the so-called 'capitalist certificate';[26] he reiterated that he was ready to work as a labourer anywhere,[27] and that he had to leave Austria by 31 January 1939 at the latest.[28] Barb referred to Leo Aryeh Mayer's letter to Bing,[29] which Bing replied to by asking him whether he would go as a goldsmith to Australia.[30] Barb replied that he wanted to emigrate only with his wife and children,[31] upon which Bing sent him a cable referring to the British initiative of the so-called Kindertransport, for bringing children to the UK and paying for their education. Bing said Barb should write to the office of the Reich Representation of German Jews at Kantstraße 158 in Berlin.[32]

Bing was able to confirm that she had been given a sufficient sum of money to finance Barb and his wife in London for some time. All further visa applications could be settled in London.[33] Barb sent a summary to Bing of his initiatives to emigrate in January 1939: he had written to 100 people in 25 countries for assistance. He was living on a pittance of 90 marks per month in Vienna with his family and repeated that he had to leave the country by the end of January 1939 at the latest.[34]

In January 1939 Professor Alfred Mahr, Austrian archaeologist and then director of the National Museum of Ireland, Dublin, sent a letter of recommendation to Bing. Mahr stressed how efficient Barb had been to build up a new museum and that the overcoming of all initial hurdles was due to Barb. In particular he mentioned the fact that cultural matters had been neglected in the kingdom of Hungary, and therefore in Eisenstadt, and yet despite this the regional museum in Eisenstadt owned a number of important objects from archaeology to art history and from paleology to the natural sciences, thanks to Barb's efforts.[35] A job advertisement, written by Mahr for Barb, was published in the same month in *The Museums Journal*.[36]

25 WIA, GC, Bing to A.A. Barb. 15.7.1938.
26 WIA, GC, Barb to Bing, 18.9.1938.
27 WIA, GC, Barb to Bing, 15.9.1938.
28 WIA, GC, Barb to Bing, 15.10.1938.
29 WIA, GC, Barb to Bing, 16.11.1938.
30 WIA, GC, Bing to Barb, 25.11.1938.
31 WIA, GC, Barb to Bing, 1.12.1938.
32 WIA, GC, Bing to Barb, 3.12.1938.
33 WIA, GC, Bing to Barb, 9.12.1938.
34 WIA, GC, Barb to Bing, 2.1.1939.
35 WIA, GC, Mahr to Bing, 12.1.1939. Alfred Mahr, Austrian archaeologist, 1887–1951.
36 BFPP, *Journal* no. 1, 2093; *The Museums Journal*, vol. 38, no. 10, 6.

Now events were precipitating. Barb wanted to leave on 31 January 1939 and spend a few days in England until receiving the visas for his onward journey to South America. He wanted to thank Bing in person for the 'incredible success' and expressed his hope 'that sometime in the future I will be permitted to prove my gratefulness with deeds'.[37] He was upbeat about the prospect of his emigration, even if he considered himself fair game.[38] Bing again informed him that the Quakers would be able to obtain his visa to Great Britain.[39] In the meantime he was sent a Columbian visa and declared that his wife and he himself would like to be useful as domestic servants in England for a short time.[40]

It did not matter to Barb whether he would be going to Columbia or Peru; he knew that he would be content with the most modest circumstances. He sent letters of recommendation to Bing, sent to him by 'local authorities, that is authorities of national socialist Germany', about which he, commenting sarcastically, was 'very proud!'[41] Despite all of these letters his scientific interest and articles did not break off; Bing thanked him for the copy of his new book *Early Roman Graves in Burgenland* for the library of The Warburg Institute.[42]

At last, on 15 March 1939, he cabled his arrival time in London[43] and right away scheduled meeting with friends in Oxford: Professor C. G. Seligman, a British anthropologist, Paul Jacobsthal, a German-British archaeologist, and Mahr, the Austrian archaeologist, and requested an appointment with Bing to quiz her about a stay in Great Britain.[44] A document in private ownership lists Barb and his wife as living in the London Borough of Kensington: 'Barb Alphons [later added in green ink: Augustinus], m[ale], 15.4.1901, Goldsmith, Jeweller, Mounter. Barb, Ilona, f[emale], 10.2.1904, unpaid, Domestic Duties'.[45]

Barb wrote to Bing to obtain information about the cost of renting a flat, about people who would act as guarantors so that the family could move in, about contacts in the former Austrian consulate, support associations, and so on, all simply termed a 'snowball system'. In the correspondence of these months Barb seemed preoccupied, pessimistic;[46] for a short time he worked for free in the British Museum in the department of coins and medals.[47] After the outbreak of the war he asked whether The Warburg Institute would stay open,[48] but was told that the

37 WIA, GC, A.A. Barb to Bing, 15.1.1939.
38 WIA, GC, A.A. Barb to Bing, 7.2.1939.
39 WIA, GC, Bing to A.A. Barb, 9.2.1939.
40 WIA, GC, A.A. Barb to Bing, 9.2.1939.
41 WIA, GC, A.A. Barb to Bing, 4.3.1939.
42 WIA, GC, Bing to A.A. Barb, 27.2.1939. Barb, A.A. (1938).
43 BFPP, *Journal* no. 1, 2094. WIA, GC, A.A. Barb to Bing, 15.3.1939.
44 WIA, GC, A.A. Barb to Bing, 22.3.1939. Charles Gabriel Seligman, British anthropologist, 1873–1940; Paul Jacobsthal, German art historian, 1880–1957.
45 BFPP, Borough of Kensington, not dated, c. 1939, without source indication. Entry no. 93.
46 WIA, GC, A.A. Barb to Bing, undated, Box 1939–1941.
47 WIA, GC, A.A. Barb to Bing, 12.8.1939.
48 WIA, GC, A.A. Barb to Bing, 18.9.1939.

Institute would be closed and the books would be moved to the countryside.[49] The departure to South America did not come about; rumours had it that he would not be able to work as a goldsmith.[50]

He still hoped to obtain a visa for Peru but reported a conversation with the Peruvian embassy to Bing: again, 'nobody with my qualifications is wanted in Peru'.[51] He then decided to register at the labour exchange in Great Britain, knowing only too well that he had to wait for two years until he, as a so-called *enemy alien*, an undesirable foreigner, was allowed to apply for work. In the meantime, he said, he would like to work as a German and Latin tutor for anybody who would like to make conversation with him in English.[52]

The fate of an emigrant, shared by so many others at the same time. Any correspondence in 1940 is missing in The Warburg Institute Archive. According to the entry in the Austrian biographical dictionary, Barb, like all other asylum seekers, was interned for a few months on the Isle of Man in a transit camp either in 1940 or 1941. According to Barb's own entries in his diaries he was on the Isle of Man, in Douglas, the capital, and lived in House 2, Central Promenade Camp, for three months in the summer of 1941. It was there that he read the works of the church father St Augustine of Hippo.[53] More on this follows below.

Moving to Leeds

Bing next received a letter from Barb 13 months on with the news of Barb's move to Leeds in the north of England.[54] He and his wife had found work as domestic servants; his children were allowed to stay with them in the house. He described his situation as tolerable, although the work was hard for his wife.[55] Bing, who exemplarily took a stand for all asylum seekers for many years, kept him informed about Institute news. She wrote that the librarian Dr. Hans Meier had been killed by an air raid on 17 April 1941.[56] All his many years of bibliographical research was lost. The death of Meier was tragic but in the first instance had nothing to do with offering a job to Barb. However, the letter proved that Bing knew full well that Barb knew of Meier's important work and therefore understood how great a

49 WIA, GC, Bing to A.A. Barb, 19.9.1939.

50 WIA, GC, see A.A. Barb to Mr. Döry (possibly Gabor Döry), related to Fritz Saxl, 26.6.1939 and WIA, GC, A.A. Barb to Bing, 22.11.1939.

51 WIA, GC, A.A. Barb to Bing, 22.11.1939.

52 WIA, GC, A.A. Barb to Bing, 22.11.1939.

53 Urban, O.H., 'Barb, Alphons Augustinus (1901–1979), Numismatiker', 2003–2018, here 2013. See also BFPP, *Journal* no. 3, 1110: 'During internment the reading of St. Augustine's "Confessiones" and "De Civitate Dei" led me, despite resistance in my family, to convert to the Roman catholic church (1941). I have taken the name AUGUSTINUS as my confirmation name'.

54 WIA, GC, A.A. Barb to Bing, 11.1.1941.

55 WIA, GC, A.A. Barb to Bing, 12.4.1941.

56 WIA, GC, Bing to A.A. Barb, 6.5.1941. Hans Meier, German medievalist and librarian, 1900–1941.

loss Meier's death was for the Institute. Bing went even further and showed her trust in him:

> I was very happy to read that you, despite all your difficulties, which I do not underestimate, are somewhat contented and will persevere. I have expected this from you. I think I know you very well by now and I have to say, I admire how you adapt to all difficult conditions and know how to preserve that which is important to you.[57]

This was the cue Barb had been waiting for in his hope of gaining employment in The Warburg Institute.

> I can well imagine that, as long as this war lasts or at least as long as it rages on English soil with all force, any supplementary addition of personnel in the Institute will not happen; but is there a – even a very minor – possibility that you would find use for me once normal conditions have returned?

His strength lay not in the work of the free scholar, but the work of the 'diligent, conscientious, initiative-taking, resourceful scholarly employee'. He would bring to a post his knowledge of classical history and the historical auxiliary sciences. Would Bing talk to Saxl? Despite his love for England he saw no other option but to return to Austria after the war.[58] This last sentence is surprising: only very few emigrants voiced the wish to return to their country and even fewer of them did just that. Naturally, there were only very few vacancies either in the new or in the old country. Bing saw no possibility for employing Barb in The Warburg Institute at that time:

> This does not mean that we in any way undervalue your qualities as scholar or as employee and you do not need to think that this reply arises from the same error which the English authorities labour under, that is, that we think you 'too good' for the position of librarian. I know very well what it would mean to you to occupy the position, we only know too well its great importance for the Institute, and I am convinced that you would fill it extraordinarily well.

She continued that for the present moment she simply could not take a decision: Dr. Hugo Buchthal had been appointed to Meier's post for two years.[59] The argument that somebody was 'too good' for a post surfaced again and again among emigrants.

57 WIA, GC, Bing to A.A. Barb, 6.5.1941.

58 WIA, GC, A.A. Barb to Bing, 18.5.1941.

59 WIA, GC, Bing to A.A. Barb, 23.5.1941. Hugo Buchthal, German-American art historian, 1909–1996.

After a training course which Barb was allowed to complete after the abolition of the xenophobic restrictions on work,[60] the correspondence paused. He had found work in Leeds as engine fitter in the armament industry and had only little time to write. In August 1942 he got in touch again: he was earning little, but the children were flourishing and his wife had found work in a garment factory. This all was as nothing compared to the dreadful hardship experienced by Jews in Nazi Germany.[61] Bing replied, again with a very sad bit of news which shocked Barb: Saxl's son Peter had been killed by an air raid on 4 December 1941.[62]

In 1944 Barb wrote to Bing again about his plans for the future, namely that he had to stay in Leeds because of his children's schooling.[63] However, again he asked, would there be employment for him in The Warburg Institute? His work in the armament factory had ceased and he was in danger of losing his job in a sewing-machine factory.[64] Bing once more assured him she was ready to do everything she could for him so that after the end of the war he would find a decent post. Due to a lack of teachers after the war there were prospects for Latin and Greek teachers.[65]

Despite this, Barb continued to work in Leeds after the end of the war. These were difficult years. Groceries were available only with ration books; the war-time bureaucracy had yet to adapt to the post-war situation. Again Professor Mayer in Jerusalem requested Barb's address from Saxl;[66] again Barb sent family news, saying that he had acquired British citizenship and therefore had to renounce his Austrian pension, which had not been easy for him.[67] Hess clarified the situation, saying that although Barb had been initially told that his claim to a pension had been turned down, Barb did not give up his fight for many years and eventually received pension payments and a lump sum for loss of earnings during the war. His Austrian citizenship was also given back to him in July 1956.[68]

60 WIA, GC, A.A. Barb to Bing, 5.6.1941.

61 WIA, GC, A.A. Barb to Bing, 2.8.1942.

62 WIA, GC, A.A. Barb to Bing, 20.12.1942, in which he referred to a letter by Bing in September 1942, no longer extant. For information on Peter Saxl, see McEwan, D., 'Why Historiography? Saxl's Thoughts on History and Writing History', 97–107 and 224–227, here 107.

63 WIA, GC, A.A. Barb to Bing, 8.9.1944.

64 WIA, GC, A.A. Barb to Bing, 24.9.1944.

65 WIA, GC, Bing to A.A. Barb, 2.10.1944.

66 WIA, GC, W. Zander to Saxl, 16.7.1946. Walter Zander, German-British solicitor, secretary of the British Friends of the Hebrew University in Jerusalem, 1898–1993.

67 WIA, GC, A.A. Barb to Bing, 20.7.1947. Dr. Knoll, for the local government of Burgenland, to Barb, 24.11.1950, with the information that Barb, having acquired a 'foreign' citizenship on 28 June 1947, had automatically lost his Austrian citizenship and thereby 'the entitlement to a pension' despite his pension contributions from 1947 to 1950. BFPP, *Journal* no. 3, 1044. Julius Knoll, Austrian lawyer, 1904–1992. Knoll worked in the Burgenland Local Government and was in 1950 head of personnel, see Hess, M. *Braver Beamter, Opportunist, Verfolgter*.

68 Ibid., chapter on 'Alphons Barb', 415–434, here 426–429.

Employment in The Warburg Institute

In the summer of 1947 Barb travelled to London for a few days, spoke with Bing and Saxl, and sent his pamphlet 'Antichrist',[69] which Bing commented with 'not much new'. She also sent the news that Rudolf Wittkower, professor for art history at The Warburg Institute, was very interested in Barb's Michelangelo research.[70] The correspondence with Bing increased after the death of Saxl on 22 March 1948 and, as a matter of course, with the job offer from The Warburg Institute.[71] By return of post Barb accepted 'joyfully and gratefully'.[72] Discussions about conditions and possible start date – 'as early as possible' – followed.[73] Barb started as library assistant on 1 January 1949, a role which later on he called 'modest' but which, 'after useless letters' and an initial visitor's visa without a work permit, he accepted gladly.[74] He became, in due time, librarian of The Warburg Institute, his field of duties extended to research and publications in addition to the academic library service. He became honorary member of a number of academic associations, recipient of the Decoration of Honour for Services to the Province of Burgenland in 1962, recipient of the Austrian Cross of Honour for Science and Art in 1968 and recipient of the title of Professor and the Golden Doctor's Diploma from the University of Vienna in 1975.[75]

His daughter Maria Henriette read Chemistry,[76] his son Wolfgang Gerson likewise.

Barb died on 13 November 1979. Professor Joe Trapp, Director of The Warburg Institute, published an obituary in *The Times*[77] and in the *Libraries Bulletin* of the University of London.[78] Barb was acknowledged as a scholar who, after his internment as an enemy alien, had been working in factories in Leeds until 1948. He was employed by The Warburg Institute as Library Assistant in 1949, first as assistant to Otto Kurz, the Austrian-British art historian and librarian, then from 1965 to his retirement in 1966 as Librarian. He became famous for his continuous

69 WIA, GC, A.A. Barb to Bing, 8.9.1947.

70 WIA, GC, Bing to A.A. Barb, 11.11.1947. Rudolf Wittkower, German-British art historian, expert on the Italian Renaissance and the Baroque, 1901–1971.

71 WIA, GC, Bing to A.A. Barb, 6.9.1948.

72 WIA, GC, A.A. Barb to Bing, 7.9.1948.

73 WIA, GC, Bing to A.A. Barb, 16.11.1948.

74 BFPP, *Journal* no. 3, 1110, undated, after 1966.

75 Urban, O.H., 'Barb, Alphons Augustinus (1901–1979), Numismatiker'.

76 WIA, GC, D. Brittain, Tutor to Women Students, University of London, King's College, to Bing, 15.9.1950. Bing's character reference for Maria Henriette Barb, dated 16 September 1950, also referred to Barb: 'I consider Miss Barb exceptionally well qualified for admission to a University course. She is both intelligent and industrious, and well suited for intellectual studies. Her home background has contributed to this, since her father is himself a well-known scholar, a classical archaeologist and numismatist. In this connection I would mention that Dr. Barb is at present Assistant Librarian of the Warburg Institute. As far as I know Miss Barb's health is excellent'.

77 Trapp, J., 'Obituary', *The Times*, 16.

78 Idem., 'Obituary', *Libraries Bulletin*, 1.

tea-drinking and his remarkable number of exotic pipes and cigars.[79] Among his more than 250 publications the best were his works on the history of folk religion and superstition from classical antiquity to the 20th century. His great knowledge allowed him to link seemingly unlinked elements: 'In the course of an article or a lecture by Barb one might find oneself taken from a Roman charm-tablet he had excavated, via an introduction to the Devil's grandmother, to mermaids and to modern devotional images of the Virgin Mary'.[80] He embodied Warburg's point of view that what we downgrade and assess as popular beliefs or superstitions had their place in the development of the history of ideas. Warburg used the term 'rudimentary perception' to express the value of the terms superstition, astrology, folk religion, and magic, which did constitute perceptions and were deployed, but were not enough, or not enough yet, to lead to the perception of truth.[81]

The conversion of A. A. Barb to Roman Catholicism

In 1942 Barb sent a very important communication to Bing, the news of his conversion:

> I do not know whether I have told you that I became a Catholic one year ago (only I, not my family, which may be sufficient evidence that it was an absolute spiritual imperative for me); I have always gained much strength, de facto all necessary strength, from this inexhaustible reservoir and do not understand that I hesitated for so long (the thought of conversion struck me for the first time more than 20 years ago).[82]

From the three volumes of his papers, referred to as BFPP, *Journals*, one can reconstruct some of the steps which motivated him to convert. He read the Roman Catholic weekly *The Tablet*[83] and he lived in the Sacred Heart parish in Leeds, which then was served by the Jesuits, among them Father Samuel Sebastian Myerscough, S. J., who had converted from Judaism and was one of the priests. From 1942

79 It is wholly unbelievable today, but smoking was not prohibited in The Warburg Institute for many years. Otto Kurz, Austrian-British art historian, 1908–1975.

80 Joe Trapp, 'Obituary', *Libraries Bulletin*, London: University of London, Oct.-Dec. 1979, no. 17, 1.

81 WIA, III, 10.2. Diary, 13.8.1901, 60. On 'Erkenntnisrudiment', 'rudimentary perception', see also Chapter 15, note 17. Warburg used the term when discussing the double portrait which the Dutch painter Jan Veth had painted of Warburg's parents, Moritz and Charlotte Warburg, today exhibited in the Deutsche Museum in Berlin. Warburg had drawn up a statement of expenditure for Veth's expenses and commented, 'Veth makes portraits, I count; primitive societies have a superstitious dislike against both: superstition is rudimentary perception – wanting to be painted and wanting to be counted is a symptom of consciously crossing the zenith'.

82 WIA, GC, A.A. Barb to Bing, 20.12.1942.

83 BFPP, *Journal* no. 3, 1092, with excerpts of articles and cut-out and pasted articles.

onwards he was the parish priest.[84] Barb entered in his *Journal* no. *2* that he had a conversation with him on 14 September 1941, on 27 November 1941 he wrote in capital letters that he had had his first confession, and a day later his first holy communion. On 30 November he entered 'I am baptised' and on 14 December 1941 'I am confirmed'.[85] Sydney Joseph Rix and Mary Rix were mentioned in the baptismal register as godparents.[86]

A word on the chronology of the conversion: Barb never mentioned the day of baptism, which would have been before confession and communion. He only stated on 30 November that he was baptised. Nowhere in Barb's writings is there further reference to his conversion. His reasons remained unexplained, both before his baptism as well as during his religious practice afterwards. Only the facts were entered into his *Journal* no. *2*. Admittedly, the *Österreichisches Biographisches Lexikon* (the *Austrian Biographical Dictionary*) mentioned that he converted after having studied the writings of Augustine in the time of his internment.[87] In this context it is interesting to note that Heinrich Alfred Barb, a Galician Orientalist who began his legal studies in Vienna in 1844, had converted to Roman Catholicism in 1844.[88] Further documents about this are missing. Heinrich's cousin was Isaac Barb, who made a name for himself for his revival of the Hebrew language. Isaac was the father of Moriz Barb and the grandfather of Alphons Barb.[89] Was there talk about the conversion in the family? Was it a topic about which the family was reticent, since it was known that Heinrich Alfred Barb wanted to pursue the career of a civil servant in the Austrian monarchy, which at long last earned him the title of court counsellor after his conversion? This title was an extraordinary honour and even more so for a converted Jew. Or was Barb's conversion a purely personal matter, as he made it out to be in his letter to Bing and as it did not bring any advantage to Barb? In Vienna the attitude of the composer and conductor Gustav Mahler was well-known: after his successes in the opera houses of Europe, Mahler wanted to be employed in Vienna and pragmatically converted in 1897

84 Obituary in *The Cottonian*, see 'Obituary of Fr. Myerscough, Samuel Sebastian, S.J.', 2–3. Myerscough was baptised Roman Catholic together with his father Samuel in 1898. The name Sebastian is of Greek origin and means 'venerable'. In its Latin translation, Augustus, it became the title of the Roman emperors. Barb chose Augustinus at his baptism for his second Christian name, possibly with regard to his studies of St Augustine or with regard to the name of the priest who baptised him. Samuel Sebastian Myerscough, British Jesuit, 1879–1954.

85 BFPP, *Journal* no. 2, 1042.

86 I am grateful for the information by Robert Finnigan, 6 March 2020, with details from the baptismal register of the Sacred Heart parish in Leeds, today in the archive of the Roman Catholic diocese of Leeds. Sydney Joseph Rix worked in a cloth factory in Leeds, possibly the same factory where Barb's wife had found work. He was buried in the Roman Catholic cemetery of Killingbrock in North Yorkshire in 1954.

87 Urban, O. H, 'Barb, Alphons Augustinus (1901–1979), Numismatiker', n.p.

88 Heinrich Alfred Barb, Galician Orientalist, 1826–1883.

89 Isaac Barb, Galician Jewish educator, 1827–1903. Moriz Barb, Austro-Hungarian engineer, 1867–1929.

in order to be eligible for the position. The aspired social adjustment helped his career.

The news of Barb's conversion came out of the blue for Bing. She reacted very quickly:

> The news of your conversion to Roman Catholicism touched me very deeply. I now understand a great deal more of your personality which earlier on I admired, but could not explain. If you say that you had been thinking about it for twenty years, then a great deal of your bearing must have come from there. I find it beautiful that you, who are in every respect the authority in the family, have avoided persuading your wife and children to convert with you. The strong influence which you have on the education of your children will in all probability increase, because you will feel strengthened in your own being by the authority which now stands behind you. I personally still think that much strength can be drawn out of human nature alone and I think I see in you one of these rare natures. But the question which follows, that is, where such a nature comes from which enables you, as a human being, to endure all the great misfortunes you had in your life with such bearing, on this we can agree only in a conversation and I do not want to write more about it in this letter.[90]

Only in the spring in 1943 did Barb confirm Bing's reaction, saying it had been a 'blessed' letter in a bad winter:

> I would really like to speak with you at length about the questions you touch upon in your letter. The thesis that human nature really is NATURA CHRISTIANA (which to me is CATHOLICA) has grown in me to an absolute and firm conviction and I can only say that I, when I (as I thought) had reason to decide on my conversion based on the great and recognised treasures, had no idea of the real glory and splendour which waited for me inside the church, [inserted by Barb: among others the complete fulfilment and perfection of my being Jewish, so that I feel as a Catholic to be more of a Jew and a better Jew than ever before].[91]

He closed with Easter wishes. What must Bing have thought when reading Barb's letters of December 1942 and April 1943? Did she feel she was deceived or was she disappointed? Did she want to express that all her efforts to aid Jews had changed with Barb's conversion to Roman Catholicism, which she found strange?

90 WIA, GC, Bing to A.A. Barb, 1.1.1943. Contrary to Bing's view, Barb stated in BFPP, *Journal* no. 3, 1110, undated, after 1966, that he had converted 'despite resistance in my family'. See also note 53. Gustav Mahler, Austrian conductor and composer, 1860–1911.

91 WIA, A.A. Barb to Bing, 26.4.1943.

Bing's reply has to be understood as an echo of another letter by her, of which Barb had no idea. I refer to Bing's letter to Hanns Swarzenski in 1933, in which Bing explained her views on why she, as a Jewish woman, wanted to stand with her religious and inherited community. In order to understand Bing's reply, it is important to summarise this correspondence.

On Bing's understanding of 'Being Jewish'

Hanns Swarzenski, a medievalist and art historian at the Berlin State Museums, had been brought up a Protestant, but learnt in April 1933, after the introduction of the civil service system in Germany, that both his grandmothers had been Jewish.[92] He corresponded with Bing and told her that he would come to Hamburg in May 1933 and wanted to talk to her.[93] They met and exchanged views on what it meant in the prevailing situation to be a German and a Jew. After Swarzenski's departure, Bing wanted to continue this profound discussion and so she wrote to him on the morning after his departure from Hamburg on 29 May 1933.[94] Times were tense; Saxl was frantically looking for a place outside Germany for the library. The reality of being German and a Jewish man or woman had become threatening to both their lives.

Bing, as a philosopher, having been awarded her doctorate from Professor Ernst Cassirer[95] in 1921 on her research into Lessing, composed in her letter a veritable article on 'Being a German' and 'Being a Jew', a topic which had for centuries in the German-speaking countries drawn a distinction between cultural identity and religious identity.[96] She wrote that 'with Jews the ancestry coincides with their history and thereby becomes their destiny, as it represents itself to me'.[97] She touched on the topic of assimilation, also an important issue in the first quarter of the 20th century, stressing that it was easier 'to believe in the possibility or desirability of complete assimilation', but history had taught her

> that the eternal Jew has to tread the path of suffering again and again and the only salvation which the single individual can find therein is that he

92 See Vorholt, H., '"Das was ich als Jude vertrete, kann ich auch in England oder Frankreich sein". A Letter by Gertrud Bing to Hanns Swarzenski of 29 May 1933', 23–37 and 204–210. Hanns Swarzenski, German-American art historian, 1903–1985.

93 WIA, GC, H. Swarzenski to Bing, 19.5.1933.

94 The letter by Bing to H. Swarzenski, 29.5.1933, is kept in the Staatsbibliothek zu Berlin – Preußischer Kulturbesitz, Nachl. 270 (G.U.H. Swarzenski), Mp. 423.

95 Bing, G., *Der Begriff des Notwendigen bei Lessing*. Ernst Cassirer, German philosopher, 1874–1945; Lessing, German writer, 1729–1781.

96 Vorholt, H., '"Das was ich als Jude vertrete, kann ich auch in England oder Frankreich sein". A Letter by Gertrud Bing to Hanns Swarzenski of 29 May 1933', 25.

97 Vorholt, H., '"Das was ich als Jude vertrete, kann ich auch in England oder Frankreich sein". A Letter by Gertrud Bing to Hanns Swarzenski of 29 May 1933', 32.

> is clear about being set apart, the proud curse to which he is subjected, that he affirms it and draws his consequences from it.[98]

This examination has to be worth one's while, so that she could say, 'What I can represent as Jew, I can also be in England and France; what I have become through my German surroundings, is not lost in the process . . .'.[99]

She then turned to his personal decision as to whether to choose to be Jewish or not. 'As I have to bear all the distress tied up for me with being Jewish, so you have to include in all honesty the current development in your concept of being German'.[100] His two Jewish grandmothers could justify him rejecting his being German, he would be entitled to do so, because then he would be deprived of the shared responsibility. If he wanted this, then he would know 'that there is only either/or':

> either you stick to what was dear to you so far, as far as you can manage it without collaborating with the state; in this case you could make it dependent on further developments, if better opportunities seem to be available abroad, or if you want to continue working in Germany . . . but not on Germany and only indirectly for Germany. Or you relinquish much of what you have so far represented, in order not to have to forgo your service of co-responsibility.[101]

Bing knew that for her being Jewish was existentially significant. She begged Swarzenski to accept her letter as 'a sign of sympathy, of compassion in shared difficulties',[102] which Swarzenski accepted: he had chosen the 'or' option. He was able to emigrate in 1936, and went to Princeton, to the Institute for Advanced Study, and stayed in the USA until his retirement and subsequent return to Germany in 1973. There was only one more reference to Bing's letter of 1933, when it was clear that Swarzenski would go to Princeton in 1936. It was the same year in which funding for The Warburg Institute in London was extended for a second time, after the first three difficult years. She sent Swarzenski this information:

> as continuation of the memorable discussion . . . which we, you and I, had in the early summer of 1933. The experiments, and I cannot formulate them in any other way, which we were about to enter into, have stopped:

98 Vorholt, H., '"Das was ich als Jude vertrete, kann ich auch in England oder Frankreich sein". A Letter by Gertrud Bing to Hanns Swarzenski of 29 May 1933', 33.
99 Vorholt, H., '"Das was ich als Jude vertrete, kann ich auch in England oder Frankreich sein". A Letter by Gertrud Bing to Hanns Swarzenski of 29 May 1933', 33.
100 Vorholt, H., '"Das was ich als Jude vertrete, kann ich auch in England oder Frankreich sein". A Letter by Gertrud Bing to Hanns Swarzenski of 29 May 1933', 33.
101 Vorholt, H., '"Das was ich als Jude vertrete, kann ich auch in England oder Frankreich sein". A Letter by Gertrud Bing to Hanns Swarzenski of 29 May 1933', 33–34.
102 Vorholt, H., '"Das was ich als Jude vertrete, kann ich auch in England oder Frankreich sein". A Letter by Gertrud Bing to Hanns Swarzenski of 29 May 1933', 34.

> You are going to America and we are staying in England. Let us hope that the new way of life will in both cases turn out satisfactorily.[103]

The summary of Bing's correspondence with Swarzenski shines a light on Bing's views. However, with Barb's letter of December 1942 she was confronted with the news of his conversion, not an 'either/or' decision, but another way out which she had not considered possible earlier on. How could or should she herself deal with such a turn of events? It goes without saying that Barb's decision in no way tarnished Barb's relationship with Saxl and Bing, but it had been important to Bing to apprise Barb of her views in the reply on 1 January 1943.

On Barb's understanding of 'Being Jewish'

What the reasons were for Barb is not completely transparent from the correspondence. In order to understand the process a little bit better, a process which ultimately has to be inscrutable for outsiders, it is necessary to look for further signs which help us to comprehend his decision. I wish to divide the topic into three discussions:

1. 'Being Jewish'
2. Research on authors from classical antiquity
3. Barb's letter to Sandor and his sister Frida Wolf (married name Löwy).

1. 'Being Jewish'

Barb, having been brought up as Jew, knew the Hebrew Bible as well as the writings of the authors of the Greek Bible. As a Catholic, he valued the tradition of both books, which made sense to him, perhaps even taught him about keeping the tradition. In 1941 he could not know that his hope of being employed at The Warburg Institute would come to pass, nor that he would meet Jewish colleagues on a daily basis. For the researcher today his 'going over to Rome' is an object of fascination; for Barb it was the proof of the veracity of his long-cherished view, the fulfilment of his belief. It is possible that he, as a student in Vienna after World War I, with an eye to employment possibilities, might have already been thinking of it, as civil service posts were the only career prospects. It may have been that his colleagues talked about it and such a sober pragmatic act for a young man made sense to him. A life as a private scholar was only open to eminently well-to-do scholars.

One document is extant, the list of books which Barb took with him to the internment camp (see figure 14.4). In first place it lists the Greek Bible, in Greek, and three books by St Augustine, *Confessions*, *The City of God* and *Meditations*.[104] He

103 WIA, GC, Bing to H. Swarzenski, 9.9.1936.

104 BFPP, *Journal* no. 2, 1056. Immediately in front of this page is Barb's list of his belongings in the internment camp, *Journal* no. 2, 1055.

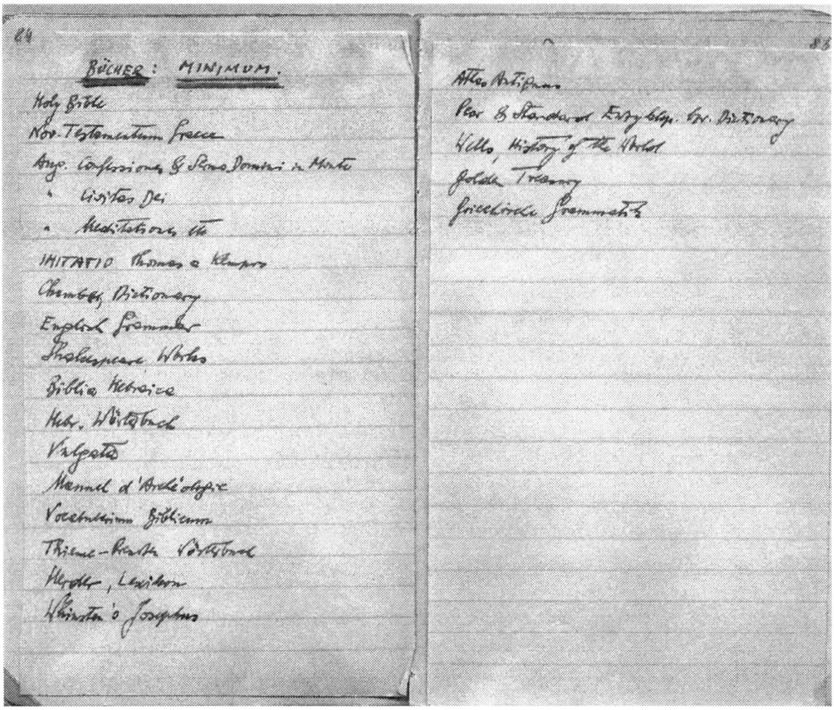

Figure 14.4 Book list.

Source: © Private collection, Barb Family, *Journal* no. 2, 1056.

also listed *Imitation of Christ*, the Hebrew Bible, an English grammar, the works of Shakespeare, art dictionaries and more, which attest to Barb's interests and possibly the notion that he would have lots of time for private reading in the internment camp.

This list corroborates the detail in the *Austrian Biographical Dictionary* that after studying St Augustine he converted.[105] Reading St Augustine might have given the last impetus for conversion after his release from the camp. He entered a few quotes by Augustine in the *Journals*, however without any further explanations on his selection and comments.

2. Research on authors from classical antiquity

Many of Barb's articles dealt with interpreting thus far unsolved words or characters on excavated objects. As a student of classical languages Barb read the Greek Bible in its original language as well as patristic writings. In order to explain them

105 See this Chapter, note 53.

he compared many scriptures from classical antiquity and Christianity. In the same way he was able to present textual and artistic developments in the centuries-old course of Christian history with new and conclusive interpretations. The following examples will explain Barb's working method.

A.) In 1933, therefore long before his conversion but within the time span he gave for thinking about it, he published a booklet on witches and magic, *The craft of witches in classical antiquity originating from the decay of classical religions.*[106] The topic of this text was revisited by Barb a few times in his Antaura research. Antaura was the harmful south wind which was credited in a number of cultures as the reason for migraines. Barb identified the Antaura wind with the Scirocco, the wind which brings illnesses. Antaura, the female demon who caused migraines, could be counteracted with the written text of a prayer or curse, wrapped up in an amulet and placed on the temples and forehead.[107] Such meteorological phenomena as hot winds were known in classical antiquity and still occur nowadays. The south wind called the Alpine Föhn in Austria, the hot autumn wind which blows from Italy over the Alps, is credited with causing headaches and migraines even today. In the series of lectures in The Warburg Institute on the 'Conflict between paganism and Christianity in the Fourth Century' Barb did not talk about this wind, but about the antique magic prayers, their prophetic mobilisation and application in many cultures.[108]

What is striking is the word 'decay' in the title of his 1933 booklet. Can one deduce from this Barb's mindset vis-à-vis the religions of antiquity? The term 'decay' describes a process and condition of decomposition, degradation, putrefaction. Antique religions have neither a salvation myth nor afterlife in their theologies, God or the Gods do not live among humans, but far distant, for instance on Mount Olympus, from where they intervene in the destiny of mortals. This is diametrically opposed to Christianity which always addresses the living God. Can one therefore draw one's conclusions about Barb's views? A similarly depreciatory word, 'rotten', can be found in stanza 8 of the poem *Du bist beglückt* by Friedrich Rückert,[109] which Barb copied into his *Journal* no. 3:

> From every depth of space, from all dimensions of time
> Humanity's spirit greets those who learn from him in their prime.
> Thoughts emerge from the rotten tomb of books
> Whilst others dwindle in the air like floral scented looks.
> But none was ever lost to a truly thinking mind

106 Barb, A.A., 'Klassische Hexenkunst aus der Verwesung antiker Religionen: Ein antikes Zaubergebet gegen die Migräne und sein Fortleben', 1–32. See also note 7.

107 See also Barb, 'Griechische Zaubertexte vom Gräberfelde westlich des Lagers: (Carnuntum)', 57–67, here 62–64.

108 Idem, 'The Survival of Magic Arts', 100–125. BFPP, *Journal* no. 3, 1157.

109 Friedrich Rückert, German poet, 1788–1866. Rückert, F., 'Du bist beglückt', 37–39. One of Rückert's poems, *Kindertotenlieder*, was set to music by Gustav Mahler.

And no new one will ever be born if not first divined.
Thus, you may comfort yourself when thought turns into light
For it will not be lost to the world even though it might
Not be what you would like to share with people. Let them argue about
Whose thought came first; it is the spirit of humanity that has more clout.[110]

Barb came back to the copied poem by Rückert in his article 'Diva matrix'[111] about the pictorial representation of a womb on a gemstone, which to Barb could be ascribed to rebirth and heaven. Like L. Thorndike,[112] Barb stressed the significance of all writings of classical antiquity for recognising patterns of argumentation, for only consenting opinions could bring about meaningful explanations. The thoughts which rose from the 'rotten tomb of books' were ambivalent but significant, like every idea which, once born, would not get lost in the world and for this reason belonged to the topic of myths, the 'spirit of humanity'.

B.) In 1971 Barb published an evaluation and addition to two articles of the medical doctor Vladimir Gurewich,[113] who had written about the iconography of the wound of Christ in Christian art in 1957 and 1963.[114] Gurewich stated in his first article that in the medieval tradition the wound of Christ had always been painted on the right side of the body, in defiance of the nascent naturalistic tendencies to paint the stab wound correctly on the left side of the body, where the heart was.[115] In his second article Gurewich added an appendix to his analysis, citing Rubens. In Rubens' drafts to his painting *Descent from the Cross*,[116] the wound is on the left side; on the finished painting, however, it is on the right side of the body.[117] Barb now commented that Gurewich saw in the style of painting on the right side of the body 'an unbroken Catholic tradition, which continued with this old custom'[118] in contrast to the presentation on the left side of the body, which presented more the exception to the rule. Even 250 years after Rubens, Edouard Manet[119] risked a similar charge as, according to Gurewich, 'it would

110 BFPP, *Journal* no. 1, 2072B. Translation by Rüdiger Goerner.
111 Barb, A.A., 'Diva Matrix, A Faked Gnostic Intaglio in the Possession of P.P. Rubens and the Iconology of a Symbol', 193–238, here 203.
112 Edward Lee Thorndike, American psychologist, 1874–1949, who worked on the theory of 'connectionism'.
113 Barb, A.A., 'The Wound in Christ's Side', 320–321. Vladimir Gurewich, Swiss medical doctor, 1901–1975.
114 Vladimir Gurewich's first article was in 1957, Gurewich, V., 'Observations on the Iconography of the Wound in Christ's Side', 358–362. His second article was in 1963, idem, 'Rubens and the Wound in Christ's Side. A Postscript', 358.
115 Idem, 'Observations on the Iconography of the Wound in Christ's Side', 358–362.
116 Peter Paul Rubens, oil sketch for the painting *Descent from the Cross*. 1612–1614. Antwerp cathedral, Belgium. Today in the Lee Collection at the Courtauld Institute Galleries, London. Peter Paul Rubens, Flemish artist, 1577–1640.
117 Gurewich, 'Rubens and the Wound in Christ's Side. A Postscript', 358.
118 Barb, A.A., 'The Wound in Christ's Side', 320.
119 Edouard Manet, French painter, 1832–1883.

have been considered heretical to point out openly a contempt of tradition'.[120] Barb asked himself how this 'strong and persistent Roman Catholic tradition' could be explained. The painting tradition was neither based on the gospel nor on a vague reference to 'Hellenistic and Early Christian notions of the primacy of "right" over "left"', which, as Gurewich himself had already found, 'had lost their force long before the time of Rubens'. Barb found an explanation which he called simple: the explanation could be found in every missal, at least in those missals which were printed before the radical change in the liturgy in the wake of the second Vatican Council. The Easter hymn of Ezechiel, verse XLVII, 1–12, mentioned the right side of the Temple and thereby became the prophetic application for the crucifixion scene and the stab wound in the side of Christ. Christian art was full of symbolism at first and only very slowly did the influence of artistic realism establish itself through exegetical strategies. The persistence of this view, which was expressed in the shortened paraphrase of the Ezechiel text and stressed the word of the prophet, gave witness to the orthodox belief in a transcendental, even mystical and miracle-filled truth, as the word of God in each single element of the biblical prophecies:

> If . . . the aggiornamento of the Roman church might allow the old Easter Anthem to disappear from the liturgy, artists will then be freed from the restrictions imposed by Hebrew prophets and medieval symbolism to follow, uninhibited, their anatomical realism – that is, unless eager for still more freedom, they might prefer to turn to properly 'demythologised' abstract art.[121]

Barb demonstrated here his reasoning for the orthodox, deeply religious or even ancient exegesis in contrast to all modernising trends of the Vatican Council. It was a clear statement against modern Bible translations and interpretations. At the time of writing he had been a member of the Roman Catholic church for many years, and highlighted with exclamation marks his quotes from modern Bible translations whose assertions he did not want to accept. To him, every Roman Catholic Mass confirmed to the faithful that he heard the word of God and in the confession of faith the Holy Spirit, who had spoken through the prophets, was invoked. He finished his analysis by writing 'who will watch the custodians?', meaning 'who will check the church leaders, who cancel the word of God?'[122]

Two years later Barb continued his deeply religious biblical exegesis,[123] in which he made a scathing attack against any further deconstruction of the traditional catholic liturgy. He denounced the falsifications of the new Bible translation of 1966 by quoting examples for the transcendental significance of the wound of

120 Barb, A.A., 'The Wound in Christ's Side', 320.
121 Barb, A.A., 'The Wound in Christ's Side', 321.
122 Barb, A.A., 'The Wound in Christ's Side', 321.
123 Idem, '"Vidi Aquam . . ." and the Wounded Christ, 20–21.

Christ being on the right side of the body, for instance Christ seated at the right hand of God.[124] He railed against the abolition of the hymn 'Hide thy face from my sins, and blot out all mine iniquities', which created only a revised, shortened version of the word of God.[125]

Barb's strict interpretations are the signs of a true convert, fastidiously zealous in keeping to the rules and furthermore, as a traditionalist, adverse to anything perceived to be modern. Throughout the centuries there were movements in Roman Catholicism which either led to a narrow national church, like the Old Catholics, or to communities which favoured their own biblical exegesis and interpretation of ministry, like the right-wing Society of Saint Pius X headed by Marcel Lefebvre.[126]

Barb's godson Giles MacDonogh called him the archetypical Central European professor, deeply religious, who did not want to accept mass in the vernacular and remained faithful to the Latin Tridentine mass. Barb always sent Christmas cards with the message of Christmas, 'Hodie Christus natus est',[127] which he bought from the Latin Mass Society in Great Britain. Even his love of the music by Anton Bruckner was influenced by the old Roman Catholic mass.[128]

C.) Finally, an example from Barb's late work 'Poison',[129] which discussed the practices, toxicological knowledge and dosages of drugs, and the application of healing methods of various products termed poisons or medicines. In Greek the word 'pharmakon' is used in its dual meaning of drug and medicine, that is, causing sickness as well as curing it, also antidote. Again, one sentence is surprising, in which Barb talks about 'doctors, priests, magicians' in Ancient Egypt, 'who all were available to the seekers of healing'.[130] In Christianity the serving of demons, 'the dispensing of lethal poison, even if somebody requests them', for instance in the case of suicide, and witchcraft were damnable.[131] The practice of doctors in antiquity applying witchcraft lived on into the Middle Ages with the persecution of witches and lives on today in so-called 'black magic',[132] with its fetishes and curses. Origen of Alexandria exhorted the baptismal candidates 'to expel the poison of snakes from their hearts',[133] that is not to follow the sorcerer, the wizard

124 A.A. Barb complained about the 1966 translation, *Holy Bible. Revised Standard Version, Catholic Edition*, 870.

125 Only sung from Easter until Pentecost Psalm 51, verse 9, 'Thou shalt sprinkle', is augmented with 'Hide thy face', referring to the more lengthy and florid antiphon, *Vidi aqua*, Ezekiel 47:1. Ezekiel, Hebrew prophet, 622–570 BC.

126 Marcel Lefebvre, French churchman, 1905–1991.

127 'Today Christ is Born'.

128 I thank Giles MacDonogh for his communication, 19.3.2020. Anton Bruckner, Austrian composer, 1824–1896.

129 Barb, A.A., 'Gift', 1209–1247.

130 Barb, A.A., 'Gift', 1211.

131 Barb, A.A., 'Gift', 1219.

132 Barb, A.A., 'Gift', 1223.

133 Origenes, *Homiliae. Die griechischen christlichen Schriftsteller (GCS)* 9, 136. Origen of Alexandria, Egyptian theologian, c. 185–c. 254.

and the poisoner. Barb ended his article with examples from pagan authors, from different times and cultures, who mixed 'truth with error as if lethal poison is mixed with honey and wine'.[134]

Again, in Barb's remarks, one finds views of 'decay' in antiquity and in them Barb's pursuit not of the old practices, but of the practices of the living God. The fact that he did not elaborate further about it in his writing is on the one hand astonishing, if one wants to believe his statement that he had been thinking about conversion for twenty years. On the other hand, however, it is not surprising: so long as Barb had employment and a career in the 1920s and 1930s, the need for conversion had not become acute. It had only become acute when Barb as a Jew 'was pushed by the Secret Police of the State to emigrate'.[135]

Or had Barb's conversion roots in other thoughts? His *Journals* contain excerpts from books, for instance Hilaire Belloc's *The Jews*.[136] Belloc, who went to school in John Henry Newman's Oratory School in Edgbaston, Birmingham,[137] was a Christian apologist, a representative of Christianity as a religion of reason, whose views of Judaism were controversial. While Barb agreed with what Belloc had written about Alfred Dreyfuß,[138] he did not conform to his explanations of the secrecy and superiority of the Jews. On the other hand, he found Belloc's chapter on antisemitism 'excellent. Brilliant description of the metropolitan press and stunning prognosis of Nazi activity in this matter'. In some instances he found Jacques Maritain's book *Antisemitism*[139] 'going deeper than Belloc and a good contrast (although not stressing the Jews' own guilt enough)'.[140] Did Barb here juxtapose the guilt or innocence of the Jews? It would be great to read more about these views, but Barb did not go into further details.

3. Barb's letter to Sandor and his sister Frida Wolf

Frida Löwy Wolf, sister of Sandor Wolf in Eisenstadt, wrote a letter of recommendation for Barb in December 1938, at the time when Barb was requesting such letters from his friends and colleagues in order to find work abroad.[141] It is an excellent testimonial for Barb and his whole family. It therefore is not surprising that Barb wrote a letter to Sandor Wolf and his sister Frida, friends from his time in Burgenland, and told them about his conversion on 26 April 1943, one day after he had informed Bing.[142] After initial questions about their health and family news, he felt compelled to share his 'very important news':

134 Barb, A.A., 'Gift', 1235.
135 BFPP, *Journal* no. 3, 1111.
136 Belloc, H., *Die Juden*. Hilaire Belloc, French-English writer, 1870–1953.
137 John Henry Newman, English theologian, 1801–1890.
138 Alfred Dreyfuß, French artillery officer, 1859–1935.
139 Maritain, J., *Antisemitism*. Jacques Maritain, French philosopher, 1882–1973.
140 BFPP, *Journal* no. 2, 1082–1083.
141 BFPP, *Journal* no. 3, EA 1022. Frida Löwy Wolf in Vienna to A.A. Barb, 14.12.1938.
142 BFPP, *Journal* no. 2, 1053–1054.

Now to one, at least for me, important disclosure and I admit being anxious about how you will receive it. I have converted to Roman Catholicism. Two facts which I wish to underline may explain why this was not a step of utilitarian calculation: 1, it was against the wish of my wife and children, who all continue with the 'Mosaic' creed. 2, I have chosen the Roman Catholic church, which in England is not very socially acceptable, although any Protestant creed might have promised far more material advantages. You might in all probability interpret my step as 'eccentricity', although I believe that so far you have thought me as rather clear thinking. A few words about it: I come, as you know, from the liberal Viennese milieu which amounted to nothing more than celebrating Pesach, New Year and Yom Kippur, very often really only Massir and Yahrzeit;[143] I was not satisfied by this, I found my Judaism to be a sort of nationalism, not very different from French or Italian, Hungarian or Czech chauvinism. I became aware of this somewhat unclear feeling for the first time some twenty years ago, and I remember that you, Mr. Sandor, assisted me in this matter indirectly. You invited me to a lecture by a rabbi – Taglicht? –[144] in B'nai B'rith[145] in Vienna – Universitätsstraße? – on the prophet Isaiah. It was there that I heard for the first time the parable of the vineyard (cap. 5)[146] and I thought to myself: And this is what he tells liberal Zionists? Isn't it clear to everybody that the expected grapes are RELIGIOSITY, that is divine service, service for God and not for the nation? And if the vineyard could speak and say, I do not produce wine, but my wood is as good as that of other forests? . . . Ever since my early youth, at least since my Bar Mitzwa,[147] I tried to find a way back to Jewish orthodoxy. I had, I have even today and will always have, the highest admiration for miracles, as I found them embodied recently in your blessed mother. But my attempt to find a way back was a total failure. One might say, the milieu was the reason; I might have had success in Palestine, in another profession, in another society; but today I no longer believe it. The branch of a tree normally never becomes root or stem. It can stay what it is, it can wither, it can have blossoms and bear fruit – the lifeblood in it decides all this.

143 'Massir', recte 'Ma'aser', tithe, a welfare tax. 'Yahrzeit', the German word used for the day of remembrance or the anniversary of the day of death of a relative.

144 Dr. Israel Taglicht, chief rabbi of Vienna, 1862–1943.

145 B'nai B'rith, Jewish organisation to promote tolerance, welfare and education within Jewry.

146 Isaiah, chap. 5, 1–7: 'Let me sing to my friend the song of his love for his vineyard. My friend had a vineyard on a fertile hillside, he dug the soil, cleared it of stones, and planted choice vines in it . . .' The parable pointed to the fact that the men of Judah had only harvested sour grapes. For the prophet the vineyard was the house of Israel and the men the chosen plants. God 'expected justice, but found bloodshed . . .'. Isaiah, Israelite prophet, 8th century–7th century.

147 Bar Mitzvah, the Jewish ritual of the coming of age of a 3-year-old boy.

I do not want to tire you with further explanations and do not want to raise the suspicion that this letter might be a badly applied attempt at conversion. I have written a long letter because I value your friendship too highly. I wanted at least with my attempt at justification to counter the danger of unheard damnation. It is a fact that I am much happier as a member of the R. C. church than ever before, a better son to my parents – who by the grace of God might understand today – , a better husband and better father, even if my wife and children do not understand this explicitly – but also more and more intensive as a Jew, in body and spirit the heir to Abraham, Isaac and Jacob – even if this sounds strange to those who have not experienced it. I still wear my 'Jewish beard', although it is much more conspicuous in England than in Austria, among my contemporaries who are nearly without exception clean-shaven. Best wishes also from my wife and children and best wishes for your welfare, Your ever grateful[148]

This letter is the only document in which Barb offers some sort of explanation for his personal reasons for conversion. However, his words do not reveal much. His decision to convert was, in his words, not 'socially acceptable' or rather not socially acceptable enough. It was the middle ground which was more understandable in Great Britain than in Austria. He made a pretext of the liberal Jewish Viennese milieu, which only brought him a few Jewish holidays that had to be kept. This statement was not satisfactory; nobody would have stopped him taking part in more ritual practices. His own first name, Alphons, and the names of his children, Wolfgang and Maria Henriette, were conventional Christian names in Austria. Had he really wanted to find a way back to orthodoxy; what did he understand by orthodoxy? He partially blamed Sandor Wolf for his conversion or for opening his eyes, because he had invited him to a lecture. Wolf, one of the most important Jews in Eisenstadt, a wine merchant, art collector, and philanthropist, whose art collections made up the core of the Burgenland Regional Museum, knew Barb, valued his archaeological knowledge and might have had a say in Barb's appointment at the museum. Barb's explanations sound like he is fishing for good will, craving attention. Were they delivered as a somewhat stark hint at involving Wolf in his decision? The argument of the passage in Isaiah of the parable of the vineyard is not surprising: it had long been circulating as an explanation for the incomprehension of Jews toward their God. The reference to Abraham, Isaac and Jacob was an embellishment; the information about his 'Jewish beard' simply cannot be taken seriously.

Many years later Barb wrote a similarly vindicating letter to Professor Robert Göbl, numismatist at the University of Vienna. The letter provided a short

148 BFPP, *Journal* no.2, 1053–1054. The copy of the letter was not signed. Barb, A.A. to Wolf, S. and his sister Löwy, F., 27.4.1943. Abraham, Isaac and Jacob, spiritual forefathers of the Israelites.

curriculum vitae: 'as a displaced person' he gave the books he was able to take with him in 1939 to the *Society of Antiquaries*, to The Warburg Institute and to other libraries. He and his wife worked as domestic servants; Barb also worked as an engineer for eight years until he was offered a post in The Warburg Institute: 'I could resume my scholarly interests'. The Institute was 'with the exception of the non-historical parts of mathematical-scientific fields a small "Universitas Litterarum"'.[149] Barb was aware that with his appointment at The Warburg Institute he had come home. He did not mention his conversion to Göbl: was it no longer necessary or was it no longer important?

On Barb's understanding of Roman Catholicism

Barb must have had his reasons for conversion, but they did not really surface in his important letter to Sandor Wolf. The title of this chapter, 'What I can represent as a Jew, I can also represent as a Catholic' is, of course, a variant form of Bing's message to Swarzenski. As a Jew Barb had been a member of the Austrian educated middle-class, neither upper class, nor lower class, but part of the middle level, which was diverse and could not be narrowed down by religion, language, or ethnic origin. In Great Britain he found himself facing a totally different world. The Church of England was the state religion, in Barb's time comprising still the majority of the population. After the Reformation and the establishment of a state religion, a Roman Catholic hierarchy was re-established only in the middle of the 19th century. Many missionary orders, which gained a foothold in Britain after the French Revolution, educated fairly ordinary Catholics initially, so that gradually a local Catholic intelligentsia was created. John Henry Newman, a so-called 'high' Church of England priest, with leanings towards Roman Catholicism, was parish priest of St Mary's in Oxford from 1828 to 1830. He was the president of the so-called *Oxford Movement*, an influential movement among the Anglicans which pleaded for a middle course for the Church of England between false Protestant doctrines and Roman Catholic exaggerations.[150] Newman, who ever since his youth had contemplated conversion to Roman Catholicism, converted in 1845, became, after initial difficulties and notably contempt from the Anglicans, a Cardinal and was declared a Saint of the Roman Catholic church in 2019.[151] Barb's development is mirrored in his thoughts, if not in his career. Barb was a gifted intellectual, like Newman, and had been like Newman thinking about his conversion for many years. Newman's motivation for establishing a middle ground did not apply to Barb. However, studying Augustine might have been the trigger, contributing to Barb's decision in 1940, at the time of his internment, and in 1941, after his release from the camp. The number of Catholics had steadily increased,

149 University of Vienna, Department of Numismatics, Barb, A.A. to Göbl, R. 11.2.1974. Robert Göbl, Austrian numismatist, 1919–1997.

150 Strange, R., 'Lessons from a Journey to Faith', 4.

151 Newman, J.H., *Apologia Pro Vita Sua*, 4.

mostly through immigrants from Ireland. For this reason the Anglicans, the larger group, comprised the royal family and aristocracy and predominantly the bulk of people in the middle and upper classes, whereas the Catholics, the smaller group, were made up of workers and people from the lower classes. The Jewish population, which in Great Britain shared the fate of Jews in many other European countries over the centuries, namely settlement and then expulsion, was a small group. And in this situation Barb opted for Roman Catholicism, the smaller group, outsiders for many years, who slowly but surely no longer encountered religious restrictions or racial hatred in the 1940s.

Did Barb's research, reading and understanding of the script on gemstones from classical antiquity, the gnostic stones,[152] influence his decision – leaving what to him were the dead gods of antiquity behind and acknowledging the living God of Christianity? In his many scientific articles before and after his conversion, Barb occupied himself again and again with the topics with which early Christianity had been faced and had to distance itself from, the Roman emperor cult, Greek polytheism, Mesopotamian and Egyptian imperial cults, as well as eschatological and salvific notions and magic practices, as mentioned above. At his baptism he added Augustinus to his name in its Latin form and signed nearly all his correspondence 'A. A. Barb'. His requiem mass was celebrated in Latin.[153]

A pen drawing in black ink by Barb is extant, possibly a design for his bookplate (see figure 14.5).[154] It is not dated, the word 'Exlibris' or something similar is missing, but Barb's signature is below the drawing. A short vertical wooden beam is topped by a crossbeam, twice as long. On the vertical beam we can make out characters or decorations. On the crossbeam sits a bird with its wings spread, sharpening its beak. A black ribbon winds itself loosely around the cross beam, its end pieces widening into broad tassels, reminiscent of the end pieces of baroque stoles worn by Roman Catholic priests.

Bookplates were often embellished with drawings in order to signal the research interests of a scholar or to give the reader some additional information

152 Betty Burn's (1925–1938), 'Catalogue of the "Gnostic Gems" in the British Museum'. Typescript, pressmark in The Warburg Institute FCB 585. Commented, corrected and annotated by A.A. Barb (1971). The Betty Burn – A.A. Barb correspondence is pasted into volume I of the three-volume oeuvre. On 25 April 1971 Betty Burn sent him her catalogue and her notes to the 'Catalogue of the "Gnostic Stones" in the British Museum'. Barb thanked her warmly on 27 April 1971 but confessed that he would like to know more about her. She replied on 11 May 1971, giving him the reasons for her gift: she had to look after her parents and she would be happy if her life's work were kept in The Warburg Institute. She possibly had read Barb's articles on gnostic stones and of the magic word Abraxas, a term from Greek mysticism, which was often rendered on gnostic stones by the image of a creature, part human and part serpent. See Barb, A.A., 'Abraxas-Studien'. *Hommages à Waldemar Deonna*, 207–208. From 2009 onwards the periodical *Abraxas. International Journal of Esoteric Studies* is published in London: Fulgur, with contributions on mystery cults, mythology and occultism.

153 I am grateful to Simon Barb, grandson of A.A. Barb, for this communication. London, 12 March 2020.

154 BFPP, *Journal* no. 3, 1118.

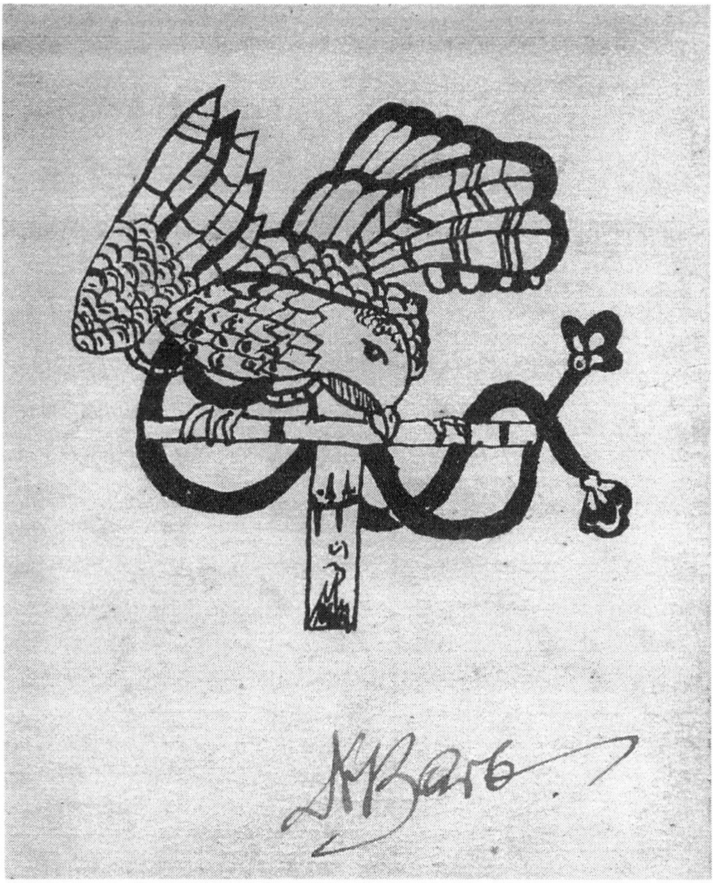

Figure 14.5 Exlibris. Private collection.
Photo: BFPP, Barb family, *Journal* no.3, 1118.

on the owner of the bookplate, or even a riddle to solve. Barb's drawing here is no exception; its interpretation is tentative. Might the two beams forming the tau cross refer to the symbol of Christianity? Might the bird be a dove, a religious symbol in Christian antiquity, symbol of the Holy Spirit and of peace? Might the wavy black ribbon signify that the bird is no longer chained to the beam? Might the pointed decorations or characters standing next to each show 'A. A.' and might below them, somewhat less clearly visible, the 'B' refer to Barb's initials? Might the whole drawing refer to the English word 'barb', which means 'spine' as well as 'quill pen'? One species of pigeon is called the 'barb pigeon' or 'Darwin's pigeon' in English, but they do not look like the bird drawn by Barb. A dove was mentioned in the first book of Moses, when Noah sent out a dove twice in order to see whether the dove could see land anywhere. The second time the dove brought back an olive leaf, and Noah knew that the flood was receding.[155] According to Emile Mâle, who traced the symmetry of topics in the Hebrew and Greek Bibles, Noah's ark did not sink 'so that the people were taught that the church finds its protection in the water of baptism'.[156] The return of the dove could therefore be understood as God having kept his word and salvation having become a reality.[157]

Ultimately, it remains unclear what the drawing is supposed to express. The many hypothetical questions offer a cluster of possible explanations. The reply to my request to the Natural History Museum in London was inconclusive. The illustration is a bird, possibly a dove; the illustrator had applied his artistic freedom in order to draw a beautiful bird, which did not really represent a recognisable species.[158] At least the bookplate, if it was supposed to present Barb, the Roman Catholic man, shows a dove-like bird, spreading its wings, free and no longer chained, sitting on a perch mounted on a pole, which could be interpreted as a tau cross with Barb's initials.

The article on 'St. Zacharias the Prophet and Martyr. A Study in Charms and Incantations'[159] possibly comes nearest to the source of Barb's conversion. The article, sparkling with examples and cross-references, is a study of the Saint as a prophet and martyr and a faith healer of nose bleeds. Blood magic and incantations were ubiquitous in all ages so that Barb wanted to go beyond them:

> It is not my intention to furnish additional material for that obsolete, if not discarded, evolutionist theory, which purports that religion is somehow the product of some sublimation of primeval magic. I am rather inclined to see in magic practices an antithesis to revealed religion and, as such, a not unimportant proof of the reality of the thesis – the divine revelation.[160]

In his pivotal studies on gnosticism, incantations and decayed antiquity, dismissed as 'Florilegium of Absurdities',[161] Barb went along the same lines as Aby Warburg's dictum 'Superstition is rudimentary perception':[162] one might present it as discarded or overruled, but it was part of the history of ideas of humanity,

155 Hebrew Bible, 1st book of Moses, Genesis, 8: 6–12.

156 Mâle, E., *Gothic Image: Religious Art in France of the Thirteenth Century*, 154: 'The ark was built by Noah, the only just man of the ancient world, as the Church was built by Christ, the supremely just man. Lastly the ark floated on the waters of the deluge to teach men that the Church finds her safety in the waters of baptism . . .'. Emile Mâle, French art historian, 1862–1954.

157 I am grateful to Dr. Timothy Jackson for this interpretation.

158 I am grateful to Florin Feneru for his explanation, 1 May 2020.

159 Barb, A.A., 'St Zacharias the Prophet and Martyr. A Study in Charms and Incantations', 35–67.

160 Barb, A.A., 'St Zacharias the Prophet and Martyr. A Study in Charms and Incantations', 35.

161 Barb, A.A., 'St Zacharias the Prophet and Martyr. A Study in Charms and Incantations', 47.

162 see Chapter 15, note 17, WIA, III, 10.2. Diary, 13.8.1901, 60. on 'rudimentary perception'.

of the conceptual appropriation of thinking and scientific experiments. When praying to the Saint for help with bleeding one could expect success. Magical practices constituted the antithesis to revealed religion and were, therefore, not insignificant proof of the reality of the thesis – the divine revelation.

Was it possible to appreciate sufficiently Barb's 'going over to Rome' with examples from Newman? Certainly in part. They can contribute to indicating Barb's scientific knowledge, his personal friendships, possibly also a good measure of his 'knowing better'. In addition to the studies on the emergence of decay in antiquity, historical examples of conversion from Judaism to Christianity, the topic of fulfilment or succession theology, might have played a role. Examples are, for instance, Heinrich Heine[163] or the former Chief Rabbi of Rome, Israel Anton Zoller, who was baptised on 13 February 1945 by Mgr. Luigi Traglia, Vice-Regent of Rome and thereby representative of Pope Pius XII, and who had added the name of the pope, Eugenio Pacelli, as his baptismal name.[164] A main factor might have been Barb's reading of works by St Augustine – as much pointers to Newman's conversion – just as much as the overall faith praxis in Great Britain, which had strengthened his views for conversion. For Newman his conversion initially brought the loss of intellectual influence, but later a more diffuse acceptance. For Barb his conversion meant leaving behind the limited Mosaic practice and acceptance of the interpretation of a living God, possibly the mystery of Christianity. For Warburg it was the way from magic to logic, without accepting a Christian faith practice.[165]

For Barb as well as for Warburg there were two focal points which were diametrically opposed, in mathematics expressed by an ellipse, which triggers tensions and depressions, a construct often quoted by Warburg. Both exist for Barb and both pose puzzles. Was Judaism, a religion of classical antiquity, in his view a religion of decay, and was – powerful – Christianity, likewise a religion from

163 Heinrich Heine, German poet, 1797–1856, author of *Die Lorelei*.

164 I am grateful to Dr. Mordechay Lewy, 11.4.2020, and Fr. Philippe Luisier SJ, 26.4.2020, for this information. Israel Anton Zoller, later Eugenio Maria Zolli, Austro-Hungarian Italian rabbi, from Brody, today Ukraine, 1881–1956. While Zoller's conversion took place after Barb's conversion, it is a pointer to the discussion of conversion among intellectuals.

165 Aby Warburg's interdisciplinary research approach in art history, the natural sciences and history of religion was well-known to Barb. WIA, GC, the mediaevalist Lenel, W. to Warburg, 22.12.1924, congratulating Warburg on the phrase 'Vom Greiftier zum Begriffsmenschen', which Warburg had coined introducing the lecture by Karl Reinhardt on Ovid's Metamorphoses on 24 October 1924 in the KBW. See Warburg, A., 'Zum Vortrage von Karl Reinhardt über "Ovids Metamorphosen"', Preface to Reinhardt's lecture in the KBW on 24 October 1924. Warburg, by using the phrase 'Vom Greiftier zum Begriffsmenschen', tried to explain the haptic experience, the development from the predatory animal which grips its prey with a clear intention of its purpose to the human being which no longer needs to kill and destroy in order to live. It is all but untranslatable in its precision, a possible translation might be 'from grasping by physical force to grasping by the intellect' or 'from physical mastery to mental mastery' or 'from prehension to comprehension'. See also Stimilli and Wedepohl, *Aby M. Warburg "Per Monstra and Sphaeram"*, 59–61. See also Chapter 7.

classical antiquity, still part of it or not? Ultimately, these two questions cannot conclusively be answered without further source material. But a quote by Theodor Georg von Hippel might show most clearly Barb's belief. He stuck it into his *Journal* no. 1 like many other devotional texts:[166] 'Being in a foreign country means falling into the hand of God'.[167]

166 BFPP, *Journal*, e.g. no. 1, 2100–2110.

167 BFPP, *Journal*, no. 3, 1111, undated curriculum vitae. 'In der Fremde sein, heisst in die Hand Gottes fallen'. Quote by Hippel, *Lebensläufe nach aufsteigenden Linien*, 9. Theodor Georg von Hippel, German satirist, 1775–1843.

Part V

STRUWWELPETER AND ITS MANY PARODIES

15

ABY WARBURG'S INTERPRETATION OF THE RUSSIAN TRANSLATION OF *STRUWWELPETER* AND THE POLITICAL PARODIES *STRUWWELHITLER – A NAZI STORYBOOK* AND *SCHICKLGRÜBER*[1]

Warburg's objective of charting the metamorphoses of ideas in words and images is the topic of this chapter on a children's book, which has become a pioneer in children's literature: *Struwwelpeter*, a book it is said should always – or never – be given to children.

Stories for children, whether in words or images, are a socialisation tool, portraying the world in strong black-and-white contrast and presenting grossly exaggerated stereotypes. The evil man or anti-hero is really frightfully bad, while the good man, initially weak, is eventually always victorious. The goal of any pedagogical literature is making clear to children the ethical signposts for what is or is not allowed, which dispositions should be nurtured or rebuked, controlled and eventually even suppressed. Frequently these signposts are exaggerated, parodied, in order to be more easily understood by children. In contrast to children's books, political parodies do not suppress inclinations – that is, punish the enemy – but hold the politician up to ridicule, pulling out all the stops to mock a pompous, bombastic politician and show his ideologies as cruel because of the contempt with which he treats human rights.

The methods used for educating children in the nursery and for making a public spectacle of one's enemies well as defamations of enemies with a view to public appeal follow the same emblematic model: firstly, bad behaviour is criticised; secondly, appeals are made directly to the misbehaving child or the politician with their lack of understanding, threatening to make their misdeeds public; thirdly, if the child or politicians do not stop their bad behaviour they are severely punished and the politician is made into a laughing stock.

1 Originally published in McEwan, D., 'Der gute Bischof Nikolaus. Aby Warburgs Interpretation der russischen Übersetzung von *Struwwelpeter* und die politischen Parodien *Struwwelhitler – A Nazi Story Book* und *Schicklgrüber*', 67–90. The present Chapter was slightly extended with material from eadem, 'Aby Warburg und die Figur des Nikolaus im "Russischen Struwwelpeter"', 354–364.

DOI: 10.4324/9781003169024-20

One of the most famous, and at the same time most infamous, primers is the collection of stories published under the title *Struwwelpeter* ('shock-headed Peter'), the name of the naughty boy who neither combs his hair nor cuts his nails. It was penned and illustrated by the medical doctor Heinrich Hoffmann in Frankfurt am Main.[2] He wanted to read funny and morally edifying stories to his children, but achieved with the publication of his book something remarkable for a German writer of his time: his texts were neither bombastic nor romantic, and the stories had a surrealist denouement. He wrote in rhyming couplets, disobedience was exaggerated, the nursery or house was presented as a torture chamber, the punishment, which followed immediately, was overkill – it was unrealistic or incomprehensible – and therefore became really funny.

The book, subtitled 'Pretty Stories and Funny Pictures', contains an introductory poem and nine stories, which amounted, according to the education standards in the mid-19th century, to a catalogue of infantile disobedience, lack of manners and mobbing. The behaviour of the parents was equally questionable; they were unmasked as highly incompetent. Indeed, the story of the tailor, with the tailor's scissors cutting off the child's thumb, does not really offer a solution for thumb-sucking. Admittedly, the pedagogical aim to educate children to become responsible adults is discernible, but the methods used are more than suspect. With the exception of the story of the good bishop Nicholas, who attempts to talk to the naughty boys, no other story shows any attempt by the parents to back down. The adults only utter commands and threats; they do not think it worth their while to find out why the children are naughty. Both groups, adults as well as children, are in a hierarchical relationship, which makes communicative conduct impossible and necessitates punishment.

Heinrich Hoffmann's *Struwwelpeter* has seen more than 1,000 editions since its first as well as dozens of translations. The first English translation was published in 1848, *The English Struwwelpeter or Pretty Stories and Funny Pictures*, and became so popular that the stories were regarded as a 'freak of acclimatization' and thereby present an extraordinary transfer of a German book into the English context.[3] The most famous translation into English is by Hilaire Belloc in 1907 but expresses in the cautionary tales a *reductio ad absurdum* of the original stories.[4]

From a letter in 1924 by Warburg to his brother Fritz it becomes clear that Warburg had been focused on the *Struwwelpeter* topic for a long time:

> Your comment last night about the chanson by Yvette Gilbert on St Nicholas coincided really well with my comment on Struwwelpeter. I do not doubt that the song by Yvette is a litany, used by seafarers

2 Heinrich Hoffmann, German psychiatrist, 1809–1894.

3 Darton, F.J.H., *Children's Books in England. Five Centuries of Social Life*, 250.

4 Belloc, H., *Cautionary Tales for Children*. Illustrated by Edward Gorey.

> in distress at sea when invoking help from St Nicholas. I would be grateful it you could send me precise dates of this chanson. It is really amusing to note that we sit in the same boat: this time under the sign of Holy Nicholas.[5]

Three months later he thanked Fritz for sending him the 'Chansons des trois petits enfants', adding that he had filed it with the papers on St Nicholas.[6]

Yvette Guilbert was a famous chansons singer, who delighted in choosing 'medieval' topics. Warburg wrote to his friend Jacques Mesnil that Yvette thought the origin of the legend of St Nicholas was to be found in a Latin version of seven or eight miracles performed by St Nicholas.[7] Mesnil replied by sending him the French text of the legend of St Nicholas, in which three little boys were killed by a butcher, their flesh salted, but brought to life again by St Nicholas.[8] In Warburg's index card boxes, his subject catalogue, his box [10] labelled 'Ikonologie Probleme' contains a list documenting the iterations of the idea of St Nicholas's miracles. Warburg here had divided the topic into four columns; the first three are headed History, Psychology and Transformation respectively, while the fourth column does not have a heading. Under 'History' his entries included: 'Soter (= saviour), 3 girls, 3 innocents, Myra, Bari, the well-behaved child'; under 'Psychology' he listed 'Hierodalen/sic!/[holy slaves],[9] Maniac'; under 'Transformation' we find the words 'fresco, Worms, Frankfurt, the saviour as avenger, "moral"'; in the fourth column he wrote 'rod, with arrow on 3 innocents, Struwwelpeter, inkwell, set a warning example, Max and Moritz, Fritz/song, Yvette Guilbert'.[10]

With this list Warburg showed how the topic of Nicholas was one of those topics which lent itself to different options of interpretation because they went back to multifarious traditions of Christian and magical patterns of behaviour.

The good bishop Nicholas and Aby Warburg's interpretation of the figure of Nicholas in *Stepka-Rastrepka*

On closer analysis the figure of Bishop Nicholas proves an excellent example of a topic's visual and textual metamorphosis. The story itself is well-known: in the original *Struwwelpeter* version three white boys ridicule an unnamed black boy, who is generically called 'Moor'. A black person was certainly a rarity in Frankfurt in the 19th century and, because unusual, also a figure of fun. The derision,

5 WIA, GC, Warburg to Fritz Warburg, 13.12.1924. Yvette Guilbert, French singer and actress, 1865–1944.

6 WIA, GC, Warburg to Fritz Warburg, 14. 3.1925.

7 WIA, III.2.1., index card box [10], 066/038 949. Warburg to Mesnil, 4.2.1925. Jean-Jacques Dwelshauvers, known as Jacques Mesnil, Belgian art historian, 1872–1940.

8 WIA, III.2.1. Index card box [10], 066/038 952, Mesnil to Warburg, 12.2.1925.

9 Hierodule, from Greek, holy slave, a slave in the service of a deity.

10 WIA, III.2.1., Index card box [10], 066/038 954. Warburg Note, 5.12.1925.

however, triggers the admonishing words of the bishop, who is loved by all children – and who still brings gifts to them or admonishes them on 6 December every year in Germany and Austria. He became the model for the American Santa Claus. Nicholas tried to advise the boys:

> 'Don't laugh', he said, 'it isn't right
> To scoff at skins as black as night.
> The Moor is not as white as you,
> But did not choose his darksome hue'.[11]

The boys, however, did not listen to the bishop. Nicholas flew into a rage and dunked them in a huge black inkwell. And when he fished them out again, they were 'much blacker black' than the Moor and now they had turned into objects of derision.[12]

The core of the legend of St Nicholas – the name in the original Greek means victor of the people or over the people – is the story of a man and his role in a critical moment in the life and death of children. The veneration of a saint, that is a person living on in the memory of other people as a guide or exemplar for behaviour, is a core practice in a number of religions. In time, facts from the life of the saint became linked to or intertwined with fable, local stories became enriched with additional facts or fiction and kept alive through songs, images and symbols. The veneration of ancestors, whose names were repeated in succeeding generations, and the cult of saints, whose names were invoked in baptism, were two mechanisms which upheld their memory. According to the place and time, these memories were codified and embroidered with general attributes and local colour. The story was furnished with a number of interpretations: the man could be a giant, a sage, a saint, a magician, a benefactor; the children could be girls or boys, innocents, sailors, or children to be baptised, etc. What the people believed, and most importantly how this was expressed, was often not what was taught by the church. Popular devotion and official church doctrine often went different ways, came together again and sat alongside each other. And precisely the figure of St Nicholas in general, and in *Struwwelpeter* in particular, manifested a multiplicity and diversity of facts about the Saint's life and the fiction that lived on of his help and miracles.

Warburg, who researched the influence of classical antiquity on the European visual memory,[13] was therefore interested in *Struwwelpeter*, a story itself told in words and pictures. What was important to him in this respect was how people dealt with fear and the linking of obedience to threats.[14] In his research of popular superstition in Luther's time, with the prognoses of comets and monstrous freaks

11 Gibson, E.K., 'Tousled-headed Peter', 45–52, here 45.
12 Gibson, E.K., 'Tousled-headed Peter', 45–52, here 52.
13 cf. Warburg, A, 'Orientalisierende Astrologie', Britt, D., 'Astrology under Oriental Influence', 699–702 and 775.
14 McEwan, D., 'Aby Warburg und die Figur des Nikolaus im "Russischen Struwwelpeter"', 354–364.

of nature,[15] Warburg had tried to understand manifestations which instilled or banished fear. Other examples were studied by Warburg, for instance the brazen serpent – those standing in front of its portrayal could no longer be harmed by it – and likewise the complex dance rituals, with which dancers and their populations could achieve power over the animals (for instance poisonous snakes).[16] Another mechanism of banning fear by images was astrology, a practice or method for forecasting and interpreting the future. By throwing light on the future the sage or priest used 'rudimentary perception' which, as precursor to astronomy, filled an important scientific position.[17]

Fear and disgrace were the important driving forces in the story of St Nicholas. Warburg saw in the figure of the bishop the continued existence of a medieval tradition of images telling the story of the evil innkeeper or butcher who cuts up three young students and puts them into a barrel of brine. However, Nicholas found them, pieced them together and brought them to life again. Nicholas is turned into the miracle worker, justice personified. Warburg finds variants of this story, with people who are helped by St Nicholas. One version tells of children who were imprisoned by a Byzantine general in a tower, from where Nicholas liberates them. Another version deals with seafarers, whose ship is tossed by a storm on the high seas. They pray to St Nicholas and are promptly saved. The images of three young men in a large baptismal font present a Christianised version of the story of the seafarers in distress. However, this particular story harks back to a different story: a mother leaves her child in a tub of hot water and hurries to attend the solemn enthronement of Nicholas as bishop of Myra, in modern-day Turkey. On her return she sees that the bishop has saved the child from certain death by scalding.[18]

The figure of St Nicholas offered seemingly endless possibilities of variations on the theme of benefactor and just, kindly helper. When Warburg in 1925 heard about a court case, the so-called 'Denke affair' in Silesia (today Ziębice in Poland), he wanted to find out whether the accused had read stories of cannibalism and whether in his town there was a church dedicated to St Nicholas with pictures showing the innkeeper cutting up the boys.[19] To Warburg this story was the example of the ur-motif of the man-eating monster, which must have been most frightening to a

15 Warburg, A, *Heidnisch-antike Weissagung in Wort und Bild zu Luthers Zeiten*; Britt, D., 'Pagan-Antique Prophecy in Words and Images in the Age of Luther', 597–697 and 760–775.

16 Warburg, A, 'A Lecture on Serpent Ritual', 222–292.

17 WIA, III, 10.2. Diary, 13.8.1901, 60. For Warburg's explanation of the quote of 'rudimentary perception' see also Chapter 14, notes 81 and 162.

18 Meisen, K., *Nikolauskult und Nikolausbrauch im Abendlande*, 261 on the version about the mother who puts her little child into a tub of hot water.

19 WIA, GC, A. Warburg to the Public Prosecutor, Prussia, 9.1.1925. The 'Denke affair' was the court case against the serial murderer Karl Denke from Münsterberg, today Ziębice, Silesia, Poland, who was said to have killed between 30 and 40 people. On top of this accusation he was said to have been a cannibal and to have sold human flesh. See Bialy, L., articles [titles unknown] about the Denke affair.

child's imagination. Warburg wrote to Eduard Hessenberg, a solicitor in Frankfurt am Main and grandson of the *Struwwelpeter* author Heinrich Hoffmann, thanking him for a Christmas present, and then continued with *Struwwelpeter*:

> In my assessment the image tradition of the Middle Ages somehow continued to have an effect in the figure of the great Nicholas and the three naughty boys. The legend was frequently illustrated and showed how the Saint brought back to life the three young students who had been dismembered by the innkeeper and packed into a barrel. The cult of the Saint was very common in German cities. Frankfurt also has its church dedicated to St Nicholas. Would it have been possible that Dr. Hoffmann had seen such images of the legend of St Nicholas? Did he live in the vicinity of this church? The Cossack-style apparel of the Saint caused a colleague to observe that Tsar Nicholas was hinted at, an assumption which to me is somewhat absurd and forced.[20]

Hessenberg obliged with a full reply:

> Now to 'Nicholas!' I am convinced that no medieval image tradition had continued to have an effect on the origin of this figure, certainly not consciously . . . But even unconsciously I do not believe in such an influence. I do not know of any such images in Frankfurt, the Church of St Nicholas does not have one.
>
> I know from my grandfather himself that the figure had nothing to do with Tsar Nicholas. In the first years after its publication the book *Struwwelpeter* was forbidden in Russia, because St Nicholas as well as *Struwwelpeter* were seen to correlate to the Tsars Nicholas and Peter. But then in 1849 *Struwwelpeter* was published in a Russian translation after the names and drawings had been changed to accommodate an appropriate Russianisation. I still own the edition. My grandfather always dismissed any relationship either of *Struwwelpeter* or St Nicholas to Russian Tsars and ridiculed such ideas.
>
> According to your opinion the figure of the great Nicholas can simply be traced back to the old custom in Frankfurt, whereby Nicholas visits families as 'Nickelos' on the evening of 5th November, that is the day before the feast of St Nicholas on 6th November. He resembles the figure of Servant Rupert in other regions. He is dressed in a brown monk's habit or a fur coat and fur hat, because he comes from the north or from Russia. In his hand he holds a rod or stick and on his back he carries a sack full of apples, nuts and sweets. He punishes the naughty children and rewards

20 WIA, GC, A. Warburg to Eduard Hessenberg, p.a. Frankfurt am Main: Literarische Anstalt Rätten & Löning, 15.1.1925.

> the well-behaved children. According to an old custom he brings a special gift, a little toy donkey for the children. – The story with the inkwell was obviously freely made up by my grandfather and only invented to have a device in order to make the naughty boys even blacker than the Moor.
>
> Of course, I cannot exclude the possibility that my grandfather once saw an image as you mentioned, but I can hardly believe it, because he surely would have told us.[21]

So, Hessenberg, like his grandfather, did not want to see Tsar Nicholas I in the punishment meted out by the Saint in the German version. He could not convince Warburg. Four years later Warburg was convinced that Nicholas, the 'German bishop of pedagogic gentleness', had turned into the evil Tsar, 'the monster of tyrannical malice', in the Russian edition.[22]

The – anonymous – translator kept to the German original, however the illustrations differed quite substantially from Heinrich Hoffmann's illustrations. As a matter of course the German stories were transposed to fit the Russian situation by using Russian names and Cossack shirts, held together by belts according to Russian fashion. In addition, Georgy V. Hohenfelden of the publishing house Moritz Ossipowitsch Wolff and illustrator Ludwig Bohnstedt further developed the illustrations which originally had been sketched out only in outlines by Heinrich Hoffmann and added decorations and details to the sceneries, furniture, outfits, posture.[23]

The Russian translation left out the name of Nicholas in order not to get into difficulties with censorship, as the name Nicholas was the name of the absolutist, authoritarian Tsar, symbol of an unenlightened cruel ruler. The bad-tempered old man is called 'toiporoi', 'bogyman', that is, a man who frightened children.

21 WIA, III.2.1.10, 066/038970. E. Hessenberg to A. Warburg, 22.1.1925. In the following year, WIA, GC, Hessenberg to Warburg, 10.10.1926, Hessenberg asked Warburg to review Hessenberg's book about his grandfather: Hessenberg, E., *"Struwwelpeter-Hoffmann" erzählt aus seinem Leben: Lebenserinnerungen seines Großvaters Dr. Heinrich Hoffmann*. WIA, GC, Warburg to Hessenberg, 12.10.1926, Warburg thanked him, he had ordered the book already, and found it very interesting, but could not review it due to being overworked. The first Russian translation, *Stepka-Rastrepka*, was published in 1849, see WIA, GC, Warburg to Saxl, 1.2.1929 and Sauer, W., 'Der *Struwwelpeter* und *Stepka-Rastrepka*. Zur Ikonographie der 2. *Struwwelpeter* fassung', 20–34. The images in the Russian version were copied by the following *Struwwelpeter* editions in Germany and abroad. See Sauer, W., 'Nachwort', 121–126, here 122. Eduard Hessenberg, German lawyer, 1873–1933.

22 WIA, GC, Warburg to Saxl, 21.3.1929.

23 For Sauer, W., 'Der *Struwwelpeter* und *Stepka-Rastrepka*. Zur Ikonographie der 2. Struwwelpeterfassung', 20–34, here 26, the drawings in the Russian *Struwwelpeter* are 'artistically markedly superior' ['künstlerisch deutlich überlegen'] to the German drawings. He could also prove that the images in the *Struwwelpeter* editions from the second German edition onwards were all based on the Russian illustrations. See Sauer, W., 'Der *Struwwelpeter* und *Stepka-Rastrepka*. Zur Ikonographie der 2. Struwwelpeterfassung', 32, on the question of whether Hoffmann could be called a plagiarist because he was silent about the origin of the images in his autobiography. Georgy Vasiljevich Hohenfelden, Russian publisher, 1838–1934; Moritz Ossipowitsch Wolff, Polish-Russian publisher, 1825–1883; Franz Ludwig Carl Bohnstedt, Russian-German architect, 1822–1885.

He put the boys into the inkwell like in the German version, but he did not look like the Saint in the German version with his beard and long gown, accessories of imagination, not reality.

When Warburg stayed in Rome in the spring of 1929, he once more touched upon the *Struwwelpeter* topic. He wanted to study the strangely medieval motifs, in particular the transposition of the figure of Nicholas. He got in touch with D. N. Jegoroff, director of the Lenin library in Moscow,[24] because he wanted to study the first Russian translation of 1849. Warburg also mentioned his initiative to Saxl, as well as his conversation with the Russian general Piotr Nikolayevich Baron Wrangel, and the Diary entry of his conversation with Duke Bülow, where he revised Hesssenberg's view of the figure of Nicholas.[25]

Wrangel, the Russian general and leader of the anti-Bolshevik White Army, explained the Russian version of *Struwwelpeter* to Warburg. In contrast to the German edition of 1845, where Nicholas was portrayed in a monk's habit and pointed hat, the Saint in the Russian version did not appear as a friend of children, but as a grey-haired giant, a demonic and nameless bogyman. To Wrangel it was totally clear that the person was supposed to be Tsar Nicholas I (1796–1855), who hoped to improve the behaviour of young people by punishing them (see figures 15.1 and 15.2). Duke Bernhard von Bülow – politician, diplomat, German chancellor from 1900 to 1909, German ambassador to Italy in 1929 at the time Warburg stayed in Rome, and a close friend of Warburg's – confirmed Wrangel's explanation. He told Warburg that he remembered when he was a small child and visiting his relatives in Frankfurt am Main having heard talk about Tsar Nicholas, who was feared as the incarnation of the 'freedom devouring tyrant'.[26] Warburg also wrote in his Diary on 19 March 1929 about the breakfast at Bülow's: 'when Bülow was a young boy Tsar Nicholas was viewed as the incarnation of a tyrant'. These statements justified Warburg in hypothesising that the Russian *Struwwelpeter* presented, in fact, a thematic and iconological metamorphosis.

The Russian translation, therefore, could be understood as allusion to Tsar Nicholas, but this in itself was not yet political parody. Warburg's iconological research directed him to investigate the development and distribution of the *Struwwelpeter* literature with its shift in meaning, which led the Frankfurt children's book to become a vehicle for political parody. In time more metamorphoses followed, which mirrored the politics of the day with its tyrants and busy-bodies.

24 WIA, GC, Clara Hertz to Lenin Library, 14.5.1929, covering letter with return of the booklet. It had been sent to Hamburg to be photographed and is still kept in the library of the Warburg Institute. Warburg mentioned Jegoroff's and Director Nevski's visit in the KBW on 30.7.1928; they were boasting about the number of books and visitors they had in Moscow, Warburg called them 'positivists of the most recent stamp'. D N. Jegoroff, Russian librarian and philatelist; Bernhard von Bülow, German statesman, 1849–1929; Piotr Nikolayevich Baron Wrangel, Russian general, 1878–1928.

25 WIA, GC, Warburg to Saxl, 1.2.1929.

26 WIA, GC, Warburg to Saxl, 21.3.1929.

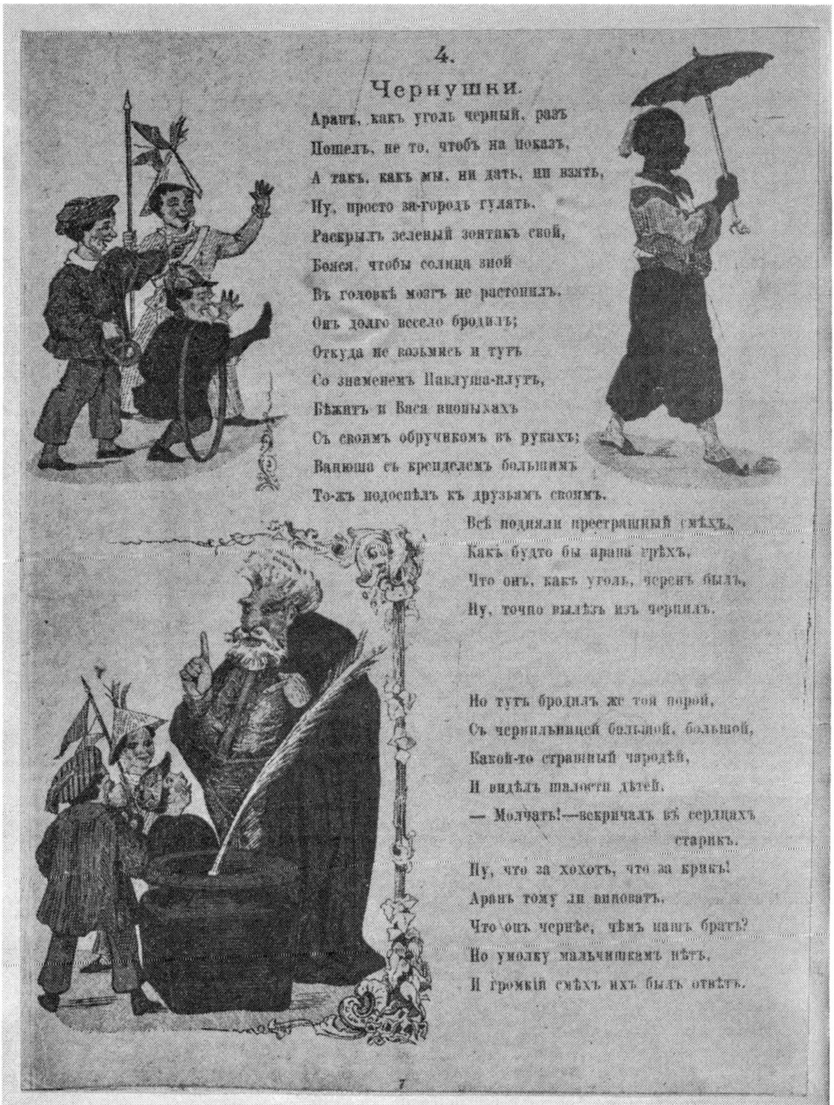

4.

Чернушки.

Арапъ, какъ уголь черный, разъ
Пошелъ, не то, чтобъ на показъ,
А такъ, какъ мы, ни дать, ни взять,
Ну, просто за-городъ гулять.
Раскрылъ зеленый зонтикъ свой,
Боясь, чтобы солнца зной
Въ головкѣ мозгъ не растопилъ.
Онъ долго весело бродилъ;
Откуда не возьмись и тутъ
Со знаменемъ Павлуша-плутъ,
Бѣжитъ и Вася впопыхахъ
Съ своимъ обручикомъ въ рукахъ;
Ванюша съ кренделемъ большимъ
То-жъ подоспѣлъ къ друзьямъ своимъ.
Всѣ подняли престрашный смѣхъ,
Какъ будто бы арапъ грѣхъ,
Что онъ, какъ уголь, черенъ былъ,
Ну, точно вылѣзъ изъ чернилъ.

Но тутъ бродилъ же той порой,
Съ чернильницей большой, большой,
Какой-то странный чародѣй,
И видѣлъ шалости дѣтей.
— Молчать!—вскричалъ въ сердцахъ
старикъ.
Ну, что за хохотъ, что за крикъ!
Арапъ тому ли виноватъ,
Что онъ чернѣе, чѣмъ нашъ братъ?
Но умолку мальчишкамъ нѣтъ,
И громкій смѣхъ ихъ былъ отвѣтъ.

7

Figure 15.1 G. V. Hohenfelden and L. Bohnstedt (1849), 'The Story of the Black Boys', *Stepka-Rastrepka*, 25.

Source: © Georg V. Hohenfelden and Ludwig Bohnstedt. 1849, 25.

Photo: The Warburg Institute.

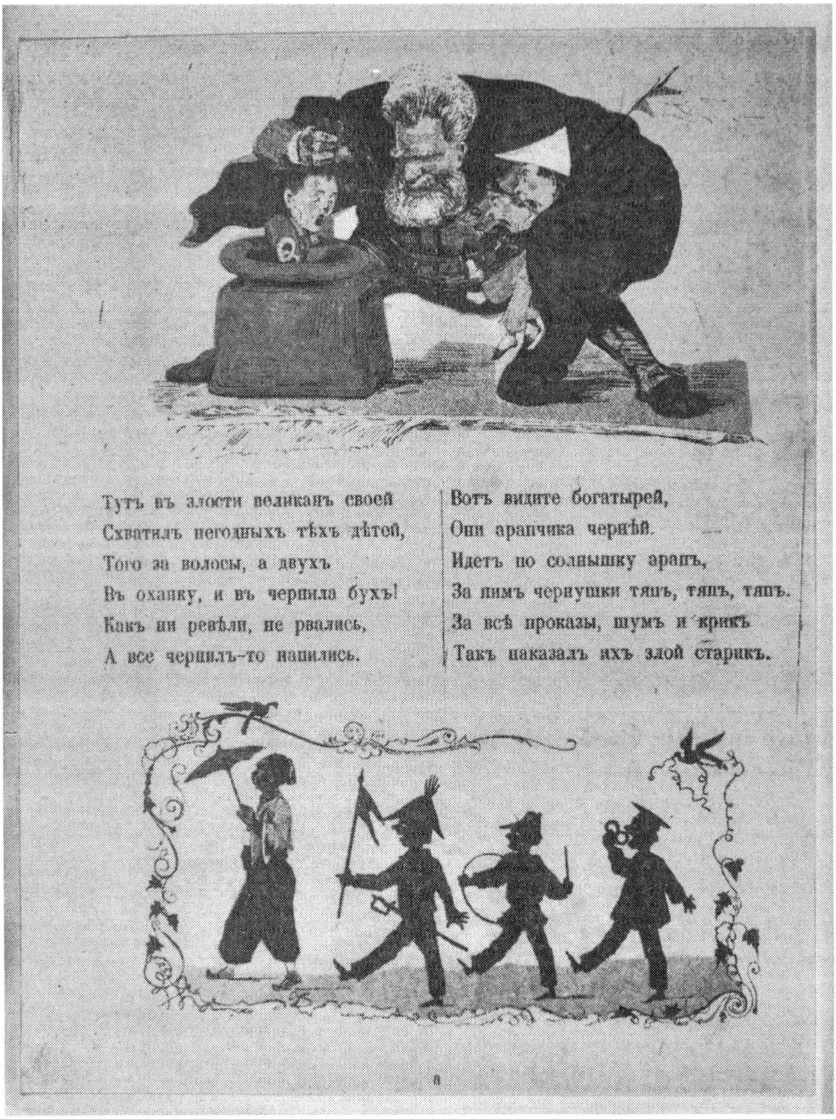

Figure 15.2 G. V. Hohenfelden and L. Bohnstedt (1849), 'The Story of the Black Boys', *Stepka-Rastrepka*, 26.

Source: © Georg V. Hohenfelden and Ludwig Bohnstedt. 1849, 26.

Photo: The Warburg Institute.

Political parodies

What was the immediate reason for Warburg's ordering a copy of the Russian *Struwwelpeter* in 1929? 'The Story of the Black Boys' in the Russian *Struwwelpeter* was not yet a political caricature of Tsar Nicholas I, but the first intermediate stage of words and images to supply a key to a 'political' reading of this story. Political parodies ridicule the powerful and thereby divest them of their power. The didactic used in children's books proved very suitable for the literary genre of parody: admonition, the threat of punishment and finally the punishment meted out, with their pious and sanctimonious undertones.[27] It was easy to rework *Struwwelpeter* following this format because it was widely known as a classic of children's literature, and one could be certain that everybody who understood the moral of the original stories would understand the reworked stories. The parodies as derivatives were particularly effective because they suggested that the politician, pulled to pieces, did not have to be taken seriously. The reader of a political parody could not help but smile when they saw that the politicians behaved like children and were heading to their certain end as demagogues or crooks.

Fully political transpositions of the message of *Struwwelpeter* appeared only at the turn of the 20th century. Now, the texts did not want to educate the children but, by denouncing the politicians, wanted to instil loathing of the anti-hero. They set in motion a formation of opinion, which in a dictatorship like in Russia could not be set in motion easily. The many political versions of the *Struwwelpeter* stories, which used the formulae of children's literature with admonitions, threats of punishment and satire, all pilloried tyrants in words and images, ridiculed them and achieved a change of opinion. *The Political Struwwelpeter* by Harold Begbie, published in 1898 in London, showed the dark side of British politics to the British public; the *Swollen-Headed William* by E. V. Lucas, with illustrations by G. Morrow, lampooned the German Emperor William II in 1914, substituting Struwwelpeter's comb and scissors on the plinth of the frontispiece with militaristic hardware like war ships and cannons.[28] The first anti-Nazi satire was *The Truffle Eater* in 1933, where master propagandist Goebbels burnt down the Reichstag building, or where the three naughty boys were the foreign journalists who had to be punished, or where Göring carried out anti-Jewish excesses.[29]

The afterlife or reincarnation of *Struwwelpeter* in the political parodies – so far some 50 are known – is astonishing. The two Nazi parodies *Struwwelhitler. A Nazi Story Book by Doktor Schrecklichkeit* (see figure 15.3) and *Schicklgrüber* (see figure 15.4) showed the spiteful and pretentious behaviour of the Nazis – in analogy to the

27 Cf. also McEwan, D., 'Struwwelhitler: A Nazi Story Book', 221–235.

28 Doderer, K., 'Panoptikum der Struwwelköpfe', 27–35, here 30; Begbie, H., *The Political Struwwelpeter*. Harold Begbie, English journalist, 1871–1929; Edward Verrall Lucas, British humorist, 1868–1938; George Morrow, British cartoonist, 1869–1855.

29 Wolfe, H., alias Oistros, *Truffle Eater, Pretty Stories and Funny Pictures*. Humbert Wolfe, Italian-British poet, 1885–1940.

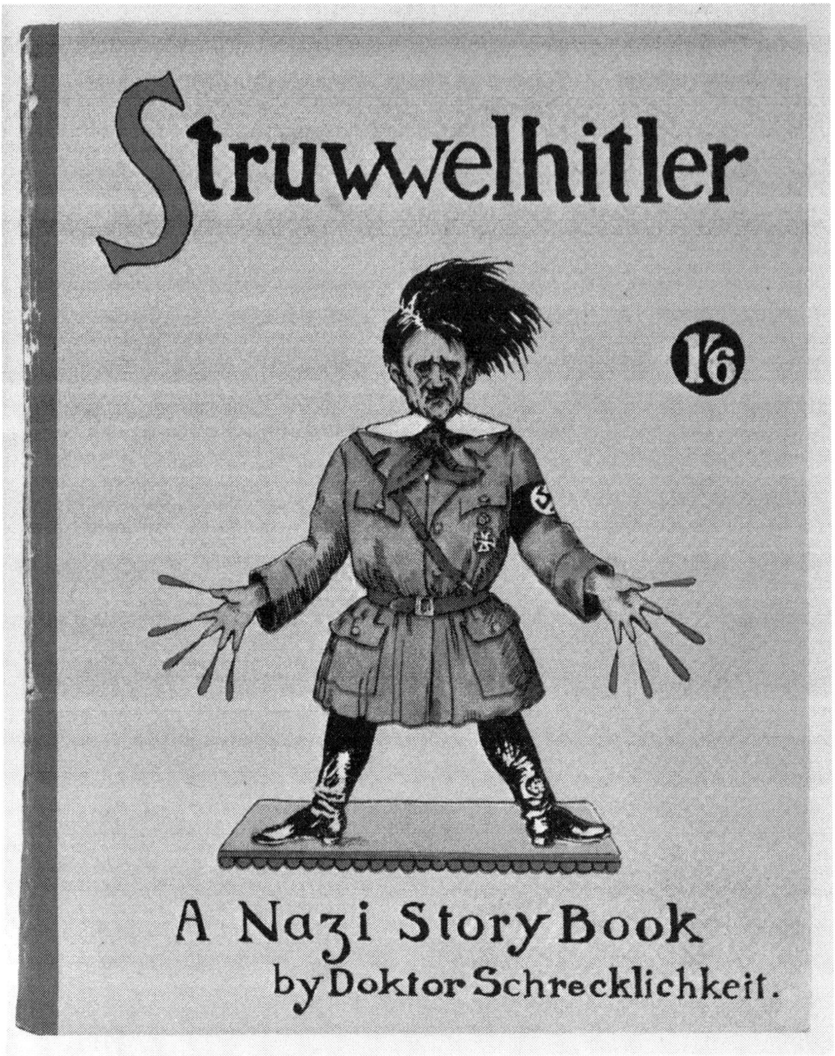

Figure 15.3 Title illustration *Struwwelhitler*.

Source: © Robert Spence and Philip Spence. 1984. Photo: Public domain.

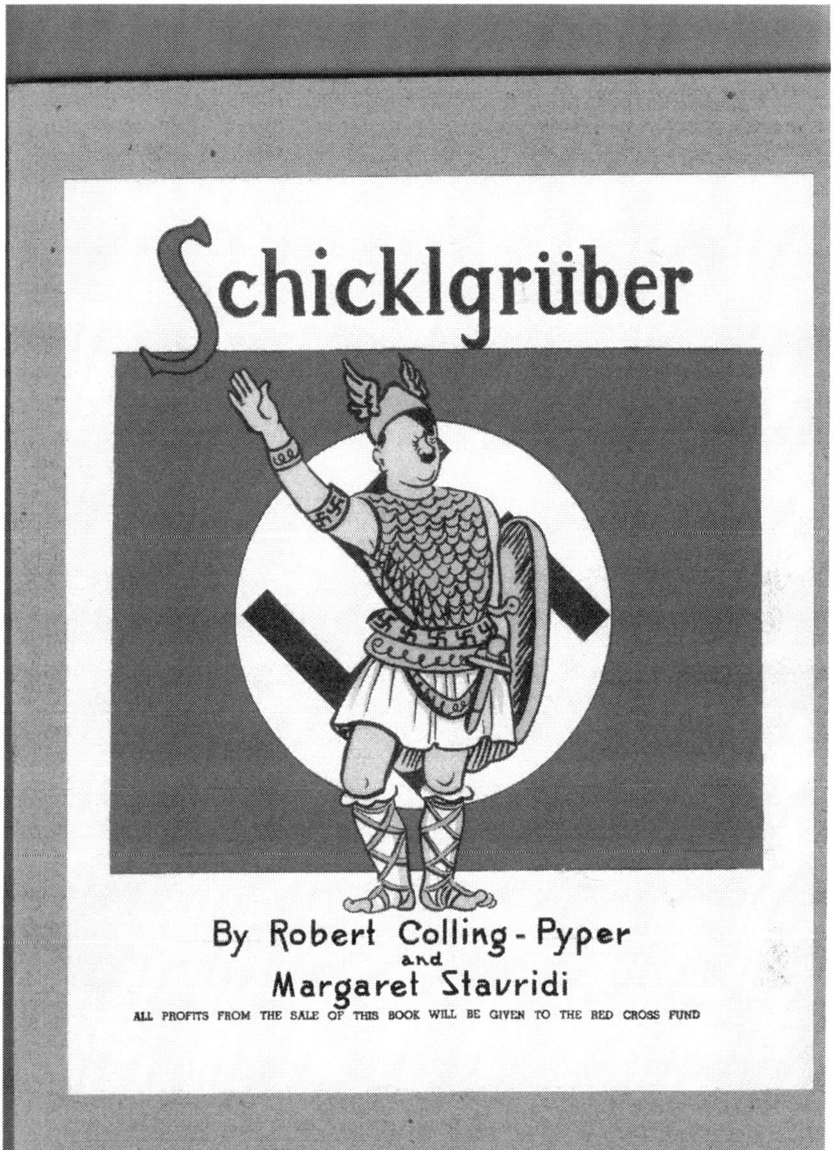

Figure 15.4 Title illustration *Schicklgrüber*.

Source: © Robert Colling-Pyper and Margaret Stavridi. 2000. Courtesy of Dr. Walter Sauer. Photo: Walter Sauer.

manners of children, but they did not instil fear; on the contrary, they produced laughter. In the first,[30] we see on the frontispiece Hitler, the stern-looking loathsome 'Führer', blood squirting out of his fingers and his hair standing on end, terror personified:

> Just look at him! There he stands
> With his nasty hair and hands.
> See! The horrid blood drops drip
> From each dirty finger tip;
> And the sloven, I declare,
> Never once has combed his hair.

The final rhyming couplet is inspirational: a favoured British dish, a pie, is used to hint at how hard but liable to break were the words of this seemingly almighty tyrant in reality:

> Piecrust never could be brittler
> Than the word of Adolf Hitler.[31]

The story of St Nicholas was called *The Story of the Nazi Boys*, in which Comrade Joseph Stalin, a large man and here a just ruler, who had no time for the naughty Nazi boys Hitler, Ribbentrop and Goebbels, unceremoniously plunged them into his red inkwell, the great patriotic war. The drawing mirrors the original version, but now the children emerged dyed red. Comrade Stalin would certainly have liked to export his political philosophy to Germany and make all Germans into 'red' Germans. From the Nazis' point of view this would have been an unthinkable outcome, but from the Allied powers' perspective it would have been a deserved, but possibly dreadful, punishment.

Robert and Philip Spence[32] from Northern Ireland kept to the format of the original *Struwwelpeter*. The nine chapters of text imitated the rhythm of the German rhyming couplets beautifully. The original stories of misdemeanours seemed to fit incredibly well for the transgressions of the Nazi bigwigs. Rudolf Heß, Deputy Führer, flew, like Robert, not with an umbrella but with a small aeroplane to Scotland. The overweight boy, Hermann Göring, president of the Reichstag and designated successor of Hitler,

30 See McEwan, D., 'Struwwelhitler: A Nazi Story Book', 221–235, and eadem, 'Der gute Bischof Nikolaus: Aby Warburgs Interpretation der russischen Übersetzung von *Struwwelpeter* und die politischen Parodien *Struwwelhitler – A Nazi Story Book* und *Schicklgrüber*', 67–90. Adolf Hitler, Austrian-German politician, 1889–1945; Joachim von Ribbentrop, German politician, 1893–1946; Paul Joseph Goebbels, German politician, 1897–1945; Joseph Stalin, Georgian Russian politician, 1878–1953.

31 McEwan, D., 'Der gute Bischof Nikolaus', 77–78.

32 Robert Spence and his brother Philip Spence produced the text and images for *Struwwelhitler* (1941). See Riha, K., *Satire und Macht*, 7. See also Fest, J., *Eine englische Struwwelpeter-Parodie aus dem Jahre 1941*. Robert Spence, British engraver; Philip Spence, alias Dr. Schrecklichkeit, British illustrator.

air force supremo, lost weight and died because he, like the original Kaspar, who did not want to swallow the soup, did not want to swallow the bad news.[33]

The British conservative and popular daily *The Daily Sketch* (merged with the *Daily Mail* in 1971) published the book in 1941. The price was the equivalent of a meal; with the profits radios were purchased, games, warm underwear for soldiers, clothing, bedding and food for the victims of air raids. *Struwwelhitler* was used for good causes and was read with pleasure. To Ernst H. Gombrich it was 'this rather fatuous sense of superiority to which pictorial satire has contributed by reinforcing the stereotype any group has of itself and of the others'.[34] How much money was raised, or how many copies were sold, is unknown.

In the second parody St Nicholas metamorphosed into the just figure of the BBC newsreader. The *Schicklgrüber* version was published in Calcutta in 1943.[35] This publication was also for a good cause, with profits to go to the Indian Red Cross and the field hospitals in Bengal. The idea for the *Schicklgrüber* version came from businessman Robert Colling-Pyper, who was living in Calcutta, and the illustrator Margaret Stavridi, wife of Alick Stavridi, employed by the *East India Railway* in Calcutta. Stavridi was a designer of stage sets and had collaborated with Colling-Pyper for a performance of the *Bengal Entertainments for the Services Association* in 1942. She also supplied drawings to the British army newspaper *Victory*. Colling-Pyper, who wanted to change the naughty boys into naughty Nazis, put an advertisement into newspapers in Calcutta, asking whether anybody had a *Struwwelpeter* copy in India, and Stavridi replied that she had one.

He commissioned her to make the drawings, keeping as much as possible to the original. Stavridi took images of Nazi leaders from newspapers and chose as title *Schicklgrüber*, the name of Hitler's grandmother, Anna-Maria Schicklgruber, and her illegitimate son Alois, the father of Hitler. Hitler's illegitimate descent would, she hoped, show how particularly contemptuous Hitler's family relations were, and she added diacritics signs on the 'u' to make it into a 'ü', a cause for the English speaking public to laugh at such a name. In addition, the number of letters was exactly the number of letters for *Struwwelpeter*, one more reason to remind readers of *Schicklgrüber*'s ancestry. In her last letter to me in January 2001 she stressed that she and Colling-Pyper had written the book simply for fun and without any propaganda motives,[36] and 'what was fun for us helped the Red Cross'.[37] Thacker's Press in Calcutta printed the book in a small edition of 1,500 copies. It was 'a clever parody', which entertained everybody who bought it for the price of 2.8 rupees.[38]

33 Rudolf Heß, German politician, 1894–1987; Hermann Göring, German politician, 1893–1946.

34 Gombrich, E. H., 'Magic, Myth and Metaphor. Reflections on Pictorial Satire', 23–66, here 39.

35 Colling-Pyper and Stavridi, *Schicklgrüber*.

36 I am grateful to Margaret Stavridi, London, for her communication on 3.1.2001.

37 McEwan, D., private archive, M. Stavridi to McEwan, D. 15.12.2000.

38 From the excerpt of a review by the journalist Sidney Isaacs, who wrote under the pseudonym *The Ditcher*. Archive copy, not dated, no name of newspaper.

The Vicereine Doreen Lady Linlithgow in New Delhi wrote a preface; Stavridi designed a very striking poster, 'Hitler Helps the Red Cross' (see figure 15.5), on which the 'Führer' took a gallant bow, lifted his hat and put a big banknote into the collection box of the Red Cross Nurse. The poster and a copy of the book were sent to New Delhi. However, the army command vetoed it,

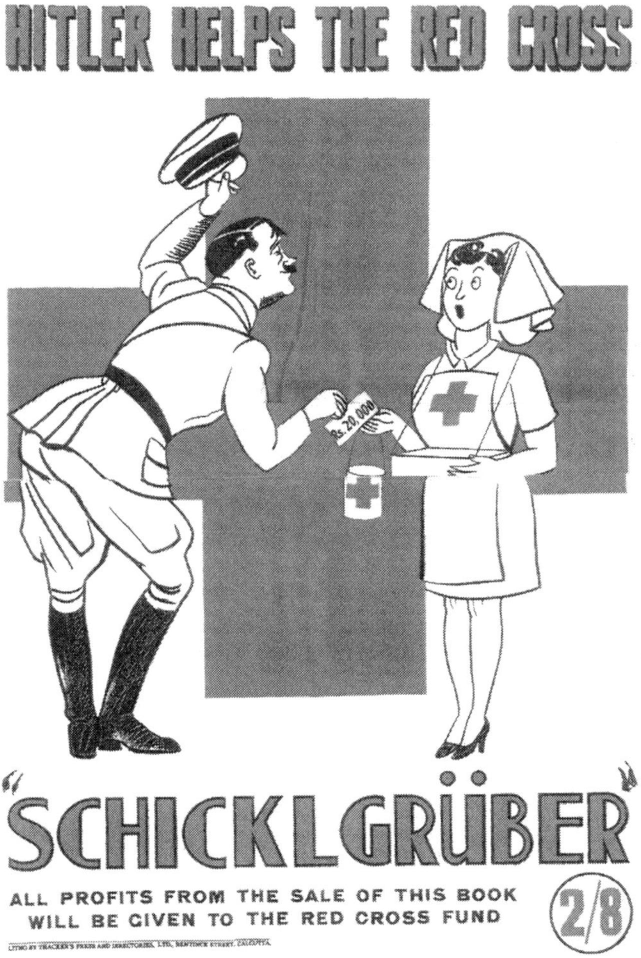

Figure 15.5 Schicklgrüber. Poster.

Source: © Private Collection.

claiming the Indians would not understand the joke so that the intended effect would fizzle out.[39]

The Calcutta version was a new interpretation of old misdemeanours, a warning to those tyrants whom Jacob Burckhardt had called 'terrible simplifiers'.[40] The introductory poem of *Schicklgrüber* hints at such a description:

> Just look at him! See him stand!
> Blood drips from his upraised hand
> See! His face with features harsh
> And his stupid small moustache;
> Hated man! From pole to pole
> None has such a blackenned (sic!) soul!
> Sound his doom on trump and tuba!
> Bloodstained monster Schicklgruber![41]

The *Schicklgrüber* version deals skilfully with the nine stories. The story of St Nicholas, here called the 'Story of the Propaganda Boys', introduces a totally new figure, an out-and-out good man, the BBC newsreader (see figures 15.6 and 15.7). This is a striking solution and gives the author the freedom to bring into play the global reputation of the BBC as the platform of truth, which enables both sides to state their arguments. The newsreader counted as impartial and had the right to call out the misdemeanours of the evildoers: the German propaganda minister Joseph Goebbels, the Italian foreign minister and Mussolini's son-in-law Count Galeazzo Ciano, and the Japanese prime minister Tojo Hideki.[42] Their anti-Churchill propaganda landed them in a big truth washing machine which looked like a radio set. With the radio set, the trio of liars could on the one hand spread their attacks, but on the other hand were exposed as a band of liars and crooks. In the original story St Nicholas took the liberty of punishing the naughty children. The same role is played by a man in a modern profession, the BBC newsreader and furthermore, truth is not represented by one person, but by a media organisation with the avowed aim of establishing the truth – or so we are told.

39 I am grateful to William Kaczynski, London, who kindly permitted me to read his collection of Stavridi papers and to quote from them. December 2000. Cf. also McEwan, D., '"Struwwelhitler" – A Nazi Story Book' and 'Schicklgrüber', 511–532.

40 Jacob Burckhardt, Swiss art historian, 1818–1897. J. Burckhardt used the phrase 'terrible simplifiers' in his letter to F. v. Preen, 24.7.1889. Friedrich von Preen, German lawyer, 1823–1894.

41 Colling-Pyper and Stavridi, *Schicklgrüber*, n.p.

42 Count Galeazzo Ciano, Italian diplomat and politician, 1903–1944; Tojo Hideki, Japanese statesman, 1884–1948; Winston Churchill, British statesman, 1874–1965.

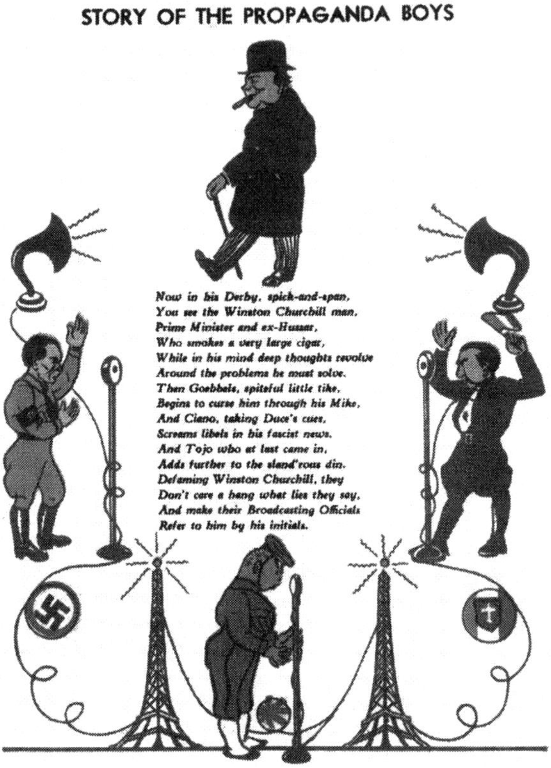

Figure 15.6 R. Colling-Pyper and M. Stavridi (1943), 'The Story of the Propaganda Boys', *Schicklgrüber*, 7.

Source: © Robert Colling-Pyper and Margaret Stavridi. 2000, 7. Courtesy of Dr. Walter Sauer.

> Now in his Derby, spick-and-span, you see the Winston Churchill man, Prime Minister and ex-Hussar, who smokes a very large cigar, while in his mind deep thoughts revolve around the problems he must solve. Then Goebbels, spiteful little tike, begins to curse him through his mike, and Ciano, taking Duce's cues, screams libels in his fascist news. And Tojo who at last came in, adds further to the sland'rous din. Defaming Winston Churchill, they don't care a hang what lies they say, and make their broadcasting officials refer to him by his initials.

Critical interpretation

The misdemeanours of the naughty children in *Struwwelpeter* were translated into the bad behaviour of the enemies in the ensuing *Struwwelpeter* parodies. Both had to expect punishment; in the reworked political, satirical versions the punishments were plausible and instantly obvious to the readership. What remains unclear is

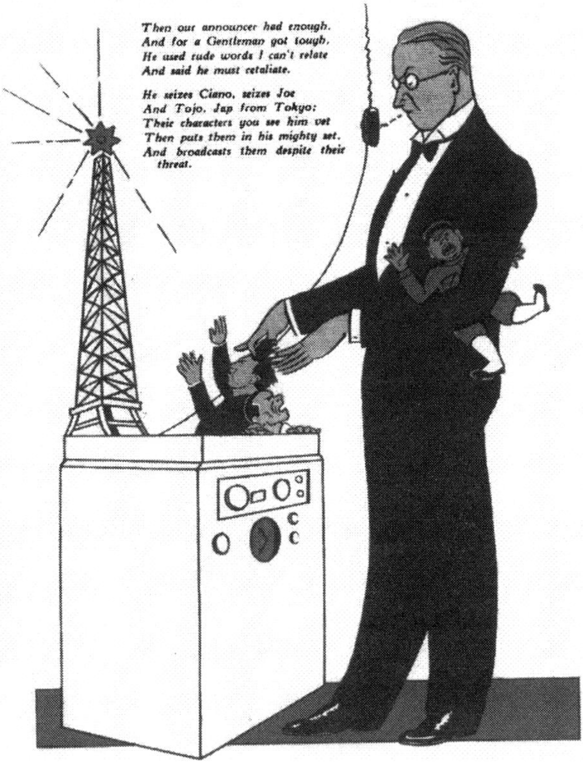

Figure 15.7 R. Colling-Pyper and M. Stavridi (1943), 'The Story of the Propaganda Boys', *Schicklgrüber*, 9.

Source: © Robert Colling-Pyper and Margaret Stavridi. 2000, 9. Courtesy of Dr. Walter Sauer.

whether understanding the political parodies was helped or not by knowing the original children's story.

There are no parodies by the Nazis of their own offences, with possibly Jews or evil politicians playing the role of the naughty children. In the years after World War II and a time when anti-authoritarian movements were gaining ground many new versions appeared,[43] for instance the *Anti-Struwwelpeter* in 1968, or in 1974 the anti-Richard Nixon text *Tricky Dick and His Pals*: 'Look at this child so clean and slick, He's called Obnoxious Tricky Dick!'[44] More political parodies will surely follow in future, because the scenarios covered by the *Struwwelpeter*

43 As, for instance, the Colling-Pyper and Stavridi version of 2000.

44 Wortis and Arkin, *Tricky Dick and His Pals: Comical Stories, All in the Manner of Dr. Heinrich Hoffmann's Der Struwwelpeter*.

repertoire, as well as the oversupply of dictatorial politicians, is inexhaustible. The method itself, as became clear, was not new, but the application of the method, to ridicule the enemy in words and images, shows joy, enthusiasm and freshness.

The two anti-Hitler versions could not have been written in more dissimilar environments, but the authors and illustrators shared the same convictions and educational milieu, which was also the reason why they knew the original *Struwwelpeter* in the first place. It was their ambition to give a new twist to old stories, which surprised and cheered up the readers in contrast to the famous sentence by Karl Kraus that 'Hitler brings nothing to my mind!'[45] Precisely this, a new twist, was demonstrated by the two Nazi parodies, as the source material was nearly infinitely expandable.

What captivates the reader of these two Nazi parodies is the way in which the melody of the German original was imitated and the English rhyming meter skilfully reflected the German verses. In the Nicholas/Stalin story is a particularly beautiful example in the final verse, when the translation for 'Buben', German for boys, rendered as 'boobies', simply funnily rhymes with 'rubies':

> See there they are and there they run!
> The Bolshevik enjoys the fun.
> They have been made as red as rubies
> Since Comrade Joseph dipped the boobies.
> Now, branded like the Bolshevik,
> They wonder if they've dropped a brick.

The illustrations of both parodies are sometimes near identical, sometimes quite different, but in any case producing a strong effect, which makes the readers smile and makes them draw conclusions. One cannot pronounce a judgement as to which versions were 'better' or 'worse' at making the readers smile; certainly, the quality of the illustrations was superior compared to the German original. They represent a raspberry to the master race, a scathing review, in particular when St Nicholas appeared as BBC newsreader.

Warburg's lifelong analysis of the methods used for banning fear was, in the *Struwwelpeter* repertoire, augmented and expanded by satire. Warburg ended his letter to Saxl about his conversation with Duke Bülow with a quote by Alexandre Dumas: 'Life is magical, you just have to see it through the right glasses'.[46] The right glasses enable the clear understanding of connections, and this was precisely what Warburg was after. The text lives in the context; the changed context became 'the right glasses' with which you could enjoy a great view. The interpretation of

45 Karl Kraus, the unerring cultural critic, introduced his book *The Third Walpurgis Night* (1952) with these words. In 1933 he started with his analysis and unmasking of National Socialists and their sympathisers, but the book was only published in 1952. Karl Kraus, Austrian writer, 1874–1936.

46 WIA, GC, Warburg to Saxl, 21.3.1929. Wilhelm Busch, German writer, 1832–1908. Alexandre Dumas, French writer, 1802–1870.

St Nicholas as the magician in the Russian version did not prove that the translator and illustrator wanted to see in him the Russian Tsar. What it did show, however, was that Warburg was right in seeing the Tsar in the magician. Therefore, the format of the *Struwwelpeter* book, with its threefold step of threats, showed that further developments were possible. They cannot yet be seen in the Russian version, but in new versions of political parodies in many different countries.

Part VI

ABY WARBURG AND MARY WARBURG

16

THE 'PALAZZO POTETJE'

Mary Warburg's triptych[1]

The triptych by the Hamburg artist Mary Warburg, wife of Aby Warburg, is kept in the Kunsthalle, the art museum in Hamburg. The archive of The Warburg Institute owns the letters and photographs which explain this triptych in greater detail. The chapter will put the genesis of this work of art and the joy it brought to the families in Hamburg into the context of the life of the young couple, then living in Florence.[2]

Aby Warburg married the painter and sculptor Mary Hertz in October 1897 in Wiesbaden. The young couple travelled from there to Florence, where they stayed until 1902 and with breaks for summer holidays in Hamburg until 1904.

Aby Warburg rented a flat in the house at Viale Principessa Margherita 42, that is, in the centre of the city and the immediate vicinity of the new German art history institute, which was housed on the same road at number 21, in the private apartment of Heinrich Brockhaus, director of the institute. Today the road is called Viale Spartaco Lavagnini; the house at number 42 has been torn down and replaced by a new building.

Florence at the turn of the 20th century was a magnet for well-to-do art lovers from the whole of Europe.[3] The establishment of the German art history institute made its presence felt in the cultural life of the city. In the winter term 1888–1889, Warburg was one of the first nine students of the Institute, which was founded by his teacher August Schmarsow. Warburg remained associated with the Institute all his life.[4]

Mary was the daughter of the Hamburg senator Adolph Ferdinand Hertz and his wife Maria Hertz, née Goßler. Both families were members of the Hamburg grande bourgeoisie, leading families in the politics, economy and culture of the city. As befitted her social status Mary went to a private school; her artistic talent

1 Originally published in McEwan, D., 'Der Palazzo Potetje. Zum Triptychon von Mary Warburg', 75–95.

2 I am grateful to Dr. Georg Syamken and Dr. Hans-Michael Schäfer, both in Hamburg, for their assistance in correcting the original article.

3 For a presentation on the social life of the Warburgs in Florence see Roeck, B., *Florenz 1900. Die Suche nach Arkadien*.

4 Courses were taught from 1888 onwards; the German art history Institute in Florence was founded in 1897. See Hubert, H.W., *Das Kunsthistorische Institut in Florenz*.

DOI: 10.4324/9781003169024-22

was recognised early and promoted. She went on to study with the Hamburg painters Adolf K. H. Mosengel, Johann Theobald Riefesell, Friedrich W. Schwinge as well as the landscape painter Hans von Bartels,[5] to whom the Hertz family was related. A range of travels enriched her artistic development further. From the substantial correspondence of Mary Warburg in the Archive of The Warburg Institute it becomes clear that the Hamburg-Munich-based painter Wilhelmine Niels was her teacher and friend. The Warburg family would support Niels throughout her life.[6]

Introduction to Mary's oeuvre

Mary Warburg's oeuvre comprises painting, sculpture, portraits, landscapes, book ornamentation, architecture, graphic art, portrait busts, small-scale sculpture, reliefs, designs and sepulchral monuments.[7] Some of Mary's works were made publicly available, for instance the design for an exhibition poster was published in the *Jahrbuch der Gesellschaft Hamburgischer Kunstfreunde* in 1895,[8] in which exhibition Mary Warburg showed pastel drawings and water colours as well as vases and figures in bronze and clay. Mary Warburg published vignettes in the *Hamburger Weihnachtsbuch* of 1892.[9] In 1899, for the first edition of the Hertz family history *Die Urgroßeltern Beets*, Mary Warburg contributed borders and vignettes, which, however, were not printed in the second edition in 1905.[10]

5 See Ghandchi, S., *Die Hamburger Künstlerin Mary Warburg, geb. Hertz*; see Hedinger et al., Mary Warburg. *Porträt einer Künstlerin*. Adolph Ferdinand Hertz, German merchant and senator, 1831–1902; Maria Hertz, née Goßler, 1844–1915; Adolf K.H. Mosengel, Hamburg painter, 1836–1885; Johann Theobald Riefesell, Hamburg painter, 1836–1895; Friedrich W. Schwinge, Hamburg painter, 1852–1913; Hans von Bartels, Hamburg painter, 1856–1913.

6 Niels was helped by Mary selling her works and by receiving financial support, particularly in her old age, from the Warburg family. See Schwindrazheim, 'Wilhelmine Niels – eine Hamburg-Münchner Malerin', 161–188. Wilhemine Niels, German painter, 1866–1943.

7 See Syamken, G., *Die dritte Dimension*, 441–446; see Vollmer, H., 'Warburg, Mary.' For a comprehensive appreciation of Mary Warburg as an artist in Hamburg see Hedinger et al., *Mary Warburg. Porträt einer Künstlerin*.

8 Hedinger et al., *Mary Warburg. Porträt einer Künstlerin*, D 2, 431.

9 *Hamburger Weihnachtsbuch*, four drawings of Neukloster near Buxtehude by Mary Warburg, Mary, 227–229. The income from the sale of the book was used to help victims of the cholera epidemic. See also Hedinger et al., *Mary Warburg. Porträt einer Künstlerin*, 32–34.

10 WIA, GC, Gustav Schiefler to Aby Warburg, 6.6.1904. The *Gesellschaft Hamburgischer Kunstfreunde* had published the book *Unser Elternhaus* by Mary Warburg's uncle Hans Hertz in 1903 in the *Hamburgische Hausbibliothek* series. Another book about the Hertz family was published in Hertz, E.D., *Die Urgroßeltern Beets*, set in German type, with book ornamentations by Mary Warburg. Gustav Schiefler, German art collector, 1857–1835, asked Aby Warburg to obtain Mary Warburg's permission for inclusion of book ornamentations by her in the second edition, either the original ones or 'new decorations' ['neuer Zierleisten']. Schiefler suggested the Warburg family make a down payment of 1,800 Reichsmarks for the printing costs, which would be recovered by the sale of the book. Between 16,000 and 18,000 copies had been sold in the first edition. The second edition was published in *Hamburgischen Hausbibliothek* in 1905, but without Mary Warburg's illustrations, possibly because the type face had been changed to Antiqua and the book lacked a careful bibliophilic presentation.

In November 1902 Mary Warburg choreographed 'tableaux vivants' on the occasion of the Schillerfest festivities in Hamburg; most notably the tableau which she and Amalie Engel-Reimers produced with scenery and costumes was praised by everybody.[11] In 1910 Mary Warburg submitted a number of her works of art to the Secession in Vienna; however, they were not exhibited – the reason given was that they arrived too late in Vienna.[12]

Today, a large part of her artistic estate is kept in the Kunsthalle Hamburg. The memorial plaque with the title *Christel* was acquired by Alfred Lichtwark in the 1890s for the Kunsthalle;[13] all other works of art were given to the Kunsthalle either as donations or permanent loans after Mary's death.[14]

The best-known bust by Mary Warburg is the bronze portrait of her husband Aby Warburg, made between 1929 and 1934, today in the Reading Room of The Warburg Institute in London. Further beautiful examples are the bust of author and family friend Lili du Bois-Reymond[15] and the bust of son-in-law Peter Paul Braden (see figure 16.1).[16] The porcelain figure of a seated woman shows Amalie Goldschmidt, known as 'Aunt Malchen', sister of Aby Warburg's father, Moritz Warburg. She was a widow from 1857 onwards and as she had no children of her own she took an active interest in the family life of her five nephews and two nieces.[17] The smiling expression around her mouth hinted at her humorous personality as well as the effect she had on the members of the family, as an old somewhat comical aunt.[18]

11 Cf. the correspondence between Mary Warburg in Hamburg and Aby Warburg in Florence in November 1902. WIA, FC, Mary Warburg to Warburg, 8.11.1902, mentioned that the photographs for the Schillerfest, the tableaux vivants, had been taken in the Restaurant Sagebiel in Blankenese. The Schillerfest marked the anniversary of the birth of German playwright, poet and philosopher Friedrich Schiller, 1759–1805.

12 WIA, GC, Vereinigung Bildender Künstler Österreichs, Secession Wien to Mary Warburg, 5.10.1910 and WIA, GC, Warburg's reply to Secession Wien, 7.10.1910.

13 Mary's friend Christine Noeldchen, born 1874. Cf. Ghandchi, *Die Hamburger Künstlerin Mary Warburg*, 26; Hedinger et al., *Mary Warburg*, P 4, 441–442. Bronze plaque, 1893. Bought by A. Lichtwark in the 1890s, today in Hamburger Kunsthalle, M-1504. Alfred Lichtwark, German art historian and curator, 1852–1914.

14 Cf. Syamken, *Die dritte Dimension*, 441. Her son-in-law, Peter Paul Braden (1900–1975), donated the estate to the Kunsthalle. Peter Paul Braden married Marietta Warburg (1899–1973) in 1927. Marietta was born in Florence; her brother Max Adolf (1902–1974) and her sister Frede (1904–2004) were born in Hamburg.

15 WIA, Photo Archive, Mary Warburg at work on the bust of Lili du Bois-Reymond, undated, location unknown. See Hedinger et al., *Mary Warburg*, P 36, 460–461. Lili du Bois-Reymond, née Hensel, German writer, 1864–1948.

16 WIA, Photo Archive: Mary Warburg at work on the bust of Peter Paul Braden, not dated, location unknown, see Figure 6.1. See Hedinger et al., *Mary Warburg*, P 38, 46–462. The photograph most probably shows Mary Warburg's studio, which for some time was located on the second floor of the KWB building, Heilwigstrasse 116.

17 See Chernow, R., *The Warburgs: A Family Saga*, for information on the Warburg family. Amalie Goldschmidt, aunt of Aby Warburg, 1831–1911.

18 WIA, Photo Archive: Amalie Goldschmidt, not dated, private collection. See Hedinger et al., *Mary Warburg*, P 33, 458–459.

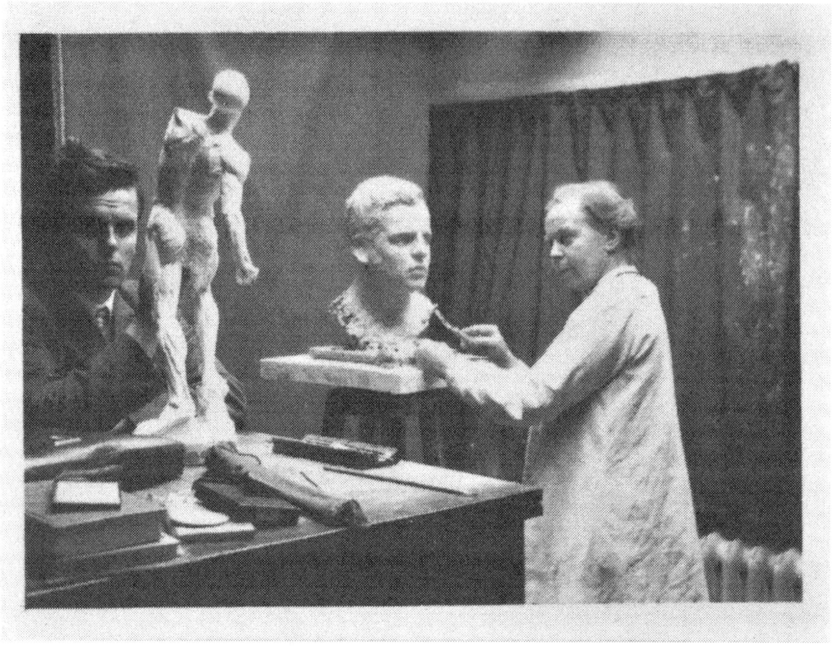

Figure 16.1 Mary Warburg sculpting the bust of Peter Paul Braden, her son-in-law, 1928. WIA, Portrait collection.

Source: © Photo: The Warburg Institute.

The 'Palazzo Potetje' triptych

Mary's relations were not only her models, but often also the recipients of her works of art. Precisely at the time when she was separated from her family, living with Aby Warburg in Florence during the first years of their marriage, Mary put her impressions on paper, to the delight of her family and friends in Hamburg. A letter to her parents was decorated with a scene from their domestic life: Aby seated at a table, in front of him an open book, with Mary standing next to him and looking over his shoulder (see figure 16.2).[19]

In one of Warburg's first letters from Florence he wrote to his mother on 28 October 1897:

> [. . .] today I went to the Arazzi-galleries with her [Mary] and looked at the four carpets, which will be the topic of my next labours; right away her clever and affectionate interest brought me a good step further than

19 WIA, FC, Mary Warburg to her parents, 4.3.1898. Cut-out of a photograph stuck onto a dark background, painted in watercolours on the letter paper.

I had been before; only now do I truly know, when the difficult and serious time of sensing and seeking approaches again, what a strong support Mary is to me. My old Florentine contacts have greeted me with great joy and I feel really more at home here or even better, 'in place', than anywhere else in the word [. . .].[20]

Warburg knew Florence from his months-long stays during and after his studies; in December 1888 he had met Mary in Florence and was happy that he could, at 31 years of age, set up his own home in Florence in 1897.

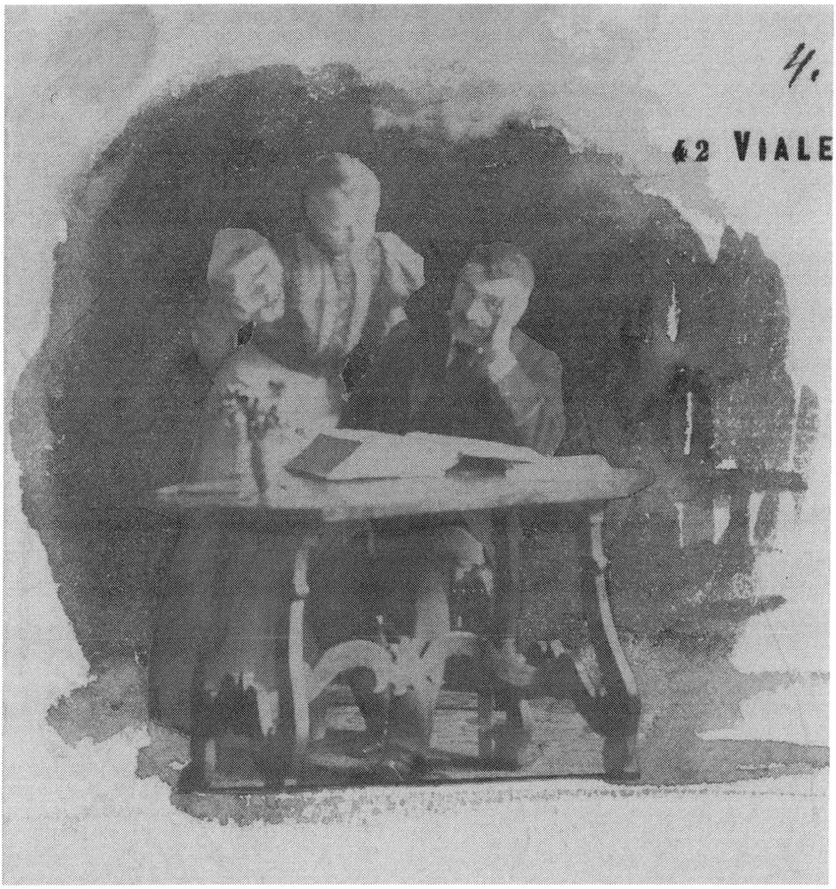

Figure 16.2 WIA, GC, cut out, Mary Warburg to her parents, 4.3.1898.

Source: © Photo: The Warburg Institute.

20 WIA, FC, Warburg to Charlotte Warburg, 28.10.1897.

His father-in-law Senator Adolph F. Hertz thanked him for describing their apartment: 'You depicted your domesticity admirably and in such lively colours that I saw in my mind's eye everything in front of me – and more than that – our happy children in their home'. It is just possible that this letter was the trigger for Mary to paint their home, a project which developed into the triptych.[21]

A well-known document from this time is the collection of paintings on paper of their apartment in Florence. Boldly put together as a triptych, it shows the protagonists and the cosy ambience in which they lived. With its nod to the triptychs of sacred paintings it was a fabulously successful joke, which was enthusiastically welcomed by the family. It was shown for the first time in an exhibition in the Hamburg Kunsthalle only in 1985.[22]

Mary produced the 'Palazzo Potetje' triptych as a Christmas present for her parents, so that they could better see and appreciate their apartment. Mary's letters about the triptych are not extant, but in their stead are the descriptions of the artwork in letters from the Warburg and Hertz families. The title refers to Warburg's nickname in the family, 'Pott', 'Putje', 'Potetje', 'Pettich', derived from the French word 'petit', meaning 'little', alluding to Warburg's short stature. The second part of the name, 'etje', possibly alluded to another malapropism from French, which even today is in general use in German as 'etepetete', possibly from 'peut-être', meaning 'maybe', in the sense of pedantic or ponderous.[23] It is conceivable that Aby Warburg appeared to the Hertz family as somewhat finicky or exaggeratedly choosy, which would explain the nickname.

Family correspondence

In the correspondence of November and December 1897 there is no mention of the designs or the making of the triptych. The little work of art was the best Christmas present and surprise from Mary to her parents in 1897. Mary's brother Wilhelm was the first who thanked his 'Putje-Bäsen' on Christmas Day:

> You little Putje-Bäsen![24]
>
> This is really nice of you and Aby, that you have thought of us so kindly. I can only say that your gifts, in particular the Palazzo Potetje, as a matter of fact, were the highlights of the evening and have decisively boosted mother's mood.[25] She had

21 WIA, FC, A.F. Hertz to Mary Warburg, 21.11.1897.

22 Cf. leaflet accompanying the exhibition by Georg Syamken, 'Mary Warburg'. *Zur Sache 11*, Hamburg 1985. See also Hedinger et al, *Mary Warburg*, 81–82 and 519 with three of the four gouaches on paper of Mary Warburg's 'Palazzo Potetje'. For the four gouaches see Z88, 343–345.

23 I am grateful to Georg Syamken for his private communications of January and February 2004 on the syllables 'etje' in 'Potetje'. The syllables might derive from French 'être, peut-être' ('being, maybe') with 'etje' referring to Warburg's 'pernickety' character.

24 The second part of this word might not be the German word 'Base', meaning 'cousin', but rather the loan word 'bas' from Dutch for 'boss'. Wilhelm Hertz, 1873–1939.

25 Mary's mother was ailing and cared for by a nurse.

come down only on Tuesday [21 December] and was not yet fully recovered. But once she was seated in her chair in the Christmas room, she was content. When, as usual, Pappus's[26] table was carried in, it was beautiful to see how mother looked at Pappus a little bit askance and how her whole face started to glow – like in younger years. And then came your gifts with the splendid poems.[27]

Our parents were really touched by both and were delighted to see how cosy your home was. The found the idea of Palazzo Potetje really lovely. Papa in particular likes very much the amusing picture with Etje in his study;[28] he also said when looking at the picture with the lamp: there sits my little girl and writes so faithfully letters back home.[29] – Also your photograph was liked by everybody. – I can assure you that you were here with us last night, we all felt it.

Mother has asked me to tell you that you made the evening beautiful for all of us; only, you have done too much, she does not like you spending so much money. She sends you a 'fat' kiss.

All of us thank you very much for your beautifully thought-out presents! I, in particular, thank you for the very useful, well, downright necessary walking stick. – The 'fat one'[30] is sorry that the 'King',[31] who was supposed to deliver the spice cakes to Naples, was delayed for two days and that the presents arrived too late for Christmas.

Even after distributing your presents the atmosphere was very happy last night. By skilfully drawing out the time to empty the basket of presents to more than half an hour, time went quickly until mother had to go to bed. The nurse and I did our best with our poems and were successful.[32] Details will be added by the nurse at the end.

Mother is tolerably well today.

We toasted your very good health at lunch yesterday and will do so again today with Aby's favourite wine, Jesuitengarten. You have deserved it with your beautiful presents.

Adieu, you two, be cheerful, we are also cheerful.
Wilhelm.[33]

26 'Pappus' was Senator Adolph Ferdinand Hertz, Mary Warburg's father.

27 The poems and letters by Mary to her parents are not extant.

28 See figure 16.3. Hamburger Kunsthalle: Aby Warburg in his study. View of the interior left wing. See also Hedinger et al., *Mary Warburg*, Z 88b. Gouache on paper, mounted on card. 'Viale Margherita 42. Weihnacht 1897'. Artistic estate Mary Warburg, Hamburger Kunsthalle.

29 Hamburger Kunsthalle: Mary and Aby Warburg seated in front of the bookshelves. View of the interior right wing. See Hedinger et al., *Mary Warburg*, Z 88d, 345.

For comparison here see Figure 16.4., WIA, Portrait collection, Mary and Aby Warburg and Heinrich and Else Brockhaus in front of the bookshelves in their apartment in Florence. See also Hedinger et al., *Mary Warburg*, 43, image no. 21; Heinrich Brockhaus, German art historian, 1858–1941; Else Brockhaus, née Brüxner.

30 Mary's brother Adolph F. Hertz was called 'the fat one'. Adolph Ferdinand Hertz, Hamburg senator, 1865–1912.

31 Adolph F. Hertz was in transit on the liner *König* ['King'] to India.

32 The poems are not extant.

33 WIA, FC, Wilhelm Hertz [Mary's brother] to Mary Warburg, 25.12.1897. Wilhelm Hertz, German lawyer, 1873–1939.

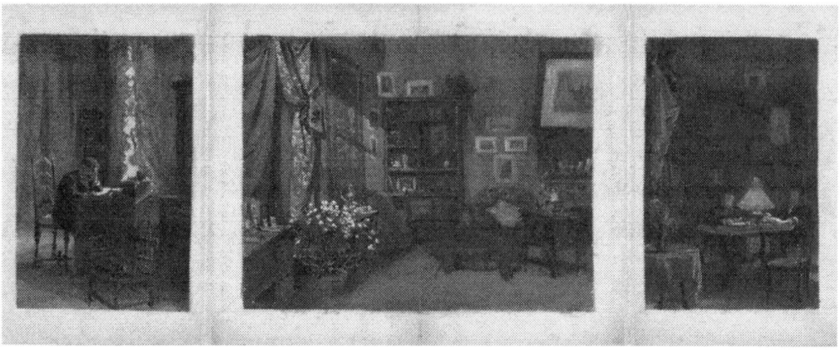

Figure 16.3 Triptych, interior view. Gouache on paper, mounted on card. 'Viale Margherita 42. Weihnacht 1897'. Artistic estate Mary Warburg.

Source: © Hamburger Kunsthalle.

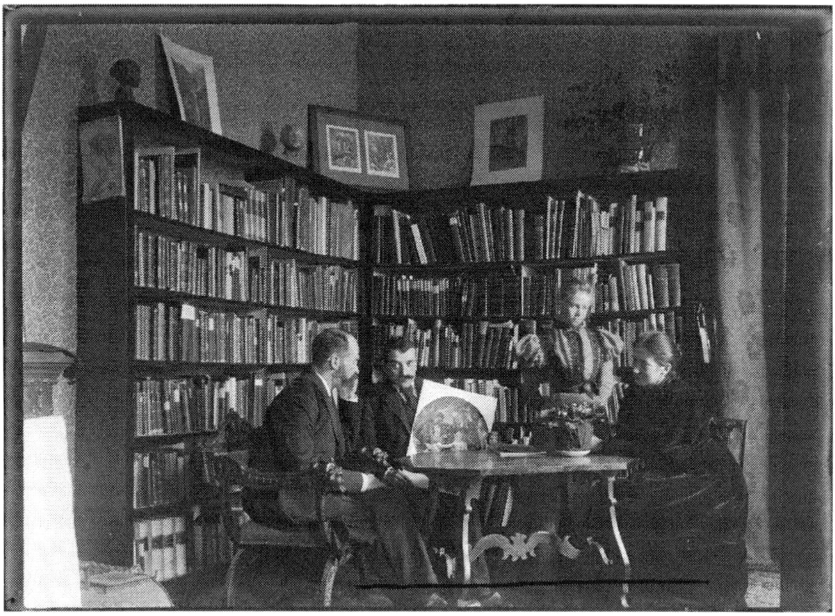

Figure 16.4 Florence, drawing room. The guests in the seating area are Else and Heinrich Brockhaus. WIA, Portrait collection.

Source: © Photo: The Warburg Institute.

On the same day Charlotte Warburg, Mary's mother-in-law, wrote to Aby and Mary:

> Beloved children
>
> This morning the post brought something which the children wanted to hide, because they put their heads together and looked at a photograph, which they thought very good, but which would be given to me only on New Year's Day. But I said, why not enjoy the picture today and this argument worked, so that Olga[34] handed me the photograph and we are looking at your dear picture already today.
>
> You, dear children, delighted us greatly with the wonderful photograph for which we thank you very much. For a long time I wanted to have a picture from you, dear Mary, and find you as well as Aby very well photographed. In contrast to it, the photograph with the hat is really not good. But another second surprise arrived today: soon after breakfast your good father appeared with a huge envelope with the cardboard Palazzo Potetje; it was charming on the outside, with the door glittering in gold bronze, the torch holders and the handles which we have often seen in Florence, but on the inside! We were totally captivated by your work of art, dearest Mary. Not only have you shown us your cosy home which you have created for yourselves, but you have also shown us you two looking very well. I can see my Aby from afar, in exactly the same reading pose. Also in the light of the lamp you look so natural and your sitting room seems to be simply ideal and cosy.[35] How charming is the bunch of marguerites! We could not admire the charming work of art enough and your dear father looked at your affectionate work proudly and happily, my dear Mary, and also your dear mother is said to have been very happy with it. Your dear father, who looked very well today and was in a good mood, stayed a little bit, then packed up his little treasure, but I can still see the charming Palazzo Potetje in my mind's eye. May you live in it happily, my dear children. I wish you a happy New Year already and thank you very much for the great joy you have given us.
>
> I love you,
> your Mama.[36]

Warburg's father Moritz also wrote on the same day about the touching scene in the morning:

> Senator Hertz was so very kind to show us your picture immediately and when one saw how lovingly your dear father unwrapped and wrapped the picture, one could see the tender love of a father.[37]

34 Olga Charlotte Kohn-Speyer, née Warburg, 1873–1904.

35 Hamburger Kunsthalle: View of the interior, middle panel. See Hedinger at al., *Mary Warburg*, Z 88c, 345.

36 WIA, FC, Charlotte Warburg to Aby and Mary Warburg, 25.12.1897.

37 WIA, FC, Moritz Warburg to Aby and Mary Warburg, 25.12.1897.

The only detailed description of the making of the triptych is in Warburg's letter to his mother:

> Dear Mama,
>
> Three of your dear letters are lying in front of me, for which we thank you whole-heartedly; we are always filled with joy when we hear from home and, when we read between the lines so much joy about our happiness, then such letters are the most beautiful festive gifts for us.
>
> The scene of how my good father-in-law showed you Mary's little watercolour, stood vividly in front of our eyes; it is a pity that we were not able to see it with you. For me it was highly amusing to see how Palazzo Potetje gradually took shape over the last few weeks. Mary painted in the mornings and evenings and she sat with her most serious little painter's face (the big pince-nez, which never stays in place, and two little steep furrows above the nose) and painted me first during the day, then in the evening; then I also had to be the model for Mary herself, which was unsatisfactory due to the differences in our size. When painting the façade, Mary officially

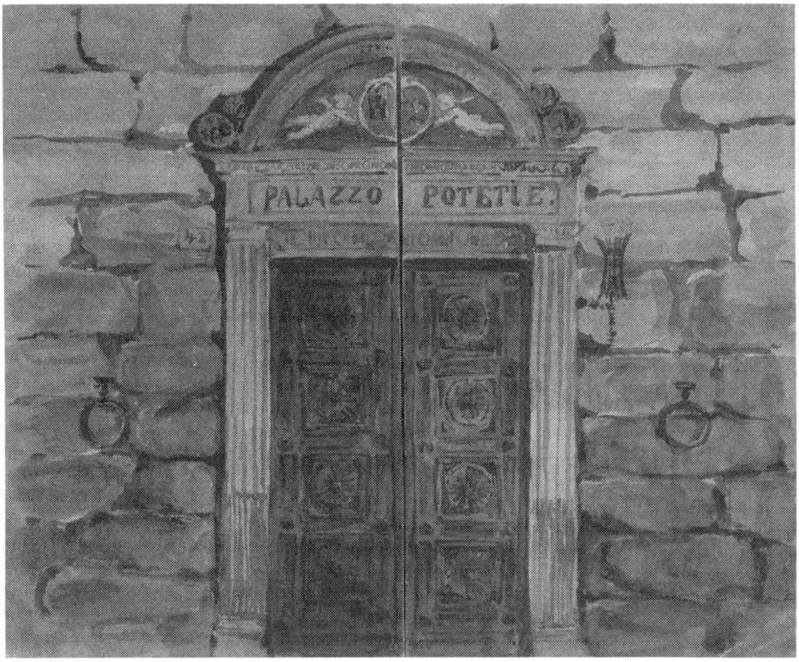

Figure 16.5 Triptych, façade of Palazzo Potetje. The two closed wings, exterior view.

Source: © Hamburger Kunsthalle.

asked me for my advice and I have to confess that we appropriated Brunelleschi's portal in the cloister of S. Croce[38] as the façade of the palazzo.[39]

The new green chairs were delivered some days ago[40] and I have to say, our sitting room can easily be compared to any creation of Schneider und Hanau.[41] Of course, we were not able to change the carpets and wallpaper, which does feel rather annoying. The best aspect of the whole setup is the two of us, which I find very fitting, and who at times still feel unused to so much inner peace. They are very grateful for the happy turn of events in their fate in 1897.

However, you must not spoil us and send us boxes of all sorts of things and port wine; I know, because of my slight hint about port wine, I myself may be guilty and hope to feel compunctions, if only weakly.

By the way, we both are careful not to become too flabby; sometimes we have to consider whether our life here is not too good for us. First and foremost, we have the most interesting contacts here and my wife neither has to run the household nor I the entire Florentine art. I want to ask you, dear mother, to send me a box of books, I really need to have the following books:

1. the volumes of Giornale Storico della Letteratura Italiana
2. the Archivio Storico dell'Arte
3. the French book on the collection in Chantilly
4. Müntz, Les Primitifs, which I regret I cannot leave in the hands of Olga.[42]

I have written to Dr. Heylbut[43] as well as to the Kunsthistorische Gesellschaft. When will Aby S.[44] return? It is possible that we will send him a Robbia copy.

Dear mother, we send you heartfelt greetings and wish you a happy New Year,

Your faithful children

Aby and Mary.[45]

Mary Warburg wrote to her mother-in-law somewhat guiltily:

38 Cappella dei Pazzi.

39 Hamburger Kunsthalle, *Façade Palazzo Potetje*. Outside view with closed wings. See Hedinger et al., *Mary Warburg*, Z 88a. Filippo Brunelleschi, Italian architect, 1377–1446.

40 Since the young couple initially had only three chairs, Mary's father sent them money to purchase more chairs.

41 Hamburg furnishers.

42 The two periodicals mentioned are in the Warburg Institute. The 'French book' on the collection in Musée Condé in the Château Chantilly is most probably a catalogue. Müntz, E., *Histoire de l'art pendant la Renaissance*. Gustave Macon, French archivist, 1865–1930; Eugène Müntz, French art historian, 1845–1902.

43 Warburg was not speaking about the philosopher Gustav Heylbut (1852–1914), but the critic and art historian Emil Heilbut (1861–1921), member of the selection commission of the art appreciation society Gesellschaft Hamburgischer Kunstfreunde. Luca della Robbia, Italian ceramicist, 1400–1482.

44 Aby S. Warburg was on his honeymoon with his second wife Elly, née Simon (1873–1931). Aby Salomon Warburg, cousin of Warburg, 1864–1933.

45 WIA, FC, Warburg to Charlotte Warburg, 29.12.1897.

> Gradually you will have formed a very bad impression of your 'youngest' daughter-in-law, either of her blackest thanklessness or most appalling laziness, because she has not written anything sensible for such a long time. My conscience has tortured me already for a long time; however, the obstacles were greater than my most serious intentions; [. . .] Dearest Mama, thank you so very much for all your kindness and your dear letters and please shift part of my debt to Christmas, which lately has taken up so much of my time. The little jokes which we have sent to Ernst Merckstrasse[46] have, with the associated poems, fulfilled their purpose and made up for our absence as much as possible.[47]

Charlotte Warburg sent her reply on a postcard:

> My dear Mary,
>
> I have neither imputed you with the blackest thanklessness nor the 'most appalling laziness', but simply told myself that if you do not write you are busy with Christmas surprises – and this was the case! If then such charming ideas in such superb execution like the 'Palazzo Potetje' appear, they are worth more than a letter – at least the joy over your little work of art is long lasting. Dear Mary, today you have compensated me with your very dear detailed letter which, thank goodness, only tells me that everything is fine. Don't you want to put a piece of paper, cut like the sole of your boots, into your boots? It is supposed to be a good remedy for cold feet. I enclose the place card for Sunday,[48] in all the turbulence of Christmas it did not turn out very well, the print is too faint. Once more cheers and a Happy New Year and a kiss to you and Aby from your
>
> Mama.[49]

Warburg mentioned the triptych once more in his letter to his father:

> Dear father,
>
> Mary and I thank you very much for your kind wishes for the New Year; we reply to them most warmly and hope that the coming year brings you, and thereby us, nothing but happiness. In 1898 you will celebrate the jubilee of M. M. Warburg and Co; with you, I am proud of looking back on one hundred years of honest work and wish you and my brothers many more years of happy and successful

46 Mary's parents lived in Hamburg at Ernst-Merck-Straße 28.

47 WIA, FC, Mary Warburg to Charlotte Warburg, 27.12.1897.

48 Traditionally Warburg's parents celebrated New Year with a large lunch party.

49 WIA, FC, Charlotte Warburg to Mary Warburg, 30.12.1897.

> work together.[50] We are sending you flowers and hope that they will arrive in time and be fresh enough to adorn the table on 2 January, if only partly, as there are not very many. We are very happy that you liked our photograph as well as Mary's little painting of our home.[51]

The correspondence reveals a very warm family relationship between the young couple and both sets of parents. Mary's present, the 'little joke', the 'Palazzo Potetje' triptych, was a very thoughtful and playful present. Behind the dramatic façade the parents could see the cosy home, Mary's gift to soothe the pain of separation, which her parents, in particular, would feel at Christmas. The 'little joke' does not only show Mary's strong artistic expression, but also her love of her family. The years in Florence would be the happiest of her life.

50 On 2 January 1898 the centenary of the Warburg Bank was celebrated.

51 WIA, FC, Aby Warburg to Moritz Warburg, 29.12.1897.

Part VII

INTERVIEW WITH DOROTHEA MCEWAN

17

THE *KULTURWISSENSCHAFTLICHE BIBLIOTHEK WARBURG* AS SEEN THROUGH ITS ARCHIVE IN LONDON AND DOROTHEA MCEWAN'S OTHER RESEARCH INTERESTS. INTERVIEW BY CÉLINE TRAUTMANN-WALLER WITH DOROTHEA MCEWAN, 2 AUGUST 2018[1]

Dorothea McEwan worked in the archive of The Warburg Institute in London for many years, and its present organisation is largely due to her. She is the author of three books and many articles on Aby Warburg and the scholars in contact with him, and she catalogued the correspondence of Aby Warburg, some 37,000 letters and postcards that are kept in the archive of The Warburg Institute. In this interview I wanted to understand what she had learnt from Warburg's work while cataloguing the archive holdings. Her own journey as an intellectual historian – from her native Austria to Great Britain, where she now lives – and her research in Egypt, Jordan and, for over twenty years, in Ethiopia – is equally of interest to understand McEwan.

How did you first get to know The Warburg Institute?

I studied history in Vienna before moving to London in 1973 with my British husband. I worked at the British Library in the Department of Manuscripts, joining a large cataloguing project for the John Churchill, First Duke of Marlborough papers.[2] From 1978 to 1993 I then worked as the archivist for Fischer Fine Art, an Austrian art gallery in Piccadilly, London, specialising in the Austrian classical modern painters Klimt, Schiele and Kokoschka. Wolfgang Georg Fischer (1933–2021) was an art historian and a man of letters who introduced the

1 Originally published in McEwan, D., 'La *Kulturwissenschaftliche Bibliothek Warburg* à la lumière de ses archives. Entretien avec Dorothea McEwan', 199–209.

2 John Churchill, First Duke of Marlborough, English statesman, 1650–1722.

DOI: 10.4324/9781003169024-24

Austrian classical modern painters to Britain.[3] He was a friend of Ernst H. Gombrich (1909–2001), director of The Warburg Institute, London. When Gombrich retired and was looking for a personal research assistant, Fischer recommended me to Gombrich and I took on this position for ten years from 1983 to 1993.

In 1991, Martin Warnke,[4] professor of art history at the Institute of the History of Art at the University of Hamburg, was awarded the prestigious Gottfried Wilhelm Leibniz prize, with which he funded a two-year research position at The Warburg Institute. I was lucky to be appointed head archivist to organise the archive and to create an online catalogue of the Aby Warburg correspondence. Of course, I knew Aby Warburg's and Fritz Saxl's books and articles primarily due to my work as intellectual historian and because of my work with Ernst H. Gombrich.

What condition was the archive in at this time?

The famous library of The Warburg Institute was very well run, thanks to the work of its specialised librarians. The library operated an open access service; readers continued to be able to choose the books themselves without having to fill in forms, etc. However, the archive did not operate a system of open access. Users needed to have letters of recommendation or introduction. Annemarie Meier, the Secretary of the Institute, who had looked after archival matters for some time after her retirement, allowed a few qualified researchers archive access. There was what was known as a 'rough register', basically a subject catalogue, but there was nothing more detailed which facilitated research. As the number of researchers interested in the Warburg archive had increased, it became clear that an archivist was needed.

How did the work of the archive develop during the years in which you were in charge?

I designed a database and started to catalogue the very extensive Warburg correspondence while at the same time helping archive users. Warburg corresponded with scholars and family members, and all this in seven languages. The archive contains an impressively large number of handwritten letters, cards, cables and postcards from and to Warburg, as well as numerous letters typed for him by Fritz Saxl and Gertrud Bing. Warburg's handwriting is not easy to read, which meant my services were frequently requested by archive users. Alongside carrying out the general work of head archivist, my task of completing the catalogue, producing English-language abstracts of every piece of writing from 1881 to 1929, took

3 Wolfgang Georg Fischer, Austrian writer and art expert, 1833–2021; Gustav Klimt, Austrian painter, 1862–1918; Egon Schiele, Austrian painter, 1890–1918; Oskar Kokoschka, Austrian artist, 1886–1980.

4 Martin Warnke, German art historian, 1937–2019.

seventeen years. The Institute took the decision to produce an English-language digital catalogue with free access via a dedicated website, https://wi-calm.sas.ac.uk/calmview/, which has been available since 2010. Over time I managed to engage colleagues and assistant archivists to start cataloguing the other holdings in The Warburg Institute Archive.

I have used this catalogue and I have also consulted the summaries of different letters. It's really helpful.

I'm grateful to you for this comment. You are not the first person to remark upon the usefulness of having the abstracts written in English. The decision to produce English-language abstracts was totally understandable, but it caused quite a few headaches. Warburg's language was precise, clipped; he used technical terms which did not have equivalents in English, and which therefore posed problems for translation. He also invented many neologisms to formulate his ideas more precisely. I had to find adequate translations or descriptions to transpose German concepts and terms into English, and I sometimes had to leave the German technical term in brackets. Both this work, the explanations for concepts used by Warburg and the digitising of the correspondence, gave researchers ease of access to the archive.

What do you think are the most important discoveries made through [the Warburg] archival research?

They are, on the one hand, the connections, the links, the – if I may say so – hypertextual links, to use an expression from internet technology. On the other hand, my work in the Archive brought to light the depth and breadth of the networks of a private scholar. Aby Warburg was a particularly important thinker in his epoch. I formed the opinion that the history of ideas of the first third of the 20th century needs to be rewritten, which, thanks to academic research in many countries, is now underway.

I was surprised to see quite how much Aby Warburg identified with his library and with his institute. In your opinion how far is this reflected in different sources as well, to wit, his private diaries, his index card boxes, his library journal?

This is an important question. With Warburg it is not that he identified with his library; I would rather say that he could not live without it. The mission he gave himself was to create this research tool, initially for his own work, and then for others who engaged in similar areas of research. At the beginning it was impossible to know what would become of this library, right up to the time when Fritz Saxl became librarian in 1914. He immediately recognised the need to open it up to the public, in order to continue the fundamental research underlying the academic work of Warburg and some other scholars, on the one hand, and on the other, to assure the library's organic growth.

The creation of the archive constituted the logical next step to this work. Warburg was someone who refused to throw away even the smallest scrap of paper. He kept ephemera, ticket receipts, the menus from his trans-Atlantic crossings, etc. as well as letters with detailed research questions, research results and organisational instructions. The entire correspondence section was very important to him as source material for queries, which at some point were moved from the correspondence collection, kept year by year in chronological and alphabetical order, to subject catalogues, the over 100 index card boxes. From very early on he started to make and keep copies of handwritten outgoing letters; from 1905 to 1918 they were kept in six volumes of so-called Copy books. As the son of a banker, he knew about the value of keeping outgoing correspondence. In 1870 German banking laws obliged the banks to keep copies of their transactions. Warburg had seen such thin-leafed Copy Books at his father's bank and had understood their value. After 1918, letters were typed and saved in the form of *duplicata*. This did not include everything, not the cards and postcards, but did include the majority of the letters.

Warburg wrote a diary throughout his life; the archive holds more than eighty volumes of diaries. Each one contains a key, a summary in key words on the last pages of each volume, under the date. They are very interesting, often repeating table talks, impressions of people, political news, but they are very difficult to read. It is practically impossible to edit and publish them all, some are in the process of publication, for instance the diary volumes during World War I.

I have mentioned the index card boxes, a method which every university library knew and used at Warburg's time. In the course of my work, a number of letters have been taken out of the index card boxes and added to the General Correspondence collection. Very often they enlarged on a topic which otherwise was discussed in the General Correspondence collection and therefore complemented this collection. The titles of each index card box, Superstition, Sfera (see Boll's *Sphaera*), History, War or Astrology, to name but a few, indicated bibliographical references for subject or specialised literature.

Finally, the so-called Library *Journal*, written by Fritz Saxl, Gertrud Bing and Aby Warburg from 1926 to 1929, is a rich source for following the organisational agenda of the KBW, the discussions with and research queries of visitors, the public discussions, seminars, and much more. The Library *Journal* is the product of the very tightly knit collaboration between Warburg and his librarians. Their collaborative work shaped the work of the Library.[5]

Would you say that Warburg contributed to an evolution in the concept of an archive?

Warburg certainly worked in many archives, in Florence in particular, and understood and valued the collection of source materials. Right from the start, he knew about the importance of keeping his papers together and collecting papers as sources for future use.

5 See Michel/Schoell-Glass, 2001.

What, in your opinion, are the most important general missions for The Warburg Institute – that is to say, as a centre of learning and research, as a library, as an archive – for the future?

The general mission of The Warburg Institute is to research the legacy of classical antiquity, to explore the European mind, and to do so through its collections, the Library, the Photographic Collection and the Archive. The Institute has proved itself as a research library thanks to its principle of good neighbourliness, which allows books with similar subject matter to sit side by side on the free access shelves. This is a great help, which all researchers continue to praise today. The Photographic Collection's holdings on paper are being digitised and equipped with new research tools. The Archive contains the important Warburg working papers and papers of scholars in contact with Warburg and academics after Warburg's death. The mission will obviously be pursued in the future thanks to the work carried out at the heart of The Warburg Institute.

As you have just mentioned the Photographic Collection, could you tell us briefly of its contents and its role in research into Warburg's research interests and all things Warburgian?

Aby Warburg was a researcher who worked on the image and the word right from the start. That is quite normal for an art historian. You present an image accompanied by a written source which more or less interprets it, drawing attention to the connections, identifying evolutions and potentially changes. Even as a student, Warburg would buy books and ask his parents for an allowance to buy more books. From the time of his Italian trips in the 1880s he bought black and white photographs, including the famous photographs by Fratelli Alinari,[6] historical prints made at a time when photography was considered a work of art. This formed the beginning of his photographic collection. He also dabbled in photography, particularly on his trip to the USA, with a small and very simple box camera. His black and white photographs from America have often been published. The Photographic Collection was progressively added to, and naturally came to include colour photographs, and these collections are in the process of being digitised today.

I would now like to come to Warburg's circle, his family, his friends, his colleagues, the Institute, the State. You have written about Mary Warburg and her art. How would you describe her, her personality as well as her work as an artist, and how do you consider her role at the heart of Aby Warburg's entourage?

Mary Warburg was an artist. A superb volume on Mary Warburg, the sculptor and painter, was published in 2020, the commented *catalogue raisonée* by Hedinger et al.[7] Mary Warburg, née Hertz, the daughter of a member of the Hamburg

6 The firm Fratelli Alinari is one of the oldest photographic firms, founded in Florence, in 1852.

7 Hedinger et al., *Mary Warburg*.

Senate, was a well-known artist, but as a young mother she put her family and her children first. As Aby Warburg's wife she was an integral part of his family and the social fabric of the city. Throughout her life she sculpted and painted.

As Aby Warburg had two sisters and four brothers, the family was large and the family contacts impressive. In time he met and worked with like-minded scholars who used the library in the way it was intended, as a 'laboratory', as an 'arsenal', in Warburg's words. After the establishment of the University of Hamburg in 1919 his library doubled up as a seminar room for the History of Art department.

The phrase 'Warburg circle' is appropriate when considering the large number of colleagues and academics, friends and family members who sought his opinion and were welcomed in the library.

I now have two questions on Saxl and the Viennese school. Warburg's family recruited Saxl to continue his work as librarian during Warburg's absence from Hamburg in 1920. It is always said that it was thanks to him that the library was transferred to and set up in England. How would you describe his role vis-à-vis that of Aby Warburg and the Institute in just a few words? To what extent would you say that the Institute is also his work?

Fritz Saxl was an art historian, who had studied in Vienna, and for one semester in Berlin. It was there that he received an invitation to visit Warburg in Hamburg in 1910. The two scholars were impressed with each other's work; Saxl recognised in Warburg a kindred spirit. After having been awarded his PhD in 1912, Saxl was helped by Warburg to obtain a research scholarship form the Heidelberg Academy of Sciences and was afterwards employed by Warburg in Hamburg in 1914. This looked so promising but came quickly to an end, when Saxl had to join the Austrian army that autumn. He served for four years, mostly on the Italian front.

The correspondence during those years shows clearly that Warburg appreciated Saxl enormously and gladly accepted his recommendations and his proposals regarding their common areas of research. Saxl had always made it quite clear that after the war he wanted to work as an art historian, but he was not sure that the new state of Austria would offer a young man like him a job dealing with the key issues in art history. After the war, Saxl worked for one year in the field of public education in Vienna before receiving the letter of recruitment from the Warburg family and moving to Hamburg. He became deputy director of the Warburg library while Warburg was recuperating at a sanatorium in Kreuzlingen, Switzerland. Saxl worked with Warburg; he visited him frequently in Kreuzlingen, and he kept up their correspondence until Warburg's return to Hamburg in 1924. In their letters, they discussed academic topics together; Saxl very often sent additional special literature, and, as a matter of course, sent news of library visitors, the developments of the University of Hamburg and Saxl's establishment of library seminars and two publication series. Theirs was, in fact, a discussion without end on all the intellectual issues which mattered to both of them, and which they pursued passionately. Their cooperation proved so strong and continuative that

Warburg, after his return from Switzerland, spoke of Saxl as his friend. Saxl was a generation younger than Warburg, and at the beginning their relationship was more like one of teacher and student. As to Saxl's innovative work, Saxl himself observed much later on that the Warburg library stimulated his work as much as he stimulated the activities in the library. The establishment of Warburg's library as the organisational entity known as the KBW brought Saxl's and Warburg's work into an institutional framework. Saxl's work on behalf of Warburg and the Warburg library was pioneering.

And what about Gertrud Bing?

Her position was central to running the library and to support Warburg in his research topics, among which the Mnemosyne Atlas ranked as the most important. She had a PhD in Philosophy, and it is well-known that Warburg appreciated her greatly, not just as an academic, but as a colleague. He always refers to her as 'my colleague Bing', using the masculine form of the word in German. In late 1933 she moved to London with Saxl and the other colleagues who had all helped with running the library after Warburg's death in 1929 and during the difficult years until the momentous move in 1933.

The 55,000 books and instruments, tools and images were packed up in Hamburg and freighted to London where the library operations began in a very short space of time – and all in English – without ever losing sight of Warburg's objectives. Saxl, Bing and many of their colleagues from Germany continued their research into the main research topic, dubbed 'The Problem', that is to say the survival of classical antiquity. The years after Warburg's death, with the economic uncertainties worldwide and the political developments in Germany, must have been very difficult years, without a doubt. One can see in the Institute correspondence that the transfer of the library to different countries – Italy, the Netherlands, the USA – had been discussed for a long time. The establishment of the Warburg library, now called The Warburg Institute, brought an academic impetus to Great Britain, which was very welcome at a time when the study of art history was just taking off there. Bing held a particularly important position: she looked after the day-to-day agenda of the Institute as well as the steeply increasing number of letters for help by colleagues from Germany and Austria. The advantages for starting in Great Britain were financial, with pledges of support by the Warburg family until The Warburg Institute became incorporated into the University of London in 1944.

The academics of The Warburg library in Hamburg had not only brought with them the library, but more importantly, a ready-made institute with its very own academic structures already in place. The Warburg Institute offered teaching and conferences, and it started the two German-language publication series *Vorträge* and *Studien* – and later in English as *Lectures* and *Studies*. In time more series were added. The Institute offered courses on its own premises just like any other university institute. Soon, the academic operations in London outstripped those on offer in Hamburg.

Fritz Saxl, who had studied in the Institute of Art History at the University of Vienna, had planned to write a biography of Warburg (just as Gertrud Bing had), but never did. The first biography published was that by Professor Ernst H. Gombrich in 1970, who was also a graduate of the Viennese Institute. You are the first archivist of The Warburg Institute and you are also from Vienna. Could one modify the title of one of your essays to 'A Tale of Three Cities' (Hamburg, London, Vienna)?

Yes, one could very well say this, but I do not see it like that. I am convinced that The Warburg Institute did not recruit me because of my Viennese origins, but because I was a historian, specialising in intellectual history, an archivist, a polyglot palaeographer, the professional they were looking for at the time. I studied in Vienna, I went to school in Vienna, but that to me is not a good enough a reason to speak of a 'Tale of Three Cities'.

Another explanation might be added: Gombrich never worked in Hamburg and Saxl had remained unknown in Vienna for decades. He had left Vienna for Hamburg, first in 1914, then again in 1920, and had built his academic career in that city. Due to political circumstances, he went to Britain and not Austria. It took years before Saxl's research work was discussed in Viennese academic circles and at the Institute of Art History of the University of Vienna. He was certainly originally from Vienna, but in the midst of political madness the city had forgotten Saxl. It was not until the 1990s, as a result of research dedicated to the history of persecuted Jewish art historians, that he became known again. However, Saxl himself never felt that he had been a persecuted Jewish Austrian, as he had left Austria long before the Anschluss in 1938.

Can Saxl be considered a representative of the Vienna School of Art History? Would that more likely be the case for Julius von Schlosser?

The Warburg library and the KBW were in contact with members of the Vienna School of Art History: Saxl visited Vienna regularly and he knew a number of art historians who had studied in Vienna and then either moved on or remained in Vienna. Some of his Austrian colleagues tried repeatedly to address him as 'one of us', but although he stayed in touch with them, he was, like Warburg, more interested in intellectual history and less in attribution history. He certainly was a graduate from the Institute of Art History in Vienna, but not a representative of the Vienna School. This was not the case for Julius von Schlosser.[8] In fact, Schlosser always presented himself as a member of the Vienna School. He was invited by Warburg to give lectures at the KBW in Hamburg, as other Austrian colleagues had been, but a closer cooperation was not attempted, nor did it occur.

In an article on Saxl and Warburg you explained that the latter refused to allow his Institute to become a 'school' in the sense of the Vienna School of Art History: '. . . the KBW went further, it pursued the "Wanderstrassen der

8 Julius von Schlosser, Austrian art historian, 1866–1938.

Kultur", which were Warburg's and Saxl's metaphor for breaking out of thinking in categories and schools'. How can we understand this complex relationship towards the creation of 'schools' which contributes perhaps to the unique position of this institute in academic and intellectual life? How far can it be taken to mean a separation of the private and the public, and the will to distinguish itself from the State – a will which, on the one hand saved the institute (because it could leave the country), but which, on the other hand, weakens it today?

Warburg, his circle of academics, his work in the library and the KBW, might have been called a school; however, it certainly never existed. The Vienna School was something completely different. It is a generic term to describe methods in art history which have benefitted from a solid academic base. Aby Warburg refused this; he did not want to be constricted or circumscribed. He wanted to pursue his programme of research without the limitations which a school, tied to an institution like in Vienna, would have brought. The Warburg library, and from 1926 onwards the KBW, was a very flexible institution. It offered conferences and seminars (at the library) for the new University of Hamburg, but that did not transform the library into a school in the narrowest sense of the term. What was important to Warburg was the exploration of the global problem of the survival of classical antiquity. The academics who corresponded with him, who held conferences there, who worked at the heart of the Warburg library, all formed a network – I would call it an academic republic with its own separate interests, which might have coincided and were related with others, but which did not pursue only one line of research.

I would also not speak of a straightforward and clear-cut demarcation between the exigencies of a state-run institution and a private institution. The work accomplished by a series of researchers at the heart of the Warburg library was a different form of collaboration from a hierarchically established state enterprise. Certainly, the work by scholars and thereby the collection of sources in the library which enabled their research may be even called something like a symbiosis of researchers. Your notion that The Warburg Institute is weakened today needs to be unpacked. Who says it is weakened? And what are the criteria? It is true, a succession of directors put their very own stamp on proceedings, but this is normal with any organisation and institution. Now that The Warburg Institute is no longer a private enterprise, but a founder member of the School of Advanced Study, a postgraduate institution of the University of London, one might be tempted to say that the Institute had been weakened by losing its 'private' status. But how does such a development manifest itself? To speak of a weakening of the singular position which The Warburg Institute did have in the academic and intellectual life of a profession is, in my view, an untenable assertion.

A symbiosis of researchers? Between the researchers at The Warburg Institute or between the Institute and its scholarly community?

Both. It always goes both ways. Specialists come to the three departments of the Institute, the Library, the Photographic Collection and the Archive, because the topics they are concerned with might also be found in these departments. Warburg had a very finely honed sense of that which would be of interest to the Library and its scholars and of who at the time merited or needed support. All these considerations were expressed within the great panorama of his library. I want to remind you of the topic of the 'Wanderstrassen der Kultur', the maps tracking the paths of culture, starting out from numerous subjects studied. How do images go from A to B; how do ideas unceasingly disappear and come to the surface again, in different epochs, in different places, in different forms; how do visual elements divide up only to reform? This was just one example, one question, which occupied Warburg and scholars around him.

The history of the Institute is a sort of history of pathways itself, from Florence to Hamburg, then contact with different European countries and finally the emigration to London. Isn't it also like a history of Europe in miniature?

I completely agree with you on this. This is an extremely important point, and it is important that it is understood as such.

I now want to come on to your research on religious conflicts, religion and imagery, and Ethiopia. To start with, you have published a lot in Britain on German topics, and you have also translated from German into English. Do you consider yourself a mediator between England/Britain on the one hand, and Germany/Austria on the other?

That's a really interesting question that I have never considered. I see myself first and foremost as a cosmopolitan, a European, and only then as a woman working transculturally, and I suppose that qualifies me to call myself a mediator. My husband had Scottish origins, and my parents grew up in the multi-cultural Habsburg monarchy. My four grandparents were born in four different countries of the empire, which are now independent states. It is chance that I was born in what is now Austria. My paternal grandfather was a military doctor, and each of his children was born in a different garrison. I could have just as well been born in Kraków or the South Tyrol, where my father was born. I certainly consider myself to be Austrian, but now I also consider myself to be cosmopolitan, as I have already said. That's one thing. The other point was regarding the religious conflicts. Even at high school this fascinated me: the question of minorities, those in the shadow of politics and its mechanism of marginalisation. One day I wrote a long article about the Jews and the Christians, on how the majority had treated and treats the minority, the way in which the Catholic church has for centuries treated the Jews. This subject was reflected in my writing and in my relationship with the people who shared the same ideas as me.

My work on Ethiopia is based on quite a separate area of research. The first post I had after gaining my PhD at Vienna University was as a researcher on the cultural influences of the Habsburg monarchy on Egypt and Jordan. I worked on the religious practices of the Christians in the Ottoman Empire, and hence also Sudan, and I was always interested in the Horn of Africa, East and North-East Africa. My husband's studies on Ethiopian art at the University of London led me back to that part of the world. Consequently, I dedicated a lot of time to Ethiopian art and I specialised in its church art, focusing on how an idea is transformed into an image. I was nominated to become a member of the Academy of Ethiopian Sciences quite by surprise in 2018, which I am very proud of, as this is in recognition of my academic approach.

Do you see a connection between your research at The Warburg Institute and your contribution to scholarship as a feminist theologian, as studying illuminated Ethiopian sacred manuscripts and wall paintings, in particular the frescos of the coronation church of Däräsge Maryam Church in North Ethiopia and the botanical research of George Wilhelm Schimper?

My work on feminist theology stems from my research on minorities. How does an established religion treat new ideas, which in certain circumstances challenge ancient certitudes? This is a subject that I am passionate about, particularly as a woman. How does the dominant group in the Roman Catholic church, here I'm talking about the clergy, treat its female members who would like to become priests and bishops? This is a question which cuts to the heart of traditional views and, in certain circumstances, questions those very views. The Warburg Institute explores the triad of religion, literature, and art, but not the modern preoccupations of feminism. The research into the ways feminist theological ideas are blocked or enter the mainstream of theological interpretation is part of my ethical make-up and forms part of my personal research on minorities.

My work in Ethiopia, the field work, as well as the work on Ethiopian illuminations in many archives of Europe, has developed from my knowledge of the country. My late husband worked on his PhD on Ethiopian illuminations, and together we travelled extensively in Ethiopia and became involved with a number of research projects. While people still remembered names of Europeans living in Ethiopia in the 19th centuries, but nothing else, I was able to find archival sources in European archives about some German painters and scientists, and was able to publish their works of art and literary estates, to wit Georg Wilhelm Schimper and Eduard Zander.[9]

Research on the history of religions has played a large role in the history of The Warburg Institute, as shown by Roland Kany's summary.[10]How

9 Georg Wilhelm Schimper, German Ethiopian botanist, 1804–1878; Eduard Zander, German painter and draughtsman, 1813–1868.

10 Kany, R., *Die religionsgeschichtliche Forschung an der kulturwissenschaftlichen Bibliothek Warburg*.

would you describe Warburg's relationship towards religion and the history of religions? What are your feelings about the place this research holds at the heart of the Institute as it currently stands? And how did this research interact with British traditions?

I would say that Warburg's relationship with religion was twofold. He personally refused to follow religious injunctions, rituals or practices in his or any other religion, while at the same time recognising the importance of religion as a vector for ideas. Certainly, lived practices were for him the guardians of ideas, and in this way religion was understood as a science to be studied. Warburg corresponded with German Protestant colleagues, with Jewish friends, with Roman Catholic scholars, he bought their books for the library, etc. The study of religion and religions maintains its importance to this day. In Great Britain, the science of religion, theology and divinity is a vast and well-established research domain.

In an article you wrote that the expression 'science of culture', 'Kulturwissenschaft', did not mean anything to the British at the time of Warburg (and possibly not today either) as there are other traditions in Britain such as that of 'intellectual history'.

The issue of how to translate *Kulturwissenschaftliche Bibliothek Warburg* has always been problematic. *Bibliothek* and *Warburg* do not present any difficulties – 'library' and, of course, 'Warburg' – but the expression *Kulturwissenschaft* does. *Kulturwissenschaft* goes further than 'cultural history', it is a human science, a history of ideas. The term 'culture' in English encompasses many things, from agriculture to intellectual culture just like in German. But *Kulturwissenschaft* has a more restricted meaning and refers to everything that has to do with intellectual problems. Nowadays this concept is translated as 'intellectual history', that is to say, the history of ideas, or if you like, the history of the mind, which brings us closer to the sense of *Kulturwissenschaft.*

I would like to ask you one last question: do you have the impression that in your own way you are continuing Warburg's work?

That's a nice but ultimately problematic question. As the archivist of the Institute I have naturally continued Warburg's work because I was able to point all researchers in the right direction or provide them with tools. Without a doubt this is a way of pursuing Warburg's work. But if we take a wider look at the situation and at the work in which Warburg was interested – the exploration of subjects in the history of religions, of literature and of art – I only pursued them in my interest in the science of religions and in the analysis of Ethiopian illuminated manuscripts, which are research areas positioned somewhere equally between the domains of science and religion. I would be happy to hear that this body of work can be considered as a continuation of Warburg's work.

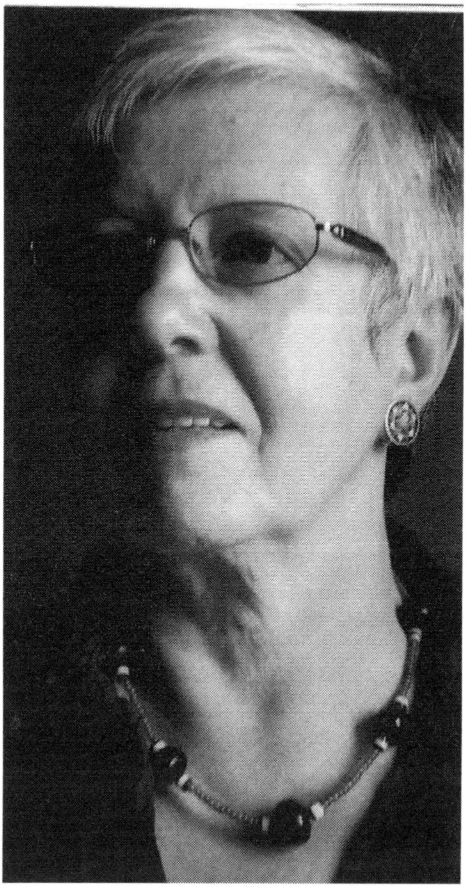

Figure 17.1 Portrait photograph of Dorothea McEwan.
Source: © Hilda Uccusic, 2016.

Maybe some of Warburg's ideas have played a role in your research, for example that of the illuminated manuscripts?

Yes, certainly, for example, I co-wrote with my late husband a volume on an illuminated Ethiopian Book of Revelation, written, illustrated and painted in an Ethiopian imperial workshop. What interested us was the question of the presentation: what was the model for producing such a volume in early 18th century Ethiopia? On the other hand, over many years I focused on some of the questions that became important to Warburg, as well as publishing the first biography of Fritz Saxl. It would have been odd had I not done so.

BIBLIOGRAPHY

Anderson, Willliam Scovil (ed.), *P. Ovidii Nasonis Metamorphoses*. Stuttgart: B. G. Teubner, 1993

Avenarius, Ferdinand, *Max Klingers Griffelkunst: Ein Begleiter durch ihre Phantasiewelt*. Berlin: Amsler & Ruthardt, 1895

Baechtold, Jacques M., *Geschichte der deutschen Literatur in der Schweiz*. Frauenfeld: T. Huber, 1892

Barb, A. A., *Die kaiserlichen Münzen der Stadt Tarsos in Kilikien*. PhD Dissertation, University of Vienna, 1924

Barb, A. A., 'Griechische Zaubertexte vom Gräberfelde westlich des Lagers: (Carnuntum)'. *Der römische Limes in Österreich*. Heft 16, 57–67. Vienna: Österreichische Akademie der Wissenschaften, 1926

Barb, A. A., 'Klassische Hexenkunst aus der Verwesung antiker Religionen: Ein antikes Zaubergebet gegen die Migräne und sein Fortleben'. *Jedermann-Hefte*, Heft 3, 1–32. Vienna, 1933

Barb, A. A., 'Österreich zur Römerzeit'. *Jedermann-Hefte*, Heft 6, 1–33. Vienna, 1934

Barb, A. A., *Frührömische Gräber von Burgenland*. Offprint from Dissertationes Pannonicae, Budapest: Königl. Ungarische Universitäts Druckerei. 2.6, 1938

Barb, A. A., 'St Zacharias the Prophet and Martyr. A Study in Charms and Incantations'. *Journal of the Warburg and Courtauld Institutes*, vol. 11, 35–67. London, 1948

Barb, A. A., 'Diva Matrix, A Faked Gnostic Intaglio in the Possession of P. P. Rubens and the Iconology of a Symbol'. *Journal of the Warburg and Courtauld Institutes*, vol. 16, no. 3/4, 193–238. London, 1953

Barb, A. A., 'Abraxas-studien'. *Hommages à Waldemar Deonna*. Collection Latomus, Brussels: Collection Latomus, 28, 207–208. 1957

Barb, A. A., 'The Survival of Magic Arts'. *The Conflict between Paganism and Christianity in the Fourth Century*, edited by Arnaldo Momigliano, 100–125. Oxford: At the Clarendon, 1963

Barb, A. A., 'The Wound in Christ's Side'. *Journal of the Warburg and Courtauld Institutes*, vol. 34, 320–321. London, 1971

Barb, A. A., '"Vidi Aquam…" and the Wounded Christ'. *Faith*, vol. 5, no. 1, 20–21, Jan/Feb. 1973

Barb, A. A., 'Gift'. *Reallexikon für Antike und Christentum*, vol. 10, 1209–1247. Stuttgart: Anton Hiersemann Verlag, 1978

Barb, A. A., *Journals*, three volumes of manuscript and typed material, letters, papers, newspaper cuttings, drawings, jottings. Private property of the Barb Family, London

Begbie, Harold, *The Political Struwwelpeter*. 1898. London: Grant Richards, 1899

Behn, Friedrich, *Das Mithrasheiligtum zu Dieburg*. Berlin and Leipzig: W. de Gruyter & Co, 1928

Belloc, Hilaire, *Cautionary Tales for Children*. Illustrated by Edward Gorey. [Reprint: San Diego: Harcourt, 2002], 1907

Belloc, Hilaire, *Die Juden*. Translation and Afterword by Theodor Haecker. Munich: J. Kösel & F. Pustet, 1927

Bender, Cora, Thomas Hensel, and Erhard Schüttpelz (eds), *Schlangenritual. Der Transfer der Wissensform vom Tsu'ti'kive der Hopi bis zu Aby Warburgs Kreuzlinger Vortrag*. Forschungskolleg 435 der Deutschen Forschungsgemeinschaft 'Wissenskultur und gesellschaftlicher Wandel', vol. 16. Berlin:Akademie Verlag, 59–61

Berezowski, Alexander, *Handbuch der Luftpostkunde. Katalog sämtlicher Marken und Abstempelungen der Luftposten*. Neustadt/Orla: Druck und Verlag der J. K. G. Wagner'schen Buchdruckerei, 1925

Bezold, Carl, *Zenit- und Aequatorialgestirne am babylonischen Fixsternhimmel. Mit Zusätzen von Franz Boll*. Heidelberg: C. Winter, 1913

Bezold, Carl (ed.), *Zeitschrift für Assyriologie*, XXX. Strasbourg: Verlag Karl J. Trüber, 1916. See sp. 139–162 for Theodor Nöldeke's review of Lidzbarski's *Das Johannesbuch der Mandäer* (1915)

Bezold, Carl (ed.), *Zeitschrift für Assyriologie*, XXXIII. Berlin and Leipzig: Walter de Gruyter & Co., 1920. See esp. 72–80 for Theodor Nöldeke's review of Lidzbarski's *Mandäische Liturgien* (1920)

Bialy, Lucyna, *Articles [titles unknown] about the Denke Affair*. Wroclaw: Gazeta Wroclawska, 30.07.1999; Wroclaw: *Stowo Polski*, 2.8.1999

Biester, Björn, *Der innere Beruf zur Wissenschaft: Paul Ruben (1866–1943). Studien zur deutsch-jüdischen Wissenschaftsgeschichte*. Mit einem Anhang: Edition und Kommentierung des Briefwechsels mit Aby M. Warburg, Hermann Usener, Ludwig Binswanger, Fritz Saxl, Gertrud Bing, Alfred Vagts, Hans Meier, Fritz M. Warburg und Carl A. Rathjens, Hamburger Beiträge zur Wissenschaftsgeschichte, vol. 14. Berlin: Reimer, 2001

Biester, Björn, and Hans-Michael Schäfer, *Carl Georg Heise – Persönliche Erinnerungen an Aby Warburg*. Wiesbaden: Gratia 43. Bamberger Schriften zur Renaissanceforschung, 2005

Bing, Gertrud, *Der Begriff des Notwendigen bei Lessing: ein Beitrag zum geistesgeschichtlichen Problem Leibniz-Lessing*. Hamburg: University, Doctoral dissertation, typescript, 1921

Bing, Gertrud, and Fritz Rougemont (eds.), *A. Warburg. Gesammelte Schriften. Die Erneuerung der heidnischen Antike*. 2 vols. Leipzig and Berlin: B. G. Teubner, 1932

Boll, Franz, *Sphaera. Neue griechische Texte und Untersuchungen zur Geschichte der Sternbilder. Mit einem Beitrag von Karl Dyroff*. Leipzig: B. G. Teubner, 1903

Boll, Franz, *Sternglaube und Sterndeutung: Die Geschichte und das Wesen der Astrologie. Unter Mitwirkung von Professor Dr. Carl Bezold*. Leipzig and Berlin: B. G. Teubner, 1919

Boll, Franz, and Carl Bezold, *Sternglaube und Sterndeutung: die Geschichte und das Wesen der Astrologie*. 3rd ed. prepared by W. Gundel. Leipzig: B. G. Teubner, 1926

Bousset, Wilhelm, 'Die Religion der Mandäer'. Review of Lidzbarski (1915). *Theologische Rundschau*, 20, 185–205. Tübingen: Mohr Siebeck Verlag, 1917

Bowen, C. P., and E. G. Sinckler, *Royal visits to Barbados*. Barbados: Herald, 1887

Brandt, Wilhelm, *Die Mandäer. Ihre Religion und ihre Geschichte*. Amsterdam, Verhandelingen der Koninklijke Akademie van Wetenschappen te Amsterdam, XVI, no. 3. Amsterdam: J. Müller, 1915

Britt, David (transl.), *Aby Warburg. The Renewal of Pagan Antiquity*. Introduction by Kurt W. Forster. Los Angeles: Getty Research Institute for the History of Art and the Humanities, 1999. See esp. the following chapters:

'Airship and Submarine in the Medieval Imagination', 332–337 and 487–490

'American Chapbooks', 703–710 and 776

'The Art of Portraiture and the Florentine Bourgeoisie', 185–221 and 435–450

'Artistic Exchanges between North and South in the Fifteenth Century', 275–280 and 468–469

'Astrology under Oriental Influence', 699–702 and 775

'Church and Court Art at Landshut', 561 and 732

'The Emergence of the Antique as a Stylistic Ideal in Early Renaissance Painting', 271–273 and 468–469

'Flemish Art and the Florentine Early Renaissance', 281–303 and 483

'Francesco Sassetti's Last Injunctions to His Sons', 223–262 and 451–466

'Italian Art and International Astrology in the Palazzo Schifanoia, Ferrara'. 563–591 and 732–758

'Pagan-Antique Prophecy in Words and Images in the Age of Luther'. 597–697 and 760–775

'Peasants at Work in Burgundian Tapestries', 315–323 and 484–485

'Piero della Francesca's *Battle of Constantine* in the Watercolor Copy by Johann Anton Ramboux', 339–342 and 490–493

'Sandro Botticelli's *Birth of Venus* and *Spring*', 89–157 and 405–431

Bungerz, Alexander, *Grosses Lexikon der Philatelie*. Munich: Kürz, 1923

Burgmair, Wolfgang, and Matthias M. Weber (eds.), '"...daß er sich nirgends wohler als in Murnau fühle..." James Loeb als Förderer der Wissenschaft und philanthropischer Mäzen'. In *Jahrbuch des Historischen Vereins*, 77–128. Bendiktbeuern: Rieß-Druck u. Verlags GmbH, 1997

Carrington, Philip, *The Early Christian Church*. Vol. 1. Cambridge: Cambridge University Press, 2011

Cassirer, Ernst, *Die Begriffsform im mythischen Denken*. Saxl, Fritz (ed.), *Studien der Bibliothek Warburg I*. Leipzig and Berlin: B. G. Teubner, 1922

Cassirer, Ernst, *Philosophie der symbolischen Formen*. Berlin: B. Cassirer, 1923–1931

Cassirer, Ernst, with contribution by Roger Hinds (1958), 'Microcosm and Memory', review of F. Saxl's *Lectures* (1957). London: The Times Literary Supplement, 23 May 1958, 277

Census Reports. United States Census Office, 1900

'-Ch'. Berlin: Vossische Zeitung, no. 536, 18 November 1933

Chavannes, Éduard, and Paul Pelliot, 'Un traité manichéen retrouvé en Chine traduit et annoté'. *Journal Asiatique*, vol. X, no. 18, 499–617, 1911

Chernow, Ron, *The Warburgs: A Family Saga*. London: Chatto & Windus, c. 1993

Colling-Pyper, Robert, and Margaret Stavridi, *Schicklgrüber*. Calcutta: Thacker's Press and Directories Ltd, 1943. Facsimile edition in 'Neudrucke von Struwwelpetriaden' edited by Walter Sauer, Andernach: Kari-Verlag, 2000

Colpe, Carsten, *Die religionsgeschichtliche Schule. Darstellung und Kritik ihres Bildes vom gnostischen Erlösermytho*. Göttingen: Vandenhoeck & Ruprecht, 1961

Cooper, James Fenimore, *Lederstrumpf-Erzählungen*. Translated by K. Federn, illustrated with lithographs by Max Slevogt. Berlin: Paul Cassirer, 1909

Cooper, Ray, *Retrospective Sympathetic Affection. A Tribute to the Academic Community*. Leeds: Moorland Books, 1996

Cumont, Franz, *Die Mysterien des Mithra: ein Beitrag zur Religionsgeschichte der römischen Kaiserzeit*. Leipzig: B. G. Teubner, 1903

Cumont, Franz, *La Théologie Solaire du Paganisme Romain. Extrait des Mémoires présentés par divers savants à l'Académie des Inscriptions et Belles-Lettres*. 12, part 2. Paris: Imprimerie Nationale, 1909

Cushing, Frank Hamilton, *Zuñi Breadstuff*. New York: Museum of the American Indian, Heye Foundation, 1920

Danzel, Theodor Wilhelm, *Mexiko I: Grundzüge der altmexikanischen Geisteskultur. Bildteil. Altmexikanische Bilderschriften*. Hagen i. W. and Darmstadt: Folkwang Verlag, 1922

Danzel, Theodor Wilhelm, *Mexiko II. Textteil: Kultur und Leben im alten Mexiko. Bildteil: Mexikanische Plastik*. Hagen i. W. and Darmstadt: Folkwang Verlag, 1922

Darton, Frederick J. H., *Children's Books in England. Five Centuries of Social Life*. Cambridge: Cambridge University Press, 1932

Deutsch, Otto Erich, 'Kunstblatt. Der internationale Kunsthistorikerkongreß in Darmstadt'. *Vienna: Neue Freie Presse*, no. 15552, 7 December 1907

Diers, Michael, *Warburg aus Briefen. Kommentare zu den Kopierbüchern der Jahre 1905–1918*. Weinheim: VCH, Acta Humaniora, 1991

Diers, Michael (ed.), *Porträt aus Büchern. Bibliothek Warburg & Warburg Institute, Hamburg 1933 – London 1993*. Kleine Schriften des Warburg-Archivs im Kunstgeschichtlichen Seminr der Universität Hamburg. Heft 1. Hamburg: Dölling und Galitz Verlag, 1993

Diers, Michael, *Schlagbilder: Zur politischen Ikonologie der Gegenwart*. Frankfurt am Main: Fischer Taschenbuch Verlag, 1997

Dilly, Heinrich (ed.), *Altmeister moderner Kunstgeschichte*. Berlin: Dietrich Reimer Verlag, 1990

Doderer, Klaus, 'Panoptikum der Struwwelköpfe'. *Struwwelpeter-Hoffmann. Texte, Bilder, Dokumentation*, edited by G. H. Herzog and Helmut Siefert, 27–35. Frankfurt am Main: Verlag Heinrich-Hoffmann-Museum, 1978

Dowden, Edward, *The Tragedy of Hamlet*. London: Methuen, 1899

Dvořákova, Hana (ed.), *Hanák na Pacifiku. Zapomenutá osobnost Františka Pospíšila. A Man from Haná on the Pacific Coast. The forgotten figure of František Pospíšil*. Brno: Moravské zemské museum, 197–206

Eckener, Hugo, *Die Amerikafahrt des "Graf Zeppelin"*. Berlin: Verlag August Scherl G.m.b.H, 1928

Eminger, Stefan, 'Theresianisten, CVer, Burschenschafter. Spitzenbeamte in Niederösterreich 1918 – 1934 – 1938 – 1945'. *Biographien und Zäsuren. Österreich und seine Länder 1918 – 1933 – 1938*, edited by W. Weber and W. Schuster, 239–270. Linz: Historisches Jahrbuch der Stadt Linz 2010/2011, 2011

Fendt, Leonhard, *Gnostische Mysterien: Ein Beitrag zur Geschichte des christlichen Gottesdienstes*. Munich: C. Kaiser, 1922

Fest, Joachim (ed.), *Eine englische Struwwelpeter-Parodie aus dem Jahre 1941*. Berlin: Autorenhaus Verlag, 2005

Fewkes, Jesse Walter, 'A Comparison of Sia and Tusayan Snake Ceremonials'. *The American Anthropologist*, vol. 8, 118–141. Washington, DC, 1895

Fewkes, Jesse Walter, 'Tusayan Snake Ceremonies'. *Extract from the Sixteenth Annual Report of the Bureau of American Ethnology*, 273–326. Washington, DC: Government Printing Office, 1897

Fleckner, Uwe (ed.), *Aby Warburg: Bildersammlung zur Geschichte von Sternglaube und Sternkunde im Hamburger Planetarium. Katalog der Ausstellung "Aby Warburg, Mnemosyne", Akademie der Bildenden Künste Wien, 25 Jan. – 13 März 1993*. Hamburg: Dölling und Galitz, 1993

Fleckner, Uwe (ed.), *Aby Warburg. Bilder aus dem Gebiet der Pueblo-Indianer: Vorträge und Fotografien*. Berlin: De Gruyter, 2018

Fliess, Selma, *Wilhelm Raabe: étude en quatre parties*. PhD Thesis, Grenoble: G. Guirimand, 1912

Fondation Eugène Piot, *Monuments et mémoires de la Fondation Eugène Piot*. Paris: Académie des Inscriptions et Belles Lettres

Fuchs, Bruno Archibald, *Die Ikonographie der sieben Planeten in der Kunst Italiens bis zum Ausgang des Mittelalters*. Munich: s. n., 1909

Fuchs, Eduard, *Die Frau in der Karikatur*. Munich: A. Langen, 1906

Fuchs, Eduard, *Der Weltkrieg in der Karikatur*. Munich: A. Langen, 1916

Galitz, Robert, and Brita Reimers (eds.), *Aby M. Warburg. 'Ekstatische Nymphe... trauernder Flußgott'. Portrait eines Gelehrten*. Schriftenreihe der hamburgischen Kulturstiftung, vol. 2. Hamburg: Dölling und Galitz Verlag, 1995

Ghandchi, Sabina, *Die Hamburger Künstlerin Mary Warburg, geb. Hertz: Werkliste*. Unpublished Master's Thesis, Hamburg University, 1986

Gibson, Evan K. (trans.), 'Tousled-headed Peter'. *Heinrich Hoffmann: Der Struwwelpeter polyglott*, edited by Walter Sauer. With pictures of the second edition and translations into English, French, Spanish, Italian and Latin and epilogue by Walter Sauer, 3rd ed., 45–52. Munich: Deutscher Taschenbuch Verlag G. m. b. H. & Co., 1994

Goerke, Franz, '"Projektionsabend – A. Warburg, Eine Reise durch das Gebiet der Pueblo-Indiane in Neu-Mexiko und Arizona". Bilder aus dem Leben der Pueblo-Indianer in Nordamerika'. *Photographische Rundschau. Zeitschrift für Freunde der Photographie*. vol. XI. Halle: Wilhelm Knapp, 1897

Goethe, Johann Wolfgang von, *Zahme Xenien*, vol. III. Weimar: H. Böhlau, 1893

Goldschmidt, Adolph, Rudolf Kautzsch, Karl Koetschau, and Aby Warburg, 'Ergebnisse des VII. [sic] internationalen Kunsthistorischen Kongresses zu Darmstadt'. *Kunstchronik. Wochenschrift für Kunst und Kunstgewerbe*. Leipzig, Neue Folge, vol. XIX, Nr. 29, 1907/1908. Jahrgang, 17. Juli 1908

Goldschmidt, Günther, and Richard Reitzenstein (eds.), *Helidori carmina quattuor ad fidem codicis casselani / Alchemistische Lehrschriften und Märchen bei den Arabern. Mit Unterstützung der Notgemeinschaft der Deutschen Wissenschaft*. Gießen: A. Töpelmann, 1923

Gombrich, Ernst H., 'Lessing'. *Henriette Hertz Trust of the British Academy, Proceedings of the British Academy*, vol. XLIII, 133–156. London: Oxford University Press, 1958

Gombrich, Ernst H., 'Gertrud Bing zum Gedenken'. *Jahrbuch der Hamburger Kunstsammlungen* 7–12, 1965

Gombrich, Ernst H., 'Festvortrag'. *Aby Warburg zum Gedächtnis. Gedenkfeier anläßlich der 100. Wiederkehr seines Geburtstages*, edited by K. H. Schäfer, E. H. Gombrich, and C. G. Heise, 15–36. Hamburg: Im Selbstverlag der Universität, 1966

Gombrich, Ernst H., *In Search of Cultural History. The Philip Maurice Deneke Lecture 1967*. Oxford: Clarendon Press, 1969

Gombrich, Ernst H., 'Introduction'. *A Heritage of Images. A Selection of Lectures by Fritz Saxl*, edited by Hugh Honour and John Fleming, 9–12. Harmondsworth: Penguin, 1970

Gombrich, Ernst H., *Aby Warburg. An Intellectual Biography with a Memoir of the History of the Library by F. Saxl*. Oxford: Phaidon, 1986

Gombrich, Ernst H., 'Magic, Myth and Metaphor: Reflections on Pictorial Satire'. In *L'Art et les Révolutions. Conférences plénières*, 23–66. Strasbourg: 27e Congrès International d'Histoire de l'Art, 1990

Gombrich, Ernst H., 'Magie, Mythos und Metapher: Betrachtungen über die satirische Graphik'. *Wilhelm-Busch-Gesellschaft, Wilhelm-Busch-Jahrbuch*, vol. 60, 35–77. Hannover: Hahn-Druckerei, 1994

Grabbe, Christian Dietrich, *Scherz, Satire, Ironie und tiefere Bedeutung*. Leipzig: Insel Verlag, 1822

Guidi, Benedetta Cestelli (trans.), '"Idea Vincit", la volante e vittoriosa Idea. Una commissione artistica di Aby Warburg'. *Lo sguardo di Giano. Aby Warburg fra tempo e memoria*, edited by Claudia Cieri Via and Pietro Monzani, 345–375. Torino: Nino Aragno Editore, 2004

Guidi, Benedetta Cestelli, and Nicholas Mann (eds.), *Photographs at the Frontier. Aby Warburg in America 1895–1896*. London: Merrell Holberton Publishers in association with The Warburg Institute, 1998

Guidi, Benedetta Cestelli, and Nicholas Mann (eds.), *Grenzerweiterungen. Aby Warburg in Amerika 1895–1896*. Hamburg and Munich: Dölling und Galitz Verlag in cooperation with The Warburg Institute, London, 1999

Gurewich, Vladimir, 'Observations on the Iconography of the Wound in Christ's Side'. *Journal of the Warburg and Courtauld Institutes*, vol. 20, 358–362. London, 1957

Gurewich, Vladimir, 'Rubens and the Wound in Christ's Side. A Postscript'. *Journal of the Warburg and Courtauld Institutes*, vol. 26, 358. London, 1963

Hamburger Echo, 21 May 1915

Hamburger Fremdenblatt. Illustrierte Rundschau, vol. 85, no. 52, 2 March 1913

Hamburger Weihnachtsbuch. Four drawings by Mary Warburg, Neukloster bei Buxtehude, 227–229. Hamburg: Verlag Otto Meissner, 1892

Haug, Steffen, 'Bildpropaganda im Ersten Weltkrieg: Aby Warburg als Redakteur der Illustrierten Zeitschrift *La Guerra del 1914*'. *John Heartfield: Fotografie plus Dynamit*, edited by Angela Lammert, Rosa von der Schulenburg, and Anna Schultz, 104–109. Exhibition Catalogue, Munich: Berlin, Akademie der Künste, 2020

Haug, Steffen and Wedekind, Gregor, 'Max Slevogt's Gesichte. Mit einem Nachtrag zu Aby Warburg', in press

Heckscher, William S., 'The Genesis of Iconology'. *Art and Literature. Studies in Relationship*, edited by Egon Verheyen, 2nd ed., 529–547. Baden-Baden: Verlag Valentin Koerner (Saecula Spiritualia, Bd. 17), N.C. (Duke University Press), 1994

Hedinger, Bärbel, Michael Diers, Andrea Völker, and Steffen Haug, *Mary Warburg. Porträt einer Künstlerin*. Munich: Hirmer Verlag, 2020

Heinrich-Jost, Ingrid (ed.), *Kladderadatsch: Die Geschichte eines Berliner Witzblattes von 1848 bis ins Dritte Reich*. Cologne: Informationspresse C. W. Leske, 1982

Heise, Carl Georg, *Persönliche Erinnerungen an Aby Warburg*. Hamburg: Gesellschaft der Bücherfreunde, 1959

Hensel, Paul, 'Montaigne und die Antike'. *Vorträge der Bibliothek Warburg 1925–1926*, edited by Fritz Saxl, 67–94. Leipzig and Berlin: B. G. Teubner, 1928

Hermanin, F., *La Farnesina*. Bergamo: Istituto italiano d'arti grafiche, 1927

Hertz, Emma Dina, née Beets, *Die Urgroßeltern Beets*. Hamburg: Hamburgische Liebhaberbibliothek, 1899

Hertz, Hans, *Unser Elternhaus*. Hamburg: Gesellschaft Hamburgischer Kunstfreunde, Reihe *Hamburgische Hausbibliothek*, 1903

Hess, Michael, *Braver Beamter, Opportunist, Verfolgter: die burgenländischen Spitzenbeamten von 1923 bis 1938; mit besonderem Blick auf die Zäsuren der Jahre 1934, 1938 und 1945*. Burgenländische Forschungen, vol. 110. Eisenstadt: Burgendländisches Archiv, 2017. See esp. chapter on A. A. Barb, 415–434

Hessenberg, Eduard (ed.), *"Struwwelpeter-Hoffmann" erzählt aus seinem Leben: Lebenserinnerungen seines Großvaters Dr. Heinrich Hoffmann*. Frankfurt am Main: Englert and Schlosser, 1926

Hinnells, John (ed.), *Studies in Mithraism*. Rome: 'L'Erma' di Bretschneider, 1994

Hippel, Theodor Georg von, *Lebensläufe nach aufsteigenden Linien*, vol. 1. Berlin: G. Reimer, 1828

Hofmann, Werner, 'Was bleibt von der "Wiener Schule"?'. *Kunsthistoriker. Mitteilungen des österreichischen Kunsthistorikerverbandes*, Jg. I, Nr. 4, 1984

Holy Bible, *Revised Standard Version*, Catholic ed. London: Catholic Truth Society, 1966

Hubert, Hans W., *Das Kunsthistorische Institut in Florenz. Von der Gründung bis zum hundertjährigen Jubiläum, 1897–1997*. Florence: Il Ventilabro, 1997

Internationale Wochenschrift für Wissenschaft, Kunst und Technik. Berlin, Verlag August Scherl, 3 August 1907

Italiaander, Rolf, *Gleise und Nebengleise des O. H. Strohmeyer*. Hamburg: Akademie der Freien Künste, 1964

The Jerusalem Bible. London: Darton, Longman, Todd, 1966

Johanning, Klaus, *Der Bibel-Babel-Streit. Eine forschungsgeschichtliche Studie*. Europäische Hochschulschriften, Reihe 23: Theologie 343. Frankfurt am Main: P. Lang, 1988

Johnson, Christopher D., and C. Wedepohl C., *From the Arsenal to the Laboratory*, 106–124. Chicago: University of Chicago Press, 2012

Jones, Henry Stuart (ed.), *A Catalogue of the Ancient Sculptures Preserved in the Municipal Collections of Rome: The Sculptures of the Palazzo dei Conservatori*, 2 vols. Oxford: The Clarendon Press, 1926

Junker, Heinrich, 'Über iranische Quellen der hellenistischen Aion-Vorstellung'. *Vorträge der Bibliothek Warburg 1921–22*, edited by Fritz Saxl, 125–178. Leipzig and Berlin: B. G. Teubner, 1923

Kany, Robert, *Die religionsgeschichtliche Forschung an der kulturwissenschaftlichen Bibliothek Warburg*. Bamberg: S. Wendel, 1989

Kaplan, S., 'Tə'əzazä Sänbät'. *Encyclopaedia Aethiopica*, edited by S. Uhlig, et al., vol. 4, 885a–885b. Wiesbaden: Harrassowitz, 2010

Kessner, L. (ed.), *Aby Warburg. Porozumět dějinám umění a kulturní historii*. Brno: Barrister a Principal, FF MU, Seminář dějin umění, 2017

Kladderadatsch, Satirical German Weekly. Berlin

Koch, Carsten, 'Richard Reitzensteins Beiträge zur Mandäerforschung'. *Zeitschrift für Religionswissenschaft*, vol. 95, 49–80, 1995

Kolbe, Jürgen, and Karl Heinz Bittel, *Heller Zauber. Thomas Mann in München 1894–1933*. Munich: Siedler Verlag, 1987

Kowalewski, Gustav, 'Der Schwerttanz'. *Akademische Turnbundsblätter*. Special issue for Years 16 and 17, 1–19. Berlin: Lüdtke, 1904

Kraus, Karl, *The Third Walpurgis Night*. Munich: Heinrich Fischer, 1952

Kunnnert, Heinrich, 'Alphons A. Barb. 75 Jahre'. *Volk und Heimat, Monatszeitschrift für Kultur und Bildung*, vol. XXVIIII, no. 8, 3–6. Eisenstadt: Burgenländisches Volksbildungswerk, 1975/1976

Kürschners Deutscher Gelehrten-Kalender (1928/29). Berlin: Walter de Gruyer, 1929

Landauer, Carl Hollis, *The Survival of Antiquity: The German Years of the Warburg Institute*. Unpublished PhD, Yale University, 1984

Le Coq, Albert von, *Die buddhistische Spätantike in Mittelasien*, 7 vols. Letterkunde. Nieuwe Reeks. Deel XVI, N° 3. Berlin: D. Reimer, 1922–1933

Lessing, Gotthold Ephraim, *Hamburgische Dramaturgie*, vol. XLIII, 209, 19.04.1768

Lidzbarski, Mark, 'Uthra und Malakha'. *Orientalische Studien Theodor Nöldeke zum siebzigsten Geburtstag (2. März 1906)*, edited by Carl Bezold. Gießen: Alfred Töpelmann, 1906

Lidzbarski, Mark, 'Ein mandäisches Amulett'. *Vogüé, Charles Jean Melchior, marquis de, Florilegium ou recueil de travaux d'érudition didiés à M. Melchior de Vogüé*, 349–373. Paris: Imprimerie nationale, 1909

Lidzbarski, Mark, *Das Johannesbuch der Mandäer. Text, Einleitung, Übersetzung und Kommentar*. Gießen: Alfred Töpelmann. [Reprint: Berlin 1966], 1915

Lidzbarski, Mark, *Mandäische Liturgien*. Berlin: Weidmannsche Buchhandlung, 1920 [1st Reprint: Berlin/Hildesheim, 1962, 2nd Reprint: Hildesheim/New York, 1971]

Lidzbarski, Mark, *Ginzā. Der Schatz oder das große Buch der Mandäer*. Göttinger Akademie der Wissenschaften. Quellen der Religionsgeschichte, vol. 13, Group 4. Göttingen: Vandenhoek & Ruprecht, 1925

Liebeschütz, Hans, *Das allegorische Weltbild der heiligen Hildegard von Bingen*. Leipzig and Berlin: B. G. Teubner, 1933

Liebeschütz, Hans, 'Aby Warburg (1866-1929) as Interpreter of Civilisation'. *Year Book of the Leo Baeck Institute*, vol. 16, 225–236. Oxford: Berghahn Books. Published for the Institute. London / Jerusalem / New York, 1972

Loeb Classical Library 194. Horace, *Epistulae*. Translated by H. R. Fairclough. Cambridge, Mass.: Harvard University Press, 1929

Loeb Classical Library 186, *Josephus*. Translated by St. H. J. Thackeray. London: W. Heinemann, New York: G. P. Putnam's Sons, 1926

Lohmann, Ingrid, 'Siegfried Bernfeld: Sisyphos oder die Grenzen der Erziehung. Der geheime Zweifel der Pädagogik'. *Klassiker und Außenseiter. Pädagogische Veröffentlichungen des 20. Jahrhunderts*, edited by Klaus-Peter Horn and Christian Ritzi, 180–192. Hohengchren: Schneider Verlag, 2001

Lucas, Edward Verrall, *Swollen-headed William*. With illustrations by George Morrow. London: Methuen & Co., 1914

Mâle, Emile, *Gothic Image: Religious Art in France of the Thirteenth Century*. New York: Harper, 1958

Maritain, Jacques, *Antisemitism*. London: The Centenary Press, 1939

Mayer, August L., *Dominico Theotocopuli El Greco: kritisches und illustriertes Verzeichnis des Gesamtwerkes*. Munich: F. Hanfstängel, 1926

Mayer, Hermann, Brigitte Salmen, and James Loeb Gesellschaft e.V. (eds.), *James Loeb. Sammler und Mäzen in München, Murnau und weltweit – Collector and Patron in Munich, Murnau and Beyond*. Munich: Hirmer Verlag, 2018

Mazal, Otto, *Bibliotheca Eugeniana: die Sammlungen des Prinzen Eugen von Savoyen. Ausstellung der Österreichischen Nationalbibliothek und der Graphischen Sammlung Albertina*. Vienna: Die Nationalbibliothek, 1986

McEwan, Dorothea, 'Struwwelhitler: A Nazi Story Book'. *Children's Literature, Bulletin of the John Rylands University Library*, edited by David Blamires, vol. 76, no. 3, Autumn, 221–235. Manchester: Manchester University Library, 1994

McEwan, Dorothea, 'Arch and Flag: Leitmotifs for the Aby Warburg Bookplate'. *Bookplate International*, vol. 3, no. 2, 95–110. London: The Primrose Academy, 1996

McEwan, Dorothea, 'Aby Warburg und die Figur des Nikolaus im "Russischen Struwwelpeter"'. *German Life and Letters*, vol. L, no. 3, 354–364. Oxford: Blackwell, 1997

McEwan, Dorothea, *Ausreiten der Ecken. Die Aby Warburg – Fritz Saxl Korrespondenz 1910–1919*. Hamburg: Dölling und Galitz Verlag, 1998

McEwan, Dorothea, 'Millennium-feuilles from Half-eaten Wafers'. London: The Warburg Institute Newsletter, 8 (Summer edition 1998): 2

McEwan, Dorothea, 'A Tale of One Institute and Two Cities: The Warburg Institute'. *German-Speaking Exiles in Great Britain. The Yearbook of the Research Centre for German and Austrian Exile Studies*, edited by Ian Wallace, vol. 1, 25–42. Amsterdam: Rodopi, 1999

McEwan, Dorothea, '"...wahrscheinlich latenter Antisemitismus"'. *Montfort. Vierteljahresschrift für Geschichte und Gegenwart Vorarlbergs*, 51.Jg., Heft 2, 197–198. Dornbirn: Vorarlberger Landesverlag, 1999

McEwan, Dorothea, 'Façetten einer Freundschaft: Aby Warburg und James Loeb. Verwandte, Freunde,Wissenschaftler, Mäzene'. *James Loeb, 1867–1933: Kunstsammler und Mäzen*, edited by Brigitte Salmen, 75–98. Exhibition Catalogue. Murnau: Schlossmuseum des Marktes Murnau, 2000

McEwan, Dorothea, 'Making a Reception for Warburg: Fritz Saxl and Warburg's Book *Heidnisch-antike Weissagung in Wort und Bild zu Luthers Zeiten*'. *Art History as Cultural History. Warburg's Projects*, edited by R. Woodfield, 93–120. Amsterdam: G+B Arts International, 2001

McEwan, Dorothea, 'Corrispondenze zodiacali e personali. I commenti di Warburg in margine alla conferenza su Palazzo Schifanoia'. *Aby Warburg e le metamorfosi degli antichi dei*, edited by Marco Bertozzi, 99–113. Ferrara: Franco Cosimo Panini Editore, 2002.

McEwan, Dorothea, '"Struwwelhitler" – A Nazi Story Book' and 'Schickelgrüber'. *German Studies Review*, vol. 25, no. 3, 511–532. Carleton College, Northfield, Minnesota, USA, October 2002

McEwan, Dorothea, 'Mapping the Traderoutes of the Mind: The Warburg Institute'. *Intellectual Migration and Cultural Transformation. Refugees from National Socialism in the English-Speaking World*, edited by Ed Timms and J. Hughes, vol. 12, 37–50. Vienna and New York: Springer Verlag, Veröffentlichungen des Instituts Wiener Kreis, 2003

McEwan, Dorothea, 'Der Palazzo Potetje. Zum Triptychon von Mary Warburg'. *Zeitschrift des Vereins für hamburgische Geschichte*, vol. 90, 75–95. Hamburg, 2004

McEwan, Dorothea, '"The Enemy of Hypothesis": Fritz Saxl as Acting Director of the Warburg Library'. *Leo Baeck Institute: Year Book 2004*, 75–86. Oxford, London, Jerusalem, and New York: Berghahn Books, 2004

McEwan, Dorothea, 'Fritz Saxl und Aby Warburg: Würdigung einer Zusammenarbeit'. *Wiener Schule. Erinnerung und Perspektiven*, edited by Bundesdenkmalamt Wien und Institut für Kunstgeschichte der Universität Wien. Wiener Jahrbuch für Kunstgeschichte. vol. LIII, 139–151. Vienna, Cologne, and Weimar: Böhlau Verlag, 2004

McEwan, Dorothea, 'Gegen die Pioniere der Diesseitigkeit'. *Trajekte*, edited by Sigrid Weigel, no. 8, Year 4, April, 9–11. Berlin: Zeitschrift des Zentrums für Literaturforschung, 2004

McEwan, Dorothea, *Wanderstrassen der Kultur. Die Aby Warburg – Fritz Saxl Korrespondenz von 1920 bis 1929. Mit einem Vorwort von Martin Warnke*. Kleine Schriften des Warburg Institute London und des Warburg Archivs im Warburg-Haus Hamburg, edited by Nicholas Mann and Martin Warnke, Heft 2. Munich and Hamburg: Dölling und Galitz Verlag, 2004

McEwan, Dorothea, 'IDEA VINCIT – "Die siegende, fliegende 'Idea'". Ein künstlerischer Auftrag von Aby Warburg. *Der Bilderatlas im Wechsel der Künste und Medien*, edited by Sabine Flach, Inge Münz-Koenen and Marianne Streisand, 121–151. Munich: Wilhelm Fink Verlag, 2005. For the translation into Italian, see Guidi, Benedetta Cestelli, '"Idea Vincit", la volante e vittoriosa Idea. Una commissione artistica di Aby Warburg'. *Lo sguardo di Giano. Aby Warburg fra tempo e memoria*, edited by Claudia Cieri Via and Pietro Monzani, 345–375. Torino: Nino Aragno Editore, 2004

McEwan, Dorothea, 'Aby Warburg's (1866–1929) Dots and Lines. Mapping the Diffusion of Astrological Motifs in Art History'. *German Studies Review*, vol. 29, no. 2, 243–268. Carleton College, Northfield, Minnesota, USA, May 2006

McEwan, Dorothea, 'Der gute Bischof Nikolaus: Aby Warburgs Interpretation der russischen Übersetzung von *Struwwelpeter* und die politischen Parodien *Struwwelhitler – A Nazi Story Book* und *Schicklgrüber*'. *Zeitschrift für Volkskunde*, vol. 102, 67–90. Münster, 2006

McEwan, Dorothea, 'Ein Kampf gegen Windmühlen. Warburgs pro-italienische publizistische Initiative'. *Kasten 117. Aby Warburg und der Aberglaube im Großen Krieg*, edited by Gottfried Korff. Untersuchungen des Ludwig-Uhland-Instituts der Universität Tübingen im Auftrag der Tübinger Vereinigung für Volkskunde, vol. 105, 135–163. Tübingen: Tübinger Vereinigung für Volkskunde, 2007

McEwan, Dorothea, 'Zur Entstehung des Vortrages über das Schlangenritual, Motiv und Motivation / Heilung durch Erinnerung'. *Schlangenritual. Der Transfer der Wissensform vom Tsu'ti'kive der Hopi bis zu Aby Warburgs Kreuzlinger Vortrag*, edited by Cora Bender, Thomas Hensel, and Erhard Schüttpelz. Forschungskolleg 435 der Deutschen Forschungsgemeinschaft 'Wissenskultur und gesellschaftlicher Wandel', vol. 16, 267–281. Berlin: Akademie Verlag, 2007

McEwan, Dorothea, 'Die Pospíšil – Warburg Korrespondenz im Warburg Institute'. *Hanák na Pacifiku. Zapomenutá osobnost Františka Pospíšila. A Man from Haná on the Pacific Coast. The Forgotten Figure of František Pospíšil*, edited by Hana Dvořákova, 197–206. Brno: Moravské zemské museum, 2008. (The additional Czech translation by *Hana Dvořákova* 'Korespondence Pospíšil – Warburg uložená ve Warburgově institute,' 183–196, with the text of his lecture to the Folklore Society in London, untitled, English and Czech, 207–218)

McEwan, Dorothea, *Correspondence of Aby Warburg, General Correspondence and Family Correspondence, from 1882 to 1929*. London: The Warburg Institute, 2010. Online database available at http://calmview.warburg.sas.ac.uk/calmview/ (accessed June 2022)

McEwan, Dorothea, 'Saxl and Boll'. *Journal of Art Historiography*, edited by R. Woodfield, vol. 5, December 2011. https://arthistoriography.wordpress.com/number-5-december-2011 (accessed May 2022)

McEwan, Dorothea, *Fritz Saxl. Eine Biografie*. Vienna, Cologne, and Weimar: Böhlau Verlag, 2012

McEwan, Dorothea, 'Due missioni politiche di Aby Warburg in Italia nel 1914–15'. *I molti Rinascimenti di Aby Warburg. Schifanoia*, edited by M. Bertozzi and G. Venturi. A cura dell'Istituto di Studi Rinascimentali di Ferrara, vol. 42–43, 2012, 57–79. Pisa-Roma: Fabbrizio Serra Editore, 2013

McEwan, Dorothea, 'Bringing Light into Darkness. Aby Warburg and Fritz Saxl in Conversation on Mithras'. *Aisthesis. Pratiche, Linguaggi E Saperi dell'estetico 8*, vol. 2, 27–39, November 2015. https://doi.org/10.13128/Aisthesis-17563. Translated into Italian by Alice Barale, 'Far luce nel buio. Aby Warburg e Fritz Saxl discutono su Mitra', 119–132 (see McEwan, Dorothea)

McEwan, Dorothea, 'Strzygowski im Spiegel der Aby Warburg Korrespondenz. Der Strzygowski-Briefbestand im Warburg Institute London'. *Von Biala nach Wien. Josef Strzygowski und die Kunstwissenschaften. Zum 150. Geburtstag von Josef Strzygowski. Akten der Konferenz Bielsko-Biala (27.–30.3.2012) und Wien (12.10.2012)*, edited by Piotr Scholz and Magdalena Dlugosz, 53–69. Vienna: European University Press, Dept. für Vergleichende Kunstgeschichte am Kulturwissenschaftlichen Institute an der Maria Curie-Sklodowska Universität in Lublin and Gesellschaft für Vergleichende Kunstforschung in Vienna, 2015

McEwan, Dorothea, 'Why Historiography? Saxl's Thoughts on History and Writing History'. *Vorträge aus dem Warburg-Haus, Band 12, The Afterlife of the Kulturwissenschaftliche Bibliothek Warburg. The Migration and the Early Years of the Warburg Institute in London*, edited by Peter Mack and Uwe Fleckner, 97–107 and 224–227. Berlin: De Gruyter, 2015

McEwan, Dorothea, 'Far luce nel buio. Aby Warburg e Fritz Saxl discutono su Mitra'. *Energia e rappresentazione. Warburg, Panofsky, Wind*, edited by Alice Barale, Fabrizio Desideri, and Silvia Ferretti, 119–132. Milano: Mimesis, 2016. Italian translation of McEwan, Dorothea, 'Bringing light into darkness. Aby Warburg and Fritz Saxl in conversation on Mithras' by Alice Barala

McEwan, Dorothea, 'La *Kulturwissenschaftliche Bibliothek Warburg à la lumière de ses archives. Entretien avec Dorothea McEwan*'. *La Kulturwissenschaftliche Bibliothek Warburg comme laboratoire*, edited by Carole Maigné, Audrey Lieber, and Céline Trautmann-Waller, vol. 28, 199–209. Paris: Revue germanique internationale, 2018

McEwan, Dorothea, '"Das, was ich als Jude vertrete, kann ich auch als Katholik vertreten". Zu Alfons Augustinus Barbs wissenschaftlicher Laufbahn und seinem Glaubenswechsel'. *Burgenländische Heimatblätter*, 82. Jg., nos. 3 and 4, 102–147. Eisenstadt: Burgenländisches Landesarchiv und Burgenländische Landesbibliothek, 2020

McEwan, Dorothea, 'Karikatur als Kriegsdienst: Aby Warburgs "neuer Stil in Wort und Bild", 1914–1918'. *Zeitschrift für Kunstgeschichte*, vol. 84, no. 1, 78–95. Berlin: De Gruyter, 2021

McEwan, Dorothea, and Martin Treml, 'Aby an Gisela'. *Trajekte*, edited by Sigrid Weigel, no. 8, Year 4, April, 4–8. Berlin: Zeitschrift des Zentrums für Literaturforschung, 2004

McEwan, Dorothea, and Bogdan Burtea, 'Eine Trouvaille aus dem Warburg Institute Archive zu Mandäismus und Gnosis'. In *"Durch Dein Wort Ward Jegliches Ding!" "Through Thy Word All Things Were Made!" 2. Mandäistische und samaritanistische Tagung / 2nd International Conference of Mandaic and Samaritan Studies. Zum Gedenken an Rudolf Macuch (1919–1993) / in Honour of Rudolf Macuch (1919–1993)*, edited by Rainer Voigt, Mandäistische Forschungen, vol. 4, 137–153. Wiesbaden: Harrassowitz Verlag, 2013

McEwan, Dorothea, and Alessandro Scafi, 'Warburg and D'Annunzio in Defence of Truth: On Modern Literature and Alleged Jewishness'. *Schifanoia. A cura dell'Istituto di Studi Rinascimentali di Ferrara 52-53. Scritti in Honore di Marco Bertozzi*, edited by

S. Caroti, A. Ghinato, and M. Inverti, 259–279. Pisa and Rome: Fabrizio Serra Editore, 2017

Meier, Hans, Richard Newald, and Edgar Wind (eds.), *Kulturwissenschaftliche Bibliographie zum Nachleben der Antike*, vol. 2. London: Cassell, 1934–39

Meisen, Karl, *Nikolauskult und Nikolausbrauch im Abendlande. Eine kultgeographisch-volkskundliche Untersuchung*. Düsseldorf: L. Schwann, 1931

Meschke, Kurt, *Schwerttanz und Schwerttanzspiel im germanischen Kulturkreis*. Leipzig and Berlin: B. G. Teubner, 1931

Michalski, Sergiusz, 'Zur methodologischen Stellung der Wiener Schule in den zwanziger und dreißiger Jahren'. *Akten des XXV. Internationalen Kongresses für Kunstgeschichte, Wien 1983. Wien und die Entwicklung des kunsthistorischen Methode*, vol. 1. Boehlau: Vienna, Cologne, and Graz, 1984

Michels, Karen, and Charlotte Schoell-Glass, *Aby Warburg. Tagebuch der Kulturwissenschaftlichen Bibliothek Warburg. Mit Einträgen von Gertrud Bing und Fritz Saxl*. Berlin: Akademie Verlag, 2001

Michels, Karen, and Charlotte Schoell-Glass, 'Aby Warburg et les timbres. En tant que document culturel'. *Protée. Revue internationale de théories et de pratique sémiotiques*, vol. 30, no. 2, 85–92, 2002

Morel, Richard Scott, 'From Neptune to Trident. How the Colonial Deputed Seal for Barbados Evolved into a National Symbol'. *British Library Blog*, July 2018, available at https://blogs.bl.uk/americas/2018/07/from-neptune-to-trident-how-the-colonial-deputed-seal-for-barbados-evolved-into-a-national-symbol.html (accessed May 2022)

Müller, Josef (ed.), *Vorschule der Ästhetik*. Leipzig: Felix Meiner, 2023

Müller, Mathias F., 'Die positivistisch-politische Kunstgeschichtsschreibung von Josef Strzygowski. Eine kritische Analyse seines chauvinistischen Denkens'. *Von Biala nach Wien. Josef Strzygowski und die Kunstwissenschaften. Zum 150. Geburtstag von Josef Strzygowski. Akten der Konferenz Bielsko-Biala (27.–30.3.2012) und Wien (12.10.2012)*, edited by Piotr Scholz and Magdalena Dlugosz, 308–320. Vienna: European University Press, Dept. für Vergleichende Kunstgeschichte am Kulturwissenschaftlichen Institute an der Maria Curie-Sklodowska Universität in Lublin and Gesellschaft für Vergleichende Kunstforschung in Vienna, 2015

Müntz, E., *Histoire de l'art pendant la Renaissance. Italie. Les Primitifs*, 3 vols. Paris: Hachette, 1889–1895

The Museums Journal, Job Advertisement for A. A. Barb by Adolf Mahr. London, vol. 38, no. 10 (1939): 6

National – Zeitung, Berlin, 20 July 1906

Naumann, Hans, *Primitive Gemeinschaftskultur. Beiträge zur Vokskunde und Mythologie*. Jena: E. Diederichs, 1921

Neumann, Carl, 'Zur Theorie der Geschichte und Kunstgeschichte'. *Die Methode der Kunstgeschichte. Ein Versuch*, edited by Hans Tietze. Leipzig: E. A. Seemann. *Historische Zeitschrift*, 116 (=3. F., 20), 484–494, 1917

Newman, John Henry, *Apologia Pro Vita Sua*. London: Longman, Green, 1864

Nöldeke, Theodor, review of Lidzbarski's *Das Johannesbuch der Mandäer* (1915). Bezold, Carl (ed.), *Zeitschrift für Assyriologie*, XXX, 139–162. Strasbourg: Verlag von Karl J. Trübner, 1916

Nöldeke, Theodor, review of Lidzbarski's *Mandäische Liturgien* (1920) in Bezold, Carl (ed.), *Zeitschrift für Assyriologie*, XXXIII, 72–80. Berlin und Leipzig: Walter de Gryuter & Co., 1920

Norberg, Matthias, *Codex Nasaraeus. Liber Adami appellatus*, Syriace transscriptus, loco vocalium, ubi vicem literarum gutturalium praestiterint, his substitutis, Latineque redditus, 2 vols. Londini Gothorum [Lund], Literis Berlingianis 1815, 1815–1816

Norden, Eduard, *Die Geburt des Kindes. Geschichte einer religiösen Idee.* Leipzig and Berlin: B. G. Teubner, 1924

'Obituary of Fr. Myerscough, Samuel Sebastian, S. J.'. *The Cottonian*, vol. XLIII, no. 92, 2–3. Stoke on Trent: Cotton College, 1954

Ohrt, Roberto, and Axel Heil (eds.), *Aby Warburg: Bilderatlas Mnemosyne: The Original.* Curated with the Warburg Institute, London in collaboration with the 'Bundeskunsthalle' of the Federal Republic of Germany, Bonn; Concept Axel Heil, Roberto Ohrt, Eva Kraus and Katharina Chrubasik; photographs Ian Jones (The Warburg Institute), Paul Taylor (The Warburg Institute), Tobias Wootton (London, Karlsruhe), Dieter Schleicher (Karlsruhe). Cologne: Verlag der Buchhandlung Walther und Franz König, 2020

Ollendorff, Oscar, *Andacht in der Malerei: Beiträge zur Psychologie der Grossmeister.* Leipzig: J. Zeitler, 1912

Ollendorff, Oscar, *Liebe in der Malerei: neue Beiträge zur Psychologie der grossen Meister.* Leipzig: Dieterich, 1926

Origenes, *Homiliae. Die griechischen christlichen Schriftsteller (GCS)* 9, 136. Posen: J. C. Hinrichs

Ovid, *Metamorphoses* IV, see Anderson, W. S. Leipzig: Teubner Verlagsgesellschaft, 1993

Paul, Jean, *Jean Pauls Werke*. Berlin: Bong, n.d. [1910]

Petermann, Julius Heinrich (ed.), *Thesaurus sive Liber Magnus, vulgo 'Liber Adami' appellatus, opus Mandaeorum summi ponderis*, tom. I (text. continens) and tom. II (lect. codd. Additamenda et corrig. continens), 2 vols. Leipzig: P. O: Weigel, 1867

Pliny the Younger, see Carrington, Philip

Pospišíl, František, 'Mečový (zbrojný) tanec naslovanské půdě'. *Národopisný věstník československý*, vol. 6, 25–55, 1911

Preuss, Hans (ed.), *Von der Freiheit eines Christenmenschen / Martin Luther*. Leipzig: Drei Rosen-Verlag, 1917

Propertius, *Elegiarum liber 2. Die Elegien des Sextus Propertius, erklärt von Max Rothstein.* Berlin: Weidmannsche Buchhandlung, 1898.

Rappl, Werner, 'Fritz Saxls Ausstellungen nach dem Ersten Weltkrieg in Wien'. *Politik der Präsentation. Museum und Ausstellung in Österreich 1918–1945*, edited by Herbert Posch and Gottfried Fliedl, 40–52. Vienna: Turia und Kant, 1996

Raulff, Ulrich, *Wilde Energien. Vier Versuche zu Aby Warburg.* Göttinger Gespräche zur Geschichtswissenschaft, vol. 19. Göttingen: Wallstein Verlag, 2003

Reclam, Philipp jun., *Grabbe, Christian Dietrich. Scherz, Satire, Ironie und tiefere Bedeutung.* Leipzig: Reclams Universal-Bibliothek, Nr. 397, 1872

Reitzenstein, Erich, *Theophrast bei Epikur und Lukrez*. Heidelberg: C. Winter, 1924

Reitzenstein, Richard, *Das mandäische Buch des Herrn der Größe und die Evangelienüberlieferung.* Heidelberg: Sitzungsberichte der Heidelberger Akademie der Wissenschaften, phil.-hist. Klasse 12, 1919

Reitzenstein, Richard, *Das iranische Erlösungsmysterium. Religionsgeschichtliche Untersuchungen.* Bonn: A. Marcus & E. Weber, 1921

Reitzenstein, Richard, *Helidori carmina quattuor ad fidem codicis casselani edidit Günther Goldschmidt. Alchemistische Lehrschriften und Märchen bei den Arabern.* Mit

Unterstützung der Notgemeinschaft der Deutschen Wissenschaft. Religionsgeschichtliche Versuche und Vorarbeiten, XIX, 19, 2 vols. Gießen: A. Töpelmann, 1923

Reitzenstein, Richard, 'Augustin als antiker und als mittelalterlicher Mensch'. *Vorträge der Bibliothek Warburg 1922–23*, edited by Fritz Saxl, 38–75. Leipzig and Berlin: G. B. Teubner, 1924

Reitzenstein, Richard, 'Alt-griechische Theologie und ihre Quellen'. *Vorträge der Bibliothek Warburg 1924–1925*, edited by Fritz Saxl, 1–19. Leipzig and Berlin: G. B. Teubner, 1927

Reitzenstein, Richard, 'Plato und Zarathustra'. *Vorträge der Bibliothek Warburg 1924–1925*, edited by Fritz Saxl, 20–37. Leipzig and Berlin: G. B. Teubner, 1927

Reitzenstein, Richard, *Die Vorgeschichte der christlichen Taufe, mit Beiträgen von Luise Troje*. Leipzig and Berlin: B. G. Teubner, 1929

Reitzenstein, Richard, 'Heilige Handlung'. *Vorträge der Bibliothek Warburg 1928–1929*, edited by Fritz Saxl, 21–41. Leipzig and Berlin: B. G. Teubner, 1930

Reuters News Agency, 'Disarmament and Peace. Mr. MacDonald's Speech at Geneva'. London: The Times. London, 4 September 1929, 11 c–d.

Riegl, Alois, *Die spätrömische Kunst-Industrie nach den Funden in Österreich-Ungarn*. Vienna: K. K. Hof- und Staatsdruckerei, 1901

Riha, Karl (ed.), *Satire und Macht. Struwwelhitler. Eine englische Struwwelpeter-Parodie aus dem Jahre 1941 von Robert und Philip Spence (alias Dr. Schrecklichkeit)*. Translated into German by Wolf Dieter Bach and Dieter H. Stündel. Cologne: Informationspresse – c.w.leske verlag, 1984

Ritter, Hellmut (ed.), *Picatrix. Das Ziel des Weisen, von Pseudo-Maǧrīṭī*. Leipzig and Berlin: B. G. Teuber, 1933

Ritter, Hellmut, and Martin Plessner (eds.), *Das Ziel des Weisen von Pseudo-Magriti*. Translated from the Arabic into German. Saxl, Fritz (ed.), *Studien der Bibliothek Warburg*, 12. Leipzig: B. G. Teubner. 1933 and *Studies of the Warburg Institute* 27, 1962

Roeck, Bernd, *Der junge Aby Warburg*. Munich: C. H. Beck, 1997

Roeck, Bernd, *Florenz 1900. Die Suche nach Arkadien*. Munich: C. H. Beck, 2001

Röhrich, Lutz, *Lexikon der sprichwörtlichen Redensarten*, 4th ed., vol. 2. Freiburg, Basle, and Vienna: Herder KG, 1973

Roth, Eugen, *Simplicissimus: Ein Rückblick auf die satirische Zeitschrift*, 4th ed. Hannover: Fackelträger, 1954

Rückert, Friedrich, 'Du bist beglückt'. *Die Weisheit des Brahmanen: Ein Lehrgedicht*, 37–39. Leipzig, 1838

Russell, James R., *Zoroastrianism in Armenia*. Cambridge, MA: Harvard University Press, Department of Near Eastern Languages and Civilizations. National Association for Armenian Studies and Research, 1987

Russell, James R., 'On the Armeno-Iranian Roots of Mithraism'. *Studies in Mithraism*, edited by John Hinnells, 183–193. Rome: 'L'Erma' di Bretschneider, 1994

Sauer, Walter, 'Der *Struwwelpeter* und *Stepka-Rastrepka*. Zur Ikonographie der 2. *Struwwelpeterfassung*'. *Schiefertafel*, Year VIII, Heft 1 (May 1985): 20–34. Pinneberg: Verlag Renate Raecke, 1985

Sauer, Walter, 'Nachwort'. *Heinrich Hoffmann: Der Struwwelpeter Polyglott*, edited by Walter Sauer, 3rd ed., 121–126. Munich: Deutscher Taschenbuch Verlag G. m. b. H. & Co., 1994

Saxl, Fritz, 'Beiträge zu einer Geschichte der Planetendarstellungen im Orient und im Okzident'. *Islam: Zeitschrift für Geschichte und Kultur des islamischen Orient*, vol. 3, 151–177. K. J. Trübner: Strasbourg, 1912

Saxl, Fritz, 'Ein neues Buch von Carl Larsson'. *Die graphischen Künste*, vol. 35, 96–99. Vienna: Selbstverlag der Gesellschaft für vervielfältigende Kunst, 1912

Saxl, Fritz, 'Kunstgeschichte und künstlerische Erziehung'. *Wiener Zeitung*, Nr. 186, 15 August 1912

Saxl, Fritz, *Rembrandt-Studien*. PhD Dissertation, University of Vienna, 1912

Saxl, Fritz, *Verzeichnis astrologischer und mythologischer illustrierter Handschriften des lateinischen Mittelalters in römischen Bibliotheken. 1*. First printed in *Sitzungsberichte der Heidelberger Akademie der Wissenschaften. Phil.-hist. Klasse, Abhandlungen 6 – 7*. Heidelberg: Carl Winters, 1915

Saxl, Fritz, *Das Nachleben der Antike: zur Einführung in die Bibliothek Warburg*, vol. 2, 244–247. Hamburg: Hamburger Universitäts-Zeitung, 1920

Saxl, Fritz, 'Rinascimento dell'Antichità. Studien zu den Arbeiten A. Warburgs'. *Repertorium für Kunstwissenschaft*, vol. 63, 220–272. Stuttgart – Berlin, 1922

Saxl, Fritz, 'Die Bibliothek Warburg und ihr Ziel'. *Vorträge der Bibliothek Warburg 1921–22*, edited by Fritz Saxl, 1–10. Leipzig and Berlin: B. G. Teubner, 1923

Saxl, Fritz, 'Frühes Christentum und spätes Heidentum in ihren künstlerischen Ausdrucksformen'. *Wiener Jahrbuch für Kunstgeschichte*, vol. 2, no. 16. Special issue, 63–121. Vienna: Krystall-Verlag, 1923

Saxl, Fritz, 'Studien über Hans Holbein d. J: I. Die Karlsruher Kreuztragung I. Vorgeschichte und Vorbilder'. *Vienna: Belvedere*, vol. 9, no. 10, 139–154, 1926

Saxl, Fritz, 'Verzeichnis astrologischer und mythologischer illustrierter Handschriften des lateinischen Mittelalters. 2. Die Handschriften der Nationalbibliothek in Wien'. *Sitzungsberichte der Heidelberger Akademie der Wissenschaften. Phil.-hist. Klasse, Abhandlungen 2*, 2 vols. Heidelberg: Karl Winters Universitätsbuchhandlung, 1925–1926

Saxl, Fritz, 'Aller Tugenden und Laster Abbildung'. *Festschrift für Julius Schlosser*, edited by Arpad Weixlgärtner and Leo Planiscig, 104–121. Zurich: Amalthea Verlag, c. 1927

Saxl, Fritz, *Antike Götter in der Spätrenaissance. Ein Freskenzyklus und ein Discorso des Jacopo Zucchi*. Saxl, Fritz (ed.), *Studien der Bibliothek Warburg, 8. I*. Leipzig: B. G. Tennber, 1927

Saxl, Fritz, 'Review of August Mayer's *Dominico Theotocopuli El Greco*'. Munich, 1926. *Kritische Berichte zur kunstgeschichtlichen Literatur*, vol. 1–2, 86–96, 1927/1928

Saxl, Fritz, *Die Karlsruher Kreuztragung des Meisters H. H. (Hans Holbein d. J.?)*, vol. 9 [15], 205–215. Vienna: Belvedere, 1930

Saxl, Fritz, 'Die kulturwissenschaftliche Bibliothek Warburg in Hamburg'. *Forschungsinstitute, ihre Geschichte, Organisation und Ziele*, edited by Ludolph Brauer, Albrecht Mendelssohn Bartholdy, and Adolph Meyer, vol. II, 355–358. Hamburg: Paul Hartung Verlag, 1930

Saxl, Fritz, *Mithras: Typengeschichtliche Untersuchungen*. Berlin: Heinrich Keller, 1931

Saxl, Fritz (posthum), *Verzeichnis astrologischer und mythologischer illustrierter Handschriften des lateinischen Mittelalters / Catalogue of Astrological and Mythological Illuminated Manuscripts of the Latin Middle Ages, Vol. 3. Handschriften in englischen Bibliotheken / Manuscripts in English Libraries*, with Hans Meier, edited by Harry Bober. London: The Warburg Institute, 1953

Saxl, Fritz, 'The History of Warburg's Library, 1886–1944'. *Aby Warburg. An Intellectual Biography with a Memoir on the History of the Library by F. Saxl*, edited by Ernst H. Gombrich, 325–338. Oxford: Phaidon Press, 1986

Saxl, Fritz and Erwin Panofsky, *Dürers 'Melencolia I'. Eine quellen- und typengeschichtliche Untersuchung*. Saxl, Fritz (ed.), , *Studien der Bibliothek Warburg 2*. Leipzig: B. G. Teubner, 1923

Schaeder, Hans Heinrich, 'Urform und Fortbildungen des manichäischen Systems'. *Vorträge der Bibliothek Warbur 1924–1925*, edited by Fritz Sxl, 65–157. Leipzig and Berlin: B. G. Teubner, 1927

Schaeder, Hans Heinrich, 'Nazarenos, Nazoraios'. *Der Mandäismus*, edited by G. Widengren, 167, 161–165. Darmstadt: Wege der Forschung, 1982

Schindler, Thomas, *Zwischen Empfinden und Denken. Aspekte zur Kulturpsychologie von Aby Warburg*. Münster: LIT Verlag, 1999

Schlosser, Julius von, 'Vom modernen Denkmalkultus'. *Vorträge der Bibliothek Warburg 1926–27*, edited by Fritz Saxl, 1–21. Leipzig and Berlin: B. G. Teubner, 1930

Schoell-Glass, Charlotte, *Aby Warburg und der Antisemitismus. Kulturwissenchaft als Geistespolitik*. Frankfurt am Main: Fischer Taschenbuch, 1998

Scholz, P., and Magdalena Dlugosz (eds.), *Von Biala nach Wien. Josef Strzygowski und die Kunstwissenschaften. Zum 150. Geburtstag von Josef Strzygowski. Akten der Konferenz Bielsko-Biala (27.–30.3.2012) und Wien (12.10.2012)*. Vienna: European University Press, Dept. für Vergleichende Kunstgeschichte am Kulturwissenschaftlichen Institute an der Maria Curie-Sklodowska Universität in Lublin and Gesellschaft für Vergleichende Kunstforschung in Vienna, 2015

Schöner, R., 'Von den römischen Kongressen'. *Finanz-Handelsblatt der Vossischen Zeitung*, 7, 26 October 1912

Schwartz, Peter J., 'Aby Warburgs Kriegskartothek: Vorbericht einer Rekonstruktion'. *Kasten 117: Aby Warburg und der Aberglaube im Ersten Weltkrieg*, edited by Gottfried Korff, 39–69. Tübingen: Tübinger Vereinigung für Volkskunde e. V., 2007

Schwartz, Peter J., 'Aby Warburg and Cinema Revisited'. *New German Critique*, vol. 47, no. 1 (139), 105–140. New York: NY Telos Press, 2020

Schwindrazheim, Hildamarie, 'Wilhelmine Niels – eine Hamburg-Münchner Malerin'. *Zeitschrift des Vereins für hamburgische Geschichte*, vol. 65, 161–188. Hamburg, 1979

Sedlmayr, Hans, *Fischer von Erlach der Ältere*. Munich: R. Piper, 1925

Sedlmayr, Hans, *Die Architektur Borrominis*. Berlin: Frankfurter Verlags-Anstalt A.G., 1930.

Seiler, Martin, 'Aspekte theoretischer Kongruenz von Wiener Schule und Warburg-Kreis: Edgar Wind und Julius von Schlosser'. *Kunsthistoriker, Mitteilungen des österreichischen Kunsthistorikerverbandes*, Jg. V (1988), Nr. 3/4. 44–50. Wien, 1988

Seiler, Martin, 'Empiristische Motive im Denken und Forschen der Wiener Schule der Kunstgeschichte'. *Kunst, Kunsttheorie und Kunstforschung im wissenschaftlichen Diskurs. In memoriam Kurt Blaukopf (1914–1999)*, edited by Martin Seiler and Friedrich Stadler, Wissenschaftliche Weltauffassung und Kunst, vol. 5. Vienna: bv&hpt Verlagsgesellschaft, 2000

Settis, Salvatore, 'Warburg continuatus. Description d'une bibliothèque'. *Le pouvoir des bibliothèques. La mémoire des livres en Occident*, edited by Marc Baratin and Christian Jacob, 122–169. Paris: Bibliothèque Albin Michel Histoire, c. 1996

Simplicissimus, Satirical German weekly. Munich

Slevogt, Max, *Gesichte. 21 Stein- und Zinkdrucke*. Berlin: Panpresse, 1917

Spence, Robert, and Philip Pence (alias Dr. Schrecklichkeit), *Struwwelhitler*. London: Daily Sketch and Sunday Graphic Ltd., 1941

Spinelli, Ingrid Warburg, *Die Dringlichkeit des Mitleids und die Einsamkeit nein zu sagen. Erinnerungen 1910–1989*. Hamburg: Döllling & Galitz, 1990

Stevenson, Robert Louis, *The Strange Case of Dr. Jekyll and Mr. Hyde*. London: Longmann, Green, and Co., 1886

Stimilli, David, and Claudia Wedepohl, *Aby M. Warburg "Per Monstra and Sphaeram". Sternglaube und Bilddeutung. Vortrag in Gedenken an Franz Boll und andere Schriften 1923 bis 1925*. Kleine Schriften des Warburg Institute London and des Warburg Archivs im Warburg Haus Hamburg, Heft 3. Munich and Hamburg: Dölling und Galitz Verlag, 2008

Stockhausen, Tilmann von, *Die Kulturwissenschaftliche Bibliothek Warburg. Architektur, Einrichtung und Organisation*. Hamburg: Dölling und Galitz Verlag, 1992

Strange, Roderick, 'Lessons from a Journey to Faith'. *The Tablet. The International Catholic Weekly*, 12 October 2019

Strauss, Herrmann, *Kreuzlinger Mosaik. Berichte und Bilder aus Vergangenheit und Gegenwart; ein Quellenbuch der Grenzstadt Kreuzlingen bis ca. 1960*. Keuzlingen: Stadtrat, 1991

Strzygowski, Josef, 'Nationale Kunstgeschichte und internationale Kunstwissenschaft'. *Internationale Wochenschrift für Wissenschaft, Kunst und Technik*, vol. 3, no. 8, 573–578. Berlin, 1907

Suhr, Norbert, 'Max Slevogt als Graphiker'. *Max Slevogt: Gemälde, Aquarelle, Zeichnungen*, edited by Ernst-Gerhard Güse, Imiela Hans-Jürgen, and Berthold Roland. Exhibition catalogue Saarbrücken, Saarland Museum, 75–93. Stuttgart: Hatje, 1992

Sukenik, Eleazar Lipa, *The Ancient Synagogue of Beth Alpha*. Jerusalem: The University Press / London: Oxford University Press, 1932 [Reprint: Hildesheim/New York 1975]

Sutton, Eric (ed. and trans.), *Gustav Stresemann. His Diaries, Letters and Papers*, vol. 8. London: Macmillan & Co., 1940

Syamken, Georg, 'Mary Warburg'. *Zur Sache 11*. Hamburg: Hamburger Kunsthalle, 1985

Syamken, Georg, *Die dritte Dimension. Plastiken, Konstruktionen, Objekte. Bestandskatalog der Skulpturenabteilung der Hamburger Kunsthalle*. Hamburg: Die Kunsthalle, 1988

Szönyi, György, 'Warburg's Intuitions in Light of Postmodern Challenges'. *Umění, Art 1*, vol. XLIX, no. 4, 2001. Prague

Thieme, Ulrich, and Felix Becker (eds.), *Allgemeines Lexikon der bildenden Künstler : von der Antike bis zur Gegenwart: unter Mitwirkung von 300 Fachgelehrten des In- und Auslandes*. Leipzig: Engelman, 1907–1950

Tietze, Hans, *Die Methode der Kunstgeschichte. Ein Versuch*. Leipzig: E. A. Seemann, 1913

Tietze, Hans, 'Romanische Kunst und Renaissance'. *Vorträge der Bibliothek Warburg 1926–27*, edited by Fritz Saxl, 43–57. Leipzig: B. G. Teubner, 1930

Tietze-Conrat, Erika, *Die Bronzen der fürstlich Liechtensteinschen Kunstkammer*, vol. 11. Vienna: Jahrbuch des kunsthistorischen Institutes der k.k. Zentral-Kommission für Denkmalpflege, 1917

Tietze-Conrat, Erika, 'Zur höfischen Allegorie der Renaissance'. *Vienna: Jahrbuch der Kunsthistorischen Sammlungen des Allerhöchsten Kaiserhauses*, vol. 34, no.1, 25–32, 1917

The Times, 'Disarmament and Peace. Mr. MacDonald's Speech at Geneva', London, 4 September 1929, 11c–d

Trapp, Joe, 'Obituary'. *Libraries Bulletin*. No. 17 (October–December 1979): 1. London: University of London, 1979

Trapp, Joe, 'Obituary'. *The Times*, 17 November 1979: 16

Treml, Martin, Sigrid Weigel, and Perdita Ladwig (eds.), *Werke in einem Band. Aby Warburg, auf der Grundlage der Manuskripte und Handexemplare*. Berlin: Suhrkamp Verlag, 2010

Troje, Luise, *Adam und Zoe. Eine Szene der altchristlichen Kunst in ihrem religionsgeschichtlichen Zusammenhange*. Sitzungsberichte der Heidelberger Akademie der Wissenschaften. Heidelberg: Carl Winters Universitätsbuchhandlung, 1916

Troje, Luise, *Die Geburt des Aion – ein altes Mysterium*. Leipzig and Berlin: Archiv für Religionswissenschaft, 22, 1924

Troje, Luise, *Die dreizehn und die zwölf im Traktat Pelliot (Dogmen in Zahlenformeln). Ein Beitrag zu den Grundlagen des Manichäismus*. Leipzig: E. Pfeiffer, 1925

Uffenbach, Philipp, *Bericht und Erklärung zweier beigefügten Kupferstücken, oder Zeitweiser der Sonnen über die ganze Welt*. Frankfurt am Main: Matthes Becker, Paul Brauchfeldts, 1598

Urban, Otto H., 'Barb, Alphons Augustinus (1901–1979), Numismatiker'. *Österreichisches Biographisches Lexikon ab 1815 (2. Überarbeitete Auflage – online)*. Institut für Neuzeit- und Zeitgeschichtsforschung 2003–2020, n. p. Vienna: Verlag der Österreichischen Akademie der Wissenschaften, 2013

Usener, Hermann, *Heilige Handlung*. Leipzig: B. G. Teubner, *Archiv für Religionswissenschaft*, vol. 7, 1904

Voigt, Rainer (ed.), *"Durch Dein Wort ward jegliches Ding!" "Through Thy Word All Things were Made!" 2. Mandäistische und samaritanistische Tagung / 2nd International Conference of Mandaic and Samaritan Studies. Zum Gedenken an Rudolf Macuch (1919–1993) / In Honour of Rudolf Macuch (1919–1993)*. Mandäistische Forschungen, vol. 4. Wiesbaden: Harrassowitz Verlag, 2013

Vollmer, Hans (ed.), 'Warburg, Mary'. *Allgemeines Lexikon der bildenden Künstler des 20. Jahrhunderts*. Vol. 6, Nachträge H–Z, 468. Leipzig: E. A. Seemann Verlag, 1962

Vondel, Joost van den, *Batavische Gebroeders; of, Onderdruckte vryheit: treurspel*. Amsterdam: Voor J. de Wees, 1690

Vorholt, Hanna, '"Das was ich als Jude vertrete, kann ich auch in England oder Frankreich sein". A Letter by Gertrud Bing to Hanns Swarzenski of May 1933'. *The Afterlife of the Kulturwissenschaftliche Bibliothek Warburg. The Emigration and the Early Years of the Warburg Institute in London*, edited by Uwe Fleckner and Peter Mack, 23–37 and 204–210. Berlin and Boston: Walter de Gruyter, 2015

Wackenroder, Wilhelm Heinrich, *Herzensergiessungen eines kunstliebendesn Klosterbruders*, edited by J. L. Tieck. Berlin, 1797

Warburg, Aby, *Sandro Botticellis "Geburt der Venus" und "Frühling"*. Hamburg: Leopold Voss, 1893. Translated into English in Britt, David, 'Sandro Botticelli's *Birth of Venus* and *Spring*', 89–157 and 405–431. 1999

Warburg, Aby, 'Bildersprache des Weltverkehrs'. Summaries of lecture in *Hamburgische Nachrichten* on 15.8.1927 and in *Hamburger Fremdenblatt* on 14.08.1927

Warburg, Aby, 'Amerikanische Chap-Books'. *Pan*. Berlin, Year 2, no. 4, 1896, 345–348. Reprinted in *A. Warburg. Gesammelte Schriften. Die Erneuerung der heidnischen Antike*, edited by Gertrud Bing, and Fritz Rougemont, vol. 2, 569–577 and 658. Leipzig / Berlin: B. G. Teubner, 1932. Translated into English in Britt, David, 'American Chapbooks', 703–710 and 776 (see Britt, David).

Warburg, Aby, 'Italienische Kunst und internationale Astrologie im Palazzo Schifanoja zu Ferrara'. *Italia e l'Arte Straniera, Atti del X. Congresso internazionale di storia dell'Arte, 16–21 October 1912*, 179–193 and plates XXXVII–XLVII. Rome: Maglione & Strini (succ. to E. Loescher), 1922

Warburg, Aby, 'Arbeitende Bauern auf Burgundischen Teppichen' (1907). *A. Warburg. Gesammelte Schriften. Die Erneuerung der heidnischen Antike*, edited by Gertrud Bing and Fritz Rougemont, vol. 1, 221–229 and 383. Leipzig: B. G. Teubner, 1932. Translated into English in Britt, David, 'Peasants at Work in Burgundian Tapestries', 315–323 and 484–485 (see Britt, David).

Warburg, Aby, 'Austausch künstlerischer Kultur zwischen Norden und Süden im 15. Jahrhundert' (1905). *A. Warburg. Gesammelte Schriften. Die Erneuerung der heidnischen Antike*, edited by Gertrud Bing, and Fritz Rougemont, vol. I, 177–184 and 368–369. Leipzig: B. G. Teubner, 1932. Translated into English in Britt, David, 'Artistic Exchanges between North and South in the Fifteenth Century', 275–280 and 468–469 (see Britt, David)

Warburg, Aby, 'Bildniskunst und florentinisches Bürgertum' (1902). *A. Warburg. Gesammelte Schriften. Die Erneuerung der heidnischen Antike*, edited by Gertrud Bing and Fritz Rougemont, vol. I, 89–126 and 340–352. Leipzig: B. G. Teubner, 1932. Translated into English in Britt, David, 'The Art of Portraiture and the Florentine Bourgeoisie', 185–221 and 435–450 (see Britt, David)

Warburg, Aby, 'Der Eintritt des antikisierenden Idealstils in die Malerei der Frührenaissance' (1914). *Gesammelte Schriften. Die Erneuerung der heidnischen Antike*, vol. 1, edited by Gertrud Bing and Fritz Rougemont, vol. 1, 173–176 and 367. Leipzig: B. G. Teubner, 1932. Translated into English in Britt, David, 'The Emergence of the Antique as a Stylistic Ideal in Early Renaissance Painting', 271–273 and 468–469 (see Britt, David)

Warburg, Aby, 'Flandrische und florentinische Kunst im Kreise des Lorenzo Medici um 1480' (1901). *A. Warburg. Gesammelte Schriften. Die Erneuerung der heidnischen Antike*, edited by Gertrud Bing and Fritz Rougemont, vol. 1, 185–212 and 370–380. Leipzig: B. G. Teubner, 1932. Translated into English in Britt, David, 'Flemish Art and the Florentine Early Renaissance', 281–303 and 483 (see Britt, David)

Warburg, Aby, 'Francesco Sassettis letztwillige Verfügung'. First printed in *Kunstwissenschaftliche Beiträge August Schmarsow gewidmet*, edited by H. Weizsäcker, et al., 129–152. Leipzig: K. W. Hiersemann, 1907. Reprinted in *A. Warburg. Gesammelte Schriften. Die Erneuerung der heidnischen Antike*, edited by Gertrud Bing and Fritz Rougemont, vol. I, 127–158 and 353–365. Leipzig: B. G. Teubner, 1932. Translated into English in Britt, David, 'Francesco Sassetti's Last Injunctions to His Sons', 223–262 and 451–466 (see Britt, David)

Warburg, Aby, 'Heidnisch-antike Weissagung in Wort und Bild zu Luthers Zeiten'. *A. Warburg. Gesammelte Schriften*, edited by Gertrud Bing and Fritz Rougemont, Fritz, vol. II, 487–558 and 647–656. Leipzig: B. G. Teubner, 1932. Translated into English in Britt, David, 'Pagan-Antique Prophecy in Words and Images in the Age of Luther', 597–697 and 760–775 (see Britt, David)

Warburg, Aby, 'Italienische Kunst und internationale Astrologie im Palazzo Schifanoja zu Ferrara'. (1912) *A. Warburg. Gesammelte Schriften. Die Erneuerung der heidnischen Antike*, edited by Gertrud Bing and Fritz Rougemont, vol. II, 459–481 and 626–644. Leipzig: B. G. Teubner, 1932. Translated into English in Britt, David, 'Italian Art and International Astrology in the Palazzo Schifanoia, Ferrara', 563–591 and 732–758 (see Britt, David)

Warburg, Aby, 'Kirchliche und höfische Kunst in Landshut' (1909). *A. Warburg. Gesammelte Schriften. Die Erneuerung der heidnischen Antike*, edited by Gertrud Bing and Fritz Rougemont, vol. II, 457 and 626. Leipzig: B. G. Teubner, 1932. Translated into English in Britt, D. 'Church and Court Art at Landshut', 561 and 732 (see Britt, David)

Warburg, Aby (1913), 'Luftschiff und Tauchboot in der mittelalterlichen Vorstellungswelt'. *A. Warburg. Gesammelte Schriften. Die Erneuerung der heidnischen Antike*, edited by Gertrud Bing and Fritz Rougemont, vol. I, 241–249 and 386–388. Leipzig: B. G.Teubner, 1932.

Translated into English in Britt, David, 'Airship and Submarine in the Medieval Imagination', 332–337 and 487–490 (see Britt, David)

Warburg, Aby, 'Orientalisierende Astrologie' (1926). *A. Warburg: Gesammelte Schriften. Die Erneuerung der heidnischen Antike*, edited by Gertrud Bing and Fritz Rougemont, vol. II, 559–565 and 657. Leipzig: B. G. Teubner, 1932. Translated into English in Britt, David, 'Astrology under Oriental Influence', 699–702 and 775 (see Britt, David)

Warburg, Aby, 'Piero della Francescas Constantinschlacht in der Aquarellkopie des Johann Anton Ramboux' (1912). *A. Warburg. Gesammelte Schriften. Die Erneuerung der heidnischen Antike*, edited by Gertrud Bing and Fritz Rougemont, vol. I, 251–254 and 389–391. Leipzig: B. G. Teubner, 1932. Translated into English in Britt, David, 'Piero della Francesca's *Battle of Constantine* in the Watercolor Copy by Johann Anton Ramboux', 339–342 and 490–493 (see Britt, David)

Warburg, Aby, 'A Lecture on Serpent Ritual'. *Journal of the Warburg Institute*, edited by Gertrud Bing, translated by W. F. Mainland, vol. 2, 222–292, 1938–39

Warburg, Aby, 'Zum Vortrag von Karl Reinhardt über "Ovids Metamorphosen" in der Bibliothek Warburg am 24. Oktober 1924'. *Vorträge 1924–1925*, edited by Fritz Saxl. Preface on a loose leaf inserted into *Vorträge*, with Reinhardt's lecture 'Ovids Metamorphosen' in KBW on 24 October 1924. See also Stimilli, David and Claudia Wedepohl, *Aby M. Warburg "Per Monstra and Sphaeram". Sternglaube und Bilddeutung. Vortrag in Gedenken an Franz Boll und andere Schriften 1923 bis 1925.* Kleine Schriften des Warburg Institute London and des Warburg Archivs im Warburg Haus Hamburg, Heft 3, 59–61. Munich/Hamburg: Dölling und Galitz Verlag, 2008°

Warburg, Aby, *Schlangenritual: Ein Reisebericht. Mit einem Nachwort von Ulrich Raulff.* Berlin: Klaus Wagenbach, 1988

Warburg, Aby, and Erwin Redslob, 'Die Briefmarke als Kulturdokument'. *Philatelisten-Zeitung*, Gössnitz, Heft 9, 01.09.1927, 118

Warburg, Aby, and Fritz Saxl, *Die Indianer beschwören den Regen. Großes Fest bei den Pueblo-Indianern.* Berlin: Jugendbücher Verlag. Issue 4, 1926: correction of the article by Else Hildebrandt

Warburg, Aby, Georg Thilenius, and Giulio Panconcelli-Calzia (eds.), *La Guerra del 1914. Rivista Illustrata dei primi tre mesi Agosto, Settembre, Ottobre*. Hamburg: Druckerei des Hamburger Fremdenblattes, 1914

Warburg, Aby, Georg Thilenius, and Giulio Panconcelli-Calzia (eds.), *La Guerra del 1914–15. Rivista Illustrata dei mesi Novembre, Dicembre, Gennaio, Febbraio*. Hamburg: Druckerei des Hamburger Fremdenblattes, 1915

Warburg, Max, *Die Judenfrage im Rahmen der deutschen Gesamtpolitik*. Private print. 1916

Warnke, Martin, and Claudia Brinck (eds.), *Aby Warburg (1866–1929). Gesammelte Schriften. Studienausgabe. 2. Abt. Band 2.1. Der Bilderatlas MNEMOSYNE*. Berlin: Akademie Verlag, 2000

Weber, Otto, *Altorientalische Siegelbilder*. Leipzig: J. C. Hinrichs, 1920

Wedepohl, Claudia, '"Agitationsmittel für die Bearbeitung der Ungelehrten": Warburgs Reformationsstudien zwischen Kriegsbeobachtung, historisch-kritischer Forschung und Verfolgungswahn'. *Kasten 117: Aby Warburg und der Aberglaube im Ersten Weltkrieg*, edited by Gottfried Korff, 325–368. Tübingen: Tübinger Vereinigung für Volkskunde e.V., 2007

Weigel, Sigrid, *Aby Warburg. Werke in einem Band. In collaboration with Martin Treml und Perdita Ladwig*. Berlin: Suhrkamp, 2010

Weizsäcker, H., et al., *Kunstwissenschaftliche Beiträge. August Schmarsow gewidmet zum fünfzigsten Semester seiner akademischen Lehrtätigkeit*. Leipzig: K. W. Hiersemann, 1907

Whiston, William (trans.), *Flavius Josephus, Jewish Antiquities* 6, 91–111. Ware: Wordsworth Editions, 2006

Wickhoff, Franz, 'Die Hochzeitsbilder Sandro Botticellis'. *Jahrbuch der k. Preussischen Kunstsammlungen*, col. XXVII, 198–207. Berlin, 1906

Wickhoff, Franz, *Römische Kunst: die Wiener Genesis*. Berlin: Meyer & Jessen, 1912

Widengren, George, 'Einleitung'. In *Der Mandäismus*, edited by George Widengren, 1–17. Darmstadt: Wege der Forschung 167, 1982

Wieser, F. Freiherr von, 'Die Lehren des Krieges'. *Flugschriften für Österreich-Ungarns Erwachen. 1*. Heft. Warnsdorf in Böhmen: Verlag Ed. Stracke, 1915

Wind, Edgar, 'Einleitung'. *Kulturwissenschaftliche Bibliographie zum Nachleben der Antike*; 1. Bd. *Die Erscheinungen des Jahres 1931*, edited by Hans Meier, Richard Newald, and Edgar Wind, v–xvii. Berlin: B.G.Teubner, 1934

Wolfe, Humbert, and Alias Oistros, *Truffle Eater, Pretty Stories and Funny Pictures*. London: Arthur Barker, 1933

Wortis, Joseph, and David Arkin, *Tricky Dick and His Pals: Comical Stories, All in the Manner of Dr. Heinrich Hoffmann's Der Struwwelpeter*. New York: Quadrangle, 1974

Wuttke, Dieter (ed.), *Erwin Panofsky. Korrespondenz 1910 – 1968: Eine kommentierte Auswahl in fünf Bänden*. Wiesbaden: Harrassowitz Verlag, 2001–2011

Yeats, William Butler, 'Among School Children'. *The Collected Poems of W. B. Yeats*, 242–245. London: Macmillan; New York: St. Martin's Press, 1958

INDEX

Made in the USA
Las Vegas, NV
24 October 2024

f0fc5605-6051-4a0d-9b1b-a111a4b080c7R01